Brain-Friendly Teaching
Tools, Tips, & Structures

Dr. Spencer Kagan

Kagan

Kagan

Kagan Publishing
981 Calle Amanecer
San Clemente, CA 92673
1 (800) 933-2667
www.KaganOnline.com

ISBN: 978-1-933445-35-9

What's Inside?

▶ Principle 1: Nourishment

To function optimally, brains are dependent on a constant, plentiful supply of nutrients. The question for us as educators becomes, what can we do to optimally nourish the brains of our students? It turns out, we have six powerful tools available to ensure the brains of our students are primed to function at their best.

▶ Principle 2: Safety

For the brains of our students to function optimally, our students need to feel safe. No put-downs, embarrassments, bullies, exclusions, or threats of any kind. Music; cooperative, inclusive teams; and exercise are among the fourteen tools to create safety.

▶ Principle 3: Social

The brain is a social organ. Humans are wired to cooperate. Cooperation is biologically rewarding. A cooperative classroom activates the social cognition network, creates an inclusive class, carefully structures cooperative interaction, and promotes cooperative play. The results: safety, peer encouragement and tutoring, and creative thinking. Implementing Principle 3 allows the brains of our students to function the ways they function best.

▶ Principle 4: Emotion

We can harness emotion in our classrooms to create a passion for learning, to make our content more memorable, to motivate, and to improve problem solving and thinking. Just as fear constricts the ability to think, positive emotions broaden thinking. By eliciting positive emotion in our classrooms, we actually make students measurably smarter!

▶ Principle 5: Attention

Attention yields retention. To the extent we focus students' attention on what we want them to learn, we facilitate learning. How can they remember something they never attended to in the first place? Here we explore fourteen tools to capture and hold attention.

▶ Principle 6: Stimuli

Brains naturally attend to certain kinds of stimuli and ignore others. By teaching with novelty, relevance, illustrations, and multimodal stimuli, we present the ways brains want to learn. Here, we examine thirteen types of stimuli that are candy for the brain!

Foreword
by Dr. Robert Sylwester

When you come right down to it, schools educate student cognitive systems that should then activate culturally appropriate behavioral responses.

Scientists historically lacked the technology they needed to understand how instructing student thought could result in culturally appropriate behavior, so educators simply perceived of our brain as a mysterious Black Box. Conversely, behavior was out in the open. When I became a teacher midway through the 20th century, Behaviorism was the dominant instructional perspective. Teachers were expected to shape student behavior so that it met cultural expectations. Whatever might occur within a student's brain was and would remain a mystery.

Some of us, however, were fascinated by the beginnings of neuroscience. Scientists were making intriguing discoveries that seemed to explain why some forms of instruction worked better than others. We excitedly told colleagues but alas, we were often wrong about the educational implications of the discoveries.

When scientists discover something that's different from what they formerly believed, they simply abandon the incorrect belief and embrace the new. Over time, educators caught that spirit of discovery. We gradually began to develop the level of understanding of neurobiological systems that would help us appropriately incorporate cognitive neuroscience discoveries into educational policy and practice.

The book assumes that 21st century teachers will have developed a basic understanding of the terms that cognitive neuroscientists use, and many of you have that knowledge. Others don't yet. Nothing to be ashamed of. We all had to learn them, and in it's much easier to do it now than it was several decades ago. Do what I did just now: type in glossary of brain terms in Google (or in some other search engine), and you'll get dozens of nontechnical glossaries (many with related illustrations). Identify one that seems especially helpful and then run off a copy that you can have immediately available as you read the book. You'll discover that you'll soon master the terms. Given what's currently occurring in cognitive neuroscience research, you'll need to understand the developments that are making education an increasingly fascinating profession.

And teachers being teachers, when you're comfortable with the terms, you'll start to use them with your students and so also help them begin to understand their own cognitive systems.

We educate young people in groups. It's less expensive but it's also cognitively better. We're a social species and so a major task for young people is to learn how to get along with others, and especially with those with whom we're not related. One of the delights of Kagan's book is how well it incorporates the social kinds of learning that so define human life. Although much of school has been historically individualized, much of adult life is basically social. We live with friends and work with colleagues. The book strongly suggests that teaching isn't about a teacher talking to a couple dozen students but rather, it's more about getting students to work together in the solution of intriguing learning tasks—and to enjoy doing it. A spirit of play thus permeates the book, just as a sense of play should permeate life.

You and then your students will appreciate the book.

It was a pleasure to read Spencer Kagan's new book, **Brain-Friendly Teaching.** *It exemplifies a solid research-based book. One of the delights of Kagan's book is how well it incorporates the social kinds of learning that so define human life.*

Robert Sylwester is an Emeritus Professor of Education at the University of Oregon and co-editor of the *Information Age Education Newsletter*.

Dr. Sylwester is the author of 20 books. His most recent books include:
   A Child's Brain: The Need for Nurture (2010, Corwin Press.)

   The Adolescent Brain: Reaching for Autonomy (2007, Corwin Press.)

   How to Explain a Brain: An Educator's Handbook of Brain Terms and Cognitive Processes (2005, Corwin Press.)

Contact information: bobsyl@uoregon.edu

Book Highlights

▶ **6 Tools to Nourish the Brain**

Grouping Structures and Interactions Structures that nourish the brain while we teach. With no time off the curriculum, we prime our students' brains for optimal functioning.

Principle 1: Nourishment, pp. 1.28–1.30.

▶ **14 Tools to Foster Safety**

Ways to build inclusive teams and classrooms. When students know they are part of a team and feel accepted by their peers, their brains solve problems more quickly and more accurately!

Principle 2: Safety, pp. 2.15–2.18.

▶ **5 Tools to Promote Social Cognition and Cooperation**

Dozens of ways to stimulate social cognition and release the social encoding advantage to improve test scores and retention of content across the range of academic content.

Principle 3: Social, pp. 3.21–3.26.

▶ **7 Tools to Improve Achievement by Harnessing the Power of Emotion**

Thirty-seven ways to elicit positive emotions that improve problem solving, increase creativity, and improve thinking skills.

Principle 4: Emotion, pp. 4.19–4.45.

▶ **14 Tools to Capture and Hold Students' Attention**

Ways to clear both short-term and working memory through frequent processing, leading to better focus, improved note-taking, retention of content, and higher test scores.

Principle 5: Attention, pp. 5.25–5.38.

▶ **13 Tools to Teach with the Stimuli Brains Seek**

Dozens of ways to teach with images, tunes, and gestures—research-proven ways to accelerate comprehension and retention.

Principle 6: Stimuli, pp. 6.53–6.88.

6 Principles

1 Nourishment

Better Nourished Brains Learn More Efficiently
6 Tools to Nourish the Brain

2 Safety

Safe Brains Think Better
15 Tools to Foster Safety

6 Stimuli

Brains Seek and Retain Specific Stimuli
13 Tools to Teach with Stimuli Brains Seek

Brain-Friendly Teaching

3 Social

Social Interaction & Social Cognition Improve Learning
5 Tools to Teach to the Social Brain

5 Attention

Attention Produces Retention of Content
14 Tools To Capture and Hold Attention

4 Emotion

Positive Emotion Promotes Thinking, Creativity & Learning
7 Tools to Teach with Emotion

Introduction

Brain-Friendly Teaching: Teaching in Ways Brains Best Learn

We have a choice. We can teach in ways that align with how brains naturally learn. If we do, our students learn more, learn more quickly, retain and recall more, and enjoy learning more. And, we are not as tired at the end of the day. Teaching becomes more joyful. It is like swimming with the current. On the other hand, we can teach in ways that do not align with how brains naturally learn. If we do, our students learn less and like learning less. And, we are more exhausted at the end of the day. It is like swimming against the current.

Many traditional teaching methods do not align well with how brains most easily learn. Without changing what we teach, we can change how we teach in ways that make teaching and learning dramatically more efficient. And it is not difficult. The tools in this book transform both teaching and learning. Brain-friendly teaching and learning is more fun and more efficient.

Let's Do a Thought Experiment

After reading this paragraph and before reading on, close your eyes and recall what you had for dinner last night. Picture as fully as you can what you ate. Recall the flavor of the food. Remember whom you were with, what the table looked like, and even some of the things in the surroundings. Don't read on until you have closed your eyes and recalled last night's dinner in as much detail as possible.

The information about last night's dinner, and there was a lot of it, came back very easily. You memorized all that content without even being aware that you were doing so! It was effortless. Now, contrast that with how difficult it is to have our students memorize our academic content, whether it is math facts or formulas, science information, spelling words or vocabulary, or history dates and events. Why? Why are our students able to memorize some information effortlessly and other information only with a struggle?

6 Principles to Enrich the Brain

1 Principle 1
Nourishment

2 Principle 2
Safety

3 Principle 3
Social

4 Principle 4
Emotion

5 Principle 5
Attention

6 Principle 6
Stimuli

The brain is designed to attend to, process, retain, and recall certain kinds of information and, information presented in specific ways. When we understand how brains best function, we can align how we teach with how brains best learn.

What Is Brain-Friendly Teaching?

Brain-friendly teaching is teaching aligned with how brains best function—with how brains best attend to, process, retain, and recall information. The concept is simple and powerful. For example, if we know from cognitive neuroscience that brains naturally attend to and retain novel stimuli, then we can apply that finding to the way we teach to promote learning. A teacher who lectures for an hour in monotone, providing no novel stimuli, is not teaching the way brains best learn. In contrast, if a teacher punctuates the same lecture with unexpected movement among students to form novel pairs, and structures social interaction over the content within pairs in novel ways—that teacher is aligning how she teaches with how brains best learn. Her teaching is more brain-friendly. Students not only retain more of the lecture, they like class, content, and teacher more. Novel stimuli is one of many types of stimuli we can provide to make our teaching more brain-friendly. Brain-friendly stimuli are presented in Principle 6: Stimuli.

When we understand how brains best function, we can align how we teach with how brains best learn.

There has been an explosion of research on the brain in the past few decades. Some of it quite closely links teaching and learning to brain processes. This explosion of brain research has led to a new view of the brain. Not very many years ago we thought brain organization was fixed, and as a result we viewed certain abilities of our students as unchangeable. Now we know the brain is amazingly plastic, rewiring itself on a moment-to-moment basis. The research on neuroplasticity is pushing us to re-examine our assumptions. We no longer accept IQ and ADD as givens. How we teach can actually increase IQ and can focus students who otherwise would be labeled ADD.

We now know how to train the brain. In fact, teaching is the only profession that on a daily basis has the primary responsibility for rewiring a group of brains! And if we apply the findings of brain science, we can do our jobs more efficiently. We can unlock potential among our students, improving their performance for a lifetime.

Teaching is the only profession that on a daily basis has the responsibility for rewiring a group of brains!

Some of the brain-science research that is most relevant for improving teaching and learning comes from the work of cognitive neuroscientists that are not themselves applying their work to education. Nevertheless, applying those findings to teaching and learning empowers us to create more brain-friendly learning environments. For example, the work on mirror neurons demonstrates that when we watch someone perform an action, our brains fire as if we were performing that action (see Principle 3: Social). This finding has a number of direct applications for us as teachers. To take two examples: We are more likely to be successful modeling our instructions rather than just giving verbal instructions, and we are more likely to be successful calming our class by responding to disruptive behavior with a calm voice and a composed face, rather than letting our own agitation show.

How Is this Book Organized?

This book is designed to present simple, but very powerful ways we can structure our classrooms and teach based on the understanding of brain function. This book contains five ingredients to help teachers make their classrooms and instruction more brain friendly: (1) Principles, (2) Tools, (3) Tips, (4) Brainiac Boxes, and (5) Structures.

Six Principles

Instead of many detailed and complicated principles of brain-based teaching, this book provides just six easy-to-understand principles. Any teacher or presenter that implements these six principles will reap dramatic benefits for themselves and for their students.

The book is organized around the 6 principles. Each principle begins with a full-page divider that gives a thumbnail sketch of the principle. The dividers look like this:

For each of the six principles of brain-friendly teaching we begin with a discussion of the theoretical and empirical rationale for that principle. For example, in introducing Principle 2: Safety, we begin with a discussion of how the brain functions under threat and how it functions in a safe environment, providing the rationale for creating threat-free classrooms.

The Six Principles:

Nourishment

1. Nourish the Brain. As the neurons in the brain talk to each other, they consume a huge percent of the nutrients in the body. Well-nourished brains learn better. Here we learn how to create well-nourished brains.

> ▶ **Interesting Finding:** Two high-intensity sprints of less than three minutes each led to a greater release of epinephrine and norepinephrine and to 20% faster acquisition of new vocabulary words compared to 40 minutes of low impact running!

Safety

2. Foster Safety. In the presence of threat, cognition and perception narrow, making learning difficult or impossible. Here we learn many ways to facilitate thinking and learning by creating brain-safe classrooms and schools.

> ▶ **Interesting Finding:** High-anxiety students score below low-anxiety students on a multiple-choice test when administered in the typical way, but when the same multiple-choice items are worded in a humorous way, high-anxiety students score as well as low-anxiety students!

Social

3. Promote Social Cognition and Cooperation. The brain is a social organ. There is a distinct social cognition network in the brain, which, when activated, makes our academic content more memorable. Here we learn how to reap the benefits of the social encoding advantage. The brain is never more engaged than when in social interaction, and never more positively engaged than when in cooperative social interaction. So, to have our students more engaged, we learn to structure positive, cooperative activities for our students. We explore three keys to structuring for successful cooperative learning.

> ▶ **Interesting Finding:** When told to memorize for a test a list of accomplishments of a person, students do not score as well on the test as when there is no mention of a test and students are told only to form an impression of the person based on their list of accomplishments. Entirely different parts of the brain are engaged under the two sets of instructions!

Emotion

4. Release the Power of Emotion. Emotion can facilitate or inhibit learning. It can turn off the ability to think and to be creative, or it can facilitate thinking, creativity, and the cementing of enduring memory for content. New research reveals the power of positive emotion to facilitate thinking and creativity. Thus we provide 37 ways any teacher with little effort can elicit positive emotion in their students. The discovery of *retrograde memory enhancement*—that anything followed by emotion is better remembered—has huge implications for teaching. Here we learn how to avoid downshifting and teach for memory by teaching with emotion.

▶ **Interesting Finding:** Following a good laugh, students have greater fluency, flexibility, and creativity of ideas. Eliciting positive emotion in any way broadens perception, increases creativity, and enhances problem solving!

Attention

5. Capture and Hold Attention. By capturing and holding attention, we radically increase retention. If the minds of our students are wandering, they have little chance of acquiring the skills and knowledge we offer. Attention yields retention. As obvious as this is, educators have failed to apply what we know about capturing and holding attention. Here we learn how to manage attention to radically improve learning.

▶ **Interesting Finding:** Mind-wandering is the default mode of the brain and occurs about 50% of the time throughout our day. Mind-wandering begins within 30 seconds of the start of a lecture, and increases in frequency as a lecture progresses!

Stimuli

6. Supply Stimuli Brains Seek. Brains seek, attend to, and retain certain kinds of information far better than other kinds. Here we learn to teach our content in ways brains are most likely to attend to and remember—to teach in the ways brains naturally seek to learn.

▶ **Interesting Finding:** Lecturers who gesture inspire more confidence among students. Teacher gestures during instruction increase performance on immediate posttests, delayed posttests, and transfer of concepts to new content! Teaching students to gesture improves their achievement!

60 Tools

For each of the six principles, after a presentation of the rationale for the principle, you will find tools to implement the principle. For example, after seeing why a threat-free environment is critical for optimal brain functioning, you will find 14 Tools to create safety, including how to provide safe forms of evaluation, and ways to ensure that every student feels included. Each of the six principles contains from 5 to 14 tools, many of

which any teacher can implement immediately with little effort. There are 60 tools in all. For each tool, look for the following icon:

Theoretical and Empirical Rationale for the Tools. The rationale for each tool is provided. The tools are all based on brain research. Some spring from theory, others have a direct empirical basis, and some have both. For example, we know from brain research that exercise increases the nutrients in the brain. This would give us a theoretical basis for advocating more exercise for students. We also have direct empirical evidence demonstrating that the more exercise students get, the better they score academically. This gives us not just a theoretical basis for advocating exercise—it gives us an empirical rationale as well. Exercise, then, is an important tool to create brain-friendly instruction.

Let's take another example: eliciting positive emotion. Theoretical support: Positive emotions release dopamine that stimulates the motivation, attention, and reward centers in the brain. On a theoretical basis alone, we would do well to elicit positive emotions in our students. Empirical support: Just prior to a math test, half of a group of students were randomly assigned to think of a positive experience. Those students assigned to the positive emotion group finished more problems and solved more problems correctly than those in whom positive emotion was not elicited. Given this and a number of other true experiments showing that eliciting positive emotion improves problem solving, creativity, and test taking, I include 37 ways to elicit positive emotion.

Experimental v. Correlational Studies. In deciding which empirical research to present, I have had a strong bias. I give little weight to correlation studies, favoring instead experimental studies. For example, there is a correlation between students having positive emotions and doing better in school. I don't present that research. From that correlation we can't tell if positive emotion causes better achievement, better achievement causes positive emotion, or some third variable causes both. I present correlation studies only rarely and only if they are consistent with the findings of theoretical and/or experimental studies.

Hundreds of Tips

Within each tool there are numerous tips to make implementation easy and successful. Tips look like this:

> ### Tip
>
> To promote performance, celebrate or praise before performance. To cement memory, celebrate or praise after performance.

For example, in Principle 3: Social, I provide the following tip: When creating teams, group students in pairs or in groups of four. Avoid groups of three. Groups of three too often become a pair and one student who is painfully isolated. Useful tips are sprinkled throughout the 60 tools. Any teacher can implement the simple tips to make a more brain-friendly class. There are hundreds of tips in all.

21 Brainiac Boxes

A fourth ingredient in this book is the inclusion of Brainiac Boxes. Would you like to know which brain structure is responsible for the experience of disgust? How activation of working memory and short-term memory light up different parts of the brain? How the four attention systems in the brain differ? For those who want to locate brain structures and functions and deepen their understanding of the brain, the book provides Brainiac Boxes—quick reference boxes that explain the brain and provide referenced research for those who would like to explore deeper. Those who would prefer to focus only on tools and tips are free to skip the Brainiac Boxes, focusing on

practical techniques to align how we teach with how brains best learn. Brainiac Boxes look like this:

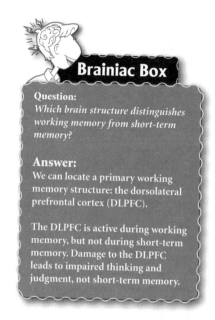

> ### Brainiac Box
>
> **Question:**
> *Which brain structure distinguishes working memory from short-term memory?*
>
> **Answer:**
> We can locate a primary working memory structure: the dorsolateral prefrontal cortex (DLPFC).
>
> The DLPFC is active during working memory, but not during short-term memory. Damage to the DLPFC leads to impaired thinking and judgment, not short-term memory.

27 Structures

The final section of the book provides 27 structures. Structures are instructional strategies you can use tomorrow as part of any lesson. Structures are step-by-step ways to structure the interaction of students with the curriculum, with each other, and with the teacher. After you have used a structure just once, you and your students become familiar with the steps of the structure and you can use it again and again as part of any lesson to align your teaching with how the brains of your students best learn.

For those of you experienced with Kagan Structures, you will find new structures like **Swap Talk**, **Traveling RallyInterview**, and **Number Group Mania!** You will deepen your understanding of what is happening in the brains of your students as you use the 27 structures. For example, new brain research reveals **Paraphrase Passport** activates the social cognition network that dramatically enhances memory. For those of you new to Kagan Structures, you will find a way of teaching that produces intense engagement and indelible learning. Structures open up a world of success and joy in both teaching and learning.

The steps of each of the 27 structures are provided in the Structures section that follows the six principles. For easy reference, throughout the book, you will find the names of the structures in bold (like this: **Celebrity Interview**) and you will find an icon with the number of the structure so you can easily locate the structure in the structure section. The structure icon looks like:

See Structures Section
3. Celebrity Interview

Why include 27 Kagan Structures in a book on brain-friendly instruction? The Kagan Structures were developed before the concept of brain-friendly instruction. They were not designed as a way to align instruction with how brains best learn. Nevertheless, Kagan Structures are among the most powerful tools we have for implementing each of the six principles of brain-friendly instruction:

Nourishment: Kagan Structures integrate frequent movement into daily instruction, increasing the supply of nutrients to the brain. Movement is part of the reason students feel energized by the structures.

Safety: Kagan Structures include positive interdependence—students are on the same side, encouraging, tutoring, and praising each other. They feel included as part of a team. All of this creates a threat-free, safe social network quite in contrast to the isolation and competition common in most traditional classrooms. With threat reduced, the prefrontal cortex is freer to think and learn.

Social: The brain is never more engaged than during social interaction, and the Kagan Cooperative Learning Structures all involve cooperative social interaction. The structures release the power of the social encoding advantage.

Emotion: Kagan Structures include encouragement, praise, challenges, and celebrations that elicit positive emotion. The positive emotion makes content more memorable and opens brains to be more perceptive, thoughtful, and creative.

Attention: Brains do not process or retain that to which they do not attend. Heightened attention leads to increased memory of content. The Kagan Structures focus attention. There is no opportunity for students' minds to wander as they interact over the content. The Kagan Structures keep each student accountable for responding on a very frequent basis, in contrast to the call-on-one-at-a-time traditional approach that allows for the minds of many to wander. Attention yields retention.

Stimuli: Brains seek both novelty and predictability. This creates a dilemma for traditional teachers—should I emphasize procedures and routines, sacrificing novelty, or should I abandon procedures and routines, for the sake of novelty? The Kagan Structures are a unique solution to this dilemma. The structures are routines, satisfying the brain's need for a predictable world, but within the structures are plenty of novel stimuli as students interact. Further, using a variety of structures creates novelty as they provide different ways to interact—with partners, teammates, and classmates.

Attention yields retention and Kagan Structures focus attention.

When teachers use Kagan Structures, they align how they teach with how brains best learn. Because Kagan Structures are so flexible and repeatable, they are empowering. Once you know one structure, you can use it to generate an infinite number of activities for your class—just plug in your own content.

What Is Not Included?
The Memory Systems

There is a very important, large area of brain research with direct implications for brain-friendly instruction that is not included in this book: The research on the memory systems. We now know that very different parts of the brain process different types of memories. For example, when we learn a new procedure (the steps of long division) we are acquiring a procedural memory. In contrast, when we memorize something (7 x 6 = 42), we are acquiring a semantic memory and a very different part of the brain is involved. Further, we know that certain instructional strategies are efficient for acquiring procedural memories whereas different instructional strategies are efficient for acquiring semantic memories.

Brain-Friendly Teaching • Dr. Spencer Kagan
Kagan Publishing • 800.933.2667 • www.KaganOnline.com

There are distinct memory systems, each most efficiently addressed with very different instructional strategies. The implications of this for educators are tremendous. We greatly improve efficiency in teaching and learning if at any moment we know which kind of memory we wish to create, and which instructional strategies will best accomplish that. This area of brain-friendly instruction is so important and so large, I have decided to address it in a second book: *Memorable Teaching: Engaging the Brain's Memory Systems.*

How to Use this Book

This book will be read and used differently by each educator. For example, I provide the details of what happens in the social cognition network of the brain when, preceding an encounter, a host greets a guest with a handshake and a smile. The research is clear: A handshake and a smile signal the brain to "approach," making class more attractive, and learning more likely. Some educators may want to read the brain research on the power of handshakes, and perhaps even follow up by reading the referenced articles that explain that research in depth. Others may want to simply read and apply the tip: *Greet students with a handshake and a smile.* Others yet might feel that greeting students with a handshake is not for them. Not all tools or tips will be useful to all teachers. The book is designed to be useful to you whether you want to learn more about the brain, whether you are simply looking for practical ways to make teaching and learning more successful and enjoyable, or both. It is up to each educator to pick and choose. I am certain, however, you will find many easy-to-use strategies that will make your classroom more brain-friendly.

In part, the book is written in the spirit of a cookbook. Included are many delightful recipes for making teaching more brain-friendly. Cookbooks, however, are not read cover-to-cover. We turn to them again and again as we seek new recipes or as we want to be reminded of old favorites. You will not want to try all the recipes included here, but I am certain you will find many that will delight you and your students.

Some educators when reviewing the research will go wherever the evidence leads. Others for a variety of reasons might balk at instituting some or even many of the brain-friendly tools. The book includes many brain-based strategies that are simple for any teacher to apply. The book also includes strategies that are not yet common practice among educators (including a prework cheer, encouraging students to drink water frequently, engaging social cognition while presenting curriculum…). Admittedly, many teachers will find some of the strategies too "way out," even if those strategies are supported by theoretical and empirical data, and rooted in solid brain science: *"My job is to teach geometry; not meditation!"* In creating this book, my job has been to evaluate the theory and research, present the best of it, and then provide tools and tips to implement the principles that spring from brain research. No teacher could possibly implement all the tools and tips presented here. What each of you does with the research, which tools, tips, and structures you choose to add to your pedagogical toolbox, is up to you.

My Recommendation

Pick tools and structures that fit your style and that of your students. Experiment with them. When you find success, make those tools and structures part of your instructional repertoire. You can, and should, start slow. Adopt and experiment with just one tool or structure. Make it your own. See the benefits. Having expanded your instructional repertoire, come back to this resource to find another tool, tip, or structure to try.

My Hope

My hope is that each of you will draw from this set of brain-friendly strategies in your own unique way, creating your own unique approach to brain-friendly teaching and learning.

Acknowledgments and Dedication

This book has been made possible by the efforts of many people. I am extremely grateful.

Miguel Kagan contributed in many ways, including cover design, formative suggestions to reorganize and to cut sections, suggestions to include a number of elements that have strengthened the book, including the links between Kagan Structures and the six principles, and design of the chapter mind-maps. By creating the chapter mind-maps, Miguel has made this book on brain-friendly instruction a bit more brain friendly! In addition, Miguel made innumerable editing suggestions that have increased readability and accuracy.

Alex Core was primarily responsible for page design, design of tables and graphics, and selection and placement of art. His skills elevated the book from a dry manuscript to a lively, brain-friendly book. His patience in dealing with input from Miguel, Me, and Becky has made the process a dream.

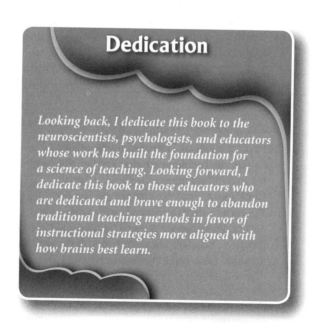

Becky Herrington has overseen every aspect of the book production. She has been my cheerleader as well as an invaluable guide and critic. She never trades expedience for excellence and the book has benefited greatly from her constant questioning if something could be done better.

Catherine Shaheen, my executive assistant became my research assistant during the writing of this book. The thousand plus references cited in the book are only a portion of the studies Catherine uncovered for my research. Catherine tirelessly set off each day to search the archives for studies I requested in brain-science, psychology, and education, meticulously cataloging and storing them for back reference. In addition, she read and edited large portions of the book, making many useful suggestions.

Erin Kant did the delightful original artwork for the book. Her work allows the book to speak to the right hemisphere—a basic tool in brain-friendly teaching!

Dean Doug Mitchell of the School of Education, University of California, Riverside graciously opened up for me the UC library system, making the work possible.

Many teachers have contributed directly and indirectly—too many to name here. I am especially appreciative of those who responded to my call to submit statements about how they have applied brain-friendly teaching principles in their own classrooms. You will find their names throughout the book.

I want to thank also Ginny Harvey who edited the book. Thanks go as well to Cristina Haley who did the indexing. Their contributions have made the book more readable, accurate, and user-friendly.

My wife, Laurie Kagan, in an important way has made the book possible. She is the one who suggested I take time from consulting and office management as well as from our time together, to write the book. Her patience, understanding, and support throughout has been unwavering.

Lastly, I want to express my appreciation and debt to the thousands of researchers whose work has made this book possible. I have cited over 1,000 research studies, but all of those studies stand on the shoulders of 1,000s of other researchers, so the debt is immeasurable. Through their combined work, we can now say with certainty: Our students will learn more, and like learning, others, and themselves more, when we align how we teach with brain science.

Thank you.

Dedication

Looking back, I dedicate this book to the neuroscientists, psychologists, and educators whose work has built the foundation for a science of teaching. Looking forward, I dedicate this book to those educators who are dedicated and brave enough to abandon traditional teaching methods in favor of instructional strategies more aligned with how brains best learn.

Brain-Friendly Teaching • Dr. Spencer Kagan
Kagan Publishing • 800.933.2667 • www.KaganOnline.com

Where to Find It

Brainiac Box Questions

Principle	Question	Page #
Principle 1	How does missing a meal impact on brain chemistry and behavior?	1.16
Principle 2	How does exercise reduce stress?	2.20
Principle 2	How does a good laugh change brain chemistry?	2.22
Principle 3	Which parts of the brain go into action when we try to figure out what someone else is thinking?	3.5
Principle 3	Where in the brain is social pain processed? Where is the dACC? What happens if we remove the dACC?	3.13
Principle 3	What is the role of the amygdalae in evaluating social stimuli?	3.15
Principle 4	Why do we love music?	4.30
Principle 4	Why do we feel good after a massage?	4.37
Principle 4	When do testosterone and cortisol levels raise and fall?	4.43
Principle 5	What is the Cortical Homunculus?	5.5
Principle 5	How does playing a virtual reality game reduce the experience of pain?	5.7
Principle 5	Which brain structure distinguishes working memory from short-term memory?	5.26
Principle 5	Why do we have such a limited capacity for short-term memory?	5.27
Principle 5	What happens in the brain during mind-wandering?	5.33
Principle 5	What does IQ measure? Where are these four intelligence factors located in the brain?	5.68
Principle 5	Which structures in the brain are engaged by short-term v. working memory?	5.69
Principle 6	What structures in the brain responds to novel stimuli?	6.5
Principle 6	How does the hippocampus respond differently to unexpected and predictable events?	6.7
Principle 6	How does the brain compensate for saccades, which give us a new picture of the world three times a second?	6.14
Principle 6	Where is the ability to deal with color located in the brain?	6.88
Principle 6	Where in the brain do visual and auditory learners process information?	6.89
Principle 6	When we look at a large L made up of small D's, which parts of the brain process the big L and which parts process the small D's?	6.92

Brain-Friendly Teaching Tools

Principle	Tool	Page #
Principle 1	**Tool 1:** Encourage Exercise	1.6
	Tool 2: Promote Play	1.12
	Tool 3: Improve Diet	1.16
	Tool 4: Supply Hydration	1.22
	Tool 5: Train Proper Breathing	1.24
	Tool 6: Teach with Movement Structures	1.27
Principle 2	**Tool 1:** Construct a Safe Context for Learning	2.12
	Tool 2: Celebrate Diversity	2.14
	Tool 3: Offer Safe Evaluations	2.14
	Tool 4: Build Inclusive Teams	2.15
	Tool 5: Form Inclusive Classrooms	2.16
	Tool 6: Play Background Music	2.19
	Tool 7: Encourage Exercise	2.20
	Tool 8: Promote Play	2.20
	Tool 9: Incorporate Humor	2.22
	Tool 10: Provide Hydration	2.25
	Tool 11: Foster Positive Social Interaction	2.25
	Tool 12: Teach Relaxation Breathing	2.28
	Tool 13: Practice Progressive Muscle Relaxation	2.28
	Tool 14: Advocate Meditation	2.31
Principle 3	**Tool 1:** Activate Social Cognition	3.21
	Tool 2: Include Classbuilding	3.24
	Tool 3: Structure Cooperative Interaction	3.26
	Tool 4: Teach Social Skills	3.36
	Tool 5: Promote Cooperative Play	3.39
Principle 4	**Tool 1:** Teach with Passion	4.6
	Tool 2: Elicit Passion	4.6
	Tool 3: Link Emotion to Content	4.7
	Tool 4: Provide Praise	4.15
	Tool 5: Celebrate Success	4.18
	Tool 6: Elicit Positive Emotion	4.19
	Tool 7: Promote Play	4.45

Brain-Friendly Teaching • Dr. Spencer Kagan
Kagan Publishing • 800.933.2667 • www.KaganOnline.com

Brain-Friendly Teaching Tools

Silly Sports & Goofy Games

Brain-Friendly Blackline Masters

Brain-Friendly Teaching • Dr. Spencer Kagan
Kagan Publishing • 800.933.2667 • www.KaganOnline.com

Structures at a Glance

Table *of* Contents

Principle 1 : Nourishment

Brain-Friendly Teaching • Dr. Spencer Kagan
Kagan Publishing • 800.933.2667 • www.KaganOnline.com

Principle 2: Safety

Table of Contents

Principle 3: Social

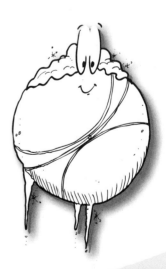

Table of Contents

Principle 4: Emotion

Brain-Friendly Teaching • Dr. Spencer Kagan
Kagan Publishing • 800.933.2667 • www.KaganOnline.com

Principle 5: Attention

Table of Contents

Table of Contents

Principle 6: Stimuli

Table of Contents

Table of Contents

Structures

Nourishment

To function optimally, brains are dependent on a constant, plentiful supply of nutrients. The question for us as educators becomes, what can we do to optimally nourish the brains of our students? It turns out, we have six powerful tools available to ensure the brains of our students are primed to function at their best.

1 Encourage
Exercise

2 Promote
Play

6 Teach with
Movement
Structures

Principle 1
Nourishment

3 Improve
Diet

5 Train Proper
Breathing

4 Supply
Hydration

Principle 1
Nourish the Brain

It's almost self-evident that a well-nourished brain is better able to attend to, process, retain, and recall new learning. What is not as self-evident is why brains are so incredibly dependent on a constant supply of nutrients, and the ways in which we as teachers can ensure the brains of our students are well nourished. Here we first examine how the structure of the brain makes nourishment the first principle of brain-friendly teaching, and then we explore six powerful tools we can use to better nourish the brains of our students.

Why Does the Brain Need Constant Nourishment?

The brain weighs about three pounds. That's a little over 2% of average body weight, yet among adults it consumes about 20% of the all the calories consumed. When learning a new skill, the brain consumes far more energy than when exercising a practiced skill. For example, after 4 to 8 weeks of practice of the visual/spatial computer game Tetris, there is a seven-fold increase in performance, but the brain consumes far less energy while playing.[1] This finding—practice leads to efficiency and lower energy consumption—is a general principle. It holds true as well for performance on logic tests,[2] verbal fluency,[3] and memory tests.[4] As brains master skills, they don't work harder, they work more efficiently, actually consuming less energy. Consistent with this finding: Babies are constantly learning new skills and the brains of babies consume about 65% of all the calories babies consume![5]

The brain receives more than its share of blood flow in the body (about 15% of all cardiac output), but it consumes an even greater share of the nutrients in the body (up to a full 25% of the oxygen)! Almost all of the oxygen consumed by the brain (94%) is consumed by the grey matter, where sensing and learning takes place. The higher the brain function, the more oxygen that portion of the brain consumes. For example, the midbrain and cerebellum consume far less than the cerebral cortex.

6 Tools to Nourish the Brain

1. **Encourage Exercise** 1.6
2. **Promote Play** 1.12
3. **Improve Diet** 1.16
4. **Supply Hydration** 1.22
5. **Train Proper Breathing** 1.24
6. **Teach with Movement Structures** 1.27

The brain is so dependent on a constant supply of oxygen and glucose, if we fully cut off the supply for but a few minutes, brain functioning deteriorates rapidly. After about 5 minutes without nutrients, neurons begin to die. Within minutes without oxygen, a person experiences drowsiness, apathy, and impaired judgment. Focused learning becomes impossible. These are symptoms commonly experienced when a person who lives at sea level travels to high altitudes where the oxygen supply is decreased. Clearly, if we want our students to be alert and exercise good judgment, we want their brains to have a constant, plentiful supply of nutrients, especially oxygen.

Connections Consume Energy. How can 2% of body weight consume up to 25% of the oxygen? Why is our brain so dependent on a constant, very large flow of oxygen? Why is the brain so hungry? The answer lies in brain structure. It is not what goes on *inside of* neurons that consume most of the energy—that's only about 20%. It is what goes on *among* neurons that burn most of the energy. About 80% of the energy consumed by the brain is consumed as neurons interact! Every neuron in the brain is connected to every other neuron in the brain within several synapses! Communication among neurons is what creates intelligence. Neurons in the brain have an average of about 2,000 connections each—some have up to 10,000 dendrite connections! Each neuron fires on the average 100 times a second! And there are almost 100 billion neurons in the human brain. Imagine 100 billion neurons, each with an average of 2,000 connections, and each firing an average of 100 times a second. It takes a huge amount of fuel to run all that activity!

100 Billion Networked Computers! The 100 billion neurons in the brain do not fire as a simple result of how many inputs they receive. It is far more complex than that. Each neuron has feedback loops; they pass along the neural message in part as a function of what has happened in the past. Each neuron weighs new inputs against what has happened in the past in that configuration. Neurons fire or fail to fire depending on the feedback they have received in the past. If firing produced no difference in the past, neurons don't fire again in the same configuration. We are actually talking about 100 billion networked computers! The brain is the most complex entity in the known universe.

Glial Cells Contribute to Intelligence. The plethora of neurons and their many interconnections is only part of the story. For each of the 100 billion neurons, there are an average of 10 glial cells. Glial cells have various functions including support, repair, nourishment, and protection of neurons. In addition, they lay down myelin, allowing neurons to fire more efficiently. New research shows the trillion glial cells actually learn; they modulate the firing of neurons, contributing to intelligence.[6]

Computer Simulations. IBM built Compass, a supercomputer-based program to simulate roughly 10 billion neurons—10% of a human brain.[7] To run Compass requires several megawatts of power compared to only 20 watts used by a real brain. Compass runs 1,500 times slower than an actual brain. To run at the speed of an actual brain, Compass would need the amount of electrical power it takes to run both San Francisco and New York! Even at the enormous efficiency of a human brain, the brain consumes an inordinate proportion of the body's nutrients, and a poorly nourished brain functions poorly.

The dendrite connections are electrical circuits, making the brain digital: On/Off. The thousands of receptors on the cell walls of each neuron are chemical, making the brain analog: The brain responds to degrees of chemical stimulation, not just on/off electrical stimulation!

Brains Are Analog and Digital! So far, we are talking about the brain as if it were only a very elaborate electrical switchboard. But the brain is far more complex than that. Whether or not a neuron fires depends not only on the electrical input coming in, but also it depends, to a tremendous degree, on the chemical make up of the brain at a given time. There are receptors on the cell walls of neurons that respond to neurotransmitters, steroids, and peptides. Each receptor is a single, very large, complex amino acid chain molecule—some approach 3,000 times the size of a water molecule. More than seventy types of receptors have been identified to date and more are yet to be discovered. Each receptor responds to only one type of molecule. For example, some receptors respond to opiates (endorphins, morphine, and heroine, which dampen pain and make us feel euphoric), others respond to stress peptides (like cortisol, which makes us feel stressed and anxious). A neuron may have millions of receptors on its surface, different numbers of different types—perhaps 10,000 of one type of receptor and 100,000 of another. Thus a particular neuron may be quite sensitive to one type of molecule, but relatively insensitive to another. And neurons fire depending on how many and which of these receptors are stimulated!

The brain is so complex, that if it were simple enough for us to comprehend, we couldn't!

Just as our eyes and ears sense different types of stimuli in the external world, through the receptors on their cell walls, neurons sense different types of stimuli in the internal world of our bodies—neurochemical stimuli. Our brains are constantly bathed in these neurochemicals and each neuron is responding to the degree of their presence or absence! Candace Pert aptly calls these neurochemicals, *"Molecules of Emotion."*[8] From moment-to-moment in the classroom, we are changing the chemical composition of brains, releasing more stress peptides by giving embarrassing public feedback or releasing more endorphins by having students do a supportive teambuilding activity.

To function optimally, this unimaginably complex organ is dependent on a constant, plentiful supply of nutrients.

Thus we can derive the first principle of brain-friendly learning:

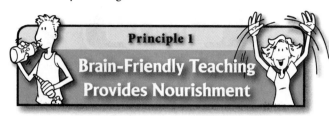

Principle 1

Brain-Friendly Teaching Provides Nourishment

Therefore, the question for us as educators becomes: *What can we do to nourish the brains of our students?* We have available six powerful tools to ensure the brains of our students are primed to function at their best.

Six Tools to Nourish the Brain

Brains function better when well nourished. We have the power to better nourish the brains of our students by using simple tools in our schools and in our classrooms. It is now beyond question that students who exercise regularly have better nourished brains and higher achievement. Simple tag games get heart and lungs pumping faster, nourishing the brain. We can teach students a habit of diaphragmatic breathing so their brains are better nourished for a lifetime. Within a few minutes of drinking water, there is a measurable increase in oxygen in the brain and cells are better able to make connections—to learn! Our schools need to be vigilant about what is in the cafeteria and in the vending machines; we can place students on a roller coaster of ups and downs, inhibiting learning, or we can put them on a steady course for thinking and learning by the snacks and meals we encourage and provide. Kagan Structures make movement an integral part of every lesson; better nourishing brains. Let's explore these six tools:

Six Tools to Nourish the Brain

1. Encourage Exercise
2. Promote Play
3. Improve Diet
4. Supply Hydration
5. Train Proper Breathing
6. Teach with Movement Structures

Tool 1

Encourage Exercise

Regular aerobic exercise improves brain functioning in a number of ways. It has been known for a long time that blood flow to the brain increases during exercise.[9] But regular aerobic exercise impacts the brain in a far more important way. The influence goes beyond the moment of exercise. Regular aerobic exercise actually promotes the development of new blood pathways in the brain. This vascular development ensures a more ample ongoing supply of nutrients to the brain, even during rest.[10] Regular exercise increases blood flow as we age, and decreases cognitive decline.[11] Further, in humans and other animals, exercise increases the supply of brain-derived neurotrophic factor (BDNF) and insulin growth factors that increase the growth of new neurons (neurogenesis), and the number of synaptic connections in the hypothalamus—the center for learning and memory.[12]

Exercise Improves Brain Growth and Brain Function

In perhaps the most comprehensive review of the effect of exercise on the brain, researchers concluded that exercise promoted brain growth and brain function in many ways, including the stimulation of new neural connections and growth of new neurons in the hippocampus, the structure critical for learning and memory. They concluded,

> Human and animal studies indicate that exercise targets many aspects of brain function and has broad effects on overall brain health, resilience, learning and memory, and depression, particularly in elderly populations. Exercise sets into motion an interactive cascade of growth factors that has the net effect of stimulating plasticity, enhancing cognitive function, attenuating the mechanisms driving depression, stimulating neurogenesis, and improving cerebrovascular perfusion.[13]

Intense Exercise Boosts Learning.

Experimenters contrasted the effects of two types of exercise and a control condition of learning of new vocabulary words.[14] To ensure the vocabulary words were new to all students, the experimenters presented a picture of a familiar object with a new name, a pseudo-word. For example, a picture of a bike was paired with the word "glump." The male students (aged 19 to 27) were assigned to each of three conditions: High-impact anaerobic sprints, low-impact aerobic running, or rest. The low-impact consisted of 40 minutes of running at a fixed target heart rate based on physical fitness (mean heart rate 140 beats per minute). The high-impact condition consisted of two sprints of 3 minutes each separated by a 2-minute break (mean heart rate 184 beats per minute). Each sprint began at 8 km/h and increased by 2 km/h every 10 seconds until exhaustion. To test for retention of learning, subjects were tested immediately after the three conditions, at 1 week and at 8 months. To test for transfer, subjects were tested on their ability to pair the new pseudo-word with the actual word for that object.

> **Tip**
> Incorporate intense brief exercise into every student's school day. Two 3-minute exhausting sprints improve brain function!

Results: The most important result of the study is the value of intense exercise. After just two sprints of less than 3-minutes each, subjects learned 20% faster compared to moderate exercise or being sedentary. Moderate exercise did not increase learning speed or retention compared to being sedentary. This finding is quite remarkable because the moderate exercise lasted 40 minutes compared to just two sprints of less than 3-minutes each!

The superiority of intense exercise paralleled changes in neurotransmitters. Epinephrine and norepinephrine were greater following intense sprints than the other two conditions, which did not differ significantly. Epinephrine concentration following intense sprints correlated with both 1-week and 8-month retention. Those who showed the greatest increases in epinephrine following exercise showed the greatest 1-week and 8-month retention. Dopamine concentrations during learning were correlated with both immediate learning and 1-week retention. Brain-derived neurotrophic factor (BDNF), associated with brain growth and development, was significantly greater for the intense sprints than the relaxed condition, and those who sustained the highest BDNF levels after intense exercise showed the greatest immediate learning success. Ratings of mood were highest after intense exercise and were correlated with learning success.

Exercise Improves Academic Achievement.

Simple experiments prove the power of a bout of exercise. John J. Ratey, MD randomly divided students into two groups before taking a standardized reading test. One group sat for 20 minutes before the test. The other group took a power walk for 20 minutes. The group that took the power walk scored a full grade higher on the reading test![15] Brain scans revealed that students who took the power walk had far more brain activity. An earlier, somewhat similar study looked at the performance of twins aged 11–14, immediately following either aerobic exercise or nonexercise. When tested on a computerized design-matching task, those assigned to a 25-minute treadmill run did significantly better than their twin sibling. Aerobic exercise did better than standard physical education exercise, but both groups were significantly better in both speed and accuracy compared to the control group.[16]

Exercise Increases Focus.
In a study directly linking exercise to brain function and academic achievement, 9-year-old boys and girls were tested after 20 minutes of intense walking on a treadmill v. 20 minutes of resting. Students were outfitted with a cap to measure electroencephalographic (EEG) activity while they did discrimination tasks to measure "attentional resource allocation." That is, the test measured ability not to be distracted by irrelevant stimuli. The research found:

> Following acute bouts of walking, children had a larger P3 amplitude, suggesting that they are better able to allocate attentional resources, and this effect is greater in the more difficult conditions…

To measure the relation of exercises to academic performance, the researchers administered tests of reading, spelling, and math. The students were tested on reading first, and that showed the largest positive outcome:

> The effect was largest in reading comprehension. If you go by the guidelines set forth by the Wide Range Achievement Test, the increase in reading comprehension following exercise equated to approximately a full grade level.[17]

Some reviews conclude the positive correlation of general amount of physical exercise and academic achievement is relatively weak.[18] While some studies have found either no correlation or a very weak correlation,[19] other large-scale studies have shown a large correlation.[20] Across all studies and reviews, the relationship of exercise to cognitive skills is quite robust.

Fitness Correlates with Achievement.
In one of the most extensive and intensive studies of the relation of physical activity to scholastic ability, a nationally representative sample of 7,961 Australian schoolchildren aged 7–15 years were rated on scholastic ability on a five-point scale.[21] The children were intensively studied using measures of amount of physical activity in and out of school, as well as the following tests of physical fitness:

▶ Large muscle power: standing long jump
▶ Large muscle force and endurance: sit-up and push-up challenges
▶ Small muscle power: right and left hand grip force (dynamometry)
▶ Joint mobility: sit and reach
▶ Lung function: Vitalograph single-breath wedge spirometer
▶ Physical work capacity: Monark cycle ergometer

The results demonstrate consistent correlations of scholastic ability with amount and type of physical activity. Students were rated on the amount of time and intensity they engaged in walking, cycling, and played sports. Further, they were rated on what they did during morning recess (sit, talk with friends, walk, run, play a sport). Children who were less active physically performed significantly lower academically.

The data strongly supports the conclusion: Academic performance is related to amount of physical fitness. Physical Fitness = Mental Fitness!

Various measures of physical fitness and capacity were also related to academic performance. Consistent relations were found with muscular force, endurance, and power. For example, students with higher scholastic ratings ran the 50-meter run faster, completed more sit-ups, and leapt greater distances in the standing long jump. The relation of scholastic ability with joint mobility was weaker. The measures of force and power were generally stronger than the measures of cardio-respiratory endurance. Perhaps most impressive is the strong, consistent relation of muscular force and endurance to academic performance for both boys and girls as measured by the number of sit-ups a student could do when challenged. See Box: Sit-Ups Correlate with Academic Achievement.

Exercise During Academics Boosts Achievement. In an extremely creative study, pediatric residents Kathryn King and Carly Scahill examined the impact of having students learn academic concepts *while* exercising:[22]

▶ First- and second-grade students moved through stations to learn academic skills while moving. For example, they traced shapes on the ground while sitting on scooters and hopped through ladders while naming colors on each rung.

▶ Third- through sixth-grade students used exercise equipment designed to teach. For example, they ran a treadmill that had a monitor that played geography lessons as the student ran through the scene. Their rock-climbing wall had numbered pegs so students worked on math skills as they climbed. Even though students took time out of regular classrooms for these exercise/academic activities, the activities resulted in improved academic achievement: The percentage of students reaching their goal on the state tests increased from 55% before the program was initiated to 68.5% after the program was initiated.

"The CDE (California Department of Education) correlated scores from standard achievement tests with scores from the FitnessGram, the state-mandated physical assessment, for more than one million students…In 2001 fit kids scored twice as well on academic tests as their unfit peers."[23]
—*John J. Ratey, MD*

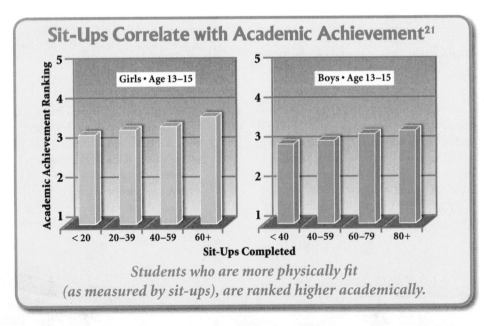

Sit-Ups Correlate with Academic Achievement[21]

Girls • Age 13–15

Boys • Age 13–15

Academic Achievement Ranking

Sit-Ups Completed

Girls: < 20, 20–39, 40–59, 60+
Boys: < 40, 40–59, 60–79, 80+

Students who are more physically fit (as measured by sit-ups), are ranked higher academically.

Exercise Immediately Prior to Academics Increases Achievement. Naperville Central High School in Naperville, Illinois, emphasizes getting the heartbeat of students elevated prior to academics, and taking frequent exercise breaks within academic classes. After about 20 minutes of academic work, students take a very brief bout of physical activity. Naperville reports dramatic academic achievement gains, and attributes the gains primarily to the physical activity. Their data, however, is difficult to interpret because those students who self-select for the program, are lower-achieving students at the outset of the program, and the program includes homework monitoring, small class sizes, one-on-one attention. Thus the results are best interpreted as the consequence of a package of interventions, rather than the outcome of exercise alone. Nevertheless, the package is producing very impressive data year after year.[24]

> *"When we run, we get more done!"*
> —*Student Quote*

Exercise After School Accelerates Achievement. Studies show increased activation of the prefrontal cortex following exercise as well as increased academic achievement. The greater the amount of exercise, the greater the executive function in the brain and the higher the achievement.[25] The students who exercised for 40 minutes a day after school showed math achievement gains about twice those who exercised 20 minutes a day after school. Those who exercised 20 minutes a day after school showed gains about twice those who did not exercise after school. The exercise consisted of tag and other active games designed by the researchers. This "staircasing" paralleled increases in executive function, and demonstrates an extremely strong causal relationship. See Box: Exercise Boosts Executive Function and Math Achievement.

Tip
Exercise during academics—have students walk as they study their vocabulary words.

Exercise Boosts Executive Function and Math Achievement[25]

Students who exercise more minutes per day have improved executive function and math achievement.

Exercise Improves Cognitive Functioning, IQ. Many research studies demonstrate exercise improves cognitive functioning and learning in children and adults.[26] A review of the literature supports the conclusion that both aerobic and resistance training are important for maintaining cognitive and brain health.[27] Regular exercise improves academic achievement,[28] intellectual performance, concentration, and memory,[29] self-esteem,[30] creativity,[31] as well as classroom behavior.[32] Highly fit children and adults have faster reaction times and superior neuroelectric indices of attention and working memory, as well as cognitive processing speed.[33] A meta-analysis of 44 studies yielding 125 comparisons concluded physical activity improves cognition in children (overall effect size = .32).[34] The analysis revealed positive effects for resistance training, motor skills training, aerobic training, and physical education. Type of training did not make a difference. Positive impact was found for perceptual skills, IQ, academic achievement, math, and verbal tasks. The positive impact was greater on math than verbal measures, and was greater yet for overall achievement and IQ.

For exercises to develop cardio fitness and strength during class, see Blackline: Exercises Within the Classroom, p. 1.10.

Display this page for students when calling for exercises within the classroom.

Exercises Within the Classroom
Exercises that Require No Equipment and Little Space

Cardio/Aerobic

Jumping Jacks

High Knee Jog in Place

Sprint in Place

Mountain Climbers

Strength

Squats

Sit-Ups

Push-Ups

Chair Dips

Brain-Friendly Teaching • Dr. Spencer Kagan
Kagan Publishing • 800.933.2667 • www.KaganOnline.com

Exercise Slows Cognitive Decline. Leisure-time physical activity at midlife at least twice a week is associated with a reduced risk of dementia and Alzheimer's disease.[35] A 2-year follow-up of elderly persons enrolled in programs of moderate activity (less than three times a week) or high activity (more than three times a week) decreased the rate of dementia and cognitive impairment compared to controls.[36] Not all exercise is equal. Previously sedentary adults, 60–70 years of age were assigned to either aerobic exercise (walking) or anaerobic exercise (stretching and toning). Those who engaged in aerobic exercise improved significantly in three measures of executive function associated with the integrity of the prefrontal and frontal cortex. Those who engaged in the toning condition did not.[37]

Exercise Anytime

In examining the data, it appears that exercise before, during, or after academics is beneficial. Contrary to the assertions of some, timing does not appear to be the critical variable. Contrary to the assertions of others, type of exercise (aerobic v. strength and resistance training) is not a critical variable. Rather, it appears that the frequency and duration of exercise is what leads to academic gains. This interpretation is consistent with the greater vascular development of the brain associated with exercise. Exercise produces vascular development of the brain that results in an ongoing better supply of nutrients to the brain, so brains are better able to learn. Clearly, more controlled research is needed to examine timing, type, and duration of exercise optimum to improve fitness and cognitive functions, but the existing research is sufficient to conclude that fitness programs should be mandatory in all schools. We need to abandon the narrow emphasis on academic achievement as an outcome of schooling. The positive consequence would include better academic achievement, enormous savings in health care costs, and a happier and healthier nation.

The data is clear: Fitness programs should be mandatory in all schools.

Encourage Exercise

Exercise boosts cognitive development and academic achievement. Research reveals positive outcomes of treadmill running and jogging, and improved brain functioning following very brief, highly exhausting sprints. Further, those students with greater strength and endurance perform better academically. Further research will reveal exactly which types of exercise programs most efficiently build brain capacity and achievement, but at this point, there can be little doubt that we would serve our students well by encouraging more exercise. Some possibilities:

- ▶ Elementary school teachers can take their students out for a run or jog.
- ▶ Schools can invest in treadmills and heart monitors.
- ▶ Teachers can challenge their students to beat their personal best records for sit-ups and pull-ups as well as speed on 50- and 100-meter dashes.
- ▶ Classes can chart the distance they run during PE, and attempt to beat their class record.
- ▶ Students can create exercise logs to record and celebrate after-school and before-school exercise.
- ▶ Teachers can include exercise breaks during lessons, calling for students to jog in place or do jumping jacks or mountain climbers.
- ▶ PE programs can transition from sports oriented to exercise oriented programs. (During a baseball game, students sit on the bench half the time, and even when in the field, only the pitcher and catcher get regular exercise.)

Administrator Tip

Evaluate schools not just on academics, but also on the physical fitness of their students.

Tool 2

Promote Play

For many teachers, the word "play" has negative connotations. We want students to be serious—to focus on their learning. Not to "play around." While I would be among the last to argue against serious, focused learning, one goal of this book is to have us reexamine our attitude toward play. *Play is a powerful tool in creating a brain-friendly classroom, and in promoting learning*. In fact, play is the only tool that helps us implement all six of the principles of brain-friendly teaching. Here in Principle 1: Nourishment, we examine the role of play in nourishing the brain. When we turn to Principle 2: Safety, we examine how play changes brain chemistry in ways that free the prefrontal cortex for thinking and learning. In Principle 3: Social, we analyze how play allows students to meet a fundamental need and to explore the curriculum in ways that are brain friendly. In Principle 4: Emotion, we discover that play creates a positive emotional tone in the classroom promoting memory for content, and that brains of all animals are hard wired for play. Play, as we will see in Principle 5: Attention, helps focuses the attention of our students. Finally, in Principle 6: Stimuli, we overview evidence that brains naturally seek play to promote creativity, and even survival. Further, play provides novelty, so the brains of our students become more alert. For now, let's limit ourselves to looking at how play nourishes the brain.

Tag Games Nourish the Brain

We can avoid sedentary recess time and ensure aerobic exercise for all students easily, and in a way students say is fun. All we need to do is have the students learn and play the thirty tag games from *Silly Sports & Goofy Games*.[38] The games are simple and can be student directed, without adult supervision. While playing these tag games, students are in constant motion: At every

moment, they are attempting to tag others while avoiding getting tagged.

One of my favorite tag games is **Everyone's IT!** Rather than having just one person "IT," the game starts with all students "IT." If an "IT" tags someone, that person is frozen. When everyone but the last person is frozen, there is applause and students can play another round. Another favorite that promotes both movement and deep breathing is **Hum Tag**. Students are in triads and take a deep breath, humming together. Why? If they run out of breath they are fair game for the ITs to tag them. See Blackline: Hum Tag, p. 1.13.

While playing these simple tag games, students' heart rate and volume as well as breathing rate and volume increase dramatically. They are not only pumping more blood to the brain, the blood that is being sent to the brain is more fully oxygenated. For students who are old enough to read, it is sufficient to simply copy a new tag game from the *Silly Sports & Goofy Games* book and hand the description to the students before they go to recess. Challenge your class to play the game and to report on the results. The tag games are simple to learn and play, but work well to pump nourishment to the brain.

Having students play tag at recess is not a substitute for a well-designed exercise program. No existing research demonstrates that increased executive function or increased academic achievement result from having students play Silly Sports and Goofy Games. Nevertheless, there is no question that students playing the tag games get aerobic exercise. They are out of breath, with hearts beating fast. All of the Silly Sports and Goofy Games energize students, whether or not they involve aerobic exercise. Teachers who include the games in their classrooms, as well as Kagan trainers who include the games in their workshops, all can testify the games energize participants. Following these brief games, many of which take less than 5 minutes, students and workshop participants return to work with more focused, alert attention. This, of course, occurs for reasons in addition to the brief experience of pumping more nourishment to the brain. There has been a state change, novelty, humor, fun, and a release of tensions—all of which contribute to

hum tag

A safe port in a storm is two others to hold hands with and hum!

1 Form Triads
All players get into groups of three.

2 Select ITs
The leader breaks up some of the groups of three to become ITs, so there is about one IT for each two groups of three. At all times ITs hold one hand above their head so everyone knows who they are.

3 Want Safety? Hold Hands and Hum!
Players are safe from the ITs if they are in a circle of three, all holding hands and humming. Want safety? Find two others who are not IT, hold hands in a circle, take a deep breath, and begin humming. You are safe, but only until someone runs out of air.

4 Run Out of Air? Break and Run!
When anyone in a group of three runs out of air, everyone must break apart and dash to find two new partners. IT can tag anyone who is not in a group of three and humming.

5 Tagged? Become an IT
If you are tagged by an IT, you become an IT and the IT is free. No tag-backs: If you are tagged, when you become an IT, you cannot turn around and tag the person who just tagged you.

6 ITness Transfers
If you are IT and you tag someone, ITness transfers to that player. Care must be taken, however, to be sure the tagged player knows they are now IT. When an IT tags a player, the IT holds up that player's arm for the count of five, looking into their eyes to be sure they know they are now IT. After counting to five, and making sure the tagged player knows they are IT and that they cannot put their hand down until they tag someone else, the old IT is free to seek two others looking to be safe. The tagged player must keep his/her hand up until he/she passes the ITness to someone else by making a tag.

Source: Dr. Spencer Kagan • *Silly Sports & Goofy Games*
Kagan Publishing
1 (800) 933-2667
www.KaganOnline.com

the higher energy and greater focus that follows participation in one of the Silly Sports or Goofy Games.

Tag Games Release Instinctual Energy

For years, I wondered why tag games release such tremendous energy. At workshops, I introduce the tag games with adults by having them play one of the simple tag games like **Everyone's IT!** or **Freezer-Unfreezer Tag**. Without exception, anywhere in the world where I am giving the workshop, otherwise reserved adults break into riotous action attempting to tag others while not being tagged.

> **Tip**
>
> Have your class try a new Silly Sport or Goofy Game at least once a week.

It took me some years to understand why tag games are so engaging and release so much primal energy. Tag games tap into deep instinctual predator-prey responses in the brain. There are two bits of evidence for this: cross-cultural observations of child play, and observations of animal play in the wild and in zoos. Children worldwide play tag. If they are not introduced to tag, they invent a tag game. Tag games, however, are not limited to humans. Researchers have observed gorillas playing tag in the very same way as do children.[39] One of the researchers, Davila Ross, stated, *"Not only did the gorillas in our study hit their playmates and then run away—chased by their playmates—they also switched their roles when hit, so the chaser became the chased and vice versa."*[40] Other animals including lion cubs play tag in the same way.

We have known for years that students love the Silly Sports and Goofy Games and that these simple activities transform the tone of the classroom and boost achievement. It is only now, with advances in comparative psychology and brain science, that we understand why

these simple activities have such a profound positive impact. Silly and goofy? From a student's perspective, yes! From the perspective of brain science, not at all!

Play as a Brain Stimulant

The power of Silly Sports to nourish the brain is not limited to the playground. Imagine your classroom is lagging. It is after lunch or during a lengthy presentation. You have students get up and do a brief tag game in the classroom. The Silly Sports and Goofy Games activities create excitement, releasing dopamine in the brain. Dopamine in turn stimulates the attention and motivation centers in the brain. Thus, after a quick Silly Sport, students return to their academic content with renewed interest and motivation. They are more alert and refreshed, ready to process new information. Teachers who do frequent brain breaks not only have a more interesting, fun class—their class achieves at a higher level academically. Silly Sports and Goofy Games nourish and stimulate the brains of students so they are more alert and motivated.

Silly Sports
A Quiet Sponge Activity

"As the Assessment coordinator, I give teachers a different Silly Sport to use every day after our TCAP (state test) sessions. We have some groups with extended time, and the regular testing group teachers need sponges for their classes. Activities that work perfectly in the classroom and are quiet enough that they don't interrupt the other testing sessions, include Pretzel, Unpretzel, Four Up, Magic 11, Ten Count, Willow-in-the-Wind, and Shoe Scramble. After the whole school is done, we take them all outside and do several of the relays in the book."

—*Krissi Hunter*
4th–8th Grade
Corwin International Magnet School
Pueblo, CO

Silly Sports and Goofy Games Create a Brain-Friendly Classroom

Silly Sport	Brain Function
Tag Games, Relays	Principle 1: Nourishment
Helping Games	Principle 2: Safety
Helping, Coordination, and Balance Games	Principle 3: Social
Meaningful Movement Games	Principle 4: Emotion
Tag, Balance, and Challenge Games	Principle 5: Attention
Challenge Games	Principle 6: Stimuli

Nine Types of Games

In the book, *Silly Sports & Goofy Games*,[41] the sports and games are categorized into nine types:

1. Tag Games
2. Helping Games
3. Balance Games
4. Coordination Games
5. Movement Games
6. Challenge Games
7. Relays
8. Silly Sports
9. Goofy Games

Each of these different types of sports and games helps us create a brain-friendly classroom, but each in different ways. For examples, the primary function of the tag games is to enhance nourishment. The helping games foster positive, supportive social interaction that create brain safety. The challenge games stimulate the prefrontal cortex. See Table: Silly Sports and Goofy Games Create a Brain-Friendly Classroom.

Silly Sports and Goofy Games: Tools to Optimize Brain States

Silly Sports and Goofy Games also help align the classroom environment with the state of relaxed alertness optimal for brain functioning. If students are too relaxed or drowsy, they do not learn well. If they are too aroused or anxious, they do not learn well. Good classroom management includes monitoring student energy levels. The goal of monitoring energy levels is to move the class into the optimal state of relaxed alertness. If the class is lagging, it is the job of the teacher to energize the class; if the class is too excited, it is the job of the teacher to provide a calming activity; if the class is too distracted, the good teacher provides focus. Silly Sports and Goofy Games can help in all these goals, helping students maintain a state in which they are relaxed but alert. Some Silly Sports and Goofy Games are energizers (e.g., **Everyone's IT!**, **Moon Jump**, **Home Run Relay**), picking up the class when energy levels sag. Other Silly Sports and Goofy Games are calming (**Willow-in-the-Wind**, **Care Lift**, **Move & Be**). Yet other games create focus (**Magic 11**, **Ten Count**, **Show Me, Don't Show Me**). All of the Silly Sports and Goofy Games create a safe environment—there are no winners or losers. Students experience excitement in a safe context with the absence of threat. Thus, Silly Sports help the teacher manage energy and attention, moving the class to the state of relaxed alertness optimal for learning.

Moon Jump
Silly Sports & Goofy Games

Tool 3

Improve Diet

What our students eat profoundly impacts brain function.

Breaking the High-Low Cycle

If a student loads up on sugar doughnuts, candy bars, pastries, or syrup-laden pancakes for breakfast, they are headed for a high followed by a low.[43] The carbohydrates are turned into glucose by stomach acid. The glucose goes quickly into the blood stream resulting in the "sugar high." Students in this state find it hard to concentrate. Depending on how many carbohydrates and sugars are consumed, students will become either hyper (sugar high) or sleepy and lethargic (like after a very big meal). The body, in an attempt to maintain homeostasis, reacts to high blood sugar: The pancreas releases insulin to take the sugar out of the blood stream and stores it in cell bodies as fat. In the short run, this often leads to irritability, fidgeting, lack of concentration, and hunger. In the long run, it leads to weight gain. When the blood sugar level dips, the uninformed student responds to the hunger by consuming another dose of sugar or carbohydrates, repeating the cycle.

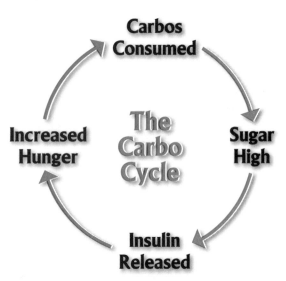

Carbos Consumed

Increased Hunger

The Carbo Cycle

Sugar High

Insulin Released

To break this high-low cycle, students need to consume proteins: eggs, chicken, meat, cheese, fish, cottage cheese, tofu, and/or seeds and nuts. Protein and fiber cause a slow release of glucose, evening out the high-low cycle. Further, protein is necessary as a source of amino acids to build neurotransmitters necessary for optimal brain function. Neurotransmitters, like norepinephrine and dopamine, increase alertness, focus, and motivation to complete tasks. See Blackline: Breaking the High-Low Cycle, p. 1.17.

Brainiac Box

Question:
How does missing a meal impact on brain chemistry and behavior?

Answer:[42]
When we miss a meal, our serotonin (5-HT) levels drop. When we have lower 5-HT, we are far more likely to be disagreeable, argumentative, competitive, and aggressive.

To test the effects of low 5-HT, researchers had people play the ultimatum game after lowering their serotonin levels. Participants could accept or reject an offer to split a monetary reward. If they rejected the offer, they received nothing, as did the person making the offer. They were offered either a 45%, 30%, or only 20% share of the money. Those with lowered serotonin retaliated by rejecting the two lower offers significantly more often than control groups.

The ventral prefrontal cortex (VPFC) inhibits impulse control. Those with VPFC damage behave like those with lowered serotonin, rejecting more offers. The findings are consistent with other research showing lowering serotonin weakens impulse control.

Breaking the High-Low Cycle
Energy Released by Carbos v. Protein

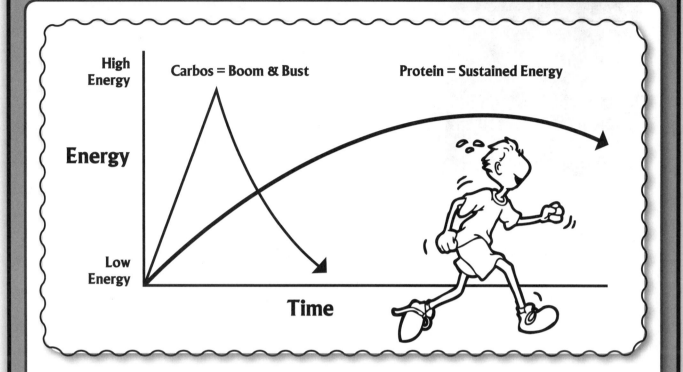

Carbos = Boom & Bust   Protein = Sustained Energy

Energy — High Energy / Low Energy / Time

Carbo Crashers (v.) Protein Power

Carbo Crashers	Protein Power
▶ Donuts	▶ Eggs
▶ Candy Bars	▶ Chicken
▶ Cookies	▶ Cottage Cheese
▶ Cakes	▶ Nuts
▶ Pancakes	▶ Cheese
▶ Waffles	▶ Ham

> **Tip**
> Teach your students to categorize foods into the food groups. Have students fill in the form, "What Did You Eat for Breakfast?"

Breakfast Boosts Achievement

Lack of nutrients for the brain results not just from what our students eat. It results also from simply not eating. A survey of 1,151 second-through fifth-grade students from low-income families found 12% to 26% attend school each day without eating anything.[44] The researchers found more than one-third of the students who failed to eat breakfast consumed less than 50% of the recommended dietary allowance for vitamins A, E, B6, and folacin, and nearly one-fourth consumed less than 50% of the recommended dietary allowance for calories, vitamin C, calcium, and iron. Other researchers have reported percentages ranging from 20% to 30% for students coming to school without eating.[45]

In a review of 47 studies focusing on the importance of breakfast, the researchers found that compared to students who skipped breakfast, those who ate breakfast had improved memory, higher test grades, and improved school attendance.[46] Missing a meal dramatically increases the probability of aggression.[47]

A good breakfast, however, may just be a marker for parental involvement and care. For example, perhaps students with poor diet also have parents who are less likely to encourage them to do their homework. Does the breakfast itself contribute to improved brain function and achievement or is lack of breakfast a marker for many variables? The answer is probably both. That is, students who have a nutritious breakfast probably have more involved, informed, and caring parents, which partially explains the improved school performance and attendance, but a nutritious breakfast almost certainly contributes to enhanced brain function.

Experimental studies provide additional strong support for the importance of a nutritious breakfast. A review of 45 research studies revealed that providing a school breakfast resulted in improved academic achievement.[48] Even with this more experimental approach, some questions remain regarding causation. The studies found that providing school breakfast resulted also in improved school attendance, so the question remains how much the improved school achievement was due to the better breakfast versus the improved attendance. While this question may be theoretically important, from a practical point of view, we can conclude providing a school breakfast is beneficial for students, regardless of the reason it leads to improved academic performance.

To help students track their protein and carbo consumption, see Blackline: What Did You Eat for Breakfast?, p. 1.19.

Diet Quality Correlates with Academic Achievement

Research supports a positive relationship between quality of diet and academic achievement. For example, in a study of 5,200 fifth-grade students, those with decreased diet quality were significantly more likely to perform poorly academically.[49] Again, however, correlation does not prove causation. Poor diet is probably associated with other factors that impair school achievement. The relationship of diet quality to school achievement, however, did remain when socioeconomic characteristics of parents and residential demographics were statistically controlled.

> **Administrator Tip**
> If possible, provide school breakfast. If not, institute a schoolwide campaign to encourage students to have a nutritious breakfast.

What Did You Eat for Breakfast?

Directions: Track your protein/carbo ratio. Each day, list the proteins and carbos you ate. Tally the number of proteins and carbos for the day. At the end of the week, total your proteins and carbos to check your ratio.

Day	Date	Proteins	Carbos
Monday		Total	Total
Tuesday		Total	Total
Wednesday		Total	Total
Thursday		Total	Total
Friday		Total	Total
Saturday		Total	Total
Sunday		Total	Total
Week Totals:			

Combining Exercise and Diet

After instituting a program called, "Making the Grade with Diet and Exercise (MGDE)," educators in Springfield Elementary school in New Middletown, Ohio, saw dramatic improvements in attendance, achievement, health, and behavior among students.[50] The program had just three simple components: (1) 10 to 20 minutes of physical activity each morning; (2) free breakfast for all students; and (3) reversing the order of lunch and recess. The morning exercise activities were chosen by and led by classroom teachers with their own class and consisted of walking, running, exercise videos, calisthenics, resistance training, and/or gymnasium and playground games. To carve out time for the physical activity, subsequent activities throughout the school day were shortened by only 2–3 minutes each. Free breakfast usually consisted of cereal and/or another bread product, milk, and juice. Having lunch follow rather than precede recess was done for two reasons: When recess follows lunch, students rush through lunch to get to recess and often do not complete their lunch. Further, when students return to class directly after recess they are often over-excited and/or quarrelling with peers so academic time is lost calming them down.

Results of the MGDE program are impressive on all measures administered. Attendance improved slightly (from 94.3% to 95.9%); discipline referrals decreased dramatically (58%); nurse visitations decreased even more dramatically (67%); teachers reported "buy in" to the program, and standardized test scores improved. Prior to the intervention, students at the school passed only one of the three mandated proficiency tests (writing). In the first year following the intervention, students improved their writing proficiency by 19% and passed all three state mandated tests (writing, reading, and math).

The MGDE program was initiated following the 1999–2000 school year. As pictured in the graph, gains began in the following school year and increased in subsequent years, approaching 100% of students passing all three proficiency tests by years 2004–2006! See Graph: Gains from Diet and Exercise.

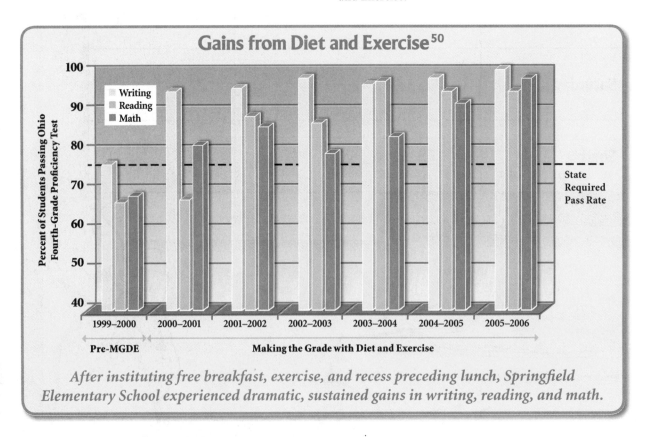

After instituting free breakfast, exercise, and recess preceding lunch, Springfield Elementary School experienced dramatic, sustained gains in writing, reading, and math.

Brain-Friendly Teaching • Dr. Spencer Kagan
Kagan Publishing • 800.933.2667 • www.KaganOnline.com

Although it may be of academic interest to ask if the improved exercise or the improved diet was responsible for the improved achievement and behavior, or to ask about the relative contribution of each, from a practical perspective, schools would do well to implement both. As we have seen in the research on exercise, numerous reviews establish a positive relationship between exercise and cognitive performance. Further numerous studies show poor diet is associated with poor school performance and test performance.[51]

Schools—Part of the Problem or Part of The Solution?

Presently, United States schools substantially contribute to the poor diet and poor health of students by making unhealthy foods readily available. The Food and Nutrition Service of the U.S. Department of Agriculture documents the following facts:[52]

- ▶ Between 18%–20% of calories consumed by children and adolescents come from added sugars.
- ▶ Almost 9 million children and adolescents in the United States are overweight.
- ▶ Prevalence of overweight among children aged 6–11 more than doubled from 1980–2002.
- ▶ Prevalence of overweight among adolescents aged 12–19 more than tippled from 1980 to 2002.
- ▶ Overweight is associated with numerous health and psychological problems including high blood pressure, bone and joint problems, low self-esteem, heart disease, gallbladder disease, anorexia, and bulimia, and higher mortality rates.
- ▶ School vending machines and/or other sources of nonschool-meal foods and beverages are provided in 98% of high schools; 74% of middle/junior high schools; and 43% of elementary schools.
- ▶ Of those schools providing nonschool-meal foods and beverages, most are high in fat and/or added sugars and portion sizes of salty snacks (e.g., potato chips) and soft drinks has increased dramatically.[53] These foods are consumed instead of healthier choices.

The Department of Agriculture together with the Department of Education have produced a comprehensive resource for schools wishing to promote a more brain-friendly diet for students.[54] The book documents six approaches schools have used successfully to transform the diet of students:

1. **Establish Nutrition Standards**
2. **Influence food and beverage contracts**
3. **Make healthy foods and beverages available**
4. **Promote healthful choices**
5. **Limit access to unhealthy choices**
6. **Use funding activities and rewards to support student health**

Administrator Tips

Renegotiate contracts with food vendors. Have vendors:

- Provide healthier food choices (shaker salads instead of candy and chips).
- Price healthier choices more attractively than less healthy choices.
- Substitute images of young people engaged in physical activity, replacing company logos on beverage machine facades.
- Offer prizes for fitness challenges.

Healthy School Nutrition Saves Schools Money!

Schools and districts have found it financially profitable to adopt healthier foods. In some cases, contracts for exclusive rights to multiyear beverage sales have been increased from $500,000 to $900,000, and many contracts are contingent on healthy-choice terms. In many cases, the money earned by the renegotiated contracts with vendors has been used to provide exercise equipment—a double win for better nourishing students' brains.

Tool 4

Supply Hydration

We generally don't think of water as nourishment. It turns out, though, that keeping the body well hydrated actually nourishes the brain!

Dehydration Shrinks Brain Cells

In an adult of normal weight, the body is about 60%–70% water. Brain cells like other nerve cells are about 85% water. In addition, the brain is cushioned by and surrounded by water. When water levels drop, cells cannot receive the nutrients they need; they shrink, decreasing their ability to function.

> In prolonged dehydration, brain cells begin to shrink. Imagine a plum gradually turning into a prune. Unfortunately, in a dehydrated state, many, many functions of the brain cells begin to get lost, such as the transport system that delivers neurotransmitters to nerve endings.[55]

Hydration Improves Health

Keeping the brain well hydrated serves a number of critical functions. In his classic book on the body's need for water, *Your Body's Many Cries for Water*,[56] F. Batmanghelidj, MD, documents how many bodily diseases originate from dehydration. Dehydration reduces the capacity of the brain

to attend to and retain information, to learn. When the body does not get enough water from the outside to keep functioning, it gathers water from internal organs including the respiratory track, digestive track, and even fluid in the joints. This increases physical fatigue and mental fatigue. Dehydration leads to a lack of ability to concentrate.

Most directly related to learning is the ability of neurons to communicate. When we talk about making learning connections, we are referring to neurons wiring together. Neurons that fire together, wire together. This process is dependent on efficient neuronal transmission. Water ionizes salts in the brain, increasing cell polarity that improves neuronal transmission. Drinking water has yet an additional benefit: Hydration increases the affinity of hemoglobin for oxygen, so our blood can carry and deliver a better supply of oxygen to the brain. With more oxygen, the brains of our students are more alert. Students are more prepared to make learning connections. A well-hydrated brain is actually better able to learn![57] To help students monitor their daily hydration, see Blackline: Daily Hydration Log, p. 1.23.

Tips
Hydrate Frequently

- Teach students about the importance of hydration.

- Have water stations and/or drinking fountains within classrooms.

- Have water breaks.

- Encourage students to drink at the outset and end of recess and passing periods.

- Allow students to keep water bottles at their desks.

- Encourage students to eat hydrating foods such as fruits and vegetables.

- Advocate that students avoid caffeine.

- Have sudents keep a Hydration Log (see blackline).

Daily Hydration Log

Directions: Circle a glass for each 8oz. of water you drink each day. Total the ounces for the day. At the end of the week, total the ounces for the week.

Total

Monday | 8 oz. | 8 oz. | 8 oz. | 8 oz. | 8 oz. | 8 oz. | 8 oz. | 8 oz.

Tuesday | 8 oz. | 8 oz. | 8 oz. | 8 oz. | 8 oz. | 8 oz. | 8 oz. | 8 oz.

Wednesday | 8 oz. | 8 oz. | 8 oz. | 8 oz. | 8 oz. | 8 oz. | 8 oz.

Thursday | 8 oz. | 8 oz. | 8 oz. | 8 oz. | 8 oz. | 8 oz. | 8 oz. | 8 oz.

Friday | 8 oz. | 8 oz. | 8 oz. | 8 oz. | 8 oz. | 8 oz. | 8 oz. | 8 oz.

Saturday | 8 oz. | 8 oz. | 8 oz. | 8 oz. | 8 oz. | 8 oz. | 8 oz. | 8 oz.

Sunday | 8 oz. | 8 oz. | 8 oz. | 8 oz. | 8 oz. | 8 oz. | 8 oz. | 8 oz.

Weekly Total

Tool 5

Train Proper Breathing

As we have seen, exercise increases oxygen to the brain, and regular aerobic exercise promotes vascular development so there is an ongoing improved supply of oxygen to the brain. Another way students can create an ongoing improved supply of oxygen to their brains is to cultivate a habit of proper breathing: Slow, steady, diaphragmatic breathing. Hyperventilation is the opposite of slow diaphragmatic breathing and results in a paradox: Plenty of Oxygen (O_2) in the bloodstream while the brain is starving for O_2.

The Hyperventilation Paradox

If you take 100 fast and deep breaths in rapid succession, you are hyperventilating. The result: You are likely to faint due to hypoxia (lack of oxygen) in the brain. The dizziness we experience when we hyperventilate is a result of oxygen depletion in the brain; it is the same experience we have at very high altitudes when we do not get enough oxygen.

This apparent paradox—deep, rapid breathing resulting in lack of oxygen—is explained by how oxygen is released from hemoglobin. Actually, during hyperventilation, you have plenty of oxygen in your blood stream; the problem is that the oxygen is not being released to the brain where it is needed. Why isn't oxygen released to the brain if there is plenty of oxygen in the blood stream? Hemoglobin carries oxygen in the blood and releases the oxygen where it is most needed. It releases the oxygen where there is a high concentration of carbon dioxide (CO_2). When we hyperventilate, we exhale so much CO_2, oxygen is not released from the hemoglobin. This binding of oxygen to hemoglobin, called the Bohr effect, occurs for a second reason when we hyperventilate: Hyperventilation leads the blood to be more alkaline, and the more alkaline the blood, the more oxygen binds to hemoglobin.

Hyperventilation

A person who is hyperventilating feels as though he or she is not getting enough oxygen so the person breathes deeper and more rapidly, gasping for air. It is a dreadful feeling—like being underwater and running out of air. But gasping for air makes the problem worse because it expels even more CO_2.

Breathing into a paper bag, the traditional treatment for hyperventilation, does have the effect of rebreathing CO_2, but is not recommended.[58] Breathing into a paper bag increases CO_2 intake, but it also restricts intake of oxygen. Oxygen depletion is counter indicated for a person already experiencing oxygen depletion to the cells. A better intervention is to do what is called, "7–11" breathing," see Tip.

Tip

To treat hyperventilation, have the person do "7-11 breathing." The person slows his or her breathing by gently inhaling for the slow count of seven and then exhales to a slow count of 11.

Ten Benefits of Diaphragmatic Breathing

Deep, slow diaphragmatic breathing produces optimum ongoing oxygenation of the brain. In addition, it has a number of health benefits: It not only better nourishes the brain, but also, it has a positive impact on most bodily functions. See Table: 10 Benefits of Diaphragmatic Breathing, p. 1.25.

Teaching 4-4-8 Breathing

There are many approaches to teaching proper breathing. My favorite is to teach students a simple method of relaxation breathing, or "4-4-8 Breathing." In preparation, student are to sit comfortably in a chair with their back straight and feet flat on the floor with their eyes closed.

10 Benefits of Diaphragmatic Breathing

Benefit	Explanation
1. Oxygen to Brain	Too shallow breathing does not provide enough oxygen. Too rapid breathing depletes CO_2 so oxygen is not released to the brain. Slow, diaphragmatic breathing optimizes oxygen to the brain.
2. Relaxation Response; Reduced Tension and Anxiety	Slow diaphragmatic breathing stimulates the vagus nerve, stimulating the parasympathetic nervous system and the relaxation response. It inhibits sympathetic nervous system arousal, lowering blood pressure, and lowering blood lactate, reducing anxiety, and promoting a feeling of calm.
3. Improved Creativity and Concentration	The relaxation response produces relaxed alertness, the optimal state for creativity and concentration.
4. Enhanced Energy, Stamina	Optimal delivery of O_2 to muscles and transportation of CO_2 from muscles optimizes energy and stamina.
5. Improved Blood Circulation to Vital Organs	Upper movement of diaphragm massages the heart. Massage improves circulation.
6. Improved Digestion	Deep diaphragmatic breathing massages the stomach, small intestine, liver, and pancreas, and improves digestion. Improved oxygenation of the stomach leads to improved function and assimilation of food.
7. Weight Loss	Increased oxygen burns excess fat more efficiently.
8. Elimination of Toxins; Improved Immune System	70% of toxins are expelled through breathing; improved breathing improves elimination of toxins. The lymphatic system eliminates cellular waste. Breathing is the pump for the lymphatic system; improved circulation of lymph improves the immune system.
9. Strengthened Lungs	Deep breathing strengthens lungs.
10. Strengthened Heart	With more oxygen delivered by the lungs, the heart does not have to work as hard. Also deep breathing leads to greater pressure differential in the lungs, increasing circulation so the heart does not have to work as hard.

Students then do the following:

4–Inhale. Place a hand on their stomach. They inhale deeply through their nose to the count of four, feeling their hand over their stomach move out as they inhale. They are to expand their stomach for three counts and then fill and expand their chest on the fourth count, inhaling completely.

4–Hold. Hold their breath for the count of four.

8–Exhale. Exhale very slowly through a small hole in their mouth for the count of eight, feeling their hand over their stomach move in as they exhale. On the last count, they are to exhale completely. Students repeat this 4-4-8 breathing pattern for 2 or 3 minutes.

A key element in relaxation breathing is the hand on the stomach. Have students be sure that their stomach expands as they inhale and contracts as they exhale. This ensures diaphragmatic, or deep, breathing that stimulates the vagus nerve, triggering the relaxation response. A number of good books describe in detail both the many benefits and the various methods of diaphragmatic breathing.[59] See Blackline: 4-4-8 Breathing, p. 1.26.

4-4-8 Breathing
A Simple Method of Relaxation Breathing

❹–Inhale

▶ Inhale through nose
▶ Hand on stomach
▶ Expand stomach to count of three
▶ Expand chest on count of four

❹–Hold

▶ Hold breath to count of four

❽–Exhale

▶ Exhale to count of eight
▶ Small hole in mouth
▶ Exhale completely on last count of eight

Making Diaphragmatic Breathing a Habit

This deep, slow diaphragmatic breathing relaxes a person in the moment. To help us reach our goal of increasing the *ongoing* supply of oxygen to the brain, we make slow diaphragmatic breathing a habit. How are habits formed? Repetition. Thus, to make diaphragmatic breathing habitual, we can take a few minutes to practice in class each day and we encourage students to practice on their own outside of school. The few minutes that it takes away from our academic curriculum each day pays off with greater rather than less academic achievement, as we will see in Tool 12: Teach Relaxation Breathing, Principle 2: Safety, where we examine the impact of breathing on brain functioning. When students practice diaphragmatic breathing, they enter a state of relaxed alertness, the optimal state for learning.

Tool 6

Teach with Movement Structures

The instructional strategies we use moment to moment in our classrooms partially determine the extent to which the brains of our students are well nourished. Major muscle movement increases heart rate and volume as well as breathing rate and volume. Thus, not only is more blood pumped to the brain, the blood that is pumped is more fully oxygenated. Although walking within the classroom to find a partner, to form teams, or to report to another team, does not have the same benefits as exercise, it does increase heart rate and breathing rate somewhat, and so improves nourishment to the brain.

Walking increases blood flow via leg valves. The valves in the legs are unidirectional, allowing blood to flow only upwards. Leg muscles actually act as secondary hearts. As we

> **Tip**
> Have students do 4-4-8 Breathing when they first enter class, before doing their board work, and before tests.

contract our leg muscles, we send more blood upward, toward the brain! Teachers who include regular movement in their classroom teach to better-nourished brains. Students are more alert, attentive, concentrate better, and more fully process, retain, and recall information.

Let's take a concrete example. Two teachers teach in classrooms next door to each other. They are at the same place in a lesson, doing a review, calling on students to answer questions. One teacher uses the traditional method and has the students raise their hands to be called on if they know the answer. The other teacher does something more brain friendly: For each question, the teacher says *"Everyone stand up. Remain standing if you know the answer."* The teacher then calls on standing students to respond. Although it takes about the same amount of time for the question/answer in each classroom, after only three or four questions, the teacher who has all the students standing and sitting has a classroom of students who are more alert and with better-nourished brains!

Kagan Structures Include Movement and Nourish Brains

In a cooperative learning classroom, students are seated in teams. Three types of Kagan Cooperative Learning Structures nourish the brain through movement: classbuilding structures, grouping structures, and interaction structures.[60]

Classbuilding Structures. Classbuilding structures have students get up from their teams to interact with others in the class. All of the classbuilding structures involve getting

Major muscle movement increases heart rate and volume as well as breathing rate and volume. Thus, not only is more blood pumped to the brain, the blood that is pumped is more fully oxygenated.

Tip

If energy dips in the classroom, use a classbuilding structure to have students interact over the content.

up and regrouping; they are designed to create class cohesion by having students interact with classmates rather than teammates. For example, during **Corners** students get up from their team and go to one corner of the room. The corner may represent alternatives that help students get to know each other (Walk to the corner that represents your favorite season: Fall, Winter, Spring, or Summer) or may represent alternatives that correspond to the academic curriculum (Walk to the corner that represents the constitutional amendment you feel is the most important: First, Second, Third, or Fourth). Because all classbuilding structures involve moving in the classroom, they serve to nourish the brain. Some of the classbuilding structures involve mixing in the room to music. If fast-beat music is played and/or students are encouraged to mix rapidly, the result is greater brain nourishment.

Ten classbuilding structures that involve movement are described in detail in the book, *Kagan Cooperative Learning*:[61]

- ▶ **Carousel Feedback**
- ▶ **Find Someone Who**
- ▶ **Find-the-Fiction**
- ▶ **Inside-Outside Circle**
- ▶ **Mix-Freeze-Group**
- ▶ **Mix-Pair-Share**
- ▶ **One Stray**
- ▶ **Quiz-Quiz-Trade**
- ▶ **StandUp–HandUp–PairUp**
- ▶ **Stir-the-Class**

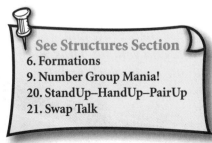

See Structures Section
6. Formations
9. Number Group Mania!
20. StandUp–HandUp–PairUp
21. Swap Talk

Numerous academic and classbuilding activities for ten of the classbuilding structures are provided in the book, *Cooperative Learning Structures for Classbuilding*.[62] Structures included in the classbuilding book that are not included in *Kagan Cooperative Learning* book include:

- ▶ **Corners**
- ▶ **Formations**
- ▶ **Line-Ups**
- ▶ **Mix-N-Match**
- ▶ **Similarity Groups**
- ▶ **Who Am I?**

Grouping Structures. Grouping structures do not have an academic focus; they are simply used to regroup students. For example, if we want students to interact in pairs with a classmate who is not a teammate, we might do a **StandUp–HandUp–PairUp**. Like it sounds, students stand up, put a hand up to indicate they are looking for a partner and to help others find them, and then pair up with another student who has a hand up. When students pair up, they do a high five and lower their hands, so only students still looking for a partner have a hand up and can easily find each other. **StandUp–HandUp–PairUp** is designed to group students; once the students are all in pairs, depending on the content and the objectives of the teacher, students might be directed to interact in any of dozens of ways using an interaction structure such as **RallyRobin**, **Timed Pair Share**, or **Pair Interview**. See Table: Sample Grouping Structures, p. 1.29.

Ways to Group Students. There are many ways to group students. In the structure **Number Group Mania!**, the teacher announces two things: the size of the group to be formed and which numbers are to join each group. Students are seated in groups of four, each with a number, 1, 2, 3, or 4. To group students using **Number Group Mania!**, the teacher calls for a breakout into one of a number of different-sized groups. For examples:

- ▶ *"When I say, 'Go,' form groups of four, everyone with a different number."*
- ▶ *"When I say, 'Go,' pair up with someone with your number."*
- ▶ *"When I say, 'Go,' form groups of three, everyone with a different number."*
- ▶ *"When I say, 'Go,' pair up, 1s with 2s and 3s with 4s."*
- ▶ *"When I say, 'Go,' form groups of eight, two students with each number."*

Students display their own number by holding up a hand with fingers raised as they walk to form groups.

Interaction Structures. In contrast to grouping structures, interaction structures are designed to direct the interaction of students. Many interaction structures do not provide additional nourishment to the brain because they do not involve major muscle movement. For example, students might do a simple **RoundRobin** seated with their teammates.

Sample Grouping Structures

Structure	Resulting Group Size
Forming Pairs	
StandUp–HandUp–PairUp	2
Forming Teams	
Pairs Pair	4
Forming Larger Groups	
Team Up!	8

Interaction Structures that Nourish the Brain. Some interaction structures, however, involve major muscle movement. They call for students to get up, group, and then interact with classmates. Some interaction structures are designed to have students repeatedly move, fostering greater brain nourishment. For example, in **Quiz-Quiz-Trade**, students find a partner, quiz each other on the academic content, and then move to find a different partner, repeatedly moving after each student in the pair has quizzed the other.

One structure that involves major muscle movement, but which does not involve face-to-face interaction among students is **TakeOff–TouchDown**. Rather than raising their hands to show agreement with a statement the teacher has made, students stand up. In the same amount of time the traditional teacher has students raise their hand, the teacher using **TakeOff–TouchDown** has students stand and sit, providing a bit more nourishment to the brain.

See Structures Section
11. PairUp Review
13. Quiz-Quiz-Trade
22. TakeOff–TouchDown
26. Traveling Heads Together
27. Traveling RallyInterview

Embedding Movement Into Structures

"When I was a classroom teacher, instead of rotating materials in Fan-N-Pick, I had students stand and rotate to the next seat and begin the next round. Sometimes I had the students rotate and stay standing the entire structure.

"As a signal that students were finished with a Single RoundRobin, I would have students stand and wait to allow them to stretch and get more O_2 to the brain."

—*Rachel Treaster*
2nd Grade, Linwood Elementary
Wichita Public Schools USD 259
Wichita, KS

Interaction Structures that Move Students into Breakout Groups. Three rounds of **Traveling Heads Together** result in new, random teams. In the process of forming these new teams, students are moving, nourishing their brains. **Traveling Heads Together** is **Numbered Heads Together** with a twist. After teammates have put their heads together to tutor each other on the correct answer or to reach consensus on a quality response, the teacher calls on a student number to travel. The student with that number travels to another team, to share his or her answer. If we do three rounds of **Traveling Heads Together** calling a different number each time and having students move each time to teams where there are no teammates from their base team, we have formed random teams: each team has all new teammates. At that point, without spending any time away from the curriculum, the teacher can have students do an activity in their new, random teams. The movement, of course, ensures that the brains of students are energized as they sit down to work in their new teams. See Table: Sample Interaction Structures That Form Breakout Groups.

Mix-Freeze-Group results in groups of different sizes depending on the number the teacher calls. The teacher has students mixing about the room. Then the teacher calls, *"Freeze!"* Next, the teacher gives a question with a number as the solution. For example, *"How many blind mice were there?"* Students quickly form groups of three. If the question had been, *"How many hydrogen atoms are there in three water molecules?"* students would form groups of six. Students hurry to join a group as they don't want to be in the "Lost and Found"—the group of students left over. As students rush to form groups, hearts and lungs pump faster and their brains receive more nourishment.

Sample Interaction Structures That Form Breakout Groups

Structure	Resulting Group Size
Forming Pairs	
Quiz-Quiz-Trade	2
Forming Teams	
Traveling Heads Together (3 rounds)	4
Forming Groups of Various Sizes	
Mix-Freeze-Group	Various Sizes

Brain-Friendly Teaching • Dr. Spencer Kagan
Kagan Publishing • 800.933.2667 • www.KaganOnline.com

Conclusion

The choice is ours. We can have students whose brains function optimally because they are well nourished, or we can work with students whose brains are not fully charged. With six simple tools in place, we can go a long way toward optimal brain functioning, which in turn leads to improved concentration, brain growth, and development, learning, and achievement. By better nourishing the brains of our students we do more: We instill in our students more joy in learning and healthy habits for life. We have the power to create a healthier, happier, more fully functioning society.

Six Tools to Nourish the Brain
1. Encourage Exercise
2. Promote Play
3. Improve Diet
4. Supply Hydration
5. Train Proper Breathing
6. Teach with Movement Structures

References

[1] Haier, R.J., Siegel, B.V.Jr., MacLachlan, A., Soderling, E., Lottenberg, S. & Buchsbaum, M.S. *Regional glucose metabolic changes after learning a complex visuospatial/motor task: a positron emission tomographic study.* **Brain Research**, 1992, 570(1), 134–143.

Haier, R.J., Siegel, B.V.Jr., Tang, C., Abel, L. & Buchsbaum, M.S. *Intelligence and changes in regional cerebral glucose metabolic rate following learning.* **Intelligence**, 1992, 16(3), 415–426.

[2] Haier, R.J., Siegel, B.V., Nuechterlein, K.H., Hazlett, E., Wu, J.C., Paek, J., Browning, H.L. & Buchsbaum, M.S. *Cortical glucose metabolic rate correlates of abstract reasoning and attention studied with positron emission tomography,* **Intelligence**, 1988, 12(2), 199-217.

[3] Parks, R.W., Crockett, D.J., Tuokko, H., Beattie, B.L., Ashford, J.W., Coburn, K.L., Zec, R.F., Becker, R.E., McGeer, P.L. & McGeer, E.G. *Neuropsychological "systems efficiency" and positron emission tomography.* **Journal of Neuropsychiatry**, 1989, 1(3), 269–282.

[4] Berent, S., Giordani, B., Lehtinen, S., Markel, D., Penney, J.B., Buchtel, H.A., Starosta-Rubin- stein, S., Hichwa, R. & Young, A.B. *Positron emission tomographic scan investigations of Huntington's disease: Cerebral metabolic correlates of cognitive function.* **Annals of Neurology**, 1988, 23(6), 541–546.

[5] Potts, R. *Evolution: Big brains explained.* **Nature**, 2011, 480(7375), 43–44.

[6] Fields, D.R. **The Other Brain**. New York, NY: Simon & Schuster, 2009.

[7] Esser, S.K., Andreopoulos, A., Appuswamy, R., Datta, P., Barch, D., Amir, A., Arthur, J., Cassidy, A., Flickner, M., Merolla, P., Chandra, S., Basilico, N., Carpin, S., Zimmerman, T., Zee, F., Alvarez-Icaza, R., Kusnitz, J.A., Wong, T.M., Risk W.P., McQuinn, E., Nayak, T.K., Singh, R. & Modha, D.S. *Cognitive computing systems: Algorithms and applications for networks of neurosynaptic cores.* **International Joint Conference on Neural Networks (IJCNN)**. IEEE, 2013.

Preissl, R., Wong, T.M., Datta, P., Flickner, M., Singh, R., Esser, S.K., Risk, W.P., Simon, H.D. & Modha, D.S. *Compass: A scalable simulator for an architecture for cognitive computing.* **Proceedings of the International Conference for High Performance Computing, Networking, Storage, and Analysis** (SC 2012), Nov. 2012.

[8] Perth, C.B. **Molecules of Emotions. Why You Feel the Way You Feel**. New York, NY: Scribner, 1997.

[9] Hedlund, S., Nylin, G. & Regnstrom, O. *The behavior of the cerebral circulation during muscular exercise.* **Acta Physiologica Scandinavica**, 1962, 54(3–4), 316–324.

Thomas, S.N., Schroeder, T., Secher, N.H. & Mitchell, J.H. *Cerebral blood flow during submaximal and maximal dynamic exercise in humans.* **Journal of Applied Physiology**, 1989, 67(2), 744–748.

[10] Shibata, S., Hastings, J.L., Prasad, A., Fu, Q., Okazaki, K., Palmer, M.D., Zhang, R. & Levine, B.D. *Dynamic Starling mechanism: effects of aging and physical fitness on ventricular-arterial coupling.* **Journal of Physiology**, 2008, 586(7), 1951–1962.

Zhang, R. *Aerobic exercise training increases brain perfusion in elderly women.* Washington, D.C. **Experimental Biology Meeting**, 2011.

[11] Middleton, L.E., Manini, T.M., Simonsick, E.M., Harris, T.B., Barnes, D.E., Tylavsky, F., Brach J.S, Everhart, J.E. & Yaffe, K. *Activity energy expenditure and incident cognitive impairment in older adults.* **Archives of Internal Medicine**, 2011, 171(14), 1251–1257.

Vercambre, M-N., Grodstein, F., Manson, J.E., Stampfer, M.J. & Kang, J.H. *Physical activity and cognition in women with vascular conditions.* **Archives of Internal Medicine**, 2011, 171(14), 1244–1250.

[12] Adlard, P.A. & Cotman, C.W. *Voluntary exercise protects against stress-induced decreases in brain-derived neurotrophic protein expression.* **The Journal of Neuroscience**, 2004, 124(4), 985–992.

Trejo, J.L., Carro, E. & Torres-Aleman. *Circulating insulin-like growth factor I mediates exercise-induced increases in the number of new neurons in the adult hippocampus.* **The Journal of Neuroscience**, 2001, 21(5), 1628–1634.

[13] Cotman, C.W., Berchtold, N.C. & Christie, L-A. *Exercise builds brain health: key roles of growth factor cascades and inflammation.* **Trends in Neurosciences**, 2007, 30(9), 464–471.

[14] Winter, B., Breitenstein, C., Mooren, F.C., Voelker, K., Fobker, M., Lechtermann, A., Krueger, K., Fromme, A., Korsukewitz, C., Floel, A. & Knecht, S. *High impact running improves learning.* **Neurobiology of Learning and Memory**, 2007, 87(4), 597–609.

[15] Ratey, J. **Spark: The Revolutionary New Science of Exercise and the Brain.** New York, NY: Little, Brown and Company, 2008.

[16] Zervas, Y., Apostolos, D. & Klissouras, V. *Influence of physical exertion on mental performance with reference to training.* **Perceptual and Motor Skills**, 1991, 73(3c), 1215–1221.

[17] Hillman, C.H., Castelli, D.M. & Buck, S.M. *Aerobic fitness and neurocognitive function in healthy preadolescent children.* **Medicine and Science in Sports and Exercise**, 2005, 37(11), 1967–1974.

[18] Tremblay, M.S., Inman, J.W. & Willms, J.D. *The relationship between physical activity, self-esteem, and academic achievement in 12-year-old children.* **Pediatric Exercise Science**, 2000, 12(3), 312–323.

[19] Coe, D.P., Pivarnik, J.M., Womack, C.J., Reeves, M.J. & Malina, R.M. *Effect of physical education and activity levels on academic achievement in children.* **Medicine and Science in Sports and Exercise**, 2006, 38(8), 1515–1519.

Ismail, A.H. *The effects of a well-organized physical education programme on intellectual performance.* **Research in Physical Education**, 1967, 1(2), 31–38.

[20] California Department of Education. **A Study of the Relationship between Physical Fitness and Academic Achievement in California Using 2004 Test Results.** Sacramento, CA: California Department of Education, 2005.

[21] Dwyer, T., Sallis, J.F., Blizzard, L., Lazarus, R. & Dean, K. *Relations of academic performance to physical activity and fitness in children.* **Pediatric Exercise Science**, 2001, 13(3), 225–237.

[22] King, K., Scahill, C., McEllingott, J. & Randazzo, W. *Implementing a physical activity program in a public elementary school and its effect on academic achievement. Paper presented at the* **Pediatric Academic Societies and Asian Society for Pediatric Research 2011 Annual Meeting**, May 1, 2011.

[23] Ratey, J. Spark: **The Revolutionary New Science of Exercise and the Brain.** New York, NY: Little, Brown and Company, 2008.

[24] Viadero, D. *Exercise seen as priming the pump for students' academic success.* **Education Week**, 2008, 27(23), 14–15.

See also the Naperville Website, **Naperville Central High School's Learning Readiness Physical Education Program**: http://www.learningreadinesspe.com/index.html

[25] Davis, C.L., Tomporowski, P.D., McDowell, J.E., Austin B.P., Miller, P.H., Yanasak, N.E., Allison J.D. & Naglieri, J.A. *Exercise improves executive function and achievement and alters brain activation in overweight children: A randomized controlled trial.* **Health Psychology**, 2011, 30(1), 91–98.

[26] Brisswalter, J., Collardeau, M. & Arcelin, R. *Effects of acute physical exercise characteristics on cognitive performance.* **Sports Medicine**, 2002, 32(9), 555–566.

Colcombe, S. & Kramer, A.F. *Fitness effects on the cognitive function of older adults: A meta-analytic study.* **Psychological Science**, 2003, 14(2), 125–130.

Etnier, J.L., Salazar, W., Landers, D.M., Petruzello, S.J., Han, M. & Nowell, P. *The influence of physical fitness and exercise upon cognitive functioning: A meta-analysis.* **Journal of Sport and Exercise Psychology**, 1997, 19(3), 249–277.

Sibley, B.A. & Etnier, J.L. *The relationship between physical activity and cognition in children: A meta-analysis.* **Pediatric Exercise Science**, 2003, 15(3), 243–256.

Tomporowski, P.D. *Cognitive and behavioral responses to acute exercise in youths: A review.* **Pediatric Exercise Science**, 2003a, 15(4), 348–359.

Tomporowski, P.D. *Effects of acute bouts of exercise on cognition.* **Acta Psychologica**, 2003b, 112(3), 297–324.

Tomporowski, P.D., Davis, C.L., Miller, P.H. & Naglieri, J.A. *Exercise and children's intelligence, cognition, and academic achievement.* **Educational Psychology Review**, 2008, 20(2), 111–131.

[27] Voss, M.W., Nagamatsu, L.S., Liu-Ambrose, T. & Kramer, A.F. *Exercise, brain, and cognition across the lifespan.* **Journal of Applied Physiology**, 2011, 111(5), 1505–1513.

[28] Dwyer, T., Sallis, J.F., Blizzard, L., Lazarus, R. & Dean, K. *Relation of academic performance to physical activity and fitness in children.* **Pediatric Exercise Science**, 2001, 13(3), 225–237.

Field, T., Diego, M. & Sanders, C.E. *Exercise is positively related to adolescents' relationships and academics.* **Adolescence**, 2001, 36(141), 105–110.

Kim, H.Y., Frongillo, E.A., Han, S.S., Oh, S.Y., Kim, W.K., Jang, Y.A., Won, H.S., Lee, H.S. & Kim, H.E. *Academic performance of Korean children is associated with dietary behaviours and physical status.* **Asia Pacific Journal of Clinical Nutrition**, 2003, 12(2), 186–192.

Shephard, R.J. *Curricular physical activity and academic performance.* **Pediatric Exercise Science**, 1997, 9(2), 113–126.

Shephard, R.J., Volle, M., Lavallee, H., LaBarre, R., Jequier, J.C. & Rajic, M. *Required physical activity and academic grades: A controlled study.* In J. Ilmarinen & I. Valimaki (Eds.), **Children and Sport**, 58–63. Berlin, DE: Springer-Verlag, 1984.

Sibley, B.A. & Etnier, J.L. *The relationship between physical activity and cognition in children: a meta-analysis.* **Pediatric Exercise Science**, 2003, 15(3), 243–256.

[29] Brisswalter, J., Collardeau, M. & Rene, A. *Effects of acute physical exercise characteristics on cognitive performance*. **Sports Medicine**, 2002, 32(9), 555–566.

Caterino, M.C. & Polak, E.D. *Effects of two types of activity on the performance of second-, third-, and fourth-grade students on a test of concentration*. **Perceptual and Motor Skills**, 1999, 89(1), 245–248.

Cotman, C.W. & Berchtold, N.C. *Exercise: a behavioral intervention to enhance brain health and plasticity*. **Trends in Neurosciences**, 2002, 25(6), 295–301.

Klein, S.A. & Deffenbacher, J.L. *Relaxation and exercise for hyperactive impulsive children*. **Perceptual and Motor Skills**, 1977, 45(3f), 1159–1162.

McNaughten, D. & Gabbard, C. *Physical exertion and immediate mental performance of sixth-grade children*. **Perceptual and Motor Skills**, 1993, 77(3f), 1155–1559.

Tomporowsi, P.D. *Cognitive and behavioral responses to acute exercise in youths: a review*. **Pediatric Exercise Science**, 2003, 15(4), 348–359.

Wittberg, R.A., Northrup, K.L. & Cottrell, L.A. *Children's aerobic fitness and academic achievement: A longitudinal examination of students during their fifth and seventh grade years*. **American Journal of Public Health**, 2012, 102(12), 2303–2307.

Zervas, Y., Danis, A. & Klissouras, V. *Influence of physical exertion on mental performance with reference to training*. **Perceptual and Motor Skills**, 1991, 72(3c), 1215–1221.

[30] Tremblay, M.S., Inman, J.W. & Willms, J.D. *The relationship between physical activity, self-esteem, and academic achievement in 12-year-old children*. **Pediatric Exercise Science**, 2000, 12(3), 312–323.

[31] Hinkle, J.S., Tuckman, B.W. & Sampson, J.P. *The psychology, physiology, and the creativity of middle school aerobic exercises*. **Elementary School Guidance & Counseling**, 1993, 28(2), 133–145.

Tuckman, B.W. & Hinkle, J.S. *An experimental study of the physical and psychological effects of aerobic exercise on schoolchildren*. **Health Psychology**, 1986, 5(3), 197–207.

[32] Keays J.J. & Allison, K.R. *The effects of regular moderate to vigorous physical activity on student outcomes: A review*. **Canadian Journal Public Health**, 1995, 86(1), 62–65.

[33] Hillman, C.H., Castelli, D.M. & Buck, S.M. *Aerobic fitness and neurocognitive function in healthy preadolescent children*. **Medicine and Science in Sports and Exercise**, 2005, 37(11), 1967–1974.

[34] Sibley, B.A. & Etnier, J.L. *The relationship between physical activity and cognition in children: A meta-analysis*. **Pediatric Exercise Science**, 2003, 15(3), 243–256.

[35] Rovio, S., Kåreholt, I., Helkala, E.L., Viitanen, M., Winblad, B., Tuomilehto, J., Soininen, H., Nissinen, A. & Kivipelto, M. *Leisure-time physical activity at midlife and the risk of dementia and Alzheimer's disease*. **The Lancet Neurology**, 2005, 4(11), 705–711.

[36] Etgen, T., Sander, D., Huntgeburth, U., Poppert, H., Forstl, H. & Bickel, H. *Physical activity and incident cognitive impairment in elderly persons: the INVADE study*. **Archives of Internal Medicine**, 2010, 170(2), 186.

[37] Kramer, A.F., Hahn, S., Cohen, N.J., Banich, M.T., McAuley, E., Harrison, C.R., Chason, J., Vakil, E., Bardell, L., Boileau1, R.A. & Colcombe, A. *Ageing, fitness and neurocognitive function*. **Nature**, 1999, 400(6743), 418–419.

[38] Kagan, S. **Silly Sports & Goofy Games**. San Clemente, CA: Kagan Publishing, 2000.

[39] Leeuwen, E., Zimmermann, E. & Davila-Ross, M. *Responding to inequities: Gorillas try to maintain their competitive advantage during play fights*. **Biology Letters**, 2011, 7(1), 39–42.

[40] Sample, I. (July 13, 2010). *Gorillas learn about injustice and revenge by playing tag* [text]. **The Guardian**. http://www.guardian.co.uk/science/2010/jul/14/gorillas-injustic-revenge-playing-tag.

[41] Kagan, S. **Silly Sports & Goofy Games**. San Clemente, CA: Kagan Publishing, 2000.

[42] Crockett, M.J., Clark, L., Tabibnia, G., Lieberman, M.D. & Robbins, T.W. *Serotonin modulates behavioral reactions to unfairness*. **Science**, 2008, 320(5884), 1739–1739.

[43] Baumann, S. **Feed Your Brain for Learning**. Farmington, MI: Emerging Free Press, 2005.

[44] Sampson, A.E., Dixit, S., Meyers, A.F. & Houser Jr., R. *The nutritional impact of breakfast consumption on the diets of inner-city African-American elementary school children*. **Journal of the National Medical Association**, 1995, 87(3), 195–202.

[45] Sampson, A.E., Dixit, S., Meyers, A.F. & Houser Jr., R. *The nutritional impact of breakfast consumption on the diets of inner-city African-American elementary school children*. **Journal of the National Medical Association**, 1995, 87(3), 195–202.

Siega-Riz, A.M., Popkin, B.M. & Carson, T. *Trends in breakfast consumption for children in the United States from 1965–1991*. **American Journal of Clinical Nutrition**, 1998, 67(4), 748S–756S.

[46] Rampersaud G.C., Pereira M.A., Girard B.L., Adams J. & Metzl, J.D. *Breakfast habits, nutritional status, body weight, and academic performance in children and adolescents*. **Journal of the American Dietetic Association**, 2005, 105(5), 743–760.

[47] Crockett, M.J., Clark, L., Robbins, T.W., Tabibnia, G. & Lieberman, M.D. *Serotonin modulates behavioural reactions to unfairness*. **Science**, 2008, 320(5884), 1739.

[48] Hoyland, A., Dye, L. & Lawton, C.L. *A systematic review of the effect of breakfast on the cognitive performance of children and adolescents*. **Nutrition Research Reviews**, 2009, 22(2), 220–243.

49 Florence, M.D., Asbridge, M. & Veugelers, P. *Diet quality and academic performance.* **Journal of School Health**, 2008, 78(4), 209–215.

Taras, H.L. *Nutrition and student performance at school.* **Journal of School Health**, 2005, 75(6), 199–213.

50 Sibley, B.A., Ward, R.M., Yazvac, T.S., Zullig, K. & Potteiger, J.A. *Making the grade with diet and exercise.* **AASA Journal of Scholarship & Practice**, 2008, 5(2), 23–45.

51 Kleinman, R.E., Hall, S., Green, H. Korzeck-Ramirez, K., Patton, K., Pagano, M.E. & Murphy, J.M. *Diet, breakfast, and academic performance in children.* **Annals of Nutrition and Metabolism**, 2001, 46(1), 24–30.

Meyers, A.F., Sampson, A.E., Weitzman, M., Rogers, B.L. & Kayne, H. *School breakfast program and school performance.* **American Journal of Disadvantaged Children**, 1989, 143(10), 1234–1239.

Pollitt, E., Leibel, R.L. & Greenfield, D. *Brief fasting, stress, and cognition in children.* **American Journal of Clinical Nutrition**, 1981, 34(8), 1526–1533.

Pollitt, E., Lewis, N.L., Garza, C. & Shulman, R.J. *Fasting and cognitive function.* **Journal of Psychiatric Research**, 1982, 17(2), 169–174.

Pollitt, E. & Mathews, R. *Breakfast and cognition: An integrative summary.* **American Journal of Clinical Nutrition**. 1998, 67(4), 804S–813S.

52 Food and Nutrition Service, U.S. Department of Agriculture, Centers for Disease Control and Prevention, US Department of Health and Human Services, & US Department of Education. FNS-374. *Making It Happen! School Nutrition Success Stories.* Alexandria, VA, 2005.

53 Nielsen, S.J. & Popkin, B.M. *Patterns and trends in food portion sizes, 1977–1998.* **Journal of the American Medical Association**, 2003, 289(4), 450–453.

54 Food and Nutrition Service, US Department of Agriculture, Centers for Disease Control and Prevention, US Department of Health and Human Services, & US Department of Education. FNS-374. *Making It Happen! School Nutrition Success Stories.* Alexandria, VA, 2005.

55 Batmanghelidj, F. *Your Body's Many Cries for Water.* Vienna, VA: Global Health Solutions, 1997, 35.

56 Batmanghelidj, F. *Your Body's Many Cries for Water.* Vienna, VA: Global Health Solutions, 1997.

57 Rogers, P.J. *A drink of water can improve or impair mental performance depending on small differences in thirst.* **Appetite**, 2001, 36(1), 57–58.

58 Bergeron, J.D. & Le Baudour, C. Chapter 9: *Caring for medical emergencies.* In **First Responder** (8 ed.), 262. New Jersey: Pearson Prentice Hall, 2006.

59 Brown, R.P. & Gerbarg, P.L. *The Healing Power of the Breath.* Boston, MA: Shambhala Publications, 2012.

Farhi, D. *The Breathing Book: Vitality and Good Health through Essential Breath Work.* New York, NY: Henry Holt & Co., 1996.

Lewis, D. *Free Your Breath, Free Your Life.* Boston, MA: Shambhala Press, 2004.

Lewis, D. *The Tao of Natural Breathing: For Health, Well-Being, and Inner Growth.* Berkeley, CA: Rodmell Press, 1997.

60 Kagan, S. *Breakouts to energize brains and boost achievement.* San Clemente, CA: Kagan Publishing. **Kagan Online Magazine**, Fall 2012/ Winter 2013. www.KaganOnline.com.

61 Kagan, S. & Kagan, M. *Kagan Cooperative Learning.* San Clemente, CA: Kagan Publishing, 2009.

62 Kagan, M., Kagan, L. & Kagan, S. *Cooperative Learning Structures for Classbuilding.* San Clemente, CA: Kagan Publishing, 2012.

Safety

For the brains of our students to function optimally, our students need to feel safe. No put-downs, embarrassments, bullies, exclusions, or threats of any kind. Music; cooperative, inclusive teams; and exercise are among the fourteen tools to create safety.

Principle 2
Foster Safety

The brain is designed to keep us alive. One way it does that is to respond efficiently to threats. In the center of the brain are two structures each about the size and shape of an almond. When discovered, they were named the amygdalae after the Latin word for almond, *amygdalus*. These two structures, the right amygdala and the left amygdala, have a number of functions, but perhaps their most important function is acting as threat sensors. They allow us to respond quickly to threats. If we perceive a threat, the amygdalae fire, setting off a cascade of involuntary reactions that keep us focused on the threat and prepared to respond.

If we *hear* an angry voice, the left amygdala begins firing above base rate initiating a cascade of reactions in the brain that prepare us to fight, flee, or freeze. If we *see* an angry face, the right amygdala sets off the fight-or-flight defense alarm reaction. Brain scans teach us a great deal about when the amygdalae fire. We can pipe in voices or show faces to people during active brain imaging to see when the amygdalae go into action. The amygdalae begin to fire when we see the face of a stranger, someone not of our own race,[1] an angry face or gesture, or a fearful face. Amazingly, the amygdalae fire when an angry face is projected so fast, the person is not even aware anything has been projected! This process of unconsciously distinguishing between safety and threat is called *neuroception*, in contrast to *perception*, which is conscious.[2] We give off cues to our genuine feelings below our conscious awareness, and we detect and respond to the cues others give off, again without being aware of either the cues or how we are reacting. Each time we are in conversation with another person, we are having an unconscious conversation, below conscious awareness![3]

The Fight-or-Flight Defense Alarm

When the amygdalae fire, they set off the fight-or-flight defense alarm, preparing us to fight or flee. The fight-or-flight defense alarm reaction was detailed by Walter B. Cannon of Harvard Medical

14
Tools to Foster Safety

> ## Tip
>
> If we are angry or upset with a student, we cannot tell the student we like him or her and expect to be believed. The student's autonomic nervous system reacts to the feelings we actually have, the subtle, unconscious messages our tone of voice, body language, and facial expressions give off—not the conscious verbal message. If we want to be believed when we tell a student we like him or her, we need to find something in the student we genuinely like, and focus on that!

When the fear center of the hypothalamus is stimulated, the hypothalamus sets off the fight-or-flight reaction in two ways. First, it sends messages to the sympathetic nervous system via direct nerve pathways. Second, it releases corticotropin-releasing factor to the pituitary, which then releases ACTH (commonly called a "stress hormone"), which in turn stimulates the adrenal cortex and the release of approximately 30 other hormones, including cortisol (another "stress hormone"), adrenalin (epinephrine), noradrenalin (norepinephrine), and related arousal hormones that set off the fight-or-flight defense reaction. See Table: The Fight-or-Flight Defense Alarm Reaction, p. 2.5.

Threat Narrows Perception and Cognition.

Part of the fight-or-flight reaction is a narrowing of both perceptions and cognitions. The amygdalae have a massive number of direct connections to our prefrontal cortex where we do our thinking and planning.[6] When we perceive a threat, the amygdalae send inhibitory

School about 100 years ago.[4] Picture a startled or frightened cat with a fixed gaze, hair standing up, back arched, ready to attack or run. As humans, our hair may not stand straight up, but we react to threats with sympathetic nervous system arousal.

The fight-or-flight reaction is mediated by a specific part of the hypothalamus.[5] Animals produce the response in the absence of an external threat if there is electrical stimulation of the fear parts of the hypothalamus. It is amazing to watch a cat with an electrode in the hypothalamus. The cat can be walking around calmly or eating, but when the experimenter presses a lever to give stimulation to the part of the hypothalamus that controls the fight-or-flight response, immediately the cat goes into the classic fight-or-flight stance preparing to fight or flee from an imaginary foe! If the electrode is placed in a different part of the hypothalamus, the cat relaxes when stimulated.

> ## Tips
>
> - Create a threat-free classroom.
>
> - Frequently check for understanding.
>
> - Give private feedback and corrections.
>
> - Use cooperative structures that allow encouragement, tutoring, and praise.
>
> - Avoid timed tests and calling on non-volunteers to answer in front of the class.
>
> - Create a "We" environment in which students support each other in working for a common goal: "If everyone scores above 80, we will play a Silly Sport to celebrate."

The Fight-or-Flight[4,5] Defense Alarm Reaction

Reaction	Function
Blood pressure increases; blood is shunted away from the extremities and digestive system and toward the deep muscle groups	To send blood to the major muscles to fight or flee; to reduce blood loss if we are cut; to conserve energy, not wasting it on digestion
Heart rate increases	To pump more nutrients to the muscles
Breathing rate increases and breathing becomes shallow	To accelerate the Oxygen-CO_2 exchange
Muscle tension increases	To flex muscles, preparing to fight or flee
Perspiration	To reduce heat buildup. (Have you ever had sweaty palms when nervous?)
Pupils dilate	To take in more light, better to see the threat
Frowning or threatening facial expressions	To ward off the threat
Perception becomes more narrowly focused; tunnel vision	To keep our eye on the threat
Impaired ability to think, plan, and inhibit impulses	To keep our mind narrowly focused on the threat

messages to the prefrontal cortex. The result: Our ability to think and reason becomes limited. In addition, our perceptual field is narrowed; we get tunnel vision. We become unable to perceive subtle internal and external stimuli. In the face of a real threat, these are very adaptive reactions. We need to keep narrowly focused on the threat; we do not want our minds wandering. Picture yourself where you are now and suddenly a growling lion walks in. You are immediately consumed with thoughts of safety. Reading this book is the last thing on your mind. The same is true for students who perceive threat—their thoughts narrow, focusing on the threat to the exclusion of learning.

Threat Weakens Impulse Control. We have all had the experience of being angry and saying or doing something we later regret. After the amygdalae have calmed down and the prefrontal cortex is fully functioning, we ask ourselves,

"How could I have done or said that?" "How could I have been so dumb?" Actually, we were dumb! The amygdalae shut down the part of the brain that does the reasoning, planning, and impulse control. In young students, the prefrontal cortex is not fully developed, and the amygdalae have more sway, explaining students' impulsiveness and lack of consideration of consequences. As students get older, increasingly, the prefrontal cortex is capable of dampening down the amygdalae reaction. We call this *emotional maturity.*

Prefrontal Cortex Controls Impulses. The role of the prefrontal cortex in controlling impulses is dramatically illustrated by the tragic fate of Phineas Gage. When his left frontal lobe was destroyed in an accident, Phineas went from

The Tragic Fate of Phineas Gage

A most dramatic example of how the thinking part of the brain inhibits the expression of impulse-driven actions is the case of Phineas Gage. Prior to his accident, Phineas was a foreman on a construction crew, and was viewed as a good leader, respected by those who worked under him. He was described as having "a well-balanced mind, being a shrewd, smart businessman, very energetic and persistent in executing all his plans of operation."[8] At 25 years of age, Phineas was working with a tamping iron to prepare a blasting charge. The blast accidentally discharged and drove his tamping bar all the way through Phineas' head. His three and a half foot long iron tamping bar landed some 80 feet away! The bar destroyed a substantial portion of Phineas' left frontal lobe. Remarkably, Phineas could walk and talk immediately after the accident, and after some time, recovered.

Given that the prefrontal cortex is the seat of impulse control, rational decision making, and planning, destroying much of that part of the brain profoundly changed Phineas. His friends claimed Phineas was no longer Phineas. This methodical, well-respected leader was described as:

> fitful, irreverent, indulging at times in the grossest profanity (which was not previously his custom), manifesting but little deference for his fellows, impatient of restraint or advice when it conflicts with his desires, at times pertinaciously obstinate, yet capricious and vacillating, devising many plans of future operations, which are no sooner arranged than they are abandoned in turn for others appearing more feasible.[8]

well-controlled to impulse dominated. There is debate regarding how completely Phineas lost his ability to control impulses and carry out plans, and the extent to which with time, he was able to recover, but this tragic accident dramatically demonstrates how the prefrontal cortex serves to inhibit impulses which otherwise would be expressed. Famed neurologist Antonio Damasio takes the case of Phineas Gage as an illustration of the link between the frontal lobes, emotion, and practical decision making.[7] See Box: The Tragic Fate of Phineas Gage.

Threat Inhibits Thinking. To keep us focused on the threat, the amygdalae send inhibitory signals to the prefrontal cortex responsible for thinking. In the face of a threat, we need to prepare for action, not cognition! Think of the amygdalae and prefrontal cortex as sitting on opposite ends of a teeter-totter. Both animal and human studies demonstrate a reciprocal relation between these structures: As neural activity in the prefrontal cortex increases, activity in the amygdalae decreases, and vice versa.[9] Intense feeling leaves us incapable of thinking rationally; thinking decreases the probability of emotion-driven, irrational behavior. When the amygdalae are up, the thinking part of the brain is down! That is, when the amygdalae are firing, the prefrontal cortex is inhibited. See the diagram below.

> *Everyone is familiar with how threat and the amygdalae firing can interfere with thinking. Remember a time you were very anxious going into an important test. Possible failure was the threat. You were so nervous you felt, "I can't even think straight." That was the action of the amygdalae sending inhibitory signals to your prefrontal cortex, actually shutting down your ability to think.*

Inhibition of the prefrontal cortex is disastrous for students. They cannot solve problems as well, and are less able to think broadly and creatively.

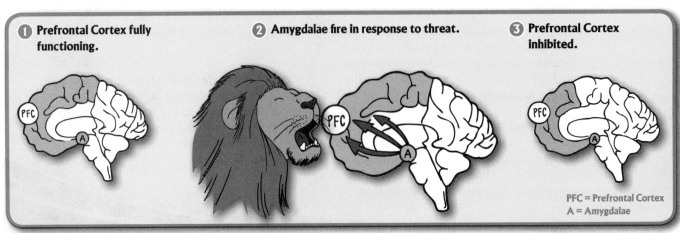

1 Prefrontal Cortex fully functioning.

2 Amygdalae fire in response to threat.

3 Prefrontal Cortex inhibited.

PFC = Prefrontal Cortex
A = Amygdalae

Threat Interferes with Achievement and Learning. Although the fight-or-flight reaction, including the narrowing of thinking and perception, is adaptive in the face of a predator, it is exactly the opposite of what we want in our classrooms. The part of the fight-or-flight reaction that most interferes with the ability to learn is the narrowing of cognition and perception. To the extent students sense any threat, their brains become less able to learn.

The negative effects of stress are not just temporary: Chronically high cortisol levels lead to the death of brain cells in the hippocampus, a structure essential for laying down new memories.[10] The hippocampus of Vietnam veterans suffering from post-traumatic stress disorder (PTSD) atrophied from 8% to 24% and was associated with impaired ability to recall old memories and lay down new memories.[11]

A series of scans conducted while second- and third-grade students did addition and subtraction revealed that those who felt panicky about doing math had increased activity in brain regions associated with fear, which caused decreased activity in parts of the brain involved in problem solving. The two groups also showed differences in performance: Children with high math anxiety were less accurate and significantly slower at solving math problems than children with low math anxiety. The results suggest that math anxiety is a math-specific fear that interferes with the brain's information-processing capacity and its ability to reason through a math problem.[12]

In one revealing experiment, Dr. Brod had students subtract 17 from a large number and then 17 from the remainder and to continue that to the background beat of a metronome. If, while subjects were performing the mental math, others who were watching made comments like, *"I did better than that,"* the subject had increased blood pressure, increased heart rate, and increased blood flow to the major muscles, preparing for fight or flight.[13]

Thus we can derive the second principle of brain-friendly learning:

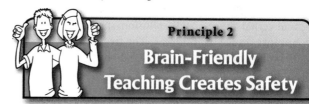

Principle 2

Brain-Friendly Teaching Creates Safety

When there is any threat at all, our students have narrowed cognition and become less able to engage in calm reflection, creative thinking, and learning.

Classroom Threats. It does not take a roaring lion to set off the amygdalae. Even small threats, all too common in classrooms, set off the sympathetic nervous system and narrow perception and cognition. There are many perceived threats that, unfortunately, occur in our classrooms.[14] See Box: Common Classroom Threats.

Whenever there is a perceived threat, the brain's ability to think, plan, problem solve, and control impulses is inhibited or shut down. Learning becomes more difficult or impossible.

Threats Before and After Class. Many students have their amygdalae firing before they even enter class. Rejection on the playground or in the hall during passing period, a comment or an incident at home or on the way to school, abuse experienced or witnessed, and violence on television or in a violent video game, are all capable of causing the amygdalae to fire, constricting cognition.

Common Classroom Threats

- Being called on to perform
- Being excluded by peers
- Bullying
- Competition
- Disapproving glance from teacher or peer
- Falling behind in work
- Fights
- Not understanding an assignment

- Oral reports
- Performing in front of peers
- Pop quizzes
- Preparation for tests
- Public correction
- Public feedback on tests and quizzes
- Put downs
- Social comparison
- Timed tests

Bullying. Bullying takes many forms: Physical and verbal abuse, social exclusion, spreading rumors, and cyber bullying. The frequency of bullying in U.S. schools is a national embarrassment: As many as 40% of adolescents report being the victims of some form of bullying.[15] Schools with more bullying score significantly lower on academic tests after controlling for poverty, minority population, and school size.[16] With the amygdalae firing, there is constricted cognition, perception, and attention, hindering the ability to perform academically. The amygdalae continue firing for some time after a threatening experience. After a school shooting, the amygdalae of all the students are firing the next day. For some, the amygdalae don't quiet down even after a week. Prolonged firing of the amygdalae is called post-traumatic stress disorder (PTSD).

Victim Responses. Bullying can result in extreme reactions among victims—suicide on the one hand and explosive violence on the other. In examining 37 incidents of extreme school violence involving 41 perpetrators, the Secret Service National Threat Assessment Center concluded three-fourths of those who had resorted to extreme school violence had a grievance and two-thirds of all attackers felt persecuted, harassed, or bullied. Motives for the violence were revenge or to simply end the harassment.

> Attackers described experiences of being bullied in terms that approached torment. They told of behaviors that, if they occurred in the workplace, would meet the legal definitions of harassment.[17]

Fellow students described the treatment of freshman Andy Williams who, following having been the victim of bullying, opened fire on classmates in a Santee, California, high school: *"They'd walk up to him and sock him in the face for no reason."* Kids would burn their lighters and then press the hot metal against his neck.[18]

Stress and the Immune System. Stress weakens the immune system making us more vulnerable to illness. Researchers distinguish naturalistic stressors (an exam) from chronic stressor (exclusion, financial worries). Naturalistic stressors suppress cellular immunity, increasing vulnerability to illness.[19]

Parasympathetic Arousal: Relaxation Response

The autonomic nervous system has two components: (1) The sympathetic nervous system which, when aroused sets off the fight-or-flight defense alarm reaction; and (2) the parasympathetic nervous system which, when aroused, releases the relaxation response.

Parasympathetic Arousal. Picture the sympathetic and parasympathetic nervous systems on opposite ends of a teeter-totter. When one is up, the other is down. When we turn on parasympathetic arousal, our breathing and heart rate slow; our digestive system relaxes, hypertension is reduced, blood pressure lowers, blood lactate (a correlate of anxiety) is reduced, and our facial muscles relax into a smile. Most importantly, because the amygdalae are not sending inhibitory signals to the frontal cortex, we can think more clearly and creatively. We can make more learning connections.

Parasympathetic arousal, like sympathetic arousal, is mediated by the hypothalamus, but a different part of that structure.[20] It is also mediated by one of the vagus nerves. There are three vagus nerves, each with different functions.[21] One of the vagus nerves, the myelinated vagus (ventral vagal complex), which originates in an area of the brainstem known as the nucleus ambiguus, sets off parasympathetic nervous system arousal,[22] inhibiting the sympathetic nervous system, turning off the fight, flight, or freeze reaction. This vagus nerve carries signals directly to the heart, lungs, intestines, and facial muscles. When it is activated, heart rate and breathing rate slow, blood pressure drops, we feel relaxed. We smile, and the body enters a state of physical calm.[23]

The Relaxation Response. Everyone is familiar with the experience of parasympathetic arousal. It is that calm, safe, all-is-good-with-the-world feeling we get during and after a warm bath, following a massage, while sitting by a bubbling brook in the quiet shade of a tall tree, and in the afterglow following making love. This parasympathetic arousal can be set off in different ways in different people. For some, it is the calm feeling after a good workout or the happiness we experience during and after a supportive conversation with a friend. Some people experience this tranquil feeling at church or temple, others via dance, yet others from singing. It is a feeling of threat-free, relaxed alertness. For many of us, the feelings come while we are engaged in some activity in which we "lose ourselves." For one person, it might be arts and crafts, for another while repairing a motor, for yet another, the feeling is released while pasting stamps in a stamp book. All of us are different: The same activity, say, dance, that sets off a parasympathetic arousal in one person sets off sympathetic arousal in another because that person feels awkward or embarrassed, or has had an anxiety-producing experience associated with dancing.

Parasympathetic Arousal Facilitates Thinking and Learning.

When we do have parasympathetic arousal, the amygdalae are at rest. The prefrontal cortex is not inhibited. We can make learning and thinking connections that are not possible when under stress. Think of the times you were taking a nice warm shower or bath and a creative thought sprung to mind. What is going on? Showers and baths don't think. Why do we have creative thoughts when we relax in warm water? When we are in warm water, we feel safe. The amygdalae stop firing. There is no inhibition of the prefrontal cortex. We are free to make cognitive connections we would not make if we were on guard.

What does all this have to do with teaching the way brains best learn? A great deal. In our

classrooms, we do not want narrow cognitions and perceptions. And for sure, we do not want to contend with impulse-dominated behaviors. We want exactly the opposite. We want students who are perceptive, who can make cognitive connections, and who consider consequences before acting. With narrowed perceptions and cognitions and inability to control impulses, ability to learn is severely hampered. Ability to control impulses is what separates students who persist in the face of a difficult learning task from those who give up.

When we feel safe, the amygdalae are quiescent and we are able to think clearly and learn more. The more we are relaxed, the more we are able to perceive all that is around us and to make cognitive connections.

> **Tip**
> **Threat and Relaxation Are Incompatible**
> Arouse students' parasympathetic nervous systems to turn off threat and facilitate learning and thinking.

Thus, if we want to create a learning environment that promotes perception, cognition, and learning, we need to create safe classrooms. The questions then become: How do we create safe classrooms? How do we put the amygdalae to rest? How do we release the relaxation response in our students? There are many ways to create safety in our classrooms. Most of the rest of this chapter catalogs and describes tools to create a safe classroom. Before we turn to those tools, let's examine an exception: In some cases, relaxation and absence of anxiety actually reduce optimal performance.

Optimal Stress: Not Too Much; Not Too Little

Although as teachers we are most concerned with reducing stress that interferes with thinking and learning, sometimes a bit of stress in the classroom can help. If students show no interest or motivation, raising their level of concern may boost their performance. This is explained by the Yerkes-Dodson Law.

The Yerkes-Dodson Law. Before turning to all the things we can do to turn off the fight-or-fight defense alarm and create a brain-safe classroom, it is important to note, we are not calling for a totally relaxed classroom. We do not want a classroom in which there is no level of concern among students—a classroom where there is no challenge, no motivation. On the contrary, as we will see, brains respond to challenge. There is a well-established curvilinear relation between challenge and achievement. Too little challenge lowers achievement just as does overwhelming challenge.

A long history of research on the question of the effect of stress on performance began with the publication of the Yerkes–Dodson Law in 1908. In studying discrimination learning in mice, Robert Yerkes and John Dodson found "Both weak stimuli and strong stimuli result in slow habit-formation."[24] This finding became extensively researched.

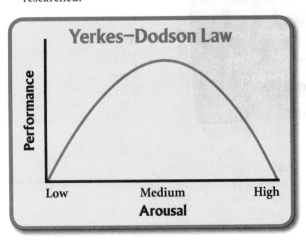

The Yerkes–Dodson Law is intuitively appealing. At very low levels of arousal (boredom), alertness is low, so performance is poor ("*I am so bored, I can't concentrate.*") At the other end of the curve, very high levels of arousal (stress) interfere with task performance ("*I am so nervous, I can't concentrate.*") See Box: Yerkes–Dodson Law.

Arousal Helps or Hurts Depending on Task. Humans aren't mice. What is true for mice doing discrimination tasks, does not always hold for humans doing different types of learning and

performance tasks. Human studies reveal the Yerkes–Dodson Law holds for some cases and not for others, depending on the type of learning or performance and depending on the student.

Memorization Tasks. Memorization tasks follow the Yerkes–Dodson Law quite well. Mildly elevated levels of glucocorticoids (stress hormones) are associated with optimal performance. When stress is too low or too high, performance on memorization tasks suffers.[25]

Highly Practiced Tasks. If it is a task that a student has done many times or that takes little mental effort, arousal must be kept high or else the student will become bored and lose interest.

Athletic and Stamina Performances. Tasks that involve stamina or persistence are best performed with high levels of arousal that keep motivation high.

Unfamiliar and Intellectual Tasks. Tasks that are unfamiliar, cognitively demanding, and that involve concentration are performed best in a relaxed state.

Thus, in general, to optimize performance, we want a relaxed state while students are engaged in problem solving, creative writing, or creating projects. In contrast, we want high arousal (a competitive tournament, or a timed test) for physical performance (running for speed) and for completion of mundane tasks that do not involve concentration.

Individual Differences. The relation of stress to performance is further complicated by individual differences. Amount of working memory and math anxiety interact with amount of stress to predict math performance.[26] That is, for students with low working memory capacity, neither amount of stress (as measured by cortisol, a stress hormone) nor amount of math anxiety predicts performance. In contrast, for students with high working memory capacity, the effect of stress works in opposite directions, depending on their math anxiety. For students high in math anxiety, additional stress leads to poorer performance. For students who are low in math anxiety, greater stress improves performance. This finding fits nicely with the Yerkes–Dodson Law: Too much or too little stress leads to less than optimum performance. Too much stress can lead students to choke; additional stress for those who are not aroused can lead students to thrive. While the interaction of working memory, math anxiety, and stress is far too complicated to easily apply directly to the classroom setting, we can infer a general rule that is applicable: Don't put additional stress on students who are already anxious; and a bit of additional arousal may be helpful for students who are too nonchalant about a learning task.

Raising Arousal. Many ways exist to raise the level of concern or arousal. See Box: Raising Arousal.

Stress and Memory

As teachers, we are in the business of creating memories. All learning is memory. Sometimes we want to have students remember a fact, sometimes a procedure, sometimes an experience, and sometimes we want students to figure out the solution to a problem. These different types of learning involve different memory systems that engage different parts of the brain in very different ways. Facts are processed by the semantic memory system; procedures are processed by the procedural memory system; incidents are processed by the episodic memory system; and figuring out solutions involves the working memory system.

Stress impacts the different memory systems in different ways. When administered high doses of cortisol, a stress hormone, semantic memory is impaired, but procedural memory is not.[28] (When stressed we can't remember a person's name, but we still know how to shake their hand or drive a car.) In contrast, when administered doses of cortisol while being presented pictures with emotional content, memory for the pictures is enhanced.[29] In general, enhanced arousal enhances episodic memory. (We remember where we were when we first heard of planes crashing into the Twin Towers on 9/11, but we don't remember where we were the day before.) Finally, high stress has the worst impact on working memory. It interferes with working memory even more than it interferes with semantic memory.[30] (Almost all of us have had the experience of going into a test or a job interview so stressed we felt we couldn't think straight.) See Table: Functions of Memory Systems, p. 2.12.

Raising Arousal

If individuals, teams, or the entire class has low motivation or seem bored with a task, there are many ways to raise their arousal:

- ▶ Remind students they will be tested on the content.
- ▶ Post task-completion time and challenge students to beat their record.
- ▶ Post percent correct and challenge students to beat the record.
- ▶ Tell students that performance will be made public (to parents or peers).
- ▶ Inform students that success on a future project depends on skill being mastered.
- ▶ Create team or individual competitions for correctness or completion time.
- ▶ Provide extrinsic rewards.
- ▶ Engage students in a Silly Sport or Goofy Game[27] to energize the class.
- ▶ Play upbeat music (around 120 beats per minute).
- ▶ Provide a fun task for individuals or teams who finish early.
- ▶ Redesign the task so it is more interesting or challenging.
- ▶ Challenge individuals or teams to find alternative, faster ways to complete the task.

Functions of Memory Systems

Memory System	Function
Semantic	Memory for Facts
Procedural	Memory for Procedures
Episodic	Memory for Incidents
Working	Manipulation of Data
Spatial	Navigation
Short Term	Immediate Recall

Focus on the Big Picture

Although mild amounts of stress may facilitate rote learning and high levels of stress may facilitate athletic performance and, in some cases, test performance for those low in anxiety, we are concerned primarily with optimizing thinking and creativity. Therefore, the rest of the chapter will focus on ways to reduce anxiety and stress in the classroom. In short—to create a classroom safe for brains to think.

Creating the Relaxed, Threat-Free Classroom

We have a choice: We can have the amygdalae of students' brains firing, inhibiting full functioning of the prefrontal cortex. Or we can put the amygdalae to rest, allowing students to be more creative and to better learn our content. In this section, we explore fourteen ways to put the amygdalae to rest. Our job as teachers is not to implement all fourteen tools—they are provided in the spirit of a smorgasbord. Pick what fits your style and that of your students. By putting in place just a few of these powerful tools, we can increase dramatically the optimal functioning of our students' brains. Here are fourteen tools to create schools and classrooms in which brains are safe to think and learn:

Fourteen Tools to Create Safety

1. Construct a Safe Context for Learning
2. Celebrate Diversity
3. Offer Safe Evaluations
4. Build Inclusive Teams
5. Form Inclusive Classrooms
6. Play Background Music
7. Encourage Exercise
8. Promote Play
9. Incorporate Humor
10. Provide Hydration
11. Foster Positive Social Interaction
12. Teach Relaxation Breathing
13. Practice Progressive Muscle Relaxation
14. Advocate Meditation

Tool 1

Construct a Safe Context for Learning

We can create a safe context for learning in a variety of ways. Some examples of things we can do:

▶ We do not announce grades or performance publicly to avoid embarrassing low-achieving students.

▶ We establish private signals so students can ask for help without public embarrassment.

▶ We create class norms respecting personal possessions and respect for personal space.

▶ We communicate predetermined consequences so students do not have to guess what will happen to them if they violate expectations.

▶ We adopt a win-win discipline style that avoids public embarrassment and punishment; focuses on learning responsible ways to behave.[31]

▶ We do not make students perform in front of the entire class without practice and preparation.

- ▶ We do not surprise students with unexpected pop quizzes.
- ▶ We establish predictable routines and procedures so students feel comfortable.

Traditional Teaching Methods Create Stress

Some traditional classroom practices create stress that can be avoided if we use cooperative learning structures. For example, following a demonstration of a new skill at the board, the traditional teacher hands students worksheets to practice the skill. A student who does not understand how to do the problem may feel too embarrassed to raise a hand to ask for help. Thus, it is common to see students struggling, practicing the skill wrong, or just giving up. If the worksheet practice is assigned as homework, some students who know they do not know the skill don't do the homework. Some rationalize: *"This assignment is dumb."* It is easier on the ego to say the assignment is dumb than to admit not understanding how to do the work.

Kagan Structures Create Safety

Kagan Cooperative Learning Structures scaffold for support and sidestep stress. For example, instead of independent worksheet work, the teacher can use the Cooperative Learning Structures like, **Flashcard Game**, **RallyQuiz**, **Sage-N-Scribe**, **Team Pair Solo**, or **Timed Pair Share**.

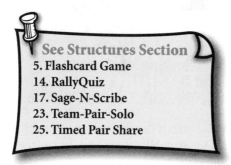

See Structures Section
5. Flashcard Game
14. RallyQuiz
17. Sage-N-Scribe
23. Team-Pair-Solo
25. Timed Pair Share

Flashcard Game. The **Flashcard Game** provides peer support as students memorize any content. A student feels safe because the three rounds of the game are structured for success. On the first round, a student has just seen and heard the answer, and is only asked to repeat the answer from short-term memory. Students feel it is "too easy" and that they "cannot miss," creating a sense of safety. As the rounds progress, students build on their successes. Knowing they will receive peer praise for every item and coaching if necessary also creates a sense of safety.

RallyQuiz. Whereas the **Flashcard Game** is ideal for placing content into semantic memory, **RallyQuiz** works well for problems that involve working memory. Students in pairs take turns presenting questions to each other, providing praise or coaching depending on whether their partner answers correctly or needs help. Because each student knows that he or she will get the answer correct, either right away or after coaching, there is a sense of safety.

Sage-N-Scribe. Students work in pairs, one is the Sage, and the other, the Scribe. For each problem, the Sage tells the Scribe how to do the problem while the Scribe records the solution. Students alternate roles for each problem. Partners encourage, tutor when necessary, and praise. No student is working alone, struggling. **Sage-N-Scribe** is a safe context for learning.

Team-Pair-Solo. In the first step of this structure, students are working in heterogeneous teams, so they have someone to turn to for help. When they are successful, they advance to pair work, and only when successful at pair work do they safely move to working alone. If students have difficulty with pair work, they can return to teamwork, and if they have difficulty with solo work, they can return to pair work. Thus, there is always a safety net. The scaffolding for success provides safety. **Team-Pair-Solo** is in contrast to first doing problems alone, which creates a much higher level of anxiety and probability of failure.

Timed Pair Share. Students have the support of sharing their ideas with a sympathetic, attentive peer, rather than taking the risk of sharing their ideas in front of the whole class. Students who would be too anxious to raise their hand to be called upon to share in front of the whole class readily share with a partner. Training students in active listening is one of the social skill components of the structure, and having a sympathetic listener increases safety.

All of the cooperative learning structures create safety because they place students on the same side. Students are hoping for the success of their peers and encourage and tutor each other. The cooperative learning structures are in contrast to traditional competitive ways classrooms are structured. In traditional classrooms, students hope a classmate does poorly so they can shine by comparison. In traditional classrooms, when a number of students raise their hands to be called on and a teacher calls on one, the others make a sound of disappointment as they lower their hands. They were in competition with each other to be called on so the success of one is associated with the failure of the others. If the student who was called upon misses, the others become animated. The failure of their classmate is an opportunity to shine, so students learn to hope for the failure of their classmates.

Social Skill Structures Create Safety. When students are polite and respectful toward each other, they are in a safe context. Some Kagan Structures are explicitly designed to promote social skills, contributing to safety. For example, during a pairs team or class discussion, the instructor might use **Paraphrase Passport**. The rule is simple: The right to speak is earned by accurately paraphrasing the opinion or idea of the person who spoke just beforehand.

See Structures Section
12. Paraphrase Passport

Because of this structure, every student knows his or her ideas will be listened to and validated, creating a caring, safe context for the exchange of ideas. **Paraphrase Passport** reduces the risk students experience as they share. Each student knows his or her ideas will meet a sympathetic paraphrase rather than an argument or put-down. This reduction of fear frees the brain for higher-level cerebral functioning. Safe students think more clearly and more deeply.

By using just a few of the Kagan Cooperative Learning Structures, we can go a long way toward enhancing social skills and creating a safe classroom. No teacher will use all Kagan Structures: Each teacher will pick from the over 200-plus Kagan Structures[32] to build their own unique instructional repertoire. As they do, the structures reduce amygdalae activation and put student brains closer to a state of relaxed alertness, the optimal state for cognitive functioning.

Tool 2
Celebrate Diversity

We create safety by respecting and celebrating individual differences. Different students learn in different ways and have different strengths. Rather than measuring all students with the same yardstick, at least some of the time, we allow students to learn in their preferred ways, and to focus on their preferred content. Allow multiple ways for students to learn, using a variety of instructional strategies based on multiple intelligences,[33] modality theory, and cognitive styles.[34] Multiple Intelligences, modality theory, and cognitive styles are covered in depth in Tool 10: Make it Multimodal and Tool 11: Teach with Styles, in Principle 6: Stimuli. Allow multiple ways for students to demonstrate their learning, including oral performances, skits, videos, and other creative expressions. In the inclusive class, differences are viewed as assets, not deficits.

Tool 3
Offer Safe Evaluations

Students feel safer if they know they will not be compared unfavorably with others. To protect them from negative social comparison, we give private feedback and establish a norm against comparing grades. The focus is on improvement, not beating others. Students' work is compared to their own prior work, not to the work of others. Emphasis is placed on portfolios and performances and away from ranking on a curve. We communicate to students that we are on their side. Our job is, above all, to help them. Evaluation is framed in terms of focus on what needs help. Our goal is not to rank students, but rather to create a learning community so all students can realize their potential.

Tool 4
Build Inclusive Teams

Teambuilding structures and activities are designed explicitly to create social safety.[35] The teambuilding structures allow students to know and support each other and to accept individual differences. Through teambuilding and classbuilding, students drop their fear of social rejection and their worry about social acceptance—they are freer to focus on the academic content. No longer fearing rejection of their ideas, students are more expressive, offering and receiving feedback essential for learning.

One of the greatest threats for any student is social isolation. Students spend a great deal of their energy worrying about "being in." To the primitive part of our brain, exclusion equals threat of death. Death by predator awaits the fish that cannot keep up with the school. The same fate awaits the antelope that cannot keep up with the herd as the herd runs from a lion. Being "in" means safety.

Teambuilding Is Inclusion

We can free up a great deal of energy among students if they belong to a team. Belonging means safety, putting the amygdalae to rest. Teambuilding activities are inclusion activities. Thus we encourage team names, team handshakes, team cheers, and mutual support activities.

When we first form teams and students first sit down with their new teammates, what do they want to do? They want to talk with each other, get to know each other. At a basic brain level,

Maslow's Hierarchy of Needs
(Original Five-Stage Model)

Self-Actualization
Fulfillment

Esteem
Achievement, Status, Reputation

Love and Belonging
Family, Friends, Relationships

Safety
Security, Predictability, Stability

Physiological Needs
Air, Food, Water, Shelter, Warmth, Sleep, Sex

they want to determine if they are safe. At an unconscious level their brains are asking, *"Am I safe? Am I safe? Am I safe?"* They want to know if they are going to be put down, excluded, or embarrassed. Until they feel safe, they are not free to concentrate on the geometry lesson. We can think of this in terms of brain neurophysiology (the prefrontal cortex cannot fully function with the amygdalae firing) or we can think of this in terms of Abraham Maslow's Hierarchy of Needs[36] (we can't focus on achievement unless we first establish safety and belonging). See Illustration: Maslow's Hierarchy of Needs, p. 2.15.

Teambuilding Structures. Many Kagan teambuilding structures are designed to help students know, appreciate, and support each other.[37] Three frequently used structures designed to build team unity and support are **RoundRobin**, **Celebrity Interview**, and **Three-Step Interview**.

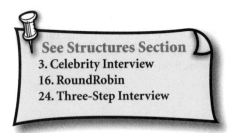

See Structures Section
3. Celebrity Interview
16. RoundRobin
24. Three-Step Interview

RoundRobin. In **RoundRobin** each student in turn shares with teammates. **RoundRobin** can be as brief as one word or phrase each: Name a movie you have enjoyed. In a **Single RoundRobin** students are finished when each has shared. In a **Continuous RoundRobin** students continue taking turns until time is called. For long answers, to equalize participation, a **Timed RoundRobin** is used—each student shares for a predetermined amount of time.

Although **RoundRobin** is most often used for academic content (*"Name inert elements, planets in the solar system, prime numbers, adjectives to describe the main character, events that led up to World War II"*), it can be used for teambuilding by having students share things about themselves, or anything enjoyable. Sample teambuilding content:

- ▸ Your dream profession
- ▸ Favorite dessert
- ▸ A present you have enjoyed receiving

- ▸ Qualities of a good friend
- ▸ Free-time activities
- ▸ If you were given $1,000 as a gift, what would you do with it?
- ▸ Who is one of your heroes? Why?
- ▸ If you could time travel for a day, would you go to the future or past? What would you want to see, do?

Celebrity Interview. Either the teacher or teammates make up a set of around eight questions, one per slip of paper. Students take turns being the celebrity. The celebrity stands and receives applause from teammates and then is given a predetermined amount of time (usually 1 to 2 minutes) to answer as many or as few of the questions as he or she wishes. For teambuilding, the questions are usually getting-acquainted questions, like those listed for **RoundRobin**.

Three-Step Interview. **Three-Step Interview** begins by forming two pairs within each team. The partners interview each other, and then students do a **RoundRobin** sharing what they learned from their partner. A benefit of **Three-Step Interview** is that it holds students accountable for listening to their partners and places heavy emphasis on acquiring the skills of active listening: facing your partner, making eye contact, showing verbal and nonverbal interest, seeking elaboration. The interview content can be focused (describe a sport or hobby you enjoy) or broad (tell me about yourself).

Tool 5

Form Inclusive Classrooms

Classbuilding is the whole-class counterpart to teambuilding. Classbuilding[38] and communitybuilding[39] structures and activities do for the class what teambuilding does for the team. To feel safe, students need to feel they are known, liked, and included not just by their teammates, but also by their classmates. A number of Kagan classbuilding structures are specifically

Classbuilding and Teambuilding
Welcoming New Students

"Our campus had two homeless shelters zoned to our school, so the classroom chemistry was changing daily as students were added and withdrawn from the class. Every time we gained a new student, we would start off the morning with a classbuilding structure like Mix-Pair-Share for students to get to know the new student a little better. Then we also did a brief teambuilder like RoundRobin to have the new student get to know his or her new teammates. Compared to the traditional methods I used before I went to a Kagan training, this was so much more effective in time management and had a more positive impact on helping the new student feel welcome, and to fit into our classroom."

—*Sarah Backner*
2nd Grade, Martinez Elementary School
North Las Vegas, NV

In the cooperative classroom, students are seated in teams of four. Each student has a number, 1, 2, 3, or 4. For **Number Group Mania!**, the teacher announces the size of the group to form and which numbers should be in each group. To encourage classbuilding, students are told not to group with a teammate. Students walk around the classroom, displaying their number with the fingers of a hand, forming groups. The teacher may play music and students are encouraged to greet their new groupmates with positive gambits such as, *"Glad to have you in my group." "We have a great group."*

Once students are in their new groups, the teacher gives them an interaction topic and a structure such as a **RoundRobin**, **RallyRobin**, **Three-Step Interview**, or **Timed Pair Interview**. Depending on the structure, they interact with, encourage, support, and tutor others, creating the feeling among themselves that they are all part of one community of learners. When this happens, the amygdalae are quiescent and the prefrontal cortex is uninhibited, free to think. See Table: Number Group Mania! Sample Groups.

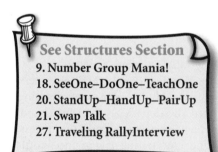

See Structures Section
9. Number Group Mania!
18. SeeOne–DoOne–TeachOne
20. StandUp–HandUp–PairUp
21. Swap Talk
27. Traveling RallyInterview

designed to help classmates know, appreciate, and support one another. Any structure that has students get up from their team and interact in positive ways with classmates serves to increase liking and bonding among classmates. Classbuilding structures include **Number Group Mania!**; **StandUp–HandUp–PairUp**; **SeeOne–DoOne–TellOne**; **Swap Talk**; and **Traveling RallyInterview**.

Number Group Mania! To allow classmates to quickly form various-sized groups, the teacher can use a very simple structure called **Number Group Mania!**

Number Group Mania!
Sample Groups

Group Size	Who Is in the Group
2	Same-Number Pairs; Odds Together and Evens Together; Different-Number Pairs: 1s with 4s and 2s with 3s
3	Same-Number Triads; Different-Number Triads; Any Three Numbers
4	Same-Number Groups; Different-Number Groups; Any Four Numbers, Two 2s with Two 4s and Two 1s with Two 3s

StandUp–HandUp–PairUp. A very quick way to form pairs in the classroom is for the teacher to say, *"When I say Go! You will stand up, put a hand up, and keep your hand up until you find someone to pair with. You will give them a high five and put your hands down, so those who are still looking for a partner can easily find them. Go!"* As with **Number Group Mania!**, once students are in pairs, they are given an interaction topic and a structure such as **Timed Pair Share**, **Timed Pair Interview**, or **RallyRobin**.

Swap Talk. To use **Swap Talk** for classbuilding, all students create a card that has three facts about themselves. Perhaps (1) Their favorite free-time activity; (2) A pet they have had or wish they had had; and (3) Their favorite fast-food restaurant and what they like to order there. Students **StandUp–HandUp–PairUp** and share the information on their cards with their partners. They then swap cards and put a hand up to find another classmate. With the new partner, they share the information on the card their old partner had given them, *"Let me introduce you to John…."* The process is repeated until time is called.

Traveling RallyInterview. Students do a **StandUp–HandUp–PairUp** and then interview each other on a predetermined set of getting-acquainted questions. They then put a hand up, find another partner, and repeat the process, continuing interviewing new partners until time is called.

SeeOne–DoOne–TeachOne. Whereas **Swap Talk** and **Traveling RallyInterview** promote classbuilding via getting acquainted, **SeeOne–DoOne–TeachOne** promotes classbuilding via mutual support. After students have learned how to solve a type of problem, they solve a similar problem on their own. Following that, they explain to a classmate how they solved their problem. As classmates tutor each other, they bond.

Choral Practice, Answer Back, and Echoing. Three related structures help classmates coordinate their efforts to promote learning. **Choral Practice, Answer Back,** and **Echoing** are different from classbuilding structures in that they do not involve classmates standing and

working together face-to-face. They do, however, involve classmates coordinating efforts and working together to master content, and to create a more cohesive class.

Choral Practice. **Choral Practice** is like it sounds. The class recites something in unison. Content ranges: Reciting the Pledge of Allegiance, the Gettesburg Address, a poem, or skip counting.

See Structures Section
4. Choral Practice

Answer Back. The teacher asks a question that has a short answer and students answer back in unison. Content might be the formula for calculating the area of a triangle, definition of a verb, formula for a salt molecule, or date of an important historical event. A kindergarten teacher might hold up a flashcard and have students name the number, letter, or color displayed. Sometimes **Answer Back** is used to have students complete a sentence: *"In 1492, Columbus…."*

Echoing. The teacher says or chants a word, phrase, definition, or rhyme, and students in unison echo the teacher.

Choral Practice, Answer Back, and Echoing are designed to create semantic memory. They are not structures that promote understanding. They should be used only in tandem with teaching for understanding. For example, it makes no sense to teach students *"Columbus sailed the ocean blue in 1492,"* if they do not also know events that led up to his voyages and their consequences.

Tool 6

Play Background Music

Background Music Elicits the Relaxation Response

Calm, predictable background music releases a parasympathetic response, lowering stress hormones, improving mood, and boosting achievement levels.

Music Reduces Stress Hormones
▶ Music increases parasympathetic activity and lowers stress hormones.[40, 41]
▶ Music with a highly rhythmic beat and greater predictability reduces cortisol and noradrenalin levels (stress hormones), whereas less rhythmic and less predictable music does not.[42]
▶ Music lowers cortisol levels during surgery[43] and lowers cortisol after a stressful announcement to patients that they will need surgery.[44]

Music Improves Relaxation, Mood
▶ Classical music played in the background one hour a day results in greater brain coherence and more time in alpha state (relaxed brain waves) among 4-year olds.[45]
▶ Preschool children relax more and engage in more prosocial behaviors when exposed to background music.[46]
▶ Asked to rate neutral facial expressions, adults rated the faces as depressed if sad music was played in the background; when upbeat music was played in the background, they rated the same faces as happy.[47]

Music Boosts Achievement
▶ Background music played in the study hall significantly increased reading comprehension scores among eighth and ninth graders.[48]
▶ Listening to music while learning vocabulary words and definitions dramatically increased vocabulary retention.[49]
▶ Stress-reducing instrumental music improves intelligence test scores among undergraduates.[50]

Background music written at about 60 beats per minute is optimal to elicit the relaxation response. There are a number of commercially available music collections specifically designed to produced relaxed alertness among students.[51]

Background Music
60 Beats per Minute Calms the Body and Mind

"When in the classroom, I used a CD player with CDs. I had a stack of 60 beats-per-minute music. As part of our classroom helpers' jobs, I had the "CD Shuffler." Each day as part of our morning routine, the CD Shuffler chose a different CD, placed it on shuffle, and was in charge of turning on and off the CD during solo work, writing time, and silent reading. It especially helped the calmness of my two students who had been diagnosed with onset childhood schizophrenia. Neither student was able to take medication on a daily basis for various reasons and the calming music helped."

—*Rachel Treaster*
Kagan Trainer

Tool 7

Encourage Exercise

Exercise reduces stress in a number of ways. It reduces cortisol, a primary stress hormone, and can release endorphins, the "feel good" hormones responsible for the runner's high. Exercise, especially during sports that command our full attention, also serves to distract us from worries, focusing our attention. Further, exercise inhibits activation of the ventral hippocampus, the part of the hippocampus which, when activated, causes us to experience stress.[52] Exercise also promotes the production and release of brain-derived neurotrophic factor (BDNF) that acts on neurons to help survival, encourage growth, and synaptic connections. BDNF is essential for learning, memory, and thinking. Stress causes a reduction of BDNF. Exercise prevents stress-produced reductions of BDNF.[53] By having our students get regular exercise, we decrease the probability of impaired brain functioning as a result of stress.

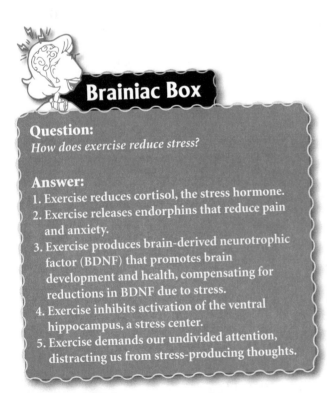

Brainiac Box

Question:
How does exercise reduce stress?

Answer:
1. Exercise reduces cortisol, the stress hormone.
2. Exercise releases endorphins that reduce pain and anxiety.
3. Exercise produces brain-derived neurotrophic factor (BDNF) that promotes brain development and health, compensating for reductions in BDNF due to stress.
4. Exercise inhibits activation of the ventral hippocampus, a stress center.
5. Exercise demands our undivided attention, distracting us from stress-producing thoughts.

We have explored in some depth the beneficial effects of exercise for the brain and learning in Tool 1: Encourage Exercise, in Principle 1: Nourishment. There, we overviewed the impressive achievement gains that result from regular exercise programs established by individual teachers for their own class and by schools for their entire student body. The work here suggests some of those achievement gains may be due to the stress-reducing impact of regular exercise.

Tool 8

Promote Play

As we saw when we explored ways to nourish the brain, Silly Sports and Goofy Games[54] get the heart and lungs moving and so pump more oxygen to the brain. At the same time as they energize brains, paradoxically, they create safety. We can be very energized, yet feel no threat.

Silly Sports and Goofy Games, unlike traditional sports and games, do not create winners and losers. They are process oriented rather than outcome oriented: Following a Silly Sport, we don't ask, *"Who won?"* but rather ask, *"Did you have fun?"* The games are inclusive; no one is ever "out." No one sits on the bench. Because of the low threat, inclusive, fun nature of the games, the amygdalae are at rest, creating a feeling of safety.

The category of Silly Sports and Goofy Games most aligned with Principle 2: Safety are the helping games. When students play the helping games, they experience mutual support, feel included, and cared for—they feel safe. Some of the helping games involve blindfolding a student who then shoots at a target with the help of teammates; others involve traditional trust activities such as falling backward into the arms of others. One of my favorites is **Air Traffic Controller**. Students are blindfolded, touring the room. But they are safe because their personal air traffic controller is giving them good guidance. See Blackline: Air Traffic Controller, p. 2.21.

Brain-Friendly Teaching • Dr. Spencer Kagan
Kagan Publishing • 800.933.2667 • www.KaganOnline.com

Source: Dr. Spencer Kagan • *Silly Sports & Goofy Games*
Kagan Publishing
1 (800) 933-2667
www.KaganOnline.com

air traffic controller

With zero visibility, if they are not to crash, Pilot or Biplane must rely on Air Traffic Controller.

1 Air Traffic Controller

Players are in pairs, one is Pilot, the other is Air Traffic Controller. Pilot simulates being in a plane by extending both arms out to form wings. Air Traffic Controller stands in one place to call out directions to Pilot.

2 Zero Visibility

Pilot has zero visibility (blindfolded or closed eyes) and must rely entirely on verbal instructions of the Air Traffic Controller to navigate the plane around the room.

3 Ground to Pilot

Air Traffic Controllers may give instructions like, "Stop! There is a plane approaching your airspace from the right; allow it to proceed before resuming acceleration."

4 Biplane

Air Traffic Controller may be played with two players forming a Biplane; they are holding hands with both arms fully extended.

Game 49

"happy helpers"

Tool 9

Incorporate Humor

Humor and laughter relieve stress. We go to a funny movie, and afterwards we feel better. What we may not know is that "all is right with the world" feeling we have when we leave the theater after a good comedy movie is because we have turned off our sympathetic nervous system arousal. Laughter is associated with parasympathetic arousal that turns off sympathetic arousal, the fight-or-flight system.

Hospital Clowns

Hospital clowns reduce anxiety and are now used in many hospitals worldwide.[55] Some hospital clowns simply entertain; others, chosen for their communication skills, compassion, and empathy, are integrated into therapy teams. The anxiety reduction of the humor and laughter produced by hospital clowns is dramatic. For example, in randomized, controlled studies, clowns are more effective than the sedative midazolam in reducing preoperative anxiety among children![56] The presence of a clown reduces pain and anxiety during otherwise painful emergency room procedures, and serves also to reduce anxiety among parents of the patients.[57]

Laughing Lowers Blood Pressure

When we are faced with a threat, our vascular system constricts to shunt blood to the deep muscle groups to prepare them to fight or flee. This is high blood pressure. Those who are in constant stress have constant high blood pressure, one of the most common causes of heart disease and death. When we experience humor, our parasympathetic system is aroused and we relax. Watching a funny movie leads to mirthful laughter that improves vascular functioning.[58] When we laugh, we relax. Could it be that our class clowns are doing more good than harm? Instead of punishing class clowns for being disruptive, we may be better off channeling

their comical creativity for the good of the class. For example, a little joke before a quiz may put students at ease.

Brainiac Box

Question:
How does a good laugh change brain chemistry?

Answer:[59]
When people sit down to watch a humorous video, before the video begins, their brain chemistry changes in beneficial ways: *"The blood drawn from experimental subjects just before they watched the humorous video had 27% more beta-endorphins and 87% more human growth hormone, compared to blood from the control group, which didn't anticipate the watching of a humorous video."* Further measurable positive changes proceed once the video begins. And the positive effects last up to 24 hours: *"Mirthful laughter diminishes the secretion of cortisol and epinephrine, while enhancing immune reactivity. In addition, mirthful laughter boosts secretion of growth hormone, an enhancer of these same key immune responses. The physiological effects of a single, one-hour session viewing a humorous video has appeared to last up to 12 to 24 hours in some individuals."*

Laughing Is Release

Why do we laugh when we watch someone else fall or get frightened? When we are watching that person, through our mirror neurons, we are experiencing what that person is experiencing. As they get hurt, we realize it is that other person, not us, that is feeling pain or embarrassment, and we feel safe. A good joke teller builds up tension until the punch line. The punch line releases tension and people laugh. Laughter is a momentary release of tension, relaxation.

Laughing Reduces Anxiety

Most people, whether they know it or not, fear flying. Some airlines have dealt with the need to relieve tension by having humorous announcements. Kulula Airlines of South Africa is famous for their humorous airline announcements. After a rough landing, the stewardess came on with this announcement:

> Ladies and Gentlemen,
> Please remain in your seats until
> Captain Crash and the Crew
> have brought the aircraft to a
> screeching halt against the gate.
> And, once the tire smoke has cleared
> and the warning bells are silenced,
> we will open the door and you can
> pick your way through the wreckage
> to the terminal...

A standard closing comment at the end of a flight:

> We'd like to thank you folks for flying
> with us today. And, the next time
> you get the insane urge to go blasting
> through the skies in a pressurized
> metal tube, we hope you'll think of
> Kulula Airways.

Most people laugh when they hear these announcements. The humor relieves the tension created by the unconscious fear of flying.

Humor
Part of a Behavior Plan

"In an effort to motivate a struggling reader, I brought in a book of jokes and allowed a student to choose a joke to tell to the class during calendar/morning meeting time each day. He would choose a joke, write it in his take-home folder, and practiced reading it with me. He read it aloud to the class the next morning."

—*Rachel Treaster*
Kagan Trainer

Humor Improves Classroom Outcomes

We can use humor in our classrooms to relieve tension; create a more relaxed, safe atmosphere; and boost creativity. Humor reduces anxiety

Tips
Incorporate Humor into Your Classroom

- Allow yourself to be silly with your students from time to time.
- Show a stand-up comic clip on a topic related to the learning topic.
- Show funny video clips for a minute or two, just for laughs.
- Tell the class a joke of the day.
- Display a comic strip for the class.
- Insert a joke between the first two questions on the test.
- Have a silly hair, silly sock, or silly hat day.
- Have students create cartoon strips of the learning content.
- Design homework questions with a key that reveals the punch line to a joke or riddle.
- Play a funny movie for a rainy day.

and increases learning among students high in anxiety.[60] Humor significantly reduces feelings of anger and hostility.[61] Humor facilitates incidental learning.[62] Watching a comedy film[63] or listening to a comedy recording[64] increases creativity.

Humor Improves Test Taking

In a simple but powerful demonstration of how humor improves test taking, experimenters designed two forms of the same 30-item, multiple-choice test. The traditional form asked questions in the typical dry academic style. The humor form of the same test assessed the same knowledge, but every third question was cast in a humorous way. The two tests formats were given to assess understanding of how genes impact on the probability of becoming schizophrenic. The possible multiple-choice answers on both forms were identical. See Box: Traditional v. Humorous Versions of a Test Question, p. 2.24.

Traditional v. Humorous Versions of a Test Question

Traditional Wording of the Question
Over the past six years, Tom's behavior has become increasingly more disturbed. He has developed a delusion that somebody is controlling his mind, and he is also having bizarre visual and auditory hallucinations. Which other member of Tom's family is most likely to exhibit bizarre behavior?

Humorous Wording of the Same Question
Claiming to be a slot machine, Julius has been standing against a wall in a Las Vegas casino for six years making bell-like sounds and occasionally complaining that he is being tilted. Which other member of Julius's family is most likely to exhibit bizarre behavior?

Alternative Answers:
a. His mother
b. His sister
c. His identical twin
d. It is impossible to make a probability statement

To determine if humor was effective in boosting the test performance of students high in test anxiety, students were divided into three groups: Low, Medium, and High in test anxiety. Results are consistent with the conclusion that humor reduces anxiety, allowing improved cognitive functioning. Those students high in test anxiety performed significantly below other students on the traditional version of the test, but scored as well as other students when humorous items were included in the test![65]

Including Humor in Our Classrooms

There are many ways to bring humor into the classroom. A joke of the day can be posted. Students can be assigned on a rotating basis to bring in and tell a clean joke. (At certain ages, and with certain classes, jokes must be cleared by the teacher before telling.) Cartoons may be used to illustrate points during academic presentations.

Short, corny jokes and riddles serve the purpose as well as long jokes, and lend themselves to being posted. One way to use them to bring a bit of levity into the classroom is to post all but the punch line, having the punch line embedded in a worksheet or a PowerPoint slide. See Table: Quick Corn.

Quick Corn

How do you stop a charging rhinoceros?	Take away his credit cards.
Is a dog better dressed in the summer or winter?	Summer In Winter: He has only a coat In Summer: He has coat and pants
Why couldn't the leopard escape from the zoo?	He was always spotted
On which side does a leopard have the most spots?	On the outside
A rooster lays an egg on the peak of a roof. Which side of the roof does the egg roll down?	Neither. Roosters don't lay eggs
What is the best way to carve wood?	Whittle by whittle
Jonny's mom had three children. The first two were named April and May. What is the name of the third child?	Jonny
Two wrongs never make a right. What did two rights make?	The first airplane
Why can't a man living in the USA be buried in China?	He is still alive
What do you call a man who shaves 15 times a day?	A barber
What has no beginning, no end, and nothing in the middle?	A doughnut

Tool 10
Provide Hydration

We have examined the role of hydration in some depth in Tool 4: Supply Hydration, in Principle 1: Nourishment. We saw how water plays an important role in keeping the brain well nourished. Water plays a role also in reducing stress, creating the feeling of safety. How? Corticoids and ACTH, the stress hormones, shut down our thinking process, narrow our cognitions, and give us the feeling of anxiety. Dehydration leads to a stress response and release of these stress hormones. After drinking a glass of water, there are measurable decreases in corticoids and ACTH.[66]

Tool 11
Foster Positive Social Interaction

Without being aware of it, we are constantly evaluating our social environment to determine if it is safe or if we need to be on guard. Subtle signals of safety or trustworthiness make the difference between triggering sympathetic (on guard, avoid) or parasympathetic (relax, approach) responses. A calm voice; a touch; a barely perceptible, gentle smile; a fleeting facial expression; a gesture from another may be experienced below consciousness, but they nevertheless profoundly influence brain function. Functional brain imaging reveals areas of the temporal cortex (the fusiform gyrus and the superior temporal sulcus) are involved in detecting subtle movements, voice inflections, and facial expressions that determine if we perceive another person as safe or trustworthy. Slight changes in these stimuli make the

difference between perceiving a person as safe or a threat.[67] If we perceive another person as safe, there is vagus nerve stimulation resulting in a parasympathetic nervous system response, reducing stress.[68] Reduced stress in turn makes students more relaxed, more observant, and better at thinking and problem solving. We will examine in some depth the important role of positive emotions in fostering thinking and problem solving in Tool 6: Elicit Positive Emotion, in Principle 4: Emotion. We explore the power of positive social interaction to create a brain-friendly classroom in Tool 4: Teach Social Skills, in Principle 3: Social. Here it is important to note that the more we can foster positive social interaction, the safer students will feel and the better they will perform.

We have reviewed ways to create more inclusive teams and classrooms. Let's focus here on two additional ways to foster positive social interaction among students: Promoting handshakes and eliminating put-downs.

Handshakes
Handshakes supply two basic needs that reduce anxiety and increase positive social contact: touch and proximity.

Touch: A Basic Need. Touch is comforting. Touching is a basic need.[69] Infants die if they are not touched—even if they have all the food and nutrients they need.[70] Compared to animal infants that are adequately touched, those lacking adequate touch differ on physiological and psychological measures. Those with sufficient touch show greater coping with stress, greater immunity, and more willingness to explore novel environments. Among humans, inadequate touch as an infant leaves the adult more susceptible to an array of diseases and symptoms as well as less able to function well in the parental role.[71] Supportive touch releases oxytocin that reduces amygdalae firing.[72] Touching communicates and calms. It creates bonds.

The pioneering research of Harry F. Harlow established touch as a basic need.[73] He raised monkeys without their mothers. In their cages were two wire surrogate mothers. One was covered with terry cloth; the other wire mother had no cloth, but had a bottle from which the

A Superior Mother Monkey

"The surrogate was made from a block of wood, covered with sponge rubber, and sheathed in tan cotton terry cloth. A lightbulb behind her radiated heat. The result was a mother, soft, warm, and tender, a mother with infinite patience, a mother available twenty-four hours a day, a mother that never scolded her infant and never struck or bit her baby in anger.... It is our opinion that we engineered a very superior monkey mother, although this position is not held universally by the monkey fathers."

—*Harry F. Harlow*

infant monkeys could feed. The baby monkeys would cling to the cloth mother and only go to the bottle for food. When they were presented with novel, frightening stimuli, the monkeys would run to the cloth mother for comfort. After comfort, they would venture out to encounter the stimuli. Those presented with the frightening stimuli without a chance to run to the cloth mother would crawl up into a ball and suck their thumb or freeze. Touch comforts.

Remarkably, the researches found monkey infants raised with surrogate mothers behaved toward their cloth mothers in much the same way as infants raised with real mothers behaved toward their real mothers:

> During the last two years, we have observed the behavior of two infants raised by their own mothers. Love for the real mother and love for the surrogate mother appear to be very similar. The baby macaque spends many hours a day clinging to its real mother. If away from the mother when frightened, it rushes to her and in her presence shows comfort and composure. As far as we can observe, the infant monkey's affection for the real mother is strong, but no stronger than that of the experimental monkey for the surrogate cloth mother, and the security that the infant gains from the presence of the real mother is no greater than the security it gains from a cloth surrogate.[74]

Tips

Release the power of touch by having students...

- High five classmates as they pair up and part.
- Give a Team Spiral Handshake.
- Create secret or unique team handshakes.
- Invent cheers that include hands touching.
- Offer classmates a pat on the back for a job well done.
- Group huddle or do a group hug to celebrate.
- Do a Sticky High Five with a partner—they do a high five and keep their palms together for the duration of their interaction.

Proximity Reduces Anxiety. It is not just touch that comforts: Simply being close to others reduces anxiety. In a series of research studies, Stanley Schachter and his coinvestigators established the "Fear-Affiliation link."[75] They demonstrated that we move closer to others to reduce anxiety. We move toward our companion in the theater during the scary part of the movie. "There is safety in numbers." Anxiety generates psychological proximity as well: Following the September 11, 2001 terrorist attack on the World Trade Center, Americans put their differences aside and pulled together.

Handshakes Transform the Brain.
Handshakes provide both touch and proximity. As we have seen, supportive touch releases oxytocin that in turn inhibits amygdalae firing.[76] Increased oxytocin levels are predictive of a range of positive social behaviors including empathy,[77] trust, and trustworthiness,[78] as well as attachment and bonding.[79] Administering a nasal spray of oxytocin, people become more trusting.[80] A firm, friendly handshake transforms brain firing in other ways as well: The nucleus accumbens, a

reward-processing region, shows greater activity as a result of handshakes. Handshakes "increase sensitivity to approach, reduce avoidance behavior in amygdalae and superior temporal sulcus."[81]

Releasing the Power of Touch in Our Classrooms. We can incorporate the beneficial outcomes of touch in our classrooms with simple handshakes, high fives, and pats on the back among our students. My favorite team handshake is the **Team Spiral Handshake**. One student extends his or her right hand toward the center of the team table, fingers curled into a fist, with thumb up. The student on that person's right, curls his or her fingers around the fingers of the fist, with thumb up. The remaining students do the same, in turn. When all hands are curled around, teammates put their thumbs down and get a good grip. To the count of three, without letting go, they shake their joined hands as if doing a handshake. Finally, at the last count, students let go, raising their hands high with thumbs up. They shout, *"great job"* or some other affirmation. For additional team handshakes, see *Kagan Cooperative Learning*.[82]

Cultures differ in preference for firmness of handshakes, and in some cultures a firm handshake is interpreted as rudeness. There are many dimensions to a handshake, and knowingly or unknowingly, we form our impression of someone by evaluating strength, grip, dryness, temperature, vigor, duration, texture, and eye contact during the handshake. Of all the variables, strength of handshake is most reliably measured. All of these variables co-vary in a very highly significant way. For example, the correlations among strength, grip, dryness, warmth, and vigor all have correlations above .80, which means, for example, if someone has a firm grip, his or her handshake is extremely likely to be dry, warm, and vigorous as well. In the United States, persons with a firm handshake are judged as being more outgoing and expressive as well as less shy and neurotic.[83]

Teacher Handshakes. Handshakes and high fives are not just for students. The teacher who occasionally greets his or her students at the door with a handshake or a high five not only communicates a welcoming friendliness, but actually aligns the brains of students with how brains best function for learning. The teacher who walks around monitoring progress on a worksheet, offering a high five when seeing a problem correctly solved, goes a long way toward creating a brain-friendly classroom.

Put-Down Free Classrooms

Put-downs are common among students, especially at certain ages. Put-downs, even if done in a playful manner, are threatening and set off the amygdalae. We can create greater safety in our classrooms if we establish a class agreement to make the classroom a "put-down free zone." Students agree to stop everything when they hear a put-down and to have the person who just gave the put-down give the other person a "put-up" (praise or compliment).

Tool 12

Teach Relaxation Breathing

Slow, deep, relaxed diaphragmatic breathing (4-4-8 Breathing) described in Tool 5: Train Proper Breathing, in Principle 1: Nourishment, is one way to activate the parasympathetic nervous system, turning off the fight-or-flight sympathetic response. The exhale during the breathing stimulates the vagus nerve which inhibits the sympathetic nervous system, slowing heart rate, lowering blood pressure, lowering blood lactate (responsible for the experience of anxiety), and producing a state of calm.

Progressive 1-2-1 Breathing. Another breathing technique that oxygenates and relaxes is progressive 1-2-1 breathing. Students begin breathing in to the count of one, hold their breath for the count of two, and then exhale for the count of one. On the second round, they breathe in for the count of two, hold for the count of four, and exhale for the count of two. On successive rounds it is 3-6-3, 4-8-4, 5-10-5, etc. Inhales are through the nose, deep, and diaphragmatic, extending the stomach. Exhales are made through a small hole made by the lips. The stomach area is contracted during the complete exhale.

Tool 13

Practice Progressive Muscle Relaxation

Progressive Muscle Relaxation (PMR) is the oldest scientifically researched method of turning off the fight-or-flight defense alarm reaction. The technique developed by Edmund Jacobson based on laboratory "studies of neuromuscular tension and relaxation," begun in 1908.[84] Jacobson discovered "a method to produce an extreme degree of neuromuscular relaxation." The method was originally designed for doctors and neurologists to treat physical symptoms. In its original form, PMR was a lengthy process: "Frequently the tension only gradually disappears; it may take 15 minutes progressively to relax a single part, such as the right arm."[85] Patients would lie on their backs and progressively tense and relax every part of their body. Dozens of muscle groups were progressively relaxed including bending the head in various directions, working separately and in various ways on the eyelids, brows, eyes, and even various tongue positions.

Very simple and brief (under 10 minutes) forms of PMR can be used in the classroom to have students enter a state of relaxed alertness. The benefits to students are not just reducing anxiety in the moment. Once students learn the method, they can use it on their own at any time to enter a state more optimal for learning. Essentially, PMR turns off the fight-or-flight, sympathetic nervous system arousal that interferes with cognitive functioning.

PMR for the Classroom

Students sit comfortably and tense a muscle as tightly as they can for five seconds. They then relax the muscle to the count of eight, focusing on the sensation of relaxation that flows into the muscle as it relaxes. The key is directing the student's attention first to the sensation of tension as the muscle is flexed, and then to the sensation

alertness to focus learning. Guided PMR might sound like this:

> "Let's sit comfortably with our feet on the floor. Rest your hands in your lap. Take a deep breath through your nose and hold it. To the count of five, we are going to scrunch up our feet, making them as tight as we can. Hold your breath as you do. Concentrate on the feeling of tension. 1. Squeeze tight… 2. Tighter…3. Feel the tension… 4. Be aware of the tension in your feet…5. Now, as tight as you can!"

> "Now we are going to slowly let out our breath to the count of eight as we let go and relax our feet. 1. Relax the feet muscles…2. Feel the relaxation flowing in …3. Focus on the feeling of relaxation…4. As you let your breath out, your whole body feels more relaxed…5. More relaxed…6. Just let the feeling of relaxation flow in… 7. You feel calm as you slowly let out your breath…8. You are completely relaxed."

of relaxation as it is released. A common sequence is to begin with the feet and work upward to the head: Feet, calves, thighs, stomach, biceps, hands, eyes, and whole face. PMR is even more effective when accompanied by a form of relaxation breathing—breathing in through the nose prior to tensing the muscle group, holding the breath while tensing the muscle, and then slowly breathing out through the mouth during the relaxation phase. The teacher guides students as they are learning the technique. Later, students can use the technique on their own.

PMR allows students to gain a sense of control over tension and anxiety. Instead of feeling that tension is something that happens to them and that it is something they have to live with, students discover they can create tension and relaxation at will. PMR is empowering.

Students can easily learn the technique and teachers can have them use it before tests or whenever they want to foster the state of relaxed

PMR for Teachers

After lunch, a few minutes before re-entering class, teachers can create a more relaxed second half of the day by practicing PMR. Alternatively, at the end of the school day, to leave the stress of the day behind, a brief PMR session is in order before heading home. See Blackline: Muscle Relaxation, p. 2.30.

Muscle Relaxation
Relaxation in Three Steps

Step 1: Get Ready: Get Comfortable
Sit with feet flat on the floor, hands in your lap.

Step 2: Locate Tension
Find a part of your body that is holding some tension.
Often it is the shoulders, neck muscles, feet, or hands.

Step 3: Breathe in through your nose and hold your breath as you tense those muscles as tight as you can for 5 seconds. Slowly breathe out through your mouth for the count of eight as you relax those muscles, feeling the relaxation flow into those muscles.

Repeat with another muscle group if desired.

Sequence of Muscle Groups

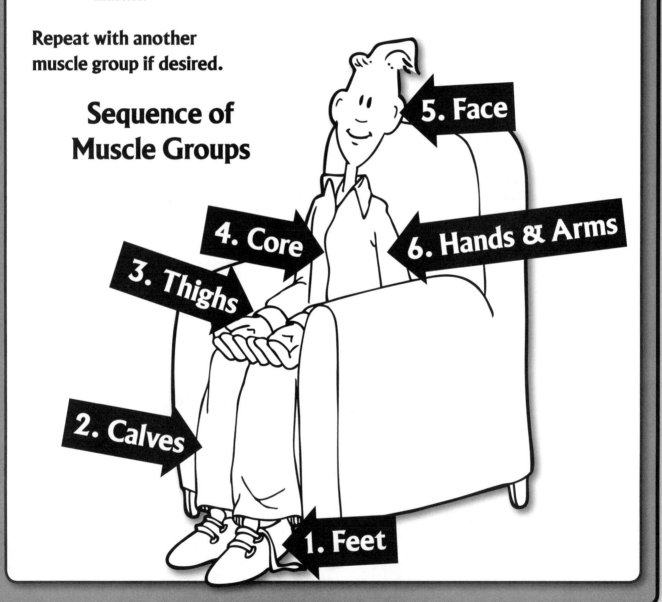

5. Face

4. Core

6. Hands & Arms

3. Thighs

2. Calves

1. Feet

Tool 14

Advocate Meditation

Meditation occupies a unique place among the techniques for producing a brain-friendly classroom. Undisputed evidence shows that regular meditation changes the function of the brain in ways aligned with learning. In addition, as we will see, it actually changes brain structure in ways that make it less likely for students to have responses that interfere with learning!

Types of Meditation

There are many forms of meditation.[86] Simple, nonmystical meditation techniques do not involve change in beliefs, values, or religion and release the relaxation response.[87] It is useful to distinguish intentional meditation techniques from transcendence techniques. Intentional meditative techniques have a goal: A person "meditates on" a topic like compassion, loving kindness, or a nonjudgmental attitude, with the goal of increasing that quality in oneself. Transcendence techniques do not have a specific goal other than to enter a state of consciousness. For example, Transcendental Meditation (TM) emphasizes effortless, spontaneous awareness: A person does not try for anything, simply observing the spontaneous changes that occur in a mantra and in the thoughts that enter consciousness. From enlivening that state, many changes flow.

Transcendental Meditation (TM) Outperforms Contemplation and PMR.

Transcendental Meditation has dramatically larger effect size in producing parasympathetic arousal and reducing anxiety than approaches to mediation that involve effortful concentration and Progressive Muscle Relaxation (PMR). See Graph: Transcendental Meditation Best at Reducing Anxiety.[88]

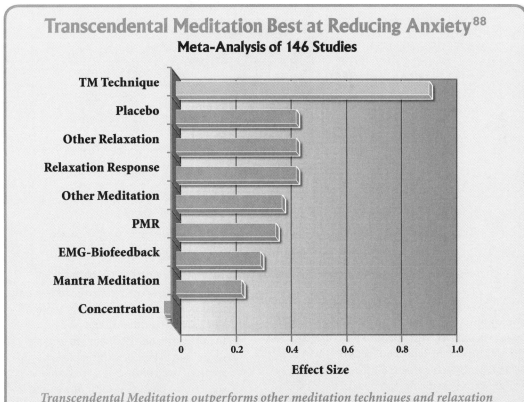

Transcendental Meditation Best at Reducing Anxiety[88]
Meta-Analysis of 146 Studies

Effect Size (x-axis, 0 to 1.0)

- TM Technique
- Placebo
- Other Relaxation
- Relaxation Response
- Other Meditation
- PMR
- EMG-Biofeedback
- Mantra Meditation
- Concentration

Transcendental Meditation outperforms other meditation techniques and relaxation techniques for reducing anxiety. Effortful concentration actually slightly increases anxiety as we attempt to direct our minds. With Transcendental Meditation, we effortlessly observe and accept the flow of our thoughts and sensations, returning to a mantra only as an anchor.

Anxiety interferes with ability to think. Thus, it is not surprising that Transcendental Meditation, which is better at reducing anxiety, is also superior in improving cognitive performance. In a series of studies including 362 high school students, Transcendental Meditation was compared with contemplation meditation and control groups using a variety of cognitive as well as emotional measures. Transcendental Meditation outperformed contemplation meditation in all comparisons and the effect sizes are extremely impressive—TM not only made students less anxious, it made them smarter and more creative! See Graph: Transcendental Meditation Increases Relaxation, Creativity, and Intelligence.[89]

> **Tip**
> Teach students a simple non-mystical meditative technique. Use the technique with students routinely to generate relaxed alertness.

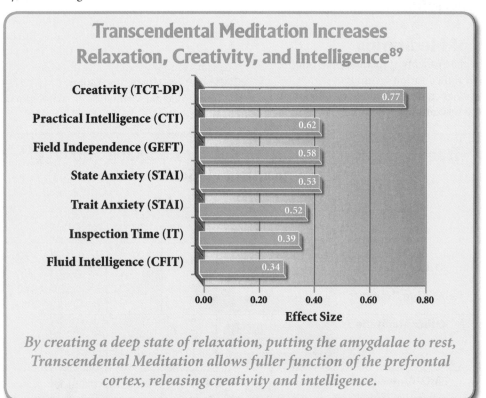

Transcendental Meditation Increases Relaxation, Creativity, and Intelligence[89]

	Effect Size
Creativity (TCT-DP)	0.77
Practical Intelligence (CTI)	0.62
Field Independence (GEFT)	0.58
State Anxiety (STAI)	0.53
Trait Anxiety (STAI)	0.52
Inspection Time (IT)	0.39
Fluid Intelligence (CFIT)	0.34

By creating a deep state of relaxation, putting the amygdalae to rest, Transcendental Meditation allows fuller function of the prefrontal cortex, releasing creativity and intelligence.

Meditation for the Classroom

A simple non-mystical meditative technique similar to Transcendental Meditation is to have students sit quietly and comfortably and focus on their breathing, gently returning their focus to their breathing whenever their mind wanders:

1. Students sit comfortably in a chair with their back straight, feet flat on the floor, hands in their lap, eyes closed.
2. As they sit, they are to pay attention to their breathing. They are to feel relaxed, but awake and alert. They are to breathe in through their nose and out through their mouth. They are to pay attention to the sound of their breath and the sensation as the air goes in and out. Their breathing may change, sometimes shallow and sometimes deep, sometimes rapid and sometimes slow, and sometimes it may pause. Students are to allow it to do whatever it wants. They are simply an observer; they are not to try to control their breathing.
3. If they become aware that their mind has wandered to something else (a memory,

Brain-Friendly Teaching • Dr. Spencer Kagan
Kagan Publishing • 800.933.2667 • www.KaganOnline.com

something to do, a desire…), this is natural. They may make a mental note of where their mind has gone, but they are to gently return their attention to their breathing. They are not to dwell on thoughts. If they have a thought, that is fine, but they are not to explore it; rather, they are to gently turn their attention back to the sound and sensation of their breath.

4. Students are encouraged to adopt a state of relaxed alertness. They are not to go to sleep; they are fully awake and alert, but totally relaxed with no goal other than to observe their breath and the contents of mind.

5. In the beginning, a 5-minute session is sufficient. The time may be increased up to 20 minutes. Students can practice this form of mindfulness on their own. Best results are obtained if the meditation is done before rather than after a meal.

The Relaxation Response. Herbert Benson developed a non-mystical approach to meditation, the Relaxation Response, in an attempt to produce the effects of Transcendental Meditation without any mystical elements. He identifies four basic elements to producing the Relaxation Response:[90]

1. **A Quiet Environment.** Nothing that will draw attention from the focus of the meditation.

2. **An Object to Dwell Upon.** The object may be internal (word or sound) or external (symbol or object).

3. **A Passive Attitude.** This is the most essential element. As focus of attention shifts from the object to dwell on, one makes note of that and gently returns attention to the object or sound. There is an accepting rather than evaluative attitude. There is nothing good or bad about attention shifting, one simply accepts that and gently returns attention to the object or sound.

4. **A Comfortable Position.** Sitting is preferred to lying down. Meditation is not sleep; it is relaxed alertness.

Physiological Changes from TM and Relaxation Response. Benson's studies of practitioners of Transcendental Meditation as well as his own non-mystical, simplified version of that meditation technique reveal that during both types of meditation, a number of physiological changes occur:

- ▶ Alpha waves, slow brain waves, increase in intensity and frequency. Alpha is associated with relaxation.
- ▶ Oxygen consumption decreases an average of 10% to 20% within the first 3 minutes.
- ▶ Blood lactate levels drop. Blood lactate is associated with anxiety. If we inject blood lactate into a normal person, he or she feels anxious. If we inject blood lactate into an anxiety neurotic, that person will have an acute anxiety attack![91]
- ▶ Heart rate slows.
- ▶ Breathing rate slows.

Blood pressure among those who consistently meditate is lowered. Among those who regularly meditate, blood pressure is lower before, during, and after meditation. They are simply more relaxed on an ongoing basis![92]

Positive Outcomes of Meditation

The largest body of research has been generated on Transcendental Meditation,[93] but positive outcomes occur regardless of type of mediation.[94] Positive outcomes include reduced anxiety and stress,[95] reduction in blood pressure and cortisol levels[96] improved memory,[97] decreased sleepiness,[98] improved academic achievement,[99] decreased absenteeism, suspensions, and rule infractions,[100] decreased aggression,[101] decreased symptoms of Attention Deficit Hyperactivity Disorder and improved executive function,[102] improved positive, constructive thinking and healthy coping,[103] improved self-esteem and strong sense of personal identity,[104] improved psychological health,[105] increased creativity,[106] increased flexibility of visual perception,[107] increased IQ and intellectual functioning,[108] improved reaction time,[109] increased brain wave coherence,[110] and reduced symptoms of posttraumatic stress.[111] Meditation is not simply eyes closed, rest, or unstructured relaxation: Meditation produces lower sympathetic nervous system arousal compared to relaxation and concentration techniques such as having people rest with their eyes closed,[112] quiet concentration,[113] and biofeedback with unstructured relaxation.[114]

Hundreds of scientific research studies have been conducted demonstrating the positive effect of various types of meditation. Meditation has the effect of synchronizing the brain.[115] Meditation as part of a school-based program reduces depression.[116] Long-term meditators show lower physiological and experienced arousal, and report greater emotional clarity.[117] Carefully controlled research demonstrates meditation produces remarkable results in a very brief time: Compared to students who were assigned to a relaxation condition, after just five days, students randomly assigned to meditate for just 20 minutes a day showed improved attention; lower anxiety, depression, anger, and fatigue; higher vigor; significant decreases in stress-related cortisol; and an increase in immune system functioning.[118] Mindfulness meditation changes gene expression in ways that reduce inflammation and stress-related symptoms, and improves immune functions.[119]

Meditation Changes Function and Structure of the Brain

Meditation not only reduces amygdalae firing during and immediately following meditation. After just 8 weeks of simple meditation for a half hour a day, the amygdalae actually shrink![120] Thus, meditation results in changes not just in brain function, but also in the actual structure of the brain. In just 8 weeks, we actually redesign our brains by simply sitting quietly and observing the contents of our mind for a half hour a day!

After just 8 weeks of simple meditation for a half hour a day, the amygdalae actually shrink!

Long-term meditation, regardless of type of meditation, is associated with increases in size of frontal lobe and hippocampus, brain structures associated with improved attention, emotional control, and memory.[121]

Not All Meditation Produces the Same Results

Brain imaging studies reveal that different types of meditation have different impact. For example, 8 weeks following meditation training, amygdalae response differed for individuals who practiced mindfulness meditation compared to those who practiced compassion meditation.[122] Mindfulness meditation reduced amygdalae reaction to all emotional stimuli; consistent with its aim, compassion meditation increased amygdalae reaction to images that showed human suffering. The researchers concluded, "Overall, these results are consistent with the overarching hypothesis that meditation may result in enduring, beneficial changes in brain function, especially in the area of emotional processing." Students lacking empathy, such as bullies or apathetic students, may benefit especially from compassion meditation.

Importantly, after just 2 months of meditation, the brains of people who had never previously meditated were systematically changed depending on the type of meditation they practiced. They reacted differently to emotional stimuli when in their normal non-meditative state. Type of meditation has predictable, systematic effects in changing brains! Of particular relevance is the differential impact of different forms of meditation. The implication is that by training in the appropriate type of meditation, we can help both students who are overreactive to emotional stimuli, and those who are underreactive, that is, who lack empathy.

A systematic review of the different effects of different types of meditation is beyond the scope of this book, but research programs establish different types of meditation impact differently on heart rate, heart breathing cohesion,[123] and differential activity in and development of different parts of the brain.[124]

Meditation for the School and Classroom.
Transcendental Meditation is being taught in hundreds of schools and many universities worldwide. It is provided to schools under various names, including Quiet Time Program,[125] Stress Free Schools,[126] and Consciousness-Based Education.[127] The results have been extremely positive as measured by academic achievement,

reduction of discipline problems and fights, as well as student and teacher reports. Teachers report students are more focused, centered, relaxed, creative, happier, and more able to achieve. They describe meditation as resulting in a quieter tone in class and more bonding among students. Students report less stress, better concentration, better relationships, and better athletic performance. Some report that as a result of meditation, for the first time, they are looking forward to coming to school. *"It calms me down and I am less likely to start a fight." "I can think about it and not just blow up." "I am a lot more cranky when I don't meditate." "You just be cool."*

Transcendental Meditation is being taught in hundreds of schools and many universities worldwide. The results have been extremely positive as measured by academic achievement, reduction of discipline problems and fights, as well as student and teacher reports.

Meditation for Teachers. Meditation is not just for students. Teachers using the technique report a greater calmness, sleeping better, and being better able to cope with stress. *"Without meditation, I would be more likely to react like the students."*

Meditation Boosts Academic Achievement. As an example of the power of meditation to improve academic achievement, let's examine a study of 253 sixth- through eighth-grade students low in English and math, who participated in a study of the effects of Transcendental Meditation (TM).[128]

Prior to the meditation experiment, all students at this high-risk, underachieving school had shown academic decline. Results indicated the usual overall academic decline among the eighth-grade students in both math (−16.93) and English (−4.91), but increases for meditating students in both math (+13.93) and English (+7.31).

These differences were highly significant ($p < .001$ math; $p < .002$ English). Among the meditating students, 40.7% gained one performance level in math and 36.8% gained one performance level in English. In contrast, among the non-meditating students, only 15% gained one performance level in math and 17.2% in English. These differences too, were highly significant ($p < .001$ math; $p < .005$ English).

Although the group of students in the meditation group were drawn from the sixth and seventh grades and the non-meditation students were drawn from the eighth grade, the overall outcomes of the study very strongly support the conclusion that meditation has a powerful positive impact on academic achievement. The results are especially impressive given that students meditated only 12 minutes twice a day—in their morning homeroom and in their last class period, yet showed substantial achievement gains in both English and math. The dependent measure was a standardized achievement test, the California Standards Test (CST) required for California State Testing and Reporting (STAR).

Ninety-two percent of faculty reported they felt the program was valuable for the school. "Observed changes in the classroom environment included students being more quiet and attentive, including a greater ability to work silently in academic activities." Faculty reported fewer student fights, less abusive language, and an overall more relaxed and calm atmosphere." A standardized measure of anxiety (State-Trait Anxiety Inventory for Children) was administered pre- and post-meditation. Results showed significant reduction in anxiety for both the sixth- and seventh-grade meditating students.

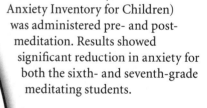

Another study of the effects of Transcendental Meditation among middle school students showed similar profound effects. Following meditating 10 minutes a day in school for a year, meditating seventh-grade African-American students reported three major outcomes: improved academic achievement, increased restful alertness, and improved emotional intelligence (self-awareness, self-control, flexibility).[129] Meditating students noted improved academic performance not just for themselves, but also for other students who meditated. In the words of one student,

> *". . . now I'm not saying all the meditators get good grades . . . but most of 'em in my class get good grades, but the ones who don't meditate, not all of 'em gonna get F's and C's and stuff, . . . but most of 'em get D's and some might get little C's, but most of 'em get bad grades."*

Students described greater relaxation, concentration, and more positive relations:

▶ *"I'm relaxed and I can concentrate more."*

▶ *"Like, I'm more nicer and mature, like toward other people. Like I can listen to them instead of me just talking all the time or something."*

▶ *"If I meditate, I feel calm and feel like I don't have to argue with anybody."*

▶ *"I used to be mad and frustrated, but now I'm just calm and happy."*

Meditation Reduces Discipline Problems.

As an example of the power of meditation to reduce disruptive behaviors, let's examine the impact of Transcendental Meditation on absenteeism, school rule infractions, and suspension days among adolescents.[130] Forty-five students were randomly assigned to one of two groups: meditation or non-meditation (lifestyle education). Each school day, the groups spent 15 minutes either meditating or in lifestyle education. The meditation group meditated for 15 minutes twice a day. During the school week, they meditated once at home on their own, and once at school; during weekends, students meditated twice a day at home. The experiment lasted 4 months.

Behaviors during the 4 months prior to the meditation were compared with behaviors 4 months following the experiment. Prior to the experiment, the meditation and lifestyle groups did not differ significantly on any of the three behavior variables: absences, rule infractions (tardy class periods, disruptive classroom behavior, fighting), and suspensions. Following the experiment, they differed on all three variables. The mean number of absences decreased in the meditating group −6.4 days compared to a mean increase of +4.8 in the non-meditating group ($p < .05$). The mean number of rule infractions decreased over the 4 months among the meditating group (−0.1) compared to an increase for the non-meditating group (+0.3), ($p < .03$). Finally, for the meditating group, there was a reduction of suspension days due to behavior-related problems (−0.3) compared to an increase in suspension days among the non-mediators (+1.2), ($p < .04$).

This study of disruptive behaviors was part of a larger study of the effect of TM on stress.[131] The larger study found a beneficial impact of TM in reducing stress as measured by cardiovascular measures. For the reasons just detailed, it is likely that the decreased stress among meditating students decreased the likelihood of their impulsive behavior that in turn decreased the probability of disruptive behaviors. Worthy of note, the improvements documented in this study were obtained with an investment of only 15 minutes a day of school time; the other 15 minutes a day of mediation were provided by the students on their own at home.

Conclusion

If we want to create a brain-friendly classroom—to optimize brain functioning and student learning—safety is a prerequisite. We need to put the amygdalae to rest. The alternative is constricted thinking and learning. Once our students are safe, our job is easier. Their brains are open to perceptions and cognitions that otherwise would be inhibited. You may feel you do not have the time or inclination to teach Progressive Muscle Relaxation or meditation, and that is fine. Each of the fourteen tools increase safety. Begin with a tool with which you feel comfortable. After adding that tool to your repertoire, experiment with a second tool to enhance safety. With some teambuilding and classbuilding, structuring to eliminate put-downs and anxiety-producing evaluations, and/or including humor, we can put the brains of our students at ease. And once we do, teaching and learning become much easier. Instead of struggling against the current, we are swimming with the current. We are teaching to brains that are functioning fully, ready to learn.

Fourteen Tools to Create Safety

1. Construct a Safe Context for Learning
2. Celebrate Diversity
3. Offer Safe Evaluations
4. Build Inclusive Teams
5. Form Inclusive Classrooms
6. Play Background Music
7. Encourage Exercise
8. Promote Play
9. Incorporate Humor
10. Provide Hydration
11. Foster Positive Social Interaction
12. Teach Relaxation Breathing
13. Practice Progressive Muscle Relaxation
14. Advocate Meditation

References

[1] Hart, A.J., Whalen, P.J., Shin, L.M., McInerney, S.C., Fischer, H. & Rauch, S.L. *Differential response in the human amygdala to racial outgroup vs ingroup face stimuli.* **NeuroReport**, 2000, 11(11), 2351–2355.

Lieberman, M.D., Hariri, A., Jarcho, J.M., Eisenberger, N.I. & Bookheimer, S.Y. *An fMRI investigation of race-related amygdala activity in African-American and Caucasian-American individuals.* **Nature Neuroscience**, 2005, 8(6), 720–722.

[2] Porges, S.W. **The Polyvagal Theory. Neurophysiological Foundations of Emotions, Attachment, Communication, and Self-Regulation.** New York, NY: W.W. Norton & Company, 2011.

[3] Goleman, D. **Social Intelligence. The New Science of Human Relationships.** New York, NY: Bantam Books, 2006.

[4] Cannon, W.B. **Bodily Changes in Pain, Hunger, Fear and Rage: An Account of Recent Researches into the Function of Emotional Excitement.** New York, NY: Appleton and Company, 1915.

[5] Hess, W.R. & Akert, K. *Experimental data on role of hypothalamus in mechanism of emotional behavior.* **Archives of Neurology and Psychiatry**, 1955, 73(2), 127-129.

[6] Young, M.P., Scannell, J.W. & Burns, G.A. **The Analysis of Cortical Connectivity.** Austin, TX: Springer, 1994.

Young, M.P., Scannell, J.W., Burns, G.A. & Blakemore, C. *Analysis of connectivity: Neural systems in the cerebral cortex.* **Reviews in the Neurosciences**, 1994, 5(3), 227-250.

[7] Damasio, A.R., Everitt, B.J. & Bishop, D. *The somatic marker hypothesis and the possible functions of the prefrontal cortex.* **Philosophical Transactions of the Royal Society of London, Series B-Biological Sciences**, 1996, 351(1346), 1413–1420.

[8] Harlow, J.M. *Recovery from the passage of an iron bar through the head.* **Publications of the Massachusetts Medical Society**, 1868, 2, 327–347.

[9] Garcia, R., Vouimba, R.M., Baudry, M. & Thompson, R.F. *The amygdala modulates prefrontal cortex activity relative to conditioned fear.* **Nature**, 1999, 402(6759), 294–296.

Kim, H., Somerville, L.H., Johnstone, T., Alexander, A.L. & Whalen, P.J. *Inverse amygdala and medial prefrontal cortex responses to surprised faces.* **NeuroReport**, 2003, 14(18), 2317–2322.

Likhtik, E., Pelletier, J.G., Paz R. & Pare, D. *Prefrontal control of the amygdala.* **The Journal of Neuroscience**, 2005, 25(32), 7429–7437.

Ochsner, K.N., Bunge, S.A., Gross, J.J. & Gabrieli, J.D. *Rethinking feelings: An fMRI study of the cognitive regulation of emotion.* **Journal of Cognitive Neuroscience**, 2002, 14(8), 1215–1229.

Quirk, G.J., Likhtik E., Pelletier, J.G. & Pare, D. *Stimulation of medial prefrontal cortex decreases the responsiveness of central amygdala output neurons.* **The Journal of Neuroscience**, 2003, 23(25), 8800–8807.

[10] Vincent, J.D. **The Biology of Emotions.** Cambridge, MA: Basil Blackwell, 1990.

[11] Bremner, J.D. *MRI-based measurement of hippocampal volume in post-traumatic stress disorder.* **Biological Psychiatry**, 1997, 41(1), 23–32.

[12] Young, C.B., Wu, S.S. & Menon, V. *The neurodevelopmental basis of math anxiety.* **Psychological Science**, 2012, 23(5), 492-501.

[13] Brod, J., Fencl, V., Hejl, Z. & Jirka, J. *Corculatory changes underlying blood pressure elevation during acute emotional stress (Mental Arithmetic) in normotensive and hypertensive subjects.* **Clinical Science**, 1959, 18, 269–279.

[14] Grannis, J.C. *Students' stress, distress, and achievement in an urban intermediate school.* **The Journal of Early Adolescence**, 1992, 12(1), 4–27.

[15] Iannotti, R.J. Luk, J.W. & Nansel, T.R. *Co-occurence of victimization from five subtypes of bullying: Physical, verbal, social exclusion, spreading rumors, and cyber.* **Journal of Pediatric Psychology**, 2010, 35(10), 1103–1112.

[16] Lacey, A. & Cornell, D. (2013). *The impact of teasing and bullying on schoolwide academic performance.* **Journal of Applied School Psychology**, 2013, 29(3), 262–283.

[17] Vossekuil, B, Reddy, M., Fein, R., Borum, R. & Modzeleski, W. *Safe school initiative. An interim report on the prevention of target violence in schools.* Washingin, DC: U.S. Secret Service National Threat Assessment Center and U.S. Department of Education, 2000, p. 7.

[18] McCarthy, T. Warning: *Andy Williams here.* **TIME**, 2001, 157(11), 24–28. (March 19, 2001)

[19] Segerstrom, S. & Miller, G. *Psychological stress and the human immune system: A meta-analytic study of 30 years of inquiry.* **Psychological Bulletin**, 2004, 130(4), 601–630.

[20] Hess, W.R. & Akert, K. *Experimental data on role of hypothalamus in mechanism of emotional behavior.* **Archives of Neurology and Psychiatry**, 1955, 73(2), 127–129.

[21] Porges, S.W. **The Polyvagal Theory. Neurophysiological Foundations of Emotions, Attachment, Communication, and Self-Regulation.** New York, NY: W.W. Norton & Company, 2011.

[22] Porges, S.W. **The Polyvagal Theory. Neurophysiological Foundations of Emotions, Attachment, Communication, and Self-Regulation.** New York, NY: W.W. Norton & Company, 2011.

[23] Gold, S. *Mind your body: A higher road to relaxation.* **Psychology Today**, 2007. Retrieved July, 2013 from: http://www.psychologytoday.com/articles/200706/mind-your-body-higher-road-relaxation

[24] Yerkes, R.M. & Dodson, J.D. *The relation of strength of stimulus to rapidity of habit-formation.* **Journal of Comparative Neurology and Psychology**, 1908, 18(5), 459–482.

[25] Lupien, S.J., Maheu, F., Tu, M., Fiocco, A. & Schramek, T.E. *The effects of stress and stress hormones on human cognition: Implications for the field of brain and cognition.* **Brain and Cognition**, 2007, 65(3), 209–237.

[26] Mattarella-Micke, A., Mateo, J., Kozak, M.N., Foster, K. & Beilock, S.L. *Choke or thrive? The relation between salivary cortisol and math performance depends on individual differences in working memory and math anxiety.* **Emotion**, 2011, 11(4), 1000–1005.

[27] Kagan, S. **Silly Sports & Goofy Games**. San Clemente, CA: Kagan Publishing, 2000.

[28] Newcomer, J.W., Selke, G., Melson, A.K., Hershey, T., Craft, S., Richards, K. & Alderson, A.L. *Decreased memory performance in healthy humans induced by stress-level cortisol treatment.* **Archives of General Psychiatry**, 1999, 56(6), 527–533.

[29] Buchanan T.W. & Lovallo, W.R. *Enhanced memory for emotional material following stress-level cortisol treatment in humans.* **Psychoneuroendocrinology**, 2001, 26(3), 307–317.

[30] Lupien, S.J., Gillin, C.J. & Hauger, R.L. *Working memory is more sensitive than declarative memory to the acute effects of corticosteroids: a dose-response study in humans.* **Behavioral Neuroscience**, 1999, 113(3), 420–430.

[31] Kagan, S., Kyle, P. & Scott, S. **Win-Win Discipline**. San Clemente, CA: Kagan Publishing, 2004.

[32] Kagan, S. & Kagan, M. **Kagan Cooperative Learning**. San Clemente, CA: Kagan Publishing, 2009.

Kagan, S. & Kagan, M. **Multiple Intelligences: The Complete MI Book**. San Clemente, CA: Kagan Publishing, 1998.

[33] Kagan, S. & Kagan, M. **Multiple Intelligences: The Complete MI Book**. San Clemente, CA: Kagan Publishing, 1998.

[34] Dunn, R. & Dunn, K. **Teaching Elementary Students through their Individual Learning Styles: Practical Approaches for Grades 3–6**. Boston, MA: Allyn & Bacon, 1992.

Riding, R. & Rayer, S. **Cognitive Styles and Learning Strategies. Understanding Style Differences in Learning and Behavior**. London, Great Britain: David Fulton Publishers, Ltd, 2001.

Stafford, R. & Dunn, K.J. **Teaching Secondary Students through Their Individual Learning Styles**. Boston, MA: Allyn & Bacon, 1993.

[35] Kagan, L., Kagan, M. & Kagan, S. **Cooperative Learning Structures for Teambuilding**. San Clemente, CA: Kagan Publishing, 1997.

[36] Maslow, A.H., Frager, R. & Fadiman, J. **Motivation and Personality**. New York, NY: Harper & Row, 1954.

[37] Kagan, L., Kagan S. & Kagan, M. **Cooperative Structures for Teambuilding**. San Clemente, CA: Kagan Publishing, 1997.

Kagan, S. & Kagan, M. **Kagan Cooperative Learning**. San Clemente, CA: Kagan Publishing, 2009.

38 Kagan, M., Robertson, L. & Kagan, S. *Cooperative Learning Structures for Classbuilding*. San Clemente, CA: Kagan Publishing, 1995.

39 Shaw, V. *Communitybuilding in the Classroom*. San Clemente, CA: Kagan Publishing, 1993.

40 McCraty, R., Atkinson, M., Rein, G. & Watkins, A.D. *Music enhances the effect of positive emotional state on salivary IgA*. *Stress Medicine*, 1996, 12(3), 67–75.

41 McClelland, D., Alexander, C. & Marks, E. *The need for power, stress, immune function, and illness among male prisoners*. *Journal of Abnormal Psychology*, 1982, 91(1), 61–70.

42 Mockel, M., Rocker, L., Stork, T. Vollert, J. Danne, O. Eichstadt, H., Muller, R. & Hochrein, H. *Immediate physiological responses of healthy volunteers to different types of music: Cardiovascular, hormonal, and mental changes*. *European Journal of Applied Physiology*, 1994, 68(6), 451–459.

43 Escher, J., Hohmann, U., Anthenien, L., Dayer, E., Bosshard, C., & Gaillard, R.C. *Music during gastroscopy*. *Schweiz Mediziniche Wochenschrift*, 1993, 123(26), 1354–1358.

44 Miluk-Kolasa, B., Obminski, S., Stupnicki, R. & Golec, L. *Effects of music treatment on salivary cortisol in patients exposed to pre-surgical stress*. *Experimental and Clinical Endocrinology*, 1994, 102(2), 118–120.

45 Malyarenko, T.N., Kuraev, G.A., Malyarenko, Y.E. & Khatova, M.V. *The development of brain electric activity in 4-year-old children by long term stimulation with music*. *Human Physiology*, 1996, 22(1), 76–81.

46 Godeli, M.R., Santana, P.R., Souza, V.H. & Marquetti, G.P. *Influence of background music on preschoolers' behavior: A naturalistic approach*. *Perceptual and Motor Skills*, 1996, 82(3c), 1123–1129.

47 Bouhuys, A.L., Bloem, G.M. & Groothuis, T.G. *Induction of depressed and elated mood by music influences the perception of facial expressions in healthy students*. *Journal of Affective Disorders*, 1995, 33(4), 215–226.

48 Hall, J. *The effect of background music on the reading comprehension of 278 eighth and ninth graders*. *Journal of Educational Research*, 1952, 45(6), 451–458.

49 Clarke, L.W. (2006). *Music soothes the soul*. *American Chronicle*. Retrieved July, 2013, from: http://calmingharp.com/2013/05/21/music-soothes-the-soul

50 Cockerton, T., Moore, S. & Norman, D. *Cognitive test performance and background music*. *Perceptual and Motor Skills*, 1997, 85(3f), 1435–1438.

51 Lamb, G. *Brain Boosters CDs: Set of 6 CDs (Code: CGBB)*. San Clemente, CA: Kagan Publishing, 2009.

Lamb, G. *Music for the Mind: Set of 6 CDs (Code: CGM)*. San Clemente, CA: Kagan Publishing, 2004.

Mozart, W.A. *The Magic of Mozart: 4 CD Combo (Code: CMZCD)*. San Clemente, CA: Kagan Publishing, 2005.

Arcangelos Chamber Ensemble. *The Sound Health Series: Set of 7 CDs (Code: DAS)*. Advanced Brain Technologies, 2003.

52 Schoenfeld, T.J., Rada, P., Pieruzzini, P.R., Hsueh, B. & Gould, E. *Physical exercise prevents stress-induced activation of granule neurons and enhances local inhibitory mechanisms in the dentate gyrus*. *The Journal of Neuroscience*, 2013, 33(18), 7770–7777.

53 Adlard, P.A. & Cotman, C.W. *Voluntary exercise protects against stress-induced decreases in brain-derived neurotropic protein expression*. *Neuroscience*, 2004, 124(4), 985–992.

54 Kagan, S. *Silly Sports & Goofy Games*. San Clemente, CA: Kagan Publishing, 2000.

55 Finlay, F., Baverstock, A. & Lenton, S. *Therapeutic clowning in pediatric practice*. *Clinical Child Psychology and Psychiatry*, 2013, 1–10.

Oppenheim, D., Simonds, C. & Hartmann, O. *Clowning on children's wards*. *Lancet*, 1997, 350(9094), 1838–1840.

Spitzer, P. Spitzer, P. *The clown doctors*. *Australian Family Physician*, 2001, 30(1), 12–16.

56 Golan, G., Tighe, P., Dobija, N., Perel, A. & Keidan, I. *Clowns for the prevention of preoperative anxiety in children: A randomized controlled trial*. *Pediatric Anesthesia*, 2009, 19(3), 262–266.

Vagnoli, L., Caprilli, S. & Messeri, A. *Parental presence, clowns or sedative premedication to treat preoperative anxiety in children: What could be the most promising option?* *Pediatric Anesthesia*, 2010, 20(10), 937–943.

57 Fernandes, S.C. & Arriaga, P. *The effects of clown intervention on worries and emotional responses in children undergoing surgery*. *Journal of Health Psychology*, 2010, 15(3), 405–415.

Wolyniez, I., Rimon, A., Scolnik, D., Gruber, A., Tavor, O., Haviv, E. & Glatstein, M. *The effect of a medical clown on pain during intravenous access in the pediatric emergency department: A randomized prospective pilot study*. *Clinical Pediatrics*, 2013, 52(12), 1168–1172.

58 Miller, M., Mangano, C., Park, Y., Goel, R., Plotnick, G.D. & Vogel, R.A. *Impact of cinematic viewing on endothelial function*. *Heart*, 2006, 92(2), 261–262.

Papousek, I. & Schulter, G. *Effects of a mood-enhancing intervention on subjective well-being and cardiovascular parameters*. *International Journal of Behavioral Medicine*, 2008, 15(4), 293–302.

Sugawara, J., Tarumi, T. & Tanaka, H. *Effect of mirthful laughter on vascular function*. *The American Journal of Cardiology*, 2010, 15(106), 6.

59 Berk, L.S., Tan, S.A. & Berk, D. *Cortisol and Catecholamine stress hormone decrease is associated with the behavior of perceptual anticipation of mirthful laughter*. *The Journal of the Federation of American Societies for Experimental Biology*, 2008, 22, 9650.

60 Smith, R.E., Ascough, J.C., Ettinger, F. & Nelson, D.A. *Humor, anxiety and task performance.* **Journal of Personality and Social Psychology**, 1971, 19(2), 243–246.

61 Dworkin, E.S. & Eeran, J.S. *The angered: Their susceptibility to varieties of humor.* **Journal of Personality and Social Psychology**, 1967, 6(2), 233–236.

Singer, D.L. *Aggression arousal, hostile humor, and catharsis.* **Journal of Personality and Social Psychology Monograph Supplement**, 1968, 8(1p2), 1–14.

62 Hauck, W.E. & Thomas, J.W. *The relationship of humor to intelligence, creativity and intentional learning.* **Journal of Experimental Education**, 1972, 40, 52–55.

63 Isen, A.M., Daubman, K.A. & Nowicki, G.P. *Positive affect facilitates creative problem solving.* **Journal of Personality and Social Psychology**, 1987, 52(6), 112–131.

64 Ziv, A. *Facilitating effects of humor on creativity.* **Journal of Educational Psychology**, 1976, 68(3), 318–432.

65 Smith, R.E., Ascough, J.C., Ettinger, F. & Nelson, D.A. *Humor, anxiety and task performance.* **Journal of Personality and Social Psychology**, 1971, 19(2), 243–246.

66 Amen, D.G. *Change Your Brain Change, Change Your Life*. New York, NY: Rivers Press, 1998.

67 Adolphs, R. *Trust in the brain.* **Nature Neuroscience**, 2002, 5(3), 192–193.

Winston, J.S., Strange, B.A., O'Doherty, J. & Dolan, R.J. *Automatic and intentional brain responses during evaluation of trustworthiness of faces.* **Nature Neuroscience**, 2002, 5(3), 277–283.

68 Porges, S.W. *The Polyvagal Theory. Neurophysiological Foundations of Emotions, Attachment, Communication, and Self-Regulation*. New York, NY: W.W. Norton & Company, 2011, 195.

69 Montegue, A. *Touching: the Human Significance of the Skin*. New York, NY: Harper & Row, 1971.

70 Bakwin, H. *Emotional deprivation in infants.* **Journal of Pediatrics**, 1949, 35(4), 512–521.

71 Montagu, A. *Touching: The Human Significance of the Skin*. New York, NY: Columbia University Press, 1971.

72 Morhenn, V.B., Park, J.W., Piper, E. & Zak, P.J. *Monetary sacrifice among strangers is mediated by endogenous oxytocin release after physical contact.* **Evolution and Human Behavior**, 2008, 29(6), 375–383.

Heinrichs, M., Baumgartner, T., Kirschbaum, C. & Ehlert, U. *Social support and oxytocin interact to suppress cortisol and subjective responses to psychosocial stress.* **Biological Psychiatry**, 2003, 54(12), 1389–1398.

Kirsch, P., Esslinger, C., Chen, Q., Mier, D., Lis, S., Siddhanti, S., Gruppe, H., Mattay, V.S., Gallhofer, B. & Meyer-Lindenberg, A. *Oxytocin modulates neural circuitry for social cognition and fear in humans.* **Journal of Neuroscience**, 2005, 25(49), 11489–11493.

73 Harlow, H.E. *The nature of love.* **American Psychologist**, 1958, 13, 673–685.

74 Harlow, H.E. *The nature of love.* **American Psychologist**, 1958, 13, 684.

75 Baker, C.R. *Defining and measuring affiliation motivation.* **European Journal of Social Psychology**, 1979, 9(1), 97–99.

Schachter, S. *The Psychology of Affiliation*. Stanford: CA: University Press, 1959.

76 Morhenn, V.B., Park, J.W., Piper, E. & Zak, P.J. *Monetary sacrifice among strangers is mediated by endogenous oxytocin release after physical contact.* **Evolution and Human Behavior**, 2008, 29(6), 375–383.

Heinrichs, M., Baumgartner, T., Kirschbaum, C. & Ehlert, U. *Social support and oxytocin interact to suppress cortisol and subjective responses to psychosocial stress.* **Biological Psychiatry**, 2003, 54(12), 1389–1398.

Kirsch, P., Esslinger, C., Chen, Q., Mier, D., Lis, S., Siddhanti, S., Gruppe, H., Mattay, V.S., Gallhofer, B. & Meyer-Lindenberg, A. *Oxytocin modulates neural circuitry for social cognition and fear in humans.* **Journal of Neuroscience**, 2005, 25(49), 11489–11493.

77 Domes, G., Heinrichs, M., Michel, A., Berger, C. & Herpertz, S.C. *Oxytocin improves "mind-reading" in humans.* **Biological Psychiatry**, 2010, 61(6), 731–733.

78 Zak, P.J. 2: *The neuroeconomics of trust.* In R. Frantz (Ed), **Renaissance in Behavioral Economics: Essays in Honour of Harvey Leibenstein**. New York, NY: Routledge, 2007, 17.

Zak, P.J., Kurzban, R. & Matzner, W.T. *Oxytocin is associated with human trustworthiness.* **Hormones and Behavior**, 2005, 48(5), 522–527.

Zak, P.J., Kurzban, R. & Matzner, W.T. *The neurobiology of trust.* **Annals of the New York Academy of Sciences**, 2004, 1032(1), 224–227.

79 Carter, C.S., Ahnert, L., Grossman, K.E., Hrdy, S.B. Lamb M.E., Porges, S.W. & Sachser, N. (Eds). *Attachment and Bonding: A New Synthesis*. Cambridge, MA: MIT Press, 2005.

Carter, C.S. *Neuroendocrine perspectives on social attachment and love.* **Psychoneuroendocrinology**, 1998, 23(8), 779–818.

Lee, H.J., Macbeth, A.H., Pagani, J.H. & Young, W.S. *Oxytocin: the great facilitator of life.* **Progress in Neurobiology**, 2009, 88(2), 127–151.

Uvnas-Moberg, K. *Oxytocin may mediate the benefits of positive social interaction and emotions.* **Psychoneuroendocrinology**, 1998, 23(8), 819–835.

80 Kosfeld, M., Heinrichs, M., Zak, P.J., Fischbacher, U. & Fehr, E. *Oxytocin increases trust in humans.* **Nature**, 2005, 435(7042), 673–676.

81 Dolcos, S., Sung, K., Argo J.J., Flor-Henry, S. & Dolcos, F. *The power of a handshake: Neural correlates of evaluative judgments in observed social interactions.* **Journal of Cognitive Neuroscience**, 2012, 24(12), 2292–2305.

82 Kagan, S. & Kagan, M. *Kagan Cooperative Learning*. San Clemente, CA: Kagan Publishing, 2009, 10–14.

83 Chaplin, W.F., Phillips, J.B., Brown, J.D., Clanton, N.R. & Stein, J.L. *Handshaking, gender, personality, and first impressions*. **Journal of Personality and Social Psychology**, 2000, 79(1), 110–117.

84 Jacobson, E. *Progressive Relaxation. A Physiological and Clinical Investigation of Muscular States and their Significance in Psychology and Medical Practice*. Chicago, IL: University of Chicago Press, 1929.

85 Jacobson, E. *Progressive relaxation. A Physiological and Clinical Investigation of Muscular States and their Significance in Psychology and Medical Practice*. Chicago, IL: University of Chicago Press, 1929, 29.

86 Goleman, D. *The Varieties of Meditative Experience*. New York, NY: Halstead Press, 1977.

Naranjo, C. & Ornstein, R.E. *The Psychology of Meditation*. New York, NY: Viking Press, 1971.

87 Benson, H. *The Relaxation Response*. New York, NY: William Morrow & Company, Inc., 1975, 67–68.

88 Eppley, K., Abrams, A.I. & Shear, J. *Differential effects of relaxation techniques on trait anxiety: A meta-analysis*. **Journal of Clinical Psychology**, 1989, 45(6), 957–974.

89 So, K.T. & Orme-Johnson, D.W. *Three randomized experiments on the longitudinal effects of the Transcendental Meditation technique on cognition*. **Intelligence**, 2001, 29(5), 419–440.

90 Benson, H. *The Relaxation Response*. New York, NY: William Morrow & Company, Inc., 1975, 67–68.

91 Pitts, F.N.Jr. & McClure, J.N.Jr. *Lactate metabolism in anxiety neurosis*. **New England Journal of Medicine**, 1967, 277(25), 1329–1336.

92 Benson, H. *The Relaxation Response*. New York, NY: Harper Collins, 2000.

93 *Scientific Research on Maharishi's Transcendental Meditation and TM-Sidhi programme. Collected Papers (Vols. 1–5)*. Fairfield, IA: Maharishi University of Management Press.

94 Luders, E., Toga, A.W., Lepore, N. & Gaser, C. *The underlying anatomical correlates of long-term meditation: Larger hippocampal and frontal volumes of gray matter*. **NeuroImage**, 2009, 45(3), 672–678.

95 Elder, C., Nidich, S., Colbert, R., Hagelin, J., Grayshield, L., Oviedo-Lim, D., Nidich, R., Rainforth, M., Jones, C. & Gerace, D. *Reduced psychological distress in racial and ethnic minority students practicing the Transcendental Meditation Program*. **Journal of Instructional Psychology**, 2011, 38(2), 109–16.

Eppley, K., Abrams, A.I. & Shear, J. *Differential effects of relaxation techniques on trait anxiety: A meta-analysis*. **Journal of Clinical Psychology**, 1989, 45(6), 957–974.

Nidich, S., Rainforth, M., Haaga, D., Hagelin, J., Salerno, J., Travis, F., Tanner, M., Gaylord-King, C., Grosswald, S. & Schneider, R. *A randomized controlled trial on effects of the Transcendental Meditation program on blood pressure, psychological distress, and coping in young adults*. **American Journal of Hypertension**, 2009, 22(12), 1326–1331.

Travis, F., Haaga, D., Hagelin, J., Tanner, M., Nidich, S., Gaylord-King, C., Grosswald, S., Rainforth M. & Schneider, R. *Effects of Transcendental Meditation Practice on Brain Functioning and Stress Reactivity in College Students*. **International Journal of Psychophysiology**, 2009, 71(2), 170–176.

96 Barnes, V., Treiber, F. & Davis, H. *Impact of Transcendental Meditation on cardiovascular function at rest and during acute stress in adolescents with high normal blood pressure*. **Journal of Psychosomatic Research**, 2001, 51(4), 597–605.

Barnes, V., Treiber, F. & Johnson, M. *Impact of Transcendental Meditation on ambulatory blood pressure in African-American adolescents*. **American Journal of Hypertension, Ltd.**, 2004, 17(4), 366–369.

Walton, K., Schneider, R. & Nidich, S. *Review of controlled research on the Transcendental Meditation program and cardiovascular disease: Risk factors, morbidity, and mortality*. **Cardiology Review**, 2004, 12(5), 262–266.

97 Miskiman, D. *The Effect of the Transcendental Meditation Program on the Organization of Thinking and Recall (Secondary Organization)*. Alberta, Canada: Graduate Department of Psychology, University of Alberta, Edmonton, 1973.

Scientific Research on the Maharishi's Transcendental Meditation and TM-Sidhi programme: Meditation Programme. **Collected Papers**, 1977, 1, 385–392.

98 Travis, F., Haaga, D., Hagelin, J., Tanner, M., Nidich, S., Gaylord-King, C., Grosswald, S., Rainforth, M. & Schneider, R. *Effects of Transcendental Meditation Practice on Brain Functioning and Stress Reactivity in College Students*. **International Journal of Psychophysiology**, 2009, 71(2), 170–176.

99 Beauchemin, J., Hutchins, T.L. & Patterson, F. *Mindfulness meditation may lessen anxiety, promote social skills, and improve academic performance among adolescents with learning disabilities*. **Journal of Evidence-Based Complementary & Alternative Medicine**, 2008, 13(1), 34–45.

Collier, R.W. **The Effect of the Transcendental Meditation Program upon University Academic Attainment**. Honolulu, HI: Department of English as a Second Language, College of Arts and Sciences, University of Hawaii, 1973.

Hall, P. *The effect of meditation on academic performance of African American college students*. **Journal of Black Studies**, 1999, 29(3), 408–415.

Heaton, D.P. & Orme-Johnson, D.W. **The Transcendental Meditation Program and Academic Achievement**. Fairfield, IA: International Center for Scientific Research Maharishi International University, 1974.

Kember, P. *The Transcendental Meditation Technique and postgraduate academic performance*. **British Journal of Educational Psychology**, 1985, 55(2), 164–166.

[100] Barnes, V., Bauza, L. & Treiber, F. *Impact of stress reduction on negative school behavior in adolescents.* **Health and Quality of Life Outcomes**, 2003, 1(10), 1–7.

[101] Shapiro J. *The relationship of the TM program to self-actualization and negative personality characteristics.* In D.W. Orme-Johnson & J.T. Farrow (Eds.), **Scientific research on the Transcendental Meditation program: Collected papers. Volume 1**, 462–467. Rheinweiler, Germany: Maharishi European Research University Press, 1976.

[102] Grosswald, S., Stixrud, W., Travis, F. & Bateh, M. *Use of the Transcendental Meditation technique to reduce symptoms of attention deficit hyperactivity disorder (ADHD) by reducing stress and anxiety: an exploratory study.* **Current Issues in Education**, 2008, 10(2), 1–15.

Travis, F., Grosswald, S. & Stixrud, W. *ADHD, Brain functioning, and transcendental meditation practice.* **Mind & Brain**, 2011, 2(1), 73–81.

[103] Nidich, S., Rainforth, M., Haaga, D., Hagelin, J., Salerno, J., Travis, F., Tanner, M., Gaylord-King, C., Grosswald, S. & Schneider, R. *A randomized controlled trial on effects of the Transcendental Meditation program on blood pressure, psychological distress, and coping in young adults.* **American Journal of Hypertension**, 2009, 22(12), 1326–1331.

[104] Dixon, C., Dillbeck, M.C., Travis, F., Msemaje, H., Clayborne, B.M., Dillbeck, S.L. & Alexander, C.N. *Accelerating cognitive and self-development: Longitudinal studies with preschool and elementary school children.* **Journal of Social Behavior and Personality**, 2005, 17(1), 65–91.

[105] Alexander, C.N., Rainforth, M.V. & Gelderloos, P. *Transcendental Meditation, self-actualization, and psychological health: A conceptual overview and statistical meta-analysis.* **Journal of Social Behavior and Personality**, 1991, 6(5), 189–248.

Gelderloos, P., Hermans, H.J.M., Ahlström, H.H. & Jacoby, R. *Transcendence and psychological health: Studies with long-term participants of the Transcendental Meditation and TM-Sidhi program.* **Journal of Psychology**, 1990, 124(2), 177–197.

Turnbull, M.J. & Norris, H. *Effects of Transcendental Meditation on self-identity indices and personality.* **British Journal of Psychology**, 1982, 73(1), 57–69.

[106] Fredrick, T. *The Transcendental Meditation technique and creativity: a longitudinal study of Cornell University undergraduates.* **The Journal of Creative Behavior**, 1979, 13(3), 169–180.

So, K.T. & Orme-Johnson, D.W. *Three randomized experiments on the longitudinal effects of the Transcendental Meditation technique on cognition.* **Intelligence**, 2001, 29(5), 419–440.

Travis, F. *Creative thinking and the Transcendental Meditation technique.* **The Journal of Creative Behavior**, 1979, 13(3), 169–180.

[107] Dillbeck, M.C. *Meditation and flexibility of visual perception and verbal problem solving.* **Memory & Cognition**, 1982, 10(3), 207–215.

[108] Cranson, R.W., Orme-Johnson, D.W., Gackenbach, J., Dillbeck, M.C., Jones, CH. & Alexander, C.N. *Transcendental Meditation and improved performance on intelligence related measures: A longitudinal study.* **Personality and Individual Differences**, 1991, 12(10), 1105–1116.

Dixon, C., Dillbeck, M.C., Travis, F., Msemaje, H., Clayborne, B.M., Dillbeck, S.L. & Alexander, C.N. *Accelerating cognitive and self-development: Longitudinal studies with preschool and elementary school children.* **Journal of Social Behavior and Personality**, 2005, 17(1), 65–91.

So, K.T. & Orme-Johnson, D.W. *Three randomized experiments on the longitudinal effects of the Transcendental Meditation technique on cognition.* **Intelligence**, 2001, 29(5), 419–440.

[109] Cranson, R.W., Orme-Johnson, D.W., Gackenbach, J., Dillbeck, M.C., Jones, C.H. & Alexander, C.N. *Transcendental Meditation and improved performance on intelligence related measures: A longitudinal study.* **Personality and Individual Differences**, 1991, 12(10), 1105–1116.

So, K.T. & Orme-Johnson, D.W. *Three randomized experiments on the longitudinal effects of the Transcendental Meditation technique on cognition.* **Intelligence**, 2001, 29(5), 419–440.

[110] Barnhofer, T., Duggan, D., Crane, C., Hepburn, S., Fennell, M. & Williams, J.M.G. *Effects of meditation on frontal alpha asymmetry in previously suicidal patients.* **NeuroReport**, 2007, 18(7), 709–712.

Orme-Johnson, D.W., Dillbeck, M.C., Wallace, R.K. & Landrith, G.S. *Intersubject EEG coherence: Is consciousness a field?* **International Journal of Neuroscience**, 1982, 16(3–4), 203–209.

Travis, F., Haaga, D., Hagelin, J., Tanner, M., Nidich, S. & Gaylord-King, C., Grosswald, S., Rainforth, M. & Schneider, R. *Effects of Transcendental Meditation Practice on brain functioning and stress reactivity in college students.* **International Journal of Psychophysiology**, 2009, 71(2), 170–176.

[111] Rees, B., Travis, F., Shapiro, D. & Chant, R. *Reduction in posttraumatic stress symptoms in Congolese refugees practicing Transcendental Meditation.* **Journal of Traumatic Stress**, 2013, 26(2), 295–298.

[112] Dillbeck, M.C. & Orme-Johnson, D.W. *Physiological differences between Transcendental Meditation and rest.* **The American Psychologist**, 1987, 42(9), 879–881.

[113] So, K.T. & Orme-Johnson, D.W. *Three randomized experiments on the longitudinal effects of the Transcendental Meditation technique on cognition.* **Intelligence**, 2001, 29(5), 419–440.

[114] Eppley, K., Abrams, A.I. & Shear, J. *Differential effects of relaxation techniques on trait anxiety: A meta-analysis.* **Journal of Clinical Psychology**, 1989, 45(6), 957–974.

[115] Lutz, A., Greischer, L.L., Rawlings, N.B., Ricard, M. & Davidson, R.J. *Long-term meditators self-induce high amplitude gamma synchrony during mental practice.* **Proceedings of the National Academy of Sciences**, 2004, 101(46), 16369–16373.

[116] Raes, F., Griffith, J.W., Gucht, K. & Williams, J.M.G. *School-based prevention and reduction of depression in adolescents: A cluster-randomized controlled trial of a mindfulness group program.* **Mindfulness**, 2013, 1–10.

117 Nielsen, L. & Kaszniak, A.W. *Awareness of subtle emotional feelings: A comparison of long-term meditators and non-meditators.* **Emotion**, 2006, 6(3), 392–405.

118 Tang, Y., Ma, Y., Wang, J., Fan, Y., Feng, S., Lu, Q., Yu, Q., Sui, D., Rothbart, M.K., Fan, M. & Posner, M.I. *Short-term meditation training improves attention and self-regulation.* **Proceedings of the National Academy of Sciences**, 2007, 104(43), 17152–17156.

119 Kaliman, P., Jesus Alvarez-Lopez, M., Cosin-Tomas, M., Rosenkranz, M.A., Lutz, A. & Davidson, R.J. *Rapid changes in histone deacetylases and inflammatory gene expression in expert meditators.* **Psychoneuroendocrinology**, 2014, 40, 96–107.

120 Lazar, S., Kerr, C.E., Wasserman, R.H., Gray, J.R., Greve, D.N., Treadway, M.T., McGarvey, M., Quinn, B.T., Dusek, J.A. Benson, H., Rauch, S.L., Moore, C.I. & Fischl, B. *Meditation experience is associated with increased cortical thickness.* **NeuroReport**, 2005, 16(17), 1893–1897.

121 Luders, E., Toga, A.W., Lepore, N. & Gaser, C. *The underlying anatomical correlates of long-term meditation: Larger hippocampal and frontal volumes of gray matter.* **NeuroImage**, 2009, 45(3), 672–678.

122 Gaëlle D., Negi, L.T., Pace, T.W.W., Wallace, A.B., Raison, C.L. & Schwartz, E.L. *Effects of mindful-attention and compassion meditation training on amygdala response to emotional stimuli in an ordinary, non-meditative state.* **Frontiers in Human Neuroscience**, 2012, 6, 292.

123 Peng, C.K., Henry, I.C., Mietus, J.E., Hausdorff, J.M., Khalsa, G., Benson, H. & Goldberger, A. *Heart rate dynamics during three forms of meditation.* **International Journal of Cardiology**, 2004, 95(1), 19–27.

124 Travis, F. *Are all meditations the same? Comparing the neural patterns of Mindfulness Meditation, Tibetan Buddhism practice "unconditional loving-kindness and compassion," and the Transcendental Meditation Technique."* **Science of Consciousness Conference**, Tucson, AZ, April, 2006. Retrieved July, 2013, from: http://www.fredtravis.com/talk.html

125 David Lynch Foundation. (2012). *TM/Quiet Time program for students* [Video Clip]. Retrieved November, 2012, from: http://www.davidlynchfoundation.org/schools.html#video=93-NzNBLCbE

126 Stress Free Schools. (2011). *Home Page: The TM Quiet Time program* [Text]. Retrieved November, 2012, from: http://stressfreeschools.org.nz/index.html

127 CBE Schools. (2008). *Home Page: Consciousness-Based Education* [Text]. Retrieved November, 2012, from: http://cbesa.org/index.html

128 Nidich, S., Mjasiri, S., Nidich, R., Rainforth, M., Grant, J., Valosek, L., Chang, W. & Zigler, R.L. *Academic achievement and transcendental meditation: A study with at-risk urban middle school students.* **Education Around the World**, 2011, 131(3), 556–564.

129 Rosaen, C. & Benn, R. *The experience of Transcendental Meditation in middle school students: a qualitative report.* **Explore**, 2006, 2(5), 422–425.

130 Barnes, V.A., Bauza, L. & Treiber, F.A. *Impact of stress reduction on negative school behavior in adolescents.* **Health and Quality of Life Outcomes**, 2003, 1(10) 1–7.

131 Barnes, V.A., Treiber, F.A. & Davis, H. *Impact of Transcendental Meditation on cardiovascular function at rest and during acute stress in adolescents with high normal blood pressure.* **Journal of Psychosomatic Research**, 2001, 51(4), 597–605.

Social

The brain is a social organ. Humans are wired to cooperate. Cooperation is biologically rewarding. A cooperative classroom activates the social cognition network, creates an inclusive class, carefully structures cooperative interaction, and promotes cooperative play. The results: safety, peer encouragement and tutoring, and creative thinking. Implementing Principle 3 allows the brains of our students to function the ways they function best.

Principle 3

1 Activate Social Cognition

2 Include Classbuilding

3 Structure Cooperative Interaction

4 Teach Social Skills

5 Promote Cooperative Play

Principle 3
Social

Principle 3

Promote Social Cognition and Cooperation

W can improve educational outcomes by aligning how students think and interact with the finding that the brain is a social organ. Brains have a social cognition network we can activate to make our content more meaningful and more memorable. Because brains are exquisitely designed to attend to and remember social content, by having students cooperate to learn, we improve academic outcomes. Here we examine the rationale for using easy-to-apply methods to increase social cognition and cooperation. We examine also the massive body of empirical data proving that cooperative learning dramatically improves academic achievement. Before turning to the five tools to teach to the social brain, let's overview the evidence that our brains are designed to attend to and remember social stimuli.

Brains Are Designed to Be Social. Our brains have distinct neural tracks dedicated to figuring out the minds of others.[1] If I ask you to memorize a list of accomplishments by Ben Franklin, one set of brain structures goes to work. If instead, I ask you to look over the same list of Ben's accomplishments and infer what kind of person Ben Franklin was, a very different set of neural tracks goes into action—the social cognition network. Whenever we attempt to understand the thoughts, feelings, or intentions of another person we activate our social cognition network, a process called *mentalizing*. Mentalizing increases memory, an effect called the social encoding advantage. Memory for the list of Ben Franklin's accomplishments is greater if we don't try to memorize it, but instead simply try to figure out what kind of person he was!

The brain structures involved in mentalizing and those for working memory are entirely independent! Brain structures for mentalizing are located mostly in the medial (midline) regions of the brain; structures responsible for working memory and fluid intelligence are located in the lateral (outer) surface of the brain. "In other words, the neuroimaging findings are telling us something we could probably never have learned by just thinking about the inner workings of our minds: Although social and nonsocial thinking feel like the same kind of process, evolution created two distinct systems to handle them."[2]

5 Tools to Teach to the Social Brain

1. **Activate Social Cognition** 3.21

2. **Include Classbuilding** 3.24

3. **Structure Cooperative Interaction** 3.26

4. **Teach Social Skills** 3.36

5. **Promote Cooperative Play** 3.39

That this social cognition network is located in a deeper part of the brain indicates it evolved earlier. We are fundamentally social beings.

These two distinct networks of brain structures actually work antagonistically.[3] Thinking about nonsocial, task-related content shuts down thinking about the thoughts, feelings, and intentions of others, and mentalizing shuts down thinking about nonsocial content. We have a social IQ and a nonsocial IQ, but we can't operate both at once!

Social Cognition Is the Brain's Default Mode. The social cognition network is our brain's default network. When we are given IQ-type test questions or try to estimate how far our car can travel on the gas remaining in the tank, our working memory and fluid intelligence go to work, shutting down the social cognition network. Brain scans reveal that as soon as we have completed nonsocial tasks, our brains reactivate the social cognition network.[4]

> The default network quiets down when we perform a specific task, such as calculating a math problem in math class or studying ancient Greek pottery in history class. But when the mind's chores are done, it returns to Old Faithful—the default mode. In other words, the brain's free time is devoted to thinking socially.[5]

We are so primed to look for thoughts, feelings, and intentions, we even impute feelings and intentions to objects. For example, when shown a motion picture of geometric figures (triangles, a circle, and an open box) moving about on the screen, normal children and adults attribute feelings and intentions to the objects: *"The big triangle is a bully that is picking on the small triangle and circle, who are running scared…."*[6] In contrast, autistic children, who have a deficit in social cognition, do not attribute feelings or intentions to inanimate objects: *"The big triangle went into the rectangle. The big triangle went out. The shapes bounce off each other…."*[7] Our normal default mode is to look for feelings and intentions, even attributing them to inanimate objects! Our default mode of cognition is social cognition. We are social creatures.

Social Cognition Predicts Successful Cooperation and Competition

Matthew Lieberman in his book, *Social*, summarizes dozens of research studies explaining how the brain's social cognition network operates. With the exception of children below 3 years of age and autistic individuals, we are all mindreaders. We gravitate to thinking about the thinking of others, and when we do, four structures in the brain become engaged and these structures are distinct from those structures associated with working memory and fluid intelligence. Lieberman calls the social network structures the *mentalizing* system.

Understanding the thinking of others is vital for all successful social interaction. Let's examine how it is prerequisite for successful cooperation as well as for successful competition.

Mindreading for Cooperation. In the video game, *Stag Hunt*, players cannot talk with each other, but must coordinate their efforts to trap a stag. For example, if a stag is headed toward a passage that has only two exits and one player intends to block one exit, to be successful in the hunt, the other player must move to block the other passage. Because the stag and the players are running, success depends on the players' ability to read the mind of the other player. Only if they can infer the intentions of each other can they coordinate efforts and trap the stag. Neuroimaging results indicate the more difficult it is to predict your partner's next move in the game, the more the mentalizing system is active.[8]

Mindreading for Competition. Imagine you are in a research study but can win real money. You are in a group and are told everyone will guess a number from 1 to 100. The winner will be the person whose guess is closest to one-half the average of all the guesses. What do you guess?

If you do not think about the thinking of others, you might guess 25. That is, you might think the average guess would be 50 (the average of all numbers) and half of that would be 25. If, on the other hand, you were more strategic and considered the minds of others, you would likely

Brainiac Box

Question:
Which parts of the brain go into action when we try to figure out what someone else is thinking?

Answer:
Remarkably, social and nonsocial reasoning are carried out by different brain structures.

When people read sentences that do not involve figuring out what someone is thinking, the lateral prefrontal regions of the brain associated with language, working memory, and fluid intelligence become engaged.

In contrast, across a number of studies, when people read sentences that involve mentalizing, thinking about the thinking of others, their social cognition network goes into action. The regions involved with working memory and fluid intelligence are quiet.

The social cognition network consists of four structures: The dorsomedial prefrontal cortex (DMPFC), the tempoparietal junction (TPJ), the posterior cingulate, and the temporal poles.

The implication: We have a social brain distinct from our nonsocial brain! Knowing what others are thinking is so important that our brains dedicate special circuits for that purpose.

guess much lower. You would think, others would figure half of an average guess would be 25 and so they would be likely to guess 25. Since the winner is the person who guesses closest to half the average guess, you might make your guess 12.5. But then, of course, if you thought others were

thinking that deeply about the game, they too might come up with a 12.5 guess, so you might come up with a guess even lower. The more you consider the minds of others, the more likely it is your guess will be lower.

Neuroimaging research demonstrates that the more individuals take into account the minds of others, making lower guesses because they understand how others will think, the greater is the activity in the mentalizing system.[9] Further, being strategic, considering the minds of others is not associated with those brain structures involved in working memory or IQ. The brain has two types of IQ: the traditional IQ and a social IQ.

Autism: Lack of Social Cognition

Many children with autism show a partial or almost complete lack of social cognition. While sitting at the dinner table, an autistic child was asked, *"Can you pass the salt?"* Instead of passing the salt, without any awareness of the intent of the person asking, and without awareness of doing something odd, the autistic child simply answered *"Yes."*[10] Failure of the social cognition network explains some of the odd behaviors of autistic children. A boy with autism, intently searched a room after hearing that someone in that room had "cried their eyes out." A 10-year-old girl with autism, who had an IQ of 100, became terrified in the doctor's office. Why? The nurse, wishing to do a simple blood test, innocently said, "give me your hand."[11] Communication breaks down when we fail to read the intent of others—when there is failure of the social cognition network.

People diagnosed with autism show above average abilities in nonsocial tests that involve analytic skills. For example, they score above average in the embedded figures test, which involves finding a simple figure hidden within a more complex illustration.[12] That persons with autism score well on tasks that do not involve social cognition demonstrates that the social cognition network is independent from nonsocial logical intelligence. It is not a failure of nonsocial intelligence that causes difficulties for persons with autism; it is a failure of the social cognition network.

The Social Encoding Advantage

Numerous studies have demonstrated that activating the social cognition network increases memory for content. In the first of these groundbreaking studies, students were given a description of a number of behaviors of a person. In one condition, they were told to memorize the behaviors. In a second condition, they were explicitly told not to memorize the behaviors. Instead, they were told to attempt to form an overall impression of the person who performed the behaviors. Students told to memorize for the test performed worse on the test than those students who were not told there would be a test but who were instead instructed to form an impression of the person based on their behaviors—basically to mentalize![13] This effect has been replicated in many studies. It is called the *social encoding advantage*.

An fMRI study revealed that distinct brain networks are engaged when people are told to "form an impression of this person" versus "remember the order in which this information is presented." When instructed to memorize the order of information (a nonsocial task), success was associated with activation of the lateral prefrontal cortex and the medial temporal lobe, the sites of working memory and fluid intelligence. In contrast, when told to form an impression of the person (a social cognition task), success was associated with activation of the dorsomedial prefrontal cortex, the core of the social cognition network.[14] The implications of these findings are enormous for us as educators. It appears that traditional educational practice actually suppresses a powerful, natural memory system. The brain naturally looks for the thoughts, feelings, and intentions of others, but traditional curriculum and instruction is relatively devoid of opportunities to mentalize. Our curriculum and instruction can be more brain friendly to the extent we engage social cognition—having students think about the thoughts, feelings, and intentions of others.

By having students work alone and focus exclusively on objective facts rather than having students work in interaction and focus also on thoughts, feelings, and intentions of actors, we are swimming against the current. We can reinvigorate education if we take these findings to heart. We will promote memory for content

"The brain has a fantastic learning system that has been largely untapped as an educational resource."[15]
—*Matthew D. Lieberman*

> ## Tip
> ### Personalize Academic Content
> Focus on the thoughts, feelings, and intentions of historical and literary characters. Put science in the context of the intentions of scientists who made discoveries. Put math in the context of intention—what can different professions do with an algorithm?

as well as liking for learning by refocusing how we have students think about academic content, and how they interact as they do. For example, instead of memorizing the accomplishments of a president, we should be having our students focus on the president's thoughts, feelings, and intentions. The facts will be acquired in that context more readily than by having students memorize. Instead of having students sit in rows facing the back of the head of the person in front of them, we should turn the chairs around and have students interact. In the process, we activate the social cognition network, boosting memory for and liking of our curriculum. We can increase the success of our students by activating their social cognition networks.

In this Principle 3: Social, we provide ways to activate the social cognition network and how best to structure cooperative learning. Before turning to those tools, let's explore the extensive evidence that the brain is a social organ.

Social Interaction: The Default Mode for Humans

Those of us who observe students in classrooms do not need brain science to tell us students are social creatures. How much energy does the traditional teacher expend trying to squelch social interaction?

Social interaction among our students is not limited to in-person interaction. Texting is the primary reason teens get a cell phone. Teens outpace all other groups in sending and receiving text messages. Teen males send and receive an average of 2,539 texts a month; teen females outpace them, sending and receiving an average of 4,050 texts a month![16]

At the time of this writing, Facebook is the most commonly viewed website in the world—ahead of Google! Facebook now has over one billion active users![17]

Seventy percent of the content of conversations is social.[18]

Social Interaction Lights Up the Brain

In *Mapping the Mind*,[19] Rita Carter displays results of active brain imaging studies that show that brains are dramatically more active while learning in interaction with others than when attempting to learn alone, learn by reading, or learn via a lecture. Opiate-like substances are released in mammalian brains during care-giving and play, explaining why these activities are so rewarding. When we help another, there is heightened activity in the caudate nucleus and anterior cingulate cortex regions of the brain, which are pleasure and reward centers.[20] Our brains, to a remarkable extent, are social organs. See Box: Interaction Lights Up the Brain!

Vigilance for Social Stimuli

Picture a primitive primate troop. Which kind of stimuli are the most important for the primates to attend to? It is the faces and body language of the other primates. Those are the cues that warn of an impending attack, or foretell kind grooming.

Sensitivity to others, knowing who dominates and who does not, who can be approached and who cannot—these are the clues that determine safety and even survival.

Our brains are exquisitely designed to tune in to and respond to social stimuli. Our social cognition network becomes active when we view any social interaction. Positive interaction activates approach parts of that network; negative interaction activates avoidance parts of the network. For example, viewing a social interaction preceded by a handshake, a smile, and an open, inviting posture activates approach areas of the social cognition network more than the

Interaction Lights Up the Brain!

Reading:
Visual Cortex

Listening to Speech:
Wernicke's Area

Speaking:
Broca's Area

Social Interaction:
Widespread Activity

Brain scans show that social interaction is the royal road to brain activation. In her book, *Mapping the Mind*, Rita Carter presents brain scans that show how different activities engage the brain. Reading, listening to a lecture, and talking all engage specific parts of the brain, but interacting with a peer over the content lights up many parts of the brain. When we interact, we have visual stimuli (the other person's face); verbal stimuli (the other person's words); and a great deal of prefrontal activity as we determine what to do with the information the other person is providing: Is it consistent with our preexisting picture of the world, or do we have to change that picture? As we interact, we attempt to understand the minds of others, activating the social cognition network. Social interaction is the royal road to brain engagement.[21]

absence of the handshake and less-inviting body language. A handshake preceding interaction causes those receiving the handshake to perceive the person offering the handshake as more competent, more interested in interacting, and more trustworthy.[22]

> ## Tip
>
> As they enter your class, greet students at the door with a smile, a handshake or high five. The touch and proximity activate the approach structures in students' social cognition network, making your class more inviting.

If brains naturally attend to and become more alert and engaged with social stimuli, brain-friendly teaching has students interact regularly over academic content. When we have students discuss, debate, and work together on the content, they become more focused, alert, and attentive. Kagan Cooperative Learning Structures involve social interaction. Thus, when we use cooperative learning, we are teaching the way brains naturally turn on. For example, rather than working on a worksheet alone, the instructor uses **Sage-N-Scribe** to have students solve problems. Because students are interacting, their brains are far more engaged.

See Structures Section
17. Sage-N-Scribe

Brains Are Designed to Attend to Faces

Additional evidence for the social nature of our brains is that our brains have specific structures designed to recognize faces. An area of the brain called the fusiform gyrus becomes active when we see a face. In fact, we are so wired to seek faces that we see faces even when none are there! Our brain turns the two headlights and the grill of a car into a face looking at us.

The fusiform gyrus is distinct from the part of the brain that responds to objects. Due to the fusiform gyrus, we recognize faces far better than inanimate objects. Not only do we seek faces, we maintain focus on faces longer than on objects. Babies at 9 minutes of age are much more likely to turn their heads toward and track with their eyes, a black and white picture if the parts of the picture are arranged to resemble a human face, than if the same parts are arranged randomly.[23] We have "socially responsive neurons!" Single neurons of humans respond selectively and preferentially to social stimuli.[24] They do not respond to an object, but respond to a face!

Because face recognition is primarily a right hemisphere function, ability to recognize faces in photos or illustrations that contain only minimal cues have been used to create tests of right hemisphere function.

A Mooney Face

Craig Mooney developed what became known as the Mooney Face Test. To test this aspect of right hemisphere function, children are presented black and white illustrations that either represent faces or not, in order to test how well they distinguish faces from non-faces. See Illustration: A Mooney Face, p. 3.8.

Prosopagnosia. Inability to recognize faces is a condition called prosopagnosia, or face blindness. The word "prosopagnosia" combines the Greek word for face (prosopon) with the medical term for recognition impairment (agnosia). Prosopagnosia occurs for either of two reasons: brain damage or heredity. Head trauma, stroke, or degenerative disease may damage the fusiform gyrus resulting in face blindness. Prosopagnosia occurs also based on genes. Hereditary prosopagnosia is far more frequent than commonly recognized. In a study of 689 randomly selected students, 2.5% had prosopagnosia, and in all cases, at least one family member had the condition as well.[25]

Children with hereditary prosopagnosia fail to develop face-recognition skills. Normally, face recognition skills develop continually until they reach adult levels in teenage years. Those with hereditary prosopagnosia often do not recognize they have a disorder because they have never been able to recognize faces and are unaware that others can. To recognize other people, students with prosopagnosia use non-facial cues such as voice, hair color, height, weight, and gait. Prosopagnosic children are sometimes mistaken for being shy or introverted and have trouble recognizing classmates. They sometimes compensate for their condition by making friends with children who have clear, distinguishing features. Adults with prosopagnosia can compensate and can function quite well: Examples include film actor Brad Pitt, primatologist Jane Goodall, and neuroscientist Oliver Sacks.

If the research on prosopagnosia holds true, one of every 40 schoolchildren cannot recognize faces! This condition is very seldom recognized or understood. Because prosopagnosia puts students at an extreme disadvantage in social relations, we would serve our student populations well by testing for face blindness. At minimum, face blindness should be considered a possibility in working with students who are shy or who behave in an odd manner in social relations.

Interestingly, although those with prosopagnosia cannot consciously recognize faces, they respond emotionally to familiar faces: their autonomic nervous system responds differently to familiar and nonfamiliar faces.[26] This indicates distinct brain systems are involved in different facets of face recognition. Brain imaging studies reveal areas other than the fusiform gyrus are also involved in face recognition.[27]

> **Tip**
> Face blindness should be a consideration in working with students who are shy, who have difficulty recognizing classmates, and/or who behave in an odd manner socially.

Single Neurons Respond to Social Stimuli

Extremely sophisticated brain research supports the conclusion that we are hardwired to respond to social stimuli. The research uses unbelievably small single-neuron electrodes that actually determine when individual neurons fire. Single-neuron electrode research overcomes the limits of brain imaging technology. There are serious limitations to even the best brain-imaging technology. Neurons fire in milliseconds but the best brain-imaging technology to date gives a 6-second snapshot of tens of thousands of neurons. It cannot tell what specific neurons are doing and when they are doing it.

Researchers placed single-neuron electrodes in different parts of the frontal cortex of macaque monkeys who were allowed to allocate rewards to themselves, to another, or to no one. Using this very advanced technology, researchers found strong support for the conclusion that "specialized social circuitry evolved a long time ago, presumably to support cooperative behavior."[28] Consistent with prior work in humans and animals, when giving a reward to oneself, the orbital frontal cortex right above the eyes is active. When giving up a reward, the anterior cingulate sulculs in the middle top of the brain is active. These two areas calculate the pros and cons of gaining or giving up a reward regardless of whether there is a social context or not. A third area, the anterior cingulate gyrus, responds to what is happening to the other monkey. This region is active when a monkey simply sees another monkey receive a reward. This same region of the brain is active in humans when we empathize with someone else. As stated by one of the authors of the single-neuron research study, "One might view these as sort of mirror neurons for the reward system."

Primate brains are exquisitely wired to respond to others. Brain areas have been found for vicarious pain perception,[29] understanding the thinking of others,[30] and empathy.[31]

Social Contact: A Biological Need

Lack of Social Interaction Causes Infant Mortality. Interaction with others is absolutely indispensable for newborn human infants. Infants who are kept clean, warm, and well nourished, but who do not receive social interaction, die. One hundred years ago, this simple fact was not yet known, and most babies placed in infant asylums younger than 1 year of age, never reached the age of 2!

The institutional mortality of infants was discussed at the annual meeting of the American Pediatric Society in 1915. Dr. Henry Chapin reported on ten infant asylums located in different cities of the United States. In all but one institution, every infant under 2 years of age died! Hamil of Philadelphia, in discussing Chapin's paper, said ironically: *"I had the honor to be connected with an institution in this city in which*

the mortality among all the infants of 1 year of age, when admitted to the institution and retained there for any length of time, was 100%. That is, no infant admitted under 1 year of age lived to be 2 years old."[32] Knox described a study in which he followed 200 infants admitted to various institutions in Baltimore. Of these, almost 90% died within a year. *"The 10% that lived,"* he said, *"did so apparently, because, for some reason or other, the babies were taken from the institutions for short times and given into the care of foster parents or relatives."*[33]

The infants placed in institutions at that time almost all developed a well-defined set of symptoms including listlessness, relative immobility, unresponsiveness to stimuli, lack of interest in stimuli, poor sucking habits, frequent stools, failure to gain weight, poor muscle tone, elevated temperature, and unhappiness. The infants would eat, but they accepted food without eagerness or interest. The clinical term used to describe this set of symptoms was "hospitalism." The symptoms are identical to what Seligman calls learned helplessness.[34] The babies learned that no matter what they did, they could not obtain the social interaction necessary for life! They gave up trying.

Some doctors understood early the need in infants for physical interaction and contact. Brennemann (1932) had a rule in his hospital: Every baby should be picked up, carried around, amused, and "mothered" several times a day.[35] In discussing hospitalism, in 1941, Friz Talbot described a visit to a children's clinic in Dusseldor around 1909. Talbot noticed a very fat old lady wandering around the ward with a very measly baby on her hip. He asked Schlossmann, the director, who she was. Talbot was told that, whenever they had a baby for whom they had done everything medically and were unsuccessful, they turned the baby over to old Anna and told her to take charge. Old Anna was always successful.[36]

By 1940, the "disease" of hospitalism had been "cured" in the United States. Practitioners had learned about infants' critical need for touch and social interaction so infants were either placed in foster homes, or if retained in institutions, large corps of volunteers were recruited to touch and play with them. Hospitalism remained common in some infant institutions in other parts of the world because of lack of understanding of infants' need for social interaction.

Skin-to-Skin Contact. Mother-infant skin-to-skin contact directly following birth has a direct, profound, and enduring impact on cognitive development! Premature infants were randomly assigned to two conditions: 73 received standard incubator treatment and 73 received incubator treatment plus Kangaroo Care. Kangaroo Care occurred for 1 hour a day for just 14 days. Infants were taken out of their incubators, undressed, and placed between their mother's breasts while the mother sat in a rocking chair.

Results were phenomenal: The infants were studied at 3, 6, 12, and 24 months of age and at 5 and 10 years of age. At all ages, infants who had received Kangaroo Care showed superior development. The early, brief skin-to-skin contact improved mental development at 6, 12, and 24 months. At 10 years of age, "infants who received skin-to-skin contact as neonates showed attenuated stress response, more mature autonomic functioning, organized sleep, cognitive control, and more reciprocal mother-child relationship."[37] Of particular interest is the improved cognitive control or executive function among the infants who received early touch. Executive function is the variable most predictive of academic achievement. Premature infants often show developmental lag or deficiency in the development of the prefrontal cortex, working memory, and executive function.[38] This deficiency was attenuated or eliminated in infants receiving Kangaroo Care!

Critical Period for Attachment. There appears to be a critical period in brain development, beyond which children lose the ability to benefit from social interaction and care. In such cases, love and care by foster parents are not enough to overcome a permanent lack of attachment. Children from Romanian orphanages were given little stimulation or attention from adults. When Western families adopted them, the parents reported inability to "reach them." As one mother reported of her 10-year-old adopted daughter,

"We have treated her exactly like our other children, who are normal and affectionate, but she has just never got the idea…. She doesn't seem to connect to us…. She's quite intelligent, but she can't learn to show concern for other people. It is not that she wants to upset us—it is more that she doesn't seem to take on board that we exist."[39]

Cooperative Interaction: Biologically Rewarding

Neuroscience research reveals cooperation is biologically rewarding: By analyzing brain activation during cooperative interaction, researchers report cooperation activates reward circuits:

During the mutually cooperative social interactions, activation was noted in those areas of the brain that are linked to reward processing: the nucleus accumbens, the caudate nucleus, the ventromedial frontal/orbitofrontal cortex, and the rostral anterior cingulate cortex. Our study shows, for the first time, that social cooperation is intrinsically rewarding to the human brain.[40]

When we structure cooperative interaction in our classrooms, students are interacting in ways their brains find rewarding. This greater enjoyment of the cooperative activity transfers to a greater liking for class and academic content. We are teaching the way brains find rewarding.

Kindness Boosts Popularity

Students who are assigned to perform acts of kindness have more friends. Nineteen classrooms of students ages 9 to 11 years old were assigned to one of two conditions: (1) Perform three acts of kindness per week for 4 weeks; or (2) Visit three places.[41] Examples of acts of kindness: "gave my mom a hug when she was stressed by her job," "gave someone some of my lunch," and "vacuumed the floor." Examples of visits: "visited grandma's house;" "went to the mall."

Results: Students in the kindness condition gained friends! At the outset and end of the experiment, peers listed who they wanted as friends. Those in the kindness condition gained

Tips

● Have students keep a kindness journal. Have them record times they have been helpful to others, and on a weekly basis share that with their teammates.

● Have the class total, post, and celebrate each week the number of kind acts performed by the class.

Tip

Be alert for social isolates or those who have suffered rejection from a peer. Find a positive quality in that student and recognize it publicly.

an average of 1.5 friends by the end of the 4-week study! Students in both conditions significantly increased their sense of well-being, but only those performing acts of kindness increased the number of students who wanted them as a friend. Further, this increased popularity was not due to the increase in well-being—they were two relatively independent outcomes.

These findings are remarkable for three reasons: (1) Preteens establish their friendship patterns over years, yet in just 4 weeks these patterns were significantly changed; (2) The study was conducted in the second half of the school year, indicating the intervention worked even after friendship patterns had been established; (3) Many of the acts of kindness were not aimed at classmates—they included things like helping mom or vacuuming. Without trying to gain more friends, and with relatively little effort, in just 4 weeks, students were chosen as friends significantly more often.

The finding is important: Being accepted and liked by peers predicts both positive adjustment and improved academic performance.[42] Well-liked preteens exhibit fewer bullying behaviors.[43] Further, when there is an even distribution of popularity in a classroom—fewer favorites and fewer isolates—the mental health of students in that classroom is improved.[44]

Social Rejection Is Painful, Literally!

One of the biggest fears among students is to be rejected socially. Being "in" is a need. Animals that can't keep up with the herd are those most likely to fall prey. Fish that can't keep up with their school are most likely to be eaten. There is safety in numbers. Brains are wired to react negatively to being "out"—being rejected.

Rejection Produces Pain. To test what happens in the brain when a person is accepted or rejected, researchers had people engage in a simulated personal dating experience.[45] First, participants selected at least 40 online profiles from a collection of 500 men and women. For each profile, participants used a seven-point scale (from "definitely no" to "definitely yes") to answer two questions: "Would I like this person?" And "Would this person like me?" Prior research had indicated that feedback from a highly rated person produces the greatest brain activation.

In the next phase of the research, while in a brain scan, participants received feedback from their highest-rated picks. The feedback was either that they were not liked (rejected) or liked (accepted). The experimenters focused on the extent the endogenous opioid system was activated in different parts of the brain in response to acceptance and rejection. Prior research has established opioid response to pain. Opioids are the brains way of dampening pain.

Brainiac Box

Question:
Where in the brain is social pain processed?

Answer:
Social pain and physical pain are processed by the same brain structure—the Dorsal Anterior Cingulate Cortex (dACC).

Question:
Where is the dACC?

Answer:
Dorsal means on top; Anterior means toward the front. The Cingulate Cortex is a long brain structure stretching from the back to the front of the brain. Cingulate means belt or girdle: The Cingulate Cortex looks like a belt hugging the corpus callosum, which connects the right and left hemispheres. The dACC is found in mammals but not reptiles.

Question:
What happens if we remove the dACC?

Answer:
In a treatment for chronic pain, a Cingulotomy, part of the dACC is removed or disconnected from other structures. Patients report they still can locate the pain and can tell the intensity of the pain, but amazingly, they no longer find the pain distressing! Apparently the dACC is what makes us respond to avoid pain.

Many results were generated for different parts of the brain, but we will focus here on the amygdalae and on other structures that respond to pain.

The study found:

▶ Rejection led to people reporting feeling more sad and rejected, less happy, less accepted, and less desire for social contact.
▶ Rejection led to greater activation of both the the right and left amygdalae.
▶ Rejection led to greater opioid release overall and especially in the amygdalae and other pain responsive structures in the brain.
▶ Opioid release suppressed norepinephrine release to the amygdale, suppressing activation of the amygdalae.
▶ Individuals who were independently assessed as more resilient produced more opioids.

> **Tip**
>
> If a student is shy, a social isolate, or has been a victim of rejection, assign a high-status, high-achieving student to be that student's buddy. Coach the buddy on what to say and do to create inclusion. Assign the buddy to be the shoulder partner of the rejected student.

The researchers concluded brains respond to social rejection in the very same way as physical pain. In the same way that opioids are released to adapt to physical pain, opioids are released to reduce the distress caused by social rejection. The researchers noted extensive research showing the same opioid release in the pain-responsive structures in response to social separation as well. In short, brains react to social rejection and

> ## Tip
> Minimize students' pain by minimizing opportunities for social rejection such as having students self-select members of a team.

social separation in the same was as they react to physical pain. Rejection is painful, literally!

Exclusion Produces Pain. While in an fMRI scanner, people played cyberball—tossing a digital ball around on a computer screen with two other people they could not see who were connected via computers. They were told the focus of the study was to determine how brains coordinate with one another to perform a simple task like tossing a ball. The actual intent of the study was to determine how brains react to social rejection. For a few minutes, the three

> ## Tip
> When a student rejects or puts down another student, intervene and have the offender empathize with the person he or she has rejected. Have students put themselves in the other person's place and say how they would feel if they were the recipient of the rejection or put-down.

participants, (one real, and the other two, unknown to the subject, and computer generated) tossed the ball about equally within the triad. Then, the other two players began tossing the ball only to each other, leaving the subject out of the play. After leaving the scanner, subjects were angry or sad. They felt rejected. Their brain scans revealed the same pattern as is elicited by physical pain: "Looking at the screens, side by side, without knowing which was an analysis of physical pain and which was an analysis of social pain, you wouldn't have been able to tell the difference."[46]

> ## Tip
> Use structures that equalize participation so no one is left out.

Social Pain and Achievement. In three different experiments, to test the impact of social pain on achievement, experimenters told students that compared to other people in the distant future, they would more likely end up alone in life. Ability to process simple information was not impacted by the manipulation, but ability to complete complex cognitive tasks was impaired. Students who were told they were more likely to be alone in life averaged 13 points lower on an IQ test and 29 points lower on a Gradual Record Exam-type test![47]

Inclusion: The Antidote to Social Pain. Because touch and support release oxytocin and oxytocin reduces amygdalae firing and the secretion of the stress hormone cortisol,[48] inclusion is an antidote to social pain. Teambuilding, classbuilding, and cooperative learning create a sense of belonging that inoculates students against the experience of social pain.

Students in the United States more than students in other countries, lack a feeling of belonging. In a study of 32,000 junior high students across a dozen countries, U.S. students rated themselves as less socially connected to their schools, teachers,

Brainiac Box

Question:
What is the role of the amygdalae in evaluating social stimuli?

Answer:
Parts of the amygdalae are active in response to potential threats—stimuli we want to avoid. The right amygdala (along with other elements in the social evaluation network) becomes active in response to stimuli we want to approach, for example, as a friendly person offering a handshake. Rather than characterizing the amygdala as a threat sensor, it is better thought of as an approach/avoid sensor.

and peers than students in most other countries. School climate in the U.S. was rated lowest of all countries—twice as negative as the country rated second to last.[49]

A Belonging Manipulation Works! A simple "belonging manipulation" led first-year college students who did not feel they belonged, to obtain significantly higher grades throughout their college career. African-American students who represented only 6% of the Yale student body were assigned to two conditions: (1) They read a statement by an older student talking about how she had been worried about fitting in but that things had turned out really well, or (2) They read a statement by an older student stating how her political views had gotten more sophisticated over

> **Tip**
> For those who are struggling, create the expectation that things get better with time.

time in college. The results: The simple belonging manipulation led to a higher GPA every semester for the following 3 years![50] Numerous studies have shown a positive relation between sense of belonging and academic achievement and school success.[51]

The Cooperation Hormone: Oxytocin

Hormone research reveals the brain is designed for social interaction. Animal research has established the hormone oxytocin as critical in promoting a wide range of prosocial behaviors including social recognition, affiliation, pair bonding, and maternal attachment.[52] In humans, oxytocin has been called the "love hormone" or the "bonding hormone." It is released during breastfeeding, childbirth, and sex.

> **Tip**
> Group students in pairs and in groups of four, and avoid triads. Groups of three are often a pair and an outsider.

Oxytocin increases generosity,[53] trust,[54] trustworthiness,[55] empathy,[56] attachment,[57] and love.[58] Oxytocin reduces the secretion of the stress hormone cortisol and down-regulates amygdalae firing,[59] so individuals feel more relaxed and are better able to approach otherwise stressful situations like public speaking or stressful social interaction. Oxytocin is released by the posterior pituitary gland, but acts at a distance. Brain structures and neural tracks activated by social behaviors are loaded with oxytocin receptors. Let's examine several research studies demonstrating that oxytocin is critical for building trust, generosity, empathy, and cooperation.

Being Trusted Boosts Oxytocin. A simple experiment revealed that being trusted by others boosts oxytocin levels.[60] Participants who did not know each other showed up for an experiment. Each was given $10 for showing up. Initially, one was randomly assigned to the role of donor and the other to the role of recipient. The donor was asked to give any amount of the $10 he or she had received ($0–$10) to the recipient, knowing that whatever amount was given would be tripled for the recipient and that the recipient would then be able to reciprocate by giving back some amount to the donor—whatever amount the recipient chose. Thus, giving money by the donor is a measure of trust (*"I will give you some of my money and trust you will reciprocate"*). Giving money back by the recipient is a measure of trustworthiness (*"I will reciprocate your trust in me"*).

In a comparison condition, the donor did not choose how much to give the recipient, rather the donor picked a ball in what appeared to be a random draw, and the ball dictated how much money the donor would give. Thus, the recipients in the first condition knew what they received was a function of the trust the donor had placed in them; in the second condition, the recipients knew the amount they received had nothing to do with the trust of the donor. The question: What did being trusted do to the generosity and oxytocin levels of the recipient? Do oxytocin levels go up when you are in a relationship where the other person trusts you?

Results are very clear. When the donor chose how much to give (placed trust in the recipient), recipients gave back 53% of what they received; when the donor did not choose, recipients gave back only 18% of what they received, even though they received the same amount of money in both conditions. The experiment demonstrated that we reciprocate the trust placed in us.

Importantly, oxytocin levels were twice as high in recipients who got the trust signal compared to those in the random draw condition. See Graph: Being Trusted Boosts Oxytocin.

Oxytocin Boosts Trust. This first experiment establishes that being trusted boosts our oxytocin level. Researchers also tested the opposite question: Does boosting oxytocin levels boost

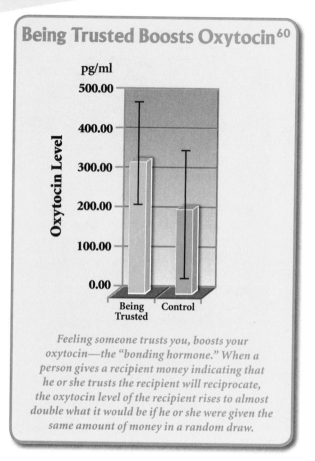

Being Trusted Boosts Oxytocin[60]

Feeling someone trusts you, boosts your oxytocin—the "bonding hormone." When a person gives a recipient money indicating that he or she trusts the recipient will reciprocate, the oxytocin level of the recipient rises to almost double what it would be if he or she were given the same amount of money in a random draw.

trust? Experimenters administered oxytocin to half the donors and half the reciprocators 50 minutes before an experiment that used the same experimental paradigm as the first experiment.

Because oxytocin passes the blood-brain barrier, it can be administered via nasal spray. In this second experiment, individuals in the experimental group were each administered an intranasal dose of 24 international units of oxytocin. The control group received the same amount of intranasal spray in the same way and at the same time, but with one exception—their spray contained no oxytocin.

Results indicated significantly higher initial donations among those receiving oxytocin compared to those who did not. Among those dosed with oxytocin, 45% showed the maximum trust level compared to only 21% of the control group. The researchers concluded, "These results concur with animal research suggesting an essential role for oxytocin as a biological basis of prosocial approach behaviour."[61]

Oxytocin Boosts Empathy. Administering oxytocin causes people to be 21% more generous.[62] Experiments reveal this increased generosity is not due to increased altruism, but rather increased empathy.[63] That oxytocin increases empathy is now well established.[64]

Primates and Infants Cooperate

Consistent with the conclusion that brains are wired to cooperate, we observe cooperation and helping in primates and infants.

Chimps Cooperate. There is approximately a 96% genetic similarity between humans and chimpanzees, although there are marked differences on 5 of the 23 chromosomes, and humans have 23 chromosome pairs whereas chimps have 24. Given our overall genetic similarity, researchers have studied cooperation among chimps with the aim of determining if cooperation is natural to our closest primate relative. Numerous findings support the conclusion that cooperation is natural for chimpanzees. Chimps:

- ▶ Coordinate efforts to defend their territory, share food, and hunt in groups[65]
- ▶ Engage in reciprocal exchanges[66]
- ▶ Refuse to participate in experiments if a partner receives a better reward for equal effort[67]
- ▶ Give their own food to another chimp who is begging[68]

In one example of peacemaking and possibly intentionally teaching youngsters about fairness and cooperation, a female chimpanzee approached two juveniles that were fighting over a leafy branch. She broke the branch in two and then handed half to each juvenile, without taking any for herself.[69]

Infants Cooperate! Consistent with the conclusion that humans are hardwired for cooperation are numerous studies that show cooperative and helpful behaviors spontaneously emerge in the first year of an infant's life.[70] Infants, with no prompting, stop playing to help an adult. If an adult drops something (a clothespin), the infant stops his or her own enjoyable play and goes over to pick up the dropped object, handing it to the adult. If the adult struggles to open a cabinet because his or her hands are full, infants stop their own play, go over to the cabinet, and open it for the adult. Infants help adults reach out-of-reach objects, remove obstacles, and even correct mistakes made by adults! Controlled experiments demonstrate this is not just "picking up clothespins" and "opening cabinet" behavior. If the adult throws down the clothespin, or just bumps the cabinet with no intention of opening it, the infants do not pick up the clothespin or open the cabinet. A few months past their first birthday, infants are doing two remarkable things: (1) perceiving the goals of others; and (2) behaving altruistically to help others.

This helping behavior appears natural, not under the control of external encouragement or reward. Controlled experiments demonstrate strong rewards or persistent adult encouragement by mothers do not increase the helping behavior. In fact, giving infants an exciting toy as a reward for helping, actually decreases the amount of helping when the infants are later tested!

Toddlers Experience Empathy. Most importantly, between a year and a half and 2 years of age, toddlers experience empathy and react accordingly. When one adult grabs and tears up a paper that another adult is working on, toddlers show facial expressions of concern (as coded by observers who see only the face, not the situation). The same toddlers do not show concern if the adult is not working on the paper when another adult walks over, grabs, and tears up the paper. Further, remarkably, the toddlers appear to bond more with the victim. That is, when the toddlers were later tested, they acted to help the victim more than the control adult.[71] These experiments establish that very early on, humans experience empathy and act helpfully—a finding consistent with the general conclusion that brains are wired for cooperative social interaction.

Empathy: Genetic or Learned?

There is a lively debate among researchers about the extent to which empathy is determined by genes v. learning. The displays of empathy in young toddlers as well as the findings that specific neural networks and hormones are associated with empathy support a genetic argument. On the other hand, abused and nonabused infants react very differently to the distress of a peer. Nonabused infants attend closely to the distressed child, show concern, and/or provide help. None of the abused infants do so.[72] Some have held up this finding as support for learning, suggesting that abused infants do not have the opportunity to learn empathy. The finding that abused infants lack empathy, however, can be interpreted in either of two ways: Abuse overrides a natural, genetically determined empathetic and cooperative nature, or empathy and cooperation are learned behaviors, learned very early in life. In either case, however, most infants are empathetic and helpful across a wide variety of situations. Regardless of whether empathy is learned early or genetic, it is strong in all but a few individuals. Thus, whenever we structure classrooms around cooperation, we are structuring in ways that allow almost all students to interact in ways that are most natural for them.

Mirror Neurons: Watching Others Wires Our Brains

The discovery of mirror neurons is a revolution in our understanding of the brain.[73] The existence of mirror neurons is additional support for the conclusion that brains are designed to be social.

If we look at someone with a certain facial expression, we make that facial expression and feel the associated emotion.[74] If we look at someone with a disgusted face, our brain fires as if we were disgusted. Looking at someone who is disgusted leads to activation of anterior sections of the insula.[75] When surgery takes out the insula, patients lose the ability to feel disgust and lose the ability to recognize disgust in others.[76] When we watch someone lift his or her hand, the part of the motor cortex responsible for lifting our own hand becomes active.

Mirror Neurons Facilitate Survival. Through mirror neurons, we are linked. This is adaptive. Picture a primitive group. Someone eats tainted meat and feels disgusted. Those who look upon that disgust and feel disgust themselves, have an advantage. They are less likely to eat the meat and less likely to get sick. Mirror neurons explain empathy. Empathy has survival value. Someone becomes afraid. Immediately we feel his or her fear and look around to see where the threat is. Without mirror neurons, we would not become vigilant and would be more likely to become a meal for a predator.

If you watch a troop of monkeys in the zoo, you can see mirror neurons in action. All the monkeys are playing randomly. Suddenly one of the monkeys senses danger and stops moving, standing alert, on guard. Immediately, the whole troop stops what they are doing, faces where the vigilant monkey is facing, and stands alert in a posture ready to fight or flee. Recently, while on a photo safari in Africa, I had the opportunity to watch a herd of impalas peacefully grazing. Unknown to them, a leopard approached in a low, hidden crouch. One impala got the scent of the leopard and became vigilant, stopping grazing and facing the hidden leopard in a stance of total alertness. Immediately, the whole herd stopped grazing and assumed the same vigilant stance, ready to flee.

Mirror Neurons Explain Contagion of Emotion. Mirror neurons help explain why some teachers have classes that get increasingly distracted whereas other teachers have classes that remain calm and focused. Let's imagine that a teacher is about to introduce some difficult material or about to give a quiz or test. One student in the class becomes anxious. Another student in the class sees the face of the first student and picks up on the anxiety via mirror neurons. Now there are two anxious faces. Others see those two and two become four, and in the blink of an eye, four become eight. Mirror neurons explain contagion of emotion.

Mirror Neurons and Class Management. Mirror neurons also explain why, when faced with a contagion of anxiety, some teachers have students who become increasingly anxious whereas other teachers in the same situation have students who calm down. A teacher who does not know about the power of mirror neurons looks out at the anxious class and becomes anxious. Students see the face of the anxious teacher and

Brain-Friendly Teaching • Dr. Spencer Kagan
Kagan Publishing • 800.933.2667 • www.KaganOnline.com

each other, telling them to be polite has little or no impact. Role-playing the desired polite behaviors provides the brain concrete visual and auditory images that are easy to emulate.

Mirror Neurons and Kagan Structures.

Mirror neurons help explain the power of Kagan Structures. For example, during **Sage-N-Scribe** students are in pairs, with one worksheet and one pencil for the pair, rotating roles for each problem they do. One student is the Sage (explaining what to do) and the other is the Scribe (carrying out the directions of the Sage). There are many advantages of this structure over working alone, including immediate reward, opportunity for immediate correction, and little opportunity for students to daydream or get off task. But mirror neurons tell us there is more to the story. Each time students observe their partner doing a problem, the observer's brain is firing as if they were doing the problem. The Sage is not only giving directions, their brain is practicing, carrying out the directions they have given as they watch their partner perform.

SeeOne–DoOne–TeachOne is another structure in which mirror neurons play a key role. Students learn by watching their teacher and then again in the last step as they observe another student teaching them.

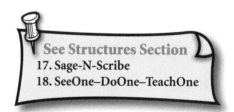

See Structures Section
17. Sage-N-Scribe
18. SeeOne–DoOne–TeachOne

As our students watch the successful performance of another student, their brains are firing as if they were performing successfully. The neurons in the observer's brain are strengthening connections necessary for successful performance. Neurons that fire together wire together—brains are rewired as neurons make new connections, a process called neuroplasticity.[77] During cooperative interaction students are wiring their brains for success.

Why Are Humans Hardwired to Cooperate?

A lively and fascinating debate rages among researchers and theorists: Why are humans so cooperative? Strong arguments can be made

---

Tips

Apply Mirror Neuron Research:

- **Giving Directions:** Model what you want students to do or have another student or team model.

- **Managing Student Emotions:** If a student or the class becomes too excited or nervous, be extra calm.

- **Managing Attention:** Use a quiet signal like a raised hand. As students raise their hands, there will be a contagion of alert attention.

- **Motivating Students:** Be passionate about your content. How you feel about the content is how your students will feel.

---

become even more anxious—anxiety escalates. In contrast, a teacher who knows about the power of mirror neurons reacts in exactly the opposite way: When faced with an anxious class, the teacher intentionally projects a very calm attitude. The students, taking their cue from the calm face of their teacher, calm down. Not a word was spoken in either scenario, but one teacher contributes to the contagion of anxiety whereas the other teacher harnesses the power of mirror neurons to calm the class.

Mirror Neurons and the Power of Modeling.
Mirror neurons explain social learning: If we look at someone doing something, our brain fires as if we were doing that thing. Observational learning is hardwired in the brain. The implication for how best to teach is profound. If we try to *explain* a procedure to our students using only words, it is uphill work and only some students will learn the procedure. If, in contrast, while we explain a procedure, we *model* how to do it, the brains of our students easily grasp the procedure. Modeling is coasting downhill with little effort; explaining with words is peddling hard, uphill. When we demonstrate the behaviors we want our students to learn, we are going with, rather than against, the way brains naturally learn. If we want students to be more polite with

Modeling is coasting downhill with little effort; explaining with words is peddling hard, uphill.

for both a genetic and learned basis for human cooperation. Several books make the case, like Charles Darwin did, that we are "born to be good: societies that cooperate and which take good care of their young and those in need, flourish."[78] Darwin stated,

> "There can be no doubt that a tribe including many members who…were always ready to give aid to each other and to sacrifice themselves for the common good, would be victorious over most other tribes; and this would be natural selection."[79]

Animals of various species cooperate to solve problems. Birds and chimps work together to get food that neither alone can obtain. In his book, *Why We Cooperate*,[80] Michael Tomasello, makes the genetic case, but in her rebuttal in that same book, Carol Dweck, provides the equally compelling case that early learning determines the propensity of humans to cooperate. Studies of primate cooperation support the genetic case that cooperation and caring is hardwired in the primate brain, but that it is also a learned behavior. Following a fight or conflict, many types of primates console the victim.[81] Juveniles are more likely to console than adults. That sensitivity to the emotions of others and the ability to provide appropriate consolatory behaviors emerges early in development, supports a genetic rather than learned argument. On the other hand, mother-reared individuals are more likely to console than orphans, highlighting the role of rearing in the development of prosocial behaviors.

If brains attend more to social stimuli than non-social stimuli, we will improve learning if we present academic content in a social context.

In speculating on why humans evolved to be more altruistic that some other species, anthropologists point out that humans needed each other to forage and hunt successfully, so there was a survival advantage for cooperation:

> Humans evolved special cooperative abilities that other apes do not possess, including dividing the spoils fairly, communicating goals and strategies, and understanding one's role in the joint activity as equivalent to another's. Good partners—who were able to coordinate well with their fellow foragers and would pull their weight in the group—were more likely to succeed.[82]

A second explanation of the evolution of cooperation in humans is that they needed to cooperate as they faced competition from other groups. Thus evolved the "group-mindedness," which causes us to identify with others in our society, even those we do not know.

Humans Are Hardwired to Compete, Too.

As anyone knows who has watched a pair of toddlers tug-of-war over a toy, from early on, we are well equipped to compete. The first half of the hardwired fight-or-flight defense alarm system is "fight." Primates who encounter another troop at the border of their territory will compete for the territory. Sometimes their shouting at each other turns to battle, and very occasionally the battle results in death. Human wars are enormously more costly, due in part to technology. The death toll in World War II exceeded 60 million people!

In arguing that humans are social and cooperative, I am not arguing that they are not also competitive and aggressive. They are. What I am arguing is that we can tap the hardwiring of the brain to attend to social stimuli in order to align how we teach with how student's best learn. We can take advantage of the fact that brains are hardwired to be social and to cooperate. If brains attend more to social stimuli than nonsocial stimuli, we will improve learning if we present academic content in a social context. If brains have a social cognition network that, when stimulated, increases memory for content, we can take advantage of that.

Logically, it can be argued that we can take advantage of brains' hardwiring to compete. In many ways traditional education has attempted that. We grade on a curve, so students know the success of one diminishes the probability of success of another. Traditionally, we discouraged sharing, telling students not to talk and not to look at the work of their neighbor. We rewarded the "best" individuals, hoping to motivate students. In fact, that approach produces for the weaker students marginalization, alienation, and eventual dropout. If our goal is to maximize academic success for as many students as possible, inclusion and cooperation trump exclusion and competition.

Cooperative Learning Is Brain Friendly

Brains are designed to attend to social stimuli, and positive social contact puts the amygdalae to rest, improving perception, thinking, problem solving, and creativity. Because oxytocin is an endogenous hormone designed to impact on neural tracks that increase bonding, trust, and cooperation, we can conclude that brains are designed for cooperation and caring. The existence of mirror neurons provides additional support: We are wired for empathy. The implication of all of this for us as educators: When we include cooperation in our classrooms, we are aligning the way we teach with how brains are designed to function. We are providing brain-friendly teaching.

Given this, we can derive the third principle of brain-friendly learning:

Principle 3

Brain-Friendly Teaching Fosters Social Cognition and Cooperation

Five Tools to Teach the Social Brain

Brains are social organs. We have a social cognition network dedicated to processing the thoughts, feelings, and intentions of others. Brains are never more engaged than when in interaction with others. To align our classrooms with how brains best function, we can engage

the social cognition network and structure for positive social interaction. The first of the five tools that follow provides ways to engage the brain's social cognition network. The remaining tools are ways to structure for a successful cooperative, inclusive classroom. The tools for promoting positive social interaction have been provided in detail in our book, *Kagan Cooperative Learning*.[83] Here we overview only briefly the most important ways to structure for cooperative classrooms.

Five Tools to Teach the Social Brain

1. Activate Social Cognition
2. Include Classbuilding
3. Structure Cooperative Interaction
4. Teach Social Skills
5. Promote Cooperative Play

Tool 1

Activate Social Cognition

The brain has two cognition systems: The social cognition system and the nonsocial cognition system. Traditional approaches to education have exercised working memory and fluid intelligence—the nonsocial cognition system. With the discovery of an independent social cognition system, we need to correct the balance. By framing our content so it involves students in inferring the thoughts, feelings, and intentions of others, we not only develop a critical neural network in the brain, but also we improve achievement. As we have seen, students told to memorize behaviors of a person for a test do not score as well on the test as do students who are not told there will be a test and are told only to infer the kind of person who would engage in those behaviors! In the context of engaging their social cognition system, students retain more

> ### Tip
> Numerous studies demonstrate activating the social cognition network increases memory for content. We can activate social cognition as we teach any content. Not only do we improve memory for content, we develop a critical brain network.

facts than if they had tried to retain the facts! This social encoding advantage is now firmly established by many research studies. It is time we activate social cognition to have the social encoding advantage work for our students.

Two Approaches to Implementing the Social Encoding Advantage

We have two ways to release the power of social encoding. We can put a twist on our curriculum and we can change our instructional practices.

The Curricular Approach.

Anytime we have students try to figure out the thoughts, feelings, and intentions of another person, the social cognition system goes into action, and we release the power of the social encoding advantage. Let's overview a few of the many possibilities:

Social Studies. Rather than having students memorize important events, their dates, and accomplishments of historical figures, we can have them mindread. For example, rather than having them memorize the accomplishments of a president, we can have students look over the president's accomplishments and try to figure out the motivation of that president. In the process, history will come alive and the accomplishments of the presidents will be retained better.

In studying a social movement like the civil rights movement, we can place emphasis on figuring out the thoughts and feelings of the actors. What were they thinking? What drove them to take the punishments they did? What did the people of the time think and feel? How do people today think and feel differently as a result? If you were Martin Luther King, Jr., how did you feel when you saw your marchers beaten at the bridge? What did you say to yourself to control your impulse to retaliate?

Language Arts. Social cognition can be activated as students write, read, and give oral reports.

Writing. The rules of grammar and the skills of paragraph construction as traditionally taught exercise the nonsocial cognition system. We try to get students to memorize grammar rules. These same skills can be taught through the social cognition system by having students focus on the question, "How will the reader react?" For example, we can show students a paragraph with no topic sentence, no concluding sentence, and jumbled supporting details. We can then contrast that paragraph with one that has all the elements of good paragraph construction, asking "How will the reader react to each paragraph?"

By engaging students in mentalizing, thinking about the thoughts and feelings of another, we engage the social cognition system. In this way, the rules of good paragraph construction are not only better remembered, they make sense! Rather than imposing the rules, we have students derive the rules via social cognition. Further, we create a habit of mind—mentalizing. It is a habit that will serve our students well throughout their lives.

For advanced students, after studying the works of an author, have students write a brief essay or story in the style of the author. Or have them role-play the author talking about his or her own work.

Reading. At all grades, students can focus on the thoughts, feelings, and intentions of characters. To increase depth of mindreading, we can pose hypothetical questions. "How would Tom have felt if Huck refused to paint the fence?" "Given what you know about Tom, what alternative strategy do you think he might have tried?"

Oral Reports. Oral reports lend themselves to engaging mindreading in two ways: Focus on audience reaction and role-playing. Prior to giving a report, we can ask students to write about how they think their audience (the class) will respond, and to list three things they will do to improve audience response, given what they know about their classmates. Another approach to incorporating mindreading is to have students give their report in role, perhaps in the role of a character or an author. How would that person present the report?

Science. As students learn any new science finding or principle, they can reflect on the impact that discovery had, has, or will have on the minds of others. How did the invention of the telephone change the way we think about time and space? Give a concrete example of how a person thought before those inventions and how people thought afterwards. Get into their mind and try to be that person. Prepare a role-play with two scenes: pre- and post-invention to illustrate the difference in how people thought.

Another approach is to have students get into the mind of an inventor. What was Edison thinking and feeling that drove him to persist after each failed attempt to find a lightbulb filament that would last? When Henry Ford said, *"They can have a Model T in any color they want, as long as it is black,"* what was he thinking? Which

created greater pride for Henry Ford: Creating the Model T, or creating the assembly line? If you were Henry Ford, how would you answer that question?

Anything that asks students to get into the mind of another activates the social cognition network and makes our content more memorable.

Math. Each time a new math skill is introduced, we can ask students to mindread. How would an architect use that skill? A cook? A teacher?

Problems and concepts can be cast in a way that promotes social cognition. We can include evaluation of feelings of others in otherwise dry content. For example, while teaching equivalent fractions, we might pose the following problem:

> **"Four of us will share a pizza. Before we cut the pizza, one of us argues to cut it in fourths and each take a piece. Another of us argues to cut it into eights and each take two pieces. Form pairs. Partner A, you will argue for dividing the pizza into four pieces; Partner B, you will argue for eight pieces. Do a RallyRobin taking turns stating arguments for your side."**

Following this activity, we can launch into an exploration of why doubling both the numerator (pieces for each) and the denominator (total pieces) creates equivalent fractions. By introducing the concept in a way that activates the social cognition network, we make the academic content more meaningful and memorable.

Thinking about the thinking of others is engaged also when we ask students to teach a concept to another student, or to write the directions to an algorithm in a way a younger student could follow them.

The Instructional Approach. How we teach either engages or fails to engage the social cognition network. Traditional seating with each student facing the back of the head of the student in front of them is exquisitely designed to prevent students from thinking about the thinking of others. Cooperative learning is perfect for

Structures for Social Cognition

Structure (See structure section)	Description	Social Cognition
Draw-What-I-Write	Students write a description of a drawing they have made and give the description to a partner who attempts to match the drawing without seeing it.	Both the author and the artist must mindread: The author thinks how the writing will be interpreted, and the artist thinks about the intention of the author.
Paraphrase Passport	The right to speak is to accurately paraphrase the person who spoke before you.	An accurate paraphrase is based on understanding the thoughts and feelings of the other.
Match Mine	The sender arranges pieces on a game board and then gives oral directions to the receiver who cannot see the pieces. The receiver attempts to arrange his or her own duplicate pieces to match the arrangement of the sender.	Both the sender and receiver must mindread. The sender must think how the receiver is interpreting the instructions; the receiver must infer the intent of the sender.
Team Interview	Each student on the team in turn is interviewed by his or her teammates.	When Team Interview is done in role, students must mindread the person they are role-playing
SeeOne–DoOne–TeachOne	Students see a demonstration of a skill, usually by the teacher. Then, they solve a problem using that skill. Finally, they teach another student the skill.	In deciding how to teach the skill and in the process of teaching the skill, a student thinks about the mind of the other. How will that person best understand? Why is that person not getting it?

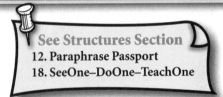

See Structures Section
12. Paraphrase Passport
18. SeeOne–DoOne–TeachOne

engaging mindreading. As students discuss and interact, they naturally think about the thoughts, feelings, and intentions of others.

All cooperative learning structures involve social cognition to some extent because they involve social interaction. Many cooperative learning structures are explicitly designed to have students take the role of the other. Since the structures are content-free and can be used as part of any lesson, they can be used to engage the social cognition network as part of any lesson. For a table that provides a thumbnail overview of a few structures to engage social cognition, see Table: Structures for Social Cognition.

Tool 2

Include Classbuilding

Classbuilding activities are designed to help students know, accept, and appreciate classmates. Most classbuilding activities involve getting up from one's team and interacting in a positive way with classmates. Many of the structures we use for academic content also serve well for classbuilding. For example, the **Flashcard Game** is usually used to have students memorize facts like the multiplication table, properties of

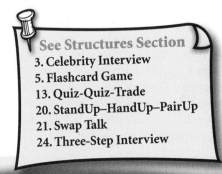

Tip

Celebrate Diversity

Have the class recognize their own diversity (some are strong in math, other with words, yet others with drawing) and have students realize we are a richer, more capable class than if we were all strong in the same way.

students do a **StandUp–HandUp–PairUp** to find a partner, and then have the pairs group with another pair to form groups of four, with no group containing two teammates. Have the groups of classmates sit down together and then use **Three-Step Interview** to get to know each other better. Topics for the interview might be student selected for more mature students, or might be teacher selected, usually on fun topics like:

- ▶ Things you like to watch on TV
- ▶ Things you're proud of
- ▶ Favorite possessions
- ▶ What you did over the weekend
- ▶ What you would do with a gift of $1,000

Celebrity Interview can be used in the same way as **Three-Step Interview** to have students get better acquainted with their classmates. Simply have students leave their teams to form groups of four with classmates and then have them use **Celebrity Interview** with getting acquainted or fun questions.

In **Swap Talk** students create cards with facts about a famous person or inanimate object and then circulate throughout the classroom repeatedly finding a partner, sharing the information on their card with their partner, trading cards, and then sharing with another partner the information on their new card. Although it is most often used for academic content, **Swap Talk** is perfect for classbuilding. Each student simply makes up a card with facts about themselves. When the game is played, each time a student shares the information on a card, the student points out to their partner the person whose card it is. **Quiz-Quiz-Trade** is like **Swap Talk** in that partners interact and then seek a new classmate with whom to interact. The difference is that **Swap Talk** is designed to share new information whereas **Quiz-Quiz-Trade** is designed to review and practice content.

chemistry elements, and capitals of states. But it can be used for classbuilding as well. To use the **Flashcard Game** for classbuilding, each student in the class makes up a card about themselves with their name on the front and three facts about themselves on the back. When the cards are completed, teams trade cards. Students then play the **Flashcard Game** to learn about the members of a different team. Cards can be rotated among teams so teams can learn about the members of various teams. Cards can be saved so the game can be played on different days until all the students know the names and facts about all of their classmates.

Three-Step Interview is usually used either for teambuilding so students get to know their teammates, or for academics as students interview their teammates on their opinion on a social issue, the progress they are making on an assignment, or in role as a historical character they have researched. To use **Three-Step Interview** as a classbuilder, simply have

The book, *Classbuilding*[84] has hundreds of classbuilding activities. For each of ten structures, it gives step-by-step instructions, hints, variations, and ready-to-use blacklines. A variety of additional classbuilding resources are available.[85] In Tool 6: Teach with Movement Structures, in Principle 1: Nourishment, sixteen classbuilding structures are listed and referenced.

Advantages of Class Meetings

1. Students learn democratic decision-making processes.
2. Students obtain a sense of control.
3. Students acquire mutual respect, caring, and social awareness.
4. Students feel peer support.
5. Students take responsibility for their decisions.
6. Commitment to class decisions is increased.
7. Students learn consensus-seeking skills.
8. Students learn planning and evaluation skills.
9. Problems and issues are aired.
10. Students are more willing to cool off in the moment of disruption, knowing a problem will be addressed in the next class meeting.
11. Many heads are better than one for problem solving.
12. The class obtains a sense of identity.
13. The teacher receives support from the class.

Class Meetings. Class meetings serve to create a sense of unity among students. Class meetings set an inclusive tone. The meta-communication: "Our class is a place where we all come together to create an environment that will benefit everyone." In effect, by having class meetings the teacher is saying, "This is not my class; this is *our* class."

Formats and step-by-step guidelines for class meetings are provided in *Win-Win Discipline.*[86] See Box: Advantages of Class Meetings.

The Agenda. Having a predetermined agenda for regular class meetings has several advantages. Students know how much time will pass until an issue is dealt with. Placing items on the class meeting agenda provides a cooling-off period. Often those items are resolved before the next meeting. The agenda takes the teacher off the spot

Agenda for Class Meetings

1. Announcements
2. Appreciations/Inspirations
3. Suggestions/Problem Solving
4. Evaluating Progress
5. Planning
6. Mutual Support Activity

of having to solve every problem in the moment of its occurrence. The teacher can add items to the agenda; students can propose items. When problems are dealt with on a regular basis and are not allowed to build up, class meetings become a time to come together to share and appreciate, not just to problem solve. See Box: Agenda for Class Meetings.

Some elementary teachers have a brief, daily end-of-the-day class meeting; others prefer a weekly or biweekly meeting. Secondary teachers gravitate to less frequent and shorter meetings, but still find advantages in a regular schedule.

Usually, rules for class meetings include (1) that to be discussed, an item must be placed on the agenda prior to the meeting; (2) nothing is placed on the agenda unless the teacher agrees; and (3) no decision can be made unless the teacher agrees.

Tool 3

Structure Cooperative Interaction

There are many approaches to structuring cooperative interaction in classrooms including collaborative learning,[87] peer tutoring,[88] and cooperative learning.[89] Within each of these broad fields, there are many different approaches, a review of which is beyond the scope of this book. Here, we will focus on one approach to cooperative learning: The Structural Approach. The approach is based on structuring the interaction among students in order to ensure that four principles are in place. The choice to focus on cooperative learning is based on it's massive positive research base and because it is implemented at all grades in all content areas. The choice to focus on the structural approach to cooperative learning is based on both empirical evidence and theoretical rationale.

PIES: The Basic Principles of Cooperative Learning

All Kagan Cooperative Learning Structures are carefully designed to put in place four basic principles of cooperative learning: *Positive Interdependence*, *Individual Accountability*, *Equal Participation*, and *Simultaneous Interaction*. Empirical research demonstrates that implementing these principles improves academic achievement. See Table: The Basic Principles of Cooperative Learning: PIES.

Positive Interdependence. Positive interdependence embodies two conditions, both of which enhance cooperation.

Positive. The word *positive* in the term "positive interdependence" derives from the mathematical term "positive correlation." A positive correlation exists whenever outcomes are positively linked. That is, if you doing well is associated with me doing better than otherwise, and you doing poorly is associated with me doing more poorly than otherwise, then our outcomes go up or down together. When our outcomes are correlated in this way, we encourage and help each other. "Your gain is my gain." For example, we tell teammates that if everyone on the team scores above 80 on a quiz, everyone on the team will have three minutes of free time. In that situation, everyone hopes their teammates will do well on the quiz and are likely to encourage and/or tutor their teammates. We experience ourselves on the same side, with a common goal.

Interdependence. The word *interdependence* in the term "positive interdependence" refers to a condition in which we can succeed only if we work together or pool our resources. Imagine we are to make a mural. The mural is to be judged by how well the final product integrates different colors. Imagine further, each teammate is given a different color and no one is allowed to touch anyone else's color. We are now in a situation of interdependence—we cannot succeed unless we cooperate. Interdependence ensures the need to cooperate.

The Basic Principles of Cooperative Learning: PIES

Acronym	Principle	Description	Determines...
P	Positive Interdependence	Students work together for mutual benefit; success requires contributions from all.	...If students feel they are on the same side with partners or teammates and success depends on the contributions of everyone, **or** if students feel isolated or in competition with others.
I	Individual Accountability	Each student is accountable for performing. No student can hide or take a free ride.	...If students take responsibility for their own work, **or** if students take a free ride based on the work of others.
E	Equal Participation	Students participate about equally.	...If all students participate about equally, **or** if some participate far less or far more than others.
S	Simultaneous Interaction	Interaction occurs in all teams or pairs at the same time.	...If students are engaged most of the time, **or** if they are engaged only a fraction of the time.

Individual Accountability. Individual accountability refers to the condition in which each individual must perform on his or her own, and the performance is viewed by at least one other. If a group is given a project and it turns in the project without specifying which student did which part, there is no individual accountability. In the absence of individual accountability, one or more members of the group can take a free ride, letting the others do all the work.

Equal Participation. To satisfy this principle, each member of the group must participate about equally. Equal participation is often satisfied by time or turns. For example, in a **RallyRobin,** each person in the pair has an equal number of turns. In a **Timed Pair Share** or a **Timed RoundRobin**, each teammate shares for an equal amount of time.

Simultaneous Interaction. Simultaneous interaction occurs when many students are actively engaged at the same time. Calling on students one at a time dramatically limits the amount of active engagement for each individual. In a class of thirty, calling on students one at a time to share for a minute each, takes 30 minutes, not counting the time it takes for the teacher to ask questions or respond to answers. In 30 minutes, each student gets less than 1 minute of active participation. In contrast, if students interact in pairs using a pair structure like **RallyRobin** or **Timed Pair Share**, interaction is simultaneous. At any moment, someone is talking in each pair. In 30 minutes, each student receives 15 minutes of active participation time, not just a minute.

Interaction that leaves out one of the PIES principles is "group work," not true cooperative learning.

PIES Ensure Success

The four PIES principles to a large extent explain why cooperative learning produces greater gains than traditional instructional approaches. With PIES in place, students are encouraging and tutoring each other, know they cannot take a free ride, are participating about equally, and are far more actively engaged.

In our own work, we have made PIES the defining principles of cooperative learning. We say any interaction that leaves out one of the PIES principles is "group work," not true cooperative learning. As simple as the PIES principles are, many teachers do not understand and apply them. They fail to recognize the difference between cooperative learning and group work. Following a workshop on Kagan Cooperative Learning, one of the most common comments by participants is, *"I thought I was doing cooperative learning, but I realize now I was just doing group work."*

Mistaking Group Work for Cooperative Learning. It is often that teachers think they are doing cooperative learning when they are doing group work. Let's take as an example the way in which many teachers have implemented **Think Pair Share**. **Think Pair Share** was developed by Frank Lyman. When implemented correctly, it is a powerful cooperative learning structure.[90] However, in a misguided attempt to implement **Think Pair Share**, many instructors fall into doing group work, not true cooperative learning. First, they have students think about a topic, then, they have the students engage in a pair discussion, and finally, they call on volunteers to share what was said in their pair discussion. When implemented this way, **Think Pair Share** violates some of the PIES principles. For example, an unmotivated student can mind-wander during Think Time, let his or her partner do all the talking during pair time, and simply not raise a hand during the share time. Thus, as commonly implemented, **Think Pair Share** violates individual accountability and equal participation. Further, during the share time, the teacher is calling on one student in the class at a time, violating the simultaneity principle as well.

> **See Structures Section**
> 25. Timed Pair Share

Kagan Structures Have PIES Built In. All of the Kagan Structures are carefully crafted to include PIES. Let's examine **Timed Pair Share** as an example. In **Timed Pair Share**, students are in pairs and one student talks for a predetermined amount of time, the partner responds, and then the two students switch roles.

Positive Interdependence. There is a positive correlation of outcomes: A good answer by one leads to learning by the other. Further, students are interdependent—neither can complete the structure without the contribution of both.

Individual Accountability. The students must perform in front of each other so an individual public performance is required.

Equal Participation. Each student participates for the same amout of time.

Simultaneous Interaction. All pairs are performing at the same time.

By carefully structuring the interaction of students to implement all four of the PIES principles, a teacher can be confident all students receive support from their teammates and are fully engaged—maximizing the probability of learning. Because all of the Kagan Structures are carefully designed to structure for PIES, teachers using the structures do not have to worry about designing lessons to include PIES. The structures ensure success.

The teacher who uses group work, who simply tells students to "turn and talk," inadvertently calls most on those who least need engagement and practice and calls least on those who most need engagement and practice. The teacher is allowing some brains to disengage.

The Cumulative Effect. It is the cumulative effect of using structures that implement the PIES principles that results in dramatic gains. Two or 3 minutes of unstructured group work v. 2 or 3 minutes of using a carefully designed structure that implements the PIES principles makes little difference. But if every time a teacher has students interact, he or she simply has students "turn and talk" without structuring for PIES, the cumulative result is some students become increasingly marginalized. It is easy and natural for the lower achieving or lower motivated student to sit back and allow her or his partner do most or even all of the talking. The result: The teacher who uses group work ends up calling most on those who least need the practice and least on those who most need the practice.

Three Keys for Success

Structures are not implemented in a vacuum. Students are in carefully designed teams; they have engaged in teambuilding to create bonding and a desire to encourage and help each other; and the teacher uses management techniques to efficiently transition students from direct instruction to student interaction and back again to direct instruction. Here, we overview these three critical keys for success: Teamformation, Teambuilding, and Management.

Key 1: Teamformation

The traditional classroom, with seats in rows, with each student facing the back of the student in front, is optimal—if we want to prevent students from interacting. But brains are most engaged when they interact. So traditional room arrangement is not brain friendly. To promote interaction, we need to rearrange the furniture, having students sit in teams. Two students on each side of a table works best. The teacher can call for teamwork, for shoulder partner pairs to work together, or for face partner pairs to work together.

Teams of Four are Magic. Why teams of four?—Primarily because teams of four maximize brain engagement.[91] As we increase the number from four, each person has less time to verbalize his or her ideas. For example during 4 minutes of interaction time, if we structure for equal participation, in teams of four, each teammate has 1 minute to express his or her ideas. In a team of six, each student has only two-thirds of a minute. In larger teams, there is more chance for a student to become disengaged. Teams of four are optimum for a second reason: they break naturally into two pairs. For maximum brain engagement, pair work is better than square work (work in groups of four)—it doubles the active engagement time. In 4 minutes, during pair work, students have an average of 2 minutes each, compared to only 1 minute each if they work as a team of four. Teams of three don't allow pair work and often lead to a pair and an outsider.

Heterogeneous Teams Maximize Learning. Teams that are heterogeneous by achievement level are optimal for a brain-friendly class. There are several advantages of a heterogeneous team.

With a high achiever, high-middle, low-middle, and low achiever on each team, we maximize the probability someone on the team can help with directions or tutoring. By having the highest achievers in the class spread out, one per team, we ensure a positive model on each team. If a student doesn't know what to do or how to do an assignment, a teammate is there to help. Further, the heterogeneous team helps reduce discipline problems. It avoids having all the low achievers grouped. If we group students by ability, we end up with high- and low-achieving teams with negative impact on the achievement and self-esteem of those in the low-achieving teams. Further, a team of all low-achieving students is more likely to get off task and/or create discipline problems.

There is another basis for advocating heterogeneous teams: empirical evidence. Well over a thousand research studies have been conducted on cooperative learning and the effects are consistently very positive. The overwhelming majority of those studies use heterogeneous groups. Thus, the empirical data supports use of heterogeneous groups. Among the over a thousand studies of cooperative learning, I have not found one that demonstrates ability grouping or student-choice grouping is superior to heterogeneous grouping! Our own research is a case in point. We have gathered a great deal of research on cooperative learning using heterogeneous groups and consistently find profound gains for the high and low achievers. I invite you to examine the data in the research section of our web page: www.kaganonline.com/free_articles/research_and_rationale. The research is summarized also in my mini book, *Kagan Cooperative Learning Structures.*[92]

How to Form Teams. There are a variety of ways of forming heterogeneous teams, but one of the simplest methods is to first create a class list rank ordered from highest to lowest achiever. Next, to form the first team, we simply take one student from the top quartile, one from the top-middle quartile, one from the bottom-middle quartile, and one from the low quartile. To form successive teams, we cross out the names of students we have already chosen and repeat the process. Details of various types of teams and methods for forming them are provided in *Kagan Cooperative Learning.*[93]

Teambuilding and Classbuilding
It Changed the Dynamics of My Class—and Me!

"Teambuilding and classbuilding were the keys to success in my classroom. Since our district has school choice, we have a wide range of socioeconomics, behavior challenges, English-language learners, as well as academic levels within a class. My first couple years of Kagan implementation, I used structures strictly with academics, but didn't see the results that Kagan proclaimed. Then I followed the Kagan recommendations, twice a week for teambuilding, once a week for classbuilding. Once I started to see increased retention of the content and learning gains, we started every day off with a teambuilding question; sometimes, I also needed to add one after lunch. I added classbuilding questions to my Find Someone Who worksheets just to add a bit of spice. I added a fun question to Mix-Pair-Share and Inside–Outside Circle.

"One of my favorites when I was teaching second grade, was doing Quiz-Quiz-Trade with 'Would You Rather…question cards?' that I found in the party section of Target. I never heard so many giggles and snickers from my students. It was awesome!!

"Classbuilding and teambuilding changed the dynamics of my classroom, but they also changed me. When I realized the power of classbuilding and teambuilding, there wasn't a day of school that I didn't truly enjoy. I laughed more, smiled more, had more energy, and enjoyed teaching like I hadn't in years."

—*Melissa Wincel*
Kindergarten, Trafalagar Elementary
Cape Coral, FL

Key 2: Teambuilding

When students first sit down in heterogeneous teams, they are not prepared to work together. The high achiever is likely to look over at the low achiever and ask herself (or if rude, blurt out), *"Do I have to work with that dummy?"* The low achiever is likely to ask himself (or if rude, blurt out), *"Do I have to work with that nerd?"* If we ignore this starting point, that students are not predisposed to work in heterogeneous teams, we are destined for resistance, sabotage, or failure.

The answer to this challenge is teambuilding. The power of teambuilding is amazing. When I first form teams in a workshop, if I do not do a bit of teambuilding, the whole day does not go nearly as well. People at all ages simply do not interact as well if they do not feel they know the people they are with, feel known, and feel a sense of mutual support. In short, as we detailed in Tool 1: Construct a Safe Context for Learning, in Principle 2: Safety, people do not function well if they do not feel safe. In my workshops, doing a simple getting-acquainted activity improves the tone of interaction all day. Following teambuilding, students feel safer to share ideas and are more supportive of each other.

Many structures are great for teambuilding. A simple **Timed RoundRobin**, in which teammates take turns for a minute each sharing things they do for fun, works extremely well. Anything that allows teammates to have a laugh together, share pleasant experiences, or get acquainted (favorite dessert, presents I have enjoyed, my dream vacation) works well to break the ice and create a feeling that we are all on the same side.

The book, *Teambuilding*,[94] contains hundreds of teambuilding activities and blackline masters for fourteen different teambuilding structures. Numerous teambuilding activities for all grade levels are provided in various Kagan resources.[95] Other teambuilding activities include creating a team name, logo, and handshake.

Key 3: Efficient Management

Management of the cooperative learning class is quite different from management of a traditional class. In the traditional classroom, the only people talking are the teacher or at times a student talking directly to the teacher. Talking is sequential: one person at a time. In the cooperative learning classroom, talking is simultaneous: Throughout the classroom, students are talking simultaneously in pairs or small groups. Thus, noise level becomes an issue. Because instructions are given to groups, we need to say who will be first in a group and we need efficient ways to stop the action to give directions for each new step of a structure or activity. A comprehensive presentation of cooperative management techniques is given in *Win-Win Discipline*.[96] Some of the most helpful management techniques include a quiet signal, student numbers, student roles, signals, and triggering.

The Quiet Signal. A teacher can use a variety of quiet signals—signals designed to focus the attention of the students back on the teacher. The best signals call for students to do something to interrupt their talking and interacting. I prefer to simply raise my hand and tell students that when they see me with a hand up, they are to do three things: (1) put their hand up; (2) give full attention to me; and, (3) if they see someone without a hand up or not giving me full attention, they are to signal that person. All I do is raise my hand and they manage the rest. Two tricks: (1) Wait for the last person to give full attention before talking, so the message is clear that everyone must give the quiet signal. If you go on without full compliance, the message to the class is you don't really have to do it and compliance will erode; (2) If the students take longer than 5 seconds, have them practice the signal. Practicing is a reminder, plus, because no one likes to practice the signal, compliance is more likely. For presentation of nine quiet signals see Tool 1: Establish a Quiet Signal, in Principle 5: Attention.

Student Numbers, Face Partners, and Shoulder Partners. By giving each student on the team a number, it becomes easy to say things like, *"Person number 3 on each team, when I say,*

Quiet Signal
For School Assemblies

"The simple act of raising my hand as a quiet signal has been an effective tool for me as the principal of our high school. At all school assemblies, I gain the attention of our entire student body in a matter of seconds…literally 2–3 seconds for the ENTIRE student body. It's simple, calm, respectful, and it works. I've had a number of community members who have been present at an assembly comment on how amazed they are that such a large group of kids can be ready to listen so quickly! Like anything, it is effective when applied *consistently.*"

—*Ty Rhodes*
Principal, Hesston High School
Hesston, KS

'Go,' you will begin the RoundRobin." Distinguish shoulder partners (the person next to you) from face partners (the person across from you). That way, it is easy to begin pair work by saying, "*Turn to your shoulder partner*" or "*Turn to your face partner.*"

Student Roles. Rather than passing papers out to students one at a time, we can have Materials Monitors from each team all come up at once and get the materials to distribute to teammates. *Advantages*: Papers are distributed more quickly, the teacher can attend to the class while papers are distributed, and Materials Monitors feel pride in their role. By assigning a range of roles like Quiet Captain, Encourager, Praiser, Cheerleader, and Recorder, students feel more important and responsible; they help manage their teams.

Signaling Completion. Rather than guessing how long a task will take, often it is better to let teams signal when they are done. For example, I might have teammates stand when they have completed a task. When between two-thirds and three-fourths of the class are finished, I ask all students to sit down. *Advantages:* The teacher gets a visual clue to know how long a task takes, early standing teams are a clue to the sitting teams that they best hurry a bit not to be last, and movement energizes students. By not waiting for the last team to finish, I have fewer students just waiting.

Triggering. In giving directions to students on what to do, it is helpful to put in place a trigger to begin the action. A simple trigger I often use is the word "*Go.*" For example, without a trigger, I might tell students, "*You are going to stand up, put a hand up, find a partner, and give the partner a high five.*" Lacking a trigger to initiate the action, before I have finished giving my directions, some students are already standing and looking around for a partner. If in contrast, with a trigger, my directions sound like, "*When I say 'Go!,' you are going to stand up, put a hand up, find a partner, and give your partner a high five,*" students listen to all my directions before acting. *Advantages*: (1) Undivided attention to all of the directions; (2) Students do not jump the gun, and so do not interfere with others hearing and processing the directions; and (3) Classmates are all on the same page, acting in unison. Some teachers use different triggers during the day to create novelty, such as "*When I clap my hands….*"

Cooperative Learning and Academic Achievement

Social interaction engages our brain's default social cognition network—what the brain most naturally attends to. Thus, during social interaction, our brains are more engaged. And engagement leads to achievement. The size and consistency of the positive outcomes of cooperative learning are among the most impressive of all educational innovations.

Social Interaction Is Processing, Enhancing Retention. Social interaction is brain-friendly teaching for yet another reason: It is a form of processing that facilitates memory. We remember dramatically more of what we say than what we hear! Let's prove that. You go to a nightclub or see a comedian on TV, and the comedian tells joke after joke. You "get" each joke and have a laugh at each. The next day someone asks, "What were some of the jokes?" You draw a blank. You heard the jokes and understood them, yet you cannot remember them. Why? You held the joke in short-term memory long enough to get the punch line, but you did not move the joke into long-term memory. To move content from short- to long-term memory, you have to process the information. You need to do something with the content—relate it to other information you already know, think about the information, put

If our content is gum and processing is chew, to have our students better understand and remember our content, we need to correct the balance. We need to stop talking and have students talk. We need more chew, not more gum.

it in your own words, process it in some way. One of the easiest ways to ensure memory is to share the information you have just heard with someone else. As we put the content into our own words, we are processing it, moving it from short- to long-term memory. If the comedian had stopped several times during his routine and had everyone turn to a partner and retell a joke he had just told, the next day almost everyone would remember those jokes. Listening is passive and engages the brain very little compared to speaking. Frequent interaction is a form of processing the content, dramatically increasing the probability of recall.

Because student brains are more engaged during social learning and because observational learning is hardwired in the brain, and because interaction cements memory, social interaction is the royal road to brain engagement and learning.

Cooperative Learning Meta-Analyses. We can make an unequivocal statement: Cooperative learning results in increased academic achievement. This statement is based on numerous meta-analyses that include over 3,000 effect sizes in controlled research studies! Although the effect sizes across meta-analyses are not all independent, the body of research on cooperative learning and academic achievement summarized in the meta-analyses represents one of the largest and strongest set of positive findings in educational research.

A meta-analysis reports the average effect size across a group of studies. Researchers have conducted a number of meta-analyses of the effects of cooperative learning on student academic achievement. See Table: Effect Size of Cooperative Learning on Achievement.

Effect Size of Cooperative Learning on Achievement

Meta-Analysis	Number of Effect Sizes	Average Effect Size	Percentile Gain
1. Cooperative Learning v. Traditional[97]	182	.78	28
2. Cooperative Learning v. Traditional[98]	414	.63	24
3. Cooperative Learning v. Traditional[99]	122	.73	27
4. Cooperative Learning v. Traditional[100]	104	.78	28
5. Cooperative Learning v. Individual Competition[101]	70	.78	28
6. Cooperative Learning v. Heterogeneous Classes[102]	829	.41	16
7. Cooperative Learning v. Individualistic Learning[103]	284	.59	22
8. Cooperative Learning v. Competitive Learning[104]	933	.54	21
9. Cooperative Learning v. Traditional[105]	49	.51	19
10. Cooperative Learning v. Traditional[106]	20	.44	17
Average	301	.62	23

Overall, the effect size of cooperative learning on academic achievement is very substantial. In every case, cooperative learning produces greater gains than comparison methods. The average effect size across the thousands of effect sizes is .62 for an average percentile gain of 23. A percentile gain of 23 is tremendous: A student who is performing at the 50th percentile in a traditional class would be scoring at the 73rd percentile in that class had he or she been taught instead using cooperative learning. Any teacher or administrator would be quite pleased to see their students jump 23 percentiles.

The string of 10 meta-analyses in the table is somewhat misleading. The meta-analyses are not all independent: some studies appear in more than one meta-analysis. Nevertheless, the overall positive impact of cooperative learning is overwhelming. The sheer number of studies and the consistency of positive effect sizes establish cooperative learning as one of the most well-researched and positive educational innovations of all time.

Peer Tutoring. Meta-analyses of the effect of peer-tutoring show positive results. In a meta-analysis of 81 studies, the average effect size was .58, equivalent to a percentile gain of 21.[107] Thus, on average, a student scoring at the 50th percentile without peer tutoring would be scoring at the 71st percentile with peer tutoring! The positive effects of being assigned the role of peer-tutor rival the effects of receiving tutoring, and in some studies, the tutors gain more than those they tutor![108] A four-month follow-up study revealed tutors retain content they tutor more than do the tutees they tutor.[109] We remember more of what we say than what we hear.

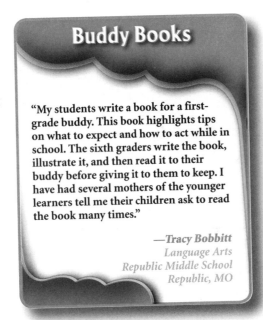

Buddy Books

"My students write a book for a first-grade buddy. This book highlights tips on what to expect and how to act while in school. The sixth graders write the book, illustrate it, and then read it to their buddy before giving it to them to keep. I have had several mothers of the younger learners tell me their children ask to read the book many times."

—*Tracy Bobbitt*
Language Arts
Republic Middle School
Republic, MO

Learning for Teaching. To test the impact of being assigned the tutoring role, experimenters assigned students to two conditions. In both conditions, students learned exactly the same content. Half were told to learn the content because a test would follow. The other half were told to learn the content in order to teach someone else. There was no mention of a test for the "learning for teaching" group. Both groups were given a test on the content following the learning session, and the group that was not studying for the test performed better on the test! There was no actual tutoring; the test was given right after the learning session. Just knowing they will be teaching someone else boosts student achievement more than studying for the test![110]

Individual Studies of Kagan Cooperative Learning.

When compared to traditional methods, Kagan Cooperative Learning methods show even stronger positive effect sizes than the average effect sizes in meta-analyses that lump many forms of cooperative learning together to calculate one average effect size. The work of a research team at State University of New York (SUNY) allows us to examine the average effect size across experiments using Kagan Structures. See Table: Effect Size of Kagan Structures on Achievement, p. 3.35.

The SUNY research team published a series of four tightly controlled, independent, peer-reviewed research studies on Kagan Structures.[111] The experiments examined the effectiveness of Kagan Structures at different grade-levels (third through eighth); with different content (science, language arts, social studies); with different student populations (high achieving, low achieving, students with disabilities); and with different Kagan Cooperative Learning Structures (**Numbered Heads Together**; **Numbered Heads Together + I***; and **Show Me**, a structure using Response Cards).

Across the four SUNY studies, the average positive effect size for Kagan Structures, was .92, an average gain from the 50th to the 82nd

* Numbered Heads Together with an incentive.

Effect Size of Kagan Structures on Achievement

Study	Effect Size	Percentile Gain
1. Numbered Heads v. Whole Class Question & Answer [112]	.95	33.0
2. Numbered Heads + I v. Whole Class Question & Answer [113]	.98	33.5
3. Numbered Heads v. Whole Class Question & Answer [114]	.78	28.2
4. Numbered Heads + I v. Whole Class Question & Answer [115]	.96	33.2
5. Show Me v. Whole Class Question & Answer [116]	.90	31.5
6. Numbered Heads v. Whole Class Question & Answer [117]	.95	33.0
7. Numbered Heads v. Whole Class Question & Answer [118]	.89	31.2
Average	.92	31.9

percentile. The size of this effect size is consistent with the average effect size found in high-quality cooperative learning studies. When categorizing meta-analyses of cooperative learning on the basis of the quality of the studies they contain, high-quality meta-analyses have an average effect size of .86; medium quality, average .56; low quality, average .49.[119] It is logical that the average effect size of Kagan Cooperative Learning Structures is greater than the average effect size in meta-analyses that include high-, medium-, and low-quality studies; weaker methods bring down the average when all effect sizes are averaged.

The higher scores for students instructed via Kagan Structures is reflected in the percent of students demonstrating mastery of the content. For example, one study examined test performance of students using the traditional Whole Class Question and Answer (WCQ&A) versus **Numbered Heads Together** (NHT).[120] Tests covered understanding of physical, chemical, and biological properties of substances and organisms. Content was new to students: Prior to instruction, the pretest class average was 18.6%. Scores using the traditional WCQ&A found 22% of the students averaged grades of 90% or above on ten-item daily quizzes. When NHT was used, 40% of students averaged 90% or above—almost doubling the performance of students taught with traditional methods! See Table: Effect Size of Kagan Structures on Achievement.

Kagan Structures Improve Time on Task. Additional support for the power of Kagan Structures was an effect size calculated on time on task. Students using the Kagan Structures were off task substantially less than those instructed with the traditional WCQ&A, effect size = .75.[121]

Students Prefer Kagan Structures. Pupils overwhelmingly prefer the Kagan Structures compared to traditional instructional strategies. Students in a class that experienced both Kagan Structures and traditional instruction were each given a hypothetical dollar to assess their satisfaction with each instructional strategy. Not every student spent their full dollar, but as a class, students spent a total of ($0.79) on Traditional Instruction; $5.89 on **Numbered Heads Together**; and $12.82 on an alternative version of **Numbered Heads Together**. Ninety-one percent of the students preferred the two Kagan Structures to traditional instruction.

Additional Studies of Kagan Structures. Many individual research studies demonstrate that, compared to traditional instructional strategies, Kagan Structures increase academic achievement across the grades and across the range of academic content, reduce discipline problems, and improve social skills among students.[122]

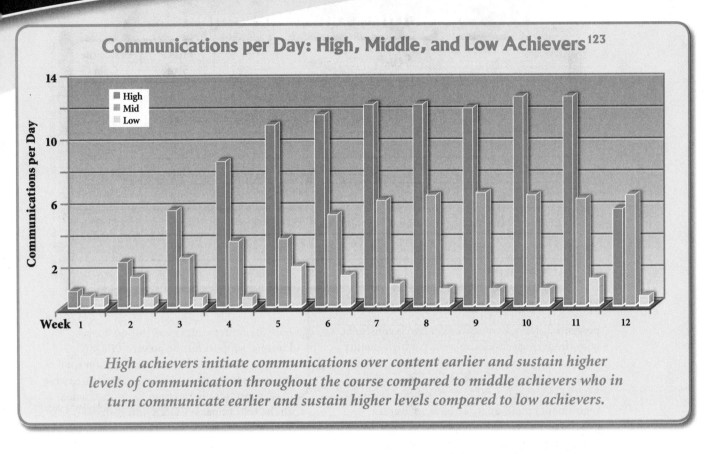

Communications per Day: High, Middle, and Low Achievers[123]

High achievers initiate communications over content earlier and sustain higher levels of communication throughout the course compared to middle achievers who in turn communicate earlier and sustain higher levels compared to low achievers.

High Achievers Choose Cooperation to Learn

The cooperative learning studies included in the meta-analyses ask what happens when a teacher uses cooperative learning v. traditional instructional strategies. A different question is how much do high- and low-achieving students spontaneously choose to cooperate to learn? A definitive answer for college students: High-achieving students choose to cooperate more than middle-achieving students who choose to cooperate more than low-achieving students.[123] Researchers found that in a college course, high-achieving students early on initiated more contacts and increased in their rate of sharing with other students at a higher rate over the 12-week course. In contrast, low-achieving students were later in initiating contacts and did so at a markedly lower rate. With regard to sharing information and initiating contacts, middle-achieving students fell between the other two groups. See Graph: Communications per Day: High, Middle, and Low Achievers.

Tool 4

Teach Social Skills

For years, cooperative learning trainers emphasized the importance of social skills and the need to do lessons on social skills. After trying that separate lesson approach, those of us using structures have found what we think is a much more effective way to have students acquire social skills. We build social-skill acquisition into every structure.

For example, during **Timed Pair Share**, we instruct students on the importance of active listening (facing the partner, eye contact, nodding, showing interest). Further, we have the listeners respond to the speakers with positive gambits such as, *"I enjoyed listening to you*

Brain-Friendly Teaching • Dr. Spencer Kagan
Kagan Publishing • 800.933.2667 • www.KaganOnline.com

because….," "Thank you for sharing," or "What I learned from you is…". Social skills are embedded into each structure and practiced as students interact.

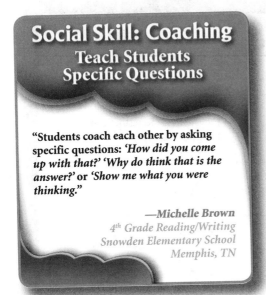

Social Skill: Coaching
Teach Students Specific Questions

"Students coach each other by asking specific questions: 'How did you come up with that?' 'Why do think that is the answer?' or 'Show me what you were thinking.'"

—*Michelle Brown*
4th Grade Reading/Writing
Snowden Elementary School
Memphis, TN

When we use structures, social skills are acquired without separate lessons on social skills. We have identified 46 social skills that are acquired via the structures. In some cases, the social skills merge with character virtues. For examples, understanding, tolerance, and honesty are virtues as well as social skills. The social skills acquired via the structures include many specific skills like accepting a compliment, checking for understanding, disagreeing politely, offering and accepting help, keeping a group on task, and using appropriate greeting and parting gambits. When structures are used, while students are learning the academic curriculum, they are acquiring a rich social skills curriculum.

Some social skills like listening and taking turns occur in most structures. Other skills like paraphrasing occur in only a few structures. See Table: Social Skills Acquired via Kagan Structures, p. 3.38. This table lists nine core social skills and their associated virtues, skills, and concepts. In the last column are listed the structures featured in this book that foster the acquisition of those skills. For example, every time students practice **Paraphrase Passport** they increase their understanding, comprehension of others, and in some cases, their compassion.

This integrated approach to social skill development has several advantages. No teacher preparation time is spent developing separate social skill lessons. By eliminating the need for separate social skill lessons, social skills are not a competing curriculum stealing time from academic skill lessons. In the structural approach, social skills are acquired as students learn their academic lessons. Students repeatedly practice the skills in a natural context, so social skills are more readily internalized and transferred to other life situations.

About half of the Kagan Structures involve turn taking. Because students are so often taking turns in pairs or teams, turn taking becomes internalized—it is just the way students behave in conversations and interactions.

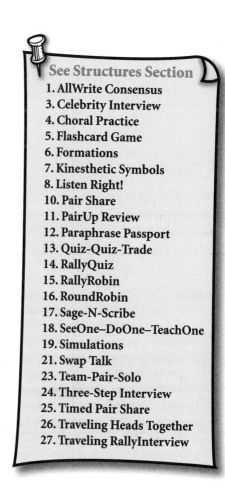

See Structures Section

1. AllWrite Consensus
3. Celebrity Interview
4. Choral Practice
5. Flashcard Game
6. Formations
7. Kinesthetic Symbols
8. Listen Right!
10. Pair Share
11. PairUp Review
12. Paraphrase Passport
13. Quiz-Quiz-Trade
14. RallyQuiz
15. RallyRobin
16. RoundRobin
17. Sage-N-Scribe
18. SeeOne–DoOne–TeachOne
19. Simulations
21. Swap Talk
23. Team-Pair-Solo
24. Three-Step Interview
25. Timed Pair Share
26. Traveling Heads Together
27. Traveling RallyInterview

Social Skills Acquired via Kagan Structures

Social Skill	Associated Virtues/ Skills/Concepts	Structures
Consensus Seeking	Tolerance, Diversity Skills, Compromise	AllWrite Consensus; Kinesthetic Symbols
Cooperation	Teamwork, Coordination of Efforts	AllWrite Consensus; Choral Practice; Formations; Kinesthetic Symbols; Simulations; Team-Pair-Solo; Traveling Heads Together
Empathy	Compassion, Understanding, Taking the Role of Others, Theory of Mind, Social Cognition	Paraphrase Passport; Simulations; Three-Step Interview
Helping	Caring, Coaching, Tutoring, Encouraging, Explaining	Flashcard Game; Formations; PairUp Review; Quiz-Quiz-Trade; RallyQuiz; Sage-N-Scribe; SeeOne–DoOne–TeachOne; Team-Pair-Solo; Traveling Heads Together
Listening	Attentiveness	AllWrite Consensus; Both Record RallyRobin; Celebrity Interview; Listen Right!; Paraphrase Passport; RallyQuiz; RallyRobin; Sage-N-Scribe; SeeOne–DoOne–TeachOne; Swap Talk; Team-Pair-Solo; Three-Step Interview; Timed Pair Share; Traveling Heads Together; Traveling RallyInterview
Paraphrasing	Compassion, Understanding, Comprehension	Listen Right!; Paraphrase Passport; Three-Step Interview
Praising	Appreciation, Complimenting, Validating, Acknowledging, Celebrating, Thanking	Celebrity Interview; Flashcard Game; Listen Right!; Quiz-Quiz-Trade; RallyQuiz; Sage-N-Scribe; Swap Talk; Timed Pair Share; Traveling Heads Together
Self-Expression	Articulation of Idea, Opinion, Point of View	AllWrite Consensus; Celebrity Interview; Pair Share; Paraphrase Passport; RallyInterview; RoundRobin; Three-Step Interview; Timed Pair Share; Traveling RallyInterview
Turn Taking	Fairness	Both Record RallyRobin; Flashcard Game; Pair Share; PairUp Review; Paraphrase Passport; Quiz-Quiz-Trade; RallyQuiz; RallyInerview; RallyRobin; RoundRobin; Sage-N-Scribe; SeeOne–DoOne–TeachOne; Swap Talk; Three-Step Interview; Timed Pair Share; Traveling Heads Together; Traveling RallyInterview

Brain-Friendly Teaching • Dr. Spencer Kagan
Kagan Publishing • 800.933.2667 • www.KaganOnline.com

Social Skills
How Did WE Do?

"I call social skills the lost art in our students. Students aren't coming into class with basic human-kindness skills. I didn't like the attitude that some students had, that they would do anything to be first in line, to get a 100% on a test. I knew I was giving these young students their foundation; I had to make a difference because it would impact their whole educational career. One of the first structures I taught my students after RallyRobin and Timed Pair Share was Inside-Outside Circle because I could cement every social skill I wanted in place from the get-go. We did a lot of echoing and copycat gambits. I filled their toolbox with different greetings, praises, and parting gambits. When I started to see that these social skills were becoming a habit and I didn't have to initiate them, then I knew they were ready for other structures. The students' attitudes also made me change how I did goals in my classroom. How the kids were doing individually was between them and me, never did I post anything individually. We had class goals and a class mission statement. They helped each other learn their math facts, sight words, and phonograms. One of their favorite sponge activities was Flashcard Game. After a weekly quiz, they would say, *'How did we do?'* not *'How did I do?'* That simple little word change warmed my heart and put a smile on my face."

—Melissa Wincel
Kindergarten, Trafalagar Elementary
Cape Coral, FL

Structures socialize students. This became very clear one day while I was watching a kindergarten class. My observation came after the students had used structures for most of the school year. The teams were making a dinosaur book, each team working on a different dinosaur. To make the covers of their books, the teacher had prepared a stylus so the students could trace the outline of their team dinosaur. The teacher asked the Materials Monitors on each team to go to the materials table and bring back for their team their team stylus. The teams began

their work, and what I saw amazed me. In each team, one student began tracing the outline of the dinosaur but then stopped about a quarter of the way through and passed the stylus and marker to the next teammate. When they were done, each teammate had done about a quarter of the tracing. I asked the teacher when she had told them to share the work of tracing. She said she did not need to instruct them to share: they had done **RoundTable** so often it was just the way they did things!

Tool 5

Promote Cooperative Play

In traditional sports, students do not play, they obey. That is, the rules of traditional sports like baseball, football, soccer, and basketball are predetermined, not created or tweaked by the students. Students are to obey the rules. Given the rules, they do battle to determine who wins and who loses. After a traditional game, we can see on player's faces and in their body language who won and who lost.

The word "play" for some educators has become synonymous with undesirable, off-task behavior—"playing around." In an era of almost exclusive focus on academic achievement, educators have become outcome oriented. Whether on the field (*Who won?*) or in the classroom (*What did the student score?*), the focus is on outcomes.

Paradoxically, we can obtain some outcomes better by not focusing on outcomes, by allowing time for non-outcome-oriented play. True play is quite in contrast to organized sports. The focus is not on winning v. losing, not on the outcome, but on the process. The question we ask after a game of baseball, football,

"In play we reveal what kind of people we are."
—*Ovid, 43 BC–17*

basketball, or soccer: *"Who won?"* The question we ask after true play: *"Did you have fun?"* True play is process rather than outcome oriented. In true play, we play with others not against others. And in the process, we release creativity and build a sense of community. Jerome Bruner, perhaps the nation's leading developmental psychologist, recognizes play as one of the most important elements in healthy development.[124]

"All work and no play makes Jack a dull boy."
— *Proverbs, 1659*

The brain is a social organ. As we have seen, the brain is more engaged in response to social stimuli than any other.[125] And, of course, most play involves social interaction. This, in part, explains why students enjoy Silly Sports and Goofy Games so much— the games allow students to attend to the type of stimuli their brains most crave.

> ## Tip
> Create an enriched classroom environment: Interactive bulletin boards, mobiles, colorful posters, distinct learning areas, and attractive seating arrangements.

There is, however, much more to the story of why play is an indispensable component of a brain-friendly diet for students. Play develops brains. Play lays down and myelinates neural tracks essential for later success. Play is so essential for brain development that we find it across the range of species in an amazing variety of forms.

Play and Social Interaction Develop the Brain

Prior to 1960, it was accepted knowledge among brain scientists that brains did not change or develop. That view became outdated as a result of classic brain-development research initiated by Marian Diamond. She and her coworkers examined the thickness of the cortex in the brains of rats after being placed alone in cages versus in cages with rat cage mates versus in cages with toys to play with. The enriched environments led to greater cortex development.[126] Rats from the enriched environment had a greater blood supply to the brain and greater development of communication between the hemispheres. Those rats that had experienced enriched environments not only had greater brain mass, they were smarter. That is, following social interaction, they could solve a variety of maze problems more quickly and more efficiently. Rats that experienced enriched environments from birth to 21 days, when tested a full year later, showed superior problem solving compared to rats that did not have the early enrichment! Early enrichment improves brain structure and function in enduring ways.[127]

Animals provided with toys to play with showed greater cortical development than those without toys.

Not surprisingly, animals that lived alone but that had a variety of toys in their cages (toys were changed several times a week) showed greater cortical development than those living alone without toys.

More important than toys for brain development is social interaction: Rats that had eleven cage mates, but no toys, showed more brain development than those that had toys but no cage mates! The research demonstrated conclusively that social stimuli are more powerful than physical stimuli for brain development. Social stimuli and physical stimuli each contribute to brain development: Rats that had cage mates and toys showed even more brain development that rats that had just toys or just cage mates.[128]

Brain structure is influenced very quickly. After only 40 minutes of exposure to an enriched environment, there is a measureable increase in the weight of the cerebral cortical tissue! One day of enrichment produces measureable increases in cortical thickness! Cerebral enrichment occurs at every age tested, from very young to very old animals.[129]

Tip

Promote brain development by allowing students frequent interaction time. When lecturing, frequently stop and have students pair up and share thoughts about the lecture content: How would you put that in your own words? How will this be useful in your life? What part of the lecture do you find most interesting? Does this relate to other things we have covered? Do you like or dislike this poem?

Almost all of the brain development documented by Diamond and her coworkers is neuroplasticity. The increased cortical development was not caused by new neurons being created, rather, existing neurons made more branches and more synaptic connections. There is, however, research

After only 40 minutes of exposure to an enriched environment, there is a measurable increase in the weight of the cerebral cortical tissue!

by Diamond and others that demonstrates that enriched environments do foster neurogenesis, that is, the development of new neurons.[130]

Play Develops the Brain. That play is associated with brain development is supported by cross-species comparisons. For example, if we rate Australian marsupial families as having (1) no play; (2) rudimentary play; or (3) frequent play, we find the amount of play is not related to body mass or metabolic rate, but is correlated with relative brain mass. Authors of the study conclude: "The distribution of play in Australian marsupials supported the hypothesis that play acts to modify brain development."[131] In another approach to determining the relation of play to brain size, fifteen orders of species were compared and brain size was significantly correlated with play complexity.[132]

Does Play Cause Brain Development or Does Brain Development Cause Play? Marian Diamond's experimental enrichment studies demonstrate play causes brain development. Play, through neuroplasticity, increases brain mass *and* makes animals smarter. Smarter animals in turn have a survival advantage so there is a selective advantage for play. Play is an essential neural track for all species.[133] It is almost certain that causality goes both ways—increased brain development leads to more complex play and more play leads to increased brain development.

Play Lays Down and Myelinates Essential Neural Tracks

Play as Preparation for Adulthood. Perhaps the most pervasive form of animal play is practice and development of skills that will be useful in adulthood. To take just one of many examples, the play of both lions and zebras reveals preparation of essential skill development:

> On the African savanna, a lion cub is wrestling with a young peer, pouncing and pawing, at one time going for the kill, and at another, playing the victim. Not too far away, a young zebra is gamboling about by itself, every so often kicking out its hind legs for no apparent reason. Years later, each animal will have matured, and the zebra may find itself desperately fleeing from the pouncing lion, and fiercely kicking back its legs in an attempt to ward off the attack.[134]

Skills of the hunt are first honed in play. Kittens pounce on balls of thread or anything that vaguely resembles a moving mouse. Play is practice:

> Groups of swallows, which prey on airborne insects, will drop a feather from high off the ground and then swoop down and catch the feather in their beaks again and again as it slowly falls to earth. Falcons and crows exhibit similar playfulness, using a wide variety of objects as toys to drop and retrieve in midair. Young kingfishers mimic catching fish by diving down and capturing small twigs floating on the surface of streams or ponds.[135]

Centuries ago, Plato recommended Greek children be given numerous toys and time to play in order to develop the skills they would need for adult life. Children naturally "play mother" or "play father" transparently practicing roles they will later adopt.

Tag is practice of predator-prey responses. Gorillas play tag. One animal initiates the game by tagging another and then scampering away. The one that is tagged chases the aggressor until making the tag. Then the two gorillas reverse roles: the chaser becomes the chased.[136] Children all over the world play tag in this same way. Without knowing it, they are honing their survival skills. Through play, we first lay down and then myelinate neural tracks that become ready to fire efficiently when needed. A myelinated neural track fires up to 200 times faster than one that is not myelinated, offering a survival advantage.

The up-and-back interactions during true play socializes. Play develops the social cognition network, fostering the development of empathy.

Play Is Pervasive Across Species

That play is essential for brain development is supported by its pervasiveness across species, as well as the many forms it takes. Perhaps the single best evidence that play provides a survival advantage is that animals risk their lives in the process of play. Unless play served vital functions, natural selection would have eliminated play long ago. What functions, then, does play serve? We can look to animal play to understand why it is essential that we write play into our curriculum. Play is a natural way to experiment, learn, and broaden our repertoire of skills, including those skills that most determine life success—social skills.

Play Socializes. Most animals engage in play fights. One is tempted to infer that this is practice designed to hone fighting skills. Surprisingly, these mock fights are more a preparation for social interaction than for actual fighting:

> …it turns out that cats that are deprived of play-fighting can hunt just fine. What they can't do—what they never learn to do—is to socialize successfully. Cats and other social mammals such as rats will, if seriously missing out on play, have an inability to clearly delineate friend from foe, miscue on social signaling, and either act excessively aggressive or retreat and not engage in normal social patterns.[137]

This tendency among animals deprived of play to respond with extreme behaviors (aggression or retreat) has a remarkable parallel in young children who have not been properly socialized. Experimenters had a team of trained observers record the responses of abused and nonabused 1- to 3-year-old children. The observers did not know which children had been abused and

Response of Abused and Nonabused Toddlers to Another Child Crying

Abused Toddlers

Nonabused Toddlers

- ■ Concern • Sadness
- ■ Interest • Looks "Mechanical" Comfort Movements
- ■ Fearful • Distress
- ■ Threats • Diffuse Anger • Physical Assaults

Abused toddlers respond with assaults, anger, or fear; nonabused toddlers respond with concern or sadness.

which had not. The observers were instructed to record all social behaviors; they were not told to look for reactions of children to another child crying. Nevertheless, later analysis revealed stark differences: When another child cried, non-abused toddlers often showed concern or sadness. In contrast, abused children never showed empathy, and more often than not, displayed fear, anger, and even physically attacked the crying child! "Eight of the nine abused toddlers, but only one of the nine controls, responded with fear, physical attack, or one of the two other types of angry behavior (nonphysical aggression, diffuse anger) to the crying of other children."[138] See Box: Response of Abused and Nonabused Toddlers to Another Child Crying.

Play Promotes Bonding, Cohesion. True play creates a same-side orientation. In traditional competitive sports, we are on the same side only with our teammates. The result: bonding with those teammates, but alienation from the players on other teams. Competitive sports fosters a "We-They" orientation. In Silly Sports and Goofy Games and other forms of true play, there is a bonding with everyone. True play

nourishes a same-side, "We" orientation. We are all in it together to have fun. It is perhaps for that reason play has the power to transform relations among students and between students and their teacher, as illustrated in Frank Lyman's Parable of Classroom Management.

Forms of Animal Play. The many forms of animal play reveal the variety of ways play develops the brain.

Play for the Joy of It. During play, there is a release of dopamine that stimulates the pleasure centers in the brain. Play is rewarding. Animals stimulate those reward centers in a wild array of types of play.

Hyenas make a substantial detour to reach a river pool, and once there, they jump in and out, splash each other, and push each other underwater. Alaskan buffalo have been seen playing on ice:

> One at a time, starting from a ridge above a frozen lake, the buffalo charged down to the shore and plunged onto the ice, bracing their legs so they spun across the ice, with their tails in the air. As each buffalo skidded to a halt, it let out a loud bellow, "a kind of gwaaa sound"—and then awkwardly picked its way back to shore to make another run....

> Adult ravens slide down a snowy slope on their backs, flying back to the top and sliding down again. Hippos in the water will do backflips over and over again.[139]

> A scientist witnessed a rhesus monkey in the wild doing a reverse flip! Young garden warblers were observed again and again picking up pebbles and marbles from the ground, flying up to a branch and dropping them into a glass, producing a sharp jingling sound. Keas, large parrots from New Zealand, are real clowns—they stand on their heads, turn somersaults on top of branches and even in deep water, land upside down, use branches as swings, and make and push around snowballs.[140]

When I was in elementary school, each classroom had a bookshelf full of games. Checkers was among my favorites. Whenever there was a rainy day, we had lunch inside. After lunch, we took games from the game bookshelf and played. I remember now, more than 60 years later, the warm glow of being inside the classroom and having time to play. That feeling transferred to liking class, the teacher, and learning.

Tip

Occasionally allow some time in class for students to play. Not with a goal, but for the sheer joy of it. The joy that springs from true play will transfer to liking of content and teacher. True play is not time lost; it is an investment in creating the emotional tone in which learning flourishes.

One of my favorite classroom games played for the pure joy of it is **Hagoo**. Teams attempt to win over members from another team by making them laugh before they do! See Blackline: Hagoo, p. 3.45.

Play for Dominance. Two grizzly bears in the Rockies were seen to wrestle for possession of a log. The bear that triumphed lay on its back and juggled the log on its feet while roaring with delight.[141]

> Young animals from across the mammalian spectrum engage their peers in bouts of wrestling and other physical activities. Elephants slap and wrestle each other with their trunks. Giraffes use their long necks to spar gently, necko a necko. Moose calves may practice their head-butting on unsuspecting trees when a peer is unavailable. Animals will even cross the species boundary to find play partners; juvenile chimps and baboons in the wild occasionally tussle together.[142]

Teasing. Animals tease each other, sometimes in daring forms, as when foxes mischievously come close, circle, and then sprint away from a hyena, as if to say, "can't catch me." Some have lost their life playing this dangerous game. A captive dolphin repeatedly teased a fish that lived in a rock crevice: he put bits of squid near the entrance to the fish's home. When the fish came out to get the squid, the dolphin would snatch it away.[143]

Source: Dr. Spencer Kagan • *Silly Sports & Goofy Games*
Kagan Publishing
1 (800) 933-2667
www.KaganOnline.com

hagoo

Crack a smile? You've just been won over by the other team!

1 The Scene

Two teams of about a dozen players each stand facing each other a very giant step apart. A player from one team steps to one end of the gauntlet, and a player of the other team steps to the other end. They stare at each other until one issues the challenge, "Hagoo."

2 The Challenge

The two players attempt to walk the entire gauntlet with a very stern frown. If either smiles, that person is won over by the other team and goes to the end of that team's line. It is not uncommon for both to burst into laughter, in which case each is won over.

3 The Goal

The object of the game is to win over all the other team members. Players cannot touch each other, but they make faces and say whatever might get the frowning person to crack a smile. Observers may be placed to judge if someone has cracked a smile.

4 Pair Hagoo

Pairs from opposite teams sidestep down the gauntlet, facing each other, each trying to make the other smile. The first to smile is won over. More than one pair can be walking at a time.

5 Inside/Outside Circle Hagoo

Two circles are formed, one inside the other. The inside circle members face outward, each facing a partner from the outside circle who is facing inward. At a signal, everyone at once attempts to win over their opponent from the other circle. Once you are won over, you "double team" a person from the other circle, unless you are needed to fill a vacancy in the circle you have just joined!

Note

Hagoo in its original form is a game given to us by the Tlingit Indians of Alaska. "Hagoo" means "Come here."

Game 205

goofy games

That play occurs across a wide variety of species, and that it takes such a wide variety of forms, supports the conclusion that we and other animals are hardwired for play. Given this, by allowing play into our classrooms, we are aligning classroom experiences with how the brains of our students naturally learn and develop. We are creating brain-friendly classrooms.

Keep Away. Beluga whales initiate a game by carrying stones or seaweed on their heads. Immediately, the other whales try to knock them off. Lions, both adults and cubs, may try to wrest pieces of bark or twigs from each other."[144]

Pretend Play. Not all play is social. Just as children can spend hours playing with their dolls or toy building blocks, so too can animals spend time alone, playing. Animals engage also in fantasy play, pretending something is other than what it is. Louis, a chimpanzee playing alone, put a board on his head, signing, "that's a hat."

Performance Play. Some play merges into a performance, and can be quite entertaining, artistic, creative, and/or daring. In his book documenting human interactions with whales, Peter J. Fromm cites numerous accounts of various species of whales showing off for humans.

Our third encounter with a minke took place on the final day of the passage. We had just sighted Antiqua, about 40 miles away. The "Christmas Winds" were blowing on our stern, 25–30 knots....

The swells were about 15 feet high and nicely spaced apart. It was some wild sailing, a great final day for a passage. I was at the wheel and looked behind at an approaching swell. There was another minke, body surfing down the face of the wave! This one was a youngster, about 15 feet long.

He would surf down the swell right to the boat, then dive under the stern. He would swim under us and then spyhop three or four boat lengths ahead and look right at us. Just before we were

about to run into him, he would dive. We would lose sight of him for a short while, then, "Here he comes again!"

He would be behind us, doing it all over again.

He was playing with the boat; there is no question at all about it. He did the same thing over and over again, for about an hour and a half. This was also quite a performance, thrilling, spectacular, and far beyond anything I could have imagined a minke whale ever doing.[145]

> ## Tip
> Make time for explorations. Have students play with math manipulatives, paint, clay, science equipment (with safety regulations firmly in place). Have students create word cards and move them about to create unusual sentences. Make social studies events into cards and have students sort and re-sort them, creating their own categories. Whatever our curriculum, we can make time for students to play with it!

Benefits of Classroom Play

Play, one of the primary forms of social interaction, is a natural way for students to learn and to develop their brains. As the animal anecdotes reveal, play promotes not just social development; it promotes creativity. Education has focused largely on teaching youth how to use established procedures to solve problems. Students learn to memorize the procedures and then, for practice, they are fed problems that can be solved with those procedures. They are then tested on the procedure by being fed more problems that can be solved with the same procedure. There are several shortcomings to this approach. After learning many procedures, when faced with a new problem, often students are at a loss as to which procedure to use, or worse yet, by then they have forgotten the procedure. Another, even greater, shortcoming is that students are not given the tools to discover for themselves new procedures for solving problems.

Play Fosters Creativity. Play offers a potential corrective: Play allows students to create their own "problems" and to create their own novel ways to solve them. Having created a procedure, students are far less likely to forget the procedure than if they were fed the procedure and required to memorize it. And having created their own solution, they are better set to independently solve the next problem they face. Success in the workplace more often results from discovering a new way to solve problems rather than applying procedures established by others.

Traditional sports like baseball, football, and basketball have preestablished rules. Students are to obey the fixed rules. It can be a healthy antidote and a spur to creativity to include in their diet some games that allow students to play with the rules. This is the philosophy in the "Silly Sports" section of the book, *Silly Sports & Goofy Games.*[146] For example, in **Alaskan Baseball**, after hitting the ball or balloon, batters do laps around their teammates to score points. Laps continue until all players on the opposing team have touched the ball. After playing this oddball version of baseball, students are encouraged to create their own brand-new set of rules for an alternative form of baseball. See Blackline: Alaskan Baseball, p. 3.48.

Play Promotes Thinking Out of the Box. Experience playing with the rules can break the set of how we think about things, allowing creative solutions. One of my favorite examples

Tip

Look for opportunities in the curriculum to have students role play adult roles. They can be lawyers defending opposite sides of a case, legislators proposing laws, environmentalists analyzing environmental impact, entrepreneurs creating new inventions, and scientists testing hypotheses.

of this occurred years ago when I was doing an intensive year-long training of trainers in cooperative learning. The focus was on cooperative learning structures and academic content, but in each meeting I included one or two of the Silly Sports and Goofy Games and encouraged the teachers to try them back at school. About a month and a half into the training, one of the participants said she had something to share. She said she was embarrassed to share it, but thought it was important. In her class, there was a boy (we will call Jim) who was confined to a wheel chair. At each recess Jim sat in his wheelchair and watched the other students play softball. This had gone on since the beginning of the school year. In fact, Jim was in fifth grade and his passive observing of playground play had been his norm every year. After the teacher introduced some of the Silly Sports to students and encouraged them to play with the rules, one day the students excitedly came in from recess to report they had changed the rules of baseball so Jim could play. A batter was selected to stand in for Jim who was in his wheelchair on the first base line with a teammate behind him to push him to first base when the ball was hit. From that point on, Jim was one of the players, "running" the bases. The teacher said she was embarrassed to share the story because prior to playing Silly

Source: Dr. Spencer Kagan • *Silly Sports & Goofy Games* Kagan Publishing 1 (800) 933-2667 www.KaganOnline.com

alaskan baseball

Why bother with bases when you can lap your teammates?

1 The Line Up
The team at bat forms a line.

2 Batter Up
The batter hits the ball (bats a balloon, kicks a rubber ball, throws a comet).

3 No Bases to Run
After hitting the ball, the batter immediately begins doing laps around his/her teammates!

4 Touch and Stop
The fielders must all touch the ball before they yell "Stop!" Upon the command "Stop!" the batter freezes. Players devise strategies to quickly all touch the ball – either tossing it, or running up and touching it while one player holds it.

5 Scoring
The score is the number of complete laps run.

6 Outfield Is Up
After each player has had a turn at bat, the other team is up!

Sports and Goofy Games, it had never occurred to her or her students to restructure the rules to include Jim. It was only after the students had experience playing with the rules that they discovered a more inclusive way to play.

One way to promote creativity and social development through play is to make a copy of one of the 206 games from *Silly Sports & Goofy Games* and send students to recess with the copy. Their task: First play the game the way it is described. Next, modify the game by changing the rules or equipment. The goal, discover a way to improve the game by making it more fun, more inclusive, or more challenging.

I am not advocating that play replace traditional curriculum or traditional sports. I am advocating play *supplement* traditional curriculum and traditional sports. Let's enrich the diet of our students. Play can enrich our sport and our academic curricula, allowing students to explore, manipulate, play, and invent. The result: greater creativity, improved socialization, and greater joy in learning.

Conclusion

The discovery of a deep-rooted social cognition network in the brain, which, when activated, enhances memory and has extremely important implications for us as educators. The more we engage students in mentalizing in association with our academic curriculum, thinking about the thoughts, feelings, and intentions of others, the more memorable we make our lessons. Some of the work demonstrating the social encoding advantage is counterintuitive and can serve as an antidote to an overemphasis on an outcome orientation in education. We divide our students into two groups. We tell one group they will be tested and that they should memorize for the test a list of accomplishments of a historical person. We do not tell the other group there will be a test, and merely tell them to to use the list of accomplishments to infer the personality or character of the historical person. We then test all the students. *Those not told to prepare for the test score better on the test!* By activating mentalizing, we improve memory for content. All of us can release the power of the social encoding advantage. And in the process, we can make our curriculum not only more memorable, but more enjoyable as well.

The study of the brain reveals counterintuitive findings: By taking time off academics to do teambuilding, classbuilding, and play, we improve academic achievement. In the next principle: Principle 4: Emotion, we discover how creativity, problem solving, and achievement are accelerated when we elicit positive emotions through activities like teambuilding and play.

The royal road to brain engagement is social interaction. And the royal road to social interaction is cooperative learning and true play. The trick: Structure cooperative interaction and play so all students are on the same side, accountable, participating about equally, and actively engaged. Kagan Structures and Silly Sports and Goofy Games are carefully designed to do that. But those structures and games cannot operate in a vacuum. We can't expect heterogeneous teams and classrooms to function optimally when the students don't know or like each other. Thus, we need teambuilding and classbuilding. Students aren't born with social skills; they must be taught.

When we put in place the five tools to promote social cognition and cooperation, students not only achieve more and like school and content more, they discover the power of mutual support. They become a community of engaged learners.

Five Tools to Teach the Social Brain
1. Activate Social Cognition
2. Include Classbuilding
3. Structure Cooperative Interaction
4. Teach Social Skills
5. Promote Cooperative Play

References

[1] Lieberman, M.D. *Social. Why Our Brains Are Wired to Connect.* New York, NY: Crown Publishing Group, 2013.

[2] Lieberman, M.D. *Social. Why Our Brains Are Wired to Connect.* New York, NY: Crown Publishing Group, 2013, 117–118.

[3] Van Overwalle, F. *A dissociation between social mentalizing and general reasoning.* **NeuroImage**, 2011, 54(2), 1589–1599.

[4] Harrision, B.J., Pujol, J., Lopez-Sola, M., Hernandez-Ribas, R., Deus, J., Ortiz, H., Soriano-Mas, C., Yücel, M., Pantelis, C. & Cardoner, N. *Consistency and functional specialization in the default mode brain network.* **Proceedings of the National Academy of Sciences**, 2008, 105(28), 9781–9786.

Spreng, R.N., Mar, R.A. & Kim, A.S. *The common neural basis of autobiographical memory, prospection, navigation, theory of mind, and the default mode: A quantitative meta-analysis.* **Journal of Cognitive Neuroscience**, 2009, 21(3), 489–510.

[5] Lieberman, M.D. *Social. Why Our Brains Are Wired to Connect.* New York, NY: Crown Publishing Group, 2013, 22.

[6] Heider, F. & Simmel, M. *An experimental study of apparent behavior.* **American Journal of Psychology**, 1944, 57(2), 243–259.

[7] Klin, A. *Attributing social meaning to ambiguous visual stimuli in higher-functioning autism and Asperger syndrome: The Social attribution task.* **Journal of Child Psychology and Psychiatry**, 2003, 41(7), 831–846.

[8] Yoshida, W., Seymour, B., Friston, K.J. & Dolan, R.J. *Neural mechanisms of belief inference during cooperative games.* **Journal of Neuroscience**, 2010, 30(32), 10744–10751.

[9] Coricelli, G. & Nagel, R. *Neural correlates of depth of strategic reasoning in medial prefrontal cortex.* **Proceedings of the National Academy of Sciences**, 2009, 106(23), 9163–9168.

[10] Firth, U. *Autism: Explaining the Enigma.* Blackwell Publishers, Ltd. Oxford: 1989, p. 120.

[11] Coleman, M. & Gillberg, C. *The Biology of Autistic Syndromes.* New York: Praeger, 1985.

[12] Firth, U. *Autism: Explaining the Enigma.* Blackwell Publishers, Ltd. Oxford: 1989, p. 99.

[13] Hamilton, D.L., Katz, L.B. & Leirer, V.O. *Cognitive representation of personality impressions: Organizational process in first impression formation.* **Journal of Personality and Social Psychology**, 1980, 39(6), 1050.

[14] Mitchell, J.P. Macrae, C.N. & Banaji, M.R. *Encoding-specific effects of social cognition on the neural correlates of subsequent memory.* **Journal of Neuroscience**, 2004, 24(21), 4912–4917.

[15] Lieberman, M.D. *Social. Why Our Brains Are Wired to Connect.* New York, NY: Crown Publishing Group, 2013, 285.

[16] Wire, N. (2010). *US teen mobile report: Calling yesterday, texting today, using apps tomorrow* [blog post]. *Retrieved from Nielsenwire at http://blog. nielsen.com/nielsenwire/online_mobile/us-teen-mobile-reportcalling-yesterday-texting-today-using-apps-tomorrow.*

[17] Facebook. (2013, September 30). *Newsroom: Keyfacts. Facebook. com.* Retrieved November 25, 2013, from: https://newsroom.fb.com/Key-Facts.

[18] Dunbar, R.I., Marriott, A. & Duncan, N.D. *Human conversational behavior.* **Human Nature**, 1997, 8(3), 231–246.

[19] Carter, R. *Mapping the Mind.* Berkeley, CA: University of California Press, 1999, 150.

[20] Keltner, D. *Born to Be Good.* New York, NY: W.W. Norton & Company, 2009.

[21] Carter, R. *Mapping the Brain.* Los Angeles, CA: University of California Press, 1999, 91.

[22] Dolcos, S., Sung, K., Argo, J.J., Flor-Henry, S. & Dolcos, F. *The power of a handshake: Neural correlates of evaluative judgments in observed social interactions.* **Journal of Cognitive Neuroscience**, 2012, 24(12), 2292–2305.

[23] Brothers, L. *Friday's Footprint: How Society Shapes the Human Mind.* New York, NY: Oxford University Press, 1997.

[24] Fried, I., MacDonald, K.A. & Wilson, C.L. *Single neuron activity in human hippocampus and amygdala during recognition of faces and objects.* **Neuron**, 1997, 18(5), 753–765.

[25] Kennerknecht, I., Grueter, T., Welling, B., Wentzek, S., Horst, J.R., Edwards, S. & Grueter, M. *First report of prevalence of non-syndromic hereditary prosopagnosia (HPA).* **American Journal of Medical Genetics**, 2006, 140A(15), 1617–1622.

[26] Bauer, R.M. *Autonomic recognition of names and faces in prosopagnosia: A neuropsychological application of the Guilty Knowledge Test.* **Neuropsychologia**, 1984, 22(4), 457–469.

[27] Gainotti, G. & Marra, C. *Differential contribution of right and left temporo-occipital and anterior temporal lesions to face recognition disorders.* **Frontiers in Human Neuroscience**, 2011, 5(55), 1–12.

[28] Chang, S.W.C., Gariépy, J-F. & Platt, M.L. *Neuronal reference frames for social decisions in primate frontal cortex.* **Nature Neuroscience**, 2012, 16(2), 243–250.

[29] Gu, X., Gao, Z., Wang, X., Liu, X., Knight, R.T., Hof, P.R. & Fan, J. *Anterior insular cortex is necessary for empathetic pain perception.* **Brain**, 2012, 135(9), 2726–2735.

Jeon, D., Kim, S., Chetana, M., Jo, D., Ruley, H.E., Lin, S.Y., Rabah, D., Kinet, J.P. & Shin, H.S. *Observational fear learning involves affective pain system and Cav1.2 Ca 2+ channels in ACC.* **Nature Neuroscience**, 2010, 13(4), 482–488.

[30] Hampton, A.N., Bossaerts, P. & O'Doherty, J.P. *Neural correlates of mentalizing-related computations during strategic interactions in humans.* **Proceedings of National Academy of Science**, 2008, 105(18), 6741–6746.

[31] Craig, A.D. (Bud). *How do you feel—now? The anterior insula and human awareness.* **Nature Reviews Neuroscience**, 2009, 10(1), 59–70.

Gu, X., Gao, Z., Wang, X., Liu, X., Knight, R.T., Hof, P.R. & Fan, J. *Anterior insular cortex is necessary for empathetic pain perception.* **Brain**, 2012, 135(9), 2726–2735.

Singer, T. *The neuronal basis and ontogeny of empathy and mind reading: review of literature and implications for future research.* **Neuroscience and Biobehavioral Reviews**, 2006, 30(6), 855–863.

Singer, T., Seymour, B., O'Doherty, J., Kaube, H., Dolan, R.J. & Frith, C.D. *Empathy for pain involves the affective but not sensory components of pain.* **Science**, 2004, 303(5661), 1157–1162.

[32] Bakwin, H. *Emotional deprivation in infants.* **Journal of Pediatrics**, 1949, 35(4), 512–521, 512.

[33] Bakwin, H. *Emotional deprivation in infants.* **Journal of Pediatrics**, 1949, 35(4), 512–521.

[34] Seligman, M.E.P. **Helplessness: On Depression, Development, and Death**. San Francisco, CA: W.H. Freeman, 1975.

[35] Brennemann, J. *The infant ward.* **American Journal of Disabilities in Children**, 1932, 43(3), 577–584.

[36] Bakwin, H. *Emotional deprivation in infants.* **Journal of Pediatrics**, 1949, 35(4), 512–521.

[37] Feldman, R., Rosenthal, Z. & Eidelman, A.I. *Maternal-preterm skin-to-skin contact enhances child physiologic organization and cognitive control across the first 10 years of life.* **Biological Psychiatry**, 2014, 75(1), 56–64.

[38] Aarnoudse-Moens, C.S.H., Duivenvoorden, H.J., Weisglas-Kuperus, N., Van Goudoever, J.B. & Oosterlaan, J. *The profile of executive function in very preterm children at 4 to 12 years.* **Developmental Medicine & Child Neurology**, 2012, 54(3), 247–253.

Luu, T.M., Ment, L., Allan, W., Schneider, K. & Vohr, B.R. *Executive and memory function in adolescents born very preterm.* **Pediatrics**, 2011, 127(3), e639–e646.

[39] Carter, R. **Mapping the Brain**. Los Angeles, CA: University of California Press, 1999, 91.

[40] Rilling, J.K. & Kilts, C. *Biological basis for human cooperation.* **ScienceDaily**. Retrieved August 1, 2011, from http://www.sciencedaily.com-/releases/2002/07/020718075131.htm.

[41] Layous, K., Nelson, S.K., Oberle, E., Schonert-Reichl, K.A. & Lyubomirsky, S. *Kindness counts: Prompting prosocial behavior in preadolescents boosts peer acceptance and well-being.* **Public Library of Science ONE**, 2012, 7(12), e51380, 1–3.

[42] Wentzel, K.R. *Peer relationships, motivation, and academic performance at school.* In A. Elliot & C. Dweck (Eds.), **Handbook of Competence and Motivation**, 279-296. New York, NY: Guilford, 2005.

Wentzel, K.R., Baker, S. & Russell, S. *Peer relationships and positive adjustment at school.* In R. Gilman, E.S. Huebner, & M.J. Furlong (Eds.), **Handbook of Positive Psychology in Schools**, 229-243. New York, NY: Routledge, 2009.

[43] de Bruyn, E.H. & van den Boom, D.C. *Interpersonal behavior, peer popularity, and self-esteem in early adolescence.* **Social Development**, 2005, 14(4), 555–573.

[44] Ostberg, V. *Children in classrooms: Peer status, status distribution and mental well-being.* **Social Science and Medicine**, 2003, 56(1), 17–29.

[45] Hsu, D.T., Sanford, B.J., Meyers, K.K., Love, T.M., Hazlett, K.E., Wang, H., Ni, L., Walker, S.J., Mickey, B.J., Korycinski, S.T., Koeppe, R.A., Crocker, J.K., Langenecker, S.A. & Zubieta, J-K. *Response of the μ-opioid system to social rejection and acceptance.* **Molecular Psychiatry**, 2013, 1–7.

[46] Lieberman, M.D. **Social. Why Our Brains Are Wired to Connect**. New York, NY: Crown Publishing Group, 2013, 59.

[47] Baumeister, R.F., Twenge, J.M. & Nuss, C.K. *Effects of social exclusion on cognitive processes: Anticipated aloneness reduces intelligent thought.* **Journal of Personality and Social Psychology**, 202, 83(4), 817.

[48] Heinrichs, M., Baumgartner, T., Kirschbaum, C. & Ehlert, U. *Social support and oxytocin interact to suppress cortisol and subjective responses to psychosocial stress.* **Biological Psychiatry**, 2003, 54(12), 1389–1398.

Kirsch, P., Esslinger, C., Chen, Q., Mier, D., Lis, S., Siddhanti, S., Gruppe, H., Mattay, V.S., Gallhofer, B. & Meyer-Lindenberg, A. *Oxytocin modulates neural circuitry for social cognition and fear in humans.* **Journal of Neuroscience**, 2005, 25(49), 11489–11493.

[49] Juvonen, J. **Focus on the Wonder Years: Challenges Facing the American Middle School, Vol. 139**. Santa Monica, CA: RAND Corporation, 2004.

[50] Walton. G.M. & Cohen, G.L. *A brief social-belonging intervention improves academic and health outcomes of minority students.* **Science**, 2011, 331(6023), 1457–1451.

Walton, G.M. & Cohen, G.L. *A question of belonging: Race, social fit, and achievement.* **Journal of Personality and Social Psychology**, 2007, 92(1), 82.

51 Chen, X., Rubin, K.H. & Li, D. *Relation between academic achievement and social adjustment: Evidence form Chinese children.* **Developmental Psychology**, 1997, 33(3), 518.

Furrer, C. & Skinner, E. *Sense of relatedness as a factor in children's academic engagement and performance.* **Journal of Educational Psychology**, 2003, 95(1), 148.

Wentzel, K.R. *Social relationships and motivation in middle school: The role of parents, teachers, and peers.* **Journal of Educational Psychology** 1998, 90(2), 202.

Wentzel, K.R. & Caldwell, K. *Friendships, peer acceptance, and group membership: Relations to academic achievement in middle school.* **Child Development**, 1997, 68(6), 1198–1209.

52 Carter, C.S. & Keverne, E.B. *The neurobiology of social affiliation and pair bonding. In D. Pfaff, A. Arnold, A. Etgen, S. Fahrbach & R. Rubin (Eds), **Hormones, Brain, and Behavior**.* San Diego, CA: Academic Press, 2002, 299–337.

Insel, T.R. & Young, L.J. *The neurobiology of attachment. Nature Reviews.* **Neuroscience**, 2001, 2(2), 129–135.

Pedersen, C.A. & A.J. Prange, A.J. Jr. *Induction of maternal behavior in virgin rats after intracerebroventricular administration of oxytocin.* **Proceedings of the National Academy of Sciences of the USA**, 1979, 76(12), 6661–6665.

53 Zak, P.J., Stanton, A.A., Ahmadi, S. *Oxytocin Increases Generosity in Humans.* **Public Library of Science One (PLoS)**, 2007, 2(11), 1–5.

54 Kosfeld, M., Heinrichs, M., Zak, P.J., Fischbacher, U. & Feh, E. *Oxytocin increases trust in humans.* **Nature**, 2005, 435(7042), 673–676.

55 Zak, P.J., Kurzban, R. & Matzner, W.T. *Oxytocin is associated with human trustworthiness.* **Hormones and Behavior**, 2005, 48(5), 522–527.

56 Domes, G., Heinrichs, M., Michel, A., Berger, C. & Herpertz, S.C. *Oxytocin improves "mind-reading" in humans.* **Biological Psychiatry**, 2010, 61(6), 731–733.

Hurlemann, R., Patin, A., Onur, O.A., Cohen, M.X., Baumgartner, T., Metzler, S., Dziobek, I., Gallinat, J., Wagner, M., Maier, W. & Kendrick, K.M. *Oxytocin enhances amygdala-dependent, socially reinforced learning and emotional empathy in humans.* **The Journal of Neuroscience**, 2010, 30(14), 4999–5007.

57 Zak, P.J. Trust: *A temporary human attachment facilitated by oxytocin.* **Behavioral and Brain Sciences**, 28(3), 2005, 368–369.

58 Carter, C.S. *Neuroendocrine perspectives on social attachment and love.* **Psychoneuroendocrinology**, 1998, 23(8), 779–818.

59 Heinrichs, M., Baumgartner, T., Kirschbaum, C. & Ehlert, U. *Social support and oxytocin interact to suppress cortisol and subjective responses to psychosocial stress.* **Biological Psychiatry**, 2003, 54(12), 1389–1398.

Kirsch, P., Esslinger, C., Chen, Q., Mier, D., Lis, S., Siddhanti, S., Gruppe, H., Mattay, V.S., Gallhofer, B. & Meyer-Lindenberg, A. *Oxytocin modulates neural circuitry for social cognition and fear in humans.* **Journal of Neuroscience**, 2005, 25(49), 11489–11493.

60 Zak, P.J., Kurzban, R. & Matzner, W.T. *The Neurobiology of Trust.* **Annals of the New York Academy of Sciences**, 2004, 1032(1), 224–227.

61 Zak, P.J., Kurzban, R. & Matzner, W.T. *The Neurobiology of Trust.* **Annals of the New York Academy of Sciences**, 2004, 1032(1), 224–227.

62 Zak, P.J., Stanton, A.A., Ahmadi, S. *Oxytocin Increases Generosity in Humans.* **Public Library of Science One (PLoS)**, 2007, 2(11), 1–5.

63 Zak, P.J., Stanton, A.A., Ahmadi, S. *Oxytocin Increases Generosity in Humans.* **Public Library of Science One (PLoS)**, 2007, 2(11), 1–5.

64 Domes, G., Heinrichs, M., Michel, A., Berger, C. & Herpertz, S.C. *Oxytocin improves "mind-reading" in humans.* **Biological Psychiatry**, 2010, 61(6), 731–733.

Hurlemann, R., Patin, A., Onur, O.A., Cohen, M.X., Baumgartner, T., Metzler, S., Dziobek, I., Gallinat, J., Wagner, M., Maier, W. and Kendrick, K.M. *Oxytocin enhances amygdala-dependent, socially reinforced learning and emotional empathy in humans.* **The Journal of Neuroscience**, 2010, 30(14), 4999–5007.

65 Boesch, C. *Cooperative hunting in wild chimpanzees.* **Animal Behavior**, 1994, 48(3), 653–667.

Boesch, C. & Boesch-Achermann, H. **The Chimpanzees of the Tai Forest: Behavioural Ecology and Evolution**. Oxford, UK: Oxford University Press, 2000.

Muller, M.N. & Mitani, J.C. *Conflict and cooperation in wild chimpanzees.* **Advances in the Study of Behavior**, 2005, 35, 275–331.

66 de Waal, F.B.M. *The chimpanzee's service economy: Food for grooming.* **Evolution and Human Behavior**, 1997, 18(6), 375–386.

Gomes, C.M. & Boesch, C. *Wild chimpanzees exchange meat for sex on a long-term basis.* **Public Library of Science One**, 2009, 4(4), e5116.

Mitani, J.C. *Reciprocal exchange in chimpanzees and other primates. In P.M. Kappeler & C.P. van Schaik (Eds), **Co-operation in Primates and Humans: Mechanisms and Evolution**.* Berlin: Springer, 2006, 107–119.

67 Brosnan, S.F., Schiff, H.C. & de Waal, F.B.M. *Tolerance for inequity may increase with social closeness in chimpanzees.* **Proceedings of the Royal Society B: Biological Sciences**, 2005, 272(1560), 253–258.

Brosnan, S.F. *A hypothesis of the co-evolution of cooperation and responses to inequity.* **Frontiers in Neuroscience**, 2011, 5(43), 1–12.

68 Goodall, J. **The Chimpanzees of Gombe: Patterns of Behavior.** Cambridge, MA: Belknap, 1986.

69 de Waal, F.B.M. **The Age of Empathy: Nature's Lessons for a Kinder Society.** New York, NY: Harmony Books, 2010.

70 Warneken, F. & Tomasello, M. *Extrinsic rewards undermine altruistic tendencies in 20-month-olds.* **Developmental Psychology**, 2008, 44(6), 1785–1788.

71 Vaish, A., Carpenter, M. & Tomasello, M. *Sympathy through affective perspective taking and its relation to prosocial behavior in toddlers.* **Developmental Psychology**, 2009, 45(2), 534–543.

72 Main, M. & George, C. *Responses of young abused and disadvantaged toddlers to distress in agemates: A study in the day care setting.* **Developmental Psychology**, 1985, 21(3), 407–412.

73 Iacoboni, M. ***Mirroring People: The Science of Empathy and How We Connect with Others***. New York, NY: Farrar, Straus and Giroux, 2009.

74 Hess, U., Blairy, S. & Philippot, P. *Facial mimicry*. In P. Philippot, R. Feldman, & E. Coats (Eds.), ***The Social Context of Nonverbal Behavior***, 213–241. Cambridge, UK: Cambridge University Press, 1999.

75 Wicker, B., Keysers, C., Plailly, J. & Royet, J.P., Vittorio Gallese, V. & Rizzolatti, G. *Both of us disgusted in my insula: The common neural basis of seeing and feeling disgust.* **Neuron**, 2003, 40(3), 655–664.

76 Calder, A.J., Keane, J., Manes, F., Antoun, N. & Young, A.W. *Impaired recognition and experience of disgust following brain injury.* **Nature Neuroscience**, 2000, 3(11), 1077–1078.

Adolphs, R., Tranel, D. & Damasio, A.R. *Dissociable neural systems for recognizing emotions.* **Brain and Cognition**, 2003, 52(1), 61–69.

77 Doidge, N. ***The Brain That Changes Itself: Stories of Personal Triumph from the Frontiers of Brain Science***. New York, NY: Penguin Books, 2007.

78 Keltner, D. ***Born to Be Good***. New York, NY: W.W. Norton & Company, 2009.

Nowak, M.A. ***Super Cooperators: Altruism, Evolution, and Why We Need Each Other to Succeed***. New York, NY: Free Press, 2011.

Tomasello, M., Dweck, C., Silk, J. Skyrms, B. & Spelke, E. ***Why We Cooperate***. Cambridge, MA: MIT Press, 2009.

79 Darwin, C. ***The Descent of Man***. London, UK: John Murray, 1871.

80 Tomasello, M., Dweck, C., Silk, J. Skyrms, B. & Spelke, E. ***Why We Cooperate***. Cambridge, MA: MIT Press, 2009.

81 Clay, Z. & de Waal, F.B.M. *Bonobos respond to distress in others: Consolation across the age spectrum.* **Public Library of Science ONE**, 2013, 8(1), e55206.

82 Tomasello, M., Melis, A.P., Tennie, C., Wyman, E. & Herrmann, E. *Two key steps in the evolution of human cooperation: The interdependence hypothesis.* **Current Anthropology**, 2012, 53(6), 673–692.

83 Kagan, S. and Kagan, M. ***Kagan Cooperative Learning***. San Clemente, CA: Kagan Publishing, 2009.

84 Kagan, M., Robertson, L. & Kagan, S. ***Cooperative Structures for Classbuilding***. San Clemente, CA: Kagan Publishing. 1995.

85 Kagan, M., Kagan, S. & Kagan, L. ***Classbuilding SmartCard***. San Clemente, CA: Kagan Publishing, 1995.

Kagan, M. ***Instant Classbuilding Software***. San Clemente, CA: Kagan Publishing, 2011.

Kagan, M. ***Classbuilding Questions***. San Clemente, CA: Kagan Publishing, 2012.

Forest, L. ***Crafting Creative Community***. San Clemente, CA: Kagan Publishing, 2001.

Shaw, W. ***Communitybuilding***. San Clemente, CA: Kagan Publishing, 1992.

Gibbs, J. ***Reaching All by Creating Tribes Learning Communities***. Windsor, CA: CenterSource Systems, LLC, 2001.

86 Kagan, S., Kyle, P. and Scott, S. ***Win-Win Discipline***. San Clemente, CA: Kagan Publishing, 2004.

87 Hmelo-Silver, C.E., Chinn, C.A., Chan, C.K.K. & O'Donnell, A. ***The International Handbook of Collaborative Learning***. New York, NY: Routledge, 2013.

Bruffee, K.A. ***Collaborative Learning: Higher Education, Interdependence, and the Authority of Knowledge, 2nd Edition***. Baltimore, Maryland: Johns Hopkins University Press, 1999.

88 Gillespie, P. & Lerner, N. ***Longman Guide to Peer Tutoring, 2nd Edition***. New York, NY: Longman, Inc., 2008.

Gillespie, P. & Lerner, N. ***The Allyn and Bacon Guide to Peer Tutoring***. New York, NY: Prentice Hall, 1999.

89 Kagan, S. & M. Kagan. ***Kagan Cooperative Learning***. San Clemente, CA: Kagan Publishing, 2009.

Slavin, R., S. Sharan, S. Kagan, R. Hertz-Lazarowitz, C. Webb & R. Schmuck (eds.). ***Learning to Cooperate, Cooperating to Learn***. New York: Plenum, 1985.

90 Lyman, F.T. *Think-Pair-Share, Thinktrix, Thinklinks, and Weird Facts: An interactive system for cooperative thinking*. In N. Davidson and T. Worsham (Eds), ***Enhancing Thinking through Cooperative Learning***. New York, NY: Teachers College Press, Columbia University, 1992, 169–181.

91 Kagan, S. *Teams of Four are Magic!* **Kagan Online Magazine**, Fall, 1998. www.KaganOnline.com

92 Kagan, S. ***Kagan Cooperative Learning Structures***. San Clemente, CA: Kagan Publishing, 2013.

93 Kagan, S. & Kagan, M. ***Kagan Cooperative Learning***. San Clemente, CA: Kagan Publishing, 2009.

94 Kagan, L., Kagan, S. & Kagan, M. ***Cooperative Structures for Teambuilding***. San Clemente, CA: Kagan Publishing, 1997.

95 Kagan, S. & Kagan, M. ***Kagan Cooperative Learning***. San Clemente, CA: Kagan Publishing, 2009.

Kagan, M. ***Teambuilding Questions***. San Clemente, CA: Kagan Publishing, 2012.

Kagan, M. & Kagan, S. *Teambuilding SmartCard*. San Clemente, CA: Kagan Publishing, 1995.

Kagan, M. *Instant Teambuilding Software*. San Clemente, CA: Kagan Publishing, 2012.

Craigen, J. & Ward, C. *What's This Got to Do with Anything?* San Clemente, CA: Kagan Publishing, 2004.

[96] Kagan, S., Kyle, P. & Scott, S. *Win-Win Discipline*. San Clemente, CA: Kagan Publishing, 2004.

[97] Walberg, H.J. *Productive teaching*. In H.C. Waxman & H.J. Walberg (Eds.) *New Directions for Teaching Practice and Research*, Berkeley, CA: McCutchen Publishing Corporation, 1999, 75-104.

[98] Lipsey, M.W. & Wilson, D.B. *The efficacy of psychological, educational, and behavioural treatment*. **American Psychologist**, 1993, 48(12), 1181–1209.

[99] Johnson, D., Maruyama, G., Johnson, R., Nelson, D. & Skon, L. *Effects of cooperative, competitive, and individualistic goal structure on achievement: A meta-analysis*. **Psychological Bulletin**, 1981, 89(10), 47–62.

[100] Johnson, D.W. & Johnson, R.T. *Learning Together and Alone: Cooperative, Competitive, and Individualistic Learning*. Boston, MA: Allyn & Bacon, 1999.

[101] Johnson, D.W. & Johnson, R.T. *Learning Together and Alone: Cooperative, Competitive, and Individualistic Learning*. Boston, MA: Allyn & Bacon, 1999.

[102] Hattie, J. *Visible Learning. A Synthesis of Over 800 Meta-Analyses Relating to Achievement*. New York, NY: Routledge, 2009.

[103] Hattie, J. *Visible Learning. A Synthesis of Over 800 Meta-Analyses Relating to Achievement*. New York, NY: Routledge, 2009.

[104] Hattie, J. *Visible Learning. A Synthesis of Over 800 Meta-Analyses Relating to Achievement*. New York, NY: Routledge, 2009.

[105] Springer, L., Stanne, M.E. & Donovan, S.S. *Effects of small-group learning on undergraduates in science, mathematics, engineering, and technology: A meta-analysis*. **Review of Educational Research**, 1999, 69(1), 212–251.

[106] Beesley, A.D. & Apthorp, H.S. (Eds.) *Classroom Instruction that Works, 2nd Edition Research Report, Mid-Continent Research for Education and Learning*. Denver, CO: Mid-continent Research for Education and Learning, 2010.

[107] Rohrbeck, C.A., Ginsburg-Block, M.D., Fantuzzo, J.W. & Miller, T.R. *Peer-assisted learning interventions with elementary school students: A meta-analytic review*. **Journal of Educational Psychology**, 2003, 95(2), 240–257.

[108] Greenwood, C.R., Carta, J.J. & Hall, R.V. *The use of peer tutoring strategies in classroom management and educational instruction*. **School Psychology Review**, 1988, 17, 258–275.

Arp, L. & Semb, G. *An analysis of the use of student proctors in a personalized college business course*. **Journal of Personalized Instruction**, 1977, 2, 92–95.

[109] Semb, G.B., Ellis, J.A. & Araujo, J. *Long-term memory for knowledge learned in school*. **Journal of Educational Psychology**, 1993, 85(2), 305–316.

[110] Bargh, J.A. & Schul, Y. *On the cognitive benefits of teaching*. **Journal of Educational Psychology**, 1980, 72(5), 593.

[111] Haydon, T., Maheady, L. & Hunter, W. *Effects of Numbered Heads Together on the daily quiz scores and on-task behavior of students with disabilities*. **Journal of Behavioral Education**, 2010, 19, 222–238.

Maheady, L., Michielli-Pendl, J., Harper, G.F. & Mallette, B. *The effects of Numbered Heads Together with and without an incentive package on the science test performance of a diverse group of sixth graders*. **Journal of Behavioral Education**, 2006, 15(1), 24–38.

Maheady, L., Mallette, B., Harper, G.F. & Sacca, K. *Heads together: A peer-mediated option for improving the academic achievement of heterogeneous learning groups*. **Remedial and Special Education**, 1991, 12(2), 25–33.

Maheady, L., Michielli-Pendl, J., Mallette, B. & Harper, G.F. *A collaborate research project to improve the academic performance of a diverse sixth grade class*. **Teacher Education and Special Education**, 2002, 25(1), 55–70.

[112] Haydon, T., Maheady, L. & Hunter, W. *Effects of Numbered Heads Together on the daily quiz scores and on-task behavior of students with disabilities*. **Journal of Behavioral Education**, 2010, 19(3), 222–238.

[113] Haydon, T., Maheady, L. & Hunter, W. *Effects of Numbered Heads Together on the daily quiz scores and on-task behavior of students with disabilities*. **Journal of Behavioral Education**, 2010, 19(3), 222–238.

[114] Maheady, L., Michielli-Pendl, J., Harper, G.F. & Mallette, B. *The effects of Numbered Heads Together with and without an incentive package on the science test performance of a diverse group of sixth graders*. **Journal of Behavioral Education**, 2006, 15(1), 24–38.

[115] Maheady, L., Michielli-Pendl, J., Harper, G.F. & Mallette, B. *The effects of Numbered Heads Together with and without an incentive package on the science test performance of a diverse group of sixth graders*. **Journal of Behavioral Education**, 2006, 15(1), 24–38.

[116] Maheady, L., Michielli-Pendl, J., Mallette, B. & Harper, G.F. *A collaborate research project to improve the academic performance of a diverse sixth grade class*. **Teacher Education and Special Education**, 2002, 25(1), 55–70.

[117] Maheady, L., Michielli-Pendl, J., Mallette, B. & Harper, G.F. *A collaborate research project to improve the academic performance of a diverse sixth grade class*. **Teacher Education and Special Education**, 2002, 25(1), 55–70.

[118] Maheady, L., Mallette, B., Harper, G.F. & Sacca, K. *Heads together: A peer-mediated option for improving the academic achievement of heterogeneous learning groups*. **Remedial and Special Education**, 1991, 12(2), 25–33.

[119] Johnson, D.K., & Johnson, R.T. (1989). *Cooperation and Competition Theory and Research*, Edina, Minnesota: Interaction Book Company.

[120] Maheady, L., Harper, G.F. & Mallette, B. *The effects of Numbered Heads Together with and without an incentive package on the science test performance of a diverse group of sixth graders.* *Journal of Behavioral Education*, 2006, 15(1), 24–38.

[121] Maheady, L., Mallette, B., Harper, G.F. & Sacca, K. *Heads Together: A peer-mediated option for improving the academic achievement of heterogeneous learning groups.* *Remedial and Special Education*, 1991, 12(2), 25–33.

[122] Kagan, S. *Kagan Cooperative Learning Structures*. San Clemente, CA: Kagan Publishing, 2013.

Kagan, S. & M. Kagan. *Kagan Cooperative Learning*. San Clemente, CA: Kagan Publishing, 2009.

[123] Vaquero, L.M. & Cebrian, M. *The rich club phenomenon in the classroom.* *Scientific Reports*, 2013, 3(1174), 1–8.

[124] Bruner, J.S., Jolly, A. & Silva, K. (Eds). *Play—Its role in development and evolution*. New York, NY: Basic Books, 1976.

[125] Carter, R. *Mapping the Brain*. Los Angeles, CA: University of California Press, 1999.

[126] Diamond, M. *Enriching Heredity. The Impact of the Environment on the Anatomy of the Brain*. New York, NY: Macmillian, Inc., 1988.

[127] Denenberg, V.H., Woodcock, J.M. & Rosenberg, K.M. *Long-term effects of pre-weaning and post-weaning free-environment experience on rats' problem solving.* *Journal of Comparative Physiological Psychology*, 1968, 66, 533–535.

[128] Diamond, M.C. *Response of the brain to enrichment.* *Annals of the Brazilian Academy of Science*, 2001, 73(2), 211–222.

[129] Diamond, M.C. *Response of the brain to enrichment.* *Annals of the Brazilian Academy of Science*, 2001, 73(2), 211–222.

[130] Kempermann, G. Kuhn, H.G. & Gage, F.H. *More hippocampal neurons in adult mice living in an enriched environment.* *Nature*, 1997, 386(6624), 493–495.

York, A.D., Breedlove, S.M. & Diamond, M.C. *Housing adult male rats in enriched conditions increases neurogenesis in the dentate gyrus.* *Society for Neuroscience Abstracts*, 1989, 15, 962.

[131] Byers, J.A. *The distribution of play behaviour among Australian marsupials.* *Journal of Zoology*, 1999, 247(3), 349–356.

[132] Iwaniuk, A.N., Nelson, J.E. & Pellis, S.M. *Do big-brained animals play more? Comparative analyses of play and relative brain size in mammals.* *Journal of Comparative Psychology*, 2001, 115(1), 29–41.

[133] Panksepp, J. *Affective Neuroscience. The Foundations of Human and Animal Emotions*. New York, NY: Oxford University Press, 1998, 291.

[134] Hawes, A. *Jungle Gyms: The evolution of animal play.* *Smithsonian Zoogoer*, January/February, 1996, 26(1).

[135] Hawes, A. *Jungle Gyms: The evolution of animal play.* *Smithsonian Zoogoer*, January/February, 1996, 26(1).

[136] Van Leeuwen, E.J.C., Zimmermann, E. & Davila Ross, M. *Responding to inequities: gorillas try to maintain their competitive advantage during play fights.* *Biology Letters*, 2011, 7(1), 39–42.

[137] Brown, S. *Play. How it Shapes the Brain, Opens the Imagination, and Invigorates the Soul*. New York, NY: Penguin Group, 2009, 31–32.

[138] Main, M. & George, C. *Responses of young abused and disadvantaged toddlers to distress in agemates: A study in the day care setting.* *Developmental Psychology*, 1985, 21(3), 407–412.

[139] Brown, S. *Play. How it shapes the Brain, Opens the Imagination, and Invigorates the Soul*. New York, NY: Avery, 2009, 30.

[140] Hawes, A. *Jungle Gyms: The evolution of animal play.* *Smithsonian Zoogoer*, January/February, 1996, 26(1).

[141] Masson, J.M. & McCarthy, S. *When Elephants Weep. The Emotional Lives of Animals*. New York, NY: Dell Publishing, 1995, 126.

[142] Hawes, A. *Jungle Gyms: The evolution of animal play.* *Smithsonian Zoogoer*, January/February, 1996, 26(1).

[143] Masson, J.M. & McCarthy, S. *When Elephants Weep. The Emotional Lives of Animals*. New York, NY: Dell Publishing, 1995, 127.

[144] Masson, J.M. & McCarthy, S. *When Elephants Weep. The Emotional Lives of Animals*. New York, NY: Dell Publishing, 1995, 127.

[145] Fromm, P.J. *Whale Tales: Human Interactions with Whales, Volume 1*. Friday Harbor, WA: Whale Tales Press, 1996, 30.

[146] Kagan, S. *Silly Sports & Goofy Games*. San Clemente, CA: Kagan Publishing, 2000.

Emotion

We can harness emotion in our classrooms to create a passion for learning, to make our content more memorable, to motivate, and to improve problem solving and thinking. Just as fear constricts the ability to think, positive emotions broaden thinking. By eliciting positive emotion in our classrooms, we actually make students measurably smarter!

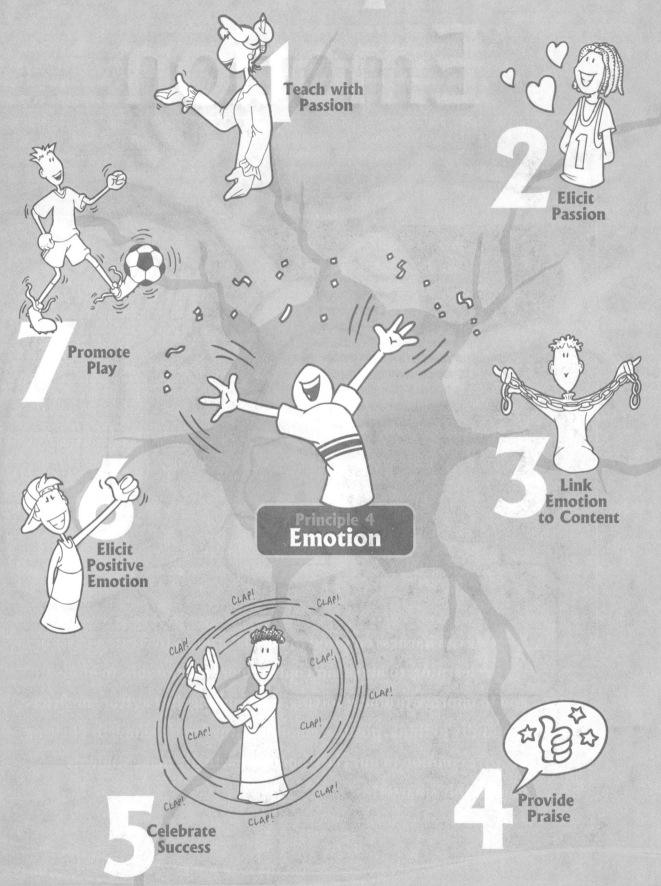

Principle 4
Emotion

1 Teach with Passion

2 Elicit Passion

3 Link Emotion to Content

4 Provide Praise

5 Celebrate Success

6 Elicit Positive Emotion

7 Promote Play

Teach with Emotion

The brain is designed to remember anything associated with emotion. We can prove this to ourselves with a simple experiment: Ask a group of people if they can remember where they were when they first heard about the two jets crashing into the Twin Towers on 9/11. Most will readily recall. Then ask if they can remember where they were the day before. Few will remember. Why? We are designed to remember events associated with emotion. This principle is called *retrograde memory enhancement*. It simply means any event followed by emotion is more likely to be cemented into memory. As teachers, we can apply this brain principle to make our content more memorable.

A very large body of research proves that positive emotion of any kind increases memory, thinking, creativity, and problem solving. It is easy to elicit positive emotion in our classrooms.

The brain research on emotion has a number of direct applications to improve instruction and to make our classrooms more brain-friendly. The emotions we generate moment to moment as we teach, either facilitate or inhibit learning. Here we will examine seven tools to teach with emotion, including ways to generate more passion for learning among students, and ways to generate more positive emotions in our classrooms.

Before examining the seven tools for teaching with emotion, let's explore how the study of emotion has revolutionized brain science.

Emotion: A Revolution in Brain Science

Our understanding of how emotion influences brain functioning has revolutionized our basic understanding of the brain. Emotions make our brains not just digital, but analog as well, and infinitely more complex. To grasp the enormity of this revolution in brain science, we need to understand a bit about neuropeptides and peptide hormones.

We now know that the probability of a neuron firing is not simply a result only of the messages received via its dendrite connections.

7 Tools to Teach with Emotion

1. **Teach with Passion** 4.6
2. **Elicit Passion** 4.6
3. **Link Emotion to Content** 4.7
4. **Provide Praise** 4.15
5. **Celebrate Success** 4.18
6. **Elicit Positive Emotion** 4.19
7. **Promote Play** 4.45

Traditionally, we thought neurons fire simply as a function of the messages they receive through their synapses. We now know neurons fire also in response to neuropeptides (that are created in cell bodies of neurons and glia cells) and by peptide hormones (that are secreted by cells all over the body). Peptide hormones are secreted from neuorendocrine cells and travel through the blood to distant tissues, allowing brain-body communication. Neuorpeptides and peptide hormones control our emotions including stress, relaxation, fear, anger, love, and caring. Candace Pert aptly calls neuropeptides "Molecules of Emotion."[1] Neuropeptides and peptide hormones also control cognitive functioning including learning, problem solving, and even test taking. Positive emotions broaden our thinking; negative emotions narrow our thinking.

Each neuron has its own set of receptors for neurotransmitters and neuropeptides: 1,000 for this one, 100 for that one, and so on. Depending on the neuropeptides present at any one moment, a neuron is more or less likely to fire. Each neuron is differentially responsive to the chemical composition of the brain at any moment.

To give a sense of the complexity of this system, consider that each neuron may have millions of receptors on its cell body surface, different numbers of different types—perhaps 10,000 of one type of receptor and 100,000 of another. Thus, a particular neuron may be quite sensitive to one type of neurotransmitter or neuropeptide, but relatively insensitive to another. Each receptor responds to only one type of neuropeptide or neurotransmitter and there are over 100 known neuropeptides, with more being discovered. For example, some receptors respond to opiates (endorphins, morphine, and heroine, which dampen pain and make us feel euphoric), other receptors on each neuron cell body respond to stress peptides (like cortisol, which makes us feel stressed and anxious).

Neurotransmitters, neuropeptides and peptide hormones each have different functions that determine our emotions. These chemical messengers regulate our heartbeat, how much we are attracted to someone, and how much we pay attention to and are motivated to complete learning tasks. Some neurotransmitters, like dopamine and norepinephrine, facilitate functions. Other neurotransmitters, like GABA, inhibit functions. They constantly influence not only how we feel, but also how well and in what ways our brains process and retain new information.

Neurons in different structures of the brain have different numbers of receptors of each type. For example, the centers for attention, motivation, and pleasure are particularly responsive to dopamine. Dopamine is released when we exercise, explaining why we are more focused and motivated following exercise. Ritalin, cocaine, and caffeine all mimic dopamine, which is why those drugs all enhance alertness, attention, and motivation. (That cocaine but not Ritalin is addictive is explained by the immediate release of cocaine compared to the slow, delayed release of Ritalin.) Just as our eyes and ears sense different types of stimuli in the external world, through the receptors on their cell walls, neurons sense different types of stimuli in the internal world of our bodies—emotional stimuli.

Peptides are produced not only by the neurons in the brain, but also in various parts of the body and these chemical messengers impact differentially on different neurons in the brain. The sensitivity of neurons to peptides and neuropeptides explains brain-body communication as well as communication among neurons. At any moment, the types of and amounts of neuropeptides our bodies are producing determines the emotions we are experiencing.

Neuropeptides are produced in the heart, spleen, bone marrow, lymph glands, dorsal horn of the spine and even the stomach, giving new meaning to the term, "Gut Feeling!"

Why is sensitivity to emotions so crucial to brain functioning? Emotions are the primitive signals that keep us alive by motivating us, keeping us from being bitten or eaten, care for and protect our progeny, and hunt for a tasty morsel. It is elegantly argued by Antonio Damasio[2] that the very origin of consciousness resides in the brain's capacity for emotion. The brain naturally focuses on and remembers stimuli associated with emotions. When strong emotion (positive or negative) is present, the amygdalae are active, and the more active they are, the greater the probability of subsequent memory of the emotion eliciting event.[3] The ability to respond to and remember what produces pain, fear, and pleasure keeps us alive. As a nation, we pay huge sums of money to keep our emotional reactions in tune, if only by exercising them vicariously through spectator movies, sports, and drama. That which makes us feel is critical for survival and so is remembered.

Emotions Inhibit or Facilitate Learning

The relation of emotion to learning and memory is much broader than simply stopping to punctuate success with praise and celebrations.

Neuropeptides Determine Learning

Emotions are the experience of the impact of neuropeptides attaching to receptors on the neuron surface, either stimulating or inhibiting an electrical charge. When we are depressed, our neurons are less likely to fire and less likely to make learning connections. When we are motivated, the opposite is true: We are disposed to attend to, process, and retain new information.

Depending on the emotions we engender in our classrooms, we inhibit or foster learning. The role emotion plays in the brain as a modifier of brain function has extreme implications for how best to structure the moment-to-moment life in our classrooms! The way we structure interaction in the classroom determines which neurotransmitters and which neuropeptides are released, and in which quantities. This in turn impacts dramatically on how likely our students are to pay attention to the learning task, how motivated they are to learn, and how free their working memory is to think and process academic content. If, for example, students are anxious, their brains release cortisol and ACTH, hormones that interfere with prefrontal cortex functioning, diminishing thinking and learning. If we do teambuilding, classbuilding, and other inclusion activities, students feel safer, release less stress hormones, and their brains think and learn better.

Thus we can derive the fourth principle of brain-friendly learning:

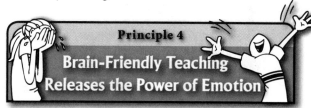

Principle 4

Brain-Friendly Teaching Releases the Power of Emotion

Seven Tools to Release the Power of Emotion

Emotion can facilitate or hinder learning. Fear inhibits the prefrontal cortex and we are less able to think, be creative, or learn. Positive emotions promote thinking and learning. Any intense emotion signals the brain to remember. If we are passionate about our content, that passion creates passion for learning among our students. If students celebrate each others' successes, they not only create a more positive, supportive classroom environment; but also they actually prime each others' brains to remember the content. Let's explore seven tools to harness the power of emotion for learning:

Seven Tools to Release the Power of Emotion

1. Teach with Passion
2. Elicit Passion
3. Link Emotion to Content
4. Provide Praise
5. Celebrate Success
6. Elicit Positive Emotion
7. Promote Play

Teach with Passion

In some workshops, I ask teachers to think back to when they were a student and to remember a teacher who really inspired them and interested them in the content of their class. I then ask them to stand if that teacher was personally passionate about the academic content. Almost all participants stand. Passion about the content is contagious. Teachers who are bored by their subject matter foster boredom; teachers who are personally excited about their content cultivate excitement among students. This is true in part because of mirror neurons: emotions are contagious.[4]

While reading a story to young students, we can exaggerate the emotions in the story, conveying with our voice, facial expressions, and gestures the surprise, fear, wonder, or love experienced by the characters. In our science class, we can conduct an experiment with a surprising outcome, exaggerating the wonder and curiosity the experiment engenders.

Tips

- Display your passion for your subject matter. The more excited you are about the content, the more excited your students will be.

- If you are bored by some content you must teach, find or create something in it that excites you!

In our history lesson, we can argue two opposite sides of an issue, each with passion, exaggerating the dilemma. Even our math lessons can be infused with emotion. We can show with great enthusiasm how an algorithm, proof, or even the mastery of the multiplication tables provides us a powerful tool.

Elicit Passion

In addition to expressing our own passion about the content, we can elicit passion for the content in our students in various ways. In Principle 6: Stimuli, we explore in some depth ways to make the content personally relevant and to have students construct meaning. Below are additional ways to make our curriculum exciting.

Choices. Giving students choices over what to study, how to study, and how to demonstrate their learning increases the probability of eliciting passion among students. When given a choice, students generally gravitate to topics that interest them.

Debates. One of the surest ways to have students become intensely involved in the content is to have students debate sides of an issue. A simple format is to break students into pairs with each student in the pair taking an opposing side of the issue. Pairs pair up so one pair watches the other pair debate, scoring for the number of arguments made and for persuasiveness. The pairs then switch roles so the judges become the debate pair. Debate content can be drawn from most academic content. For examples:

- ▶ History: Pro v. Con—Capital Punishment
- ▶ Science: Pro v. Con—Cloning
- ▶ Literature: Which of two poems or short stories is more impactful?
- ▶ Math: Which of two algorithms is more useful?
- ▶ Art: Which of two paintings has better use of composition, contrast…?
- ▶ Music: Which of two compositions evokes more emotion?

Brain-Friendly Teaching • Dr. Spencer Kagan
Kagan Publishing • 800.933.2667 • www.KaganOnline.com

Curricular Projects. Projects release passion. Students become intensely engaged in the process of creating something of their own design. Mini-projects can be infused throughout the curriculum:

- ▶ Social Studies: Have students draw a symbol that represents democracy.
- ▶ Science: Have students design an experiment that tests the inertia created by different surfaces.
- ▶ Literature: Have students write a poem in a style being studied.
- ▶ Geometry: Challenge students to create alternative proofs for a theorem.

Challenges. Passion is released when students attempt to meet a difficult challenge.

Challenging Questions. Some challenges are to find the answer to a difficult question or problem: *"How many square feet of lawn does it take to contain a million blades of grass?" "What is the sum of the numbers from 1 to 100?" "Given a paragraph, how can you rewrite it in as few words as possible without any loss of meaning?" "List as many consequences as you can of the invention of the computer." "Why do birds sing?"* Challenge students to answer intriguing questions or solve difficult problems that require out-of-the-box thinking.

Challenging Projects. Some challenges involve creating something: Propose an invention that will reduce litter. Create an economical plan that would make our city more beautiful. Design a way to improve the furniture arrangement in our class. Propose a way we can use our time in class to improve our average test scores. Add an additional layer of engagement and an enthusiasm for the content by creating team challenges and projects that require cooperation to succeed.

Field Trips. Field trips often elicit excitement. They can be made even more exciting by turning them into a scavenger hunt. Students are given a worksheet that challenges them to find certain objects and answer certain questions while on the field trip.

Tool 3

Link Emotion to Content

Our brains are designed to remember emotion-linked events. Emotion is the good stuff and the bad stuff; the painful stuff and the pleasurable stuff. If we are to survive, we must remember what hurts us (so we don't do that again) and what gives pleasure or relieves pain (so we do that again). Our brains are designed to help us survive and to help us pass along our genes. We get pleasure and happiness from those things that help us survive and pass along our genes (eating, sleeping, exercising, mating) and we get pain and sadness from those things that prevent our survival (losing a loved one, breaking a limb, going hungry, being isolated). After getting burned by touching a hot stove, we readily remember not to touch another hot stove. After tasting a unique and savory dessert, we readily remember the special restaurant that serves that great dessert.

If we are not teaching with emotion, we are not teaching for memory.

This principle, remembering things associated with emotion, in scientific lingo is called, *retrograde memory enhancement.* It is a principle discovered by James McGaugh and his co-workers, described in his classic book, *Memory and Emotion.*[5] McGaugh provides ample evidence that the brain is designed to remember anything associated with emotion. Retrograde memory enhancement is a basic principle of brain science.

As teachers, we can take advantage of this principle. All we have to do is teach in ways that link emotion to content we want our students to remember. Good teachers know that dry content is soon forgotten; exciting content is remembered. Think back to your years as a student. What

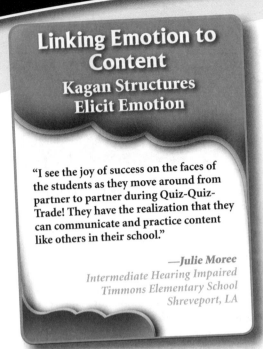

Linking Emotion to Content
Kagan Structures Elicit Emotion

"I see the joy of success on the faces of the students as they move around from partner to partner during Quiz-Quiz-Trade! They have the realization that they can communicate and practice content like others in their school."

—*Julie Moree*
Intermediate Hearing Impaired
Timmons Elementary School
Shreveport, LA

stands out in your memory? Is it the content of a lecture a teacher gave? Or is it some activity that generated emotion? If we have our students perform simulations of events we want them to remember, encouraging them to evoke emotion in the simulations, we make our content more memorable.

Emotion and Short- v. Long-Term Memory

To better understand the link between emotion and memory, we need to take a brief detour into the nature of short-term and long-term memory systems. Although a loud noise, or surprising stimuli will cause us to focus our attention on, and place something into short-term memory, it is emotion that cements the memory into long-term memory. Retrograde memory enhancement applies to long-term memory.

There is very strong evidence that short- and long-term memories are based on completely independent processes.[6] It does not surprise us to hear we can have short-term memory without long-term memory. What is shocking, though, is to learn that we can have long-term memory without short-term memory.[7] Contrary to how most people think, short-term memory does not turn into long-term memory. Injection of certain drugs *following* learning enhances long-term, but not short-term, memory. We have

independent short-term and long-term memory systems! The long-term memory system takes a longer time to consolidate (we recall better after sleeping on it). This feature is very adaptive because it allows us to give more weight to and better remember things that are followed by positive or negative consequences, even if those consequences occur well after the event. Any event that is *followed by* emotion is better remembered; this is the process called retrograde memory enhancement. Retrograde memory enhancement is adaptive: if emotion follows an experience, the brain says, "This is something worth remembering." Retrograde memory enhancement has important implications for us as teachers, indicating the need to follow important learning and task completion with emotion. Thus, it is important to include praise and celebrations following successes.

A brain-friendly classroom is one in which emotions are not avoided, but rather elicited in service of learning.

Tips

- Let students sleep on it. Memories are consolidated during sleep, especially those tagged by emotion as important.

- Introduce a skill and have students practice the skill in a brief practice session. Then, come back to the skill the next day after the students have consolidated the learning during a night's sleep.

- Teaching in several brief sessions, distributing practice, leads to greater memory than teaching a skill all in one session.

Kagan Structures Elicit Emotion

Most Kagan Structures evoke emotion. The structures have students experience praise, celebrations, expressing and defending one's point of view, disagreements, sense of accomplishment, and/or pride in mastery. In many ways, Kagan Structures link emotion to the learning of content. For examples, see Table: Kagan Structures Elicit Emotion, below and p. 4.10.

Kagan Structures Elicit Emotion

Structures	Structure Section	How Emotions Are Elicited
AllWrite Consensus	1	Emotion is generated as students express and defend their own points of view, and again when they reach consensus.
Celebrity Interview	3	Students enjoy the status of being the celebrity and receiving the applause and attention of their teammates.
Flashcard Game	5	Each time a student responds correctly, the student wins his or her flashcard back and receives "surprising, delightful" praise. Students receive praise for every card, either right away if they had the correct answer, or after the coaching helps them arrive at the correct answer.
Formations	6	Students struggle to accomplish the formation, especially if no talking is allowed. There is pride in accomplishment when they succeed.
Listen Right!	8	After students hear back from the teacher on the key points of the passage, they praise each other if they included those points in their notes.
Number Group Mania!	9	There is considerable excitement as students move to sort themselves into the required groups. Students grab others to join their group and welcome them. Students feel needed.
Paraphrase Passport	12	Students feel understood and accepted when they are correctly paraphrased.
PairUp Review Quiz-Quiz-Trade RallyQuiz Sage-N-Scribe	11 13 14 17	Correct responses receive praise or celebrations. Students are encouraged to use different praise for each question and to elicit surprise and delight.
SeeOne–DoOne–TeachOne	18	Students feel pride and a sense of accomplishment when they are able to teach a partner a new skill.
Simulations	19	Students are encouraged to evoke emotion in their classmates via their simulation to make it more memorable. Anxiety prior to performance and a sense of accomplishment after the performance are common.

(continues)

Kagan Structures Elicit Emotion continued

Structures	Structure Section	How Emotions Are Elicited
Swap Talk	21	Emotion is elicited as students thank each other for what they have shared, while looking for and greeting a new partner, and while parting.
Team-Pair-Solo	23	Students feel a sense of accomplishment when they advance to "Solo"—able to solve problems alone that before they could only solve with help.
Three-Step Interview	24	Emotion is generated as students ask and answer interview questions. They feel understood in Step 3, when they are introduced to the team.
Timed Pair Share	25	This structure is often used to have students express their own thoughts and feelings. Students enjoy the uninterrupted attention.
Traveling Heads Together	26	Excitement mounts as the spinner is spun to see who will be called on to travel. Students enjoy applause after answering.

Converting Dry Data into an Exciting Discovery

There are many ways to structure our learning activities so they evoke emotion. When teaching a lesson on the sizes and distances from Earth of the objects in the solar system, I first gave a worksheet to each student team with the raw data See Blackline: Size and Distance of Sun and Planets, p. 4.11. These cold facts evoked no emotion at all.

After giving student teams the worksheet with the raw data, I had students translate the facts into something they could relate to. They were to figure out:
1. The time it would take in a passenger jet traveling at 600 miles an hour to travel to the moon.
2. The time it would take in a passenger jet traveling at 600 miles an hour to travel to the sun.

After completing these two calculations, students were amazed! Students had no idea how close the moon is to us compared to how far the sun is from us. This amazement cemented the content into memory.

At this point in the lesson I asked, *"If these two celestial bodies are so incredibly different in distance from us, why do they look about the same size?"* This launched us into some calculations on relative size. To answer the relative size question, we did three more simple calculations:
1. The time it would take in a passenger jet traveling at 600 miles an hour to travel around the moon.
2. The time it would take in a passenger jet traveling at 600 miles an hour to travel around the earth.
3. The time it would take in a passenger jet traveling at 600 miles an hour to travel around the sun.

After completing these three calculations, students experienced amazement and a sense of wonder. For the first time, students grasped how small the moon is compared to the incredible size of the sun. At this point, their interest was piqued in the relative size of the other planets, and so students broke into pairs using **Sage-N-Scribe** to fill in the missing cells in the table, converting diameter to circumference.

The math is easy:
1. Fill in the empty cells of the table by determining the circumference of each planet in miles using the formula $C = d \times \pi$ where C= Circumference; d = Diameter; π = 3.14. (A story about Archimedes, the Greek mathematician of the 3rd century who discovered π, the ratio of circumference to diameter, adds interest.)
2. Divide the circumference in miles by 600 to determine the number of hours a trip around the planet would take.
3. Divide the number of hours by 24 to convert hours into days.

Size and Distance of Sun and Planets

Directions: Use this worksheet to record size and distance of the moon and the planets.

Solar Object	Distance from Sun	Travel Time in Jet (at 600 miles an hour)	Diameter	Circumference	Time for Jet to Circumnavigate (at 600 miles an hour)
Sun			865,000 miles 1,392,684 km		
Earth's Moon	Lunar Distance (LD)* 238,900 miles; 384,400 km		2,159 miles 3,474 km		
Mercury	36 million miles 57.9 million km		3,031 miles 4,878 km		
Venus	67.2 million miles 108.2 million km		7,521 miles 12,104 km		
Earth	93 million miles 149.6 million km		7,926 miles 12,756 km		
Mars	141.6 million miles 227.9 million km		4,222 miles 6,787 km		
Jupiter	483.6 million miles 778.3 million km		88,729 miles 142,796 km		
Saturn	886.7 million miles 1,427.0 million km		74,600 miles 120,660 km		
Uranus	1,784.0 million miles 2,871.0 million km		32,600 miles 51,118 km		
Neptune	2,794.4 million miles 4,497.1 million km		30,200 miles 48,600 km		
Pluto (dwarf planet)	3,674.5 million miles 5,913.5 million km		1,413 miles 2,274 km		

*LD = Lunar Distance: Distance of the moon from the Earth

Space Travel

In your mind, reduce the earth to the size of a grape. Hold on to that image. That is shrinking it quite a bit because each of us would be the size of an atom! But on that scale, we can grasp some relative distances.

If the earth were the size of a grape, the moon would be 1 foot from the earth, and about the size of a BB. The sun would be a city block away and have the diameter of about 6 feet, the height of a tall person. A BB compared to a person, that is the difference in size between the moon and the sun. They look about the same size to us because the moon is so much closer.

Another way to grasp relative sizes of sun, moon, and Earth: Let's say you get into a passenger jet and decide to take a trip around each one. The moon's circumference is 6,790 miles around. Earth is almost 25,000 miles around at the equator. The sun is 2,713,406, or almost 3 million, miles in circumference. Traveling at 600 miles an hour in a passenger jet, it would take you half a day to fly around the moon (11.3 hours); less than 2 days to fly around Earth (1.73 days); but more than half a year (188 days) to fly around the sun. Although the moon and the sun look about the same size to us, it would take half a day to fly around the moon, and half a year to fly around the sun!

Now let's get in our passenger jet and travel to the moon and then to the sun. It will take us 17 days to get to the moon, but we have to travel much longer to get to the sun. It will take us 17 years to get to the sun! The sun is that far away!

The solar system is really big. Earth is one of the inner planets, relatively close to the sun. In our passenger jet, it would take 17 years to travel from the earth to the sun, but to travel to Pluto, at the outer reaches of our solar system, it would take 698 years!

The moral: By translating raw data into something the students can relate to, we can create activities that generate surprise and wonder, making our content more memorable. The lesson on the size and distance of objects in our solar system as well as the content in the box on Space Travel, illustrate ways to make raw data and abstract ideas concrete. **The trick:** Convert the abstract into the concrete and translate it into something students can relate to. It is difficult to relate to a large number, but easy to relate to time spent in an airplane. See Box: Space Travel.

Attaching emotion to abstraction is an uphill battle. It is much easier to attach emotion to ideas, principles, and theories once students can relate to them in concrete terms. It is our job as teachers to present the curriculum to students in ways they can connect to in terms of their personal experience, and then to make that content more memorable by linking the curriculum to emotion when possible. For an in-depth exploration of ways to make the curriculum relevant, see Tool 12: Establish Relevance, in Principle 6: Stimuli.

Tip

Translate dry or abstract data into something students can relate to from their personal experience. Without personal relevance, it is nearly impossible to elicit emotion. Personal relevance is the key to emotion and memory.

Surprise and wonder are but two of the many emotions we can evoke to make our content more interesting and memorable. In teaching a lesson on the Great Depression, we have students do a simulation to evoke empathy, pity, and anger. We create debates so students feel competitive. We create challenges for our teams so they feel pride in accomplishment.

Teaching with Emotion: What Do Teachers Say?

When I ask teachers about integrating emotion into their academic lessons, they often report lessons that evoke emotion are among the very best they offer. Emotion is elicited via debates, simulations, role-plays, linking the content to personal concerns, and by including emotion-eliciting curriculum content. See Table: Linking Emotion to the Curriculum.

For examples, elementary teachers read with emotion children's literature (e.g., *How to Eat Fried Worms* by Thomas Rockwell) and have students debate issues raised by stories. (Should Goldilocks have gone into the Bears' house? She was cold and hungry, but it was not her house.) Having students role-play a scene from the western movement in which they must decide on only one toy they can bring with them in the covered wagon helps them feel the sacrifice made by the settlers. Having older students design and present a simulation of what the stock market crash of 1929 meant for employees and families makes the content memorable.

Secondary teachers describe a variety of ways they have linked emotion to their content:

Linking Emotion to the Curriculum

Subject Grade Teacher	Lesson Abstract
Integrated Career Unit Middle School **–Shannon Rewerts**	**Economics.** We talk about supply and demand, consuming, opportunity cost, trade-offs, types of income, and budgeting. The kids make choices by going through a monthly budget with a salary they receive for a career they are interested in researching. They do an estimate, talk to parents about budgeting for certain items, and then create an actual budget based on their salary. They have federal and state taxes taken out, which is a huge eye opener for the kids. **Language Arts.** Kids create a résumé for the project that includes degrees they would have to obtain for their careers, work experiences, and references. They write a letter of application to a place of employment. They create business cards related to their career. **Mathematics.** Kids build various graphs for their projects (e.g., bar graphs with projected earnings over a lifetime, pie graphs that depict how their household budgets are spent.)
History Middle School **–Deb Kuntz**	I did a simulation lesson: Arriving at Ellis Island. When students entered class, they received a "passport" and had to visit areas of the room before going through the door labeled New York. Once class started, I closed the door and told them a story about what it was like to be on the ship. Once we "arrived" on Ellis Island, students lined up to be seen by the "doctor" (me and the resource teacher). Each student was given a card with an X for possibly handicapped, L for lame, B for blind, or P for pregnant. All students with the same letters moved to a different part of the classroom to represent who would be sent back to their home country. We explained what the letters meant so they knew why they were being sent back. We had the number of students in each category in about the same percentage as people sent back during that time period. *(continued)*

Brain-Friendly Teaching • Dr. Spencer Kagan
Kagan Publishing • 800.933.2667 • www.KaganOnline.com

Principle 4
4.13

Linking Emotion to the Curriculum continued

Subject Grade Teacher	Lesson Abstract
Social Studies High School **—Eric Hanson**	I create congressional committees in each class to debate, revise, amend, and vote on pieces of legislation. I pick debate topics like immigration, student loans, and legalization of marijuana. I use school administrators as witnesses before the committee, and students ask questions regarding the topic.
Language Arts High School **—Vern Minor**	I had my students read Shakespeare's *Romeo and Juliet*. Every year, my students dreaded having to read the work, but it became the students' favorite. I believe it was because of the emotions it stimulated. There are several very strong themes that resonate with students: teenage suicide, young love, family conflict, mortality, fate v. free will. Our discussions were very passionate.
Science High School **—Ryan Lacson**	For many students, my Biology II course is their first honors class. With each new group, I have to move their recall-driven, black-and-white minds into the higher-level, gray-area-dwelling world of an honors course. To do this, I start the year with a short bioethics unit. Many students are used to science being purely objective, but the ethics unit forces them to apply objective facts towards a subjective topic (e.g., organ transplant lists, gender-reassignment in athletics, stem-cell research). In the process, students can get pretty heated, but many tell me it forced them to reflect on, question, and defend their beliefs.
Science High School **—Garrett Prevo**	In our unit on nuclear reactions, we describe how a nuclear reaction occurs and the unbelievable amount of energy that is released with the fission of each atom. We talk about the various uses for nuclear reactions. Inevitably, the nuclear bomb is mentioned. We then discuss how those bombs work. Finally, we talk about the ethical implications of nuclear energy. I show them videos and pictures of the destruction from Chernobyl, Hiroshima, and Nagasaki. This always elicits emotions and helps students remember concepts and implications around nuclear energy.

Tool 4

Provide Praise

If we have students praise each other when they are successful, it evokes emotion, which by the principle of retrograde memory enhancement makes lessons more memorable. The praise, however, must be surprising. If students simply say, "Good job" every time, all novelty and emotion soon wear off. Thus we teach students a variety of praise gambits and encourage them to create their own surprising and delightful praisers.

Do Rewards Undermine Intrinsic Motivation?

In his book, *Punished by Rewards*, Alfie Kohn argued that rewards erode intrinsic motivation.[8] The argument is straightforward: When we reward students for their performance, they begin working for the reward rather than the intrinsic pleasure of succeeding at a task. If we then take away the reward, students will not be motivated to perform the task. On the basis of this argument, many educators have pulled back from offering rewards for performance and even became hesitant to offer praise to students.

We must be careful not to overgeneralize. Only under very special circumstances does praise undermine intrinsic motivation. Praise far more often increases motivation. Research has firmly established that praise is a powerful positive motivator more often increasing rather than undermining motivation.[9] An extensive meta-analysis that examined the results of 96 experimental studies revealed that verbal praise does not undermine intrinsic motivation. The authors conclude: "In summary, subjects rewarded with verbal praise or positive feedback show significantly greater intrinsic motivation than non-rewarded subjects."[10]

Praise Undermines Intrinsic Motivation Only in Special Circumstances. There is one very special set of circumstances in which praise can undermine intrinsic motivation. To understand how this can come about, we need to understand the concept of an *attribution shift*. Attribution theory describes how we explain to ourselves why we do what we do. For example, if someone offers me $100 to wash his or her car and while I am washing the car, someone asks me, *"Why are you washing that car?"* I will say, *"To earn $100."* I am *attributing* my actions to earning the money.

An attribution shift can occur when someone who is performing for intrinsic rewards shifts to performing for extrinsic rewards. For example, imagine a student who really enjoys drawing and who, if given the opportunity, would gladly draw pictures for no extrinsic reward. If you ask the student why she is drawing, she likely would say, *"Because I like to draw."* The student is making an intrinsic motivation attribution; the student is attributing her motivation to internal factors, not an external reward. Now let's imagine further that we begin to pay the student $50 for each drawing the student produces. After doing a number of drawings and receiving $50 for each, someone asks the student why she is drawing. At that point the student is likely to say, *"Because I get paid for each drawing."* The student has made an attribution shift. Prior to being paid, she made an internal attribution (*"I like to draw"*); after consistently being paid for each drawing, the student shifted to making an external attribution (*"I get paid"*). The student no longer experiences herself as drawing for the intrinsic pleasure, but for the extrinsic pay. Now, let's imagine one more step to this scenario: We take away the pay. After consistently being paid for each drawing, we say to the student, *"I will no longer pay you to draw."* We then ask the student if she will draw for no pay. Some students in this situation would likely say, *"If I am not going to be paid, I won't draw."*

What has happened in this scenario is that extrinsic reward (pay) has undermined intrinsic motivation (desire to draw for the rewards intrinsic to the task). It is this possibility that is at the heart of the argument that students are punished by rewards. The argument is that by providing students extrinsic rewards, tokens, sweets, or praise, we are likely to undermine their intrinsic motivation. Note, however, intrinsic motivation is undermined only in a very special case. As we have seen, rewards can erode motivation only if two things happen: (1) students who were intrinsically motivated make an attribution shift, thinking they are now working only for the external reward, and (2) following that, the rewards are taken away. The reason the argument that praise reduces intrinsic motivation is an overgeneralization is that most rewards do not lead to an attribution shift. For example, a student is drawing and the teacher walks by and says, *"I really like the way you have used contrast in your painting."* The teacher is praising the student, but the student does not suddenly make an attribution shift saying to himself or herself, "I am only painting because the teacher praises me." Most praise does not lead to an attribution shift and does not erode intrinsic motivation. As we have seen, the empirical work lands on the other side: Praise increases motivation.

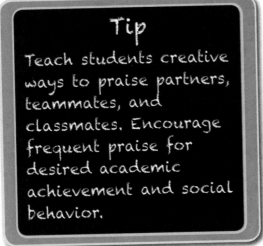

Tip

Teach students creative ways to praise partners, teammates, and classmates. Encourage frequent praise for desired academic achievement and social behavior.

Fostering Intrinsic Motivation

It is important to foster intrinsic motivation. As much as possible, we need to create learning tasks that are intrinsically motivating. There is an easy check to determine if students are intrinsically motivated: We ask them. If we ask students why they are doing a learning task and they respond, "for the points," "for the token," or "for a grade," we need to reexamine our curriculum and instruction. Students will be intrinsically motivated to the extent the learning task is appropriately challenging (not too easy; not too difficult) and to the extent we are using engaging instructional strategies.

In Praise of Praise

A great deal is to be said in favor of praise—praise from teachers and from fellow students. Praise changes brain functioning in beneficial ways, and has a number of positive psychological outcomes.

Praise and the Brain. If we examine what happens in the brain when a student receives any reward, including praise, we find a release of dopamine. Dopamine not only stimulates the pleasure centers, it stimulates the motivation and attention centers so students are more alert and more motivated to complete tasks. Because praise makes students feel supported, they feel safe. As we have seen, this puts the amygdalae to rest, allowing full function of the prefrontal context. Students in a supportive social environment can think more clearly and be more creative.[11] Their brains are closer to the optimal state for learning: relaxed alertness. We will cover in depth the influence of positive emotions on the brain in Tool 6: Elicit Positive Emotion, in Principle 4: Emotion.

Psychological Benefits of Praise. Praise helps students feel part of a positive, supportive social community. Students know they have the support of their teammates and classmates. We all enjoy praise. It helps us feel appreciated and competent, and increases our motivation.

Praise influences our self-evaluation. When we are praised for an accomplishment, our self-concept is influenced. We feel, "I am good at this." This in turn increases our motivation in two ways. Once we feel we are good at a type of task, we persist longer in the face of difficulty. We live up to our self-concept. Secondly, we persist at the task in anticipation of future praise.

Creative Praise

Cheese Grater

Alaska Hurray

Round of Applause

Truck Driver

For additional creative ways to praise, see *Kagan Cooperative Learning*.[12]

Praise is the opposite of criticism. Criticism leads us to avoid tasks, lowering our motivation. Students, whose teachers mark only the errors on their essays or math tests, become demotivated. They avoid those tasks in anticipation of future criticism and internalize a low self-evaluation, aligning their behavior with their low self-evaluation.

Thus we include plenty of praise from teammates and partners as students master new skills. See Box: Creative Praise.

Kagan Structures Include Praise

Many Kagan Structures include praise as an essential element. See Table: Kagan Structures Elicit Emotion, pp. 4.9–4.10. During the **Flashcard Game**, for example, each time a student responds correctly to the flashcard question, the student wins the card back and receives "surprising, delightful" praise. The surprise creates novelty to which brains attend, and the delightful praise is designed to elicit positive emotion. We tell students, *"If you put a smile on the face of your partner, you have given him or her a dose of dopamine which has reached the pleasure center in the brain."*

Tool 5

Celebrate Success

Student cheers and celebrations are another way to elicit positive emotion. Praise is something we give to an individual or team following a good performance. Cheers are something a team or class does to celebrate their own performance. While teaching, we include team and class cheers, fun handshakes, pats on the back, and high fives. Punctuating our activities with emotion creates a positive class tone and makes our content more memorable.

There are many cheers. Among my favorites are the unique cheers teams and classes develop themselves. I was observing a classroom in Australia when, during a lesson, a boy came up to the teacher to show her a new cheer his team had created. He first crossed his arms in front of himself to make a large letter X. Then he waved his right hand from right to left, symbolizing the motion of a stream. When the teacher asked what his cheer was, he smiled and said, *"Extreme!"* Not

missing a beat, the teacher stopped the lesson and announced the boy had a new cheer to share with the class. After the boy modeled the cheer, the teacher had everyone practice it, making the movements and simultaneously saying, *"Extreme!"*

When the Australian boy shared with his teacher and class the new cheer his team had come up with, he and the class were broadening their repertoire of cheers. The class had been shown and had practiced a number of "premade" cheers. Then they had been encouraged to come up with their own unique cheers. By increasing their repertoire of cheers, the class had more creativity, variety, and novelty. It was a more brain-friendly classroom. See Box: Creative Cheers, p. 4.19.

Praise
Business Cards in a Detergent Box!

"I printed off cheers and praises onto business cards and put them into a recycled box of 'Cheers' detergent. We would draw them out as options to praise and cheer during structures or after activities. Students became motivated to make up new cheers and praises so their idea could be added to the box."

—Rachel Treaster
2nd Grade, Linwood Elementary USD 259 Wichita, KS

Tip
Encourage teams to invent and share new cheers.

Creative Cheers

Fireworks

Team High Five

Sparkles

SNAP!
SNAP!
SNAP!

Western Wahoo

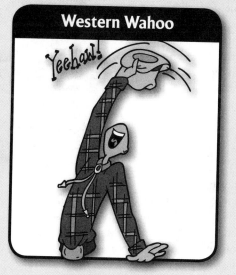

Yeehaw!

For additional creative cheers, see *Kagan Cooperative Learning*.[13]

Tool 6

Elicit Positive Emotion

A large body of research converges on one conclusion: Eliciting positive emotion is one of our easiest, most powerful, research-based tools to create a brain-friendly classroom. Nearly 300 research studies demonstrate that eliciting positive emotions improves thinking, problem solving , health, learning, energy, creativity, friendships, and even test taking.[14] Most important for us as teachers: When we elicit positive emotions in any way (think about your favorite dessert, do a team cheer, describe to a partner a present you have received that you really liked), students have broader attention and are able to think better. Taking just a few minutes to elicit positive emotions literally makes our students more perceptive and smarter!

Negative Emotions v. Positive Emotions

When we talk about "positive emotions," we are referring to emotions we are pleased to have, emotions like joy, playfulness, contentment, interest, and hope. "Negative emotions" are emotions we would rather not experience— emotions like anger, frustration, anxiety, fear, and sadness. Negative emotions, however, are not bad. Anger prepares us to counter an attack or overcome an obstacle. Fear prepares us to avoid something that might harm us. Sadness is our reaction to loss, letting us know what we value, preparing us to avoid future loss, if possible. Nevertheless, positive and negative emotions are fundamentally different in ways that explain why positive emotions open us up to think more broadly and negative emotions generally constrict our ability to think and be creative.

Negative emotions prepare us for quick action. Let's take fear for example. Even before we can think about it, we jump back from the snake in our path. In the face of threat, we don't want to be looking around and contemplating all the options. As anger intensifies, we prepare to fight and we need to keep a narrow focus on our opponent. We get tunnel vision, shutting out the irrelevant stimuli in our peripheral vision. In the face of a threat, we rely on biologically determined action responses: fight, flee, or freeze. Those organisms that didn't react to threat quickly and instinctively, didn't survive. To ponder creative new responses in the face of threat can mean death. When we are faced with stimuli that create negative emotions, it is adaptive for our cognition, perception, and behavioral options to narrow.

In her "broaden-and-build" theory of positive emotions, Barbara Fredrickson contrasts the functions of positive and negative emotions.[15] When we are happy, we do not have to prepare for immediate action. Joy does not give us impetus to act quickly in a predetermined way. We are free to think and feel—to enjoy the moment.

We look around and take it all in. When we are in a good mood, we explore; we are less likely to stick to the familiar.[16] Positive emotions broaden our perceptions and cognitions. Playfulness is a prototypic positive emotion. Joy and playfulness share the same neural tracks.[17] Play is creative, spontaneous, and often aimless. Play is a time to experiment, to try anything, to learn. We try on new responses, some of which work and some of which don't, but in the process, we broaden our response repertoire. This is adaptive. Having a broader response repertoire, we can be more adaptive in the future. The empirical research strongly supports the remarkable conclusion that when we are happy, we are smarter!

Beneficial Effects of Eliciting Positive Emotions

Eliciting positive emotions has numerous positive effects including, enhanced problem solving and creativity, broadened thinking and perception, improved test taking, as well as increased earnings and longevity. In addition, positive emotions can "undo" the negative effects of negative emotions. Some of the ways of eliciting positive emotions take but a few minutes, yet have profound and lasting impact.

Positive Emotions Promote Problem Solving and Creativity. Among adults and children, a wide range of methods converge on the same conclusion: Make people happy and they are better able to solve problems and come up with creative solutions.

> ▶ Prior to making a difficult clinical diagnosis on a liver disease case, physicians were randomly assigned to two conditions. Half were given a small bag of hard candy (only ten pieces colorfully wrapped) and were told they were not allowed to eat the candy until later. The other half of the doctors did not receive candy. Those who were given the candy just before making their diagnosis more often made the correct diagnosis. They took in more information and thought more broadly, considering all the options before settling on a diagnosis. In contrast, those not given the candy more often made their diagnosis based on their first, wrong impression.[18]

- Negotiators given a small gift prior to a difficult negotiation more often come up with win-win solutions.[19]

- In 1945, a famous test of flexible thinking and creative problem solving was developed.[20] Participants were presented with a book of matches, a small box of tacks, and a candle. (See Figure: Candle Problem.) They were given the following instructions: *Show how to fix the lit candle on the corkboard wall in a way that it won't drip on the table below.*

Candle Problem

Some people find the solution and others do not. Finding the solution depends on breaking the set of seeing the box as a container for tacks and seeing it instead as a candle stick holder that can be fastened to the wall. (See Figure: Candle Solution.) Solution depends on flexible thinking and putting ideas together in new and useful ways. In this case, creative problem solving is almost literally thinking outside the box!

Candle Solution

What is nothing short of amazing is that given the creative thinking problem to solve, eighth grade students, college students, and adults in separate experiments in different labs, all found the solution significantly more often if positive emotion is elicited before presenting the problem![21] The experiments were sophisticated. To test that positive emotion was causing the improved problem solving, not something specific about the way positive emotion was elicited, different ways of eliciting positive emotion were used (gift of small bag of candy v. watching a brief comedy film clip). The finding: It does not matter how the positive emotion is elicited, it still results in more solutions. To test that positive emotion rather than just emotional arousal caused the improvement, negative emotions were tested. Negative emotions did not work. To test that positive emotion rather than just heightened arousal caused the improvement, physical exercise was tested. That too did not work. Only eliciting positive emotion improved flexible thinking and problem solving.

Laughter Boosts Creativity. In a classic study of the effects of laughter on creativity,[22] researchers first used an audiometer to test four different recordings of audience reaction to comedians, to pick the one that produced the longest and loudest laughter among students. They then tested the effect of that comedy on the creativity of 282 tenth grade students. Half the students were given a creativity pretest, and half were not. Half of each of those two groups listened to the comedy before being retested on creativity and the other half served as controls.

> **Tip**
> Before having students take a test or perform anything that takes thinking or problem solving, have them engage in an activity that elicits positive emotions.

Tip

Have the students view a comedy clip or hear a few jokes before any project that demands creativity.

To test for creativity, researchers used the Torrance Tests of Creative Thinking that measures fluency of ideas, flexibility of ideas, and originality of ideas. Results showed that for girls and boys, and for pretested and non-pretested groups, creativity was significantly greater for students following a good laugh. See Graph: Humor Boosts Creativity.

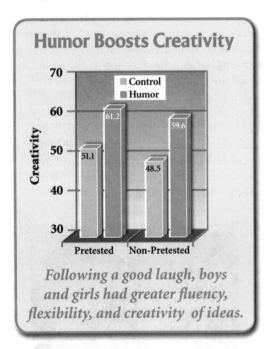

Humor Boosts Creativity

Following a good laugh, boys and girls had greater fluency, flexibility, and creativity of ideas.

There are many possible interpretations as to why humor boosts creativity. The broaden-and-build theory offers one interpretation. Other interpretations are possible. Much of humor is based on imagining the impossible and/or on hitting the audience with the unexpected. We laugh at the unusual and ridiculous. Creativity too relies on suspending the usual rules and thinking out of the box. With both humor and

creativity, we stop being practical and logical. Humor involves the unexpected; a defining characteristic of creativity is openness to the unusual and non-conventional. "Laughter is a sense of freedom from the limitations of the real world."[23] Thus it could be that listening to humor models the mindset necessary to come up with set-breaking thinking that is at the heart of creativity. However, it works. The research reveals we can boost creativity by the use of humor.

Positive Emotion Broadens Thinking.
Another series of studies found positive emotion broadens thinking: After positive emotion is elicited, people have more ideas!

▶ After viewing films that elicit positive emotions, college students write more ideas than after viewing films that elicit negative emotions.[24]

▶ After watching a comedy film or after being given a bag of candy, participants come up with more remote word associations indicating broader thinking.[25]

▶ After eliciting positive emotion in adolescent students, students increase in verbal fluency, ability to find categories, and come up with unusual examples of items for the categories—in short, they are better at thinking![26]

Tip

Prior to administering a test, call on a few students to draw a joke from the joke jar to read to the whole class.

Positive Emotion Broadens Perception.
Attention opens up after people experience positive emotions. People scan more and notice more.

▶ After viewing films that elicit amusement or contentment, perception is broader than after viewing films that elicit anger or anxiety.[27]

- When participants are presented with positive words, they are more perceptually flexible. That is, in visual tasks, they are better able to see the big picture and also better able to attend to the details. They better see both the forest and the trees.[28]
- Brain scans reveal positive affective states increase and negative affective states decrease responses to novel stimuli. "These findings collectively suggest that affective valence differentially biases gating of early visual inputs, fundamentally altering the scope of perceptual encoding."[29]
- Eye movement studies show that negative emotional states like anxiety and fear narrow attention and focus.[30]
- Participants given a small bag containing five chocolate candies before entering an eye-scanning test have broader attention and more frequently scan the visual field.[31]

> **Tip**
>
> Before a lecture or demonstration, elicit positive emotion. Have students recall in detail a positive experience.

Positive Emotion Improves Test Taking. At all grades tested, students perform better on tests after experiencing positive emotions.
- When positive emotions are elicited prior to giving people a difficult remote association test, both college students and practicing physicians score better.[32] For example, a sample question asked for a word that links the words *mower, atomic,* and *foreign.* People who experienced positive emotions prior to the test more often came up with the correct linking words, in this case: *power.*
- Positive emotion was elicited prior to a math test by telling students to "Think of a time when they were extremely happy." Students were given 5 minutes to complete as many math problems as they could

from grade-appropriate math worksheets. Those given the positive mood induction prior to the test solved significantly more problems correctly. This finding held true for all populations tested: Third through fifth grade at-risk students; third through fifth grade non-risk students; and junior and senior high school students with learning disabilities. Positive emotions raise expectations: Among the older students, those who were assigned to think of an extremely happy time predicted they would solve more problems.[33]
- Four-year-old children completed a block assembly task more quickly and with fewer errors if they were simply asked beforehand to think about something that made them happy![34]

Positive Emotion Predicts Life Earnings and Longevity. Those with positive emotions become richer and actually live longer!
- College freshmen who score higher on a test of happiness had a higher income nineteen years later, and it was not a function of their initial level of income.[35]
- Years ago, as they were about to take their final vows and leave the convent, Catholic nuns were asked to write a very brief (200 to 300 words on a single page) autobiography containing interesting, edifying, and outstanding events in their life. The nuns averaged 22 years of age. Those autobiographies were archived. By year 2000, the nuns averaged 80 years of age and 76 of them had died. To determine if there was a relation between longevity and positive emotion expressed sixty years before, their autobiographies were taken from archive and analyzed for frequency of expression of positive, negative, and neutral emotions. Very few negative emotions were expressed, but the nuns differed remarkably in number of positive emotion words and sentences they included in their autobiographies. Among the half of the nuns who had the fewest positive emotion words, 57% had died; among the half that had written the most positive emotion words only 27% had died. Given their differential

mortality rates, for the half of the nuns who had the fewest positive emotion words, the probability of being alive by age 90 was only 30%, but for those nuns who had the most positive emotion words, the probability of reaching 90 years of age was over twice that—65%![36]

Why Are Positive Emotions So Powerful?

That positive emotions result in so many different positive outcomes seems almost mystical. Eliciting positive emotions results in 4-year-olds assembling blocks with fewer errors and is correlated with nuns living dramatically longer! How is it that if we ask students to remember a happy time, a few minutes later they score significantly higher on a math test? There is something happening in the moment. But there is also something happening in a lifetime, otherwise, why would a single-page autobiography written at age 22 so eerily predict if a person will be living or dead by 80 years of age? Let's first examine these two questions separately—what happens in a lifetime, and what happens in the moment—and then look for the common thread.

Why Did the Nuns Live Longer? The nun study is particularly fascinating for two reasons. First, we all want to live longer, and if we can figure out what was going on with the nuns, it might help us reach our goal. Second, the nuns were all living a very similar lifestyle, so the study resembles a controlled experiment. That is, all of the nuns in the study were not drinking, were religious, were living in the same area of the country, had somewhat similar types of work, and lived in moderate conditions. That so many variables are controlled, narrows down our search.

In spite of their similarity in lifestyle, how frequently they expressed positive emotions at age 22 predicted their longevity. Those who expressed more positive emotion words and sentences lived much longer. How can we explain this?

There are daily stressors every person faces, even nuns. When they left the convent, the nuns went to work in low-income schools, hospitals, shelters for the homeless, and had other placements that on a daily basis create stress for caretakers. Anxiety and stress generated by seeing suffering and not always being able to help, takes a toll—especially if your vow is to alleviate suffering. Stress and anxiety set off the sympathetic nervous system fight-or-flight reaction that stresses the cardiovascular system and is a primary cause of heart disease and death.[37] Stress compromises immune system functioning, creates susceptibility to stress-related physical disease, and has been associated also with increased incidence of cancer.[38]

Given that stress created by negative emotions is inevitable, and prolonged and/or repeated stress is associated with increased probability of life-threatening disease, anything that can turn off the negative effects of stress would promote a longer life. This is where nuns who often experienced and expressed positive emotions had a decided advantage. Nuns who wrote about and experienced the most positive emotions while writing their autobiographies, in contrast to their more stoic counterparts, almost certainly experienced more positive emotions throughout their lifetime. And positive emotions undo the effects of stress and negative emotions!

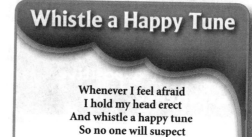

Whistle a Happy Tune

Whenever I feel afraid
I hold my head erect
And whistle a happy tune
So no one will suspect
I'm afraid…

The result of this deception
Is very strange to tell
For when I fool the people
I fear I fool myself as well!

I whistle a happy tune
And every single time
The happiness in the tune
Convinces me that I'm not afraid.

—*The King and I*
Richard Rodgers and Oscar Hammerstein

Note: Rodgers and Hammerstein composed this song about the "undoing" effect of positive emotions before the undoing effect of positive emotions was "discovered" by scientists!

In dramatic demonstrations of how positive emotions "downregulate the potentially health-damaging cardiovascular reactivity that lingers following negative emotions," researchers intentionally placed subjects in a very stressful situation, inducing high levels of stress, and then monitored their physiological functioning as they showed the subjects films designed to elicit positive, neutral, or negative emotions. The question: How long would it take to relieve the harmful effects of stress given the different film conditions? The results have been replicated and confirm that positive emotions "undo" the harmful physiological impact caused by stress.[39] See Box: The Undoing Effect of Positive Emotions.

Alternative Interpretations of Nun Longevity. A number of studies demonstrate that positive emotions predict longevity.[41] One interpretation is relatively straightforward: Those nuns who consistently elicited positive emotions throughout their lifetime had a substantial survival advantage compared to their more stoic counterparts because of their ability to turn off stress. If each time they faced stress they could turn it off more quickly by eliciting positive emotions, their cardiovascular system suffered less damage, and their immune system was less impaired. This interpretation is supported by research showing a positive attitude reduces cardiovascular stress during aging.[42] In reaction to experiencing something stressful, a twisted ankle for example, stoic acceptance (*"suffering is part of life"*) does not return physiological functioning to normal nearly as quickly as does a positive emotion like

The Undoing Effect of Positive Emotions[40]

Stress Induction: Subjects were given precisely 60 seconds to prepare a 3-minute speech and were told they had a 50–50 chance of being selected to deliver the speech which would be videotaped immediately and then shown and evaluated. Subjects were instructed that if they were selected to deliver their speech, a 3-minute timer would appear on a screen and that they were to look directly into the video camera and begin their speech, speaking clearly. Cardiovascular measures indicated this manipulation, as expected, elicited cardiovascular stress.

The Four Videos: Subjects were then shown one of four videos of equal duration.
Waves: Ocean waves breaking on a beach, elicits *contentment*.
Puppy: Small dog playing with a flower, elicits *amusement*.
Sticks: Abstract dynamic display of colored sticks piling up, elicits *no emotion*.
Cry: Young boy crying as he watches father die, elicits *sadness*.

The Results: Compared to those experiencing no emotion or the negative emotion of sadness, those experiencing positive emotions, amusement, and contentment, relieved stress and speeded the return of cardiovascular functioning to baseline levels far faster.

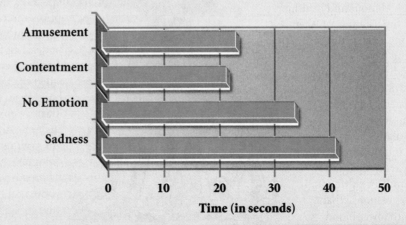

gratefulness ("*Thank God it was not worse.*") or contentment ("*It is God's will that I stay off my feet for awhile.*") Multiply these different reactions by a lifetime of responding to stress, and the longevity of the more positive nuns is no longer a mystery.

Before concluding that positive emotion leads to longevity, we must strike a note of caution. Any correlational study is open to alternative explanations. One of many possible explanations of the greater longevity of the happier nuns was that a third variable was causing both happiness and longevity. For example, it could be that positive emotion does not cause the longevity, but rather that exercise is the real cause. This interpretation would go like this: (1) Exercise elevates mood; (2) The nuns who expressed positive emotions in their early autobiography did so because they were getting regular exercise; (3) Those nuns who early learned to include exercise in their lives continued to do so throughout life; (4) People who get regular exercise live longer. In this interpretation, it was not positive emotion that led the happier nuns to live longer; rather, both positive emotions and longevity were a result of the same thing— exercise. Exercise is not the only variable that could possibly cause both longevity and a positive attitude, so we cannot with certainty infer causality from correlation.

I prefer to believe that experiencing positive emotions for a lifetime does in fact increase longevity. In support of the positive emotion interpretation, experimental work demonstrates that eliciting positive emotions via a loving kindness meditation treatment results in enhanced social relations and healthier cardiovascular functioning.[43] Other research is testing a range of health benefits resulting from positive emotions, including release of oxytocin; alterations in gene expressions related to health; improved immune system regulation of inflammatory processes; and improved vagal tone (a measure of parasympathetic system functioning, resulting in the relaxation response that is associated with lower blood pressure and a healthier heart).[44]

Why Does Recall of a Happy Experience Result in Better Performance?

The improved math scores following eliciting positive emotion occurred in a true experiment, not just a correlation study. The same is true of the doctors who made a more accurate diagnosis after receiving some candy. Thus, we can trust positive emotions cause improved performances, and this finding begs for an explanation. Why does remembering a happy experience or receiving a bag of sweets lead to better performance?

Positive Emotion Frees the Prefrontal Cortex. Some students have mild to severe math anxiety. All students have some anxiety before a test. Anxiety, as we have seen, narrows cognition. When there is stress, the amygdalae send signals to inhibit the prefrontal cortex.[45] Remembering a happy experience produces a positive emotion, and positive emotions "undo" the negative effects of stress. With stress lowered, students are better able to think broadly because the amygdala is not inhibiting the prefrontal cortex. Students become more creative, thinking of more alternatives. Positive emotion liberates the prefrontal cortex! Joy is impetus to play, explore, savor, and integrate. When we experience joy, we are not defending against a potential threat—we are encountering positive stimuli, we open up, looking for more. Our perceptions and cognitions broaden.[46] Trying on new and creative responses broadens our repertoire of responses, which increases our ability to cope in the future. The positive impact of positive emotions on perception and cognition has been proven.[47] The theory that describes the benefits of positive emotions is called the broaden-and-build theory because positive emotions cause us to broaden our range of responses in the moment and to build a broader repertoire of potential responses to use in the future.[48]

When we are happy, we are smarter!

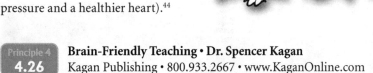

Broader perception and more fluidity of thought offer an explanation of why positive emotions resulted in a more accurate diagnosis for physicians given the bag of candy. In working toward a diagnosis, the physicians given the candy had broader thinking and perception; they did not stop at the first explanation that occurred to them. Being more relaxed, they did not jump to a quick conclusion. They took in all the data before coming to a diagnosis.

Positive Emotion Releases Beneficial Neurotransmitters and Hormones. Positive emotions release dopamine, beta-endorphins, and human growth factor.[49] All of these stimulate the brain in positive ways, increasing the feeling of well-being, stimulating the motivation and attention centers in the brain, and stimulating growth and repair of cells and tissue.

Release of dopamine is certainly at least partially responsible for improved cognitive functioning following positive affect. Dopamine, as we have seen, stimulates the motivation and attention centers in the brain. Students are more focused and more motivated to stay on task. Dopamine almost certainly causes greater cognitive flexibility. Dopamine pathways are active during periods of positive affect and dopamine stimulates the anterior cingulate, the structure most involved in flexible thinking.[50] When drugs are administered that counter the effect of dopamine or when medical conditions cause reduced levels of dopamine, both working memory and flexible thinking are impaired.

Reversing the "Success Yields Happiness" Formula

Traditionally, we have thought of the relation of happiness and success as *Success → Happiness*. Considerable research and theory supports the opposite formula: *Happiness → Success*.[51] This principle, "The Happiness Advantage," fits nicely with the brain research we have been examining. When we are happy, our amygdalae fire less, our prefrontal cortex is freer to function fully, we experience less stress, we think more clearly and creatively, we perceive more broadly, we are healthier, and we live longer. We simply function better and so are more successful.

This reversal of the traditional way of thinking about the happiness-success relationship has extreme implications for us as teachers. It should cause us to re-prioritize. Traditionally, we have operated under the assumption that if we can teach the students our content, they will be successful and happiness will follow. The evidence supports the opposite approach. If I can create a threat-free, happy classroom environment, the probability of student success will be increased.

Reversing the happiness-success formula has worked for me personally when teaching my workshops. Very early on in any workshop or presentation, I have participants do a teambuilding activity. Experience has taught me that my participants will master my content far better all day if we start by eliciting positive emotions. In the past, when I have felt rushed and wanted to "cover my content," I would sometimes leave out the initial teambuilding. Without exception, those workshops did not go nearly as well. Trying for success before happiness just doesn't work nearly as well as putting happiness first in the formula.

Ways to Elicit Positive Emotions

As teachers, we can elicit positive emotions in many ways. Given the many benefits of eliciting positive emotions, including enhanced creativity, learning, and test taking, we would do well to generate positive emotions in our students on a regular basis and in many ways. Releasing positive emotions on a regular basis has a cumulative effect, transforming class climate.

> ## Tip
> To promote performance, celebrate or praise before performance. To cement memory, celebrate or praise after performance.

Elicit Positive Emotion Prior to Performance.

In each of the research studies, positive emotions were elicited before performance. This is in contrast to giving praise for good performance or having a team celebrate an accomplishment. Thus, the research suggests we introduce praise and cheers prior to rather than after performance. Because we have been stuck in a reinforcement paradigm, we have reserved the celebrations until after the performance even in classrooms in which praise and cheers are common. The positive emotion research should lead us to turn that timetable on its head.

Praise: Before or After Performance?

An apparent contradiction exists between the principles of retrograde memory enhancement v. the happiness advantage. Retrograde memory enhancement encourages us to have praise and celebrations following performance; the happiness advantage encourages us to place praise and celebrations prior to performance. This apparent contradiction is resolved when we focus on outcomes. Retrograde memory enhancement focuses on memory as an outcome. We remember better that which is followed by emotion. The happiness advantage focuses on motivation and performance. We are more motivated and perform better when we experience positive emotions.

> ## Tip
> Surprise students with unexpected events that elicit positive emotions. Before a presentation, take a few minutes to allow students to share with a partner a present or kind act they have received that they have enjoyed.

What then, shall we do in our classrooms? The answer seems clear: Prior to performance, make sure students experience positive emotion. This can take the form of having students experience praise or any of the 37 techniques for eliciting positive emotion which we are about to explore. Following learning, cement the learning by associating it with a strong emotion. Again, this can take the form of praise or cheers, or any of the 37 techniques for eliciting positive emotion. In short: Eliciting positive emotion prior to performance is likely to boost performance, and eliciting positive emotion following learning is likely to boost memory for that learning.

Give Unanticipated Rewards.

Dopamine release is a major motor behind the positive effects of eliciting positive emotions. Brain studies reveal dopamine is released most strongly following *unanticipated* rewards.[52] This has clear implications for how we induce a positive mood. If we try to elicit positive emotion in the same way each time or at the same time each day, it will have less positive impact than if we surprise students with a positive emotion experience.

Give Noncontingent Rewards.

When our goal is to elicit positive emotion, making rewards contingent on performance is not as powerful as noncontingent rewards. For example, if we say, "*If we do well on the test, we will get to watch a funny video clip (or do a Silly Sport),*" we have made the reward contingent on performance. This makes the reward more predictable and so releases less dopamine. It also introduces some anxiety into the situation: Some students will worry about their performance and whether or not they will receive the reward. Far more powerful in eliciting positive emotions are unanticipated, noncontingent positive emotion moments like, "*I have a surprise! Before we complete the learning task, we get to watch a funny video clip (or do a Silly Sport).*" Novelty and surprise are essential elements in maximizing dopamine release that in turn releases the power of positive emotion.

37 Ways to Elicit Positive Emotions

1. Praise and Cheers Before Performance.

Traditionally, praise and celebrations follow task completion, punctuating the accomplishment. The research on eliciting positive emotions would have us reconsider. Just as sports teams give a team cheer *before* they go out onto the field, we can elicit positive emotions among students by having them give a cheer *prior* to beginning their group project. A team handshake before the test will boost test performance more than a celebration afterwards. Each team can design its own unique cheer. Prework praise is another way to elevate emotion. Students can generate praise gambits and use them before a test or a task: *"You are brilliant!" "You always come up with great ideas." "You are a great teammate."* See Box: 37 Ways to Elicit Positive Emotions.

2. Music.

Music evokes emotion. It makes us happy or sad, energetic or relaxed, romantic or angry. A consistent finding is that fast music and music in the major scale produce happy emotions; slow music and music in the minor scale produce sad emotions.[53] Interestingly, happy music without lyrics produces stronger positive emotions than does happy music with lyrics.[54] As with other emotion-eliciting stimuli, brain scans while listening to music reveal the emotional processing of music is associated with activation of the cingulate and orbiofrontal cortices.[55] Further, consistent with other stimuli that evoke positive emotions, happy music releases dopamine, explaining in part the rewarding properties of music.[56]

The Power of Music

"Music hath charms to soothe a savage beast, to soften rocks, or bend a knotted oak."

—William Congreve

> **Tip**
>
> Provide noncontingent rewards. Rather than "If... Then," try "Now that..." Instead of "If we score well on the test, we will get to...", make rewards noncontingent and unexpected: "You all did really well on the test, so let's celebrate by...."

---

37 Ways to Elicit Positive Emotions

There are many ways we can elicit positive emotions in our classrooms, and many can be implemented drop-of-the-hat, prior to or during a learning task or test. The following 37 possibilities are a sample of ways to elicit positive emotions.

1. Praise and Cheers	14. Count Blessings	27. Warm Weather Walk
2. Music	15. Positive Postcard	28. Acts of Kindness
3. Novelty	16. Success Stories	29. Recalling Helping
4. Happy Recall	17. Hobbies	30. Anticipating Helping
5. Joke Jar	18. Three Wishes	31. Visualization
6. Fun Jar	19. Curiosity, Wonder	32. Guided Imagery
7. Free Time	20. Reassurance	33. Progressive Relaxation
8. Free Reading	21. Safe Place	34. Relaxation Breathing
9. Silly Sports	22. Touch	35. Mental Retreats
10. Fantasy Time	23. Massage	36. Meditation
11. High Hopes	24. Pets	37. Power Posing
12. Anticipation of Treat	25. Plants	
13. Video Clips	26. Nature	

Tip

Create a collection of upbeat music without lyrics to play before tests, worksheet work, and projects.

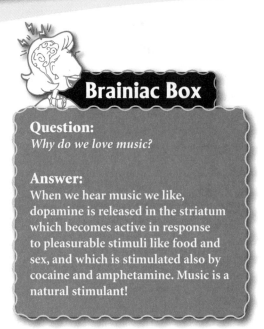

Brainiac Box

Question:
Why do we love music?

Answer:
When we hear music we like, dopamine is released in the striatum which becomes active in response to pleasurable stimuli like food and sex, and which is stimulated also by cocaine and amphetamine. Music is a natural stimulant!

In an amazing study of music preferences, participants were placed in an fMRI brain scan while they listened to previously unheard pieces of music.[57] They were then allowed to bid how much they were willing to spend to purchase the music. Activity in a very specific part of the brain, the nucleus accumbens, predicted how much people were willing to spend: The more activity in the nucleus accumbens, the more money people were willing to spend! The nucleus accumbens interacted with the auditory cortex; the more people were willing to spend, the more there was cross talk between these areas as well as other areas associated with reward. The nucleus accumbens is part of the pleasure center in the brain. Although different people chose to buy different pieces of music, the nucleus accumbens lit up when they listened to pieces they were willing to buy when later tested.

As the tempo of music rises above 60 beats a minute (the heart rate), we get increasingly energized. As it drops below 60 beats a minute, we get increasingly relaxed. Kagan offers several series of CDs for the classroom, some to sooth and relax, others to energize, and yet others selected for specific emotions such as inspiration, concentration, stress reduction, engagement, and learning.[58] Music is one of the primary tools we have to elicit positive emotions.

3. Novelty. There is actually a novelty structure in the brain linked to structures responsible for emotion and memory. Novelty activates the dopamine reward system and the hippocampus in the same way rewards do, promoting memory for the content.[59] In Tool 5: Punctuate with Processing, in Principle 5: Attention, we explore this novelty structure and examine many ways to create positive emotion through novelty. For

now, it is sufficient to say that including novel and unexpected events in our lesson plan is one of the many ways to elicit positive emotion.

4. Happy Recall. Recalling a happy event prior to a test is a research-based way to elicit positive emotion and to improve test performance.[60] Before learning tasks, projects, and tests, we can have students take a minute or two to remember any number of positive emotion events—a time they were proud, happy, content, felt cared for.... We can ask students to simply remember one of those times, take a few minutes writing about the experience, or have them turn to a partner to share one of those times, using **Timed Pair Share**.

See Structures Section
26. Timed Pair Share

Timed Pair Share is an excellent structure to elicit positive emotions via recall. In a **Timed Pair Share**, each student in a pair has the same amount of time to share with his or her partner while the partner practices active listening. First, the teacher announces a topic that elicits a positive emotion, say gratitude or amusement. Then, students spend just 1 minute each describing a time they have experienced that emotion. The leading researcher on positive

The Ten Positive Emotions

1. Amusement
2. Awe
3. Gratitude
4. Hope
5. Inspiration
6. Interest
7. Joy
8. Love
9. Pride
10. Serenity

emotions identifies ten emotions that consistently lead to positive outcomes: amusement, awe, gratitude, hope, inspiration, interest, joy, love, pride, and serenity.[61] Different emotions can be the topic each time we use **Timed Pair Share** to elicit positive emotions. For example, we might say, *"Describe to your partner one of the times you were really interested in something— really curious." "What is something you hope to accomplish in your lifetime?" "Tell your partner about something you are really proud of having made or having done."* See Box: The Ten Positive Emotions.

5. Joke Jar. As we have seen when we examined the need for safety, humor reduces anxiety. One way to integrate humor into our classrooms is to allow students to tell a joke. Two jars are created: The Joke Jar and the Name Jar. Clean jokes are submitted to the teacher prior to this activity and kept on separate slips of paper or cards in the Joke Jar. The Name Jar has cards, each containing a student name. At unanticipated times, before a test or learning activity, the teacher calls: *"It's Joke Jar time."* A student name is drawn from the Name Jar and that student draws one joke from the Joke Jar and reads that joke to the class.

Administrator Tip

Create a "Positive Emotion of the Week Program" for your school. For 10 weeks have faculty brainstorm and implement ways to elicit among students, staff, and faculty one of the ten positive emotions each week.

6. Fun Jar. In the Fun Jar are slips of paper or cards that describe fun things the class can do on the fly—things that take only a few minutes. The slips might contain names of Silly Sports, a 3-minute free-time pass, names of favorite songs that can be played, an opportunity to watch an amusing video clip, a chance to pull a joke from the Joke Jar, have funny hat day the next day, have dress up day the next day, or any other positive emotion-eliciting event. When students are not expecting it, a bell is rung or "Fun Jar" is announced and a student is called to pull a slip from the Fun Jar.

Tip

Frequently take 2 minutes to have students pair up to do a Timed Pair Share on a time they experienced one of the ten positive emotions.

7. Free Time. By gifting students 2 or 3 minutes of free time, we elicit positive emotions. For example, *"Students, I have a little gift for you. Starting when I say, 'Go!,' you will have 3 minutes of free time. You can use your free time any way you would like. You can get up and stretch. You can walk over and talk to someone. You can close your eyes and rest. You can read something you enjoy reading. You can make a note to yourself about something you don't want to forget. You can pretty much do anything you would like short of making too much noise or disturbing someone else. 'Go!'"*

8. Free Reading. In-class free reading is a step on the path to becoming a life-long reader. Reading for pleasure elicits positive emotions. Free reading is student-choice reading. Students can bring their own books, magazines, or articles to read during free reading, or reading material can be made available for students to "check out" from the in-class free reading library. Name cards are placed in books once they have been checked out, remaining in the book or article until the student is finished with that reading. Announcing a brief, unexpected, free reading time elicits positive emotions. *"Class, before we take on our next topic, we can enjoy 5 minutes of free reading."*

9. Silly Sports. Silly Sports elicit positive emotions. Students can play any of the 206 games in *Silly Sports & Goofy Games* to elicit emotion.[62] For those games in this book, see Table: Silly Sports and Goofy Games.

Silly Sports and Goofy Games

Silly Sport	Page
Air Traffic Controller	2.21
Alaskan Baseball	3.48
Balloon Bounce	4.47
Hagoo	3.45
Hum Tag	1.13
Pantomime Relay	4.48
Ten Count	6.29
Clapping Game	6.34

10. Fantasy Time. Our fantasies give us pleasure. We can elicit positive emotion in a heartbeat by allowing students to go on a brief flight of fantasy. Have them pair up and talk about where they would go for a week's vacation—all expenses paid! Other fantasy topics include how to spend $500, finishing school and having their dream profession, becoming a sports star (describe which sport and what they accomplished), being a movie star....

One of my favorite flights of fantasy is to have students pick one of several superpowers they would most like to have and then have them describe to a partner how they would use that superpower. See Box: Superpowers, p. 4.33.

11. High Hopes. Hope is a positive emotion. We can elicit hope by having students express what they hope for. This one is tricky. We don't want a D student saying they hope for an A. That will only have them focus on the discrepancy between what they want and what they can get, eliciting sadness, frustration, or a negative emotion. Perhaps the best way to elicit expressions of hope is to focus on the medium- or long-term future and have the hope be something fairly reasonable. Providing positive examples of what we hope for helps put the activity on the right footing. For example: *"Write down three things your hope for in your life. For example, I hope my family is healthy. I hope my students learn well and enjoy class. And I hope for more peace and less hunger in the world."* Another example: *"Tell your partner the work you would most like to do when you leave school."*

12. Anticipation of Treat. Mere anticipation of a positive outcome elicits positive emotion. The blood drawn from experimental subjects who were told they were about to watch a humorous video had 27% more beta-endorphins, the feel good hormone.[63] Prior to a test or a learning experience, we can spend a minute describing a future positive experience planned for the class—something we know they will enjoy. We might describe an upcoming field trip, a new silly sport we will try, or the upcoming class party. Anticipation of fun elicits positive emotions.

13. Video Clips. As we have seen in the experimental research, video clips can be used to elicit positive emotions like contentment and amusement. Brief video clips have proven power to broaden thinking and improve problem solving. There are many humorous video clips on YouTube. We can have students search for them and submit the links for teacher approval. A rule: The humor cannot be at the expense of someone else; no videos about falling, crashing, or someone being injured.

Superpowers

Choose a superpower and say,
"How you would use it?"

Ability to...
- ▶ Fly
- ▶ Time travel forward for a day
- ▶ Time travel backward for a day
- ▶ See through walls
- ▶ Read minds
- ▶ Know the future
- ▶ Change the past
- ▶ Listen at a distance
- ▶ Become invisible

17. Hobbies. Another positive emotion is interest. By having students describe a favorite hobby, we elicit the feeling of interest. A **RoundRobin** in which each student takes a minute to share about her or his hobby can elicit the feeling of interest, both in the person sharing and in those listening. *"What is something that really grabs your interest? Something you get lost in? For example, some people really like to make models. When they are making models, they tune out everything else because they are so involved.*

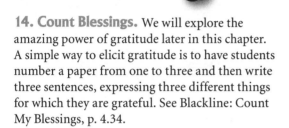

See Structures Section
16. RoundRobin

Each of us has different interests. It could be coin or stamp collecting, drawing, playing music, or reading a certain kind of book. What is your interest? Something you do that gets you so involved you tune out everything else?"

14. Count Blessings. We will explore the amazing power of gratitude later in this chapter. A simple way to elicit gratitude is to have students number a paper from one to three and then write three sentences, expressing three different things for which they are grateful. See Blackline: Count My Blessings, p. 4.34.

15. Positive Postcard. Traditionally, travelers bought a pretty picture postcard and sent it to those back home with the message, "Wish you were here." We can elicit positive emotions by having students write a positive postcard or letter saying why it is great to be them. For the young students, provide sentence starters:

I get to eat _____.
     (Favorite dessert)

I get to play _____.
     (A game you like)

I get to be with (_____).
     (A person you like)

See Blackline: Positive Postcard, p. 4.35.

16. Success Stories. Genuine pride in accomplishment (in contrast to false pride or boasting) is a positive emotion. We can elicit the feeling of pride in our students by having them talk about or write about an accomplishment that made them feel good. *"What is something you made or did, that made you feel really good? For example, I feel good when I give a lesson and I know my students have enjoyed the lesson and learned something important."*

18. Three Wishes. You announce that students have found an ancient oil lamp and when they rubbed it, a magical genie appeared. The genie grants each of them three wishes. (One wish cannot be for as many more wishes as they want.) They take out a piece of paper, number it one to three, and in one sentence for each wish, list their wishes. See Blackline: Three Wishes, p. 4.36.

19. Curiosity, Wonder. Having students share things they wonder about or are curious about is yet another way to elicit positive emotion. *"What is something you are curious about? What is a question you think about and would like to know the answer? What is something you wonder about? For example, sometimes I wonder why people are especially helpful to each other when there is a crisis. Something else that amazes me: We plant a very tiny flower seed and the seed knows to become a poppy, or a daisy, or some other flower. How can all that information be stored in that seed? Think about it—what is something that amazes you, something you wonder about."* [Pause] *"Each of you in your teams will take turns sharing something you wonder about. Anything you wonder about will be fine to share. You will each have 45 seconds to **RoundRobin** with your teammates."*

Count My Blessings

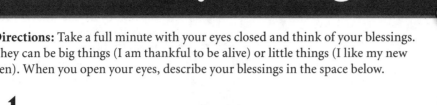

Directions: Take a full minute with your eyes closed and think of your blessings. They can be big things (I am thankful to be alive) or little things (I like my new pen). When you open your eyes, describe your blessings in the space below.

1. _____

_____

_____

_____

2. _____

_____

_____

_____

3. _____

_____

_____

_____

Brain-Friendly Teaching • Dr. Spencer Kagan
Kagan Publishing • 800.933.2667 • www.KaganOnline.com

Positive Postcard

Directions: Think of why it is great to be where you are. Pretend you are writing a postcard or letter to a friend far away. Tell him or her why you "Wish you were here." You can tell your friend about TV shows you could watch together, games you could play, things you could do together, or why you wish he or she could enjoy the great weather with you. What would you do together? Why would it be nice for your friend to be here with you?

Wish you were here because...

_____

_____

_____

_____

We could enjoy...

_____

_____

_____

_____

_____

It's great to...

_____

_____

_____

Three Wishes

Directions: You have found an ancient oil lamp. When you rubbed it, a magical genie appeared. The genie tells you to write your three wishes below and he will grant your wishes. No wishing for more wishes!

My three wishes are...

1. _____

_____

_____

_____

2. _____

_____

_____

_____

3. _____

_____

_____

_____

Brain-Friendly Teaching • Dr. Spencer Kagan
Kagan Publishing • 800.933.2667 • www.KaganOnline.com

20. Reassurance. We experience positive emotions when we know others are "there for us." Teach students to generate and use reassurance gambits like, *"I know you will do really well on the test." "You will do great in the game."*

21. Safe Place. Feeling secure is a positive emotion. Having students talk about where and when they feel safe and protected elicits this emotion. You might say something like, *"When I was a child, I use to have a favorite safe place. My grandmother and grandfather played a big grand piano, and when they were playing, I liked to crawl under the piano in the space under the piano where their feet pressed the pedals. I felt really safe there, listening to the music. It was like my own little cave. Is there a place or a time you feel really safe? What is a safe place for you?"* [Pause] *"With your partner talk about your safe places."*

22. Touch. Touch releases oxytocin, a hormone that quiets the amygdalae and produces positive emotions.[64] Cortisol, a stress hormone, is reduced by social support and by oxytocin.[65] It is most reduced by a combination of the two. Partner handshakes, high fives, and pats on the back include touch and social support. My personal favorite is the **Team Spiral Handshake**, described and pictured in Tool 11: Foster Positive Social Interaction, in Principle 2: Safety.

23. Massage. Massage quiets the amygdalae and elicits positive emotions.[66] Across a wide variety of studies, massage has been found to decrease the presence of the stress hormone cortisol by an average of 31% and increase the presence of the positive emotion neurotransmitters serotonin (28%) and dopamine (31%).[67]

Brainiac Box

Question:
Why do we feel good after a massage?

Answer:
(1) Massage lowers cortisol, often called the stress hormone. Cortisol is released when we tense for fight or flight. (2) Massage increases release of serotonin, often called the feel good hormone. The synthetic counterpart of serotonin is found in Prozac and in many anti-pain medications. It enhances the production of dopamine and inhibits the production of cortisol. (3) Massage increases the production of dopamine, a neurotransmitter that activates reward centers in the brain.

Before introducing massage into your classroom, check with your administrator. Gentle massage has worked extremely well to elicit positive emotions each time I have tried it with teachers and students. Most often, I have used it as a conclusion when using **Inside-Outside Circle**, but it can be used as a stand-alone. Students stand in a circle, all facing inward. I tell them to do a right face, so students are facing the back of the student in front of them. They take a side-step inward to make the circle tighter. They then place their hands on the shoulders of the person in front of them. At a signal, they give that person a gentle shoulder massage.

24. Pets. Petting live animals reduces anxiety. We can say this with certainty based on the results of a tightly controlled experiment.[68] First, to induce anxiety, university students were shown a tarantula spider that they were told they might be asked to hold. The experimenter then left them alone for 2 minutes with the tarantula in the jar and the jar uncovered! They were then randomly assigned to one of five groups: Pet a live rabbit, a live turtle, a toy rabbit, a toy turtle, or control (no petting). Toys were of the same size and texture as the live animals. Stress was measured three times: baseline, after being left alone with the tarantula, and after petting/control for 2 minutes. Stress was measured with a twenty-item reliable state anxiety scale that assesses feelings of tension, nervousness, worry and apprehension.

Results: (1) The tarantula manipulation raised stress a great deal; (2) Petting live animals reduced stress significantly more than not petting anything; (3) Petting live animals reduced stress significantly more than petting toys; (4) Petting

distress when a dog is present during a physical examination.[71]

Teachers who have a class pet (hamsters, gerbils, rats, guinea pigs, birds, reptiles, fish) elicit positive emotions. Pets that can be handled or cuddled (hamsters, guinea pigs) almost certainly elicit more positive emotion than those that can only be viewed (fish, most birds). But even a hardy fish such as a Betta, which is inexpensive, has a long life span, and can be kept in a simple fish bowl, elicits positive emotions, especially if students have turns feeding and changing the water. Care giving elicits positive emotions.

25. Plants. Plants, especially colorful flowering potted plants, in three ways contribute to positive emotions. First, they bring a bit of nature into the classroom, and nature has a calming effect. Second, they are aesthetically pleasing, another source of positive emotions. And third, they are air purifiers.

NASA published an unclassified study of the ability of indoor plants to remove pollutants from the air. Different plants are best at removing different types of air pollutants, but potted mum plants and Gerber daisies (also known as African daisy) are the best across the board. Fortunately, both mums and Gerber daisies are colorful and easy to care for.

Assigning students the care of plants elicits positive emotions. Mums and daisies are easy to propagate from seeds, rooted stem cuttings, and by crown division. Directions are readily available on the Web. Plant growth and propagation by various methods lend themselves nicely to science experiments. Having students care for and propagate plants offer students new skills and are a source of pride and accomplishment, additional positive emotions.

26. Nature. Spending time in nature improves mood and well-being.[72] Simply viewing slides of nature as contrasted with slides of urban environments produces positive emotion.[73] For improving attention, sitting by a mural of a nature scene, especially if the scene contains water, is better than sitting in a coffee shop.[74] The nature slides increase alpha waves in the brain that are associated with the release of serotonin, a mood elevator. Nature is curative: Compared to patients who have rooms facing a brick wall,

Tip

Have a live animal or animals in the classroom and allow students to pet them. Before a test or learning task, students with anxiety (test anxiety, speech anxiety, math anxiety...) might be allowed a brief petting time.

the hard shelled animal worked as well as petting the furry animal; (5) Petting toys did not reduce stress more than doing nothing.

These results are remarkable! After only 2 minutes of petting a live animal, anxiety is significantly reduced! The results are consistent with brain studies revealing petting an animal significantly changes brain chemistry. In five to 20 minutes after petting a dog, people experience dramatic neurophysiologic changes. Positive emotion hormones and neurotransmitters (beta-endorphin, oxytocin, prolactin, and dopamine) all increase while the stress hormone cortisol decreases.[69] The results are consistent also with studies of animal-assisted therapy. For patients with psychotic disorders and mood disorders, statistically significant reductions in anxiety result from 30 minutes of interaction with a therapy dog.[70] The effect is consistent across age groups. Three- to 6-year-old preschool children visiting a doctor show significant reductions in systolic and mean arterial pressure, heart rate, and behavioral

patients assigned to rooms with a view of nature have shorter postoperative hospital stays, receive fewer negative comments in nurses' notes, and take fewer pain killers.[75]

Although we may not have a choice about the view from our classrooms, and we may not be able to take our students out into nature on a regular basis, we can bring nature into our classrooms. Pictures on the walls, flowers, and class gardens elicit positive emotions.

27. Warm Weather Walk.
When there is pleasant weather (spring and early summer), taking a walk outside improves memory and mood, and elicits broader cognitive and perceptual styles.[76] Strolling through a park, the woods, or an arboretum increases attention, concentration, memory, and cognition.[77] Warning: This research indicates the same positive effects do not occur all year: A walk in hot summer weather actually lowers mood.

28. Acts of Kindness.
People who are assigned to do five acts of kindness in a day report feeling much happier than control groups, and that feeling lasts for many days.[78] People who keep a kindness journal—that is, keep a tally of every act of kindness they do each day for a week, become happier, kinder, and more grateful.[79] As the graph reveals, after just 1 week, people randomly assigned to keep a Kindness Journal became significantly happier than those who did not keep a journal. We can make our students and ourselves happier just by keeping a Kindness Journal!

Carrying out acts of kindness brings about positive emotion after those acts are performed, especially if a Kindness Journal is kept. In the classroom, we may want something that will elicit positive emotion in the moment, just before students take a test or engage in a learning activity. A possibility is to ask students to share with a partner or write about an entry in their Kindness Journal. Alternatively, if no Kindness Journal is kept, we can ask students to commit to an act of kindness one day, and then have them talk about their act of kindness on a following day. Simply talking about something kind we have done elicits positive emotion. See Graph: Acts of Kindness Journal.

29. Recalling Helping.
When we help someone, we elevate our own mood.[80] Positive emotions not only elicited when we care for someone, but also when we feel cared for. Recalling a moment in which we offered help or were helped brings back some of that positive emotion. Students can share these positive memories with a partner, their teammates, or in a journal.

30. Anticipating Helping.
Thinking about helping someone is another way to elicit positive emotion. Have students take a moment to think about how they might help someone in the class, in their family, in the neighborhood, or even a stranger. Have them take a full minute to imagine a concrete picture of themselves carrying out the helpful act.

31. Visualization.
Visualizations work in two ways to calm students. First, visualizations are done with eyes closed, reducing the excitement of external stimuli. Second, visualizations take students to a calmer place or time. Have students close their eyes and see a tranquil place. It can be a real place they have visited or one of their imaginations. Water is calming: A tranquil lake or bubbling brook has calming effects. Have students look around in their mind and enjoy the

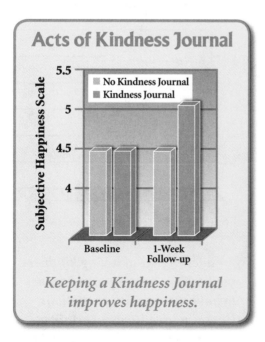

Acts of Kindness Journal

Subjective Happiness Scale

- No Kindness Journal
- Kindness Journal

5.5
5
4.5
4

Baseline   1-Week Follow-up

Keeping a Kindness Journal improves happiness.

calm view. Make the visualization auditory as well as visual: Have students listen to the sounds of nature in their mind—the sound of birds chirping or the flow of water over the rocks in a stream. Alternatively, have students listen to a CD with nature sounds during their visualization.

32. Guided Imagery. Guided imagery is just like visualization with one exception: The teacher guides the students through a script, determining what the students will visualize. You talk while the students visualize, directing their attention to various things. You may guide the students to focus on certain things by saying, *"Now look closer at..."* or, *"Turn your attention to…"*. You can even ask the students to engage in a conversation during the guided imagery: *"Ask the old wise woman for some advice. Take to heart what she tells you."*

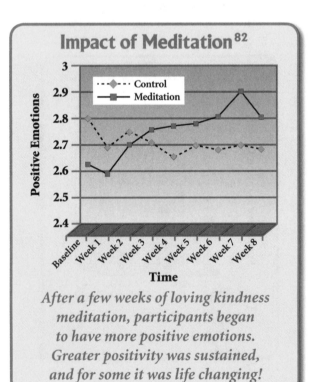

A guided imagery may take the students through a process (steps of a math problem, steps to follow in a science experiment, steps of a swimming flip turn) or an exploration of a place (what they see in Lincoln's log cabin, what they see in a pond).

It is easiest if you have a prepared script or if you are very familiar with the content. Remember, you are guiding the students to focus on things you hope they will feel or remember.

In using guided imagery to elicit positive emotion, the teacher can guide students through a script in which they experience, hope, gratitude, wonder, amusement, or any of the positive emotions. Serenity and calm are powerful positive emotions. See Box: Guided Imagery Script: A Calm Place, p. 4.41. It is from the book, *Win-Win Discipline*.[81] It is designed to elicit calm as well as enjoyment of nature.

33. Progressive Relaxation. To elicit a feeling of calm, have students do a few minutes of progressive relaxation. The technique has been described in Tool 13: Practice Progressive Muscle Relaxation, in Principle 2: Safety.

34. Relaxation Breathing. Relaxation breathing has been described in Tool 12: Teach Relaxation Breathing, in Principle 2: Safety. Once students have learned this technique, it can be used to elicit positive emotion prior to a test, performance, project, or lecture, broadening attention and thinking.

35. Mental Retreats. A brief retreat from external stimuli is yet another way to elicit positive emotion. To have students take a one- or 2-minute mental retreat, tell them to close their eyes and attend to the sound of their breath coming in and out. As simple as this is, mental retreats can be profoundly relaxing, allowing students to become far more focused.

36. Meditation. We have examined the positive results of meditation in depth in Tool 14: Advocate Meditation, in Principle 2: Safety. A brief meditative experience can be provided by having students take a "mental retreat" as just described, or by having them focus full attention on their stream of consciousness, whatever comes to mind, with an attitude of detached amusement.

Impact of Meditation[82]

Positive Emotions plotted against *Time* (Baseline, Week 1–Week 8) for Control and Meditation groups.

After a few weeks of loving kindness meditation, participants began to have more positive emotions. Greater positivity was sustained, and for some it was life changing!

Guided Imagery Script: A Calm Place

Students, we are all going to visit a calm, beautiful place. But we are going to visit this place in our mind's eye.

First, I want you to sit comfortably, with your back straight in your chair, your feet flat on the floor, and your hands resting comfortably in your lap, palms up.

Now, take a few deep breaths and let them out slowly. Breathe in through your nose as deeply as you can and then slowly let the air out through your mouth. Breathe in quickly and breathe out slowly. Be sure to get the last bit of air out when you breathe out. Don't hold any stale air. Focus on the sound and feel of the air as you let it out slowly through your mouth. That's it. Get calm and relaxed.

Now, everyone please close your eyes. In your mind's eye, I want you to see a beautiful calm lake. You are standing by the shore. There is white sand under your feet. The sand feels warm. You wiggle your toes in the sand and enjoy the feeling of the warmth. [**Pause**]

Now, look to the left. There are some green ferns and a palm tree. You walk over. You touch the fern and feel its fuzzy leaf. You let the leaf run slowly over your hand, enjoying the touch. [**Pause**]

Now, look up at the leaves of the palm tree. It is a coconut palm and has three coconuts in a cluster. You notice how pretty they are. You are enjoying the peacefulness of this place. [**Pause**]

Not far away, you hear the sound of a bird chirping. You listen carefully. You can hear some crickets. And occasionally, there is a frog croaking. Listen with all your attention. Enjoy it. You hear the sound of the water gently lapping on the shore. [**Pause**]

You turn and walk toward the water. It's so very blue. It stretches out in front of you flat and calm. You dip your warm feet into the cool water and enjoy the refreshing feeling. This seems like such a perfect place. Take a few moments to enjoy it and look around. [**Pause**]

Now, please don't open your eyes quite yet. I want you to focus on the calm, safe feeling you have. Notice how you are breathing easily. You feel perfectly comfortable. In a moment, I will ask you to open your eyes. When I do, don't jump out of the calm feeling. Let it stay with you.

Now, slowly open your eyes. Don't say anything yet. Just look around and feel very calm, relaxed, and very alert. What do you see or hear?

Source: Guided Imagery Script: A Calm Place, p. 12.42, *Win-Win Discipline*. Kagan Publishing, 2004.

To test the impact of meditation on the experience of positive emotions, Barbara Fredrickson and her co-workers randomly assigned half of 139 Compuware employees to a "loving kindness meditation" condition; the other half served as controls. Participants learned how to meditate during seven group training sessions conducted during employee lunch hours. They learned first to direct love and compassion toward themselves, later to loved ones, and finally to acquaintances, strangers, and all living beings. They practiced at home 5 days a week. The experiment lasted for 9 weeks. No differences emerged in their positivity until after the third week, and emerged at different rates for different individuals, but overall, was revealed. See Graph: Impact of Meditation, p. 4.40. In contrast to the control participants who showed no change, meditators became increasingly positive, showing significant increases in joy, gratitude, serenity, interest, hope, pride, amusement, and love.[82] The experiment radically transformed the lives of some participants, as described in Barbara's book, *Positivity*.[83]

37. Power Posing. We all know that emotion affects our posture. We stand tall with confidence; we collapse with grief; we hold our head high with pride; we look down with shame. Remarkably, research reveals the opposite is true as well: Our posture affects our emotions.[84]

To test this hypothesis, participants (26 females and 16 males) were tested before and after assuming two, 1-minute *high-power poses* as opposed to two, 1-minute *low-power poses*. Based on prior research, high-power poses were defined as expansive, open-body positions, and low-power poses were defined as contractive, closed-body positions. The two high-power poses were (1) seated on a chair with

High-Power Poses

Low-Power Poses

feet up on a table, leaning back with hands behind the neck, elbows expanded outward; and (2) standing, leaning forward with hands spread wide on a table and with feet spread wide. The two low-power poses were (1) seated on a chair with feet close together, both hands between the thighs with one hand on top of the other; and (2) standing with legs crossed and hands tightly gripping the body. See illustrations.

The participants did not know what was being tested; they were told they were to pose in different positions "To test accuracy of physiological responses as a function of sensor placement relative to your heart." To make this believable, the experimenter placed an electrocardiography lead on the back of each participant's calf and the underside of the left arm. In fact, the experimenters were testing whether these simple 1-minute poses would impact on participant emotions and hormone levels. And they did! The high- and low-power poses had a significant impact on hormone levels, risk taking, and feelings of being powerful, in charge.

Hormone Levels. Results of the experiment were clear: High-power poses caused an increase in testosterone compared to low-power poses, which caused a decrease in testosterone. Further, high-power poses caused a decrease in cortisol, and low-power poses caused an increase in cortisol.

Risk-Taking. Participants were given $2 and were told they could either keep the $2 or they could roll the dice to either double their money or lose it all. The odds were set at 50/50. After assuming high-power poses, significantly more participants (86.4%) took the risk than those who had been placed in the low-power poses (60%).

Feelings of Powerfulness. Participants rated how "powerful" and "in charge" they felt on a scale of 1 (not at all) to 4 (a lot). The power poses impacted on the subjective feeling of powerfulness in the predicted directions. Those who had been placed in the high-power positions had a mean of 2.57 on the powerfulness scale; those who had been placed in the low-power positions had a mean of 1.83, a highly significant difference.

Related Findings. Power posing results in a variety of positive outcomes, including:

▶ Greater tolerance for pain and a firmer handshake[85]
▶ Thinking of more power words in a word-completion task
▶ Feeling a greater sense of personal power
▶ Taking more action (speaking in a debate, helping someone in need, seeking help)
▶ Functioning better cognitively (ability to identify the object in a fragmented picture)[86]
▶ Feeling a greater sense of fulfillment of basic needs; displaying a more negative response to social exclusion[87]

When I was in elementary school over sixty years ago, it was standard practice for all students to

have their posture assessed and for those with poor posture (slumped shoulders and back) to receive corrective feedback and exercises to improve their posture. Given the science of posture posing and the feelings of well-being that follow two simple, 1-minute power posture poses, wouldn't we do well for our students to reinstitute this simple practice?

Eliciting Positive Emotions v. Providing Incentives

Most of us have offered our students incentives of one kind or another.

▶ "If we all get our permission slips in tomorrow, we will have 5 minutes of free time."
▶ "If you score 90% or more, you will get an A."
▶ "When all desks are clear, we can line up for recess."
▶ "If everyone on the team scores above 80%, everyone on that team will get 5 bonus points."
▶ "If the class has a tardy-free month, we can celebrate with ice cream!"

Providing incentives is very different from eliciting positive emotion. See Table: Providing Incentives v. Eliciting Positive Emotions, p. 4.44.

Contingency. Incentives are contingent: If you do X, you will receive Y. Eliciting positive emotion is noncontingent: We surprise our students with a treat or in some way elicit positive emotion, not based on what they have done. Eliciting positive emotion is like dropping some good fortune on our students. For no particular reason, we show a funny video or give them 3 minutes of free time.

Reward Size. Incentives may offer any size reward. Big: If the class reads X number of books this month, we will have a professional reader come in. Small: If everyone has a clean desk before I count to five, we will have 3 minutes of extra recess time. In contrast, eliciting positive emotion as described in the research usually involves a small reward: finding a coin in the coin slot, receiving a few candies, or taking a moment to remember a positive experience.

Brainiac Box

Question:
When do testosterone and cortisol levels raise and fall?

Answer:
In humans and other animals, testosterone levels are higher in those who are more dominant. Levels rise following a win and lower following a loss. Testosterone levels rise in anticipation of competition. Higher levels predict willingness to compete. Higher levels are associated with leadership.

Cortisol is often called the stress hormone. In response to stimuli, cortisol levels rise and fall in the opposite direction compared to testosterone. For example, those in power have lower cortisol levels. Cortisol levels drop as power or dominance increases. Chronically high levels of cortisol are associated with impaired immune functioning, stress-related illness, hypertension, and memory loss.

When Given. Incentives follow performance; eliciting positive emotion precedes performance. This is something we may want to take to heart if our goal is to boost test scores. Telling students they will receive a reward if they score well may increase anxiety, diminishing their ability to think. In contrast, telling students to take 2 minutes to remember a great present they have received, diminishes anxiety and increases the ability to think.

Time Frame. Incentives may be for something in the moment (*"If everyone lines up quietly by the time I count three, we can go to recess 2 minutes early."*) or something far in the future (*"If everyone gets their homework in on time this month, we will have cupcakes."*) In contrast, eliciting positive emotion usually involves something spontaneous in the moment. (*"Everyone **StandUp–HandUp–PairUp**. Think of something fun you do after school. In three sentences or less, tell your partner."*)

Attitude. Incentives produce anticipation, and may engender doubt (*"Will we get the reward or not?"*). Eliciting positive emotion produces

> ## Tip
> Have students experiment with their posture, assuming high- and low-power posture positions and introspecting on how the different positions make them feel. Encourage students to adopt posture that gives them a greater sense of well-being.

surprise and pleasure. For no reason at all, we get this unexpected benefit.

Impact. Incentives and eliciting positive emotion have quite different impact on students. **Incentives** usually increase motivation and induce students to work harder toward the goal. They often narrow the focus of students: the goal becomes the objective. Incentives may be given to individuals. If, however, incentives are given to a team or the class as a whole, they serve as teambuilding or classbuilding activities. We are positively interdependent;

Providing Incentives v. Eliciting Positive Emotions

	Incentives	Eliciting Positive Emotion
Contingency	Contingent	Noncontingent
Reward Size	Big or Small	Usually Small
When Given	Following Performance	Preceding Performance
Time Frame	Short or Long	In the Moment
Attitude	Anticipation and Doubt	Surprise and Pleasure
Impact	▶ Increased Motivation ▶ Narrow Focus on Goal ▶ Teambuilding ▶ Can Erode Intrinsic Motivation ▶ Can Be Seen as a Bribe	▶ Broaden Cognition and Perception ▶ Lower Stress, Happier ▶ More Charitable ▶ Health Benefits ▶ Improved Test Taking

we succeed or fail together. Pulling together to reach the goal increases cohesion and a sense of accomplishment. There can be down sides to incentives. If we fail to reach the goal, we become disheartened. Incentives can undermine intrinsic motivation (I am working for the reward, not for the learning). Finally, incentives can make it appear like the teacher is trying to manipulate or bribe us. (*"Oh, this work is so boring, you have to bribe us to do it"*).

Eliciting positive emotion, unlike incentives, broadens rather than narrows perceptions and cognitions. There is no anxiety; no way to fail to receive the reward. Stress is reduced rather than increased. Eliciting positive emotion has a number of positive side effects, including the feeling of gratefulness, happiness, and a sense of well-being. Students feel the teacher cares about them in a noncontingent way. We are accepted for who we are, not just if we perform well.

Tool 7

Promote Play

The brain better remembers anything associated with emotion. When there is emotion, the neurons in the brain actually fire at an increased rate signaling the hippocampus that "this stimuli is worth remembering." This makes sense in terms of evolution. Anything that creates fear, pleasure, or any of the other emotions has survival implications; remembering emotionally laden events gives us an advantage.

Many of the Silly Sports and Goofy Games elicit emotion. For example, when emotion cards are the content for **Pantomime Relay**, students develop emotional intelligence. Each student in turn guesses the emotion being acted out by a teammate and then runs up

to turn over the next emotion card to see which emotion they are to act out for the next teammate in line. When that heightened emotional state transfers to classroom activities, academic activities are better remembered. See Blackline: Pantomime Relay, p. 4.48.

Play also releases dopamine that stimulates the attention and motivation centers in the brain. Following play, students pay closer attention and are more motivated to finish tasks.

A dramatic example of play transforming student motivation occurred the very first time Dan Kuzma tried a Silly Sport, **Balloon Bounce**. See Blackline: Balloon Bounce, p. 4.47. Play transforms a class. We can't attribute the enhanced motivation of Dan's class simply to a dose of dopamine stimulating the attention and motivation centers. It could be that students simply saw Dan as a source of rewards and did not want to cross him. Or perhaps they got out all their tension and pent up energy and so were happy to sit down and work. Or was it all of these things in a perfect storm? Whatever the reasons, we have to stand in awe of the power of a simple Silly Sport to transform a classroom!

Play Transforms a Class

Years ago, I attended a trainers' meeting Spencer Kagan and Laurie Kagan conducted in Reno, NV. The purpose of the meeting was to train trainers to facilitate Multiple Intelligences workshops. We were introduced to the theory and practice of Brain Breaks.

I flew home on a red eye and went directly to my school to teach. I had a "free period" first period that year, and was looking forward to using the free time to "gather" myself for the school day. As I walked into the front office, one of the assistant principals, a friend and colleague for many years, asked me to "cover" a class first period for a teacher who was absent that day. He said that it would be a very difficult class to cover, and that he would do it if I declined. I was kind of put off that he didn't think I could cover a class as a substitute for one period. I asked him how many students were in the class. He said, seven, six freshman and one sophomore. (That further perturbed me.)

It was a World Language class. We had a new World Language Supervisor and up to that time, Special Services students were not allowed to take World Language courses. She wanted to change that, and this was a class that was made up of all Special Services students, six freshmen and a sophomore who failed every class they took their freshman year.

I walked into the class. There were detailed lesson plans and worksheets for the students to complete. I passed out the worksheets and asked the "kids" to get to work. It was as if I wasn't in the room and/or they had heard nothing that I said. There wasn't anything that I did that could get them to sit down and get to work.

I noticed some blown-up balloons in the corner of the room. I asked what they were for. One of the girls in the class said it was her brother's birthday and his teacher said she could decorate the room. I remembered "Balloon Bounce" from the training in Reno and asked her if I could use the balloons. She said yes, and I implemented Balloon Bounce.

When we were finished, I asked them to sit down and get to work. To my amazement, they sat down and completed the assignment. That was the first time I ever used a Brain Break.

The next day between classes, the young sophomore boy who hadn't passed a class the year before, excitedly ran up to me in the hallway. He said, "Mr. Kuzma, Mr. Kuzma, we showed our teacher what you did with us yesterday in class. But, don't worry, you wont get in trouble, we didn't tell her who showed us how to do it!"

That was one of the most amazing experiences I have had in a classroom.

—*Dan Kuzma*
Indian Hills Regional High School
Oakland, NJ

Brain-Friendly Teaching • Dr. Spencer Kagan
Kagan Publishing • 800.933.2667 • www.KaganOnline.com

Source: Dr. Spencer Kagan • *Silly Sports & Goofy Games*
Kagan Publishing
1 (800) 933-2667
www.KaganOnline.com

balloon bounce

This all-time favorite is guaranteed to bring laughs and high spirits to any group.

1 Form Groups
Players form groups of four.

2 Inflate Balloons
Each group inflates and ties off two balloons, preferably of different colors.

3 Hold Hands
Players hold hands in a circle, holding the balloons in their hands.

4 Balloon Bounce
Players bounce a balloon in the air without letting go of their hands. They use hands, heads, elbows, feet, or any body part to keep the balloon afloat.

5 Experts? Bounce Two
When the group feels confident, they release the second balloon and try to keep two balloons in the air at once. If a balloon lands on the ground, players must pick it up and get it bouncing again without letting go of their hands.

for variety...

Feather Float
A feather is used instead of a balloon. Instead of hitting it, to keep the feather afloat everyone blows.

creative coordination

Game 10

Source: Dr. Spencer Kagan • *Silly Sports & Goofy Games*
Kagan Publishing
1 (800) 933-2667
www.KaganOnline.com

pantomime relay

From the pantomime box each player races to communicate, becoming "angry," "changing a flat tire," or just being a "digital clock."

1 Getting Ready

Pantomime slips: slips of paper, one per player, have written on them things to pantomime. Pantomime Box: 10 paces from the start/finish line is a box drawn on the ground with chalk or masking tape.

2 Pantomime Slips Distributed

Each player pulls from a hat a pantomime slip and reads it, being careful not to let anyone else see it.

3 Players Form Teams

Players stand in teams behind the start/finish line. Each team has an equal number of players.

4 The Relay Is On

At a signal from the leader, the first player from each team runs to the pantomime box, stands in it, and pantomimes what is on their slip. The teammates take turns guessing what is being pantomimed. Each in turn must make a guess, continuing until a correct guess is made. When the action is correctly guessed, the pantomimer runs back to tag the next in line. The first team to have all players return is congratulated by all the other teams.

What to Pantomime?
Easy:
- Athletes: baseball player, swimmer, football player, tennis player, basketball player, wrestler, boxer
- Emotions: sad, happy, angry, disgusted, fearful, love, embarrassment, playfulness

Harder:
- Actions: Operating a jackhammer, directing traffic, gardening, sewing, cooking, vacuuming, washing a car, changing a tire, making a bed
- Things: a television, a CD player, a digital clock, a chest of drawers, a tire, a mailbox

Harder Yet:
- Character Traits: Fairness, Honesty, Responsibility, Respect, Reliability

ridiculous relays

Game 137

Conclusion

Emotion can either interfere with or facilitate teaching and learning. By understanding emotion, we can harness the power of emotion to promote learning. Emotion research is not only revolutionizing our understanding of the brain, it is debunking many long-standing beliefs and turning on their head assumptions about causality. Smiles and body language are a cause as well as a consequence of positive emotion. Happiness is a cause as well as a consequence of success. When we experience positive emotions, we become smarter and more creative. Contrary to common practice, for many students, offering rewards contingent on performance is likely to create anxiety and diminish rather than accelerate performance and learning. Contrary to common practice, to boost performance, praise and celebrations do more good prior to rather than following performance. Because strong negative emotion cements memory as effectively as does strong positive emotion, it appears that the ability of praise following performance to boost retention is not explained by reinforcement theory, but rather by a basic brain process: retrograde memory enhancement. What can we conclude? We want to elicit positive emotions frequently: Prior to learning to reduce stress and increase performance; following performance to cement learning in memory. The findings of brain-science and psychology demand we reevaluate the role of emotion in our classrooms and schools. If we are not teaching with emotion, we are not harnessing some of the most powerful tools available to increase positive outcomes for our students.

Seven Tools to Release the Power of Emotion

1. Teach with Passion
2. Elicit Passion
3. Link Emotion to Content
4. Provide Praise
5. Celebrate Success
6. Elicit Positive Emotion
7. Promote Play

References

[1] Perth, C.B. *Molecules of Emotions. Why You Feel the Way You Feel.* New York, NY: Scribner, 1997.

[2] Damasio, A. *The Feeling of What Happens. Body and Emotion in the Making of Consciousness.* New York, NY: Harcourt Brace & Co., 1999.

[3] Adolphs, R., Tranel, D., Buchanan, T.W. *Amygdala damage impairs emotional memory for gist but not for details of complex stimuli.* **Nature Neuroscience**, 2005, 8, 512–518. DOI:10.1038/nn1413.

Dolcos, F., LaBar, K.S. and Cabeza, R. *Interaction between the amygdala and the medial temporal lobe memory system predicts better memory for emotional events.* **Neuron**, 2004, 42, 855–863. DOI:10.1016/S0896-6273(04)00289-2.

LaBar, K.S. and Cabeza, R. *Cognitive neuroscience of emotional memory.* **Nature Reviews Neuroscience**, 2006, 7, 54–64. DOI:10.1038/nrn1825.

McGaugh, J.L. *The amygdala modulates the consolidation of memories of emotionally arousing experiences.* **Annual Reviews of Neuroscience**, 2004, 27, 1–28. DOI: 10.1146/annurev.neuro.27.070203.144157.

[4] Iacoboni, M. *Mirroring People. The Science of Empathy and How We Connect with Others.* New York, NY: Picador, 2009.

[5] McGaugh, J.L. *Memory and Emotion.* New York, NY: Columbia University Press, 2003.

[6] McGaugh, J.L. *Memory and Emotion. The Making of Lasting Memories.* New York, NY: Columbia University Press, 2003.

[7] Izqauierdo, I., Baros, D.M., e Souza, T.M., de Souza, M.M., Izquierdo, L.A. & Medina, J.H. *Mechanisms for memory types differ.* **Nature**, 1998, 393(6686), 635–636.

[8] Kohn, A. *Punished by Rewards.* Boston, MA: Houghton Mifflin Company, 1993.

[9] Kagan, S. *In Praise of Praise.* San Clemente, CA: Kagan Publishing. **Kagan Online Magazine**, Spring 2007. www.KaganOnline.com.

[10] Cameron, J. and Pierce, W.D. *Reinforcement, reward, and intrinsic motivation: A meta-analysis.* **Review of Educational Research**, 1994, 64(3), 363–423.

11 Isen, A.M., Daubman, K.A., & Nowicki, G.P. *Positive affect facilitates creative problem solving.* **Journal of Personality and Social Psychology**, 1987, 52, 1122–1131.

12 Kagan, S. & Kagan, M. **Kagan Cooperative Learning.** San Clemente, CA: Kagan Publishing, 2009, 10.15.

13 Kagan, S. & Kagan, M. **Kagan Cooperative Learning.** San Clemente, CA: Kagan Publishing, 2009, p. 10.15.

14 Lyubomirsky, S., King, L. & Diener, E. *The benefits of frequent positive affect: Does happiness lead to success?* **Psychological Bulletin**, 2005, 131(6), 803–855.

15 Fredrickson, B.L. *Cultivating positive emotions to optimize health and well-being.* **Prevention and Treatment**, 2000, 3(1), 1a.

Fredrickson, B.L. *The role of positive emotions in positive psychology: the broaden-and-build theory of positive emotions.* **American Psychologist**, 2001, 56(3), 218–226.

16 deVries, M., Holland, R.W., Chenier, T., Starr, M.J. & Winkielman, P. *Happiness cools the warm glow of familiarity. Psychophysiological evidence that mood modulates the familiarity-affect link.* **Psychological Science**, 2010, 21(3), 321–328.

17 Panksepp, J. **Affective Neuroscience. The Foundations of Human and Animal Emotions.** New York, NY: Oxford University Press, 1998, 281–282.

18 Isen, A.M., Rosenzweig, A.S. & Young, M.J. *The influence of positive affect on clinical problem solving.* **Medical Decision Making**, 1991, 11(3), 221–227.

19 Carnevale, P.J.D. & Isen, A.M. *The influence of positive mood and visual access on the discovery of integrative solutions in bilateral negotiation.* **Organizational Behavior and Human Decision Processes**. 1986, 37(1), 1–13.

20 Duncker, K. *On problem solving.* **Psychological MonoGraphs**, 1945, 58(5), 270.

21 Greene, T.R. & Noice, H. *Influence of positive affect upon creative thinking and problem solving in children.* **Psychological Reports**, 1988, 63(3), 895–898.

Isen, A.M., Daubman, K.A., & Nowicki, G.P. *Positive affect facilitates creative problem solving.* **Journal of Personality and Social Psychology**, 1987, 52(6), 1122–1131.

22 Ziv, A. *Facilitating effects of humor on creativity.* **Journal of Educational Psychology**, 1976, 68(3), 318–432.

23 Dugas, J. **Psychologic du Rire.** Paris, FR: Hachette, 1902.

24 Fredrickson, B.L. & Branigan, C. *Positive emotions broaden the scope of attention and thought-action repertoires.* **Cognition and Emotion**, 2005, 19(3), 313–332.

25 Isen, A.M., Daubman, K.A. & Nowicki, G.P. *Positive affect facilitates creative problem solving.* **Journal of Personality and Social Psychology**, 1987, 52(6), 1122–1131.

Isen, A.M., Johnson, M.M.S., Mertz, E. & Robinson, G.F. *The influence of positive affect on the unusualness of word associations.* **Journal of Personality and Social Psychology**, 1985, 48(6), 1413–1426.

26 Greene, T.R. & Noice, H. *Influence of positive affect upon creative thinking and problem solving in children.* **Psychological Reports**, 1988, 63(3), 895–898.

27 Fredrickson, B.L. & Branigan, C. *Positive emotions broaden the scope of attention and thought-action repertoires.* **Cognition and Emotion**, 2005, 19(3), 313–332.

28 Baumann, N. & Kuhl, J. *Positive Affect and Flexibility: Overcoming the Precedence of Global over Local Processing of Visual Information.* **Motivation and Emotion**, 2005, 29(2), 123–134.

29 Schmitz, T.W., DeRosa, E. & Anderson, A.K. *Opposing influences of affective state valence on visual cortical encoding.* **Journal of Neuroscience**, 2009, 29(22), 7199–7207.

30 Derryberry, D. & Tucker, D.M. *Motivating the focus of attention.* In P.M. Neidenthal & S. Kitayama (Eds.), **The Heart's Eye: Emotional Influences in Perception and Attention**, 167–196. San Diego, CA: Academic Press, 1994.

Mogg, K., McNamara, J., Powys, M., Rawlinson, H., Seiffer, A. & Bradley, B.P. *Selective attention to threat: A test of two cognitive models of anxiety.* **Cognition and Emotion**. 2000, 14(3), 375–399.

Mogg, K., Millar, N. & Bradley, B.P. *Biases in eye movements to threatening facial expressions in generalized anxiety disorder and depressive disorder.* **Journal of Abnormal Psychology**, 2002, 109(4), 695–704.

31 Wadlinger, H.A. & Isaacowitz, D.M. *Positive mood broadens visual attention to positive stimuli.* **Motivation and Emotion**, 2006, 30(1), 87–99.

32 Estrada, C., Young, M. & Isen, A.M. *Positive affect influences creative problem solving and reported source of practice satisfaction among physicians.* **Motivation and Emotion**, 1994, 18(4), 285–299.

33 Bryan, T. & Bryan, J. *Positive mood and math performance.* **Journal of Learning Disabilities**. 1991, 24(8), 490–494.

34 Master, J.C., Barden, R.C. & Ford, M.E. *Affective states, expressive behavior, and learning in children.* **Journal of Personality and Social Psychology**, 1979, 37(3), 380–90.

35 Diener, E. Nickerson, C. Lucas, R.E. & Sandvik, E. *Dispositional affect and job outcomes.* **Social Indicators Research**, 2002, 59(3), 229–259.

36 Danner, D.D., Snowdon, D.A. & Friesen, W.V. *Positive Emotions in Early Life and Longevity: Findings from the Nun Study.* **Journal of Personality and Social Psychology**, 2001, 80(5), 804–813.

37 Barefoot, J.C., Dahlstrom, W.G. & Williams, R.B., Jr. *Hostility, CHD incidence, and total mortality: A 25-year follow-up study of 255 physicians.* **Psychosomatic Medicine**, 1983, 45(1), 59–63.

Benson, H. **The Relaxation Response.** New York, NY: William Morrow and Company, Inc., 1975.

Fredrickson, B.L., Maynard, K.E., Helms, M.J., Haney, T.L., Siegler, I.C. & Barefoot, J.C. *Hostility predicts magnitude and duration of blood pressure response to anger.* **Journal of Behavioral Medicine**, 2000, 23(3), 229–243.

Scheier, M.F. & Bridges, M.W. *Person variables and health: Personality predispositions and acute psychological states as shared determinants of disease.* **Psychosomatic Medicine**, 1995, 57(3), 255–268.

[38] Eysenck, H.J. *Cancer, personality and stress: Predictions and prevention.* **Advances in Behavioral Research and Therapy**, 1994, 16(3), 167–215.

Greer, S. & Morris, T. *Psychological attributes of women who develop breast cancer: A controlled study.* **Journal of Psychosomatic Research**, 1975, 19(2), 147–153.

[39] Fredrickson, B.L., Mancso, R.A. Branigan, C. & Tugade, M.M. *The undoing effect of positive emotions.* **Motivation and Emotion**, 2000, 24(4), 237–258.

Fredrickson, B.L. & Levenson, R.W. *Positive emotions speed recovery from the cardiovascular sequelae of negative emotions.* **Cognition and Emotion**, 1998, 12(2), 191–220.

[40] Fredrickson, B.L., Mancso, R.A. Branigan, C. & Tugade, M.M. *The undoing effect of positive emotions.* **Motivation and Emotion**, 2000, 24(4), 237–258.

[41] Levy, B.R., Slade, M.D., Kunkel, S.R. & Kasl, S.V. *Longevity increased by positive self-perceptions of aging.* **Journal of Personality and Social Psychology**, 2002, 83(2), 261–270.

Moskowitz, J.T. *Positive affect predicts lower risk of AIDS mortality.* **Psychosomatic Medicine**, 2003, 65(4), 620–626.

Ostir, G.V., Markides, K.S., Black, S.A. & Goodwin, J.S. *Emotional well-being predicts subsequent functional independence and survival.* **Journal of the American Geriatrics Society**, 2000, 48(5), 473–478.

[42] Levy, B.R., Hausdorff, J., Hencke, R. & Wei, J. *Reducing Cardiovascular Stress with Positive Self-Stereotypes of Aging.* **Journal of Gerontology: Psychological Sciences and Social Sciences**, 2000, 55(4), 1–9.

[43] Kok, B.E., Coffey, K.A., Cohn, M.A., Catalino, L.I., Vacharkulksemsuk, T., Algoe, S.B., Brantley, M. & Fredrickson, B.L. *How positive emotions build physical health: Perceived positive social connections account for the upward spiral between positive emotions and vagal tone.* **Psychological Science**, 2013, 24(7), 1123–1132.

[44] Fredrickson, B.L. *Positive emotions broaden and build,* 1-57. In E. Ashby Plant & P.G. Devine (Eds.), **Advances on Experimental Social Psychology**, 2013, 47.

[45] Garcia, R., Vouimba R.M., Baudry M. & Thompson R.F. *The amygdala modulates prefrontal cortex activity relative to conditioned fear.* **Nature**, 1999, 402(6759), 294–296.

Kim, H., Somerville L.H., Johnstone T., Alexander A.L. & Whalen P.J. *Inverse amygdala and medial prefrontal cortex responses to surprised faces.* **NeuroReport**, 2003, 14(18), 2317–2322.

Young, M.P., Scannell, J.W., Burns, G. & Blakemore, C. *Analysis of connectivity: Neural systems in the cerebral cortex.* **Reviews in the Neurosciences**, 1994, 5(3), 227–250.

Young, M.P., Scannell, J.W. & Burns, G. **The Analysis of Cortical Connectivity.** Austin, TX: R.G. Landes, Springer, 1994.

[46] Fredrickson, B.L. *The role of positive emotions in positive psychology: the broaden-and-build theory of positive emotions.* **American Psychologist**, 2001, 56(3), 218–226.

Fredrickson, B.L. *What good are positive emotions?* **Review of General Psychology**, 1998, 2(3), 300–319.

[47] Fredrickson, B.L. *What good are positive emotions?* **Review of General Psychology**, 1998, 2(2), 300–319.

[48] Fredrickson, B.L. *The role of positive emotions in positive psychology: The broaden-and-build theory of positive emotions.* **American Psychologist**, 2001, 56(3), 218–226.

[49] Berk, L.S. & Tan, S.A. *[beta]-Endorphin and HGH increase are associated with both the anticipation and experience of mirthful laughter.* **The Journal of the Federation of American Societies for Experimental Biology**, 2006, 20(4), A382.

[50] Ashby, F.G., Isen, A.M. & Turken, U. *A neuropsychological theory of positive affect and its influence on cognition.* **Psychological Review**, 1999, 106(3), 529–550.

[51] Achor, S. **The Happiness Advantage: The Seven Principles of Positive Psychology that Fuel Success and Performance at Work**. New York, NY: Crown Publishing, 2010.

[52] Mirenowicz, J. & Schultz, W. *Importance of unpredictability for reward responses in primate dopamine neurons.* **Journal of Neurophysiology**, 1994, 72(2), 1024–1027.

Schultz, W. *Activity of dopamine neurons in the behaving primate.* **Seminars in Neuroscience**, 1992, 4(2), 129–138.

[53] Khalfa, S., Schon, D., Liegeois-Chauvel, J-L. A. & Liegeois-Chauvel, C. *Brain regions involved in the recognition of happiness and sadness in music.* **NeuroReport**, 2005, 16(18), 1981–1984.

[54] Brattico, E., Alluri, V., Bogert, B., Jacobsen, T., Vartiainen, N., Nieminen, S. & Tervaniemi, M. *A functional MRI study of happy and sad emotions in music with and without lyrics.* **Frontiers in Psychology**, 2011, 2, 308.

[55] Khalfa, S., Schon, D., Liegeois-Chauvel, J-L. A. & Liegeois-Chauvel, C. *Brain regions involved in the recognition of happiness and sadness in music.* **NeuroReport**, 2005, 16(18), 1981–1984.

[56] Salimpoor, V.N., Benovoy, M., Larcher, K., Dagher, A. & Zatorre, R.J. *Anatomically distinct dopamine release during anticipation and experience of peak emotion to music.* **Nature Neuroscience**, 2011, 14(2), 257–262.

[57] Salimpoor, V.N., van den Bosch, I., Kovacevic, N., McIntosh, A.R., Dagher, A. & Zatorre, R.J. *Interactions between the nucleus accumbens and auditory cortices predict music reward value.* **Science**, 2013, 340(6129), 216–219.

[58] Kagan Publishing. **Music for the Mind, Energizing 60's Music, Sound Health Series, The Magic of Mozart.** http://www.kaganonline.com/catalog/music_2.php#CEM

59 Wittmann, B.C., Bunzeck, N., Dolan, R.J. & Duzel, E. *Anticipation of novelty recruits reward system and hippocampus while promoting recollection.* **Neuroimage**, 2007, 38(1), 194–202.

Bunzeck, N., Doeller, C.F., Dolan, R.J & Duzel, E. *Contextual interaction between novelty and rewards processing within the mesolimbic system.* **Human Brain Mapping**, 2012, 33(6), 1309–1324.

60 Bryan, T. & Bryan, J. *Positive mood and math performance.* **Journal of Learning Disabilities.** 1991, 24(8), 490–494.

61 Fredrickson, B. *Positivity.* New York, NY: Crown Publishers, 2009.

62 Kagan, S. *Silly Sports & Goofy Games.* San Clemente, CA: Kagan Publishing, 2000.

63 Berk, L.S. & Tan, S.A. *[beta]-Endorphin and HGH increase are associated with both the anticipation and experience of mirthful laughter.* **The Journal of the Federation of American Societies for Experimental Biology**, 2006, 20(4), A382.

64 Kirsch, P., Esslinger, C., Chen, Q., Mier, D., Lis, S., Siddhanti, S., Gruppe, H., Mattay, V.S., Gallhofer, B. & Meyer-Lindenberg, A. *Oxytocin modulates neural circuitry for social cognition and fear in humans.* **Journal of Neuroscience**, 2005, 25(49), 11489–11493.

Morhenn, V.B., Park, J.W., Piper, E. & Zak, P.J. *Monetary sacrifice among strangers is mediated by endogenous oxytocin release after physical contact.* **Evolution and Human Behavior**, 2008, 29(6), 375–383.

65 Heinrichs, M., Baumgartner, T., Kirschbaum, C. & Ehlert, U. *Social support and oxytocin interact to suppress cortisol and subjective responses to psychosocial stress.* **Biological Psychiatry**, 2003, 54(12), 1389–1398.

66 Hui, K.K., Marina, O., Liu, J., Rosen, B.R. & Kwong, K.K. *Acupuncture, the limbic system, and the anticorrelated networks of the brain.* **Autonomic Neuroscience**, 2010, 157(1), 81–90.

67 Field, T., Hernandez-Reif, M., Diego, M., Schanberg, S. & Kuhn, C. *Cortisol decreases and serotonin and dopamine increase following massage therapy.* **International Journal of Neuroscience**, 2005, 115(10), 1397–1413.

68 Shiloh, S., Sorek, G. & Terkel, J. *Reduction of state-anxiety by petting animals in a controlled laboratory experiment.* **Anxiety, Stress & Coping: An International Journal**, 2003, 16(4), 2003.

69 Odendaal, J.S.J. & Meintjes, R.A. *Neurophysiological correlates of affiliative behaviour between humans and dogs.* **Veterinary Journal London England**, 1997, 165(3), 296–301.

70 Barker, S.B. & Dawson, K.S. *The effects of animal-assisted therapy on anxiety ratings of hospitalized psychiatric patients.* **Psychiatric Services**, 1998, 49(6), 797–801.

71 Nagengast, S.L., Baun, M.M., Megel, M. & Leibowitz, J.M. *The effects of the presence of a companion animal on physiological arousal and behavioral distress in children during a physical examination.* **Journal of Pediatric Nursing**, 1997, 12(6), 323–330.

72 Franklin, H. *Beyond toxicity: Human health and the natural environment.* **American Journal of Preventative Medicine**, 2001, 20(3), 234–239.

73 Ulrich, R.S. *Natural versus urban scenes: Some psychophysiological effects.* **Environment and Behavior**, 1981, 13(5), 523–556.

74 Felsten, G. *Where to Take a Study Break on the College Campus: An Attention Restoration Theory Perspective.* **Journal of Environmental Psychology**, 2009, 29(1), 160–167.

75 Ulrich, R.S. *View through a window may influence recovery from surgery.* **Science**, 1984, 224(4647), 42–421.

76 Keller, M.C., Fredrickson, B.L., Ybarra, O., Côté, S., Johnson, K., Mikels, J., Conway, A. & Wager, T. *A warm heart and a clear head: the contingent effects of mood and weather on cognition.* **Psychological Science**, 2005, 16(9), 724–731.

77 Berman, M. Jonides, J. & Kaplan, S. *The cognitive benefits of interacting with nature.* **Psychological Science**, 2008, 19(12), 1207–1212.

78 Lyubomirsky, S. *The How of Happiness.* New York, NY: Penguin, 2007.

79 Otake, K., Shimai, S., Tanaka-Matsumi, J., Otsui, K. & Fredrickson, B.L. *Happy people become happier through kindness: A counting kindnesses intervention.* **Journal of Happiness Studies**, 2006, 7(3), 361–375.

80 Post, S.G. *Altruism, happiness, and health: It's good to be good.* **International Journal of Behavioral Medicine**, 2005, 12(2), 66–77.

81 Kagan, S., Kyle, P. & Scott, S. *Win-Win Discipline.* San Clemente, CA: Kagan Publishing, 2004, 13.42.

82 Fredrickson, B.L., Cohn, M.A., Coffee, K.A., Pek, J. & Finkel, S.M. *Open hearts build lives: Positive emotions, induced through loving-kindness meditation, build consequential personal resources.* **Journal of Personality and Social Psychology**, 2008, 95(5), 1045–1062.

83 Fredrickson, B. *Positivity.* New York, NY: Crown Publishers, 2009, 75–90.

84 Carney, D., Cuddy, A.J.C. & Yap, A. *Power posing: Brief nonverbal displays affect neuroendocrine levels and risk tolerance.* **Psychological Science**, 2010, 21(10), 1363–1368.

85 Bohns, V.K. & Wiltermuth, S.S. *It hurts when I do this (or you do that): Posture and pain tolerance.* **Journal of Experimental Social Psychology**, 48(1), 2012, 341–345.

86 Huang, L., Galinsky, A.D., Gruenfeld, D.H. & Guillory, L.E. *Powerful postures versus powerful roles: Which is the proximate correlate of thought and behavior?* **Psychological Science**, 2011, 22(1), 95–102.

87 Welker, K.M., Oberleitner, D.E., Cain, S. & Carré, J.M. *Upright and left out: Posture moderates the effects of social exclusion on mood and threats to basic needs.* **European Journal of Social Psychology**, 2013, 43(5), 355–361.

Attention

Attention yields retention. To the extent we focus students' attention on what we want them to learn, we facilitate learning. How can they remember something they never attended to in the first place? Here we explore fourteen tools to capture and hold attention.

Capture and Hold Attention

We are very concerned with attention deficit. We label those students with unfocused attention as having ADD, (Attention Deficit Disorder), and then we give them a drug to help them focus. We know that without focused attention, learning is impaired or impossible. The brain can't retain what is not perceived, and it can retain only little of what is only little perceived. Fleeting, scattered attention is a prescription for poor learning. Unfocused attention is associated also with inability to complete tasks in a timely way. The question then becomes, "How can we as teachers produce among our students sustained, focused attention?"

"When attention is impaired, it detracts from everything we do, and when it is well focused, it enhances everything we do."[1]
—B. Alan Wallace

Scattered attention is a modern malady. Daniel Goleman talks about "the chronic distractibility that has become the norm in modern life, an addiction to splitting our focus between email and iPod, between the person we are with and the one on the cell phone, and between the present moment and our planning for the next one.[2] "How do we cure this malady, both in our classrooms and in our society?"

In this Principle, we will explore some of what we know about attention, ways we can capture and hold the attention of our students, and then we will examine a concept that holds tremendous, untapped potential for our students: training attention.

Having or not having focused attention was once thought of as a given. You were either good at or poor at concentrating. Today, however, we know the brain is extraordinarily malleable. We can apply what we know about neuroplasticity to help all students better focus their attention.

Wouldn't it be a better world if we could teach all of our students how to focus their minds, not just so they can acquire more of the content of our courses, but so they can have ongoing focused

14 Tools to Capture and Hold Attention

attention throughout life? Work, relationships, scientific discoveries, creativity, appreciation of the beauty that surrounds us, and spirituality are all improved in proportion to the degree we have focused attention. We have the ability to focus the attention of our students in the moment of instruction and also to teach them to manage their attention for a more focused and successful life. Before examining those exciting tools, let's turn to some of what we know about attention.

What Do We Know About Attention?

Neuroscientists distinguish distinct attention systems in the brain, each activated by different stimuli and mediated by different neurotransmitters. Yet our conscious experience of attention is unified. At any moment, we are aware of some stimuli and unaware of others. We want students to "pay attention" to our lesson and tune out distractions.

When it comes to defining the conscious experience of attention, I don't think anyone has done a better job than William James over 100 years ago:

> "Everyone knows what attention is. It is the taking possession of the mind, in clear and vivid form, of one out of what seem several simultaneously possible objects or trains of thought. Focalization, concentration of consciousness are of its essence. It implies withdrawal from some things in order to deal effectively with others…".[3]

One thing I especially like about James' definition of attention is that he places core to the definition the acknowledgment that to focus on something, to give it our full attention, we must withdraw our focus from other things. We have selective attention. To focus on one thing, we stop focusing on other things. Two implications: We have selective attention, and efficient multitasking is a myth. Let's examine each of these implications in turn.

Selective Attention. Our brains are designed to "tune in" to some things while "tuning out" others. The brain is hardwired to give more attention to some things than others. As illustrated by the cortical homunculus, the brain devotes considerable real estate to what the hands and face feel, but little to the back, calves, and shoulders—even though those each cover a much larger area.[4]

We simply cannot function if we attend to all the stimuli that impinge on us moment to moment. As you read this paragraph, to attend to, understand, and later remember it, you have to "tune out" the feeling your clothes create on your skin, the background sound of an air conditioner or passing airplane, a thought about what you will have for dinner, the feeling of a passing breeze, the temperature of the room, the feeling of this book in your hands, and a bit of tension you feel in the back of your neck. If you attended equally to all of those and the myriad other internal and external stimuli your brain receives moment to moment, you could not function— let alone understand and retain the meaning of what you are now reading. We need selective attention to survive. Given a limited number of resources, the brain allocates attention to the most important stimuli.[5]

We only remember the things we focus on. Selective Attention yields Selective Retention.

Part of our job while we teach is to create selective attention. Students simply will not remember what they do not attend to. Our job in part is to help students tune out distractors and to create full, undivided attention on what we want them to remember.

We know the link between attention and memory from our own personal experience: You come home exhausted. As you enter the house, someone begins a conversation with you. You attend to the conversation while absentmindedly setting down your car keys nearby, but in a place that you usually don't set them. Later, you can't find your keys. If, in contrast, in the moment you placed down your keys you had focused on that act—had placed your undivided attention on where you were placing the keys, later you would know exactly where they were.

We only remember the things we focus on. *Selective Attention Yields Selective Retention.* We do not recall the things we tune out. The brain has to tune out some things in order to attend to others, and only those things that receive fairly full attention are well remembered.

Dichotic Listening. The inability to attend to two things at once was established over a half century ago in classic dichotic listening experiments.[6] The experimenters used earphones to broadcast a different message to each ear of people being tested. The results: People can tune out one message and tune in to the other message. But there is a cost: *Subjects can remember almost nothing of the message they have not focused on!* Thus, we can formulate an extremely important principle of brain-friendly teaching:

Attention Yields Retention

If we want students to remember the skill or the content we are teaching, we need to first capture and then hold their attention. An obvious corollary of the principle that *Attention Yields Retention Is Lack of Attention Yields Lack of Retention.*

The Power of Selective Attention.
Holding your hands in ice water is painful. Try it sometime and you will discover you can only last a few minutes before the pain becomes intolerable! To test the power of selective attention, experimenters had people hold their hands in ice water as long as they could under different conditions. The conditions were designed to prime them for mild or severe discomfort and to direct their attention toward or away from the sensation.

Participants were in five conditions. They were told: (1) They *may* find it uncomfortable; (2) They *will* find it *very* uncomfortable; (3) They were to describe their moment-to-moment sensations; (4) They were to use a clock to set goals for themselves, as they tried to keep their hands in the water as long as they could; and (5) They were to view travel slides and to push a button to change slides.[7]

Brainiac Box

Question:
What is the Cortical Homunculus?

Answer:
The brain is hardwired to devote a great deal of attention to some stimuli and ignore other stimuli. In the sensory homunculus, far more signals reach the brain from the tongue, lips, and fingers than from the calves, shoulders, and back, even though the tongue, lips, and fingers represent smaller areas. The areas of the body we need to give more attention to send more signals to the brain and are represented by larger areas in the brain, as illustrated by the sensory and motor homunculi.

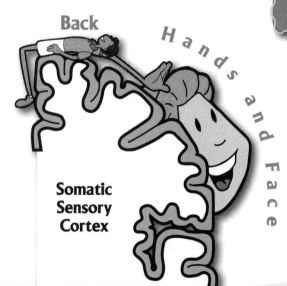

Back

Hands and Face

Somatic Sensory Cortex

◀ *The illustration depicts the amount of space the brain devotes to different body areas. Lips and tongue get as much space as chest, leg, foot, and toes combined. The brain devotes more space to more important areas. It is hardwired for selective attention.*

Selective Attention
A Simple Experiment

You are going to read this entire paragraph and then do what it says to do. **Do not act until after reading this whole paragraph, and do not read beyond this paragraph until you have done what it says to do.** You will simply reach up with one hand and scratch the very top of your head with all five fingernails at once. As you do, you are going to focus fully on the sensation you get from each finger. Which finger seems to press hardest, and which finger presses lightest? Can you rank the pressure from each finger? Be ready to report back on "finger pressures" after you scratch your head. Don't read further. **Scratch Now.**

Let's call that Scratch 1. Now, after reading the next paragraph, you will do Scratch 2.

You are going to read this entire paragraph and then do what it says to do. **Do not act until after reading this whole paragraph.** When you finish reading this paragraph, once again you will scratch the top of your head with the same five fingers in exactly the same way you did the first time. This time, however, rather than being ready to report on finger pressures, you will attend very closely to the sound you hear as you scratch your head. Locate the sound: Determine if it appears to be inside your head or outside. Be ready to describe the sound in detail. Focus fully on the rhythm of the sound and the sound itself. Don't read further. **Scratch Now.**

If you are like most people, with Scratch 1, you were mainly aware of pressure and not sound, and with Scratch 2 you were mainly aware of sound, but not pressure. Why? By directing attention to the sound and rhythm of the scratching and away from the pressure, the sound and the rhythm were magnified in your field of attention.

By directing attention away from one thing and toward another, we not only create selective attention, we create selective memory. Our students will remember only that to which they attend. And because teaching is the attempt to create memory for our content, good teaching is to a large extent the management of attention.

The results: A dramatic confirmation of the power of selective attention. Being told it *might* be uncomfortable or that it *will* be very uncomfortable made no difference. In contrast, directing attention toward or away from the pain created by the ice water made a huge difference: When people were directed to describe their moment-to-moment sensations, they lasted about half as long as when their attention was directed toward viewing and controlling the travel slides! Directing one's attention toward one thing, causes us to ignore other things. See Graph: How Many Seconds Can You Keep Your Hands in Ice Water?, p. 5.7.

Distraction for Pain Management. Among the most dramatic examples of the power of attention management is in the clinical treatment of pain. Daily wound care treatment of burn victims involves the cleaning and removal of dead skin, which is an excruciating process.

Even the administration of opioids (morphine-related analgesics) cannot eliminate the pain. Using virtual reality games as an adjunct to opioids to distract patients during wound care dramatically reduces the experience of pain far beyond the use of opioids alone. For example, in one study, seven children with acute burn injuries underwent eleven extremely painful treatments with standard pharmacologic analgesia with and without attending to a virtual reality program to distract them. Pain was measured on a scale of 0–5. With the analgesia alone, pain was rated at an average of 4.1 compared to 1.3 when the children were distracted playing a virtual reality game![8]

Attention management is a critical teaching skill. Success as a teacher is determined in part by the ability to direct the attention of students toward academic content and away from distractions.

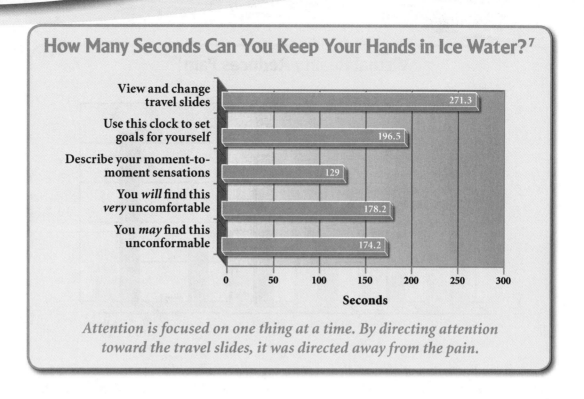

How Many Seconds Can You Keep Your Hands in Ice Water?[7]

Category	Seconds
View and change travel slides	271.3
Use this clock to set goals for yourself	196.5
Describe your moment-to-moment sensations	129
You *will* find this *very* uncomfortable	178.2
You *may* find this unconformable	174.2

Attention is focused on one thing at a time. By directing attention toward the travel slides, it was directed away from the pain.

Similar results have been obtained in a number of studies. Twelve burn patients reported less than half as much pain when engaged in a virtual reality game as when only administered traditional opioid medication.[10] A study compared four conditions in the treatment of nine subjects experiencing pain: (1) Opioids only; (2) Virtual reality game playing only; (3) Opioids plus virtual reality; and (4) Neither opioids nor virtual reality. Results: Opioids alone reduced pain and reduced activity in the insula and thalamus. Virtual reality game playing alone was slightly more effective than opioids alone in reducing pain unpleasantness! Opioids plus virtual reality was the most effective condition on all measures.[11] That simply redirecting attention away from pain is even slightly more effective than administering opioids is an incredible testimony to the power of attention management.

The completeness of distraction is strongly related to the amount of pain experienced during burn care. Playing Nintendo does not distract attention nearly as much as being engaged in a virtual reality game in which there is almost no possibility of visual or auditory input from anything but the game. Thus, we would predict that playing a virtual reality game would be a more effective distraction from pain than would be playing a Nintendo game. A study of two teenage boys with severe burns confirmed that prediction: Playing a virtual reality game reduced the experience of pain about twice as much as playing a Nintendo game.[12] See Graph: Virtual Reality Reduces Pain, p. 5.8.

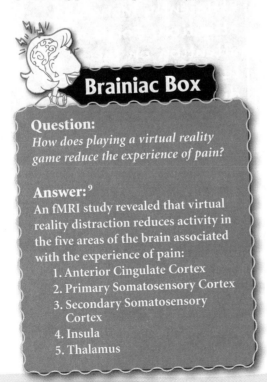

Brainiac Box

Question:
How does playing a virtual reality game reduce the experience of pain?

Answer:[9]
An fMRI study revealed that virtual reality distraction reduces activity in the five areas of the brain associated with the experience of pain:
1. Anterior Cingulate Cortex
2. Primary Somatosensory Cortex
3. Secondary Somatosensory Cortex
4. Insula
5. Thalamus

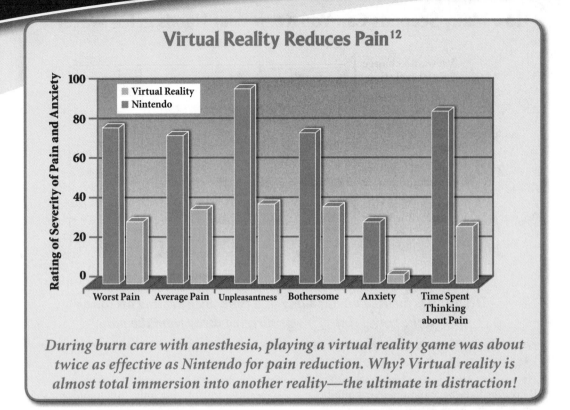

Virtual Reality Reduces Pain[12]

During burn care with anesthesia, playing a virtual reality game was about twice as effective as Nintendo for pain reduction. Why? Virtual reality is almost total immersion into another reality—the ultimate in distraction!

Managing Attention

Magicians and pickpockets regularly perform feats that seem impossible. How? By managing attention. As teachers, we too can do some magic by managing attention. Ability to manage attention well is a core competency of the successful teacher.

Magicians Manage Attention. Every time he performs close-up work, a master magician proves the power of managing attention. The magician at a party walks up to a small group of people, say four or five. He offers to do a coin trick or a card trick. In the middle of his trick, he reaches into his pocket and pulls out the watch of someone in the small group and asks, *"Does this by chance belong to anyone?"* The owner of the watch gasps. He or she has not felt or seen a thing as the magician unbuckled the watch and put it in his pocket. How is this possible? *Management of attention.*

The magician is a master of misdirection. By having everyone focus on his right hand while doing the card trick, his left hand is free to steal the watch and place it in his pocket, undetected. We only have a limited amount of attention

> **Tip**
> Maximize learning by efficiently managing attention: Focus all attention on the lesson and away from distractions.

resources. The more the magician has us use up our attention resources on anything other than the deception he is performing (his talk, his touch, some other attention grabber), the freer he is to perform his deception undetected.

There is no better example of the power of attention management than the astounding performances of magician, Apollo Robbins.

> **Apollo Robbins is sweeping his hands around the body of the fellow he has just chosen from the audience. "What I'm doing now is fanning you," the master pickpocket from Las Vegas informs his mark….**

Brain-Friendly Teaching • Dr. Spencer Kagan
Kagan Publishing • 800.933.2667 • www.KaganOnline.com

Apollo is demonstrating his kleptic arts to a roomful of neuroscientists who have come to Las Vegas for the 2007 Magic of Consciousness symposium….

Apollo has dared everyone in the auditorium to try to catch him pilfering this man's belongings up on stage in plain view. We watch intently just like everyone else, but none of us really stands a chance….

Apollo tells George one thing while doing two other things with his hands. This means that in the best-case scenario, George has only a one in three chance of noticing when something of his gets snatched. His real chances are actually far below one in three: In the psychic sparring ring of attention management, Apollo is a tenth-degree black belt. By continually touching George in various places—his shoulder, wrist, breast pocket, outer thigh—he jerks George's attention around the way a magnet draws a compass needle….

Apollo steals George's pen, notes, digital recorder, some receipts, loose cash, wallet, and, very early on, his watch…. We notice the watch when we see Apollo folding his arms behind his back, buckling it onto his own wrist as his patter leads George down some new garden path of attention.[13]

Street Thieves Manage Attention. Common street thieves work in pairs using the same principle of misdirection. One bumps into and distracts the mark while his or her partner reaches into the mark's pocket to pinch the wallet. As teachers, our job is the opposite. Instead of misdirecting the attention of our students, our job is to direct their attention like a laser beam on the content or skill we want our students to remember or master. We are successful as teachers to a large degree to the extent we are masters of managing attention.

Good Teachers Manage Attention. In doing hundreds of classroom observations, I have been struck by the variance among teachers in how well they manage attention. Sometimes I walk into a classroom and the attention of the students is diffuse. Some students are listening to the teacher, but others are looking at their desk, some have their eyes wandering around the room, and yet others appear somewhat dazed. I can predict with a great deal of certainty there will be little learning in that class. On the other hand, if I walk into a classroom and all students are alert and all eyes are riveted on the teacher, it is almost certain there will be a great deal of learning.

The art of teaching is to an important extent the art of managing attention.

Our students remember only that to which they attend. And because teaching is the attempt to create memory for content, good teaching is to a large extent the management of attention.

The Myth of Multitasking

This call to narrowly focus the attention of our students on the content to be mastered seems to fly in the face of the idea that some people are good at multitasking and that the brain is a parallel processor able to do many things at once. It is true that the brain does many things at once, but the bulk of what the brain does never reaches our consciousness. At any moment, the brain is involved in regulating many internal bodily processes, scanning the environment for threats and opportunities, deciding which of all the stimuli it is processing should reach consciousness, and of those that reach consciousness, which should be tagged for memory storage. But these processes occur outside of our conscious awareness. If they did not, our attention would be so divided, we could not function. To function, our awareness needs to be focused. Only what we focus on, what we become consciously aware of, has a chance to be remembered.

Regarding multitasking: One of the best examples of our inability to multitask is what happens when we try to do two things at once, like driving and talking on a cell phone.[14] Experiments show our ability to drive is dramatically impaired while talking on a mobile phone. In-person conversations, cell phone conversations, texting while driving, and even listening to music while driving are dangerous! We simply cannot multitask as well as we think we can.

Conversations Disrupt Driving.

Using drivers in real cars on actual highways, researchers found complex conversations captured drivers' attention so fully, their ability to respond to visual targets was reduced by as much as 30%![15] When interviewed, the drivers could verbalize their inattention blindness, saying things like, *"I looked, but failed to see."* Results indicated that simple tasks that do not demand much of our attention (listening to the radio, listening to a conversation) do not produce as negative an effect. Complex cognitive tasks like responding in a conversation significantly impair our driving ability. Talking on a cell phone had a similar effect as did having a conversation with a passenger. There is only a finite capacity in working memory, so when it is taxed by one task, there is less left for another task. We are not good at multitasking.

Mobile Phone Calls Cause Accidents! To test if in fact mobile phone calls while driving cause actual accidents, researchers did a detailed analysis of phone records of people involved in accidents. They compared the time of 26,798 cell phone calls with the time of car accidents involving 699 drivers in Toronto, Canada, over a 14-month period.[16] The risk of an actual collision was four times as great when talking on a cell phone! Apparently it was the distracting influence of thinking about the conversation, not the handling of the cell phone that increased the risk of an accident: The risk of an accident using hands-free v. handheld phones was not significantly different. The heightened

The risk of an actual collision was four times as great when talking on a cell phone!

risk of an accident while talking on the cell phone was true for experienced drivers as well as less experienced drivers, and for all ages tested.

Texting Disrupts Driving.

Texting while driving is a common form of multitasking. A survey of 2,000 Facebook users found 45% engage in texting while driving.[17] Texting while driving results in a 35% slower reaction time—greater reduction in reaction time than that caused by alcohol consumption to the legal limit (12% greater) and marijuana use (21% greater)![18] Reading and writing text messages caused a significant increase in number of lane departures: Reading messages results in a 12.7% increase in lateral position variability whereas writing a message increased variability by 91.4%.[19]

These findings are very consistent with cognitive load theory: The more the brain is occupied by one thing, the less it can do another. Using a high-fidelity driving simulator, researchers found people engaged in texting while driving respond more slowly to the onset of braking lights, are impaired in forward and lateral control, and are involved in more accidents.[20] When engaged in high cognitive load texting (alphabetizing a five-letter string), participants driving in a simulator are less likely to identify and appropriately respond to events that would result in a collision.[21]

Texting as an Addiction.

Texting while driving is more distracting than conversing and so is almost certainly more dangerous. A frightening finding is that people who text while driving know it is dangerous, but choose to text anyway.[22] Given the persistence in texting and cell phone use in spite of general knowledge that these are potentially life threatening, we would do well to treat these behaviors as addictions. Like all addictions, the behavior is rewarding in the short run but damaging in the long run. The immediate reward is stronger in determining behavior than is the knowledge of a long-run potential or actual negative consequences—even if the potential consequence is to cripple or kill self and/or others!

Preferred Music Increases Violations[25]

Violation	No Music	Safe Music	Preferred Music
Frequency	10.12	10.09	11.93
Severity	158	157	189

Listening to Music Disrupts Driving. Young, novice drivers are ten times more likely to be in an accident during their first 500 miles. Their most common violations: speeding (37%) and lane weaving (20%), both of which correlate with listening to music while driving.[23] While listening to higher-tempo music, driving speed increases.[24]

To test the impact of music on driving, researchers had 85 young drivers take six trips each, in three different conditions: (1) listening to their own choice of music; (2) listening to music designed to maintain focused attention and to not distract; and (3) with no music playing.[25] The drivers allowed to select their own music chose Pop, Rock, Pop-Rock, Hip-Hop, Reggae, Ethnic, and Soul music (82%) and Classical, Movie Soundtracks, Reggae, and World Music (18%). Almost all of the participants (96%) rated the music they chose for the experiment as similar to the music they drive with every day. The experimenter-supplied alternative music was carefully designed for vehicle safety.[26] They were pieces designed to furnish "an optimal acoustic background for improved vehicular driving." The music is "a blend of easy-listening, soft-rock, and light, snappy, up-beat smooth jazz, with a touch of ethnic world-music flavor; the tracks do not include vocal performances involving lyrics, nor instrumental cover versions of well-known popular tunes." In the safe music, there is no specified melody line to sing along with.

The cars used in the experiment were rigged with in-vehicle data recorders that measured 27 behaviors of the car and driver, including: speeding (3-levels); braking (7-levels); turning with acceleration; turning with braking; and rpms in acceleration. The in-vehicle data recorded frequency of violations and severity of violations.

Among these young drivers, at-risk driving was significantly greater when drivers listened to music they selected. Listening to either no music or music designed not to distract was far less likely to cause at-risk driving. See Table: Preferred Music Increases Violations.

Mind-Wandering Causes Car Accidents.

A study of 1,000 drivers injured in car accidents found mind-wandering just before the accident was involved in half the accidents and that more intense mind-wandering was associated with the driver being the cause of the accident.[27]

Multitasking Impairs Performance on Even Simple Tasks.

A number of experiments demonstrate that performance is impaired when doing two tasks at once, even when the two tasks are simple and when people believe the tasks don't interfere with each other.[28] Studies show that even simple tasks take longer and are completed with more errors when done simultaneously than sequentially. The conclusion of one of the most extensive reviews of multi-tasking ever conducted: "The results show that people have surprisingly severe limitations on their ability to carry out simultaneously certain cognitive processes that seem fairly trivial from a computational standpoint."[29]

Students who multi-task have more problems with academic work.

Multitasking and Learning. Those studies examining the relation of multitasking to learning are consistent with the conclusion that focusing on a single task at a time produces better performance.[30] Students who multitask have more problems with academic work.[31] Using Facebook and text messaging while studying is associated with lower student grades.[32]

Inattention Blindness

As we have seen, participants talking on the phone fail to brake or slow down when necessary, miss traffic signs, and get in more traffic accidents. In these studies, researchers use eye-tracking devices and have discovered that when drivers are engaged in an engrossing conversation, they *look right* at the target, yet fail to *see* it. This is called "inattention blindness."[33]

Inattention blindness is another very strong demonstration of our inability to multitask. When one thing captures our attention, it simultaneously draws our attention away from other things. This is demonstrated in a number of almost unbelievable research studies:

- ▶ People walking while talking on a cell phone fail to notice a brightly colored clown riding a unicycle.[34]
- ▶ People very engaged in counting basketball passes fail to notice a gorilla walk through the middle of a basketball game.[35]
- ▶ People instructed to attend to black objects and ignore white objects on a computer monitor fail to see a bright red cross pass across a computer monitor for a full 5 seconds.[36]

Inattention Blindness Among Radiologists.
These examples of inattention blindness extend even to experts trained to detect abnormalities. In an almost unbelievable experiment, 24 radiologists who were highly trained in detecting lung-nodules were tested by inserting into the last case they examined, scans that contained a gorilla 48 times the size of the average nodule (about the size of a matchbook). The experts were to scan the slides looking for lung nodules. The gorilla appeared in five scans. Those who failed to see the gorilla viewed the scans with the gorilla an average of 5.3 seconds, providing ample opportunity to see the gorilla. Eye tracking revealed that the majority of those who missed the gorilla looked directly at its location. The gorilla was not difficult to see: following the experiment when the experts were allowed to review the slides without looking for lung-nodules, they all immediately saw the gorilla. Yet a full 83% percent of the radiologists did not see the gorilla when they were focused on looking for lung nodules![37]

Inattention Blindness Among Medical Examiners.
This failure to see the obvious has its parallel among medical examiners. A guide wire was mistakenly left in a patient during an operation. It was clearly visible on three different chest CT scans. Radiologists, emergency physicians, and internists viewed the scans repeatedly, yet it went unnoticed for 5 days![38]

Discrete Attention Systems

Brain imaging studies reveal there are independent attention systems. Our attention is captured by the backfire of a car and by an engrossing novel, but entirely different brain systems are involved.

Top-Down v. Bottom-Up Influences.
Attention is determined by types of sensory information coming in (loud bang, someone calling out our name) and by our voluntary, conscious control (refocusing attention on the reading text after realizing our mind has been wandering; consciously avoiding distractions in order to finish a task). These different influences on attention are determined by activation of different parts of the brain. Conscious, voluntary control of attention is managed in part by the top part of our brain, including the prefrontal cortex and is called top-down, or executive, function. Automatic turning of one's attention to incoming stimuli is activated by subcortical structures and is called bottom-up, or alerting and orienting.[39]

We cannot control the bottom-up structures. We see a flash of light or hear a loud bang and we automatically turn to check out the source. Something that just grabs our attention is activating the bottom-up structures. We can control the top-down structures. Active listening, for example, is a top-down function. We consciously decide to ignore our own thoughts and give full, undivided attention to the person with whom we are interacting. That we can control our attention has extreme implications for us as educators. Anything we can consciously control is something we can train. We can train students to improve their attention skills. We cover training of attention in Tool 13: Train Attention and in Tool 14: Train Working Memory.

Four Brain Systems Determine Level of Attention.
Four independent brains systems determine level and type of attention: *Arousal:* our general level of alertness; *Alerting:* how well we become alert in reaction to a new stimuli; *Orienting:* how well we detect what that new stimulus is and maintain attention on it; and

Executive Control: how well we voluntarily manage our attention, including consciously directing our attention toward some stimuli and away from others.[40] Each system has distinct functions, is located in different parts of the brain, is activated primarily by different neurotransmitters, and has a different amount of heritability. See Table: Four Attention Systems.

General Arousal Level. As teachers, we know some students enter class "bright-eyed" and focused, whereas others seem far less alert. Some are wide-awake; others are drowsy. This general level of arousal is mediated by the right hemisphere and subcortical structures, including the reticular formation.[41] How alert a student is depends on many factors including diet, exercise, and learned helplessness v. learned effectiveness. It depends also on genes. How generally outgoing v. shy a person is for life is partially determined

by genes, and outgoing people are more alert than shy people. The arousal system in the brain is complex, influenced primarily by norepinephrine, but also by acetylcholine, dopamine, and serotonin. When activated, the arousal system makes us generally more sensitive and responsive to incoming stimuli.

Alerting. Our alerting system is activated when we sense something is about to happen but we don't know what, where, or when. We are on guard.

Orienting. Our orienting system is activated when we automatically focus on one stimuli from among many—literally we orient toward a particular stimuli. A flash of light or a crack of a branch in a nearby bush automatically activates the orienting system.

Four Attention Systems[41]

Attention System	Function	Location	Neurotransmitter	Heritability	What to Do
Arousal	Maintains level of alertness.	Right hemisphere and subcortical structures including the reticular formation.	Norepinephrine	High	• Fast beat music at entrance • Colorful bulletin boards • Movement • Social interaction
Alerting	We are response ready; we know something is about to happen, but don't know when, where, or what it is.	Frontal and parietal areas of right hemisphere	Noradrenaline	Low	• Unexpected events • Novelty • Variety • Announce surprise coming
Orienting	Detects source of orienting; maintains alert attention to selected stimulus. Stimulus driven.	Parietal lobe; Pulvinar; Superior colliculus	Acetylcholine	None	• Quiet signal • Processing • Multimedia • Relevance
Executive Control	Monitors and directs attention; conscious, effortful self-regulation of attention; avoids distractions. Voluntarily controlled.	Frontal areas: Anterior cingulate; dorsal and lateral prefrontal cortex	Dopamine	High	• Train attention • Train working memory • Meta-cognition • Meta-attention

Executive Control. Conscious, effortful attention such as planning, decision making, error detection, and regulation of thoughts and feelings activate the executive attention network. Executive control allows us to consciously direct our attention toward some stimuli and away from others. It resolves conflicts regarding what to attend to. When students play "Simon Says", the teacher (Simon) asks students to focus on what he or she says, not what he or she does, creating a conflict between automatic mirror neuron responses and conscious executive control of attention. How well a student plays "Simon Says" is a measure of executive control.

ADHD and the Attention Systems. There are different types of ADHD,[42] and students with ADHD may have difficulties with any or all four of these attention systems.[43] After eight, 1-hour sessions of playing a computer game that demanded heightened attention, 11-year-old students with ADHD were better able to focus and disregard distractions. They showed significant improvements in flexibility of attention, vigilance, and ability to avoid distractions.[44] All students perform better academically, in proportion to which they can sustain attention on academic content while listening to a presentation, reading, classwork, or while doing homework. One of the most exciting areas of application of brain research to education is training attention and executive control, the last two tools of this principle.

Managing the Attention of Our Students

The evidence all points to the same conclusion: To maximize learning, we manage attention and develop attention skills. We need to focus the attention of our students on that which we want them to remember, help them sustain their attention, and to withdraw their attention from irrelevant stimuli. We are managers of attention.

Thus we can derive the fifth principle of brain-friendly teaching:

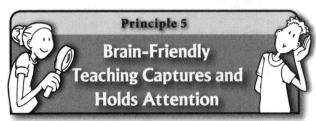

Principle 5

Brain-Friendly Teaching Captures and Holds Attention

Fourteen Tools to Capture and Hold Attention

If increased attention results in increased retention of our academic content, our skill as teachers depends on knowing ways to capture and hold student attention. How do we get students to focus on what we want them to retain and tune out that which is not relevant? The skill of managing attention is a core competency for successful teaching, regardless of the content

---

Tips
Capturing and Holding Attention

There are things we can do to capture and hold the attention of our students, corresponding to each of the four attention systems.

- **Arousal:** Create a high-stimulus environment including fast-beat music as students enter class, colorful, interactive bulletin boards, frequent movement, and social interaction.

- **Alerting:** Include frequent unexpected events, novelty, variety, and announce there will be a surprise.

- **Orienting:** Structure for full-alert attention with a quiet signal. Include frequent processing. Include multi-media presentations and make content personally relevant.

- **Executive Control:** Train attention and working memory. See the last two tools of this principle.

we teach. Here we examine fourteen powerful tools to focus attention. Most are quite simple, easily adopted by any teacher. Only the last two are complex. My suggestion: Begin with the simple tools. Master them. See the difference they make. Then, only if inclined, move up to the more complex tools. Work within your comfort level. Structure for success, for your students and yourself.

> *"The highest success in teaching depends upon the power of the teacher to command and hold the attention of her pupils."* [45]
> —*Catharine Aiken, 1895*

Fourteen Tools to Capture and Hold Attention

1. Establish a Quiet Signal
2. Teach with Kagan Structures
3. Teach with Active Listening
4. Clear Short-Term and Working Memory
5. Punctuate with Processing
6. Avoid Distractions
7. Distribute Practice
8. Create Flow
9. Respond to Attention Styles
10. Include Elements of Lesson Design
11. Encourage Exercise
12. Promote Play
13. Train Attention
14. Train Working Memory

Tool 1

Establish a Quiet Signal

Decades ago, during my first cooperative learning demonstration lesson, building off my experience as a child in the Cub Scouts, I instituted a quiet signal to manage the attention of the class. I told the students that when I raised my hand, they were to raise their hands and to give me full, alert attention. Now many schools and districts routinely use that quiet signal. The main intent of the quiet signal is not to produce quiet—it is to manage attention. By having students stop doing whatever they are doing, raise a hand, and focus fully on the teacher, we create an orienting response. This full-alert attention focuses the class.

Managing the Quiet Signal

One important trick in implementing the quiet signal is to wait until the last student raises his or her hand and gives full attention. If we don't, if we go on in spite of some students not giving full attention, the message to the class is that you don't really have to do it. In that case, compliance will erode. By being insistent, we manage the attention of all our students, increasing the probability they will remember whatever we then share.

> *The main intent of the quiet signal is not to produce quiet—it is to manage attention.*

Alternative Quiet Signals

There are many alternative quiet signals. See Box: Alternative Quiet Signals, p. 5.16. I have sorted the signals into two types: those requiring the teacher to walk over to a place or object in the room, like flipping the lights, and those the teacher can use wherever he or she is, like echo clapping. For efficiency, I advocate teaching students at least one signal that the teacher can use without needing an extra object and without having to go to a certain place in the room. When students are interacting, the most effective teachers are either observing or interacting with a team or pair. If at that moment the teacher needs to share something with the whole class (perhaps have everyone see something creative a team or

Tip
Create a quiet signal you can use at any moment, no matter where you are in the classroom.

Alternative Quiet Signals[46]

In her book, *How to Survive and Thrive in the First Three Weeks of School*,[46] Elaine McEwan describes all but the last of the following alternative quiet signals:

Quiet Signals That Require an Extra Object

Wind Chimes: Hang wind chimes and tap them when you want attention.

Lights Out: Flip the lights off and on.

Musical Attention: Play a scale on a toy xylophone.

Rain-stick: Flip over a rain-stick and expect full attention by the time the rain-stick finishes.

Quiet Signals the Teacher Can Use Anywhere

Echo Chorus: Say, *"One, two, three, eyes on me."* The class echoes back, *"One, two, eyes on you."*

Echo Clapping: Clap a pattern such as "Dun Dun Da Dun Dun" and the class claps back, "Dun Dun."

Give Me Five: Hold up your hand with five fingers up. When you see at least five students giving you full attention, begin a slow countdown with your fingers. All should be giving you full attention by the time you finish the countdown.

Sign Language: Hold up a closed fist ("S" in Sign Language for Silence).

And One to File Away...

The File Cabinet: One quiet signal that McEwan does not describe in her book was reported to me by Laurie Kagan. Laurie went into a high school chemistry class for a coaching session and noticed a rather large dent near the bottom of a metal file cabinet. When she asked the teacher about the dent, he proudly said, *"That is my Quiet Signal!"* When asked to demonstrate, the teacher had all students talking, walked over to the file cabinet, and kicked it—hard! He got immediate, full attention!

pair is doing), it is inefficient to have to walk away from the team or pair and find the rain-stick or flip the light switch. Many gym teachers know the importance of having their quiet signal with them at all times—thus, the traditional whistle on a lanyard around their necks.

Brain Processes Underpinning the Quiet Signal

Three brain processes contribute to the effectiveness of the hand-up quiet signal. Let's examine what is going on in the brain when we use the hand-up quiet signal.

Quiet Signals Are Competing Responses.

If we did a brain scan while students are talking with each other, we would find a great deal of activity in their temporal lobes where the brain processes speech. Wernicke's area is busy decoding the words of others, making meaning out of those sounds. Broca's area is busy translating students' own thoughts into words so they can communicate their thoughts. All this is going on while they are interacting. Then we give a quiet signal. As students raise their hands, their motor cortex becomes active, interrupting the temporal lobe activity. The attention system becomes alert, prepared to orient toward new stimuli—what the teacher is about to present.

Quiet Signals Create an Orienting Reflex.

Students become more alert in response to the quiet signal because the stimuli in their environment is changing (hands raising, students looking up toward the teacher). Students' brains orient toward and focus on new stimuli. When students give this orienting response (also called an *orienting reflex*),[47] their bodies and brains change in important ways: The blood vessels in the brain dilate allowing more blood flow to the brain, the blood vessels to the major muscle groups constrict, the heart beats slower, eyes dilate, focus becomes more intense, Alpha brain waves are blocked momentarily, and students become more alert.

The *Orienting Reflex* is a primary reflex. That is, it takes precedence over whatever else the body is doing. It is like the brain says, "Stop everything. Before I go on, I need to know if I am safe." The rest of the body relaxes while the brain goes into a momentary overdrive to check out the novel stimuli. Is it a threat? Is it an opportunity? Do I need to approach or avoid? When, following an orienting response, there is no danger perceived, the brain has a positive response. Arousal is lowered, and the brain prepares for approach and exploration. We explore the importance of the brain's reaction to novel stimuli in more depth in Tool 1: Stimulate with Surprise and Novelty, in Principle 6: Stimuli. Here it is important to note how the quiet signal first focuses students' attention, and then prepares them to attend to what the teacher says following the signal.

Quiet Signals Create a Contagion of Attention. The third brain process that makes the quiet signal effective is the activation of mirror neurons.[48] Because those around us are becoming more alert, we also become more alert. When we see the face of someone else experiencing an emotion, because of our mirror neurons, our brains fire as if we are having that emotion. Alertness spreads throughout the class. We explored the importance of mirror neurons in some depth in Principle 3: Social. For now, we need note only that mirror neurons are the motor of the quiet signal. A student sees another becoming attentive, and so becomes more attentive. Now there are two. Two leads to four, and soon the whole class is attentive. Mirror neurons create a contagion of emotion—in this case, a contagion of alert attention.

Tool 2

Teach with Kagan Structures

Kagan Structures help focus attention, activating all four of the attention systems. As we have seen in Principle 3: Social, social interaction lights up the brain. This fuller brain engagement increases arousal. Social interaction always involves novel stimuli, which creates alertness and orienting. Executive control is exercised as students direct their attention to each other and to the task at hand.

Because the structures are often used to punctuate lectures and presentations, they clear working memory, one of the most powerful tools we have for creating undivided attention. We explore the importance of processing and clearing short-term and working memory in Tool 4: Clear Short-Term and Working Memory and Tool 5: Punctuate with Processing, in Principle 5: Attention.

Finally, the structures are step-by-step instructional sequences. Because the teacher has the students focus on one step at a time, students don't have to think about what is coming next. This frees working memory to fully focus on the task at hand. It allows undivided attention, as students are not thinking about both the task at hand and what they are to do next.

Managing Structures: No Frontloading

While taking students through a structure, it is preferable to give one bit of instruction, let the students carry out that action, and then give the next bit of instruction. This one-step-at-a-time approach, giving bite-sized instructional bits, is preferable to telling the students all the steps of the structure at the outset. Frontloading the steps clogs working memory, causing a lack of focus.

Structures Focus Attention

Listen Right! **Listen Right!** is a powerful structure to create undivided attention. It is designed to replace the traditional way we have students take notes during a lecture. Traditionally, we have had students take notes *while* we lecture. This causes a division of attention. The students are not fully listening because they are also trying to take notes, and they are not fully focusing on their note-taking because at the same time they are trying to listen to the lecture. In **Listen Right!** students listen with undivided attention to a chunk of lecture and then stop to take notes on that chunk. In this way, they have undivided attention while listening and undivided attention while taking notes. The quality of both the listening and the note-taking is radically improved. Undivided attention improves retention.

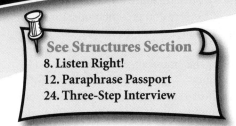

After using **Listen Right!** in a workshop or in a class, we often ask participants or students if they were listening more carefully because they were not trying to take notes while listening. Almost all emphatically agree. We then ask if their note taking was better because they were not trying to listen to the next bit of the presentation while writing their notes. Again, there is almost total, emphatic agreement.

Other forces are also at work in **Listen Right!** that focus attention. Because the students know they will share their notes after each chunk, they listen more carefully. They are held accountable for listening and note-taking. This is in contrast to the traditional lecture format in which students can take notes or not, knowing that no one will know.

Because the students are interacting after each chunk of the presentation, this processing serves to clear working memory so students listen to the next chunk with freer attention. It is perhaps the frequent processing and individual accountability built into the structure that most contributes to how **Listen Right!** captures and holds attention.

Cautionary Notes. There are probably important individual differences in the reaction of students to **Listen Right!** Some students may listen more carefully by taking notes at the same time. For these students, **Listen Right!** may not be as effective as allowing simultaneous note-taking. It is, however, for them a form of training— learning another way to listen. Another note of caution is warranted: **Listen Right!** is more appropriate for some types of content than others. Listening to a story or a description of an event is very different from taking notes on the steps of a math algorithm. There are times we want students to take notes *as we present* rather than *after* a presentation chunk.

Three-Step Interview. The third step of **Three-Step Interview** is designed to hold students accountable for listening, and so intensifies their focused attention. In the first two steps of **Three-Step Interview**, while the pairs are interviewing each other, they know Step 3 is coming. They know in Step 3 they will each be responsible for sharing what they learned during the pair interview. Knowing they will be held accountable for what they have heard, students listen more intently—they have more focused attention.

Paraphrase Passport. You earn the right to speak during **Paraphrase Passport** by accurately paraphrasing the person who spoke before you. Thus, students are held accountable for listening and listen with more focused attention. The conversation during **Paraphrase Passport** is far more intense and focused than in a typical group discussion. In group discussion, often everyone is waiting their turn to talk, giving little or even no attention to what others are saying.

Most Kagan Structures Focus Attention. **Three-Step Interview**, **Paraphrase Passport**, and **Listen Right!** are but three of the many structures that focus attention. Student behavior using the structures stands in stark contrast to student behavior in the traditional classroom. Teachers using the traditional way of structuring interaction in the classroom call on students one at a time to answer teacher-generated questions. The result: one student intensely focused on answering the question, some number of students listening, to the answer, and some number of students mind-wandering. There is no accountability for listening to the answer of a fellow student, so students are free to think about other things. When structures are used, all students are engaged simultaneously, and there is little chance for mind-wandering because often someone is asking you a question during face-to-face interaction. Students keep each other focused and engaged.

The various structures focus attention in different ways. See Table: Kagan Structures Focus Attention, p. 5.19.

Kagan Structures Focus Attention

Structures	Structure Section	How Structures Focus Attention
AllWrite Consensus	1	In the process of struggling toward consensus, students need to listen carefully to each other so they can find a solution that incorporates all concerns or ideas.
Both Record RallyRobin	2	Students listen carefully to the idea of their partner because they must record it.
Celebrity Interview	3	One student is standing, and all questions and attention are focused on that one student.
Choral Practice	4	Students must coordinate their speaking to be able to respond in unison. Thus, their minds cannot wander; they must focus on the speech of others.
Flashcard Game	5	One student is holding up a card, demanding the response of the partner. There is no opportunity for mind-wandering.
Formations	6	For each student to find a place in the formation, he or she must pay close attention to where the others are placing themselves.
Kinesthetic Symbols	7	Students in teams or as a class perform the kinesthetic symbols in unison, demanding careful attention to coordinate efforts.
Listen Right!	8	Listening is not distracted by trying to take notes at the same time. Note-taking is not distracted by attempting to listen at the same time.
Number Group Mania!	9	Students are all focused on becoming part of a group. They do not want to be last to join.
PairUp Review Quiz-Quiz-Trade RallyQuiz Traveling RallyInterview	11 13 14 27	Mind-wandering does not exist when someone is quizzing you or interviewing you.
Paraphrase Passport	12	Students listen intently because their right to speak is contingent on their ability to paraphrase the prior speaker.
RallyRobin	15	After a partner gives a brief response, the student is responsible for responding. Turns alternate quickly, focusing attention.
Traveling Heads Together	26	Students are held accountable for listening, as they will travel to another team to report.
Sage-N-Scribe	17	The Scribe must listen carefully to the Sage in order to carry out the Sage's instructions.
Three-Step Interview	24	Interviewers listen intently because they must share with the group what they have learned in the interview.
Timed Pair Share	25	Students are instructed in active listening and how to focus intently on the speaker without interrupting.

Tool 3

Teach with Active Listening

Many students have not learned the art of active listening. In many groups, each person is waiting his or her turn to talk, paying little or even no attention to the person talking. Without active listening skills among students, much of what a teacher presents is lost. In some classrooms, the teacher is talking, but only some students have their attention focused on the teacher. Some students are looking around, perhaps directing their attention to objects in their desk. Like any skill, active listening can be taught and learned.

Let's overview approaches to teaching active listening to others and active listening during note-taking.

Active Listening During Conversations

Teaching students how to fully attend to others during interaction is facilitated by a combination of modeling, practice, and reinforcement. A second approach is to use the structure **Paraphrase Passport**.

Modeling, Practice, and Reinforcement.
The most powerful approach to teaching active listening integrates modeling, practicing, and reinforcing.

> ## Tip
> Teach active-listening skills to students as if they have no idea what it is—many don't!

Define Active Listening via Modeling. We begin our mini-active listening training by inviting a student to the front of the room. We ask the student to tell us about something fun they have done in the last month. As they do, we turn our body slightly away from the student, look around, take something out of our pocket and examine it, and so on. We do not look at the student. After a bit, we ask the student how that felt. The student says, *"Not good."* We ask why. The student says, *"Because you were not listening to me."* Then we say, *"OK, let's try it again."* This time we face the student, make eye contact, nod, show facial expressions of interest, and paraphrase the student one or two times while the student is talking, checking for understanding. We then once again ask the student how it felt. We get a positive response. We define the second approach as "Active Listening." We then ask all the students in the classroom to turn to a partner and do a **RallyRobin**, naming the elements of active listening, making sure everyone knows active listening consists of facing the speaker, making eye contact, expressing interest, and paraphrasing.

Practice and Reinforcement of Active Listening. Next, we have the students turn to a partner and do a **Timed Pair Share**, each sharing for a minute while his or her partner practices active listening. While this is happening we circulate and make positive comments on their use of active listening. Afterwards, we describe to the class some of the positive active listening we heard and saw.

Ongoing Reinforcement. Once active listening has been defined, on an ongoing basis, we compliment students when we see it being used. We model, practice, and reinforce repeatedly as needed.

See Structures Section
12. Paraphrase Passport
25. Timed Pair Share

Paraphrase Passport. **Paraphrase Passport** is a Kagan Structure explicitly designed to foster active listening. It is used when students interact with a partner or during a team discussion. The rule is simple: You cannot share your idea until after you have paraphrased the person who spoke right before you, to that person's satisfaction. If a student fails to correctly paraphrase, the speaker restates or rephrases his or her idea, and the paraphraser gets a second try. It is remarkable how intently students (and adults) listen when they know they will be held accountable for listening.

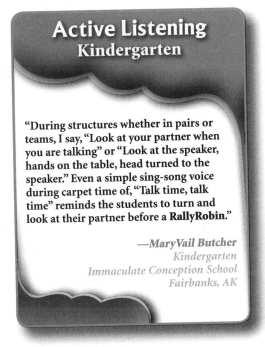

Active Listening
Kindergarten

"During structures whether in pairs or teams, I say, "Look at your partner when you are talking" or "Look at the speaker, hands on the table, head turned to the speaker." Even a simple sing-song voice during carpet time of, "Talk time, talk time" reminds the students to turn and look at their partner before a **RallyRobin**."

—*MaryVail Butcher*
Kindergarten
Immaculate Conception School
Fairbanks, AK

Paraphrasing can be facilitated by giving students paraphrase chips or by having them make up the paraphrase chips. The chips can be slips of paper. On the chips are written sentence starters for paraphrasing like:

▶ *"If I hear you right, you mean…"*
▶ *"To summarize…"*
▶ *"It seems to me you are saying…"*
▶ *"Your main point is…"*

Students draw and use one of the chips when it is their turn to paraphrase.

Teaching Active Listening During Note-Taking

We can teach students many ways to take notes, including mind mapping and word webbing (see Tool 7: Illustrate with Images, in Principle 6: Stimuli); outlining, diagraming, and creating concept maps. Here we will focus on three approaches that promote active listening by having the students listen for specific information: Cloze Note-Taking, Conceptual Pre-Questions, and Cornel Note-Taking.

Cloze Note-Taking. Students listen to a presentation far more intently if they are actively seeking specific information. A way to put students into that active search mode is to provide cloze note-taking sheets. The notes are partially written for the students, but bits of information (names, numbers, phrases) are left out—an underline is provided for students to fill in the missing information.

Without active listening skills, students lose much of what a teacher presents.

> *Sample Cloze Note-Taking Sentences:*
> *"It is better to be safe than _____."*
> *"You can lead a horse to water, but you can't _____ _____ _____."*

The Zeigarnik Effect. The brain seeks closure. We want to write in *"sorry"* where it is missing in the sentence, *"It is better to be safe than sorry."* In the same way, when students have a cloze note-taking sheet, they are motivated to actively listen for the missing words and phrases. The tendency of the brain to return to and attempt to complete uncompleted tasks is called the *Zeigarnik effect*, named after the Russian psychologist, Bluma Zeigarnik. Empirical evidence supports the Zeigarnik effect; students remember uncompleted test items better than items they have completed.[49]

Cloze sentences can be used for comprehension evaluation in a test or quiz:

Sample Cloze Recall/Compression Sentences:
A common format for using cloze to test recall or comprehension:
"In a cloze sentence, words are _____."
(omitted, underlined)

Tip
Apply the Zeigarnik effect to help end procrastination. For the student who can't get started on a task, ask only that they do the first small step (answer the first question, solve the first problem). For many students, once a task is started, they are motivated to finish.

Conceptual Pre-Questions. Students who have not been tutored in note-taking skills most often engage in some form of "verbatim note-taking." They simply write down points from the lecture or presentation with no analysis, evaluation, or interpretation. They act as a faulty tape recorder, with little or no thought, capturing some but not all of the information presented. A simple way to boost active listening in a lecture and to boost note-taking beyond the verbatim level is to include conceptual pre-questions. The Pre-Questions create active listening by having students listen for specific information or concepts.

The Power of Pre-Questions. In testing the power of conceptual pre-questions, experimenters presented a lecture on a fictional African tribe, the Mala. Included in the lecture were facts, like the following:

> The first slaves were forcibly taken from Mala to Europe in 1610. When Europeans came over to Mala to settle there, they never paid the Malans for the land they occupied. For the first 50 years of this century, foreign-controlled factories employed the Malans at deplorably low wages. Prior to the coming of the Europeans, Arab nomads frequently plundered villages in Mala.[50]

Tip
Allow students time to review before a test.

Students were assigned various conditions: *Note-Taking:* Students were assigned to take notes or not to take notes. If they took notes, they were told to take notes the way they usually did in a lecture. *Review:* Students either reviewed their notes mentally before the test, read them over, or did not review. *Pre-Questions:* During the lecture, students either attempted to answer pre-questions, or were not given pre-questions. Pre-questions focused students on themes that united the lecture facts. If given pre-questions, students were told to try to answer the pre-question while listening to the lecture. A sample pre-question

tied together the facts of the lecture, for example, *"In what ways were the Mala exploited?"*

Students were tested 24 hours later. The results:

- ▶ **Taking Notes.** Taking notes resulted in significantly higher recall that listening only.
- ▶ **Reviewing Notes.** There was a 40%–50% increase in recall if students reviewed their notes before the test.
- ▶ **Pre-Questions.** If not given pre-questions, students simply listed information directly from the lecture without deriving key concepts or integrating lecture content and prior knowledge. They recalled the concepts only 27% of the time. When given pre-questions, the key concepts appeared in student notes, concepts were more often integrated, and students recalled the key concepts 68% of the time!

Without Pre-Questions, 27% of concepts were recalled. With Pre-Questions, 68% of concepts were recalled!

Active listening is more than being a tape recorder. It involves reacting to and actively encountering the content. By attempting to answer the pre-questions, students were listening for, seeking, specific information rather than passively responding.

Cornell Notes. The Cornell note-taking system was developed for college students,[51] but is now taught at all levels. Students take and review notes using a three-part note-taking sheet. See Blackline: Cornell-Type Note-Taking Page, p. 5.23. During the lecture, students are to take notes in a telegraphic form and may use images and/or diagrams, but are encouraged not to take verbatim notes. Long ideas are to be paraphrased. During and/or following the presentation, questions and keywords are recorded in the left column. Following the lecture, a brief summary is written at the bottom of the page. To review for a test, students focus on the summary and may cover the notes section and attempt from memory to answer the questions and define the keywords.

Cornell Notes v. Cloze Notes. A study that contrasted no note-taking, Cornell Notes, and a form of cloze note-taking called Guided Notes, found both note-taking approaches superior to

Use this Cornell-Type Note-Taking Page during and immediately following lectures, and then again to review for tests.

Cornell-Type Note-Taking Page

Directions: Step 1. During Lecture: Take notes during lecture and jot down keywords and questions the lecturer answers. **Step 2. Following Lecture:** Add additional questions and keywords. Write a concise summary of the lecture. **Step 3. Before Test:** Review, rereading the summary, then attempt to summarize without viewing the summary and with the notes covered. From memory, define the keywords and answer the questions.

Topic: ______________________

Questions/Keywords: ________

Name: ______________________

Class: ______________________

Period: ______________ **Date:** ____________

Notes: ______________________

Summary: ______________________

the listen-only control.[52] Cloze note-taking was superior to Cornell Notes for recall and student comments indicated they thought they learned more using the cloze note-taking than they did using Cornell Notes. The researcher concluded that while cloze notes were significantly superior for recall, Cornell Notes may be superior for synthesis, application, or evaluation of content.

> **Tip**
>
> Intersperse pre-questions prior to and at various points in a presentation. Encourage students to find and take notes on the answers to the pre-questions.

Maximizing Recall: A Before-During-After Approach. To maximize recall, we would do well to adopt a Before-During-After approach.

Before Presenting. Prior to a lecture or presentation, we use pre-questions so students are actively seeking the answers to key questions.

We encourage note-taking and provide either cloze note-taking sheets, Cornell Notes, or some combination.

While Presenting. Frequently stop to have students talk about key points. Hold students accountable for their note-taking using structures like **Listen Right!** or **Traveling Heads Together**. Check for understanding and give students opportunities to ask questions and seek clarification. Because pictures are remembered better than words, make ample use of visuals and encourage students to take notes using visuals (see Tool 7: Illustrate with Images, in Principle 6: Stimuli).

After Presenting. Following a presentation, we have a number of options to increase recall. The most powerful options are to have students interact over the content using an interactive structure and to encourage students to review their notes in structured ways.

Structures to Cement Memory. Following a presentation, different structures are used to cement memory, depending on the type of content to be learned. Different structures are designed for simple recall, acquisition of conceptual knowledge, and for practicing procedures. See Table: Structures to Cement Learning.

Structures to Cement Learning

Recall	Conceptual Knowledge	Procedural Knowledge
Both Record RallyRobin (2)	AllWrite Consensus (1)	Sage-N-Scribe (17)
Choral Practice (4)	Paraphrase Passport (12)	SeeOne–DoOne–TeachOne (18)
Flashcard Game (5)	Simulations (19)	Team-Pair-Solo (23)
Kinesthetic Symbols (7)	Three-Step Interview (24)	
PairUp Review (11)	Timed Pair Share (25)	
Quiz-Quiz-Trade (13)	Traveling RallyInterview (27)	
RallyQuiz (14)		
Traveling Heads Together (26)		

Note-Taking Review Procedures. The best ways to have students review their notes include ways to have students attempt to reproduce from memory what they have been taught, using their notes to check for accuracy and completeness. Have students cover the notes section of their Cornell Notes and attempt to answer the questions from memory.

Overlap Maps: Students who have taken notes using a mind mapping attempt to recreate their mind map from memory. When finished, those items they left out are filled in using a red pen or marker. Thus, when they review for the test, the items they are most likely to miss stand out in red. A third approach is quite similar, using a cloze note-taking sheet. Students are provided a second copy of the cloze note-taking sheet and attempt to fill it in from memory. Missed items are filled in using a red pen or maker. That second sheet is later used to review for the test or quiz.

Tool 4

Clear Short-Term and Working Memory

Those who present workshops on the brain for educators advocate frequently clearing working memory. They generally fail, however, to distinguish clearing working memory from clearing short-term memory. Both are important, but they involve different brain structures and processes. When we understand the distinction, we discover there are different methods for clearing short-term v. working memory. Before turning to those methods, let's distinguish short-term memory and working memory.

Short-Term Memory v. Working Memory

Short-term memory is memory for information we repeat back, like memory for a telephone number we have just heard or a sign we have just seen. In contrast, working memory is information we are presently paying attention to, thinking

about, and working on. Content for working memory can be drawn from short-term memory, prior experience, imagination, or sensory input. It is information we work on as we think, create, and problem solve.

Short-term memory is temporary storage. Think of a refrigerator. We place food in the refrigerator and later take it out, unchanged. Short-term memory is like the refrigerator, holding something until we bring it out, unchanged. Working memory, in contrast, works on, changes content. Think of a frying pan on the stove above a lit burner. We put in the pan the raw ingredients for a stir fry, stir them, and a bit later, those raw ingredients are changed into a finished stir fry. We take content out of the refrigerator unchanged, whereas we change what we put in the frying pan. We bring the content out of short-term memory unchanged, whereas we manipulate content with working memory. In working memory we combine, analyze, evaluate, compare, organize, and create.

Short-Term Memory. Imagine you are in an unfamiliar town and ask someone for directions. As you drive away, you try to recall the directions just as they were told to you so you won't get lost. You are drawing from short-term memory—recalling the information without changing it. Short-term memory for words (like directions we hear) is processed in a different part of the brain than short-term memory for pictures (like a map we have looked at). People can have better short-term memory for either verbal or visual content.

We draw content out from short-term memory unchanged; we manipulate content with working memory.

Working Memory. Now imagine you are trying to find a friend's house in a strange part of town without clear directions. As you try to figure out which way to turn, you draw into consciousness all manner of information: What you know about the general layout of towns; how streets are generally numbered; and that because you are traveling toward the setting sun, you must be traveling west. To figure how much farther you have to drive, you mentally estimate how long you have been traveling and subtract that from how long you were told it would take to arrive at your friend's house. You are using your working memory—manipulating information.

This distinction between short-term memory and working memory fits with our experience, but those writing on the topic have not all supported this simple, commonsense distinction. For example, John Ratey equates working memory with what I have described as short-term memory: "Working memory holds small amounts of information for only a few seconds at a time. It gives us the ability to remember a telephone number taken from the phone book long enough to dial the phone."[53] James McGaugh equates the two: "Today the terms 'short-term memory' and 'working memory' refer to memory for recent experiences...."[54] A number of authors either blur or discount the difference between working memory and short-term memory.

> ## Short-Term v. Working Memory
>
> Short-term memory is for storage: *Can you repeat back these numbers: 10, 14, 37, 12?*
>
> Working memory is for both storage and manipulation: *Can you sum the following numbers in you head: 10, 14, 37, 12?*

Brain Imaging Distinguishes Short-Term and Working Memory.
Clever active-brain imaging studies support a clear distinction between short-term memory and working memory.[55] While taking an fMRI, people are shown a series of letters scrambled in random order. After an 8-second delay with the letters out of sight, they are asked to state the letters back in one of two ways, either in the order they were presented (maintenance) or in alphabetical order (manipulation). Simply repeating the letters is short-term memory; alphabetizing the letters involves mental manipulation; it involves working memory. The experiments reveal that when working memory is involved (alphabetizing), the dorsolateral prefrontal cortex is significantly more active than when only short-term memory is involved. Thus, we can actually

locate a primary brain structure that becomes significantly more active when we engage working memory compared to when we engage only short-term memory. Thus, our commonsense distinction between short-term and working memory is supported. Thinking, manipulating information, and exercising working memory, are different from simply recalling information.

Short-Term and Working Memory Work in Concert.
For purposes here, we will stick to this simple distinction: short-term memory is for maintenance; working memory is for manipulation. I would be remiss, however, if I didn't note this distinction is not quite as clear cut as I am making it. Short-term memory and working memory are intertwined. Part of what I am working on, the contents of working memory, is content drawn from short-term memory. Further, while exercising working memory, I may place content temporarily into short-term memory to be drawn back a bit later into working memory. The two systems often work in concert.

> *Brain science supports our commonsense distinction between short-term and working memory. Thinking, manipulating information, and exercising working memory, are different from simply recalling information.*

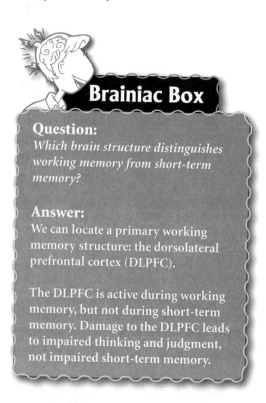

Brainiac Box

Question:
Which brain structure distinguishes working memory from short-term memory?

Answer:
We can locate a primary working memory structure: the dorsolateral prefrontal cortex (DLPFC).

The DLPFC is active during working memory, but not during short-term memory. Damage to the DLPFC leads to impaired thinking and judgment, not impaired short-term memory.

There can be no working memory without short-term memory. This has led some brain theorists to conceptualize working memory as both maintenance and manipulation—they conceptualize short-term memory as a component of working memory. There is no question, however, that working memory engages a part of the brain, the dorsolateral prefrontal cortex, that is not activated by short-term memory.

The picture gets even more complex when we dig into it: Both short-term memory and working memory have components. Short-term memory for verbal content and for visual content are processed by different parts of the brain. Working memory too has distinct components.[56] Efficient working memory depends on a collection of skills, including ability to focus and sustain attention, avoid distractions, shift tasks, and compare and manipulate the contents of consciousness. All of these components of working memory involve different sets of brain structures.

Limited Capacity of Short-Term Memory

Short-term and working memory systems have very limited capacity: We can only hold a certain amount of information in consciousness at one time.[57] A considerable amount of empirical research confirms exactly how much can be stored in short-term memory. The work began in 1956 with the publication of a classic article by George Miller, *"The magical number seven, plus or minus two: Some limits on our capacity for processing information."*[58] Research and theory have revised Miller's magical number seven; there is strong support that short-term memory can hold only four chunks of information. Chunks, however, can contain more than one item.[59] Students differ dramatically in their working memory capacity and this is a very important partial explanation of school achievement differences. Very exciting work shows that working memory capacity can be increased with training[60] and this in turn increases both intelligence and school achievement. We address this extremely important topic in Tool 14: Train Working Memory.

Depending on the content, age, and ability of the student, more or less information can be retained in short-term memory, but there is very strong agreement: What can be retained in short-term memory is very little and held only very briefly.

Limited Capacity Is Adaptive. Given the very limited capacity of short-term and working memory, we might ask why the brain is designed with such limited capacity. The limited capacities of short-term and working memory systems are very adaptive. If we were juggling 100 things in consciousness at once, our attention would be so divided, we could not function or survive.

The limited capacities of working and short-term memory systems do, however, have critical implications for us as educators. As we lecture or do a demonstration, we are filling short-term and working memory. After only four chunks of information, we have exceeded the limit of short-term memory's capacity for even the very best of our students.[61] Once short-term memory is full, to continue presenting is like pouring more water into a glass that is already full. The solution: frequent processing. As students process the content, they move it from short-term and working memory to longer-term memory. This leaves attention freer to store and process new information.

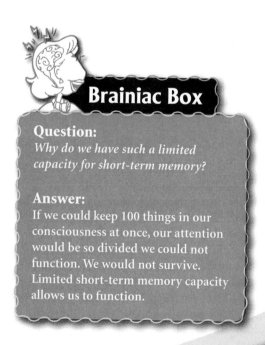

Brainiac Box

Question:
Why do we have such a limited capacity for short-term memory?

Answer:
If we could keep 100 things in our consciousness at once, our attention would be so divided we could not function. We would not survive. Limited short-term memory capacity allows us to function.

Why "To Do" Lists Work. The classic situation of filling up short-term memory is trying to keep in mind all the things we have to do. When we have many unfinished tasks, we feel as if our brain is full. We cannot concentrate. We feel overwhelmed and feel we can't take in anything more.

When we are in that situation, after we sit down and write a "To Do" list, we feel relief. Our mind feels clearer; we feel we can concentrate and focus.

Why does writing a "To Do" list have such a profound, immediate positive impact? Prior to writing the list, we were trying to hold important items in short-term memory. Since short-term memory has a limited capacity, we feel "We can't take in any more." To focus on something additional would mean forgetting something from our unfinished task list. After writing down the "To Do" list, we are free to concentrate on new content, knowing we don't have to keep the "To Do" items in mind. In effect, our "To Do" list items have moved from internal short-term memory to an external long-term storage device—a piece of paper. We no longer have to keep the items in short-term memory and our attention is free to take in more information. Our experience corroborates brain research: We have a limited capacity in short-term memory, and when short-term memory is full, we cannot take in more information.

Two Reasons Students Can't Focus on a Lesson

The simple distinction between short-term memory (storage, recall, maintenance), and working memory (thinking, processing, manipulation) is important because the ability of our students to attend fully to the content of our lessons can be diminished by either of the two processes. They are not able to focus fully on our lesson either because their short-term memory is full (*"I can't take in any more"*) or because their working memory is distracted, puzzling about something else (*"Let me weigh the evidence: Did that girl smile at me because she wants me to ask her out, or is she just a friendly girl?"*).

If we launch into a lesson while our students are still pondering unresolved problems, they have less free attention for our presentation.

Ways to Clear Short-Term and Working Memory

Given the distinction between short-term and working memory, to restore our students' brains to full-alert focused attention and increase retention of our content, we need two different processes: (1) moving content from short-term to long-term memory, or an external storage device (notes); freeing attention for the lesson, and (2) clearing working memory, so students are not preoccupied, pondering things other than the lesson. See Table: Kagan Structures to Clear Short-Term Memory, p. 5.29.

Ways to Clear Short-Term Memory.
Teachers can use many ways to have students clear short-term memory. While presenting information, we can frequently stop talking and have students:

> ▶ Jot down important points of the lecture and compare them with a partner.
> ▶ Create a mnemonic to remember a list.
> ▶ Draw a graphic organizer to hold the information.
> ▶ Do a Kagan Structure to review the content.
> ▶ Tell a partner how they will remember the content.
> ▶ Make links to prior knowledge.
> ▶ Fill in cloze words or phrases on a handout.

Anything that moves the content of short-term memory to student notes or to long-term memory helps clear short-term memory.

Kagan Structures Clear Short-Term Memory.
Many Kagan Structures can be used to clear short-term memory. The classic example is **Listen Right!** After taking in a chunk of information, students write down the key points, clearing short-term memory. Think of the notes page as a hard drive. The students are moving the content from RAM (short-term memory) to a hard drive (note paper). To take another example, the teacher has read a part of a story to the class or the students have read the portion of the story. The teacher stops and asks students to do a **RallyRobin**, taking turns to name the events of the story that have transpired so far, in chronological order. The students have just read

Kagan Structures to Clear Short-Term Memory

Structure	Structure Section	How Structures Clear Short-Term Memory
Both Record RallyRobin	2	After stating an answer, the students record it, moving it from short-term memory to their notes.
Choral Practice	4	After the teacher has presented content, the students say it in unison. By repeating the content several times, content moves from short- to long-term memory.
Flashcard Game	5	The Flashcard Game is explicitly designed to move content from short- to long-term memory. On the first round, students have just seen and heard the answer they are to give, simply drawing it from immediate short-term memory. On the second and third rounds, students are to draw the answer from long-term memory as they have not just seen or heard the answer.
Listen Right!	8	After hearing a chunk of content, students record it in their notes, clearing short-term memory.
RallyRobin	15	By repeating a list, students increase the probability it will move from short-term to long-term memory.

or heard the story, and the events are in short-term memory. As students name the events, they are moving the content from short- to long-term memory. A variety of other Kagan Structures can be used to clear short-term memory. See Table: Kagan Structures to Clear Short-Term Memory.

Ways to Clear Working Memory. Clearing working memory is different from clearing short-term memory. The contents of short-term memory are the information we have just presented to our students. The process of working memory is the manipulation of content. As we present information, students begin to analyze it, compare it with prior knowledge, evaluate the likelihood it will be personally relevant in the future, and so on. Further, students' working memory may be puzzling over nonacademic content—the advantages and disadvantages of different approaches asking parents to borrow the family car, possible ways to spend the money they received as a birthday gift, and so on.

The more our students have on their minds, the more their attention is diverted from our lesson content. Students don't enter our class with cleared working memory. Prior to entering our class, things have happened before school, in a prior class, during passing period, at lunch, and/or at recess. If we launch into a lesson while our students are still thinking about prior events or ongoing problems, they have less free attention for our presentation. For example, following a school shooting in the news or another major public or private disturbing event, students can think of little else. They have little room in working memory to think about our content. Rather than ignoring this, the wise teacher devotes some time for students to talk about the event, to "get it out." Having expressed their thoughts and feelings, the students are freer to take in new information.

Let's consider two approaches to clearing working memory prior to a lesson: (1) Closure: helping students process the content of working memory to get done with it or at least put it aside; and (2) Refocusing: creating an activity that so fully engages students that they focus completely on the activity rather than other thoughts.

Clearing Working Memory through Closure. Several ways are available to help students get closure on the things rattling around in their minds—things robbing their ability to focus on our curriculum. The goal: clear working memory so there is more attention space available to process new academic content. Anything that helps students let go of what they have been thinking of will increase attention for the new content.

To clear working memory we can have students:
▶ Make a list of things they have been thinking about and file it away.
▶ Create a worry list, crumple it up, and toss it into the waste basket.
▶ Talk to a partner about what has happened to them prior to class.

Clearing Working Memory with Kagan Structures. Many Kagan Structures are ideal for having students discuss what is on their minds, allowing them to get closure, and to clear working memory. For example, a teacher might simply begin class by having students pair up and do a **Timed Pair Share** for 2 minutes each, telling their partner all the things that have happened to them before class and things they have been thinking about. See Table: Kagan Structures to Clear Working Memory.

Clearing Working Memory through Refocusing. Anything that helps students give full attention to something in the present has the effect of helping them let go of things they have been thinking about. One of the reasons we have full-

Kagan Structures to Clear Working Memory

Structure	Structure Section	How Structures Clear Short-Term Memory
AllWrite Consensus	1	After students have been thinking about an issue, the teacher might call for an AllWrite Consensus. As they come to consensus on their response, they obtain closure.
Listen Right!	8	Students process each chunk of the presentation with peers, getting done with that piece, leaving working memory freer to think about the next chunk.
PairUp Review	11	After the teacher has presented a question, students independently write their own answers before discussing it. As they write their answers, they think through the content, getting closure on their idea.
Paraphrase Passport	12	As students express their point of view, they put their thoughts together, clearing working memory.
Traveling RallyInterview	27	Students may be asked to interview each other on "things on their mind." For examples: "Things you have been wondering about, hoping for, worried about…".
SeeOne–DoOne–TeachOne	18	Students first see a procedure and may have questions about how to do the procedure. By performing the procedure and teaching someone else the procedure, they clear up their questions and concerns, freeing working memory.
Timed Pair Share	25	Timed Pair Share is perfect for having students express and get closure on what is on their minds.
Traveling Heads Together	26	The teacher poses thought questions. As students discuss their best answers and formulate a team response, they get closure on the question.

alert attention after seeing a good movie, engrossing play, or athletic event is that those events create full, undivided, alert attention. We let go of whatever was in working memory. The more engaging the activity, the more we are distracted from other thoughts, emotions, and sensations. Remember how virtual reality serves to reduce the pain of burn victims during otherwise excruciating procedures. Immersing them in a totally engrossing experience diverts their attention. We can use this process with our students by having the class engage in an activity that demands full, alert, focused attention in the moment. Following that activity, working memory is clear, ready to focus on new content.

We can have students:
- ▶ Give a team cheer or team handshake, or create a new celebration.
- ▶ Exercise (swim in place, do a few jumping jacks).
- ▶ Move to music.
- ▶ Play a Silly Sport.
- ▶ Spend a few minutes doing relaxation breathing.
- ▶ Meditate for a few minutes.
- ▶ Practice progressive muscle relaxation.
- ▶ Experience guided imagery to let go of the past and focus on the present.

By having our students frequently clear their working and short-term memory systems while we teach, their attention is freer to take in a greater proportion of our content. They have undivided attention, rather than a "cloudy mind."

The most powerful tool we have for clearing both short-term and working memory is processing, the tool we explore next.

Frequent processing clears short-term and working memory, allowing students to give full, undivided attention to new content.

Tool 5

Punctuate with Processing

If our academic content is gum, and the discussion and thinking about the content (processing) by students is chew, then brain science gives us a clear directive: Increase the amount of chew. A lot of gum with little chew leads to little learning. Because of the ways the short-term and the working memory systems operate, frequent processing increases learning in seven powerful ways. Only with frequent processing does our content stand a chance of moving from short-term to long-term memory. We can dramatically increase retention of content in students of any age if we frequently punctuate our presentations, lectures, and demonstrations with student processing. If I had only one way to tell teachers how to increase student memory for their content, I would choose frequent processing.

"If teaching were the same as telling, we'd all be so smart we could hardly stand it."
—Mark Twain

What Is Processing?

Processing is active mental engagement with the content: thinking about, analyzing, connecting new content to prior knowledge, formulating questions about it. There are numerous ways to have students process the content. Perhaps the simplest and most powerful is for teachers to stop talking and let the students talk. The 200-plus Kagan Structures for active engagement are all forms of processing. In addition, we can have students interact in structured ways to organize, apply, analyze,

The 200-plus Kagan Structures for active engagement are all forms of processing.

synthesize, and evaluate the content. A few of the many ways to have students process the content include:

- ▶ Retelling the content in their own words
- ▶ Mind Mapping
- ▶ Creating Graphic Organizers
- ▶ Debating
- ▶ Writing an essay or letter
- ▶ Drawing a symbol or picture

Having students see how they can use the content (establish personal relevance) and make sense of the content (construct meaning) are two powerful forms of processing we deal with in Tool 10: Make It Multimodal and Tool 11: Teach with Styles, in Principle 6: Stimuli.

What Does Processing Do?

As our students process the content, seven very important things happen. Let's examine the seven ways processing enhance learning:

1. Processing Clears Short-Term and Working Memory
2. Processing Enhances Storage and Retention of Content
3. Processing Prevents Mind-Wandering
4. Processing Produces Retrograde Memory Enhancement
5. Processing Creates Episodic Memories
6. Processing Provides Novel Stimuli, Increasing Alertness
7. Processing Activates Many Parts of the Brain

> **Tip**
> Punctuate lectures and demonstrations with frequent processing.

1. Processing Clears Short-Term and Working Memory. Presentations fill short-term memory. When we are presenting via lecture, video, or demonstration, we are filling up short-term memory. After a bit, unless we have students in some way move that content into long-term memory or storage, we exceed the capacity of short-term memory to hold more content. Moving the content from short-term to

long-term memory is analogous to writing a "To Do" list—it frees space in short-term memory so new information can be stored temporarily. If we fail to free space in short-term memory, as we continue presenting, other information is lost. It is like pouring more water into a glass that is already full. Continuing to provide input beyond the capacity of short-term memory, results in a student either ignoring the next chunk of input

Presenting when short-term memory is full is like pouring more water into a glass that is full.

> **Tip**
> Increase the frequency of processing in the second half of a lecture or presentation.

because they can't take in any more, or taking in the next chunk of input at the cost of displacing something already in short-term memory. Long lectures suffer from diminishing returns: The longer the lecture, the more retention decreases. For example, when tested after a lecture on the classics, students answered correctly 70% of the test questions from the first half of the lecture, but answered correctly only 30% of the questions from the second half of the lecture![62]

2. Processing Enhances Storage and Retention of Content. Processing promotes long-term retention. If the telephone operator gives us a number to call, we hold the number in short-term memory just long enough to make our call. After making the call, if someone asks

> **Tip**
> Students remember dramatically more of what they say than of what we say. Let them talk!

Brain-Friendly Teaching • Dr. Spencer Kagan
Kagan Publishing • 800.933.2667 • www.KaganOnline.com

Only with frequent processing does our content stand a chance of moving from short-term to long-term memory.

us for the number, we can't remember it. It is gone! Why? Content does not move automatically from short- to long-term memory. The two memory systems are completely independent.[63] To remember something long term, we must process the content. Each of us has different ways of doing that. For example, to recall a telephone number, some of us look at the relation of the numbers to each other, some of us create a visual image of the number, others link the numbers to words or even make a number sentence, others yet use one of the many mnemonic devices. Whichever process is used, the numbers are placed in long-term memory through thinking about the numbers, processing them. Processing is the golden key to move content from short- to long-term memory.

Tip

Frequently stop talking. Don't do all the work. Processing enhances retention. Pause and have students each tell a partner how he or she plans to remember important content.

To process, have students discuss the content, analyze it, relate it to their own prior knowledge and to the prior knowledge provided by those with whom they are interacting. Through processing, students are actually rewiring their brains, forming dendrite connections. The information is stored in more places in the brain, and so there are more associative links. This dramatically increases the probability of later recall.

If our students don't rehearse information, chunk it, create a mnemonic, or in some other way process our presentation, they will not move the content, from short- to long-term memory, and our lesson soon will be forgotten. This

then, provides the second brain-based rationale for frequent processing: *Frequent processing stores content in long-term memory, increasing the probability of later recall.*

Through processing students are actually rewiring their brains, forming new dendrite connections.

3. Processing Prevents Mind-Wandering.

In the traditional lecture format, the professor stands before a podium and talks. Over 50 years ago when I was an undergraduate at the University of California, Berkeley, some professors gave the same word-for-word lecture year after year. Students who could afford five dollars (not a minor expense for Berkeley students at that time) bought mimeographed lecture notes prepared by graduate students. The notes were written from a prior year, but we could read the

Brainiac Box

Question:
What happens in the brain during mind-wandering?

Answer:[72]
The default state of the brain is self-generated thought or mind-wandering. The specific areas of the brain active during mind-wandering are the same areas active during social cognition—we gravitate to thinking about personal and social issues.

Because we have only limited attention resources, an external demand for attention reallocates brain processing resources from the default state to the external stimuli, deactivating those areas associated with mind-wandering.

Four areas of the brain are active during mind-wandering, and become inactive when faced with an attention-demanding external task:
- ▶ left posterior parieto-occipital cortex
- ▶ left fusiform gyrus
- ▶ left anterior cingulate gyrus
- ▶ left middle frontal gyrus.

lecture word-for-word as the professor spoke it. (Or, as some of us did, we could skip class and study the notes later.)

Lectures have changed dramatically since I was an undergraduate. Today, lectures are often punctuated by or accompanied with PowerPoint slides and projected videos. Nevertheless, even lectures sprinkled with visuals suffer from mind-wandering. Mind-wandering is variously referred to as "stimulus-independent thought (SIT),"[64] "task unrelated images and thoughts (TUIT),"[65] "task unrelated thought (TUT),"[66] "attention lapses,"[67] "zone outs,"[68] "daydreaming,"[69] "decoupling of attention from the external environment,"[70] and "mind-wandering."[71]

Mind-Wandering Is Well Researched.

Numerous studies document the pervasiveness and negative effects on achievement of mind-wandering:

- Among 2,250 adults randomly sampled during the day via an iPhone application, mind-wandering (attention to non-task-related thoughts) occurred a remarkable 46.9% of the time![73]
- The iPhone application revealed mind-wandering occurs in all but one waking activity at least 30% of the time or more. The one exception: making love![74]

> **Tip**
>
> Teach students to self-monitor for mind-wandering during reading. At the end of each sentence (very young students), paragraph (older students), page (mature readers), have students put in their own words what the passage meant and ask themselves if they were thinking about anything else.

- A bell was sounded to sample mind-wandering during college classes, and the researchers found minds wandering 54% of the time!
- Spontaneous mind-wandering occurs more often among college students with a childhood history of ADHD.[75]
- Mind-wandering occurs about 20%–40% of the time during reading, and those whose minds are wandering are often unaware they are off topic—they lack meta-cognitive skills.[76]
- Mind-wandering without awareness results in poor response inhibition.[77]
- In a major review of mind-wandering research, the authors concluded, "mind-wandering may be one of the most ubiquitous and pervasive of all cognitive phenomena."[78] Their review of different approaches to measuring mind-wandering revealed mind-wandering occurs across a diverse variety of tasks between 15% and 50% of a person's time.
- Mind-wandering is related to decreased note-taking and lower performance on course exams.[79]
- Participants whose minds wander more, fail to notice when the text they are reading has turned to gibberish and continue reading for a significant number of words before realizing that what they are reading makes no sense![80]
- Reading comprehension is lower for those whose minds wander more.[81]

Minds Wander Early and Frequently. Using a clicker device to record mind-wandering during lectures, researchers found attention lapses to be early and frequent. They disconfirm the notion that minds only begin to wander after about 10 minutes into a presentation:

> Contrary to common belief, the data in this study suggest that students do not pay attention continuously for 10–20 minutes during a lecture. Instead, their attention alternates continuously between being engaged

and nonengaged in ever-shortening cycles throughout a lecture segment.... Students report attention lapses as early as the first 30 seconds of a lecture, with the next lapse occurring approximately 4.5 minutes into a lecture and again at shorter and shorter cycles throughout the lecture segment.[82]

Additional research has disconfirmed the belief that attention declines only after 10 to 15 minutes into a lecture. Minds begin wandering right away![83]

> **Tip**
> Punctuate lectures frequently with brief interaction breaks during which students show their notes to a partner and discuss the content.

> **Tip**
> Teach students to self-monitor for mind-wandering during lectures. Allow them time to share their personal strategies for keeping focused on the lecture.

Mind-Wandering Lowers Achievement.

Experimenters measured mind-wandering in a lecture to 334 undergraduate students taking an introduction to psychology course.[84] During the 50 minute lecture, a bell rang at 8, 15, 25, 34, and 40 minutes into the lecture. Students recorded if they were focused on the lecture or on unrelated thoughts or images. Increased mind-wandering was associated with lower performance on midterm and final exams and overall course grades. It was also correlated with lower overall academic performance. To the extent the mind is wandering, the lecture is not understood or retained.[85]

The relation between mind-wandering and test performance is strong. Experimenters tested mind-wandering and test performance in three 1-hour lectures, each with different content. Individuals were probed at intervals during the lectures to report if their minds were wandering. After the lecture was over, those who self-reported mind-wandering on fewer than 50% of the probes correctly answered 77% of the questions on lecture content; those who reported mind-wandering on more than 50% of the probes correctly answered only 54% of the questions![86]

Dual Function of the Default Network. The default mode network in the brain, the posterior cingulate cortex and the anterior medial prefrontal cortex, is active during mind-wandering. Surprisingly, it is also active during reading. This apparent paradox is explained by brain studies showing that the default mode network is capable of connectivity with different parts of the brain at different times. Thus, the default network can either inhibit reading (and other task performances) or can facilitate reading, depending on the structures with which it is connected.[87]

Sitting Up Front Linked to Less Mind-Wandering. Those students seated in the front third of the lecture hall experienced less mind-wandering, but the interpretation of this finding is not clear: There may be a direct impact of seating, or perhaps students who are more interested in the course content choose to sit up front.[88]

Cooperative Learning: An Antidote to Mind-Wandering. As students interact to process the content, their attention focuses on their partners or teammates, eliminating the possibility of mind-wandering. Cooperative learning is the strongest tool we have to counter mind-wandering. Mind-wandering occurs

Tip

Rotate student seating so individual students and teams have the opportunity to be closer to the front of the room where minds wander less. When possible, circulate in the classroom or lecture hall so students are more often close to the presenter.

during unstructured small-group discussion half as much as during lecture.[89] During unstructured group discussion, however, some students can do most or even all the talking, allowing others freedom for mind-wandering. When cooperative learning is well-structured, there is no opportunity at all for mind-wandering. For example, during a simple **RallyRobin**, partners take turns stating ideas or answers. To avoid giving repeats, students must keep their attention focused on what their partner is saying.

See Structures Section
15. RallyRobin

The mind wanders to internal thoughts, memories, and feelings whenever there is not external stimuli demanding attention—mind-wandering is the default mental state. Mind-wandering occurs more often during rest than during activity, and occurs more often with easy, practiced, repetitive, and routine tasks.[90] And therein lies the rub for lecturers. As presenters, we are in competition with the inherent tendency of students' minds to wander. Given a limited

capacity for working memory, attention to internal, non-lecture-related content decreases free attention available to process the lecture. Even lectures accompanied with visuals involve students sitting, listening, and perhaps taking notes—routine, repetitive tasks especially prone to mind-wandering. Attention, heart rate, and note-taking all drop increasingly as a lecture continues,[91] and it's during this state of reduced arousal that minds are most prone to wander. Immediately following active student engagement, minds are clearer and wander less frequently.[92]

Mind-wandering is decoupling of attention from external stimuli. This, of course, leads to poor processing of academic content.

This then, provides the third brain-based rationale for frequent processing: *Frequent processing interrupts mind-wandering, increasing focus and retention.*

4. Processing Produces Retrograde Memory Enhancement.
Emotion cements memory. As we saw in Tool 3: Link Emotion to Content, in Principle 4: Emotion, retrograde memory enhancement is a basic principle of brain science: Anything followed by emotion is better remembered.[93] What does this have to do with frequent processing? Usually, more emotion is generated in a lively interaction with a peer than is generated by a lecture by a professor. By frequently punctuating the lecture with processing time, we link the content to emotion, enhancing memory.

Processing links emotion to academic content, releasing the power of retrograde memory enhancement to make the content more memorable.

5. Processing Creates Episodic Memories.
The brain has independent memory systems. An episodic memory is a memory for incidents (the time we took a roller coaster ride; the time we buried a pet). A procedural memory is memory for how to do things (how to ride a bike; how to type). A semantic memory is memory for isolated facts and information (the capital of California; the definition of a word). A good part of lectures consist of facts and information to be stored

Brain-Friendly Teaching • Dr. Spencer Kagan
Kagan Publishing • 800.933.2667 • www.KaganOnline.com

in the semantic memory system. If content for semantic memory is not processed, not put into a meaningful context and internalized, it is far less likely to be maintained. When students cram for a test, too often they are attempting to put information into the semantic memory system, but because they are not fully processing the content, at best, they retain the information only long enough to spit it back on the test. A few weeks later the information is gone.

The semantic memory system is more fragile than the episodic and procedural memory systems. Anxiety interferes with semantic memory. That is why sometimes even if we know the name of someone very well, given the anxiety associated with a social introduction, our mind goes blank when we go to introduce the person in a social setting. Procedural and episodic memories are more stable. As we get older we forget the names of things (semantic memory), but don't forget how to drive a car or brush our teeth (procedural memories) or the time we got married or the time we lost our car keys and had to walk home (episodic memories).

What does all this have to do with the desirability of frequent processing? As students interact over the content, they create an episodic memory. Why? Episodic memories are created when an event has a beginning and an end as well as a location, especially if there is emotion associated with the event. When students turn to a partner for an animated interaction, the event has a beginning and an end, a location, and is associated with emotion. Why is this important? Episodic memories are more enduring; they are the natural way the brain remembers.

We can prove this to ourselves by recalling what we had for dinner last night. With little effort, we bring back what we ate, where we sat, who was at the table, and things that were said. We memorized all that without even trying. Episodic memories are effortless and more enduring than

semantic memories. Students have to work hard to remember a list of facts, but they easily recall the time they interacted with a peer over the content.

Processing creates episodic memories that are more stable and more easily recalled than semantic memories.

6. Processing Provides Novel Stimuli, Increasing Alertness.
There is a novelty center in the brain called the substantia nigra/ventral tegmental area, the SN/VTA. Human brain scans reveal the SN/VTA becomes active whenever we encounter novel stimuli.[94] The SN/VTA is linked to both the hippocampus (critical for memory and learning) and the amygdalae (reactive to emotional stimuli). Novel stimuli make students more alert and attentive; memory for novel stimuli is enhanced and more enduring. Processing the content at different times with different partners creates novelty in two ways: (1) Processing breaks the routine of the lecture providing novel stimuli; and (2) What a partner says during the processing time often is unpredictable, novel stimuli. Processing produces novel stimuli, which makes us more alert, providing yet another brain-based rationale for frequent processing:

Processing activates the novelty center in the brain, resulting in increased student alertness enhancing the probability of storage and later recall of lecture content.

7. Processing Activates Many Parts of the Brain.
While processing content with a partner, many parts of the brain are activated. Wernicke's area decodes the words of our partner. Broca's area encodes our own words. The temporal lobe processes not only words, but also decodes tone of voice. The visual cortex processes the face of our partner as well as his or her gestures and body language. Mirror neurons decode the feelings and actions of our partner. Further, the prefrontal cortex is very active, as we must either

add the information provided by our partner to our existing cognitive framework (assimilation) or adjust our way of thinking about the world because our partner has provided information that doesn't fit with our cognitive framework (accommodation).

Processing links the content to more places in the brain, creating more associative links, enhancing memory for lecture content.

Tool 6

Avoid Distractions

As indicated at the outset of this Principle, we obtain fuller attention to the degree that we avoid distractions. The goal: undivided attention. There are a number of ways to avoid dividing attention.

Introducing a Lesson

Clear the Desk. A simple way to get students set for new learning is to have them clear their desks. By putting away everything, they have fewer distractions. They are more set to focus on new learning.

Post Lesson Maps. To avoid students being distracted by wondering what they will do next, post and explain a lesson map before launching a lesson. Students who know what is coming next are less likely to wonder about it. Some students cannot settle down into a lesson with undivided attention unless they have a map of the lesson—what they are going to do first, next, and so on. Providing that map at the outset of a lesson prevents divided attention for some students. Providing a lesson map is not in conflict with giving instructions in bite-sized pieces. First we give the big picture, where the whole lesson is going, then we settle down into taking it a bite at a time.

Bite-Sized Project Chunks. If students have a complex, multistep project to complete, it is easy for them to get overwhelmed, thinking of all they have to do. Their attention is divided. They are not thinking only about the immediate part of the task at hand, but also all the things they have to do. We

dramatically increase their probability of success by having them focus on and completing just one step at a time. For example, rather than providing the students with all the steps to complete a research project, we might lead the students through the project focusing on only one part at a time: research skills, gathering research, creating visuals, selecting quotes, creating an outline, creating a rough draft, revising, bibliography and referencing, final draft.

Bite-Sized Directions. The same principle of giving bite-sized instructions applies also to carrying students through the steps of a structure. Rather than frontloading at the outset by telling students the ten steps of **Traveling Heads Together**, we structure for success by describing just one step at a time and having the students carry out that step before describing the next step. As a rule of thumb: Do not give more instructions than students can carry out without having to ask for clarification. Students have divided attention if, while they are performing a task, they are trying to keep a complex set of instructions in their heads.

Check-Off Lists. Another solution is to give students or have students create a check-off list of steps in a task, moving the instructions from short-term memory (where they serve as a distraction) to a piece of paper where they can be accessed as needed.

During a Lesson

Avoid the Split-Attention Effect. Analysis of instructional materials reveals that those that focus attention produce better mastery than those that divide attention. This finding has been labeled the *Split-Attention Effect*.[95] The effect occurs across a variety of instructional materials. For example, if an instructional video is playing and the narration is in projected words below, there will be less retention than if the same video is playing and the narration is by a voice. By having two sources of visual input, attention is divided, and content is not as fully attended to and not as well retained. To take a different example, if students are learning to tell time, a diagram that puts the meaning of the hour hand and the meaning of the second hand right by each hand produces more learning than a diagram that shows the same clock but puts the explanation to one side or at the bottom. See Diagram: Educational Design to Avoid Split Attention, p. 5.39.

Educational Design to Avoid Split Attention

Don't Use Input Competing for the Same Modality

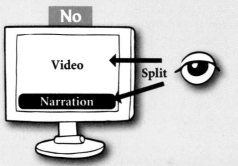

No — Two competing visual inputs

Yes — Two noncompeting inputs: visual and auditory

Tip Use multiple modalities to reinforce the content.

Don't Separate Visual Inputs

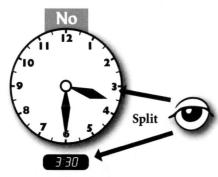 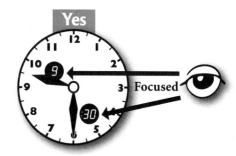

No — Clock separated from time

Yes — Time integrated with clock

Tip Physically combine separate visual elements.

Don't Separate Explanations from Visuals

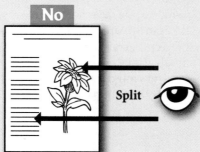 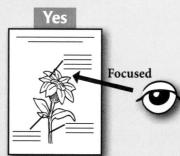

No — Explanation separate from visual

Yes — Explanation integrated with the visual

 Tips • Use captions explaining visuals.
• Use diagrams.

• Show visual aids in the same place as the explanation, not separately.

Familiar and Even-Tempo Background Music. There are two competing brain principles we must balance when asking about whether or not to play **background** music while students are studying in class or at home. On the one hand, we know the importance of undivided attention On the other hand, in Principle 2: Safety, we explored the importance of creating a stress-free, relaxed learning environment. In that principle, we provided research showing that soothing background music dramatically increases learning. How does that square with the call for undivided attention?

A great deal of research has been conducted to address this question. The research is summarized in depth by Nelson Cowan in his book, *Memory and Attention*.[96] The research demonstrates that humans are extremely good at selective attention. Central to this research are dichotic listening studies. That is, if we use earphones to play one message into one ear and a different voice with a different message into the other ear, and tell subjects to listen only to the message from one of their ears, they can do that almost completely, "tuning out" the ignored message. Almost all of the target message is retained and almost none of the ignored message is retained. Further, the more familiar the ignored message, the easier it is to tune out. The brain habituates to any stimulus that has been seen or heard many times, and that stimulus loses its ability to grab our attention. In the dichotic listening studies, if the ignored message contains novel stimuli of any sort, it "grabs" the attention of the person trying to tune it out, and some of the target message content is lost.

This gives us a clear answer regarding background music. If the music has an even and predictable rhythm and/or if is music that has been heard many times, it is not likely to interfere with concentration and is likely to contribute to greater relaxation, which facilities learning. If, in contrast, the music has unexpected changes in words, tone, beat, or if it is novel music, it is quite likely to interfere with the ability to concentrate. In practical terms, classic music with no words and an even beat will likely enhance learning, whereas rock music and music with lyrics will likely compete with learning. Baroque music played larghetto (60–66 beats a minute) is balanced and predictable and likely to enhance learning. Gary Lamb has composed and created the *"Music for the Mind"* CD series, played at around 60 beats a minute, designed as learning-enhancing background music.[97] Much of the new age music is excellent background music because it does not grab attention and provides a relaxed mood.

Kagan Structures Avoid Distractions

Mind-wandering is the most common distraction for students. In the absence of stimuli in the environment demanding attention, students gravitate to mind-wandering. When students are working alone on worksheets, it is easy for their minds to wander. There is no stimulus pulling their attention back to the task. It is easy for their minds to wander also during question-answer time—they can tune out both the question and the student answer, simply choosing not to participate by not raising their hand. In contrast, if students are in interaction while doing a worksheet or answering questions, there is little chance for mind-wandering: their partner or teammates are demanding a response. Almost all Kagan Structures reduce mind-wandering and keep students from attending to distracting stimuli via the demands of interaction. How can a student's mind wander during the **Flashcard Game** when their partner is holding up a card,

See Structures Section
5. Flashcard Game
24. Three-Step Interview

showing them the front, and asking what is on the back? How can a student get off task during **Three-Step Interview**? At each step, the student is either being interviewed; listening carefully as he or she interviews a partner because he or she will be accountable for sharing afterwards; or sharing what was just learned.

Tool 7

Distribute Practice

Distributed practice is better than massed practice. This is one of the oldest findings in modern psychology, discovered by Hermann Ebbinghaus in his pioneering memory research in 1885. The effect has been researched extensively and is very reliable.

We produce more learning by spacing learning and practice sessions rather than having them all at once. For example, three short-learning sessions of 10 minutes each will lead to more retention than one 30-minute session. The same amount of practice time broken into separate sessions and spread out over time increases learning and retention. A meta-analysis of 63 research studies with 112 effect sizes yielded an effect size of .46 favoring distributed practice.[98] That means that a student scoring at the 50th percentile in a class using massed practice would be scoring at the 68th percentile had the student

Tip

Decide what you most want students to remember from your lesson and emphasize it at both the beginning and at the end of your lesson.

been moved to a class using distributed practice and then compared to classmates using massed practice. Distributed practice leads to an average gain of 18 percentiles!

Although very infrequently used,[99] the positive impact of distributed, or spaced, practice is extremely well established, improving performance for students of all ages. It improves the performance of adults,[100] undergraduates,[101] secondary biology students,[102] elementary school students,[103] and even preschoolers and infants.[104]

The research on distributed practice is complicated. How much gain will occur varies across studies and depends on the nature of the learning task, the amount of space between learning sessions, the intervening activity, and the quality of the study. In general, longer gaps between learning sessions produce greater gains than brief gaps, especially if there is to be a long gap between the last learning session and the test.[105] For our purposes here, we can simply generalize: Spaced practice is almost always better than lumped practice.

Tip

Harness the power of distributed practice. Schedule brief, spaced practice sessions rather than one long practice session.

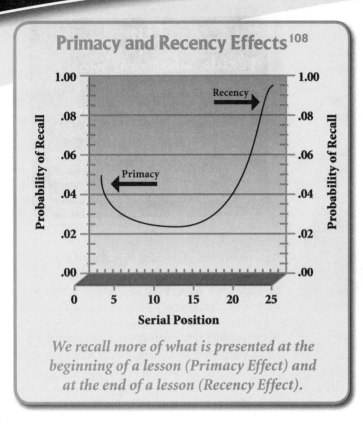

Primacy and Recency Effects[108]

We recall more of what is presented at the beginning of a lesson (Primacy Effect) and at the end of a lesson (Recency Effect).

beginning content (Primacy Effect) and the ending content (Recency Effect) are well established.[107] See Graph: Primacy and Recency Effects. Primacy can be explained because attention wanes during long learning sessions and because there is nothing in short-term memory at the outset of a learning session, so there is undivided attention. Recency can be explained because we are testing for content the person has just heard or seen, and nothing has come after the last items to displace them from short-term memory.

How do primacy and recency partially explain distributed practice? In massed practice, there is only one beginning and one end. If we break the 30-minute session into three 10-minute sessions, there are three beginnings and three endings, multiplying the primacy and recency effects.

Why Does Distributed Practice Improve Performance? There are a number of reasons for the superiority of distributed practice compared to massed practice.

Enhanced Rehearsal. By spacing practice, there is an opportunity for the brain to rehearse the skill between practice sessions. This enhanced rehearsal interpretation is supported by brain imaging studies.[106]

State-Conditioned Learning. Each time we practice a skill, we are in a different state. For example, if we learn a skill when we are hungry, before lunch, we will perform better on a test of that skill if the test is given when we are hungry, before lunch. The performance of the skill is associated with the state we are in when we acquire the skill. By distributing practice, a skill is associated with more states, and so is more likely to be performed no matter what state we are in.

Primacy and Recency. My favorite interpretation of the distributed practice effect is based on primacy and recency effects. We retain more of the beginning and the end of any learning session than what is presented or practiced in the middle. These effects, retaining more of the

Tool 8

Create Flow

All of us sometimes experience flow. It is that state where our attention and efforts are all effortlessly focused on a task. We are not trying to focus our attention; our attention is completely focused without effort. Accomplishing the task, whether it is a tennis serve, solving a problem, writing an essay, or repairing a motor, feels harmonious, in the zone. We experience no distractions and time seems to disappear as we work. We are in the flow.

The characteristics of flow and what allows us to enter the flow state have been defined.[109] *Flow occurs when we are motivated to accomplish a task and task difficulty matches our ability.* I like to explain flow with a tennis example. See Diagram: Flow, p. 5.43.

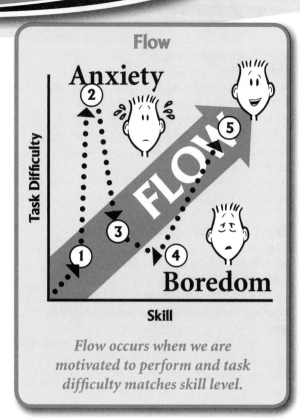

Flow

Flow occurs when we are motivated to perform and task difficulty matches skill level.

4. Boredom. Now you are getting better at keeping your eye on the ball and you are being more successful. In fact, you are acquiring more skill. The pro, however, does not realize this, and continues to send you very easy lobs. As this process continues, you begin to feel bored. This isn't fun. Your skill level now exceeds the task difficulty and you feel like doing something more challenging. You have distracting thoughts of other things. Your attention is again divided. You have fallen out of flow. See circle 4.

5. Return to Flow. The pro senses your distraction and realizes she must adjust. She begins hitting you more difficult balls that match your newly acquired higher skill level. You feel challenged. This is fun again. There are no distracting thoughts. You are fully concentrated on the task at hand. You have returned to flow because task difficulty matches your ability. See circle 5.

Creating Flow: Differentiated Instruction

We want our students to enter the flow state as they practice new skills. We want them to feel motivated, successful, and to work without distractions. We want to avoid anxiety on the one hand and boredom on the other. As we have seen, the trick is to match task difficulty to student ability. The challenge for us as teachers, of course, is that we have a room full of students with a range of ability levels. (Oh, to have the life of a tennis pro, teaching just one student!) One solution: differentiate instruction.

There are a number of ways we can differentiate to better match task difficulty with student ability:

Progressive Worksheets. Worksheets can be designed so successive problems are more difficult. If students are told "no one is expected to finish all of the problems; just complete the problems in order, finishing as many as you can in the time allotted," students all advance closer to their appropriate match of task difficulty and ability.

Challenging Sponges. A sponge activity is designed to "soak up" extra time and energy. Some students finish tasks before others. Usually, the high achievers are those to finish first. The norm in the classroom can be for those who

1. In Flow. Imagine you have never played tennis and decide to take a lesson from a pro. The pro knows you are a novice so after initial instruction on how to hold the racquet and how to stand and swing, the pro begins the practice portion of the lesson by lobbing easy shots over the net, practically aiming for your racquet. You hit them back with good consistency. You are feeling great. The low task difficulty matches your low ability level. You feel successful and have no distracting thoughts. Your attention is fully focused. You are in circle 1 in the Flow diagram.

2. Anxiety. Now the pro sees your success rate is high so asks you to back up and begins to hit more difficult shots to you. Your success rate drops. You begin to worry if you will be good at tennis. As you miss more shots, you begin to feel anxious: *"Will I be good at this? Should I really take up tennis?"* You are out of flow. Your worries divide your attention. Flow is undivided attention, but your attention is divided. You are out of flow. You are in circle 2 of the Flow diagram.

3. Back in Flow. The pro sees your distress and adjusts. She begins to hit easier shots to you. The task difficulty again matches your skill level. You begin to feel relief. This is fun. It is effortless. You feel in the zone. In the flow. See circle 3.

finish any task early to go to one of the sponge activity tables. Awaiting students as they arrive at a sponge activity table are self-directed, more challenging tasks.

Some of the sponge activities can be cooperative learning tasks. For example, the game **Spin-N-Think** can be played with any higher level thinking content and with any number of students from two to five. As additional students finish early, they join a group to play **Spin-N-Think**. A Spin Captain is chosen for each question, and after all students think about their answers, the spinner chooses who will answer, paraphrase, praise, and augment. The spinner is designed so it chooses one student each time, regardless of whether the students are working in pairs, or groups of three, four, or five.

Time Allocation. Some students or some groups can be allotted more time to finish a task.

Preteach. Via homework, aides, or differentiated activities, some students can be given advanced preparation (preinstruction instruction) for the questions or problems to be completed in class.

Buddies. Students may be assigned and sit next to a buddy who is instructed how to coach without telling answers. Homework Buddies (a teammate to call if you need assistance) ensure that students know where to turn if they discover at home they do not know how to do the homework.

Bite-Sized Pieces. Complex tasks can be broken down into "bite-sized pieces," and some students may be asked to focus on fewer pieces.

Seating. Students who are easily distracted may be seated up front where they are less distracted by others. When students are in teams of four, the numbers may correspond to ability level. For example, when the teacher calls for number 2s to respond, the teacher knows to ask a more challenging question than when asking for number 4s to respond.

Homogeneous Groups. Students may break out from their heterogeneous teams and work in teams that are homogeneous by ability level. Different teams may be assigned different tasks, different amounts of time to work on a given task, or different types of support. A warning: Homogeneous groups by ability level should be used only occasionally to avoid students internalizing and having a negative self-image (*I work in the dummy group.*)

Response Cards or Board Responses. Response cards or possible answers posted on the whiteboard can be used in a variety of ways to differentiate. When answering, weaker students can respond by choosing one of the premade response cards or selecting a posted response; more advanced students can create their own responses. Alternatively, some individuals, pairs, or teams may be provided with response cards, whereas more skilled individuals or groups are not.

Differentiated Curriculum. Individual students may be given learning tasks with different levels of difficulty. For example, although all students may be working on the same concept during math, some students may be working with manipulatives, others with drawings, and yet others with purely abstract numbers. Students may be assigned worksheets of different levels of difficulty.

Differentiation within Structures. Most of the Kagan Structures either have built-in differentiation, or can be modified for differentiation. An example of a structure with built-in differentiation is **Team-Pair-Solo**. Students work first on problems as a team. When they are sure everyone can do that type of problem they advance to pair work to do more problems of the same type. Finally, they advance to solo work. If a pair gets stuck, they move back to teamwork. Individuals that get stuck, move back to pair work. During team and pair work, teammates and partners provide the support that helps weaker students work at the appropriate level of difficulty.

For examples of ways to differentiate the structures featured in this book, see Table: Kagan Structures to Differentiate Instruction, p. 5.45.

Kagan Structures to Differentiate Instruction

Structures	Structure Section	Differentiated Instruction
Flashcard Game	5	The Flashcard Game has built-in differentiation: Students take a pretest with items with a range of difficulty. They make up cards only on the items they have missed. Bonus items are available for students who ace the pretest.
Kinesthetic Symbols	7	The teacher may circulate and provide support for individuals or groups having difficulty creating an appropriate symbol.
Listen Right!	8	Students who miss the important points in the chunk of the presentation receive help from their partner; pairs who miss an important point receive help when the teacher announces the points to remember.
Pair Share	10	Teacher may post several questions students can choose among to respond. Students gravitate to their own level of difficulty.
Quiz-Quiz-Trade	13	Students may travel with quiz cards that have questions with different levels of difficulty. They can show the questions to their partner who chooses the question to answer.
RallyQuiz	14	Students may be provided lists of questions that are color coded by difficulty. Students are instructed to find a partner with the same color question sheet.
Sage-N-Scribe	17	Different pairs may be working at different levels of difficulty. Alternatively, if the pairs are of mixed ability, the worksheet can be constructed so A works on more difficult problems than B.
Team-Pair-Solo	23	Team-Pair-Solo has built-in differentiation: Students get help from teammates until they are ready to progress to pair work and then get help from their partner until they are ready to progress to solo.
Three-Step Interview	24	Interview questions can be placed on cards. Students can choose to read a card or to make up their own question.

Tool 9

Respond to Attention Styles

I am fond of telling people that each of us can choose our world. When we look at a rose bush, we can choose to focus on the thorns or focus on the rose buds. We can choose our world. It is also true that we have attention styles: Habits determine where we focus our attention. Without conscious choice some of us automatically focus on the thorns and everything else that is ugly and wrong, whereas others focus on the rose buds and everything else that is beautiful and right. Two teachers are looking at the same student essay. One focuses on every detail that is not correct—improper punctuation, run-on sentences, lack of paragraph topic sentences, and so on. The other teacher focuses on the ideas the student wants to convey and appreciates the depth of thought. By what we focus on, we create our world and create how we respond to the world.

Our students enter our classrooms with their own attention styles. By understanding and responding to those styles, we can better capture and hold their attention. Probably the most important of all attention styles is the analytic-global dimension. Here we examine how to capture and hold the attention of students with an analytic style as well as those with a global style.

Individual Differences in Attention Style

Attention can be like a laser or like a broad floodlight. We can thread a needle or take in the beauty of a panorama. At any one moment, we can take in the forest or see only one detail of one tree. We are parallel processors, but not all that we process reaches consciousness: Although we are simultaneously responding to both the big picture and the details, at any one moment, we are conscious of only one pole of that dimension. Most of us have the ability to switch rapidly from one mode of attention to another.

Ability v. Style. Ability is one thing; style is another: What we can do is ability; what we prefer to do is style. Although our students each have the ability to focus on either the big picture or the small details, they each have their own attention style. Some students enter our classroom prepared to process the big picture; others are predisposed to focus on the details. Understanding and applying this knowledge can help us avoid frustration in our learners and help us better reach our learning objectives. We need to teach in ways that captures and holds the attention of all of our students, knowing they come to us with different attention styles.

Attention Style Experiment

Try this simple experiment to better understand attention style: After reading **ALL** the directions in this paragraph, you will be instructed to turn to a page and look at what is on that page for only 5 seconds. After looking at what is in the box on that page for only about 5 seconds, you will turn back to this page. When you look at the illustration, please be meta-perceptual. That is, be aware of what you see first, next, and so on during the 5 seconds. Make a mental note of what you see the moment you first look at what is in the box. After viewing the illustration for only 5 seconds, you will turn back to this page. Turn now to p. 5.77 and follow the instructions above the box called, *"Attention Experiment."*

Dont read on! Turn to p. 5.77 now.

Now that you have seen the figure, answer these two questions:
1. Did you first see the figure as one large letter L or as a group of many D's?
2. During the 5 seconds did you switch? That is, if you saw the figure first as one large L, did it become a group of many D's, or if you first saw it as a group of many D's did it become one large letter L?

I have done this experiment many times in workshops in different parts of the world. Every time there are the same two findings: (1) People have an attention style. That is, they approach the figure first either as one large letter L or as a collection of D's. That is, they first look for the big picture or first focus on the details. (2) Within the 5 seconds almost everyone switches so they have seen it both ways. Thus, while we do have an attention style, how we approach stimuli, we also have the ability to switch from one style to another and do so spontaneously.

Brain research has shown the right hemisphere is primarily responsible for processing the big picture whereas the left hemisphere processes the details. The right hemisphere sees one big L; the left hemisphere sees the D's.[110] People with certain kinds of right hemisphere damage, however, can focus only on the details; they fail to see the big picture and cannot process relations among things. In contrast, people with certain kinds of left hemisphere damage, fail to process details, seeing only the big picture.[111] See Table: Capture Both Attention Styles, p. 5.47.

Capture Both Attention Styles

Content	Big Picture Global	Small Details Analytic
Math	How will you find long division useful in your life?	What are the steps of the division algorithm?
Social Studies	What are ways the Civil War changed American culture?	How many troops were there from each side during the battle of Gettysburg?
Science	What are some of the costs and benefits of space exploration?	What are differences between comets and asteroids?
Language Arts	What is the moral of the story?	Which literary techniques did the author use?

Teaching to Capture Both Styles

What are the implications of this for us as teachers? As we introduce a lesson, some students are looking for the big picture. They want a lesson map. Where are we going? Others are looking to know if they will learn some interesting details. Thus, it is almost always a good idea to provide both the lesson map and one or two intriguing details at the outset of a lesson so all students feel comfortable. As we teach, we want to continue to provide both the big picture and intriguing details.

Tool 10

Include Elements of Lesson Design

Some of the elements of lesson design are particularly useful in focusing the attention of students, including sets, closures, and guided practice.

Sets

Students give fuller attention to a lesson and retain more if prior to the input of content they get set to learn. Dimensions of a good set include activating prior knowledge, making relevance salient, and creating active participation—either overtly or covertly.

Activating Prior Knowledge. One of the most fundamental principles of brain science is *"neurons that fire together, wire together."* Contiguity, neurons firing at the same time, is how we learn. Pavlov rang a bell each time he fed his dogs. Soon, to make the dogs salivate, all he had to do was ring the bell. Neurons associated with eating were activated at the sound of the bell because the sound of the bell had been consistently associated with the smell and taste of food.

Whatever we teach, students almost always have some prior knowledge about that content. By having them talk about, think about, or draw about that prior knowledge, we activate the neurons associated with that prior knowledge. If at that time, we present the new knowledge, the neurons associated with the new knowledge are firing at the same time as the neurons associated with the old knowledge. Because neurons that fire together, wire together, new dendrite connections are formed linking the new knowledge with the old. Thus, whenever the old knowledge is activated so too is the new knowledge. A more extensive neural net is formed, deepening understanding and making the new knowledge less likely to be forgotten.

Activating prior knowledge at the outset of a lesson can be covert (in the student's head) or overt (via action).

Covert Set:
"Today's lesson is on celestial objects. What do you now know about the planets and the stars? Take a moment and mentally review what you now know."

Overt Set:
"Today's lesson is on celestial objects. What do you now know about the planets and the stars? Take a moment with your shoulder partner and RallyRobin things you now know about the planets and the stars."

Prior knowledge is more fully activated by having students interact to express their prior knowledge:

We are going to do simulations to more fully understand what the stock market crash meant for families and businesses. Before teams choose their topics, let's get into what it feels like to lose something you value. Think of something important you have lost. In your teams, you will do a Timed RoundRobin describing something you have lost and how you felt.

There are a number of advantages of using overt active participation to create the set. With covert active engagement, we can never be sure there is not mind-wandering for some students. With overt active engagement, as students verbalize their thinking, they listen to themselves and this becomes another way of activating their prior knowledge. As students verbalize their prior knowledge, they provide new knowledge for their partners or teammates.

Whether the set is overt or covert, by activating prior knowledge, student attention is more focused. They know what the content relates to: They have created a mental space to contain the new content. They are set to learn: Their working memory is more highly activated as they are set to make connections between the lesson content and what they already know.

Making Relevance Salient. Another aspect of a good set for a lesson is to make students aware of how the new knowledge is relevant to them. Often this takes the form of showing students how the lesson content will be useful to them in their life now or in the future.

Tomorrow we are going to learn about multiplication. Your homework tonight is to interview an adult and find out how multiplication is useful to them. Tomorrow, we will report back to our teammates on what we found in our interviews.

Creating relevance can take the form of showing students how the new knowledge or skill will empower them.

We are going to create watercolor paintings. Let's look at some of the watercolors created by students in prior years. The sky effects were created by first painting with water! That is one of the techniques we will explore.

By establishing relevance, students are more attentive. They see the lesson as something that will empower them and so it is worth their full attention. There are many ways to create relevance. That topic is covered in detail in Tool 10: Make It Multimodal, in Principle 6: Stimuli.

Closures

Sets are at the beginning of a lesson. Closures occur at the end of sub-objectives in a lesson and also at the end of the whole lesson. Closures cement learning. Closure moves content from short-term and working memory to long-term memory. Good closures occur when students do the work.

Like sets, closures can be covert or overt.

Covert Closure:
"Pretend that tomorrow we will have a new student join our class. Think about what you would tell that student to describe the important points of today's lesson."

Overt Closure:
"Make a list of the most important things you learned from today's lesson."

Overt closure can occur in many ways, including having students verbalize their learning, draw it, write about it, or even create kinesthetic symbols to symbolize the learning. As with sets, overt closures have the advantages of holding students accountable and of providing an additional form of input rather than just thought.

Whether closures are overt or covert, they are an opportunity for students to think about their learning. As students think about their learning, neurons are firing. Students are strengthening those neural networks. The more times a neural network fires, the stronger it gets; the more likely it is to fire again. Neural networks that fire many times become myelinated and fire up to 200 times faster than those that are not myelinated. This is the rational for repetition of learning. Closure is a mini-repetition of what has been learned, strengthening neural connections.

Processing for Closure. If we have students process each piece of a project or lesson before going on to the next piece, they are not still thinking about the last piece while trying to do or learn the next piece. Closures free attention for the next bit of learning. By talking about, discussing, reviewing what they have learned, students get closure on that piece. They move the content from short- to long-term memory. The old content is more firmly stored and attention is undivided while working on the next new content.

Closure moves content from short-term and working memory to long-term memory.

Kagan Structures for Sets and Closures. Interviews are excellent for activating prior knowledge, for making relevance salient, and for obtaining closure. At the outset of a lesson, we can use **Celebrity Interview** or **Three-Step Interview** to have students interview each other about what they know about the topic we are about to present, and how they think it might be relevant to them personally. Those same structures are excellent following a lesson segment to obtain closure by having students state what they have learned. **Timed RoundRobin** and **Timed Pair Share** allow each student to share for a minute so are excellent for sets and closures.

See Structures Section
3. Celebrity Interview
16. RoundRobin
24. Three-Step Interview
25. Timed Pair Share

Guided Practice

After demonstrating a skill, teachers who skip directly to individual practice are certain to lose some students. Because we have heterogeneous classes and we cannot teach to the lowest achiever when giving a presentation, it is predictable that following direct instruction, at least some students will need guided practice.

The alternative is for some students to be lost as they work on a worksheet or project they don't understand. Students who are lost are likely to engage in mind-wandering or, worse yet, rationalization: *"I don't care about this stupid lesson."* By scaffolding support via guided practice, students stay within their comfort zone and stay focused on the learning task.

An excellent example is contrasting what happens if we follow direct instruction with solo worksheet work v. a Kagan mastery structure like **Sage-N-Scribe**. Working alone, when they come to a problem they can't do on their own, some students will have their pencil on the paper with their mind on something else. With **Sage-N-Scribe** students who need help receive it so their attention stays focused on the task.

Picture each student with a worksheet consisting of sentences lacking proper punctuation. We might have the students do **AllWrite Consensus**. Student #1 suggests the proper punctuation for the first sentence. Teammates each put a thumb up if they agree, down if they disagree, or sideways if they are in doubt. Only when they all reach agreement can each pick up his or her pencil and properly punctuate the first sentence. Next, Student #2 suggests how sentence two should be punctuated. There are many ways to use structures for guided practice. See Table: Kagan Structures for Guided Practice.

Kagan Structures for Guided Practice

Structures	Structure Section
AllWrite Consensus	1
Both Record RallyRobin	2
Choral Practice	4
Flashcard Game	5
PairUp Review	11
Quiz-Quiz-Trade	13
RallyQuiz	14
RallyRobin	15
RoundRobin	16
Sage-N-Scribe	17
SeeOne–DoOne–TeachOne	18
Team-Pair-Solo	23
Traveling Heads Together	26

Tool 11

Encourage Exercise

Exercise has a direct and immediate impact on attention. A study of 9-year-old boys and girls contrasted the impact on attention of 20 minutes of rest v. 20 minutes of exercise (walking on a treadmill).[112] The researchers examined the impact of the exercise on attention, EEG activity, and academic achievement. To test attention, they used the flanker task. Students were shown congruent and incongruent figures on a screen and were to push a button when they saw incongruent figures. In the flanker test, students have to direct their attention to the target stimulus and ignore distracting stimuli. It is a strong measure of how well a student can focus his or her attention. Results for exercise were very positive:

> "What we found is that following the acute bout of walking, children performed better on the flanker task," Hillman said. "They had a higher rate of accuracy, especially when the task was more difficult. Along with that behavioral effect, we also found that there were changes in their event-related brain potentials (ERPs)—in these neuroelectric signals that are a covert measure of attention resource allocation."

In tests of academic achievement, for those who exercised, there was a full grade-level improvement in reading as measured by the Wide Range Achievement Test. The difference was not statistically significant given the small number of students tested (20), but would be highly significant in a larger group. The spelling and math scores did not show as much improvement, but the experimenters speculate that was because those tests were administered after the reading test, when the impact of the exercise had worn off. These results are consistent with the impact of exercise on achievement reviewed in Tool 1: Encourage Exercise, in Principle 1: Nourishment. A considerable body of research shows superior cognitive functioning among students who get regular aerobic exercise.[113]

How Does Exercise Improve Attention?

Exercise induces biochemical changes including release of serotonin and brain derived neurotropic factor,[114] increases blood flow to the brain,[115] and creates a higher state of arousal.[116] How much each of these variables contributes to the positive impact of exercise on attention is a question open to investigation. Regardless of how exactly exercise improves attention, we can conclude that by including exercise programs, classrooms and schools will foster cognitive development, attention, and achievement.

Tool 12

Promote Play

Play enhances attention in a number of ways. As we have just seen, exercise enhances attention. Many of the Silly Sports and Goofy Games involve aerobic exercise. In addition, the tag games create alertness as students attempt to tag each other and not be tagged. Participants are so involved they clear working memory of anything but the moment, creating focus. In workshops, after just a few minutes of playing a Silly Sport or

Goofy Game, I ask teachers if they feel more alert and more able to concentrate. Without exception, they enthusiastically answer Yes! Play enhances attention in yet another way: Because play is fun, it elicits positive emotion which broadens attention.

Tool 13

Train Attention

Most educators treat attention as a given. It is assumed that some students have the gift of sustained concentration; others do not. Those with sustained concentration keep their focus on their work, finish early, and finish well. Students whose attention drifts, get off task, finish late if at all, and being distracted, turn in work of poor quality. If the distractibility is too great, students are referred for assessment that most often results in a label of ADD or ADHD and a prescription of methylphenidate, commonly called Ritalin.

The Ritalin Controversy

Strong arguments can be made for prescribing Ritalin for students with attention deficit disorder and powerful arguments can be made against prescribing Ritalin. There is little doubt the drug is over-prescribed. It has too often become the first line of defense rather than the last. After overviewing the pros and cons of prescribing Ritalin, we turn to a treatment option that ought to be tried before we resort to drugging our students—attention training.

The Argument for Ritalin. The argument for Ritalin is pharmacological, behavioral, and pedagogical. Animal studies reveal Ritalin stimulates the motivation and attention centers of the brain,[117] suppresses attention to nonrelevant stimuli,[118] and even enhances brain plasticity that promotes new learning.[119] Further, brain scans of humans reveal Ritalin stimulates the attention, motivation, and reward centers in the brain, promoting focused attention, motivation, and improved performance in both normal subjects and those with attention deficit disorder.[120] Dopamine is the natural neurotransmitter that stimulates the attention and motivation centers in the brain. There is strong evidence that students with true ADD have dopamine deficiency[121] and the primary effect of Ritalin is to enhance the pool of available dopamine by inhibiting the reuptake process.[122] Further, many teachers describe students who were "unteachable" until they were put on Ritalin, but who became good students after they were put on Ritalin. Those advocating Ritalin sometimes make the analogy to vitamin deficiency: Rickets, a softening of the bones, results from Vitamin D deficiency and when Vitamin D is administered, rickets is prevented. Ritalin advocates argue attention deficit results from dopamine deficiency and when Ritalin is administered, attention deficit is prevented.

The Argument Against Ritalin. The counter argument in the Ritalin debate is also pharmacological, behavioral, and pedagogical. Normal doses of Ritalin occupy more than 50% of the dopamine transporters, radically interrupting the normal dopamine uptake process.[123] In the long run, the brain responds to this excess of available dopamine by producing less dopamine,[124] making the student even more Ritalin dependent. Ritalin works in the brain in exactly the same way as does cocaine! Both Ritalin and cocaine inhibit the re-uptake of dopamine.[125] "The relationship between drug doses (milligrams of hydrochloride salt per kilogram body weight) and percentage occupancy of the dopamine transporter is indistinguishable for cocaine and methylphenidate [Ritalin], and corresponded to about 50% occupancy...."[126] Experimenters have administered Ritalin intravenously to subjects familiar with the effects of cocaine, and asked them to describe the effects of Ritalin. Their response: The effects of the two drugs are indistinguishable! "When Ritalin was administered intravenously to cocaine abusers, it induced a "high" that was reported to be

almost indistinguishable from that induced by intravenously induced cocaine."[127] However, because Ritalin is taken in pill form, it is absorbed much more slowly than cocaine, which is inhaled or injected. Thus Ritalin, taken in prescribed doses, does not result in the immediate "rush" or "high" of cocaine and so is far less likely to become addictive. Nevertheless, there is potential for Ritalin addiction by taking the drug in high doses or by taking it in ways that are absorbed rapidly. Ritalin is readily available and is abused in a number of forms, including to get high, to stay awake, to control weight gain, and to counter the depressive effects of alcohol.

Over-Prescription. There is little doubt that Ritalin is over-prescribed, See Box, Ritalin.

Ritalin
Over-Promoted, Over-Marketed, and Over-Sold

"Since 1990, prescriptions for methylphenidate have increased by 500 percent, while prescriptions for amphetamine for the same purpose have increased 400 percent. Now we see a situation in which from seven to ten percent of the nation's boys are on these drugs at some point as well as a rising percentage of girls.... These drugs have been over-promoted, over-marketed and over-sold, resulting in profits of some $450 million annually. This constitutes a potential health threat to many children and has also created a new source of drug abuse and illicit traffic. The data shows that there has been a 1,000 percent increase in drug abuse injury reports involving methylphenidate for children in the 10 to 14 year old age group. This now equals or exceeds reports for the same age group involving cocaine."

—DEA Report[128]

Side Effects of Ritalin. Another counter-argument in the Ritalin debate are the many reported side effects of Ritalin, including insomnia, tearfulness, rebound irritability, personality change, nervousness, anorexia, nausea, dizziness, headaches, heart palpitations, and cardiac arrhythmia.[129] Prominent doctors and psychologists argue that ADD is a myth, not a true disease, and that there are many non-pharmacological solutions to ADD.[130]

False Attribution. The pedagogical counterargument to the prescription of Ritalin is that lack of dopamine and associated lack of motivation and attention among students is not something the student brings to class, but rather is caused by lack of relevance and interest in our worksheets! Students with supposed "attention deficit" show intense, prolonged, undivided attention when the content interests them. In effect, the argument is that the problem is in the situation, not in the student!

Let's follow a supposed "ADD student" when he leaves school. The student switches on his home computer and spends hours in intense, uninterrupted concentration getting to the next level and then next level yet of a video game! It appears that problem is not pharmacological; it is pedagogical!

Students who are distracted and failing when working alone on worksheets blossom when allowed to work cooperatively with others on the same content. A number of carefully controlled research studies have compared Kagan Structures with traditional instructional strategies.[131] The research reveals that compared to traditional instructional strategies, Kagan Cooperative Learning Structures result in improved sustained attention (less time off task), double the number of students scoring 90% or more, and reduce the number of failing grades to zero! Students prefer the Kagan Structures twelve times as much as traditional methods. Students say traditional methods are boring and Kagan Structures are fun. (Are we reminded of the student who does not concentrate in school, but gives full concentration to video games?) Kagan Structures eliminate boredom and mind-wandering because they involve active engagement and social interaction. We can reduce the need for Ritalin by making our content more appropriately challenging and by making our instructional strategies more engaging.

Attention Training

Using more engaging content and instruction is undoubtedly an extremely powerful approach to capturing and holding the attention of our students. There is no question that motivation drives attention. Anything that increases the motivation of our students to learn will increase how well we can capture and hold their attention.

There is another side of the coin. What determines how well students concentrate on our lessons is not just a function of how engaging the lesson is. Students bring to any lesson content their personal set of attention skills. Each student in a classroom falls somewhere along an attention skills continuum—everywhere from superb powers of concentration and attention management on one end of the continuum to ADD on the other end. No matter where a student is on that continuum, they will do better academically and in life if they improve their attention skills. Thus, training attention should be, and some day will be, a part of every student's education.

Whether or not a student has true ADD, and whether or not the student is taking Ritalin, attention training holds great promise. The question is not Ritalin v. Attention Training. The more important question: Why not make attention training part of our curriculum for all students? When we want to teach the young students to print, we take time away from practicing printing to teach them how to hold the pencil. When we want to have students do a research a report, we take time off from having them do the research to teach them how to make note cards, use the library and Internet, and how to structure a successful research project. We know that in the long run, taking time off from performance to teach the skills of performance lead to better printing and better research reports. In the same way, we need to take time off lecturing to teach students how to manage their attention during a lecture. We need to take time off from assigning homework to teach our students how to manage their attention while doing their homework. In the long run, this investment in skill development will have big pay-offs for performance in our class and for performance in life.

Our reluctance to take on this task, training attention, may have its roots in the seminal work of the great American psychologist William James. Early on, James formed our thinking about attention. He recognized the importance of sustained attention, but assumed it was a "fixed characteristic"—a gift we either had or did not have:

> "The possession of such a steady faculty of attention is unquestionably a great boon. Those who have it can work more rapidly, and with less nervous wear and tear. I am inclined to think that no one who is without it naturally can by any amount of drill or discipline attain it in a very high degree. Its amount is probably a fixed characteristic of the individual."[132]

Since James penned those words over a hundred years ago, we have learned a great deal about the brain. We now know the brain is far more plastic that anyone ever dreamed.[133] By applying the principles of neuroplasticity, people who were paralyzed for years, and who the medical profession had thought would never walk, now walk. When someone goes blind and learns Braille, their brains reconfigure themselves, dedicating a great deal more real estate to their Braille reading finger than before. The brain is far more malleable and trainable than we previously imagined. Given our new understanding of neuroplasticity, James' belief in the immutability of attention style is unwarranted.

James did believe that if we could train attention, it would be *the* education *par excellence*.[134] What teacher doesn't dream of teaching a classroom of students who are fully alert, fully focused on the lesson? What would we give to teach a student who has scattered, fleeting attention how to focus and concentrate? If only that student had sustained, focused attention, his or

her learning would soar. New technology that applies neuroplasticity is now being used to train students how to increase their working memory and maintain attention. A by-product of this training is increased intelligence!

School and life success depend on ability to control one's attention (fully focus, sustain focus, ignore distractions, clear short-term and working memory). Given our new appreciation for the power of neuroplasticity, it is time we design and test programs to train attention.

In what follows, we examine seven approaches to attention training: (1) Brain Games, (2) Meditation Training, (3) Breathing Buddies, (4) Meta-Attention Training, (5) Attention Flexibility Training, (6) Aiken Methods, and (7) Attention Modification Training.

Attention Training 1: Brain Games

Computer games are a natural way to rewire the brain. We learn more when we have focused attention, and we lay down and strengthen neural tracks by repeated practice. Computer games have both components: They rivet our attention and demand we repeatedly practice certain behaviors.

Taking advantage of the natural marriage between computer games and neuroplasticity, researchers have developed games to retain the brain's attention systems. After playing a variety of attention training games for only 5 days, 4-year-old and 6-year-old students showed strong improvements in executive attention and intelligence.[135] Like many successful computer-based approaches to training the brain, the experiment used adaptive training. That is, when children were successful, difficulty was increased. The computer games included:

- ► Moving a cat to a grassy area while avoiding muddy areas
- ► Catching a moving umbrella to keep the cat dry
- ► Anticipating where a duck will emerge after it swims underwater

- ▶ Remembering items after they disappear from the screen
- ▶ Ignoring conflicting impulses: picking the larger array of digits when sometimes the larger array is of the smaller digit (picking the array of seven number 2s rather than the array of two number 9s)

> ## Tip
> Encourage students to play brain games.

A highly significant main effect revealed training increased ability of students to ignore the conflicting impulse to choose the larger number instead of the correct response (the larger array). This indicates improved executive function—ability to manage attention. Further, brain-wave analyses were as expected, revealing improved executive function: EEG brain wave data from the prefrontal and frontoparietal regions revealed that the training for 4-year-olds produced brain wave patterns similar to the untrained 6-year-olds, and training for the 6-year-olds produced brainwave patterns similar to adults! This brief attention training appears to have facilitated maturation of executive control of attention!

That a simple, brief computer game can improve a brain attention system offers great hope. As programs are developed and tested, they are certain to become commonly used tools to improve attention among students—especially for students with attention deficits. Some developers predict, "brain training games will be a standard part of schooling, with the best ones gathering data about the players as they simultaneously fine-tune themselves into the exact game needed—an empathic tutor."[136]

A number of research labs are developing brain games to train attention skills. Daniel Goleman describes a simple game called *Tenacity* that is being developed at the University of Wisconsin for the iPad. The game is designed to calm and focus the player. At the beginning level, it involves ignoring distractions while tapping the iPad screen with one finger each time the player exhales, but tapping it with two fingers on every fifth exhale. Goleman's grandchildren found the game enjoyable and wanted to play again. The 13 year-old reported, *"I feel calm and relaxed—I like this game."* The 12 year-old reported, *"I felt really focused."*[137]

Commercial programs to improve attention skills have gained worldwide followings with millions of subscribers, but some caution is warranted. Many researchers have been quite skeptical based on two kinds of findings: (1) failure for the skills acquired in the brain training programs to transfer generally to everyday skills; and (2) failure to replicate the findings of the game developers.[138] For certain, playing the brain training games improves ability to play the games themselves, and the training cannot hurt. However, how much the games can improve important cognitive skills that can be applied across situations, remains at the time of this writing an unanswered question.

Attention Training 2: Meditation

Meditation training is a form of attention training. A key attention skill is self-regulation of attention: consciously monitoring one's attention, moving attention from distractors and toward an intended object of focus. Training this skill is at the heart of most forms of meditation training. As students learn and practice meditation, they are exercising and developing critical attention skills.

> ## Tip
> Teach students a simple, non-mystical mediation technique. To avoid unwanted baggage, call it "Quiet Time" or "Focus Skills." Have a regular time in class to practice quiet time or focus skills.

There is a second way meditation improves attention. When we are anxious or stressed, the amygdalae are firing and cognition and perception are narrowed. Focused attention and concentration are dependent on absence of distractors or on our ability to ignore distractors. Anxiety is a powerful distractor. Meditation reduces anxiety. This induced calm promotes concentration.

A number of findings support the conclusion that meditation increases attention skills:

▶ Meditation improves attention[139]
▶ Meditation decreases symptoms of ADHD[140]
▶ Meditation improves executive function[141]
▶ Meditation increases flexibility of visual perception[142]
▶ Meditation makes people more engaged and attentive[143]
▶ Meditation decreases anxiety and stress, improving concentration[144]
▶ Mediation improves memory[145]

The greater attentiveness and focus caused by meditation is almost certainly a result of multiple causes:

▶ **Positive Emotions.** As we have seen, positive emotions open perception. Meditation is associated with increases in activation of the anterior left hemisphere,[146] which is a pattern associated with positive affect.

▶ **Meta-Cognition: Antidote to Mind-Wandering.** Meditation is associated with greater meta-cognition, awareness of one's own thinking. Awareness of one's own thinking is key to counteracting mind-wandering.[147] By reducing mind-wandering, meditation increases attention to class content.

▶ **Attention Restoration.** Meditation shares critical features with attention restoration therapy: both refresh attention by a temporary retreat from common mental habits and the unnecessary use of directed attention.[148]

▶ **Freeing Brain Resources.** Following 3 months of regular meditation, people show less "attentional blink" deficit. That is, in tests of attention, they are better able to detect a second target that quickly follows a first target. Scalp-recorded brain potentials reveal the improved attention of meditators in attentional blink studies is due to their less effortful attention, freeing attention resources to perceive more.[149]

▶ **Relaxation Response.** As we have seen in Tool 14: Advocate Meditation, in Principle 2: Safety, meditation leads to higher vagal tone, lower heart rate, parasympathetic arousal, and relaxation. Anxiety narrows perception; relaxation broadens perception. The greater attention of meditators is probably due in large part to reduced anxiety.

At this point, it is an open question to the extent of which meditation directly strengthens attention skills and the extent of which the improved attention of meditators is a by-product of reduced stress and anxiety, or the combination of these and other factors. In any case, meditation improves attention.

Attention Training 3: Breathing Buddies

Relaxation breathing, described in Tool 13: Practice Progressive Muscle Relaxation, in Principle 2: Safety, has a profound impact on attention. As we have seen, anxiety constricts attention and relaxation broadens attention. Relaxation breathing combined with progressive muscle relaxation has been applied in schools under the name of "Breathing Buddies." The Breathing Buddy program is described by Daniel Goleman in his book, *Focus.*[150]

The twenty-two second graders sit doing their math, three or four to a table, when Miss Emily strikes a melodious chime. On cue, the kids silently gather on a large rug, sitting in rows, cross-legged, facing the two teachers. One girl goes over to the classroom door, puts a DO NOT DISTURB sign on the outside knob, and closes it.

They follow the directions of a man's friendly voice leading them through some deep belly breathing, as they count to themselves, "One, two, three," while they take a long exhalation and inhalation. Then they squeeze and relax their eyes; stretch their mouth wide open, sticking out their tongue; and squeeze their hands into a ball, relaxing each in turn. It ends with the voice saying, "Now sit up, and feel relaxed," and as they do, they all seem to be just that.

The students and teachers testify to the power of Breathing Buddies. Students say, *"It feels nice inside." "…it calmed my body." "It made me have happy thoughts."* Without Breathing Buddies, the calm focused attention of students disappears. Goleman describes the difference, quoting their teacher:

> "We've got many kids with problems, but when we do this, they don't act out," says Miss Emily. But the week before, a glitch in the school day meant Room 302 skipped this ritual. "It was like they were a different class," says Miss Emily. "They couldn't sit still; they were all over the place."[151]

The school principal testifies as well: *"This helps them relax and focus."* The school's Breathing Buddy program is progressive. Five- to 7-year-olds practice Breathing Buddies as described. From 8 years up, they practice mindfulness of breathing: a program that increases calm and sustained attention for both students and teachers.

Attention Training 4: Meta-Attention Training

Before laying out the steps of meta-attention training we need to spend a bit of time deepening our own understanding of the dimensions of attention.

Dimensions of Attention. Let's distinguish three dimensions of attention, each of which has two poles. This three-dimensional model of attention (B, C, and D) is easily grasped. See Box: B C D Attention Dimensions.

B C D Attention Dimensions

Breadth: Narrow ←——→ Broad

Content: Internal ←——→ External

Duration: Fleeting ←——→ Sustained

These three dimensions are associated with different brain structures and functions. In general, the right hemisphere specializes in broad, big picture processing whereas the left hemisphere processes details.[152] In normal individuals, there is parallel processing so the brain simultaneously processes both the big picture and the details. Nevertheless, at any one instant, we are consciously aware of only one or the other pole of this dimension. Different brain structures and processes are active when our attention is fleeting v. sustained,[153] and when the content of our attention is external or internal.[154]

We are all somewhat familiar with these three dimensions of attention. As teachers, we know how they can promote or inhibit learning. A student will learn little, if during a class presentation his or her attention is inward (daydreaming, remembering last night's date, fantasizing about tonight's date, or reliving an upsetting event that occurred before school). The student might not even be aware that his or her attention has drifted to some internal content. The student lacks the skill of meta-attention— awareness of the **Breadth, Content,** and **Duration** of his or her attention. The student lacks also the skill of attention flexibility—the ability to shift to the attention style most adaptive for a given situation. Wouldn't it be powerful if students monitored their own attention and then shifted their style to the style most adaptive for the content to be learned? Before we turn to attention training (meta-attention and attention-flexibility training), let's examine the three dimensions of attention in a bit more detail.

Visiting the Supermarket. These three dimensions of attention are easily understood by example. Let's contrast two different ways to visit a supermarket:

Visit 1: The Last-Minute Dash. Many guests are coming over to our house within the hour for a barbecue. We discover we are missing the barbecue sauce for the ribs, a critical ingredient. We make a dash to the store. As we enter the store, our only thought is to get the barbecue sauce and get home in time. We make a beeline to the sauce isle, grab what we need, and head straight for the shortest checkout line. If later someone asks what else we saw in the supermarket while we were there, we would have no idea, we would reply, *"I didn't have time to look around; I was focused on getting the sauce I needed."* The *Breadth* of our attention **was narrow rather than broad**, like a laser beam rather than a floodlight. If they asked about any thoughts or fantasies we had as we rushed for what we needed, we might answer, *"I didn't have time to be daydreaming—I was on a mission."* The *Content* of our attention was **external rather than internal**. If they asked us to describe the label and packaging on the barbecue sauce we grabbed at the store, we might answer, *"I didn't read the label or examine the packaging; I just grabbed what I needed and ran."* We glanced at the sauce only long enough to recognize that it was indeed what we wanted. The *Duration* of our attention was **fleeting rather than sustained**.

Visit 2: The Leisurely Stroll. Let's revisit the supermarket on a different day, but this time we are in no hurry. As we casually stroll down the cereal aisle, we are struck by the vast array of cereal boxes that take up most of that aisle.

Our attention style creates our world— and to a large extent, determines who we are!

At that moment, the *Breadth* of our attention is **broad rather than narrow**—we are looking at the aisle as a whole, not focusing on any one cereal. Then our attention shifts. Somehow, one cereal box draws our attention. We have the impulse to reach for it. That one box among many seems to stand out and say, "pick me." We wonder what there is about that cereal box that is like an attention magnet. As we puzzle about how that one box captures our attention, we focus on our internal processes—what grabs my attention? At that moment the *Content* of our attention has shifted, **from external to internal**. We have shifted also **from broad external** (the whole row of cereal boxes) **to narrow internal** (wondering what exactly is it in ourself that creates the impulse to reach for the one box among many).

After puzzling over our own reaction and noticing the power of containers to attract or fail to attract attention, our attention again shifts: We begin to imagine creating a different type of container for cereal—one that would distinguish itself from all the others, one that would make everyone want to reach up and grab it. We ponder this question for awhile so the *Duration* of our **internal attention is sustained**. After fantasizing about inventing this new type of container for cereal, our fantasy becomes more elaborate: We have become rich by selling the new cereal container idea to several cereal companies as a revolutionary marketing tool. From there, our attention shifts yet again, this time hopping in quick succession from thing to thing that we will buy and do with our newfound riches! So our attention has remained *internal*, but the *Duration* of our attention has shifted **from sustained to fleeting**.

If we contrast our first and second trips to the supermarket, several things stand out. We were an entirely different person on the first trip than the second. In effect, we visited a different supermarket. We create our world by the type of attention we adopt!

There is no one right way to maintain attention. Different styles of attention serve us well for different types of tasks. If we have a very important, time-sensitive task to complete, it is an important skill to be able to rigidly maintain external, narrow, sustained attention. If on the other hand, we want to be creative, it is important to be able to shift our attention repeatedly, shifting back and forth between the big picture

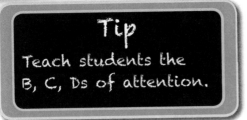

Tip
Teach students the B, C, Ds of attention.

and the details, to allow fleeting as well as sustained attention, and to repeatedly shift the content of our attention between the external aspects of the project to our internal feelings about those aspects. In short, it is adaptive to have flexible attention.

Different attention styles are adaptive in different situations. The quality of our relationships is determined to a large extent by our ability to maintain external, narrow, focused attention on another person, and then also to shift, to direct our attention internally to our own thoughts and feelings in reaction to the other person and to be able to share those. In contrast, the ability to lead a successful meeting or run a successful classroom depends on our ability to shift into broad and often fleeting attention to take in what is happening with all those at the meeting or in the classroom. This ability distinguishes good from poor teachers and has been called "withitness"—the ability to attend to and understand what is happening with all of the students in the class.

We want students to be able to maintain the type of attention that will lead to success in a given situation. To this end, students need to learn to manage their own attention first by being aware of the attention style they are adopting at a given time and then being able to turn their attention inward or outward, focus broadly or narrowly when needed, and being able to scan a situation or sustain their focus on a detail as the task requires. Because different types of attention serve us well in different situations, a goal of education should be to *train attention flexibility*—the ability to shift from one pole to another along each of the three attention dimensions. The first step toward obtaining attention flexibility is to be aware of the three dimensions of attention and to have an ongoing awareness of which pole of each dimension we are occupying at a given time. Having an ongoing awareness of the type of attention, we are using is meta-attention skill. Let's examine how we might train that skill.

Steps of Meta-Attention Training.
Meta-attention training is a two step process:
(1) Introduce the B, C, Ds of attention, and
(2) Have students practice placing themselves in each pole of each dimension.

Introducing the B, C, D's of Attention. The first step in meta-attention training is to make students aware of the three dimensions of attention. The visits to the supermarket scenarios are a helpful introduction. A second way to introduce the B, C, D's is experientially. Have students engage in an unstructured discussion on a topic to which they would all like to contribute— something like favorite TV programs. After about 4 minutes of unstructured discussion, have students identify which pole of each dimension they were occupying. Have students reflect on if they really focused on the person talking or if their attention was also on other things going on in the room (Breadth = Narrow v. Broad). Have students ask themselves how much they were focused on their own thoughts v. the thoughts of others (Content = Internal v. External). Finally, ask them to identify how long their attention stayed focus just on the speaker each time someone was speaking, or if they found their attention jumping to other things (Duration = Fleeting v. Sustained). See Box: B C D Attention Dimensions.

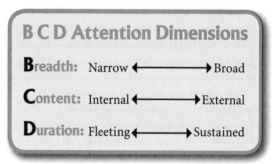

B C D Attention Dimensions

Breadth: Narrow ⟷ Broad

Content: Internal ⟷ External

Duration: Fleeting ⟷ Sustained

Define active listening in terms of the B, C, and D's. Without the skill of active listening, interaction in groups often is everyone waiting his or her turn to talk with no one listening very intently. Introduce the idea of active listening. Active listening is Narrow, Sustained, External attention.

Practice Using the B, C, and D's. The second step of meta-attention training is practice. The goal is to make meta-attention a habit of mind. As with all habits, there is just one road to success:

practice. Once students are familiar with the B, C, D's, we repeatedly have them practice paying attention to their own attention.

Practice might sound like this:

"Students please turn to a partner and describe a fun experience you have had." [Students share for a minute.] *"Now, I want you to take out a piece of paper and make two columns, one labeled Internal and the other External."* [Students comply.]

"Think back on the conversation you just had. During that conversation, what were all the ideas you heard from your partner and things you noticed about your partner? List those in the external column." [Students list ideas and observations.] *"What were all the ideas you came up with and the feelings you were aware of during the conversation? List those in the internal column."* [Students list ideas and observations.]

"Notice, during a conversation, we shift up and back from internal to external content. Now we are going to have a conversation again, but this time A's in each pair, you will maintain only external attention. Forget your own thoughts and feelings during this next conversation, and just take in what your partner shares. B's share your thoughts and feelings about fun things to do over the weekend." [B shares for 30 seconds while A listens, and then they reverse roles.]

"Students, the point of this exercise is that we can choose. At any moment, we can choose to shift our attention from internal to external. We can choose to have sustained external attention if we want."

Another way to have the students practice meta-attention is to stop at random moments during a lecture or during a pair or team interaction and have students define where they were at that moment along the poles of the B, C, D dimensions. The more students pay attention to their attention, the more meta-attention becomes a habit of mind. Our goal: Develop the skill of meta-attention—ongoing ability to direct one's

attention to one's own attention, increasing the ability to locate oneself along the poles of the B, C, D Attention Dimensions.

Attention Training 5: Attention Flexibility Training

Once students are familiar with the B, C, D Attention Dimensions, we can have them practice maintaining different positions in that matrix. The goal: ability to shift at will from one position along those dimensions. In this way, we train attention flexibility—control of attention.

Training attention flexibility can be especially helpful for some students with learning disorders. We know the student who cannot focus for any length of time, whose attention is almost always *fleeting*, even in situations in which sustained attention is necessary. These students have a rigid rather than flexible attention style; they are stuck at the fleeting end of the duration dimension. We also know the student who gets tunnel vision and gets stuck on a difficult problem; he or she focuses on that problem to the exclusion of all else and sees only one way to approach solving the problem Their attention style is rigid also, but stuck at the opposite end of the fleeting—sustained duration dimension. These students are actually sustaining attention too much. They need to take a breath and refocus their attention on some other problem or some other way of approaching the problem at hand. Awareness and flexibility of attention style are tremendous advantages in school and in life.

Attention flexibility training might sound like this:

"Today we are going to work on developing our ability to shift up and back between broad and narrow focus. At any moment, we can choose to take in the big picture or to focus on just one part of the picture."

"Everyone get relaxed. Now please look at the index finger of your right hand. Focus on just the fingernail of that finger. Notice the shape of the

nail. *Notice the moon of the fingernail. Notice the color difference between the moon and the rest of the fingernail. Now focus on just that part of the fingernail below the moon, where the fingernail meets the finger. Inspect closely the exact place where the fingernail merges from the finger.*" [Give students about 20 seconds.]

"*Now I want you to shift your attention to the whole finger.* [Pause.] *Now broaden your attention so you are looking at the back of your whole right hand.* [Pause.] *Broaden your attention even more so you can see both hands. Look at them both at once without shifting attention from one to the other.* [Pause.] *Now a real stretch: Hold your arms outstretched in front of you with the backs of your fingers pointing upward* [Teacher models.] *Broaden your attention as much as you can so you take in the backs of your hands and as much else beyond your hands as you can. Don't shift from one thing to another. Rather, without thinking, broaden your attention to take in as much as you can at once.*" [Pause.]

"*Now lets practice attention shifting. When I say 'Go,' I want you to shift your attention all the way back to just the line where the fingernail of your index finger emerges from the index finger of your right hand. Once you have done that, shift to broad attention. Shift up and back from broad to narrow several times.*" [Pause for about 15 seconds.]

"*The point of this exercise is to notice how we can shift our attention at will. Now please turn to a partner. I want you to discuss with your partner when it might be useful to have very narrow attention and when it might be better to have broad attention.*"

With exercises like this, we can have students practice shifting their attention back and forth from one end to the other along each of the three attention dimensions. When students become practiced at attention flexibility, they are more likely to be able to choose the best attention space to occupy at a given moment. Students who too

often have fleeting attention can self-monitor and choose more sustained attention. Students who too often focus only on the details can learn to shift at will to see the big picture. Others who tend to be very global can learn to shift at will to be more detail oriented.

Requesting Attention Style. Once students become quite versed in the Attention Dimensions, a teacher can call for an attention style that is adaptive at any moment in a lesson. For example, the teacher might at one point in the lesson say, "*I want you to have sustained, external, broad attention on this picture.*" Later in the lesson, the teacher might call for a different attention to the same picture: "*Let your attention shift from detail to detail in the picture.*" Yet later, the teacher might direct, "*Look at the picture for a moment and then shut your eyes. I want the direction of your attention inward. How do you react to the picture? What are your thoughts and feelings?*"

Shifting attention is not just for art class. A teacher may direct the attention of students from details of a proposed act of Congress to students' feelings and thoughts about the act and then to how they picture the society being different if the act is passed. Good science involves the ability to be analytic, focusing narrowly on the details, but then shifting to be global, focusing on how an element interacts with its ecology. As students practice different attention styles, they increase their attention flexibility and become more likely to be successful in whatever profession they adopt.

Attention Training 6: The Aiken Methods

Meta-attention and attention flexibility training are approaches to increasing attention resources. A different approach is the incredible work of Catharine Aiken. In 1895 at the age of 40,

Catharine Aiken published her book, *Methods of Mind-Training*.[155] By that time, Catharine had become principal of the Stamford Female Seminary. She was applying attention training with great success at that school, and visitors traveled from considerable distances to view Catherine's methods in action. They were amazed by what her students could do.

As a young teacher, Catharine had despaired: The results of traditional teaching methods provided her students content, but failed to provide them intelligence. They could repeat back what was taught, but had, in Catherine's words, "a lamentable want of mental power."

> ...the teacher, perhaps through no fault of her own, but of that tyrant, Custom, had been bound to the task of finding out how much or how little her scholars knew, measured by the standard of the textbook. This was the schoolteacher's occupations. Oh, what drudgery!
>
> It was in the endeavor to find a better way for the developing of youthful minds than the text-books afforded that my mind was continually exercised.[156]

It was while viewing circus performances that Miss Aiken had the insight that led her to transform her approach to teaching and to developing the minds of her students.

> ...it was a child who led me to catch a glimpse of the better way for which I had sought so earnestly. Some small friends had begged me to take them to the circus which was exhibiting in the town where I had been teaching, and I consented somewhat reluctantly. While watching various acrobatic feats, my attention was particularly drawn to a Japanese lad of but a few years, who was walking a tight-rope; the rope was stretched at a height that made the feat extremely dangerous—a single misstep as he balanced himself in midair would have proved well-

nigh fatal. Another lad also attracted my attention and filled me with amazement by his skill and agility in rapidly tossing up and catching sharp-bladed knives.

> What was it which enabled each to perform his dangerous feat without faltering or mistake? The answer was to be found in the fact that fear had caused them to rivet their attention upon their tasks absolutely, so that they were utterly oblivious to all else. This exhibition of the possibilities of concentrated attention as exemplified by the Japanese boys impressed itself upon my mind with peculiar force.
>
> It was then I realized the value of a mental power which would aid me to train the mind to a greater degree of attention....
>
> Here, then, is the important work of the teacher. It is in the schoolroom that these habits of attention should be formed.

With great passion, Catharine Aiken developed a large set of tasks to develop the powers of attention among her students. Today, we know she was doing applied neuroplasticity. Miss Aiken thought of it simply as creating habits of mind, or as she called it, "mind-training."

Most of the techniques she used to train attention involved using a handheld slate. She would show the front of the slate for as brief as 3 seconds, and then rotate the slate so the content was out of sight. She would then ask students either to recall the content verbatim or perform some operations on the content. We now know she was training short-term and working memory. Some of her techniques included:

Short-Term Memory Practice
- Briefly show two or three columns of numbers and have students recall them.
- Briefly show students history events and dates and have them recall them.
- Have students very briefly read sentences and repeat them word for word.

- For math, have students recall equivalent measurements (feet in a mile; cups in a quart) or algebraic formulas.
- For history, have students list events and their associated date.
- For vocabulary development, have students recall lists of synonyms.

Working Memory Practice

- Show students a column of numbers for only a few seconds and then, with the numbers out of sight, ask students to multiply the first number by the third, or take the root of the fifth number.
- Briefly show students figures that were similar or different and have them make discriminations with the items out of sight.

After the students had practiced Aikens' mind-training for some time, they were capable of extraordinary mental feats of both short-term and working memory. To take but one of many examples, students were exposed to a list of numbers for only 3 seconds and then "were asked but once to multiply the first number by two, to extract the cube root of the second, to square the third, to extract the square root of the fourth, to divide the fifth by two, to multiply the sixth by twenty-four, and to divide the seventh by four, and then to repeat the changed column."

Some of the accomplishments of the students resemble those of autistic savants. And this is almost certainly no accident. Without knowing it, Aikens was training students to use a different part of their brain, a part not normally developed by traditional educational methods. This is most clearly revealed in an exercise Aikens called "unconscious counting." She would expose students to arrays of up to twenty things and have students say how many items there were, without counting them.

There are presented to the eye, for example, a number of circles placed upon the revolving board. Instead of counting one, two, three, four, five, six, seven, the pupil distinguishes at a glance that the numerical value of the group is seven. The relative position of the circles should be changed, and the practice continued until the group is a quickly perceived and as certain to mean seven to the mind as a single object to mean one.

After a few weeks of practice, not exceeding 5 minutes each morning, my pupils were able to recognize instantly twenty objects without counting, seldom mistaking the group, of whatever kind, for any other number.

Although she could not know it, Miss Aikens was developing global, simultaneous right-hemisphere processing, in contrast to analytic, sequential left-hemisphere processing. The process is called *subitizing*. We all subitize to some extent. When a young child plays her first board game, she rolls the dice and then counts the dots on the dice to determine how many spaces to move. After some time, when the child rolls a 3 or 5, she does not need to count the dots. She sees the entire array as a 3 or as a 5. Subitizing feels different from counting; counting engages parts of the brain not engaged when subitizing is happening.[157]

What Aikens' students were doing is the same thing autistic savants do when they see an array of items and immediately state the number of items in the array. Oliver Wolf Sacks, the famed biologist, neurologist, and author describes

> **Tip**
> Engage students in daily mind training. Have them practice short-term and working memory skills using your academic content.

just such an incident. It occurred while he was interviewing 26-year-old twin autistic savants. Their savant skills are astounding: If you give them a date, any time in the next forty thousand years, almost instantly they will tell you the day of the week of that date. If you read three hundred digits to them, they can repeat the digits back flawlessly from memory. Nevertheless, these skills are "splinter skills." The twins cannot do simple arithmetic. They have IQs of 60.

The twins, like Miss Aikens' students, do not count the items in an array of objects—they *see* the number. The twins can instantly see large arrays as a number. Sacks describes an amazing incident in which the twins see a large array as a number:

A box of matches on their table fell, and discharged its contents on the floor: "111," they both cried simultaneously.... I counted the matches—it took me some time—and there were 111.

"How could you count the matches so quickly?" I asked. "We didn't count," they said. "We *saw* the 111."

Similar tales are told of Zacharias Dase, the number prodigy, who would instantly call out, "183" or, "79" if a pile of peas was poured out, and indicate as best he could—he was also a dullard—that he did not count the peas, but just "saw" their number as a whole, in a flash.[158]

With continued practice, Miss Aikens' students began performing astounding feats of memory: "As the pupils' power of continuous attention increased with practice, a greater number of lines of prose and poetry was read for their recalling, until they could repeat from twenty to thirty lines, and even more, of that which they had heard or read but once."

The students were not just placing content into short-term memory, to be repeated back and soon forgotten. Prose passages containing details of names and dates were read to the students. Later, "the pupils have recited, often without hesitation, the entire selection after weeks and even months have elapsed."

These prodigious feats of memory generalized. Students could apply their memory skills to a range of content. For example, students who had trained on remembering numbers, letters, dates, and numbers of items in an array could at a glance remember the notes of sheet music after an extremely brief exposure, even though they had not practiced the skill on sheet music. Their music teacher was amazed. In his words:

"Having witnessed several astonishing illustrations of Miss Aiken's mind-training, and wishing to test the principle as applicable to the reading of music, I wrote on a blackboard, out of sight of the class and without previous intimation, the following musical phrase:

"After being exposed to the view of the pupils for the short space of time of 3 seconds, it was repeated by them from memory correctly, naming note for note in the treble and the bass, together with their value and place in the measure."

—*Albert Woeltge*

Miss Aikens' work offers a critique of our traditional philosophy of education. Traditionally, it has been assumed that as students master more and more content, their cognitive development will be enhanced. Catherine Aikens thought that this puts the cart before the horse—that we need to first directly develop cognitive skills because then the mastery of content would be easy. She talks about saving time by taking time off the curriculum to teach attention skills. She demonstrated that once students mastered attention skills, they breezed through curriculum in a fraction of the time, and with fuller mastery. She likened the traditional approach to expecting a mechanic to build complex machines before mastering the tools of his trade:

> "It would be thought a strangely absurd thing to expect an unskilled mechanic to produce a piece of intricate and useful workmanship without a thorough knowledge of the use of his tools and of the machinery necessary for its construction…. More unreasonable is the exaction made of the untrained student that she shall comprehend and learn long and difficult lessons without the best use of her mental faculties."[159]
> —*Catherine Aiken, 1895*

Attention Training 7: Attention Modification Treatments

One of the clearest sets of data demonstrating that attention can be trained is a body of work called *attention modification*. Researchers have found that people have attention biases that underpin behavioral patterns. That is, obese people pay more attention to food. Drug-related pictures capture the attention of drug-addicted people. The attention of people suffering from anxiety gravitates to anxiety-producing stimuli.

In a remarkable series of experiments, these attention biases have been reversed using a simple experimental paradigm, and the results are less obesity, drug addition, and anxiety![160] The experimental paradigm is to project the attention-grabbing stimuli and a neutral stimulus for a half a second, and then train the viewer to attend less to the attention-grabbing stimuli, countering attention bias. Research demonstrates the treatment works by training the brain to disengage attention from the undesirable stimulus.[161] The effects of attention training can be long term. For example, alcohol-dependent individuals trained to overcome their attention bias showed a 10% decrease in relapse rates a year later.[162]

Although at the time of this writing, attention modification has not been applied in educational settings, it may in the future play a role. For example, those students with speech phobia or math anxiety may have their anxiety reduced via attention modification. The work in the area of attention modification provides additional proof that attention styles are malleable. One implication: We should not treat ADD as a given, treatable only by drugs. Attention can be trained.

Tool 14
Train Working Memory

Research supports the conclusion that we can make students smarter by training working memory. The ability to focus on and sustain attention may be at the heart of this work. The working memory training methods are time-consuming, computer-based programs that are beyond the capacity of individual teachers to develop or include as part of regular classroom instruction. Nevertheless, they are presently being used in many schools in many countries, and may represent an approach that will become common, especially for students with learning difficulties. The computer-based training programs run themselves using adaptive training (students get easier problems after failures and more difficult problems after successes), and have been used successfully by students working alone at home. The promise: Give these programs to students to run at home, or set up a time and place for them to run the programs at school, and students will get smarter!

Before examining this exciting work, let's review what working memory is; the links between working memory, achievement, attention, and intelligence; and brain scan studies locating the components of working memory.

What Is Working Memory?

Working memory is the ability to hold information in consciousness and to manipulate that information. Thus, working memory involves two major components: (1) maintaining, and (2) manipulating information in one's mind. To spell this out a bit, working memory capacity is (1) short-term memory: how much, how long, and how well can we hold information in our mind; and (2) executive function: how well can we manipulative that information—analyze, synthesize, evaluate, apply, and find relations among the bits of information.

For example, if I ask you to subtract 9 from 17 in your head, for success you would need short-term memory; you would need to remember those numbers. You would also need executive function: While holding the numbers in short-term memory, you would need to manipulate them. Thus, to get the right answer, you would need both components of working memory.

Let's take another example. If I ask you to repeat back some letters in order, say Q, A, B, D. You would use only short-term memory to accomplish that task. But if I ask you to repeat those letters backwards, or to repeat them in alphabetical order, you would need both short-term memory and executive function because you would be maintaining the letters while manipulating them.

Working Memory Capacity. If I asked you to subtract 438 from 711 in your head, you would need a much greater working memory capacity than when you subtracted 9 from 17. Working memory capacity is how much information you can accurately maintain and manipulate in consciousness.

Working Memory Increases with Age. Like attention span, working memory develops with age. This is true for both short-term memory and for working memory.[163] Short-term memory: When presented a series of numbers and asked to repeat them, a typical 4-year-old can handle only two to three numbers correctly. By 16 years of age, students can repeat up to 7 or 8 digits. Working

memory: When asked to repeat a list of numbers in backwards sequence, 4-year-olds can correctly state only two numbers, but average 15-year-olds can state four digits correctly.

Individual Differences in Working Memory.

There are marked differences among students in their working memory capacity. In a typical class of 7-year-old students, among the thirty pupils, three will have a working memory capacity of a 4-year-old and three will have a working memory capacity of a 10-year-old![164] These working memory differences put some students at a severe disadvantage in mastering complex academic tasks while they make achievement a breeze for others.

Working Memory and ADHD. Brain imaging studies reveal that those brain structures that show increased activity consequent to working memory training are the same brain structures that show decreased activity in students with ADHD.[165] Research shows diminished symptoms of ADHD following training working memory.[166]

Working Memory and Achievement

Working memory predicts school achievement. Among children of 7 to 14 years, working memory predicts attainment in both English and mathematics on standardized tests.[167] While short-term memory is predictive, it is executive function that is most predictive of achievement. At entry to school, working memory is predictive of children's literacy scores. Among (11- to 14-year-olds,) both verbal and nonverbal working memory predict test scores in English, mathematics, and science.[168] Working memory also predicts a range of specific types of learning and achievement, including skills like learning logic,[169] learning computer programming,[170] and regulating emotion.[171]

Students with a range of learning difficulties score low on measures of both short-term memory and working memory.[172] Working memory capacity deficits are many times more common among students classified as having special needs than in students without special needs.[173] Among 6- and 7-year-old students, low executive function predicts poor performance on tests for vocabulary, language comprehension, literacy, and mathematics.[174]

It is logical that working memory capacity would have a direct impact on learning and achievement. When working memory capacity is exceeded, there is no learning. This has been demonstrated by experiments that put increasing load on working memory. As load on working memory increases, learning decreases.[175] Students with low working memory capacity are more likely to have that capacity exceeded when presented with complex learning tasks.

Working Memory and Attention

The link between working memory and attention is extremely strong. Ability to control attention to a large extent determines the quality of both short-term memory and the ability to manipulate information.

Attention and Short-Term Memory.

Short-term memory is partially a function of quality of input and retrieval skills. Full, undivided attention increases quality of input (we don't retain what we don't attend to; we retain better that which gets full attention) and improves retrieval skills (we fail at recall if our attention drifts or is distracted).

Attention and Executive Function.

The ability to manipulate information while holding it in awareness depends to a large extent on the ability to control attention—to focus on the task at hand, sustain attention, and ignore internal and external distractions that might steal attention from the task.

Research Support: Attention-Working Memory Link.

Research strongly supports the conclusion that the ability to control attention is a key determinant of working memory capacity. When students are tested on how often their minds wander during the day while doing real-life tasks, those with low working memory capacity are off task more often.[176] When presented with challenging tasks that demand more working memory capacity, those

with low working memory more often have their minds wander. High working memory predicts the ability to concentrate on the task at hand and avoid distractions. People with low working memory have more difficulty controlling their attention in experimental tasks; they are less able to sustain attention on relevant tasks, and less able to ignore distracting stimuli.[177] Distracting tasks interfere with performance far less for those with high working memory (30% decrease) compared to those with low working memory (50% decrease).[178] A number of research studies have established that ability to control attention is a key component, if not the most important determinant, of working memory capacity.[179] Attention control is central to the relation between working memory and general intelligence.[180] Specific parts of the prefrontal cortex and parietal cortex are associated with the ability to switch focus of attention from one task to another, one of the dimensions of working memory.[181]

Does Attention Training Explain Positive Effects of Both Working Memory and Meditation Training?

An intriguing possibility is that many of the positive outcomes of training working memory and training meditation are explained by improvements in the ability to focus and maintain attention. Both working memory training and meditation training improve IQ,[182] and impulse control.[183] Training in meditation improves working memory and reduces the symptoms of ADHD.[184] It is likely that ability to control one's attention, that is, maintain focus and avoid distractions, explains these gains. Meditation training is a form of attention training; it is practice directing one's attention, either on an internal mantra or an external object.[185] Working memory training is also a form of attention training, keeping attention narrowly focused on the task, avoiding distractions.

Working Memory and IQ

IQ tests include tests of working memory. Both short-term and working memory tests are part of traditional IQ tests. Short-term memory: The

Wechsler Intelligence Scales include Digit Span (repeat the numbers I say). Working memory: the Wechsler Scales include Letter-Number Sequence (repeat randomly arranged letters and numbers back in numeric and alphabetical order). The arithmetic subscale also involves working memory.

IQ tests include a basket of skills, many of which do not involve working memory. Working memory accounts for only 25% of the variance in IQ test scores.[186] For example, being able to give correct definitions of words gives a person a higher IQ score, but that skill depends mainly on acquired knowledge, not working memory. Because IQ tests include measures of working memory, students with limited working memory generally score low on IQ tests; students with high-capacity working memory generally have higher IQ scores.

IQ tests assess much more than tests of working memory. An IQ score is partially a function of one's home and school learning environment. Researchers distinguish crystallized and fluid intelligence.[187] Crystallized intelligence, unlike fluid intelligence, measures prior acquired knowledge and experience. Fluid intelligence measures problem solving not dependent on prior knowledge. Measures of working memory are aligned with fluid intelligence. They are not dependent on prior knowledge or experience. Nevertheless, working memory and fluid intelligence are not identical; there are factors other than working memory measured by tests of fluid intelligence.[188]

It is the working memory component of IQ tests that best predicts school achievement. Working memory capacity predicts school achievement,[189] and it predicts school achievement better than does IQ.[190]

Children 7 and 11 years old tested for working memory, IQ, and school achievement were retested 2 years later. Results were clear: Working memory but not IQ significantly predicted learning gains.[192] Because IQ tests include

Brainiac Box

Question:
What does IQ measure?

Answer:[191]
Factor analyses reveal IQ tests measure four different skill sets:
  1. Verbal Comprehension (VCI)
  2. Perceptual Organization (POI)
  3. Working Memory (WMI)
  4. Processing Speed (PSI)

Question:
Where are these four intelligence factors located in the brain?

Answer:
Brain lesion mapping of 241 patients revealed distinct areas corresponding to three of the four skill sets:
VCI: Left inferior frontal cortex
POI: Right parietal cortex
WMI: Left frontal and parietal cortex
PSI: No reliable single location

acquired knowledge as well as working memory, they are a less pure measure than working memory. Working memory subscales of the IQ test better predict achievement than does the full IQ test score.[193]

Working Memory, Brain Structure, and Brain Function

Working memory training has been evaluated with functional magnetic resonance imaging.[194] The brain imaging studies examine the functioning and structure of the brains of participants during and after working memory training. Results show greater brain activity and growth as a result of the training.

Working Memory and Brain Functioning.
Results of the neuroimaging studies are consistent with the two-component model of working memory.[195] That is, simple storage is associated with activity in specific brain structures: Verbal content is associated with activation in the left

Brainiac Box

Question:
Which structures in the brain are engaged by short-term v. working memory?

Answer:[196, 200]
Short-term memory for verbal content activates the left hemisphere, Broca's area, and the premotor areas. Short-term memory for visual content activates the right hemisphere of the occipital lobe.

Working memory activates the dorsolateral prefrontal cortex and the anterior cingulate, the same areas associated with attention management and fluid intelligence.

hemisphere, Broca's area, and premotor areas; visual content is associated with right-hemisphere activation and occipital lobe. In contrast, when more than simple storage is involved, when manipulation of the content is required, activation occurs in the dorsolateral prefrontal cortex and anterior cingulate.[196] These areas are associated also with impulse control, attention management,[197] and fluid intelligence.[198] Not to oversimplify, it should be noted some executive function tasks, like goal management, are not located only in the prefrontal cortex—they are more widely distributed.[199]

Follow-up brain scan studies reveal that after training working memory, those areas activated during working memory training remain significantly more active even 2 months,[201] and 8 months later![202] Specific areas of the prefrontal cortex are more active for months. However, because working memory involves a number of different cognitive functions, it is not clear exactly which aspects of working memory are associated with the parts of the brain that become more active after training. As researchers state,

Working memory includes several cognitive components such as encoding, control of attention, maintenance of information, and resistance to interference. The specific functions of the areas where we observed training-induced increases in activity remain to be determined.[203]

Working Memory and Brain Structure.

Consistent with the general finding that greater brain activity produces brain development and myelination, working memory training changes the structure of the brain. During working memory performance, the lateral prefrontal cortex and the parietal cortex are activated.[204] To test if that activation leads to structural changes in the brain, researchers trained participants on working memory using three working memory training paradigms: (1) remembering the location and order of circles that were presented in 1-second intervals; (2) an n-back training: remembering how many stimuli back in a series a target stimulus appeared; and (3) a dual n-back task: memorizing the identity of a stimuli, its location on a line, and how many stimuli back it appeared. The n-back tests were adaptive, that is, success led to more demanding tasks; failures led to easier tasks. Measures of brain density caused by dendrite branching and myelination revealed those areas associated with working memory activation developed as a result of the working memory training.[205] The experiment also revealed growth in those areas that are responsible for communication between the right and left hemispheres. The research revealed a convincing dose-response pattern: As working memory training increased, working memory areas in the brain developed more. See Graph: Working Memory (WM) Training, p. 5.70.

For educators, these results are among the most exciting to flow from brain science. We are seeing relatively brief working memory training result in brain growth in the areas responsible for intelligence, focused attention, and school achievement. Further, the more training, the more brain growth. As the authors conclude in an understatement, *"Thus, the idea that a brain structure can be changed through short-term cognitive training may provide the basis for new insights into neural plasticity, and may have clinical applications."*[206]

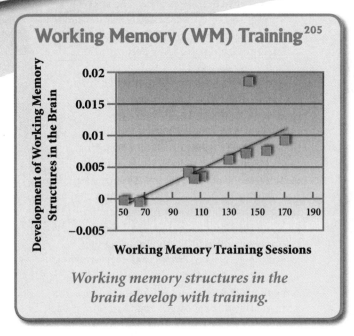

Working Memory (WM) Training[205]

Working memory structures in the brain develop with training.

The mechanism of brain growth and sustained increased activity in working memory areas as a result of working memory training is at least partially explained: As a result of training working memory, there is an increase in the density of the dopamine receptors in those prefrontal and parietal areas activated by working memory training.[207] This neuroplasticity of working memory supports the conclusion that we can improve brain structure and function by training working memory. Like with muscles, workouts make working memory stronger. The researchers note, *"The effect of training of WM is thus in several respects similar to the changes in the functional map observed in primate studies of skill learning, although the physiological effect in WM training is located in the prefrontal association cortex."*[208] Working memory training follows the pattern of neuroplasticity: Greater use leads to greater development. Working memory training rewires the brain.

Training Working Memory

The good news: Working memory, like many things that we once thought were fixed, can be trained. There are numerous studies demonstrating that training working memory results in academic improvement across a variety of content areas, including reading,[209] and math.[210] A 6-month follow-up found working memory training resulted in sustained gains in mathematical ability.[211] Numerous studies demonstrating successful training of working memory and transfer have been conducted with adults and school-aged children at all grade levels. Positive results have been found also with preschool children.[212]

The bad news: There are different approaches to training working memory and the results across studies are mixed.[213] There are now commercial programs designed to boost working memory that are widely used in schools and clinics in many countries.[214] These programs are well advertised and offer a wide range of promises, but, as we will see, they must be viewed with caution. A complete review of the large body of research on training working memory is beyond the scope of this book. What we can do here is overview some of the different approaches that have been taken to training working memory, some of the different kinds of results these approaches produce, and some critical issues. Some studies dramatically increase working memory capacity that in turn increases intelligence. This offers one of the greatest hopes for educators: We can make students smarter! Unfortunately, not all approaches to training working memory produce gains in intelligence, and only a few studies test for and/or demonstrate sustained gains or gains that transfer beyond the experimental paradigm.

Approaches to Training Working Memory.

Three different approaches to training working memory can be distinguished. Some approaches focus on increasing short-term memory span. Others focus on executive function, mental manipulation of information. Yet other training paradigms focus on increasing ability to sustain attention and avoid distractions.

Training working memory usually involves "adaptive training," that is, giving successively more difficult problems following successes and giving easier problems following failures. To accomplish this, most training programs are computer based. In almost all cases, participants improve in the training tasks with practice across studies using different approaches, improvement sometimes produces gains in intelligence, problem solving, impulse control, and academic achievement, but sometimes does not.

The Goal of Working Memory Training.

Working memory training aims at transfer. That is, we hope that following working memory training, students will be able to use their increased working memory capacity to be more successful at a wide range of tasks including academic achievement, problem solving, and creativity. The goal: Make students smarter. Given that increased working memory capacity is associated with increased achievement and a range of real life skills, this goal is reasonable.

The Digit Span Success/Failure Story.

Some types of working memory training succeed at improving performance on the training task, but fail to obtain transfer. A classic example of this kind of success/failure was a very intensive training in short-term memory.[215]

To increase short-term memory, a college student practiced repeating back numbers that were read aloud for an hour a day three to five times a week for 20 months. This training worked incredibly well, but failed completely. That is, improvement on the training task was nothing short of phenomenal, but there was no transfer.

The student developed his short-term memory strategies so well that after 230 hours of practice, he increased his digit span from 7 digits to a span of 79 digits! He could actually listen to 79 random digits and then repeat them all back in order accurately! See Graph: Training Digit Span.

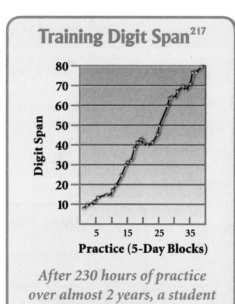

Training Digit Span[217]

After 230 hours of practice over almost 2 years, a student increased his short-term memory for numbers from 7 to 79!

How in the world had this normal college student become a wizard at short-term memory for digits? In a word, the answer is chunking. Short-term memory can hold but four chunks of information at a time.[216] But within chunks, there are items. What the student learned over time is that he could create chunks within chunks. For example, after some practice, the student could remember 18 items by remembering three chunks of 4 digits each, and keeping the last 6 digits in his memory buffer—a total of four chunks. After this method reached a plateau, the student made a major breakthrough. He learned to keep chunks of digits rather than digits in each chunk and in his memory buffer—dramatically increasing his digit span!

Although training to increase digit span was amazingly successful; the training was a complete flop with regard to developing a general short-term memory capacity. After being able to hold 79 digits in short-term memory, the experimenters tested this digit wizard with letters. Amazingly, there had been absolutely no transfer: Prior to the digit training, the student had a letter span (ability to correctly repeat back a string of letters) of about six letters. After his incredible success in increasing digit span, the student's letter span remained about six letters! Thus, we can conclude that the student had acquired a task-specific skill that did not transfer, even to a fairly similar task.

Near- and Far-Transfer.

How similar the experimental task is to the test for transfer is an extremely important question. For over 100 years, researchers have understood that near-transfer (the transfer test is very similar to the training task) is easy to obtain but that far-transfer (the transfer test is dissimilar to the training task) is difficult.[217] Obviously, the hope in training working memory is to obtain far-transfer. Ideally, we would like working memory training to improve a wide range of skills, even those very unlike the skills involved in the training.

While some studies of training working memory (like the digit span experiment just described) show no transfer at all, a number of carefully controlled studies show very large effects on far-transfer measures. Training working memory has produced far-transfer in participants young and old, with and without learning difficulties. Working memory training has improved intelligence, memory, and academic achievement, and has reduced the symptoms of ADHD.[218] In general, however, most effective training paradigms (like studies of neuroplasticity in general) are lengthy and demanding. For example, university students trained in working memory showed little or no gain in intelligence when trained for 8 or 12 days, but when trained for 17 to 19 days showed an increase in intelligence tests of 40%![219]

Duration of Effects. Another issue is how long the benefits last. Sadly, some of the studies that produce strong transfer find the advantages of training working memory fade over time. Other studies, however, demonstrate sustained improvements in intelligence and academic improvement.[220]

Sample Study: N-Back Research

Let's examine in detail a very promising approach to training working memory—one of many studies which inspire hope that we can actually make students smarter.

The Design. Experimenters randomly assigned young adults to one of five conditions: They trained working memory for 0, 8, 12, 17, or 19 days.[221] The training was very taxing. Participants were trained via a computer program. During training, on the computer monitor, every 3 seconds subjects were presented simultaneously with a visual stimulus (a white square appearing in one of eight positions on a black square) and an auditory stimulus (one of eight consonant letters). As the stimuli were presented, subjects were to indicate if the next new stimuli matched the auditory or the visual component of one of the previous stimuli, pressing one key if it was an auditory match and a different key if it was a visual match. This task is called an *n-back test* because the matching stimulus might be any number of

stimuli back. N-back level is how far back subjects can accurately detect a match. As pictured in the graph, all groups steadily improved with more days of training performance on the training task. The task trains working memory rather than just short-term memory because the participant must ignore conflicting stimuli (stimuli that occurred between the present and past stimuli), and they must do attention shifting, looking at both the auditory and visual components of the stimuli. See Graph: Training Working Memory.

Did Working Memory Training Boost Intelligence? To test if this improvement in the training task led to an improvement in fluid intelligence, two different tests of fluid intelligence were administered, shortened versions of the Raven's Advanced Progressive Matrices (RAPM) and the Bochumer Matrizen-Test (BOMAT). To avoid practice effects, odd and even items of the RAPM test and forms A and B of the BOMAT were used for the pre- and post-tests. The eight-session group was tested on the RAPM and the other groups on the BOMAT.

Both tests of fluid intelligence increased following training. Importantly, the more training sessions in working memory students received, the more their fluid intelligence increased. See Graph: Working Memory Training Increases Intelligence, p. 5.73.

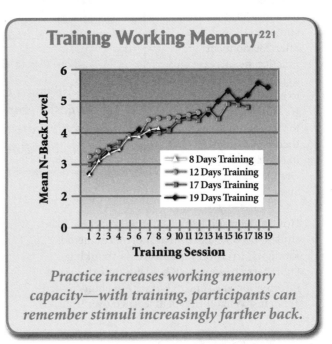

Training Working Memory[221]

Practice increases working memory capacity—with training, participants can remember stimuli increasingly farther back.

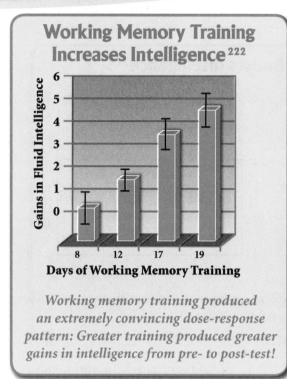

Working Memory Training Increases Intelligence [222]

Gains in Fluid Intelligence vs **Days of Working Memory Training** (8, 12, 17, 19)

Working memory training produced an extremely convincing dose-response pattern: Greater training produced greater gains in intelligence from pre- to post-test!

The improvement in fluid intelligence as a function of working memory training held for all groups tested and for students with initial high- and low-working memory. Although both high- and low-working memory groups gained in fluid intelligence following the working memory training, those students below average in initial working memory capacity showed significantly greater gains in fluid intelligence.

Replication and Extension. The positive results just described were obtained using dual n-back training. That is, participants saw letters and shapes and then had to determine if either the letter or the shape had appeared previously. To determine if a single n-back training would produce similar results, in a follow-up experiment, participants were randomly assigned to either a dual n-back (letters and shapes) or single n-back (shapes only) training.[222]

The results replicated the effects of the dual n-back study: Over training sessions, participants improved on the single n-back training even more than those faced with the more complex dual n-back task. See Graph: Working Memory Training Boosts Intelligence, p. 5.74.

To test if the training increased intelligence, two different fluid intelligence measures were administered: The Bochumer Matrizen-Test (BOMAT) and the Raven's Advanced Progressive Matrices (RAPM). On both measures, the dual and single n-back training groups improved in intelligence significantly more than the control group. The very slight improvement of the control group from pre- to post-test can be attributed to practice effects.

Critiques of Working Memory Studies

The bold and extraordinarily important claim that we can improve the intelligence of students by training working memory has received critical responses from some in the scientific community. Specific criticism of the n-back studies described here has centered on the studies' use of a time-limited version of the Raven's Progressive Matrix Test of fluid intelligence and that the training task and the test of fluid intelligence may be too similar, so the studies demonstrate near- rather than far-transfer.[223]

A broad critique of the working memory studies has been levied, using the results of a meta-analysis.[224] The authors average results across studies and find: (1) participants improve in the working memory training tasks; (2) reliable near-transfer effects for nonverbal reasoning are shown, but these effects were not sustained; and (3) there is no evidence that working memory training produces generalized gains to the other skills that have been investigated (verbal ability, word decoding, or arithmetic), even when assessments take place immediately after training. The authors make a chilling conclusion:

> Our meta-analyses show clearly that these training programs give only near-transfer effects, and there is no convincing evidence that even such near-transfer effects are durable. The absence of transfer to tasks that are unlike the training tasks shows that there is no evidence these programs are suitable as methods of treatment for children with developmental cognitive disorders or as ways of effecting general improvements in adults' or children's cognitive skills or scholastic attainments.[225]

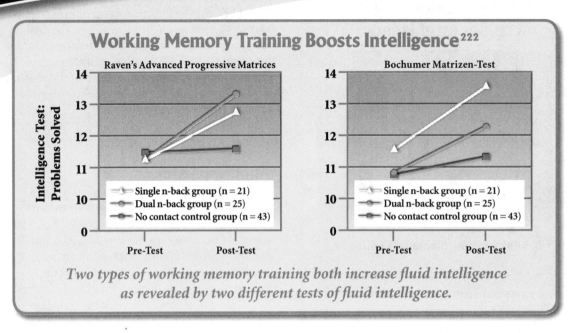

Working Memory Training Boosts Intelligence[222]

Two types of working memory training both increase fluid intelligence as revealed by two different tests of fluid intelligence.

Critique of the Critiques

This very harsh critique of working memory training is unwarranted. Many studies show improved academic performance following working memory training. The research on training working memory taken as a whole provides a coherent integration of studies of learning, intelligence, and cognitive psychology; brain activity; and development of brain structures. When students are given tasks that exercise working memory, their brains become active in predictable ways, their brains develop in corresponding ways, and they become better able to solve a range of problems that test intelligence. The ability to grow brains in ways that improve fluid intelligence is now within our reach—a goal not long ago thought impossible. The specific and general critiques of working memory training are both flawed.

The Critique of N-Back Studies Unwarranted.
The n-back studies reviewed here are remarkable. They demonstrate a clear dose-response effect, which is among the most powerful effects in psychological and brain research: At each level, the more training participants received, the better they became on the training task, which is not remarkable. What is remarkable is that each level of increased working memory training resulted in an increased score on two different standard measures of fluid intelligence. Further, the consistency of these results with studies of

brain activity and brain growth in other n-back studies paints a remarkably coherent picture. The argument that the training task was too similar to the abbreviated, timed tests of fluid intelligence, is not convincing because other research demonstrates n-back training produces gains in the full Raven Matrices along with brain activity and brain growth in the working memory structures of the brain.[226] Because the brain studies showed increased activity of the working memory centers of the brain 8 months later, the argument that working memory training effects are not sustained is also not supported.

The Meta-Analysis Critique Misguided.
There is a serious problem with basing conclusions on a meta-analysis that averages effects of very different working memory training paradigms used with very different populations. Averaging effect sizes across studies only makes sense if the studies use similar methods, which the working memory studies do not. The working memory training studies as a group are about as dissimilar as any in psychological research. They involve preschool, elementary, college, and adult samples. They test clinical populations as well normal populations. They involve a variety of ways to train working memory, and use a variety of ways to test near- and far-transfer.

To lump all these different studies together and calculate an average effect across studies is like determining the effectiveness of three different cancer drug treatments on four different types of cancer by averaging effects across all the cancer drug treatment studies. Imagine we wanted to test the effects of three different drugs on four types of cancer: bone cancer, breast cancer, liver cancer, and prostate cancer. Let's imagine further that drug two is consistently very effective, but only on bone cancer. None of the other drugs is beneficial for any kind of cancer. If we lump all the effect sizes of all the studies, we would find drugs don't improve cancer outcomes. We would throw out the baby with the bath water. The important question to ask is not whether the studies as a whole average gains. The question to ask is which methods improve which component of working memory for which kind of population.

Lumping Studies Masks Important Findings. Working memory training improved fluid intelligence and produced sustained gains in a 3-month follow-up, but only for students who improved considerably on the training task.[227] We need to understand why working memory trainings produce positive results on some tasks but not others. A promising explanation is based in neuroscience: Researchers found positive results for a task that had a shared neural mechanism (the striatum) with the training task, but no positive results for a task that did not engage that neural track.[228]

Sustained Gains. Following working memory training, individuals improve in spatial, verbal, and reasoning tests, and in some cases those gains are sustained for a considerable time. That other studies using different methods do not obtain the same positive results is not a reason to conclude, as the meta-analysis authors do, there is "no evidence these programs are suitable as methods of treatment...."

Far-Transfer. In the meta-analysis seven studies of working memory training showed significant improvement in the Stroop test whereas six did not. To lump these studies and average across studies does not further science. We need to investigate why some studies produce this impressive far-transfer and others do not. The Stroop test presents color words for subjects to read. The words are printed in different colors. For example, Red might be printed in red, or it might be printed in some other color. Subjects are told to ignore the print color and read the words. Errors occur when subjects see a color word printed in a color different from the word. For example, when the word "green" is printed in yellow ink, subjects fail to disregard the ink color and say "yellow." Errors indicate inability to direct one's attention to one kind of stimuli and ignore another. The Stroop test is very dissimilar to the working memory training tasks. That half of the studies showed this far-transfer and half did not is not reason to average those studies and conclude there is no far-transfer. It is reason to investigate why some studies show transfer and other do not. That some working memory training procedures produce such far-transfer indicates working memory training can increase a general capacity, not just a task-specific skill. That capacity might well be management of attention.

The Promise of Working Memory Research

We are on the threshold of being able to apply neuroscience research to train components of working memory so students will be more successful in school and in life. Working memory research is causing us to rethink intelligence. Traditionally, we have thought of students as gifted, smart, or slow, and have taken their intelligence as a given. We now think of the intelligence of students as a function of specific brain structures that can be trained. Intelligence is no longer fixed. Just as we take a student in the gym and build up their muscles so they can do heavier lifting, we can take a student into the mental gym and build up their intelligence so they can solve more difficult problems and achieve more in school.

Consistency with Brain Science. A consistent finding across the neuroimaging studies is that working memory training makes the working memory centers in the brain more active. Given the central importance of working memory for intelligence, problem solving, and achievement, this finding stands as one of the most promising neuroscience research findings for educators. We are on the threshold of a time when we will be able to teach all students to be smarter!

Future Research Holds Promise. Future research will determine the most effective and most efficient training methods to develop the different components of working memory—visual and verbal short-term memory, focusing and sustaining attention, and various kinds of mental manipulation of the contents of the mind. That research will need to address individual differences; it could well be that different training paradigms will work better with different individuals. There are different types of ADHD.[229] A student whose attention is like a hummingbird, flitting from one thing to another, might well need a different kind of training than a student whose obsessive ruminations don't allow broad external attention. The importance of individual differences is suggested by studies demonstrating adults show a different pattern of brain activation than do young adults in the same training paradigm.[230] That we do not at this point have all the answers is reason for excitement rather than despair. A time is coming when we will be able to better serve our students by teaching them to control their attention.

A Call for Far-Far-Transfer Studies. As educators, we need to call for research to focus on real-life educational outcomes. The field of working memory training distinguishes near- and far-transfer. Near-transfer is a test close to the training; far-transfer is a test of fluid intelligence. If that is the case, as educators we need to call for far-far-transfer! That is, rather than testing the effects of working memory training on intelligence, we need more studies to test the effects also on school-related outcomes. That research needs to broaden its scope including not just academic achievement, but also variables like discipline and social skills. Because training working memory exercises the part of the brain that helps inhibit impulses, we can predict the

training might well reduce discipline problems. Research has shown working memory training to improve self-regulation of emotion.[231] Strong working memory helps people stay goal-oriented and helps develop resistance to impulses. Given this, researchers trained alcoholics and found training working memory reduced alcohol intake even 1 month after training.[232] Given that disruptive school behavior is often impulse driven, it is reasonable to expect working memory training will help minimize disruptive behaviors.

Exercising Working Memory as We Teach

As we teach, we are exercising working memory, putting things into short-term memory and asking students to think about and manipulate that content in various ways. If the research on working memory tells us anything, it tells us that giving working memory a workout causes brain development. The question becomes, then, can we exercise working memory more efficiently as we teach? The paradigms for working involve intensive computer-based training. We can, however, efficiently exercise working memory while we teach our content.

Mental Math. At any grade level, we can give developmentally appropriate mental math problems. For the little ones, we ask them to listen carefully and sum the claps: *"Clap Clap plus Clap Clap Clap."* For somewhat older students, *"How much is 7 times Clap Clap Clap?"* For yet older students *"Close your eyes and take the square root*

of 36, divide by 2, multiply by 7. [Pause].
Give yourself a pat on the back if you have 21!"
With practice we can stretch the length and
difficulty of problems students can do in their
head.

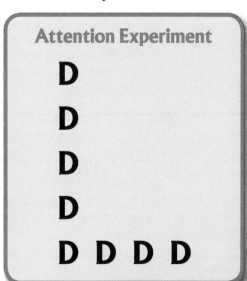

Short-Term Memory Practice.
While they are learning the names of the
colors, young students can be stretching
short-term memory. For example, we
have color cards to hold up, 2 seconds
each. After holding them up, we pause
and then on a cue, we ask students in
unison to call out the names of the
colors we have presented, in order. After
they can do two, we move up to three, and so on.
Older students can repeat the names of chemicals
after seeing cards or PowerPoint slides with
chemical symbols on them. We can use a wide
range of our academic content to stretch short-
term memory.

Avoiding Distractors.
We can insert
distractors cards and tell students to ignore them
when we do the short-term memory practice.
For example, students are
learning to distinguish
fruits from vegetables.
We hold up cards with
pictures: Apple, Orange, Broccoli, Peach, and
Grapes. We then call for students to name
only the fruits, in order. These simple
exercises don't steal time from our
academic content, but serve to give
components of working memory
a workout.

*Attention Yields
Retention.*

Over 100 years ago, an educator
who understood the importance
of developing attention skills
was able to have her ordinary
students perform extraordinary,
almost unbelievable, mental
feats. Is there a reason over 100
years later we cannot at least try
to accomplish what she did?

Instructions: Look at what is in the box
below for about 5 seconds only. Be aware of
what you see first, next, and so on. When
done, turn back to p. 5.47.

Attention Experiment

D

D

D

D

D D D D

Conclusion

We have powerful tools to capture and hold the attention of our students, greatly improving memory for our content. Many of these tools are so simple any educator can use them immediately. It is obvious that all teachers and presenters will increase their effectiveness by establishing an effective quiet signal, teaching active listening, and avoiding distractions. Prior to any brain-science rationale, researchers and educators discovered it is important to distribute practice, offer lesson maps, and include elements of lesson design. Good teachers have long understood the importance of active engagement and so have implemented cooperative learning and frequent processing to increase student engagement and achievement.

Brain science provides additional support for using those underutilized tools. What is new is a brain-based understanding of why these instructional strategies are so powerful. Understanding how frequent processing clears short-term and working memory encourages us to correct the imbalance in the ratio of student-to-teacher talk.

Fourteen Tools to Capture and Hold Attention

1. Establish a Quiet Signal
2. Teach with Kagan Structures
3. Teach with Active Listening
4. Clear Short-Term and Working Memory
5. Punctuate with Processing
6. Avoid Distractions
7. Distribute Practice
8. Create Flow
9. Respond to Attention Styles
10. Include Elements of Lesson Design
11. Encourage Exercise
12. Promote Play
13. Train Attention
14. Train Working Memory

Some new approaches to managing attention are springing from our increased understanding of the brain. Only recently, based on advances in brain science research, have we scientifically approached what was once thought impossible: training attention and working memory. The promise from these approaches is as exciting as anything in education. We are on the threshold of being able to give all students a profound gift for life: the ability at will to manage their own attention. Teachers of the future will accept as a given that intelligence is malleable and that with appropriate training, we can make all students smarter.

References

[1] Wallace, B.A. *The Attention Revolution. Unlocking the Power of the Focused Mind.* Somerville, MA: Wisdom Publications, 2006, xii–xiii.

[2] Goleman, D. Foreword. Wallace, B.A. *The Attention Revolution. Unlocking the Power of the Focused Mind.* Somerville, MA: Wisdom Publications, 2006.

[3] James, W. *The Principles of Psychology.* New York, NY: Henry Holt, 1890, 303–304.

[4] Jasper, H. and Penfield, W. *Epilepsy and the Functional Anatomy of the Human Brain. 2nd edition.* New York, NY: Little, Brown and Co., 1954.

[5] Gepshteina, S., Lesmesb, L.A. & Albright, T.D. *Sensory adaptation as optimal resource allocation.* **Proceedings of the National Academy of Sciences of the USA**, 2013, 10(11), 4368–4373.

[6] Broadbent, D. *Failures of attention in selective listening.* **Journal of Experimental Psychology**, 1952, 44(6), 428–433.

Cherry, E.C. *Some experiments on the recognition of speech, with one and with two ears.* **The Journal of the Acoustical Society of America**, 1953, 25(5), 975–979.

[7] Kanfer, F.H. & Goldeoot, D.A. *Self-control and tolerance of noxious stimulation.* **Psychological Reports**, 1966, 18(1), 79–85.

[8] Das, D.A., Grimmer, K.A., Sparnon, A.L., McRae, S.E. & Thomas, B.H. *The efficacy of playing a virtual reality game in modulating pain for children with acute burn injuries: A randomized controlled trial.* **BioMed Central Pediatrics**, 2005, 5(1), 1.

[9] Hoffman, H.G., Richards, T.L., Coda, B., Bills, A.R., Blough, D., Richards, A.L. & Sharar, S.R. *Modulation of thermal pain-related brain activity with virtual reality: evidence from fMRI.* **Neuroreport**, 2004, 15(8), 1245–1248.

[10] H.G. Hoffman. *Virtual-reality therapy.* **Scientific American-American Edition**, 2004, 291, 58–65.

[11] Hoffman, H.G., Richards, T.L., Van Oostrom, T., Coda, B.A., Jensen, M.P., Blough, D.K. & Sharar, S.R. *The analgesic effects of opioids and immersive virtual reality distraction: evidence from subjective and functional brain imaging assessments.* **Anesthesia and Analgesia**, 2007, 105(6), 1776–1783.

[12] Hoffman, H.G., Doctor, J.N., Patterson, D.R., Carrougher, G.J. & Furness, T.A.III. *Virtual reality as an adjunctive pain control during burn wound care in adolescent patients.* **Pain**, 2000, 85(1–2), 305–309.

[13] Macknik, S.L. & Martinez-Conde, S. **Sleights of Mind. What the Neuroscience of Magic Reveals about Our Everyday Deceptions.** New York, NY: Picador Books, 2010.

[14] Strayer, D.L., Drews, F.A. & Johnston, W.A. *Cell phone induced failures of visual attention during simulated driving.* **Journal of Experimental Psychology**, 2003, 9(1), 23.

Strayer, D.L. & Johnson, W.A. *Driven to distraction: Dual-task studies of simulated driving and conversing on a cellular telephone.* **Psychological Science**, 2001, 12(6), 462–466.

[15] Recarte, M.A. & Nunes, L.M. *Mental workload while driving: Effects on visual search, discrimination and decision making.* **Journal of Experimental Psychology: Applied**, 2003, 9(2), 119–137.

[16] Redelmeier, D.A. & Tibshirani, R.J. *Association between cellular-telephone calls and motor vehicle collisions.* **The New England Journal of Medicine**, 1997, 336(7), 453–458.

[17] Reed, N. & Robbins, R. *The effect of text messaging on driver behaviour.* **Published Project Report**, 2008, 367, 1–70.

[18] Reed, N. & Robbins, R. *The effect of text messaging on driver behaviour.* **Published Project Report**, 2008, 367, 1–70.

[19] Sexton, B.F., Tunbridge, R.J., Board, A., Jackson, P.G., Wright, K., Stark, M.M. & Englehart, K. **The Influence of Cannabis and Alcohol on Driving. TRL Report 543.** Crowthorne, England: Transport Research Laboratory, 2002.

Sexton, B.F., Tunbridge, R.J., Brook-Carter, N., Jackson, P.G., Wright, K., Stark, M.M. & Englehart, K. **The Influence of Cannabis on Driving. TRL Report 477.** Crowthorne, England: Transport Research Laboratory, 2000.

[20] Drews, F.A., Yazdani, H., Godfrey, C.N., Cooper, J.M. & Strayer, D.L. *Text messaging during simulated driving.* **Human Factors: The Journal of the Human Factors and Ergonomics Society**, 2009, 51(5), 762–770.

[21] Rondell, B. & Chaparro, A. *The effects of texting and driving on hazard perception.* **Proceedings of the Human Factors and Ergonomics Society Annual Meeting.** 2012, 56(1), 715–719.

[22] Lantz, G. & Loeb, S. *An exploratory study of psychological tendencies related to texting while driving.* **International Journal of Sustainable Strategic Management**, 2013, 4(1), 39–40.

[23] Brodsky, W. *The effects of music tempo on simulated driving performance and vehicular control.* **Transportation Research, Part F: Traffic Psychology and Behavior**, 2001, 4(4), 219–241.

[24] Brodsky, W. *The effects of music tempo on simulated driving performance and vehicular control.* **Transportation Research, Part F: Traffic Psychology and Behavior**, 2001, 4(4), 219–241.

[25] Brodsky, W. & Slor, Z. *Background music as a risk factor for distraction among young-novice drivers.* **Accident Analysis & Prevention**, 2013, 59, 382–393.

[26] Brodsky, W. *The effects of music tempo on simulated driving performance and vehicular control.* **Transportation Research, Part F: Traffic Psychology and Behavior**, 2001, 4(4), 219–241.

[27] Galera, C. Orriols, L., M'Bailara, K., Laborey, M., Contrand, B., Ribéreau-Gayon, R., Masson, F., Bakiri, S., Gabaude, C. Fort, A., Maury, B., Lemercier, C., Cours, M., Bouvard, M.P. & Lagarde, E. *Mind wandering and driving: Responsibility case-control study.* **British Medical Journal**, 2012, 345, 1–23.

[28] Gladstones, W.H., Regan, M.A. & Lee, R.B. *Division of attention: The single-channel hypothesis revisited.* **Quarterly Journal of Experimental Psychology: Human Experimental Psychology**, 1989, 41(1), 1–17.

[29] Pashler, H. **Psychological Bulletin**, 1994, 116(2), 220–244.

[30] Mayer, R.E. & Moreno, R. *Nine ways to reduce cognitive load in multimedia learning.* **Educational Psychologist**, 2003, 38(1), 43–52.

[31] Junco, R. & Cotten, S. *Perceived academic effects of instant messaging use.* **Computers & Education**, 2010, 56(2), 370–378.

[32] Junco, R. & Cotten, S. *No A 4 U: The relationship between multitasking and academic performance.* **Computers & Education**, 2012, 59(2), 505–514.

[33] Most, S.B. *What's "inattention" about inattention blindness?* **Consciousness and Cognition**, 2010, 19(4), 1102–1104.

Strayer, D.L., Cooper, J.M. & Drews, F.A. *What do drivers fail to see when conversing on a cell phone?* **Proceedings of the Human Factors and Ergonomics Society, 48th Annual Meeting**, 2004, 2213–2217.

[34] Hyman, I.E., Boss, S.M., Wise, B.M., McKenzie, K.E. & Caggiano, J.M. *Did you see the unicycling clown? Inattention blindness while walking and talking on a cell phone.* **Applied Cognitive Psychology**, 2009, 24(5), 597–607.

[35] Most, S.B., Simons, D.J., Scholl, B.J., Jimenez, R., Clifford, E. & Chabris, C.F. *How not to be seen: the contribution of similarity and selective ignoring to sustained inattention blindness.* **Psychological Science**, 2001, 12(1), 9–17.

[36] Carpenter, S. *Sights unseen.* **Monitor on Psychology**, 2001, 32(4), 54.

[37] Drew, T., Vo, M.L-H. & Wolfe, J.M. *The invisible gorilla strikes again: Sustained inattention blindness in expert observers.* **Psychological Science**, 2013, 24(7), 1–6.

[38] Lum, T.E., Fairbanks, R.J., Pennington, E.C. & Zwemer, F.L. *Profiles in patient safety: Misplaced femoral line guidewire and multiple failures to detect the foreign body on chest radiography.* **Academic Emergency Medicine**, 2005, 12(7), 658–662.

[39] Posner, M.I. & Petersen, S.E. *The attention system of the human brain.* **Annual Review of Neuroscience**, 1990, 13, 25–42.

Raz, A. & Buhle, J. *Typologies of attentional networks.* **Nature Reviews Neuroscience**, 2006, 7(5), 367–379.

[40] Fan, J., Wu, Y., Fossella, J.A. & Posner, M.I. *Assessing the heritability of attention networks.* **BioMed Central Neuroscience**, 2001, 2(1), 14.

Posner, M.I. & Raichle, M.E. **Images of the Mind**. New York, NY: Scientific American Library, 1994.

Serences, J.T. Shomstein, S. Leber, A.B., Egeth, G.X. & Yantis, S. *Coordination of voluntary and stimulus-driven attentional control in human cortex.* **Psychological Science**, 2005, 16(2), 114–122.

Posner, M.I. *Attention in cognitive neuroscience: An Overview.* In M.S. Gazzaniga (Ed.) **The Cognitive Neurosciences**, 615–624. Cambridge, MA: MIT Press, 1995.

[41] Raz, A. & Buhle, J. *Typologies of attentional networks.* **Nature Reviews Neuroscience**, 2006, 7(5), 367–379.

[42] Amen, D.G. **Healing ADD. The Breakthrough Program that Allows You to See and Heal the 6 Types of ADD**. New York, NY: Berkley Publishing Group, 2001.

[43] Rothbart, M.K. &Posner, M.I. *Temperament, Attention, and Developmental Psychopathology, In D. Cicchetti & D.J. Cohen (Eds.)* **Handbook of Developmental Psychopathology**, 167–188. New York, NY: Wiley, 2006.

Swaab-Barneveld, H., de Sonneville, L., Cohen-Kettenis, P., Gielen, A., Buitelaar, J. & Van Engeland, H. *Visual sustained attention in a child psychiatric population.* **Journal of American Academy of Child and Adolescence Psychiatry**, 2000, 39(5), 651–659.

[44] Tucha, O., Tucha, L. Kaumann, G., Konig, S., Lange, K.M., Stasik, D., Streather, Z., Engelschalk, T. & Lange, K.W. *Training of attention functions in children with Attention Deficit Hyperactivity Disorder.* **Attention Deficit and Hyperactivity Disorders**, 2011, 3(3), 271–283.

[45] Aiken, C. **Methods of Mind Training, Concentrated Attention and Memory**. Kindle eBook, Kindle Edition, July 2, 2012.

[46] McEwan, E.K. **How to Survive and Thrive in the First Three Weeks of School**. Thousand Oaks, CA: Corwin Press, 2006.

[47] E.N. Sokolov. *Neuronal models and the orienting reflex.* In Mary A.B. Brazier (Ed.), **The Central Nervous System and Behavior**, 187–276. New York, NY: Josiah Macy, Jr. Foundation, 1960.

[48] Iacoboni, M. **Mirroring People: the Science of Empathy and How We Connect with Others**. New York, NY: Pan Books Limited, 2009.

[49] Johnson, P.B., Mehrabian, A. & Weiner, B. *Achievement motivation and the recall of incompleted and completed exam questions.* **Journal of Educational Psychology**, 1968, 59(3), 181–185.

[50] Rickards, J.P. & McCormick, C.B. *Effects of interspersed conceptual pre-questions on note-taking in listening comprehension.* **Journal of Educational Psychology**, 1998, 80(4), 592–594.

[51] Pauk, W., Owens, R. J. Q. **How to Study in College**. Boston, MA: Wadsworth, 2014.

[52] Jacobs, K. *A comparison of two note taking methods in a secondary English classroom.* **Proceedings: 4th Annual Symposium: Graduate Research and Scholarly Projects**. Wichita State University, April 25, 2008.

[53] Ratey, J.J. **A User's Guide to the Brain**. New York, NY: Pantheon, 2001, 131.

[54] McGaugh, J.L. **Memory and Emotion. The Making of Lasting Memories**. New York, NY: Columbia University Press, 2003, 10.

[55] D'Esposito, M. Postle, B.R., Ballard, D. & Lease, J. *Maintenance versus manipulation of information held in working memory: an event-related fMRI study.* **Brain and Cognition**, 1999, 41(1), 66–86.

Postle, R.R., Berger, J.S. & D'Esposito, M. *Functional neuroanatomical double dissociation of mnemonic and executive control processes contributing to working memory performance.* **Proceedings of the National Academy of Sciences USA**, 1999, 96(22), 12959–12964.

[56] Cowan, N. **Working Memory Capacity**. New York, NY: Psychology Press, 2005.

[57] Cowan, N. **Working Memory Capacity**. New York, NY: Psychology Press, 2005.

Miller, G.A. *The magical number seven, plus or minus two: Some limits on our capacity for processing information.* **Psychological Review**, 1956, 63(2), 81–97.

[58] Miller, G.A. *The magical number seven, plus or minus two: Some limits on our capacity for processing information.* **Psychological Review**, 1956, 63(2), 81–97.

[59] Cowan, N. *The magical number 4 in short-term memory: A reconsideration of mental storage capacity.* **Behavioral and Brain Sciences**, 2001, 24(1), 97–185.

Cowan, N. **Working Memory Capacity**. New York, NY: Psychology Press, 2005.

[60] Jaeggi, S.M., Buschkuehl, M., Jonides, J. & Perrig, W.J. *Improving fluid intelligence with training on working memory.* **Proceedings of the National Academy of Sciences of the United States**, 2008, 105(19), 6829–6833.

[61] The exact capacity of working memory differs for different individuals depending on their age and the type and complexity of their encoding process. It differs also for different types of content and whether there are internal or external distractions. In all cases, however, the capacity is quite limited.

[62] Risko, E.F., Anderson, N., Sarwal, A., Engelhardt, M. & Kingstone, A. *Every attention: Variation in mind-wandering and memory in a lecture.* **Applied Cognitive Psychology**, 2012, 26(2), 234–242.

[63] McGaugh, J.L. **Memory and Emotion. The Making of Lasting Memories**, New York, NY: Columbia University Press, 2003.

[64] Mason, M.F., Norton, M.I., Van Horn, J.D., Wegner, D.M., Grafton, S.T. & Macrae, C.N. *Wandering minds: The default network and stimulus-independent thought.* **Science**, 2007, 315(5810), 393–395.

[65] Lindquist, S.I. & McLean, J.P. *Daydreaming and its correlates in an educational environment.* **Learning and Individual Differences**, 2011, 21(2), 158–167.

[66] McKiernan, K.A., D'Angelo, B.R., Kaufman, J.N. & Binder, J.R. *Interrupting the "stream of consciousness": An fMRI investigation.* **NeuroImage**, 2006, 29(4), 1185–1191.

[67] Bunce, D.M., Flens, E.A. & Neiles, K.Y. *How long can students pay attention in class? A study of student attention decline using clickers.* **Journal of Chemical Education**, 2011, 87(12), 1438–1443.

[68] Schooler, J.W. *Re-representing consciousness: Dissociations between experience and meta-consciousness.* **Trends in Cognitive Science**, 2002, 6(8), 339–344.

[69] Lindquist, S.I. & McLean, J.P. *Daydreaming and its correlates in an educational environment.* **Learning and Individual Differences**, 2011, 21(2), 158–167.

[70] Smallwood, J. & Schooler, J.W. *The restless mind.* **Psychological Bulletin**, 2006, 132(6), 946–958.

[71] Smallwood, J., Fishman, D.J., & Schooler, J.W. *Counting the cost of an absent mind: Mind wandering as an underrecognized influence on educational performance.* **Psychonomic Bulletin & Review**, 2007, 14(2), 230–236.

[72] Christoff, K., Gordon, A.M., Smallwood, J., Smith, R. & Schooler, J. W. *Experience sampling during fMRI reveals default network and executive system contributions to mind wandering.* **Proceedings of the National Academy of Sciences**, 2009, 106(21), 8719–8724.

Mason, M.F., Norton, M.I., Van Horn, J.D., Wegner, D.M., Grafton, S.T. & Macrae, C.N. *Wandering minds: The default network and stimulus-independent thought.* **Science**, 2007, 315(810), 393–395.

McKiernan, K.A., D'Angelo, B.R., Kaufman, J.N. & Binder, J.R. *Interrupting the "stream of consciousness:" An f MRI investigation.* **NeuroImage**, 2006, 29(4), 1185–1191.

[73] Killingsworth, M.A. & Gilbert, D.T. *A wandering mind is an unhappy mind.* **Science**, 2010, 330(6006), 932.

[74] Cameron, P. & Giuntoli, D. *Consciousness sampling in the college classroom or is anybody listening?* **Intellect**, 1972, 101(2343), 63–64.

[75] Shaw, G. A. & Giambra, L. M. *Task-unrelated thoughts of college students diagnosed as hyperactive in childhood.* **Developmental Neuropsychology**, 1993, 9, 17–30.

[76] Schooler, J.W., Reichle, E.D. & Halpern, D.V. *Zoning out while reading: Evidence for dissociations between experience and metaconsciousness*, 203-226. In D.T. Levin (Ed.), **Thinking and Seeing: Visual Metacognition in Adults and Children**. Cambridge, MA: MIT Press, 2004.

[77] Smallwood, J., McSpadden, M. & Schooler, J.W. *The lights are on but no one's home: Meta-awareness and the decoupling of attention when the mind wanders.* **Psychonomic Bulletin & Review**, 2007, 14(3), 527–533.

[78] Smallwood, J. & Schooler, J.W. *The restless mind.* **Psychological Bulletin**, 2006, 132(6), 946–958, 956.

[79] Lindquist, S.I. & McLean, J.P. *Daydreaming and its correlates in an educational environment.* **Learning and Individual Differences**, 2011, 21(2), 158–167.

[80] Smallwood, J., Fishman, D.J. & Schooler, J.W. *Counting the cost of an absent mind: Mind wandering as an underrecognized influence on educational performance.* **Psychonomic Bulletin & Review**, 2007, 14(2), 230–236.

[81] Schooler, J.W., Reichle, E.D. & Halpern, D.V. *Zoning out while reading: Evidence for dissociations between experience and metaconsciousness. In D.T. Levin (Ed.),* **Thinking and Seeing: Visual Metacognition in Adults and Children**, 204-226. Cambridge, MA: The MIT Press, 2004.

Smallwood, J., McSpadden, M. & Schooler, J.W. *The lights are on but no one's home: Meta-awareness and the decoupling of attention when the mind wanders.* **Psychonomic Bulletin & Review**, 2007, 14(3), 527–533.

[82] Bunce, D.M., Flens, E.A. & Neiles, K.Y. *How long can students pay attention in class? A study of student attention decline using clickers.* **Journal of Chemical Education**, 2011, 87(12), 1438–1433, 1442.

[83] Wilson, K. & Korn, J.H. *Attention during lectures: Beyond ten minutes.* **Teach Psychology**, 2007, 34(2), 85–89.

[84] Lindquist, S.I. & McLean, J.P. *Daydreaming and its correlates in an educational environment.* **Learning and Individual Differences**, 2011, 21(2), 158–167.

[85] Smallwood, J., Beech, E.M., Schooler, J.W. & Handy, T.C. *Going AWOL in the brain—mind-wandering reduces cortical analysis of the task environment.* **Journal of Cognitive Neuroscience**. 2008, 20(3), 458–469.

[86] Risko, E.F., Anderson, N., Sarwal, A., Engelhardt, M. & Kingstone, A. *Every attention: Variation in mind-wandering and memory in a lecture.* **Applied Cognitive Psychology**, 2012, 26(2), 234–242.

[87] Smallwood, J., Gorgolewski, K.J., Golchert, J., Ruby, F.J., Engen, H., Baird, B., Vinski, M.T., Schooler, J.W. & Margulies, D.S. *The default modes of reading: modulation of posterior cingulate and medial prefrontal cortex connectivity associated with comprehension and task focus while reading.* **Frontiers in Human Neuroscience**, 2013, 7. Article 134, 1–10.

[88] Lindquist, S.I. & McLean, J.P. *Daydreaming and its correlates in an educational environment.* **Learning and Individual Differences**, 2011, 21(2), 158–167.

[89] Geerligs, T. *Students' thoughts during problem-based small-group discussions.* **Instructional Science**, 1995, 22(4), 269–278.

[90] Mason, M.F., Norton, M.I., Van Horn, J.D., Wegner, D.M., Grafton, S.T. & Macrae, C.N. *Wandering minds: The default network and stimulus-independent thought.* **Science**, 2007, 315(5810), 393–395.

McKiernan, K.A., D'Angelo, B.R., Kaufman, J.N. & Binder, J.R. *Interrupting the "stream of consciousness": An fMRI investigation.* **NeuroImage**, 2006, 29(4), 1185–1191.

[91] Bligh, D.A. **What's the Use of Lectures?** San Francisco, CA: Jossey-Bass Publishers, 2000.

[92] Bunce, D.M., Flens, E.A. & Neiles, K.Y. *How long can students pay attention in class? A study of student attention decline using clickers.* **Journal of Chemical Education**, 2011, 87(12), 1438–1433.

[93] McGaugh, J.L. **Memory and Emotion. The Making of Lasting Memories**. New York, NY: Columbia University Press, 2003, 10.

[94] Bunzeck, N. & Düzel, E. *Absolute coding of stimulus novelty in the human substantia nigra/VTA.* **Neuron**, 2006, 51(3), 369–379.

[95] Chandler, P. & Sweller, J. *The Split-Attention Effect as a Factor in the Design of Instruction.* **British Journal of Educational Psychology**, 1992, 62(2), 233–246.

Kalyuga, S., Chandler, P. & Seller, J. *Managing Split-attention and Redundancy in Multimedia Instruction.* **Applied Cognitive Psychology**, 1999, 13(4), 351–371.

Mayer, R.E. & Moreno, R. *A Split-attention effect in multimedia learning: Evidence for dual processing systems in working memory.* **Journal of Educational Psychology**, 1998, 90(2), 312–320.

[96] Cowan, N. **Memory and Attention. An Integrated Framework**. Oxford: Oxford University Press, 1997.

[97] Lamb, G. **Music for the Mind CD Series**. San Clemente, CA: Kagan Publishing, 2011. http://www.kaganonline.com/catalog/music.php#CGM.

[98] Donovan, J.J & Radosevich, D.J. *A meta-analytic review of the distribution of practice effect: Now you see it, now you don't.* **Journal of Applied Psychology**, 1999, 84(5), 795–805.

[99] Dempster, F.N. *The spacing effect—a case study in the failure to apply the results of psychological research.* **American Psychologist**, 1988, 43(8), 627–364.

[100] Cepeda, N.J., Pashler, H., Vul, E., Wixted, J.T. & Rohrer, D. *Distributed practice in verbal recall tasks: A review and quantitative synthesis.* **Psychological Bulletin**, 2006, 132(3), 345–380.

[101] Bird, S. *Effects of distributed practice on the acquisition of second language English syntax.* **Applied Psycholinguist**, 2010, 31(4), 635–650.

[102] Reynolds, J.H. & Glaser, R. *Effects of repetition and spaced review upon retention of a complex learning-task.* **Journal of Educational Psychology**, 1964, 55(5), 297–308.

[103] Rea, C.P. & Modligliani, V. *The spacing effect in 4-year-old to 9-year-old children.* **Memory & Cognition**, 1987, 15, 436–443.

Seabrook, R., Brown, G.D.A & Solity, J.E. *Distributed and massed practice: From laboratory to classroom.* **Applied Cognitive Psychology**, 2005, 19(1), 107–122.

[104] Rea, C.P. & Modligliani, V. *The spacing effect in 4-year-old to 9-year-old children.* **Memory & Cognition**, 1987, 15, 436–443.

Toppino, T.C. *The spacing effect in young children's free-recall—support for automatic-process explanations.* **Memory & Cognition**, 19(2), 159–167.

Toppino, T.C. & Digeorge, W. *The spacing effect in free-recall emerges with development.* **Memory & Cognition**, 1984, 12(2), 118–122.

[105] Cepeda, N.J., Coburn, N., Rohrer, D., Wixted, J.T., Mozer, M.C. & Pashler, H. *Optimizing distributed practice, theoretical analysis and practical implications.* **Experimental Psychology**, 2009, 56(4), 236–246.

Cepeda, N.J. Vul, E. Rohrer, D., Wixted, J.T. & Pashler, H. *Spacing effects in learning: A temporal ridgeline of optimal retention.* **Psychological Science**, 2008, 19(11), 1095–1102.

[106] Callan, D.E. & Schweighofer, N. *Neural correlates of the spacing effect in explicit verbal semantic. Encoding support the deficient-processing theory.* **Human Brain Mapping**, 2010, 31(4), 645–659.

[107] Murdock, B.B., Jr. *The serial position effect of free recall,* **Journal of Experimental Psychology**, 1962, 64(5), 482–488.

[108] Murdock, B.B., Jr. *The serial position effect of free recall.* **Journal of Experimental Psychology**, 1962, 64(5), 482–488.

[109] Csikszentmihalyi, M. **Finding Flow: The Psychology of Engagement with Everyday Life**. New York, NY: Basic Books, 1997.

Csikszentmihalyi, M. **Flow: The Psychology of Optimal Experience**. New York, NY: Harper Collins Publishers, 1990.

[110] Fink, G.R. Halligan, P.W., Marshall, J.C., Frith, C.D., Frackowiak, R.S. & Dolan, R.J. *Neural mechanisms involved in the processing of global and local aspects of hierarchically organized visual stimuli.* **Brain**, 1997, 120(10), 1779–1791.

[111] Carter, R. *Mapping the Mind*, Berkeley, CA: University of California Press, 1999.

[112] Hillman, C.H., Pontifex, M.B., Raine, L.B., Castelli, D.M., Hall, E.E. & Kramer, A.F. *The effect of acute treadmill walking on cognitive control and academic achievement in preadolescent children.* **Neuroscience**, 2009, 159(3), 1044–1054.

[113] Hillman, C.H., Buck, S.M., Themanson, J.T., Pontifex, M.B. & Castelli, D.M. *Aerobic fitness and cognitive development: Event-related brain potential and task performance indices of executive control in preadolescent children.* **Developmental Psychology**, 2009, 45(1), 114–129.

Hillman, C.H., Castelli, D.M. & Buck, S.M. *Aerobic fitness and neurocognitive function in healthy preadolescent children.* **Medicine and Science in Sports and Exercise**, 2005, 37(11), 1967–1974.

[114] Brezun, J.M. & Daszuta, A. *Serotonin may stimulate granule cell proliferation in the adult hippocampus, as observed in rats grafted with foetal raphe neurons.* **European Journal of Neuroscience**, 2000, 12(1), 391–396.

Vaynman, S. & Gomez-Pinilla, F. *License to run: Exercise impacts functional plasticity in the intact and injured central nervous system by using neurotrophins.* **Neurorehabilitation and Neural Repair**, 2005, 19(4), 28 3–295.

[115] Delp, M.D., Armstrong, R.B., Godfrey, D.A., Laughlin, M.H., Ross, C.D. & Wilkerson, M.K. *Exercise increases blood flow to locomotor, vestibular, cardiorespiratory and visual regions of the brain in miniature swine.* **Journal of Physiology**, 2001, 533(3), 849–859.

Dempsey, J.A., Hanson, P.G. & Henderson, K.S. *Exercise-induced arterial hypoxaemia in healthy human subjects at sea level.* **Journal of Physiology**, 1984, 355(1), 161–175.

Jorgensen, L.G., Nowak, M., Ide, K. & Secher, N.H. *Cerebral blood flow and metabolism.* In B. Saltin, R. Boushel, N. Secher & J. Mitchell (Eds.), **Exercise and Circulation in Health and Disease**, 113–236. Champaign, IL: Human Kinetics, 2000.

[116] Kamijo, K., Nishihira, Y., Hatta, A., Kaneda, T., Wasaka, T., Kida, T. & Kuroiwa, K. *Differential influences of exercise intensity on information processing in the central nervous system.* **European Journal of Applied Physiology**. 2004, 92(3), 305–311.

[117] Brown, J.A, Xu, J., Diggs-Andrews, K.A., Wozniak, D.F., Mach, R.H. & Gutmann, D.H. *PET imaging for attention deficit preclinical drug testing in neurofibromatosis-1 mice.* **Experimental Neurology**, 2011, 232(2), 333–338.

[118] Drouin, C., Page, M. & Waterhouse, B. *Methylphenidate enhances noradrenergic transmission and suppresses mid- and long-latency sensory responses in the primary somatosensory cortex of awake rats.* **Journal of Neurophysiology**, 2006, 96(2), 622–632.

[119] Tye, K.M., Tye, L.D., Cone, J.J., Hekkelman, E.F., Janak, P.H. & Bonci, A. *Methylphenidate facilitates learning-induced amygdala plasticity.* **Nature Neuroscience**, 2010, 13(4), 475–481.

[120] Volkow, N.D. Wang, G-J., Maynard, L., Gatley, S., Gifford, A., Franceschi, D., Joanna Fowler, J., Logan, J., Gerasimov, M., & Yu-Shin Ding, Y.A. *Therapeutic doses of oral methylphenidate significantly increase extracellular dopamine in the human brain.* **Journal of Neuroscience**, 2001, 21(2), RC121.

Volkow, N.D., Wang, G-J., Tomasi, D., Kollins, S.H., Wigal, T.L., Newcorn, J.H., Telang, F.W., Fowler, J.S., Logan, J., Wong, C.T. & Swanson, J.M. *Methylphenidate-elicited dopamine increases in ventral striatum are associated with long-term symptom improvement in adults with attention deficit hyperactivity disorder.* **The Journal of Neuroscience**, 2012, 32(3), 841–884.

[121] Sagvolden, T., Johansen, E.B., Aase, H.& Russell, V.A. *A dynamic developmental theory of attention-deficit/hyperactivity disorder (adhd) predominantly hyperactive/impulsive and combined subtypes.* **Behavioral and Brain Sciences**, 2005, 28(3), 397–419.

[122] Volkow, N.D., Wang, G.J., Fowler, J.S., Logan, J., Gerasimov, M., Maynard, L., Ding, Y.-S., Gatley, S.J., Gifford A., & Franceschi, D. *Therapeutic doses of oral methylphenidate significantly increase extracellular dopamine in the human brain.* **Journal of Neuroscience**, 2001, 21(2), RC121.

[123] Volkow, N.D., Wang, G.J., Fowler, J.S., Logan, J., Angrist, B., Hitzemann, R.J., Lieberman, J. & Pappas, N.R. *Effects of methylphenidate on regional brain glucose metabolism in humans: relationship to dopamine D2 receptors.* **American Journal of Psychiatry** 1997, 154(1), 50–55.

[124] Volkow, N. & Thomas, R. *What are the long-term effects of methylphenidate treatment?* **Biological Psychiatry**, 2003, 54(12), 1307–1309.

[125] Vokow, N.D. & Fowler, J.S. **Imaging the Effects of Psychostimulants in the Human Brain**. Upton, New York: Brookhaven National Laboratory, 1973.

[126] Gatley, S.J., Volkow, N.D., Gifford, A.N., Fowler, J.S., Dewey, S.L., Ding, Y.-S. & Logan, J. *Dopamine transporter occupancy after intravenous doses of cocaine and methylphenidate in mice and humans.* **Psychopharmacology**, 1999, 146(1), 93–100.

[127] Volkow, N.D., Wang, G.J., Fowler, J.S., Gately, S.J., Logan, J., Ding, Y.S., Dewey, S. Hitzemann, R., Gifford, A. & Pappas, N.R. *Blockade of striatal dopamine transporters by intravenous methylphenidate is not sufficient to induce self-reports of "high."* **Journal of Pharmacology and Experimental Therapies**, 1999, 288(1), 14–20.

[128] Haislip, G.R. **DEA Report: ADD/ADHD Statement of Drug Enforcement Administration. San Antonio, TX: Drug Enforcement Administration**, United States Department of Justice, 1996.

[129] Stein, D.B., **At Last! A Healthy, Drug-Free Alternative to Ritalin**. San Francisco, CA: Jossey-Bass Inc., Publishers, 1999.

[130] Armstrong, T. **The Myth of the A.D.D Child: 50 Ways to Improve Your Child's Behavior and Attention Span Without Drugs, Labels, or Coercion**. New York, NY: Penguin Putnam Inc., 1997.

Baughman, F.A. Jr. & Hovey, C. *The ADHD Fraud: How Psychiatry Makes "Patients" of Normal Children*. Victoria, BC, Canada: Trafford Publishing, 2006.

[131] Haydon, T., Maheady, L. & Hunter, W. *Effects of Numbered Heads Together on the daily quiz scores and on-task behavior of students with disabilities*. **Journal of Behavioral Education**, 2010, 19, 222–238.

Maheady, L., Mallette, B., Harper, G.F. & Sacca, K. *Heads together: A peer-mediated option for improving the academic achievement of heterogeneous learning groups*. **Remedial and Special Education**, 1991, 12(2), 25–33.

Maheady, L., Michielli-Pendl, J., Harper, G.F. & Mallette, B. *The effects of Numbered Heads Together with and without an incentive package on the science test performance of a diverse group of sixth graders*. **Journal of Behavioral Education**, 2006, 15(1), 24–38.

Maheady, L., Michielli-Pendl, J., Mallette, B. & Harper, G.F. *A collaborate research project to improve the academic performance of a diverse sixth grade class*. **Teacher Education and Special Education**, 2002, 25(1), 55–70.

[132] James, W. *Talks to Teachers: On Psychology, and to Students on Some of Life's Ideals*. New York, NY: W.W. Norton, 1899/1958, 84.

[133] Doidge, N. *The Brain that Changes Itself*. New York, NY: Penguin, 2007.

Schwartz, M.J. & Begley, S. *The Mind & the Brain. Neuroplasticity and the Power of Mental Force*. New York, NY: Harper Perennial, 2002.

[134] James, W. *The Principles of Psychology*. New York, NY: Dover Publications, 1890/1958, 322.

[135] Rueda, M.R., Tothbart, M.K., McCandliss, B.D., Saccomanno, L. & Posnter, M.I. *Training, maturation, and genetic influences on the development of executive attention*. **Proceedings of the National Academy of Sciences**, 2005, 102(41), 129–140.

[136] Goleman, D. *Focus. The Hidden Driver of Excellence*. New York, NY: HarperCollins, 2013, p. 183.

[137] Goleman, D. *Focus. The Hidden Driver of Excellence*. New York, NY: HarperCollins, 2013, p. 1834

[138] Owen, A.M., Hampshire, A., Grahn, J.A., Stenton, R., Dajani, S., Burns, A.S., Howard, R.J. & Ballard, G.C. *Putting brain training to the test*. **Nature**, 2010, 465(7299), 775–778.

Smith, S.P., Stibric, M. & Smithson, D. *Exploring the effectiveness of commercial and custom-built games for cognitive training*. **Computers in Human Behavior**, 2013, 29(6), 2388–2393.

[139] Tang, Y., Ma, Y., Wang, J., Fan, Y., Feng, S., Lu, Q., Yu, Q., Sui, D., Rothbart, M.K., Fan, M. & Posner, M.I. *Short-term meditation training improves attention and self-regulation*. **Proceedings of the National Academy of Sciences**, 2007, 104(43), 17152–17156.

[140] Grosswald, S., Stixrud, W., Travis, F. & Bateh, M. *Use of the Transcendental Meditation technique to reduce symptoms of attention deficit hyperactivity disorder (ADHD) by reducing stress and anxiety: an exploratory study*. **Current Issues in Education**, 2008, 10(2), 1–15.

[141] Grosswald, S., Stixrud, W., Travis, F. & Bateh, M. *Use of the Transcendental Meditation technique to reduce symptoms of attention deficit hyperactivity disorder (ADHD) by reducing stress and anxiety: an exploratory study*. **Current Issues in Education**, 2008, 10(2), 1–15.

[142] Dillbeck, M.C. *Meditation and flexibility of visual perception and verbal problem solving*. **Memory & Cognition**, 1982, 10(3), 207–215.

[143] Siegel, D. *The Mindful Brain*. New York, NY: Norton, 2007.

[144] Elder, C., Nidich, S., Colbert, R., Hagelin, J., Grayshield, L., Oviedo-Lim, D., Nidich, R., Rainforth, M., Jones, C. & Gerace, D. *Reduced psychological distress in racial and ethnic minority students practicing the Transcendental Meditation Program*. **Journal of Instructional Psychology**, 2011, 38(2), 109–116.

Eppley, K., Abrams, A. & Shear, J. *Differential effects of relaxation techniques on trait anxiety: A meta-analysis*. **Journal of Clinical Psychology**, 1989, 45(6), 957–974.

[145] Miskiman, D. *The Effect of the Transcendental Meditation Program on the Organization of Thinking and Recall (Secondary Organization)*. Alberta, Canada: Graduate Department of Psychology, University of Alberta, Edmonton, 1973.

[146] Davidson, R.J., Kabat-Zinn, J., Schumacher, J., Rosenkranz, M. Muller, D., Santorelli, S.F., Urbanowski, F, Harrington, A., Bonus, K. & Sheridan, J.F. *Alterations in brain and immune function produced by mindfulness meditation*. **Psychosomatic Medicine**, 2003, 65, 564–570.

[147] Schooler, J. W. *Re-representing consciousness: Dissociations between experience and meta-consciousness*. **Trends in Cognitive Sciences**, 2002, 6, 339–344.

[148] Kaplan, S. *Meditation, restoration and the management of mental fatigue*. **Environment and Behavior**, 2001, 33(4), 48–505.

[149] Slagter, H.A., Greischar, L.L., Francis, A.D., Nieuwenhuis, S., Davis, J.M. & Davidson, R.J. *Mental training affects distribution of limited brain resources*. **PLOS Biology,** 2007, 5(6), e138.

[150] Goleman, D. *Focus. The Hidden Driver of Excellence*. New York, NY: HarperCollins, 2013, pp. 186–189.

[151] Lantieri, L. *Building inner resilience in students and teachers*. In G. Reevy & E. Frydenberg, eds., *Personality, Stress and Coping: Implications for Education*. Charlotte, NC: Information Age, 2011, 267–292.

[152] Ornstein, R. *The Right Mind: Making Sense of the Hemispheres*. New York, NY: Harcourt Brace & Company, 1997.

[153] LaBerge, D., Carlson, R.L., Williams, J.K. & Bunney, B.G. *Shifting attention in visual space: Tests of moving-spotlight models versus an activity-distribution model*. **Journal of Experimental Psychology: Human Perception and Performance**, 1997, 23(5), 1380–1392.

Posner, M.I. *Orienting of attention.* **Quarterly Journal of Experimental Psychology**, 1980, 32(1), 3–25.

Posner, M.I., Cohen, Y. & Rafal, R.D. *Neural systems control of spatial orienting.* **Philosophical Transactions of the Royal Society of London. Series B Biological Sciences**, 1982, 298(1089), 187–198.

[154] Cahn, B.R. & Polich, J. *Meditation states and traits: EEG, ERP, and neuroimaging studies.* **Psychological Bulletin**, 2006, 132(2), 180–211.

Graziano, M.S.A. & Kastner, S. *Human consciousness and its relationship to social neuroscience: A novel hypothesis.* **Cognitive Neuroscience**, 2011, 2(2), 98–113.

[155] Aiken, C. **Exercises in Mind Training, in Quickness of Perception, Concentrated Attention and Memory.** New York, NY: Harper & Brothers, 1899.

Aiken, C. **Methods of Mind-Training.** New York, NY: Harper and Brothers, 1895.

[156] Aiken, C. **Methods of Mind-Training.** New York, NY: Harper and Brothers, 1895.

[157] Corbetta, M., Shulman, G.L., Miezin, F.M. & Petersen, S.E. *Superior parietal cortex activation during spatial attention shifts and visual feature conjunction.* **Science**, 1995, 270(5237), 802–805.

Piazza, M., Mechelli, A., Butterworth, B. & Price, C.J. *Are subitizing and counting implemented as separate or functionally overlapping processes?* **NeuroImage**, 2002, 15(2), 435–446.

[158] Sacks, O. **The Man Who Mistook His Wife for a Hat.** New York, NY: Touchstone, 1970, 199–200.

[159] Aiken, C. **Methods of Mind-Training.** New York, NY: Harper and Brothers, 1895.

[160] Amir, N., Beard, C., Burns, M. & Bomyea, J. *Attention modification program in individuals with generalized anxiety disorder.* **Journal of Abnormal Psychology**, 2009, 118(1), 28–33.

Beard, C., Sawyer, A.T. & Hofmann, S.G. *Efficacy of attention bias modification using threat and appetitive stimuli. A meta-analytic review.* **Behavior Therapy**, 2012, 43(4), 724–740.

Boutelle, K.N., Kuckertz, J.M., Carlson, J. & Amir, N. *A pilot study evaluating a one-session attention modification training to decrease overeating in obese children.* **Appetite**, 2014, In Press.

Hakamata, Y., Lissek, S., Bar-Haim, Y., Britton, J. C., Fox, N.A., Leibenluft, E. & Pine, D.S. *Attention bias modification treatment. A meta-analysis toward the establishment of novel treatment for anxiety.* **Biological Psychiatry**, 2010, 68(11), 982–990.

Hallion, L.S. & Ruscio, A. *A meta-analysis of the effect of cognitive bias modification on anxiety and depression.* **Psychological Bulletin**, 2011, 137(6), 940–958.

Heeren, A., Reese, H.E., McNally, R.J. & Philippot, P. *Attention training toward and away from threat in social phobia: Effects on behavioural, subjective, and physiological measures of anxiety.* **Behaviour Research and Therapy**, 2012, 50(1), 30–39.

MacLeod, C., Rutherford, E., Campbell, L., Ebsworthy, G. & Holker, L. *Selective attention and emotional vulnerability: Assessing the causal basis of their association through the experimental manipulation of attentional bias.* **Journal of Abnormal Psychology**, 2002, 111(1), 107–123.

See, J., MacLeod, C. & Bridle, R. *The reduction of vulnerability through the modification of attentional bias: A real world study using a home-based cognitive bias modification procedure.* **Journal of Abnormal Psychology**, 2009, 118(1), 65–75.

[161] Amir, N., Weber, G., Beard, C., Bomyea, J. & Taylor, C.T. *The effects of a single-session attention modification program on response to a public-speaking challenge in socially anxious individuals.* **Journal of Abnormal Psychology**, 2008, 117(4), 860–868.

Heeren, A., Lievens, L. & Philippot, P. *How does attention training work in social phobia: Disengagement from threat or reengagement to non-threat?* **Journal of Anxiety Disorders**, 2011, 25(8), 1108–1115.

[162] Eberl, C., Wiers, R.W., Pawelczack, S., Rinck, M., Becker, E.S. & Lindenmeyer, J. *Approach bias modification in alcohol dependence: Do clinical effects replicate and for whom does it work best?* **Developmental Cognitive Neuroscience**, 2013, 4, 38–51.

[163] Dehn, M.J. **Working Memory and Academic Learning. Assessment and Intervention.** Hoboken, NJ: John Wiley & Sons, 2008.

Gathercole, S.E. & Alloway, T.P. **Working Memory & Learning. A Practical Guide for Teachers.** Los Angeles, CA: Sage Publications, 2008.

[164] Gathercole, S.E. & Alloway, T.P. **Working Memory & Learning. A Practical Guide for Teachers.** Los Angeles, CA: Sage, 2008.

[165] Castellanos, F.X., Giedd, J.N., Marsh, W.L., Hamburger, S.D., Vaituzis, A.C. & Dickstein, D.P. *Quantitative brain magnetic resonance imaging in attention-deficit hyperactivity disorder.* **Archives of General Psychiatry.** 1996, 53(7), 607–616.

Castellanos, F.X., Lee, P.P., Sharp, W., Jeffries, N.O., Greenstein, D.K., Clasen, L.S., Blumenthal, J.D., James, R.S., Ebens, C.L., Walter, J.M., Zijdenbos, A., Evans, A.C., Giedd, J.N. & Rapoport, J.L. *Developmental trajectories of brain volume abnormalities in children and adolescents with attention- deficit/hyperactivity disorder.* **The Journal of the American Medical Association**, 2002, 288(14), 1740–1748.

[166] Klingberg, T., Fernell, E., Olesen, P.J., Johnson, M., Gustafsson, P., Dahlström, K., Gillberg, C.G., Forssberg, H. & Westerberg, H. *Computerized training of working memory in children with ADHD: a randomized, controlled trial.* **Journal of the American Academy of Child and Adolescent Psychiatry**, 2005, 44(2), 177–186.

Klingberg, T., Forssberg, H. & Westerberg, H. *Training of working memory in children with ADHD.* **Journal of Clinical and Experimental Neuropsychology**, 2002, 24(6), 781–791.

[167] Gathercole, S.E., Brown, L. & Pickering, S.J. *Working memory assessments at school entry as longitudinal predictors of National Curriculum attainment levels.* **Educational and Child Psychology**, 2003, 20(3), 109–122.

[168] Jarvis, H.L. & Gathercole, S.E. *Verbal and non-verbal working memory and achievements on national curriculum tests at 11 and 14 years of age.* **Educational and Child Psychology**, 2003, 20(3), 123–140.

[169] Kyllonen, P.C. & Stephens, D.L. *Cognitive abilities as determinants of success in acquiring logic skill.* **Learning and Individual Differences**, 1990, 2(2), 129–160.

[170] Shute, V. *Who is likely to acquire programming skills?* **Journal of Educational Computing Research**, 1991, 7(1), 1–24.

[171] Schmeichel, B.J., Volokhov, R. & Demaree, H.A. *Working memory capacity and the self-regulation of emotional expression and experience.* **Journal of Personality and Social Psychology**, 2008, 95(6), 1526–1540.

[172] Swanson, H.L. & Siegel, L. *Learning disabilities as a working memory deficit.* **Issues in Education: Contributions from Educational Psychology**, 2001, 7(1), 1–48.

[173] Alloway, T.P., Gathercole, S.E., Adams, A.M. & Willis, C.S. *Working memory abilities in children with special educational needs.* **Educational and Child Psychology**, 2005, 22(4), 56–67.

[174] Gathercole, S.E. & Pickering, S.J. *Assessment of working memory in six- and seven-year old children.* **Journal of Educational Psychology**, 2000, 92(2), 377–390.

Gathercole, S.E. & Pickering, S.J. *Working memory deficits in children with low achievement in the national curriculum at 7 years of age.* **British Journal of Educational Psychology**, 2000, 70(2), 177–194.

[175] Reber, P.J. & Kotovksy, K. *Implicit learning in problem solving: The role of working memory capacity.* **Journal of Experimental Psychology: General**, 1997, 126(2), 178–203.

[176] Kane, M.J., Brown, L.E., Little, J.C., Silvia, P.J., Mylin-Germeys, I. & Kwapil, T.R. *For whom the mind wanders, and when: An experience-sampling study of working memory and executive control in daily life.* **Psychological Science**, 2007, 18(7), 614–621.

[177] Conway, A.R.A., Cowan, N. & Bunting, M.F. *The cocktail party phenomenon revisited: The importance of working memory capacity.* **Psychonomic Bulletin & Review**, 2001, 8(2), 331–335.

Kane, M.J., Bleckley, K.M, Conway, A.R.A. & Engle, R.W. *A controlled-attention view of working-memory capacity.* **Journal of Experimental Psychology: General**, 2001, 130(2), 169–183.

Kane, M.J. & Engle, R.W. *Working memory capacity and control of attention: The contributions of goal neglect, response competition, and task set to Stroop interference.* **Journal of Experimental Psychology: General**, 2003, 132(1), 47–70.

[178] Kane, M.J. & Engle, R.W. *Working memory capacity, proactive interference, and divided attention: Limits on long-term memory retrieval.* **Journal of Experimental Psychology: Learning, Memory, and Cognition**, 2000, 26(2), 333–358.

[179] Engle, R.W. *Working memory capacity as executive attention.* **Current Directions in Psychological Science**, 2002, 11(1), 19–23.

Kane, M.J., Conway, A.R.A., Bleckley, M.K. & Engle, R.W. *A controlled-attention view of working memory capacity.* **Journal of Experimental Psychology: General**, 2001, 130(2), 169–183.

Unsworth, N. & Engle, R.W. *The nature of individual differences in working memory capacity: Active maintenance in primary memory and controlled search from secondary memory.* **Psychological Review**, 2007, 114(1), 104–132.

[180] Conway, A.R., Kane, M.J. & Engle, R.W. *Working memory capacity and its relation to general intelligence.* **Trends in Cognitive Science**, 2003, 7(12), 547–552.

[181] Yeung, N., Nystrom, L.E., Aronson, J.A. & Cohen, J.D. *Between-task competition and cognitive control in task switching.* **Journal of Neuroscience**, 2006, 26(5), 1429–1438.

[182] Ackerman, P.L., Beier, M.E. & Boyle, M.O. *Working memory and intelligence: The same or different constructs?* **Psychological Bulletin**, 2005, 131(1), 30–60.

Cranson, R.W., Orme-Johnson, D.W., Gackenbach, J., Dillbeck, M.C., Jones, CH. & Alexander, C.N. *Transcendental Meditation and improved performance on intelligence related measures: A longitudinal study.* **Personality and Individual Differences**, 1991, 12(10), 1105–1116.

Dixon, C., Dillbeck, M.C., Travis, F., Msemaje, H., Clayborne, B.M., Dillbeck, S.L. & Alexander, C.N. *Accelerating cognitive and self-development: Longitudinal studies with preschool and elementary school children.* **Journal of Social Behavior and Personality**, 2005, 17(1), 65–91.

So, K.T. & Orme-Johnson, D.W. *Three randomized experiments on the longitudinal effects of the Transcendental Meditation technique on cognition.* **Intelligence**, 2001, 29(5), 419–440.

Cranson, R.W., Orme-Johnson, D.W., Gackenbach, J., Dillbeck, M.C., Jones, CH. & Alexander, C.N. *Transcendental Meditation and improved performance on intelligence related measures: A longitudinal study.* **Personality and Individual Differences**, 1991, 12(10), 1105–1116.

So, K. T. & Orme-Johnson, D.W. *Three randomized experiments on the longitudinal effects of the Transcendental Meditation technique on cognition.* **Intelligence**, 2001, 29(5), 419–440.

[183] Houben, K., Wiers, R.W. & Jansen, A. *Getting a grip on drinking behavior: training working memory to reduce alcohol abuse.* **Psychological Science**, 2011, 22(7), 968–975.

[184] Grosswald, S., Stixrud, W., Travis, F. & Bateh, M. *Use of the Transcendental Meditation technique to reduce symptoms of attention deficit hyperactivity disorder (ADHD) by reducing stress and anxiety: an exploratory study.* **Current Issues in Education**, 2008, 10(2), 1–15.

Travis, F. Grosswald, S. & Stixrud, W. ADHD, *Brain Functioning, and Transcendental Meditation Practice.* **Mind & Brain**, 2011, 2(1), 73–81.

[185] Naranjo, C. & Ornstein, R.E. *The Psychology of Meditation*. New York, NY: Viking Press, 1971.

[186] Ackerman, P.L., Beier, M.E. & Boyle, M.O. *Working memory and intelligence: The same or different constructs? **Psychological Bulletin**, 2005, 131(1), 30–60.

[187] Cattell, R.B. *Theory of fluid and crystallized intelligence: A critical experiment*. **Journal of Educational Psychology**, 1963, 54(1), 1–22.

[188] Conway, A.R., Kane, M.J. & Engle, R.W. *Working memory capacity and its relation to general intelligence*. **Trends in Cognitive Science**, 2003, 7(12), 547–552.

[189] Alloway, T.P., Gathercole, S.E., Adams, A.M., Willis, C., Eaglen, R. & Lamont, E. *Working memory and other cognitive skills as predictors of progress toward early learning goals at school entry*. **British Journal of Developmental Psychology**, 2005, 23(3), 417–426.

Dehn, M.J. **Working Memory and Academic Learning. Assessment and Intervention**. Hoboken, NJ: John Wiley & Sons, 2008.

Gathercole, S.E. & Alloway, T.P. **Working Memory & Learning. A Practical Guide for Teachers**. Los Angeles, CA: Sage Publications, 2008.

Gathercole, S.E., Lamont, E. & Alloway, T.P. *Working memory in the classroom*. In S.J. Pickering (Ed.), **Working Memory and Education**, 219–240. Burlington, MA: Academic Press, 2006.

Pickering, S.J. & Gathercole, S.E. *Distinctive working memory profiles in children with special educational needs*. **Educational Psychology**, 2004, 24(3), 393–408.

Swanson, H.L. Cochran, K.F. & Ewers, C.A. *Can learning disabilities be determined from working memory performance?* **Journal of Learning Disabilities**, 1990, 23(1), 59–67.

[190] Alloway, T.P. & Alloway, R.G. *Investigating the predictive roles of working memory and IQ in academic attainment*. **Journal of Experimental Child Psychology**, 2010, 106(1), 20–29.

[191] Gläscher, J., Tranel, D., Paul, L.K., Rudrauf, D., Rorden, C., Hornaday, A., Grabowski, T., Hanna Damasio, H. & Adolphs, R. *Lesion mapping of cognitive abilities linked to intelligence*. **Neuron**, 2009, 61(5), 681–691.

[192] Alloway, T.P. *Working memory, but not IQ, predicts subsequent learning in children with learning difficulties*. **European Journal of Psychological Assessment**, 2009, 25(2), 92–98.

[193] Dehn, M.J. **Working Memory and Academic Learning. Assessment and Intervention**. Hoboken, NJ: John Wiley & Sons, 2008, 201–209.

[194] Fiez, J.A., Raife, E.A., Balota, D.A., Schwarz, J.P., Raichie, M.E. & Petersen, S.E. *A positron emission tomography study of the short-term maintenance of verbal information*. **Journal of Neuroscience**, 1996, 16(2), 808–822.

Jonides, J., Smith, E.E. Marshuetz, C., Koeppe, R.A. & Reuter-Lorenz, P.A. *Inhibition in verbal working memory revealed by brain activation*. **Proceedings of the National Academy of Sciences of the United States of America**, 1998, 95(14), 8410–8413.

Olesen, P., Westerberg, H. & Klingberg, T. *Increased prefrontal and parietal brain activity after training of working memory*. **Nature Neuroscience**, 2004, 7(1), 75–79.

Westerberg, H. & Klingberg, T. *Changes in cortical activity after training of working memory—a single-subject analysis*. **Physiology and Behavior**, 2007, 92(1-2), 186–192.

Smith, E.E. & Jonides, J. *Neuroimaging analyses of human working memory*. **Proceedings of the National Academy of Sciences of the United States of America**, 1998, 95(20), 12061–12068.

[195] D'Esposito, M. Postle, B.R., Ballard, D. & Lease, J. *Maintenance versus manipulation of information held in working memory: an event-related fMRI study*. **Brain and Cognition**, 1999, 41(1), 66–86.

Postle, R.R., Berger, J.S. & D'Esposito, M. *Functional neuroanatomical double dissociation of mnemonic and executive control processes contributing to working memory performance*. **Proceedings of the National Academy of Sciences USA**, 1999, 96(22), 12959–12964.

[196] Smith, E.E. & Jonides, J. *Neuroimaging analyses of human working memory*. **Proceedings of the National Academy of Sciences of the United States of America**, 1998, 95(20), 12061–12068.

[197] Jonides, J., Smith, E.E. Marshuetz, C., Koeppe, R.A. & Reuter-Lorenz, P.A. *Inhibition in verbal working memory revealed by brain activation*. **Proceedings of the National Academies of Sciences**, 1998, 95(14), 8410–8413.

[198] Gray, J.R., Chabris, C.F. & Braver, T.S. *Neural mechanisms of general fluid intelligence*. **Nature Neuroscience**, 2003, 6(3), 316–322.

[199] Carpenter, P.A., Just, M.A. & Reichle, E.D. *Working memory and executive function: Evidence from neuroimaging*. **Current Opinion in Neurobiology**, 2000, 10(2), 195–199.

[200] D'Esposito, M. Postle, B.R., Ballard, D. & Lease, J. *Maintenance versus manipulation of information held in working memory: an event-related fMRI study*. **Brain and Cognition**, 1999, 41(1), 66–86.

Gray, J.R., Chabris, C.F. & Braver, T.S. *Neural mechanisms of general fluid intelligence*. **Nature Neuroscience**, 2003, 6(3), 316–322.

Jonides, J., Smith, E.E. Marshuetz, C., Koeppe, R.A. & Reuter-Lorenz, P.A. *Inhibition in verbal working memory revealed by brain activation*. **Proceedings of the National Academies of Sciences**, 1998, 95(14), 8410–8413.

Postle, R.R., Berger, J.S. & D'Esposito, M. *Functional neuroanatomical double dissociation of mnemonic and executive control processes contributing to working memory performance*. **Proceedings of the National Academy of Sciences USA**, 1999, 96(22), 12959–12964.

Smith, E.E. & Jonides, J. *Neuroimaging analyses of human working memory*. **Proceedings of the National Academy of Sciences of the United States of America**, 1998, 95(20), 12061–12068.

[201] Westerberg, H. & Klingberg, T. *Changes in cortical activity after training of working memory—a single-subject analysis*. **Physiology and Behavior**, 2007, 92(1–2), 186–192.

[202] Olesen, P., Westerberg, H. & Klingberg, T. *Increased prefrontal and parietal brain activity after training of working memory.* **Nature Neuroscience**, 2004, 7(1), 75–79, 78.

[203] Olesen, P., Westerberg, H. & Klingberg, T. *Increased prefrontal and parietal brain activity after training of working memory.* **Nature Neuroscience**, 2004, 7(1), 75–79, 78.

[204] Baddeley, A. *Working memory: Looking back and looking forward.* **Nature Reviews Neuroscience**, 2003, 4(10), 829–839.

Klingberg, T. *Development of a superior frontal-intraparietal network for visuo-spatial working memory.* **Neuropsychologia**, 2006, 44(11), 2171–2177.

[205] Takeuchi, H., Sekiguchi, A., Taki, Y., Yokoyama, S., Yomogida, Y., Komuro, N., Yamanouchi, T., Suzuki, S. & Kawashima, R. *Training of working memory impacts structural connectivity.* **Journal of Neuroscience**, 2010, 30(9), 3297–3303.

[206] Takeuchi, H., Sekiguchi, A., Taki, Y., Yokoyama, S., Yomogida, Y., Komuro, N., Yamanouchi, T., Suzuki, S. & Kawashima, R. *Training of working memory impacts structural connectivity.* **Journal of Neuroscience**, 2010, 30(9), 3302.

[207] Bäckman, L., Nyberg, L., Soveri, A., Johansson, J., Andersson, M., Dahlin, E., Neely, A.S., Virta, J., Laine, M. & Rinne, J.O. *Effects of working-memory training on striatal dopamine release.* **Science**, 2011, 333(6043), 718.

McNab, F., Varrone, A., Farde, L., Jucaite, A., Bystritsky, P., Forssberg, H. & Klingberg, T. *Changes in cortical dopamine D1 receptor binding associated with cognitive training.* **Science**, 2009, 323(5915), 800–802.

[208] Westerberg, H. & Klingberg, T. *Changes in cortical activity after training of working memory—a single-subject analysis.* **Physiology and Behavior**, 2007, 92(1), 186–192.

[209] Chein, J.M. & Morrison, A.B. *Expanding the mind's workspace: Training and transfer effects with a complex working memory span task.* **Psychonomic Bulletin & Review**, 2010, 17(2), 193–199.

Gathercole, S.E., Alloway, T.P., Willis, C. & Adams, A.M. *Working memory in children with reading disabilities.* **Journal of Experimental Child Psychology**, 2006, 93(3), 265–281.

Loosli, S.V., Buschkuehl, M., Perrig, W.J. & Jaeggi, S.M. *Working memory training improves reading processes in typically developing children.* **Neuropsychology: A Journal on Normal and Abnormal Development in Childhood and Adolescence**, 2012, 18(1), 62–78.

[210] Passolunghi, M.C. & Siegel, L.S. *Short-term memory, working memory, and inhibitory control in children with difficulties in arithmetic problem solving.* **Journal of Experimental Child Psychology**, 2001, 80(1), 44–57.

[211] Holmes, J., Gathercole, S.E. & Dunning, D.L. *Adaptive training leads to sustained enhancement of poor working memory in children.* **Developmental Science**, 2009, 12(4), F9–F15.

[212] Thorell, L.B., Lindqvist, S. Bergman, S. Bohlin, G. & Klingberg, T. *Training and transfer effects of executive functions in preschool children.* **Developmental Science**, 2009, 12(1), 106–113.

[213] Melby-Levag, M. & Hulme, C. *Is working memory training effective? A Meta-Analytic review.* **Developmental Psychology**, 2013, 49(2), 270–291.

Shipstead, Z., Redick ,T.S. & Engle, R.W. *Does working memory training generalize?* **Psychologica Belgica**, 2010, 50(3–4), 245–276.

[214] *Cogmed Working Memory Training Program.* **Pearson**. Retrieved January 28, 2014 from http://www.cogmed.com/

CogniFit. Retrieved January 28, 2014 from http://www.cognifit.com/

Jungle Memory. Train Your Child's Brain! Retrieved January 28, 2014 from http://www.junglememory.com/

[215] Ericcson, K.A., Chase, W.G. & Faloon, S. *Acquisition of a memory skill.* **Science** 1980, 208(4448), 118–1182.

[216] Cowan, N. *The magical number 4 in short-term memory: A reconsideration of mental storage capacity.* **Behavioral and Brain Sciences**, 2001, 24(1), 97–185.

[217] Thorndike, E.L. & Woodworth, R.S. *The influence of improvement in one mental function upon the efficiency of other functions.* **Psychological Review**, 1901, 8(3), 247–261.

[218] Dahlin, E., Neely, A.S., Larsson, A., Bäckman, L. & Nyberg, L. *Transfer of learning after updating training mediated by the striatum.* **Science**, 2008, 320(5882), 1510–1512.

Klingberg, T., Fernell, E., Olesen, P.J., Johnson, M., Gustafsson, P., Dahlström, K., Gillberg, C.G., Forssberg, H. & Westerberg, H. *Computerized training of working memory in children with ADHD: A randomized, controlled trial.* **Journal of the American Academy of Child and Adolescent Psychiatry**, 2005, 44(2), 177–186.

Klingberg, T., Forssberg, H. & Westerberg, H. *Training of working memory in children with ADHD.* **Journal of Clinical and Experimental Neuropsychology**, 2002, 24(6), 781–791.

Li, S.-C., Schmiedek, F., Huxhold, O., Röcke, C., Smith, J. & Lindenberger, U. *Working memory plasticity in old age: Practice gain, transfer, and maintenance.* **Psychology and Aging**, 2008, 23(4), 731–742.

Loosli, S.V., Buschkuehl, M., Perrig, W.J. & Jaeggi, S.M. *Working memory training improves reading processes in typically developing children.* **Neuropsychology: A Journal on Normal and Abnormal Development in Childhood and Adolescence**, 2012, 18(1), 62–78.

Westerberg, H. & Klingberg, T. *Changes in cortical activity after training of working memory—a single-subject analysis.* **Physiology and Behavior**, 2007, 92(1–2), 186–192.

[219] Jaeggi, S.M., Buschkuehl, M., Jonides, J. & Perrig, W.J. *Improving fluid intelligence with training on working memory.* **Proceedings of the National Academy of Sciences of the USA**, 2008, 105(19), 6829–6833.

[220] Holmes, J., Gathercole, S.E. & Dunning, D.L. *Adaptive training leads to sustained enhancement of poor working memory in children.* **Developmental Science**, 2009, 12(4), F9–F15.

Jaeggi, S.M., Buschkuehl, M., Jonides, J. & Shah, P. *Short- and long-term benefits of cognitive training.* **Proceedings of the National Academy of Sciences of the USA**, 2011, 108(25), 10081–10086.

[221] Jaeggi, S.M., Buschkuehl, M., Jonides, J. & Perrig, W.J. *Improving fluid intelligence with training on working memory.* **Proceedings of the National Academy of Sciences of the USA**, 2008, 105(19), 6829–6833.

[222] Studer, B.E., Jaeggi, S.M., Buschkuehl, M., Su, Y.-F., Jonides, J. & Perrig, W.J. *Improving fluid intelligence—Single n-back is as effective as dual n-back.* **Poster session presented at the 50th annual meeting of the Psychonomic Society**, Boston, MA, 2009.

[223] Moody, D.E., *Can intelligence be increased by training on a task of working memory?* **Intelligence**, 2009, 37(4), 327–328.

[224] Melby-Levag, M. & Hulme, C. *Is working memory training effective? A Meta-Analytic review.* **Developmental Psychology**, 2013, 49(2), 270–291.

[225] Melby-Levag, M. & Hulme, C. *Is working memory training effective? A Meta-Analytic review.* **Developmental Psychology**, 2013, 49(2), 283.

[226] Takeuchi, H., Sekiguchi, A., Taki, Y., Yokoyama, S., Yomogida, Y., Komuro, N., Yamanouchi, T., Suzuki, S. & Kawashima, R. *Training of working memory impacts structural connectivity. Journal of Neuroscience*, 2010, 30(9), 3297–3303.

Westerberg, H. & Klingberg, T. *Changes in cortical activity after training of working memory—a single-subject analysis.* **Physiology and Behavior**, 2007, 92(1–2), 186–192.

[227] Jaeggi, S.M., Buschkuehl, M., Jonides, J. & Shah, P. *Short- and long-term benefits of cognitive training.* **Proceedings of the National Academy of Sciences of the USA**, 2011, 108(25), 10081–10086.

[228] Dahlin, E., Neely, A.S., Larsson, A., Bäckman, L., Nyberg, L. *Transfer of learning after updating training mediated by the striatum.* **Science**, 2008, 320(5882), 1510–1512.

[229] Amen, D.G. **Healing ADD. The Breakthrough Program that Allows You to See and Heal the Six Types of ADD**. New York, NY: Berkley Publishing, 2001.

[230] Dahlin, E., Neely, A.S., Larsson, A., Bäckman, L. & Nyberg, L. *Transfer of learning after updating training mediated by the striatum.* **Science**, 2008, 320(5882), 1510–1512.

[231] Schmeichel, B.J., Volokhov, R. & Demaree, H.A. *Working memory capacity and the self-regulation of emotional expression and experience.* **Journal of Personality and Social Psychology**, 2008, 95(6), 1526–1540.

[232] Houben, K., Wiers, R.W. & Jansen, A. *Getting a grip on drinking behavior: Training working memory to reduce alcohol abuse.* **Psychological Science**, 2011, 22(7), 968–975.

Stimuli

Brains naturally attend to certain kinds of stimuli and ignore others. By teaching with novelty, relevance, illustrations, and multimodal stimuli, we present the ways brains want to learn. Here, we examine thirteen types of stimuli that are candy for the brain!

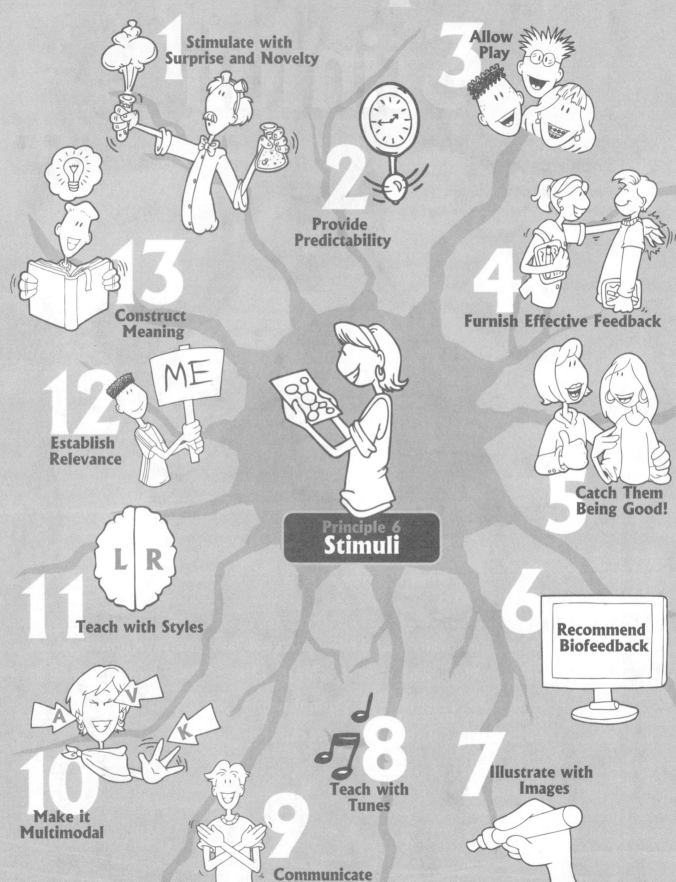

Principle 6
Supply Stimuli Brains Seek and Retain

Brains naturally seek certain kinds of stimuli and pay little or no attention to other kinds of input. Brains also retain some kinds of information far easier than others. Brain-friendly teaching presents academic content as stimuli brains naturally attend to and retain.

This principle, presenting our content as stimuli brains naturally seek, is different from simply focusing and holding the attention of our students. In Principle 5: Attention, we examined ways to manage the attention of our students regardless of our content. For example, no matter what content we teach, to focus the attention of our students, we can use a quiet signal and frequently clear working memory. Principle 5 provides content-free strategies. Here, in Principle 6, we examine the kinds of stimuli brains naturally attend to, and examine ways to present our content as that kind of stimuli.

If the brain is hungry for some kinds of stimuli but uninterested in other kinds, we will be more successful as teachers by presenting our lessons as stimuli brains seek. For example, if we know brains naturally seek personally relevant content, as we present our content, we want to make sure it is personally relevant for our students. To take a second example, if brains seek and remember concrete visual images, as we teach, we want to provide that kind of stimuli—that is, present our content with concrete visual images. The question becomes, then, which kinds of stimuli do brains naturally seek and retain?

In Principle 5: Attention, we established that our brains have selective attention. Thus, in Principle 6: Stimuli, we ask, what kind of information do our brains select? Some answers are obvious, others less so. Let's start with the obvious. Right now, after reading this paragraph, I want you to stop and focus only on all the sensations provided by your clothes touching your skin. For me right now, my collar is rubbing a bit against my neck, my jeans are putting some pressure on my thighs, the sock on my right foot feels like it has slipped a bit, and my tennis shoes feel slightly tight around my feet. What can you become aware of as you stop right now to focus on the sensations your clothes are providing?

13
Tools to Supply Brain-Friendly Stimuli

Brains are selective. We are designed to seek, attend to, and retain certain kinds of information, but we naturally tune out and quickly forget other kinds of information. This is adaptive: We cannot possibly attend to, process, retain, and recall all the information that impinges upon us. As teachers, knowing which kinds of information our students are likely to attend to and retain, we can dramatically increase the probability of learning.

If you are like most people, until I directed your attention to the sensations provided by your clothes, you were mostly or completely unaware of those sensations. Rather, (hopefully) you were focusing on the ideas provided by this writing. Why would you select the ideas over the sensations? My guess: As you are reading this, you are seeking, new ideas—ideas that are personally relevant to you as an educator. You may even be anticipating a reward (more success in teaching) by applying the ideas you find here. In contrast, you find nothing novel, interesting, personally relevant, or potentially rewarding in how your socks feel around your ankles! This is fairly obvious. But from this mundane mini-experiment we can derive some powerful principles for teaching. Our students will tune in to and more likely remember stimuli that are novel, personally relevant, and rewarding. Novelty, personal relevance, and potentially rewarding information are brain-friendly stimuli—they are the kind of stimuli brains seek and remember.

If we provide our content as stimuli brains naturally seek, it is like swimming with the current. Teaching is easier. We don't have to work as hard to capture and hold the attention of our students. We are not as exhausted at the end of the day. If, on the other hand, we ignore the simple fact that brains seek certain kinds of stimuli and ignore others, and if we don't align our teaching with that principle, our students will be less motivated, less interested. They will like class less. Teaching will be swimming against the current. We will work harder, but our students will pay less attention and retain less.

Thus we can derive the sixth principle of brain-friendly learning:

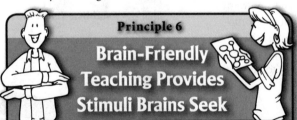

Principle 6
Brain-Friendly Teaching Provides Stimuli Brains Seek

Here, we examine thirteen types of stimuli brains attend to and retain. Knowing and applying this knowledge as we teach, we swim with the current. We dramatically increase student learning. Students like our class more—they are getting what their brains seek.

Thirteen Tools to Supply Brain-Friendly Stimuli

1. Stimulate with Surprise and Novelty
2. Provide Predictability
3. Allow Play
4. Furnish Effective Feedback
5. Catch Them Being Good!
6. Recommend Biofeedback
7. Illustrate with Images
8. Teach with Tunes
9. Communicate with Gestures
10. Make It Multimodal
11. Teach with Styles
12. Establish Relevance
13. Construct Meaning

Tool 1

Stimulate with Surprise and Novelty

The brain is designed to survive. In order to survive, we need to attend to novel and unexpected stimuli. Novel stimuli might be a threat we need to avoid, or an opportunity—something that will help us survive. There is a novelty center in the brain called the substantia nigra/ventral tegmental area, the SN/VTA. Human brain scans reveal the SN/VTA becomes active whenever we encounter novel stimuli.[1]

Brain-Friendly Teaching • Dr. Spencer Kagan
Kagan Publishing • 800.933.2667 • www.KaganOnline.com

We can capture and hold the attention of our students far more easily if we create novelty by including in our lessons things the students have never before seen—unexpected, surprising events.

Novelty lights up the brain as an absolute variable whereas reward lights up the brain as a relative variable. What do we mean by this?

Rewards Are Relative

Our brains compare rewards. A reward will light up the brain if compared to a lesser reward, but the same reward will not light up the brain when compared to a larger reward. We get excited by the larger reward.[7] It is not the absolute amount of the reward that our brains respond to; it is the relative amount of the reward compared to alternatives.

Novelty Is Absolute

Novelty does not work in the same way as rewards. We respond to novelty, not by comparison to other stimuli, but by comparison to whether we have ever seen that stimuli before. If we have not seen a stimulus before, it produces a novelty response. The more times we see that same stimulus, the less it activates the novelty response tracks. By the third and successive

To elicit the novelty response, we need to present our students with stimuli they have never previously encountered.

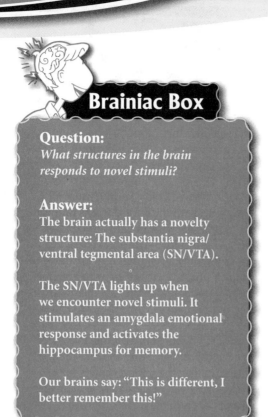

Brainiac Box

Question:
What structures in the brain responds to novel stimuli?

Answer:
The brain actually has a novelty structure: The substantia nigra/ventral tegmental area (SN/VTA).

The SN/VTA lights up when we encounter novel stimuli. It stimulates an amygdala emotional response and activates the hippocampus for memory.

Our brains say: "This is different, I better remember this!"

The SN/VTA is linked to both the hippocampus (critical for memory and learning) and the amygdalae (reactive to emotional stimuli). Individual neurons in the brain will fire or not depending on if the stimulus is novel, and novelty directly activates the hippocampus, promoting memory for novel content.[2] Novelty also activates the dopamine reward system in the same way rewards do, and this burst of emotion also promotes memory for the content.[3] Given a choice between tokens for variety of food rewards compared to tokens for the most preferred food reward each time, non-human primates choose the variety token, even if that leads to a less preferred food reward.[4] Novelty has such rewarding properties that it can be a more powerful attraction than cocaine.[5] We are born predisposed to become alert when faced with novelty. When presented with the same stimuli repeatedly, infants become bored; they habituate. In contrast, when presented with novel stimuli, infants instantly become alert.[6] The first time we hear a joke, we wait with anticipation for the novel ending. If someone starts to tell us that same joke again, we tell them, "Stop, I've heard that one." We are not interested if there is no surprise, no novelty.

A Note-Taking Tour

Allison made note-taking more novel and brain friendly by hanging pictures and maps of the Middle East all over the school. Then during class, instead of having students take notes while seated in the classroom, she had her students walk as a group from location to location taking notes. It was a novel twist on their typical routine. Students were stimulating their brains as they walked from location to location.

—*Allison Ortega*
9th Grade Geography Teacher
W.A. Todd Junior High School
Donna, TX

presentations, we habituate. That is, the stimulus is no longer novel and has lost its power to elicit the novelty response. This is true even if the stimulus is novel compared to the other stimuli we are experiencing.[8] Once the brain has encountered a stimulus several times, it loses its ability to elicit the novelty activation response, even if we have not seen that stimulus for some time. To elicit the novelty response, we need to present our students with stimuli they have never previously encountered.

The novelty structure in the brain is activated when we experience unexpected stimuli. We become more alert. We attend more carefully. We remember the event. The evolutionary basis for this is obvious: The novel information may be a threat (hungry predator) or an opportunity (something good to eat). Attending to novel stimuli helps us survive. Those animals that did not become more alert when novel or unexpected stimuli appeared did not survive to pass along their genes!

> ## Tip
> To increase memory for content, surprise your students with novelty.

Unpredictability, Surprise

Brain scans reveal there is another way to light up the brain—unpredictability. The brain lights up when there is a mismatch between expectation and experience. For example, slowly read the following list of words, focusing on the mental picture each creates in your mind:

gathering...group...meeting...conference... carrot...assembly...

When you came to the word "carrot," your anterior hippocampus fired above baseline![9] Why? After reading the first four words your brain created a set of expectations that all the words would relate to groups of people. When you came to the word "carrot," experience did not meet expectation. Researchers call this the *oddball response.* Our anterior hippocampus lights up to unexpected stimuli, stimuli that violates our expectations.

Unexpected, unpredictable stimuli cause a dopamine release to the reward tracks in the brain.[11] This is why we wait with anticipation for the punch line of a joke. The joke is designed to have an unpredictable ending. As we wait for the joke's punch line, we are waiting with anticipation for a dose of dopamine to activate the reward tracks of our brains!

If rewards are presented in a predictable fashion, they become routine and lose their ability to stimulate the reward centers in the brain. Rewards given in a predictable schedule are boring; the brain habituates, showing decreased release of dopamine to stimulate the reward centers. See Graph: How Rewarding Are Predictable v. Unpredictable Stimuli?

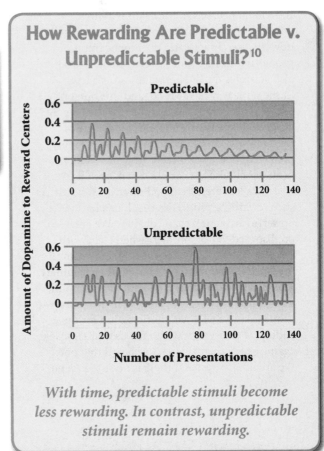

How Rewarding Are Predictable v. Unpredictable Stimuli?[10]

With time, predictable stimuli become less rewarding. In contrast, unpredictable stimuli remain rewarding.

Brainiac Box

Unexpected v. Predictable Events

Question:
How does the hippocampus respond differently to unexpected and predictable events?

Answer:
When we encounter an unexpected event, the anterior hippocampus fires, signaling the brain: *You better remember this! You need to revise your picture of the world.*

When the event becomes familiar, the anterior hippocampus doesn't fire—it is the posterior hippocampus that fires, signaling the brain: *The world works the way you thought. No need to get excited; you don't have to change your picture of the world. File this away as confirming established expectations.*

Unpredictable rewards can stimulate the reward tracks of the brain even more than does a person's subjective preference for that reward. What we say about how much we like something does not determine how much the reward tracks of the brain are stimulated as much as how unpredictable that reward is!

We always have expectations about how the world works. Whenever we encounter a situation in which the world does not behave the way we expected, we have to revise our picture of the world. This is one way we get smarter. It is the job of the anterior hippocampus to respond to novel stimuli and to code them for memory so that we can upgrade our picture of the world, change our expectations to correspond to reality. Interestingly, it is the posterior hippocampus that responds to familiar stimuli. As novel stimuli are repeatedly experienced, they become familiar stimuli and the anterior hippocampus no longer fires. It is the posterior hippocampus that fires to familiar stimuli, filing them away as confirming expectations.

Unexpected Stimuli Grab and Hold Attention

Something that does not fit with our understanding with how the world works, grabs and holds our attention. A magician has us draw a card from the deck and we see him place it in the middle of the deck. After some hocus-pocus, he has us turn over the top card of the deck and we are shocked to see it is our card! Our attention is riveted because suddenly the world is not working the way we expect. Content that does not obey the usual laws of how the world works is novel and so grabs our attention. Since we need to live in a predictable world, our brains go to work trying to figure out stimuli that confound our expectations.

Ways to Violate Student Expectations

When we present content that violates the expectations of our students, we focus their attention and they remember that content better. The brain is geared to pay special attention to and remember things that don't conform to expectations.

There are many ways to violate expectations as we teach our content, including:

Science
- ▶ Perform an experiment with an unexpected outcome. Pour one clear liquid into another clear liquid and the combined liquids turn colored. Students are suddenly interested.
- ▶ State facts that violate expectations; for example: Beer, wine, bread, cheese, and yogurt are all examples of controlled spoilage.

Tip

To focus the attention of students, and to promote memory for content, violate expectations and present something students are not expecting.

Math

▶ Have students guess how long it would take to count to a million taking one second for each number, not stopping for rest, meals, or sleep, and then have them calculate the answer (11.6 days).

▶ Have students guess how many 1-ft.-square cubes can fit into a box that is 6 ft. on a side, and then figure out the answer (216).

▶ Tell students to:

 1. Think of any number between 50 and 100.
 2. Add to that number 72.
 3. Subtract 100.
 4. Add 5.
 5. Subtract your answer from the number you started with.
 6. Then announce the answer is 23!

Have students then figure out why the answer will always be 23. After they have figured it out, have them create similar problems that have answers of 12 or 20.

Language Arts

▶ Leave out a word in a poem and have students guess the word the author used, before revealing the author's unusual word choice.

▶ Describe unusual characteristics of an author or unusual impact of a piece of literature.

▶ While reading a story, before an unexpected outcome, have students guess what will happen next.

Social Studies

▶ Have students make predictions about the outcomes of a social or economic policy that did not work as expected, and then reveal actual outcomes.

▶ Have students guess the date of the last state that voted to repeal a ban on interracial marriage (Alabama, 2001).

▶ Announce to students that Albert A. Gore got 50,999,897 votes and George W. Bush got 50,456,002 votes in the presidential election of 2000, but that Bush was elected president. Have students analyze the advantages and disadvantages of the Electoral College.

Unexpected Stimuli as a Lesson Set. Dan Kuzma, a distinguished high school social studies teacher and Kagan trainer, offers the following example of using unexpected outcomes to stimulate curiosity at the outset of a lesson. Without telling the students which war he is providing data for, he begins the lesson on the American Revolutionary War by asking students to make a prediction. Which of two countries will win the war? See Table: Who Will Win the War?

Stimuli that confound expectations provide excellent sets for lessons. Students get set to learn when their curiosity is aroused. A teacher comes into the science class with a bullwhip. She cracks the whip and it makes a very sharp sound. This is a novel stimulus at two levels. First, teachers don't usually crack bullwhips in class.

Who Will Win the War?

Country 1	Country 2
Army of 36,000 plus 30,000 supplemental recruits	Army of 20,000—often less
Army well trained and well armed	Army poorly trained, poorly armed
Army well paid	Army poorly paid
Army of full-time soldiers	Army of part-time soldiers reluctant to leave home for extended time
Army well fed	Army poorly fed, often rotten food
Experienced Navy of 131 ships—39 battle ready	No Navy—no ships
Population unanimous in support of victory	Population in conflict—half loyal to opposing country

Brain-Friendly Teaching • Dr. Spencer Kagan
Kagan Publishing • 800.933.2667 • www.KaganOnline.com

Second, the teacher asks, *"What made that loud crack?"* Things going through the air don't usually make a loud, sudden cracking sound. This stimulus is not conforming to the usual way things behave; it is novel. The teacher has our attention. We want to know. This is the introduction to a lesson on the speed of sound. (The bullwhip makes that sound because the tip of the whip has actually broken the sound barrier and we have heard a mini sonic boom).

Imponderables Arouse Curiosity.
The book, *Why Do Clocks Run Clockwise? And Other Imponderables*[12] presents 239 puzzling questions that can grab and hold the attention of our students.

- ▶ *"Why do dogs walk in circles before lying down?"*
- ▶ *"Why do some localities use salt and others use sand to treat icy roads?"*
- ▶ *"What is the purpose of the ball on top of a flagpole?"*
- ▶ *"Why don't spiders stick to their own webs?"*
- ▶ *"Why are executions in the United States held between midnight and seven AM?"*

Kagan Structures Produce Unexpected and Novel Stimuli.
Other people are among the greatest sources of novelty and unpredictability. When we interact with others, there is always new and unexpected stimuli. People say things we have not heard; they do things we do not expect. Part of the reason we find it so rewarding to interact with others is because we become more alert and engaged in the face of the novel and unexpected stimuli they present. Kagan Cooperative Learning Structures[13] ensure engagement by all students through social interaction.

The structures offer novelty and surprise in a number of ways. The structures include the use of spinners and selectors to determine who will represent their team or who will move to another team to share their team's answer. As the spinner

is spun, excitement and interest is generated because no one can know who will be selected. The outcome is unexpected. There are novel stimuli provided by peers during the social interaction. The input and feedback of a partner or teammates is often unpredictable. Since there are over 200 different Kagan Structures, each time we introduce a new structure, we elicit the novelty response. Further, Kagan Cooperative Learning Structures encourage students to use "surprising and delightful" praise, and to use different gambits as they interact to keep the stimulation high. Students in classrooms in which the structures are used regularly report the classes to be more "fun." In technical terms, students are telling us that structures respond to the brain's need for a regular input of novel and unexpected stimuli! See Table: Kagan Structures Produce Novel, Unexpected Stimuli, p. 6.10.

Play Provides Unexpected and Novel Stimuli.
Novelty is almost a defining characteristic of play. Play is a time to try on new moves, to experiment, to play with others. It is an opportunity to react to the novel responses of others. Imagine students working for some length of time on a series of problems. They become bored. What is boredom? It is a lack of novel stimuli. Their brains begin to function at lower levels. Suddenly the teacher says, *"Let's have a brain break!"* calling for students to do **Mirror Mirror** or any of the 206 Silly Sports or Goofy Games.[14] Students stand up. Quickly they become intensely engaged. Why? They are attending to novel stimuli. After a few minutes, the students return to their seats, refreshed. Their increased alertness, caused in part by the novel stimuli, is channeled toward to academic work, and achievement is increased. There is novelty in the content of the game, and there is novelty each time we introduce a new game to our students; the introduction of a Silly Sport in the middle of a lesson provides unexpected stimuli.

Kagan Structures Produce Novel, Unexpected Stimuli

Structures	Structure Section	How Structures Produce Novelty, Surprise
Celebrity Interview	3	Teammates don't know what the interviewee will share.
Three-Step Interview	24	
Timed Pair Share	25	
Formations	6	What the teacher asks the students to form is a surprise; how they form it is novel.
Kinesthetic Symbols	7	Students come up with novel ways to symbolize the content.
Simulations	19	Students come up with novel presentations.
TakeOff–TouchDown	22	Instead of always asking students to raise a hand, the teacher surprises students by asking them to raise all of themselves.
Traveling Heads Together	26	Students don't know who will be called on to travel, or who will join their team.
Flashcard Game	5	Students are encouraged to respond to correct answers with surprising and delightful praise.
Quiz-Quiz-Trade	13	
RallyQuiz	14	
Sage-N-Scribe	17	

Variety

We can keep stimulation high in our classrooms by mixing things up. Variety in the classroom can be created in many ways. We can vary the order of what is taught, the types of instructional strategies we use, who students interact with, the sources of information, room arrangement, posters on the wall, the kinds of cheers and celebrations we do, and even what we wear.

> *"Variety's the very spice of life that gives it all its flavour."*
>
> —*William Cowper (1731–1800)*

Variety is not Novelty. Variety is changing the order of things. We can do things we have done before, but in a different order or in a different way. If the stimuli are not new, we will not elicit the novelty response. Nevertheless, by mixing up our routines, we make class more interesting, enjoyable, and memorable.

A cautionary note: We must balance the need for novelty and variety with the need for predictability. For example, if we change a class routine unexpectedly, some students will become anxious. Thus, we might say something like, *"Tomorrow we are going to change our usual routine, and I will announce what that will be at the beginning of class tomorrow."* We reduce anxiety by preparing students to expect novelty.

Myriad Ways to Create Novelty and Variety

Novelty and Variety are created by teaching with a variety of structures, teaching with multiple intelligences strategies, and by mixing up classroom routines.

Structures Offer Variety. Teachers using a number of structures create variety. For example, a lesson might begin with a **RoundRobin** for

second way: Each structure engages a different set of intelligences. For examples, when we use **Formations**, we are engaging the Visual/Spatial and Bodily/Kinesthetic intelligences; when we use **Same-Different**, we are engaging the Logical/Mathematical, Visual/Spatial, and Interpersonal Intelligences. With 84 different Multiple Intelligences Structures, we can include variety all school year. And each time we introduce a new Multiple Intelligences Structure, we elicit the novelty response as well!

students to share prior knowledge on the lesson topic; progress to a **Listen Right!** or a **Swap Talk** to provide input; use **RallyRobin** or **RallyQuiz** to review the input; do a **Team-Pair-Solo** to make sure all students master a new skill, and wrap up with a **Timed Pair Share** to allow students to verbalize what they have learned.

Multiple Intelligences Provides Variety.
Multiple Intelligences Structures are content-free instructional strategies designed to engage the various intelligences while we teach our curriculum.[15] Multiple Intelligences Structures are compatible with the brain's need for variety in two ways: First, by changing our instructional strategies on an ongoing basis, we are creating variety in our classroom.

See Structures Section
8. Listen Right!
14. RallyQuiz
15. RallyRobin
16. RoundRobin
21. Swap Talk
23. Team-Pair-Solo
25. Timed Pair Share

The teacher who dresses in period costume for a history lesson has caught the attention of the students before saying a word. And because the lesson is linked to novel stimuli, the lesson will be better remembered: *That was the time Mr. Jones dressed as a Civil War soldier.* But we don't have to go to such extremes to elicit the novelty response. Anything that is new, different, or surprising will elicit the novelty or reward response. See Tips Box on the next page for a few of the many possibilities. See Table: Stimuli to Capture Attention, p. 6.13.

Our teaching style is quite in contrast to that of the teacher who always lectures or who only uses any other single mode of instruction. Multiple Intelligences Structures create variety in a

Tips

Create Novelty and Variety in many ways:

- Redecorate the room.
- Rearrange the furniture for the day.
- Pantomime an aspect of the content.
- Have students create items for the test.
- Teach from a different part of the room.
- Rearrange where students sit for the day.
- Break up the lesson with a new Silly Sport.
- Have students stand while you give initial input.
- Teach using novel cooperative learning structures.
- Create novel formats for a test (e.g., draw answers).
- Give a test on the content before teaching the content.
- Tell students to take notes only with pictures, no words.
- Begin the lesson by having students guess what they will learn.
- Provide novel sources of input (guest lecture, old-time movie...).
- Have students close their eyes and imagine a scene related to the content.
- Stop in the middle of the lesson and have students generate content-related questions.

Stimuli to Capture Attention

Novelty, Variety, and Surprise

Novel Activities	Include novel activities. On a regular basis, have students experience "something different."
Order of Events	Change the order of events; vary the routines in the class.
Voice Changes	As you lecture or give instructions, for emphasis and drama, change your voice. Sometimes whisper. Sometimes speak in a loud voice. Change the pitch.
Location of Lecture	If you have a lecture especially important for the students to remember, give your lecture from the back or side of the room. Rearrange furniture.
Dress	When appropriate for a history or literature lesson, wear a costume. Have dress up days for the class.
Sources of Information	Use a wide range of sources of information: Web; Guest Lectures; Reading; Videos; Magazines; Skype Interviews; Student Reports on Interviews, Experiments, Readings.
Manipulatives	Provide or have students make manipulatives to symbolize the content. Have them use tactile and kinesthetic senses by arranging the manipulatives to create a time line or geometric figure. Put questions on cards to play games as students review.
Vary Group Size	Mix up grouping. Have students work alone, in pairs, in teams, and as a class.
Vary Group Composition	Use fixed, carefully assigned teams, but break out occasionally into brief random teams for specific activities. Create random pairs for partner work. Alternate between shoulder partner and face partner interaction within teams.
Seating	Occasionally reassign student seating within teams. Reassign where teams sit.
Provide Choices	When appropriate, give students choices regarding what to study, how to study, and how to be evaluated.
Unexpected Outcomes	Do demonstrations or read stories that have unexpected outcomes. Have students make predictions that you know will be confounded.
Surprise	Surprise students with unexpected events: Rewards, a video, a new Silly Sport, a new structure.
Celebrations	Include class celebrations.
Cheers	Have students develop and use class and team cheers. Have them create new cheers.
Praise	Provide novel praise. Have students use surprising, delightful praise.

Tool 2

Provide Predictability

Although brains respond positively to novel stimuli, they seek predictability. We see this need for predictability in an extreme form in many autistic children. Break their routine and they throw a tantrum. Although most of us do not have such an extreme need for predictability, we all seek predictability. We adapt readily to predictable stimuli, but unpredictable stimuli interfere with our performance.[16] When faced with aversive stimuli, humans and animals prefer predictability.[17]

Seeking predictability is related to our need for safety and our need to make sense of the world. If we don't know what is coming next, it may be something bad. We need to be on guard. As we saw when we explored novelty, we are constantly making predictions about how the world will behave, and when the world doesn't conform to our expectations, the brain goes into high gear trying to reconcile predictions with reality. We have a need to understand our world. Although a bit of novelty delights us, stimulating the reward centers in the brain,[18] too much unexpected stimuli places us on guard. We do not want to live in an unpredictable world.

Individuals differ in their need for predictability. For some students, a classroom is not safe unless there are predictable routines. When students are not safe, as we have seen, their amygdalae fire, student cognitions and perceptions narrow, and little learning can occur.

We Make Predictions Every Moment

Jeff Hawkins has convincingly argued that the brain makes predictions several times every second, and that it is the very essence of intelligence.[19] To prove that our brains are constantly making predictions, he asks us to do a thought experiment. Imagine Jeff snuck over to your house while you were out, and he made a minor change in your front door. For example, he might change the placement of the door handle, the color of the door, the weight of the door, the squeak it makes or doesn't make as it opens, or any number of other features of the door. Imagine further after one of those changes, you come home and approach your front door. Immediately you notice the change Jeff has made. If Jeff changed the color of the door only slightly, something would seem odd. As you reached to open the door, if Jeff had changed the placement of the handle even slightly, it would feel out of place. If he had changed the weight of the door, you would push too hard or not hard enough as you opened it. If he changed the sound it makes when you open it, you would notice. There are a million possible ways Jeff could change the door, but no matter how Jeff changed your front door, you would notice. Why would you notice? Reality would not meet your prediction. Jeff takes this as proof that without your knowing it, your brain had made predictions about how the door should look and behave. If you hadn't made those predictions, you would not be surprised at any of the possible changes Jeff had made.

The implications of this are incredible. It means your brain makes predictions about everything you are about to see, touch, hear, smell, and even

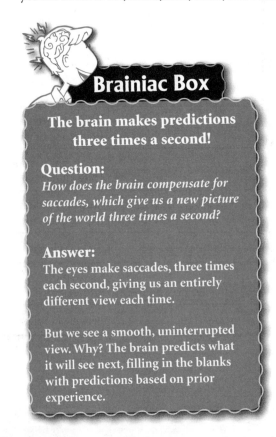

Brainiac Box

The brain makes predictions three times a second!

Question:
How does the brain compensate for saccades, which give us a new picture of the world three times a second?

Answer:
The eyes make saccades, three times each second, giving us an entirely different view each time.

But we see a smooth, uninterrupted view. Why? The brain predicts what it will see next, filling in the blanks with predictions based on prior experience.

Brain-Friendly Teaching • Dr. Spencer Kagan
Kagan Publishing • 800.933.2667 • www.KaganOnline.com

taste. All of us have gone to pick up a glass we thought was full and instead of gently raising it, have it fly up, because it was empty! Without knowing, we had made a prediction about the weight of the glass and had accordingly adjusted the strength with which to raise it. We are constantly making predictions, and when reality and prediction don't match, we are surprised.

How can the brain make so many parallel Predictions every moment? The answer: predictions are based on memory. All of our memories of how something has behaved in the past are consolidated into a prediction of how it will behave in the future. And most all of this is done unconsciously! When things don't work the way they have in the past, we go to work to reconcile the difference, and revise our model of how the world works. Jeff explains, *"The cortex is an organ of prediction."* Our senses feed information up to the top layer of the cortex to allow input, but the top layer of the cortex feeds predictions down. Because of this, we only see what we predict, unless prediction does not meet reality, in which case we revise our predictions. To function, we need to understand how the world works; we need to live in a predictable world.

Even Babies Make Predictions. At birth, infants show a startle reaction to novel stimuli, but quickly habituate. They are seeking patterns and forming expectations. In a classic experiment, babies are presented with a ball that rolls down an incline and hits a miniature bowling pin, making a loud noise when the pin falls over. For the first few trials, each time the pin falls and the baby hears the loud noise, the infants show a diffuse startle reaction. After several trials, their behavior changes: They simply watch with little excitement and do not show a startle reaction to the noise. They have habituated to the noise. However, if after the babies have habituated, the apparatus is rigged so when the

ball hits the pin, it does not fall over, the babies once again show a startle reaction. The babies fixate, searching to make meaning of this novel set of events. Why? The predictable pattern is broken; the world is no longer predictable.

Babies (and adults) are meaning makers. With no instruction, babies learn to make sense of these funny sounds we emit called words. They convert the buzzing confusion of verbal and visual stimuli into familiar objects, and predictable relations among objects.[20]

Predictability Reduces Stress

If people are subjected to aversive stimuli, it creates stress. However, if someone can predict when the aversive stimulus is to occur, or how it will occur, stress is reduced.[21] Seeking predictable patterns is one way we make sense of the world; it is related to our need for safety. For some students, a classroom is not safe unless there are predictable routines.

Unpredictability Hinders Performance. Performance following predictable stimuli is better than performance following unpredictable stimuli. For example, people perform better on a proofreading task following being exposed to predictable noise than they do following unpredictable noise.[22]

Predictability Enhances Well-Being. In an extremely intensive investigation of the effects of control and predictability, older residents in a home for the aged (mean age 81 years) were assigned to have a college student visit them over a period of 2 months, averaging 1.3 visits of a week.[23] Visits were about 50 minutes. There were four conditions, but relevant here is the effect of random v. predictable visits. Random visits were initiated by *"I decided to drop by and pay you a visit today."* In the predictable condition, residents were informed beforehand of when the visitor would be coming.

Results: Residents rated both the random and predictable visits very positively (they seldom had visitors). Nevertheless, the impact of predictable visits was significantly more positive. By the end of only 2 months, those residents that had predictable visits (something they could look forward to) were rated by the activities director as healthier; took fewer medications; were more active; were more hopeful; and had more of a future orientation. On a questionnaire, they rated themselves as happier, having more zest for life, and less lonely. This last variable is particularly interesting because residents in both conditions were visited exactly the same amount of time. It was predictability, not amount of visits or length of time of visits that significantly reduced loneliness! The researchers conclude:

> This study demonstrates that the decline in physical and psychological status and level of activity associated with increased age can be inhibited or reversed by making a predictable or controllable significant positive event available to aged individuals. The study further supports the conceptualization that the many negative consequences of aging may be mediated by increased unpredictability and uncontrollability.

Prediction and Magic

Magicians do much of their magic by taking advantage of this simple principle: We see what we predict. Magicians set up situations in which we see only our predictions, not the reality of what they are doing. *"The spooky truth is that your brain constructs reality, visual and otherwise. What you see, hear, feel, and think is based on what you expect to see, hear, feel, and think."*[24] For example, a very simple magic trick anyone can do is to make a coin disappear. While people are seated at a table the magician announces he will make a coin disappear. He places the coin on the table in front of him. With a smooth motion of his hand over the coin and sliding his hand on the table toward him, he acts as if he is picking up the coin while actually sliding it off the table into his lap. He makes a fist as if he has picked up the coin and raises his empty fist looking at it as he does. People are astonished when he opens the fist and the coin is not there. In two ways, those watching the trick have seen what they expected to see. When someone closes a fist over something as if they are picking it up, we expect the object to be in their Stand. Further, when someone's eyes follow something, our eyes follow that object.

Experience has taught us that the place to look is where others are looking. We have seen the magician pick up the coin and raise it in his fist. We have seen what we expect to see! I have performed this trick without watching my fist as I raise it, and the trick fails. If, however, I look at my fist as I raise it, all eyes follow mine and the trick always works. How I direct my attention determines how others direct theirs.

> **Tip**
> Focus your attention on that which you want your students to focus their attention.

Confirmation Bias

The need to live in a predictable world is so strong, we often abandon rationality in our attempt to align present experience with expectations. We interpret incoming data in ways that are consistent with our prior beliefs, even if there is a more rational way to interpret the data. This tendency is variously called confirmation bias, motivated reasoning, and cognitive dissonance reduction.[25]

There are many research studies demonstrating confirmation bias. Brain scans demonstrate how the brain interprets incoming information in ways to make it consistent with our predictions, even when that is not rational. Our irrationality is a measure of our need to live in a predictable, consistent world. Let's examine how confirmation bias plays out in politics, science, and education.

Confirmation Bias: Politics. Experimenters tested 15 "committed Democrats" and 15 "committed Republicans" prior to the Bush v. Kerry election. While in an fMRI scanner, participants were presented with statements and actions by each candidate that were wildly inconsistent, and then asked to rate if the statements and actions were in fact contradictory.[26] For comparison, contradictory statements and actions by a politically neutral person were included. The results demonstrate the need to align perceptions with expectations. Expecting their own candidate's actions to align with what their candidate said, participants found a way to rationalize the inconsistency in their own candidate, seeing it as not that inconsistent after all. Thus, Democrats rated Kerry's words and deeds as significantly less inconsistent than did Republicans while Republicans rated Bush as significantly less inconsistent than did Democrats. There was little difference between Democrats and Republicans in rating the neutral person. See Graph: Biased Political Reasoning.

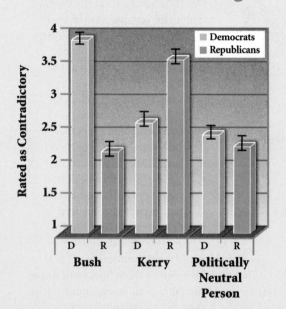

Biased Political Reasoning[26]

When presented with an action by a political candidate that wildly contradicts their verbal statement, Democrats rate the contradictory statements of Republicans as more contradictory; Republicans rate the contradictory statements of Democrats as more contradictory. They do not differ much in rating nonpolitical statements.

Brain Activation Associated with Confirmation Bias. The pattern of brain activation aligned with this process of confirmation bias. When the participants were first confronted with inconsistent statements and actions by their candidate, threat centers in the brain began firing. When they had time to rationalize away the inconsistency, the threat centers calmed down:

> The large activation of the ventral striatum that followed subjects'

processing of threatening information likely reflects reward or relief engendered by "successful" equilibration to an emotionally stable judgment. The combination of reduced negative affect (absence of activity in the insula and lateral orbital cortex) and increased positive affect or reward (ventral striatum activation) once subjects had ample time to reach biased conclusions suggests why motivated judgments may be so difficult to change (e.g., they are doubly reinforcing).

We all want a predictable world, a world that behaves in the ways we expect. If that means we have to be biased in our reasoning, that is the price we pay. We need to satisfy the drive for predictability.

Confirmation Bias: How We View a Face. In another approach to demonstrating confirmation bias in politics, researchers tested Republican leaning and Democratic leaning Ohio undergraduates before and after the 2012 election. The undergraduates were presented with 450 comparisons of two pictures of Mitt Romney's face. On each trial, they were asked to pick which of the two faces looked more like Mitt Romney. The faces were independently rated as more or less trustworthy. Republican-leaning students picked faces that looked more trustworthy far more than did the Democratic-leaning students. The researchers concluded, *"…citizens may not merely interpret political information about*

Confirmation Bias:
Self-Esteem

"I have done that—says my memory.

"I cannot have done that—says my pride, and remains adamant.

"At last, memory yields."

—*Friedrich Nietzsche*

a candidate to fit their opinion, but they may construct a political world where they literally see candidates differently."[27] How we see the world is influenced by our values and expectations! We live in different worlds!

Confirmation Bias: Science. The history of science is replete with examples of intelligent people sticking to their predictions about how things work in the face of contradictory evidence. Despite a wealth of scientific evidence to the contrary, intelligent people dismiss global warming as a hoax, based on their personal and/or political biases. Even scientists tend to seek evidence that confirms their predictions while ignoring evidence that contradicts their predictions.[28] The theory that the earth is the center of the universe prevailed since ancient times. In the face of contradictory evidence, scientists did not abandon the theory. Rather, they repeatedly adjusted the theory to reconcile it with the new observations.[29] (Persistence in this belief is strong: 18% of Americans believe the sun revolves around the earth!)[30]

Tremendous resistance is generated whenever a theory or person presents a picture of the world that contradicts the way we believe things are. Galileo, Darwin, and Freud, among others, paid the price of outrage as they proposed theories that threatened long-standing beliefs. Galileo was sentenced to indefinite imprisonment by the Roman Inquisition (a sentence later reduced to house arrest) because of his support of the Copernican idea that the earth revolved around the sun. He was ordered, "to abandon completely... the opinion that ...the earth moves, and henceforth not to hold, teach, or defend it in any way whatsoever, either orally or in writing."

It is not just non-scientists who stick to their beliefs in the face of contrary evidence: Newton refused to believe that the earth could be much older than 6,000 years based on the reasoning of Archbishop Usher that placed the date of creation at 4,004 BC. Once people, even scientists, have a picture of how the world works, they don't want that picture challenged—they want a predictable world.

Confirmation Bias: Education. Because all of us seek and find evidence that confirms our biases while ignoring evidence that contradicts our biases, as teachers we must be extremely cautious about forming opinions about the intelligence or ability of our students. Once those opinions are formed, we find ways to confirm them. Worse yet, in subtle and not so subtle ways, our opinions are communicated to our students, who in turn internalize our opinions of them and then act in ways to live up to or down to our expectations. The impact of teacher expectations on student achievement was the topic in a series of experiments by Robert Rosenthal and Lenore Jacobson.[31] The results became known as the Pygmalion effect. The researchers gave students the Test of General Ability (TOGA), an IQ test, and then informed teachers that on the basis of the IQ test, certain students were discovered to be "spurters"—that is, they would do better than expected compared to their classmates that year. In fact, those who were designated as likely to blossom were randomly selected. Nevertheless, by the end of the school year, those given the "spurter" label performed significantly better on the IQ test than those not given the label.

Explaining the Pygmalion Effect. The Pygmalion effect can be explained as a self-fulfilling prophecy: Believing a student will blossom, the teacher treats the student preferentially and communicates those expectations to the student, who in turn responds to the preferential treatment and lives up to the higher expectations. The motor that drives this self-fulfilling prophecy is confirmation bias: Believing the student is of higher ability, without knowing, the teacher finds data that supports that view, and ignores data that contradicts that view.

Teacher Expectations Influence Teacher Behavior. There has been criticism of the Rosenthal experiments,[32] but there is ample support for the finding that teacher expectations influence teacher behavior toward students.[33]

When a teacher holds low expectations for a student, the teacher:

- ▶ Calls on the student less often
- ▶ Pays less attention to the student
- ▶ Smiles at the student less
- ▶ Offers less eye contact
- ▶ Waits less time for the student to answer questions
- ▶ More often gives the student the answers rather than probing for a correct answer

When asked to rate the performance of a student, those believing the student was from a high socioeconomic background rated the student as above grade level; those believing the student was from a low socioeconomic background rated the student's performance as below grade level.

Teacher Expectations Influenced by Race and Socioeconomic Status. Teacher expectations are determined, among other things, by race and socioeconomic status of students. Teachers generally hold higher expectations for Caucasian compared to African American and Hispanic students, and for students from higher compared to lower socioeconomic status.[34]

Teacher Expectations Influence Interpretations of Student Behavior. Simply believing a student is of high or low socioeconomic status determines how we interpret their performance. To demonstrate this, before viewing a video of a student taking an academic test, experimenters told participants either that the student was from a high socioeconomic background or that the student was from a low socioeconomic background. All participants saw the same video of the same student performing an academic test. When asked to rate the performance of the student, those believing the student was from a high socioeconomic background rated the student as above grade level; those believing the student was from a low socioeconomic background rated the student's performance as below grade level.[35] The researchers interpreted the finding as "hypothesis-confirming," what we have called "confirmation bias." As soon as they were told the socioeconomic status of the student, the viewers formed expectations, and then confirmed those expectations by looking for data that supported their expectation and ignoring data that did not. We want to live in a predictable world, and adjust our perceptions accordingly.

Student Expectations Influence Teachers

In a fascinating reversal of the Pygmalion effect, researchers gave students expectations about teachers, and found students rated them accordingly, and teachers actually lived up to or down to the student expectations.[36] Student expectations were manipulated by giving them the results of a bogus survey that had rated a teacher either high or low. During the subsequent lesson, those given the positive expectations leaned forward toward the teacher more than those given low expectations. Following the lesson, those in the low expectation condition scored 52.2% on the test; those with high expectations scored 65%! Finally, students with low expectations rated the lesson as being "more difficult," "less interesting," and "less effective." In an additional experiment to demonstrate the impact of student behavior on teacher effectiveness, teachers were assigned to teach a lesson. Unknown to them, the students in the lesson were instructed to either lean forward and look interested, or to act bored. Those teachers with the more attentive students felt better about their lessons and were rated by independent judges as having given a better lesson. Our students shape our behaviors!

Providing Predictability

To feel secure, students need predictability. Some students will feel secure only if they know where they are in a lesson, and what is coming next. All students will learn and retain information better if it is within an understandable, predictable context. To the extent we make our instructional strategies, lessons, and classrooms predictable, we become brain-friendly teachers.

See Structures Section
8. Listen Right!
26. Traveling Heads Together

Kagan Structures Are Predictable Sequences. All of the more than 200 Kagan Structures are predicable sequences. The step-by-step sequence within each structure not only makes them easy for a teacher to implement; but also, it provides predictability for students. A number of times, I have done an informal experiment with teachers and with students. I have them experience for the first time a multistep structures like **Listen Right!** (a seven-step structure) or **Traveling Heads Together** (another seven-step structure) and then quiz them to see if they know the steps. They do. They know them not because I have told them the steps, but rather because they have experienced them. They know the steps because they can remember what they just did. Because the students so readily learn the steps of the structures, the structures become predictable sequences. At any moment in a structure, students are secure: They know what is coming next.

Communicating Expectations Provides Predictability. We provide predictability by clearly communicating: (1) the content and process of our academic lessons, (2) the calendar of classroom events, (3) our management procedures, and (4) our discipline policy. Let's start with the big picture, the entire course, and then work down through smaller and smaller chunks until we get to communicating what will happen next in a lesson.

Course Syllabus, Course Outline, or Course Overview. How we communicate our expectations for the big picture will depend on the grade level we teach. At secondary, we can provide and overview a course outline or a course syllabus at the outset. At elementary, we might

simply list or overview some of the major topics we will cover for the year:

> One of the exciting things you will learn this year is how to multiply large numbers. You will be able to use this important skill throughout life when you need answers. You will be able to figure out how much wood you will need to build a tree house, how much to charge for your work, and figure out how much food to order for a party.

Monthly or Weekly Calendar of Events. Knowing what is coming next serves to allay fears, get students prepared for upcoming events, and engender positive emotions as students anticipate positive events. These features are illustrated in the comments of Melissa Wincel:

> "I had two students with autism and predictability was a BIG deal. I had a small calendar that I taped to their desk and placed a different colored star for different events: red = fire drill; green = visitor was coming; blue = assembly; yellow = school event. The boys really liked the calendar: We counted down the days until the big event. When I taught younger students, I put clipart or stickers on the calendar to represent the event."

The Daily Routine. Posting a daily routine provides security. Students know where they are in the plan. The daily routine may vary and may even contain novel and unexpected elements.

Lesson Plan. To prepare students for a lesson, some teachers email, post on the class webpage, or simply display on the Smart Board the lesson plan or a visual lesson map. An important element of the lesson plan or map is the time frame; students feel more secure if they know approximately at what time they will be doing what. We have discussed how brain breaks create a brain-friendly classroom. The lesson map includes the scheduled brain breaks, perhaps indicating there will be a new Silly Sport at 10:00 a.m. Some teachers provide predictability by having scheduled brain breaks each day, say at 10:00 a.m. and 2:00 p.m.

At Capitol Elementary School in Baton Rouge, Louisiana, there is schoolwide implementation of SWBAT (Students Will Be Able To...). At the onset of each lesson, students chorally read the SWBAT. Teachers check for understanding, making sure students know what they will be learning, and why it is important.

Checking for Understanding. Whichever way we communicate our expectations, we will be more successful in creating a predictable classroom if we check for understanding among students and allow for their questions. One of my favorite ways to create engagement while checking for understanding is to have students explain to a partner the expectations. While they are talking, I listen in to see how well they understand, offering clarification if the understanding is not complete.

Bell Work. As students enter class, there is a posted problem to solve, reading assignment, or writing topic. Not only does this create a predictable beginning of class, it communicates a set of expectations: We come to class to learn.

Sets and Closures. Classic elements of lesson design are sets and closures. To get students set for what they are about to learn, we might share what is to be learned next, why it is important, and how it will be learned. The "how" makes the lesson a predictable sequence. Students feel more secure while in a lesson if they know what is coming next and how much more there is to come in the lesson. Closure defines the end of a section of a lesson or sub-objective, often with students expressing in some way what they have learned in that segment, and how they will use it. By obtaining closure on a part of a lesson before tackling the next part, students approach the new learning with a cleared working memory and can more fully focus on the new segment of the lesson.

Triggering. Triggering creates a mini-moment of predictability. A trigger lets students know they will do something at a signal, like pulling the trigger of a starting gun at the beginning of a race. For example, the teacher may say *"When I say 'Go,' you will all stand up. What you are going to do is...."* The word *"Go,"* is the trigger that starts the action. The advantage of using triggering is that students wait to hear all of the instructions before beginning the action. For example, if the

teacher had said, *"You will stand up and then you will...."* some students, but not all, will begin to stand up before the instructions are finished, making it difficult for other students to focus on the instructions, creating a fuzzy class tone. A trigger creates a predictable classroom; we know just when to do what.

Procedures and Routines
Kindergarten

"As a K teacher, routines and procedures are the basis of everything else I do. I even model for my students MANY times before they do them on their own. Without routines and procedures, I could not teach my little ones! Here are some ideas that I use daily...

"**The Quiet Signal.** I have the steps posted in my room. We go over each individual step. Even this late in the year, if they are not engaged, I use this to get their attention and get them back on track. I also make sure they are following every step, every time. If you don't do this, they get sloppy and then you've lost them!

"**Clean-Up Song.** We sing a little song for our clean-up time. This gets them motivated and thinking about cleaning. They know that when the song is done, they should be cleaned up and that we then meet on the carpet. This works wonders. Without the routine of the song...they never seem to get motivated to get in gear.

"**Lining Up, Walking.** We practice the procedure for lining up and for walking in the hall as well. I have the expectation that my K students will walk quietly in the hall with their hands to themselves. If we are not doing that properly, we simply go back to the classroom and start over until we get it right. Once they learn the routine, then you have to keep your expectations high for them to keep up the routine.

"**Glue Sticks.** We even have procedures in my room for using our glue sticks. I model, model, model at the beginning of the year and then I hold them to that expectation for the rest of the year."

—*Lisa McCroskey*
Kindergarten, Price Elementary School
Republic, MO

Luck Has Little to Do With It!

"Every time I would hand out a test, quiz, or any formal assessment, I would say this phrase: "Good luck, but, between you and me, luck has little to do with it." I found that my students looked forward to my saying it. Eventually, and without prompting, I would say the first part and they would complete the last part. I wanted to drill into their minds that effort and practice were much more useful strategies for learning, than luck. I think the unexpected side effect of repeating the phrase before a test helped calm them from any anxiety."

—*Elia Chesnoff*
9th–12th Grade Teacher
Sarasota Military Academy
Sarasota, FL

Tests. Tests create anxiety. Some of this anxiety can be reduced if students know exactly when tests will occur, the content to be covered, the format of the test, and how much the test will count toward their grade. Many schools now use online grade reporting systems that allow parents and students to view grades on assignments and tests on a daily basis. Parents and students don't need to guess how they are doing in class, or what grade they have received on an assignment, quiz, or test.

Making Classroom Events Predictable

Classroom and school events like assemblies, school plays, and charity drives, can be added to the monthly or weekly class calendar. Knowing ahead of time about upcoming events adds predictability as well as something for students to look forward to.

Class Visitors. Melissa Wincel prepared her class for visitors, modeling a proactive approach. The visit was placed on the monthly calendar, and students prepared for the visit:

> When I had a visitor coming, I tried to get a picture of the visitor for my students and then I wrote a little biography. I worked that into my lesson as a PowerPoint about him or her. I included tidbits of what he or she would present to build suspense and excitement. Sometimes, we wrote a friendly letter to the visitor and that person wrote back to the class prior to the visit.

Fire Drill. An unexpected fire drill creates anxiety. If permitted, adding the fire drill to the daily calendar reduces anxiety. Alternatively, to reduce anxiety while making the drill realistic and retaining the element of surprise, if permitted, you can announce in advance there will be a drill this week, without stating the day or time.

Field Trips. Many teachers create checklists or short-answer questions for students to mark or answer while on the field trip. Going over the worksheet prior to the tour provides predictability. Melissa, always proactive, prepared her students for field trips by taking them on a virtual tour.

Making Management Predictable

Procedures and routines are the royal road to a predictable classroom. The details of how to establish predictable procedures, routines, agreements, expectations, and rules have been presented in detail in the book, *Win-Win Discipline*.[37] With practiced procedures and routines in place, students know just how to perform, reducing anxiety as well as creating a more efficient classroom.

Procedures. A procedure is a series of steps taken to accomplish an end. For example, as students enter class, they move their name card on the role card chart from "absent" to "present." This not only saves time in taking role; it creates a predictable sequence for students as they enter class. Procedures can be established to create predictable sequences for lining up, coming in from lunch, requesting a bathroom break, and so on.

Routines. Routines are a sequence of procedures. For example, a morning routine might include: (1) move your role card to present, (2) hang up your jacket or coat, (3) go quietly to your desk, (4) place all books except your notebook in the desk or seat rack, (5) open the notebook to the bell work section, (6) write at the top of a clean page, the date and the bell work problem, (7) solve the bell work problem. Routines are predictable sequences of procedures that create security—students know just what to do.

Routines can vary in length. A morning routine may take only a few minutes. In contrast, predictability can be created by a week-long routine, as illustrated by Ryan Lacson, a high school science teacher, in Republic, Missouri:

> In Bio II, everything leading up to the exams are routine. Since exams are the most stressful part of the unit, I try to keep the days leading up to exams the same. The week of exams almost always looks like this:

> ▶ **Tuesday and Wednesday:** Work on study guides via RoundTable Consensus (last days to come in and retake quizzes before/after school)

> ▶ **Thursday:** Go over study guide answers via Three Stray (study sessions before and after school)

> ▶ **Friday:** Exam
> We also begin every class with "Tonework" which reviews the material we just covered. I guess you could say that Bio II is an exercise in routines.

Rochelle Shumaker, a middle school mathematics teacher in Republic, Missouri, provides an excellent example of a middle school routine. Her students live in a predictable world:

> Every day on my whiteboard I display: What, How, and Why. For each of those titles, I write down what we are doing, how we are going to do it, and why we are doing it. I try to have a real-life example each day, and this year I have started writing jobs that would use it.

> When class starts, I begin with roll, during which I ask teams if they have someone missing. If so, depending on the day of the week, the teammates know which teammate is responsible for gathering the homework, writing the absent student's name on it, and putting it in the tray for them. This has helped so much this year with kids getting work and turning it in.

> After roll, I start with announcements and then go into explaining what we are doing, how we are doing it, and why we are doing it, as well as discussing real-life examples.

> Once all of that has been done, I go into the lesson, usually taking notes. I provide a guided notes sheet that I have broken up into independent work, partner work, and teamwork. One structure I use a lot is Team-Pair-Solo. That one works well with guided notes and is easy to implement. I do use other structures within my notes.

A Predictable Entrance
Music

"Music is a very effective way to create specific environments for learning. I often have music playing as students enter the room in the older grades. This may be current popular music, classical, jazz, etc. The idea is to engage the older students in an immediate brain process of listening and thinking as they enter the room and begin to write the daily objectives in their planner."

—*Tricia Zinecker*
Music Teacher
Republic Middle School
Republic, MO

After notes, roughly 10–15 minutes, we do guided practice. I do different structures here and sometimes I do two. If I feel the kids are ready, we do an independent activity, which is roughly a small number of problems usually ten or less. If I have several team questions, we stop and do another guided practice activity, I try to have three or four ready to go.

Once the guided practice or independent practice is done, I implement closure most days. I need to pat myself on the back for this because it DOES make a difference with the kids in what they learn and retain.

Notebooks. Spending time with students to create their tabbed notebook has big payoffs, not just for efficient management but also for creating predictability. Elia Chesnoff describes it:

Having an organized notebook helped to provide predictability. Every student was expected to have a notebook and every notebook was to look exactly the same. Each notebook had the same tabbed sections and every time they took notes, it went into a particular section.

Making Discipline Policy Predictable

Knowing what will happen to me if I do X or Y is at the heart of living in a predictable classroom. Clear communication of discipline consequences prior to any infraction makes it far less likely that discipline consequence will have to be used.

Just Consequences. Details of establishing just consequences for irresponsible behaviors are detailed in the book, *Win-Win Discipline*.[38] Just consequences have three components: (1) Appropriate (linked and commensurate to the misbehavior), (2) Clear, and (3) Preestablished. Having clear, preestablished consequences creates a predictable classroom environment. When consequences are not clear and pre-established, some students will misbehave just to test consequences.

Types of Consequences. When to use each of four types of consequences is also detailed in *Win-Win Discipline*. The four types of consequences are: (1) Teaching responsible thinking, (2) Apology, (3) Restitution, and (4) Lost Activity, Access, or Interaction. Preestablishing with students when each type of consequence will be demanded creates predictability.

Ways to Communicate Upcoming Events

In interviewing teachers and principals to find how expectations about upcoming events are communicated, I am impressed with their range of methods. Educators have found many clever ways of making available to students their monthly and weekly calendars, their daily routines and lesson plans, and their management and discipline approaches. See Tip Box on the next page.

Principal Carol Lohkamp shares:

One of the things that helps primary students is a posted visual schedule of the day. I have seen teachers use a clothespin arrow to indicate what is happening now, and then move it to show what is coming up next. Some teachers use a star to mark where the schedule will change for a special event (e.g., special assembly instead of writing workshop).

Two-Way Communication

Having a student question time offers students the opportunity to clarify goals and procedures, increasing understanding and compliance. To the extent possible, allow student input into creating goals and procedures. Students are far more likely to understand and comply with something they have helped create. Two-way communication about class expectations creates ownership among students and makes a student's world more predictable. We can ask students to evaluate our lessons. Did the lesson go as they expected, or were there some curve balls along the way?

of novelty. One way to make variety predictable is to adjust our daily or weekly calendar when routines are to be changed. It is possible also, to schedule novelty. This is not as much of an oxymoron as it sounds. For example, we might say that every day at 2:00 p.m. (for self-contained classes) or every Wednesday at the end of class (for secondary classes), we will play a novel Silly Sport or Goofy Game.

Kagan Structures. Structures offer a unique way to solve the dilemma of balancing predictability and novelty. Kagan Structures are step-by-step predictable instructional strategies. But within those predictable sequences, there is plenty of novelty. The students never know who may be called upon, the content of the question, what a teammate may say, and even which structure the teacher might use next. There are numerous books on structures including cooperative learning structures, multiple intelligences structures, and structures for specific academic content areas and grade levels.[39]

Balancing Predictability and Novelty

A brain-friendly classroom has a good balance of predictability and novelty. Think of a balance scale. If we are too heavy on predictability and forget to include novelty, the class will be monotonous and students will become bored. If we are too heavy on novelty and forget the need for predictability, the class will be chaotic and students will become anxious. See Box: Balancing Novelty and Predictability.

Predictable Novelty. One solution is to create predictable novelty. That is, announce that there will be a surprise at 11:30 a.m. Students needing a predictable world will have their need met, yet students can all benefit from the positive effects

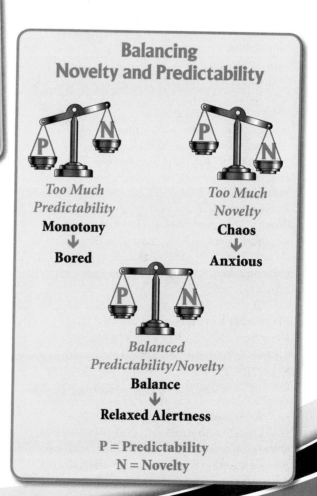

Balancing Novelty and Predictability

Too Much Predictability
Monotony
↓
Bored

Too Much Novelty
Chaos
↓
Anxious

Balanced Predictability/Novelty
Balance
↓
Relaxed Alertness

P = Predictability
N = Novelty

Learning Centers. Learning centers offer the opportunity to embed novelty into a predictable sequence. When learning centers are set up, students rotate through the centers at a predictable time and in a predictable sequence. Having center work become part of the weekly routine adds an additional layer of predictability. As Rob Jutras, a Kagan trainer, explains, when he was a classroom teacher, he always included **Fan-N-Pick** as one of his centers, to add predictability:

> Each day, in my class, there was Center Time where students would rotate throughout the week to different centers meeting different objectives. One center was always Fan-N-Pick. There was a set of cards at the table with a set of questions. The cards were always there; there was always a set of questions; the objective is what changed. Students enjoyed the predictability. They relied on it.

Fan-N-Pick is a student run, content-free structure. Once students have learned the simple rules of the game, the teacher needs only to supply the questions. Publications describe the game in detail and there is an optional **Fan-N-Pick** management mat to make the structure more game-like.[40] Like all Kagan Structures, **Fan-N-Pick** combines both predictability and novelty. The structure is a predictable set of steps so students always know what they are to do next, but the content of the questions and the interaction of students over the questions provides novelty.

Many other Kagan resources are ideal for learning centers. Each has the advantage of offering novelty within a predictable sequence of steps. **Spin-N-Think** (for higher-level thinking questions) and **Spin-N-Review** (for questions that have a correct answer) are simple student-run games ideal for learning centers.[41] The Q-Dice and Q-Spinners are manipulatives used at learning centers. The question manipulatives provide question prompts to facilitate students generating and answering their own questions about the content.[42]

Novelty within Predictability

Teachers have found clever ways to reap the benefits of both predictability and novelty. For example, Elia Chesnoff created novelty within predictability in two ways:

> Every time I would begin a new mini-lesson I would have the title page on a PowerPoint slide, include the same phrase. For example, if I were teaching a mini-lesson on sonnets, the title page would say, "Understanding Sonnets is of the Utmost Importance." Or if I would teach a mini-lesson on writing an introduction paragraph, the first slide would say, "The Ability to Write an Introduction Paragraph is of the Utmost Importance." The students would quickly catch on that I obviously thought everything I did was of the utmost importance. They began to look forward to seeing the phrase and I enjoyed the irony and feigning complaints that "not everything could be of the utmost importance." I could then create novelty by not including the phrase on the title page of a specific mini-lesson. I would then have the phrase appear in large letters on the second slide of the PowerPoint. You can imagine the effect on students of playing with class expectations.

> I kept a cymbal in my classroom and I used it as a conditioning tool. I started by telling them, "I'm going to hit the cymbal now because the next piece of information is a guaranteed test question." I would hit the cymbal and then tell them the information. Hitting the cymbal could then be used to accentuate a strong point I was trying to make. The predictability came from having a cymbal in the classroom and knowing what it meant, and yet the novelty came because they never knew when I would hit it.

Tool 3
Allow Play

The focus of Principle 6: Stimuli, is to include in our teaching the kinds of stimuli brains seek. Play is a basic need rooted in a primal emotional system. Brains seek play!

Animals Seek Play

Jaak Panksepp, a prominent neuroscientist, together with his coworkers have painstakingly documented the amount of play among mice under different conditions. If animals are deprived of play, when given the opportunity, they make up for lost time, playing at rates five times the animals that had not been deprived. Panksepp concludes,

> …play is a primary emotional function of the mammalian brain [that] was not recognized until recently, but now the existence of such brain systems is a certainty…. The impulse for play is created not from past experiences, but from the spontaneous neural urges within the brain.[43]

That play is a need is revealed by successive attempts by animals to initiate play, in the following case, across species:

> M'Bili, a young mongoose rebuffed by her mongoose playmates, ran over to a large lizard, hopping and uttering play calls, and began tossing dead leaves about. When this produced no reaction, M'Bili danced around the lizard, tapping it and pretending to nibble at the lizard's back, forefoot, and face. The lizard closed its eyes and did not respond, and M'Bili gave up.[44]

Neurotransmitters and Neuronal Tracks Govern Play. Neuroscience research provides additional support for the conclusion that play springs from a primal emotional system. Amount of play can be increased or decreased by injection of specific neurotransmitters into specific parts of the brain. For example, play is not simply part of the exploratory system: stimulants like amphetamines increase exploratory activities but very radically reduce play behaviors.[45]

As might be expected, play among mice is reduced by the odor of a cat. This effect is so strong that even when the odor is completely removed, play is reduced up to a week.[46] A very low dose of morphine increases play behavior dramatically, and can even overcome the inhibiting effect of cat smell. Clearly, play is under the influence of brain neuropeptides. Specific somatosensory projection systems of the brain mediate play; damage to those areas reduces play behavior, but not other functions such as food seeking.[47]

> ### Tip
> Use Play as a reward:
> "If everyone scores 80 or above on the quiz, we will play a new Silly Sport."

Play as a Reward. Given that play is a primary neural track, Jaak Panksepp, proposes classroom teachers use play as a reward:

> The benefits, for both classroom discipline and educational progress, might be enhanced if the availability of roughhousing was used to systematically reward scholarly achievement. But this would require us to begin viewing this ancient evolutionary brain function as a potentially desirable activity, rather than a disruptive force whose energies need to be suppressed or dissipated on the playground after the earnest business of education has been completed….
>
> It is worth considering whether it might be possible to develop maneuvers to reduce disruptive play

impulses in the classroom, while utilizing opportunities to release those impulses as a reward for scholarly achievement.[48]

Why Are We Hardwired for Play?

If purposelessness is one of the defining characteristics of play, why then has it survived in the gene pool? Why is it a need? It must have an important advantage because sometimes those that play, pay the ultimate price! Mountain goats bound playfully along rock faces thousands of feet high and sometimes fall to their death.[49] "In a study of seal pups, among the twenty-six that were killed by predators, twenty-two were killed while playing out of the protective range of their parents."[50] Hungry animals sometimes forego food for the opportunity to play. Play takes time and energy away from survival-related activities, yet bears that play the most, survive the longest![51] The answer to this puzzle is that play develops the brain. It allows the opportunity to learn how the physical and social world works. It allows us to try on new responses, making us more adaptive and better able to survive.

A biologist studying river otters documented how play allows testing new behaviors. First, the biologist rewarded the otters with food for swimming through a hoop. After having learned that reward contingency, the otters began playing with the situation, seeking feedback for each new variation they tried:

> …the animals started introducing their own twists to the task. They swam through the hoop backward and waited to see if they got a reward. They swam through and then turned around and swam back through the other way. They swam halfway through and stopped. After each variation, they waited expectantly to see if this version of the task would earn a reward or not.[52]

We could not ask for a clearer example of how play is a form of experimentation that results in cognitive development and a better understanding of one's environment! This better understanding broadens our repertoire, preparing us for a future in which we cope better, and make smarter decisions. As we saw when we examined the impact of social interaction, animals that play together develop bigger brains.[53]

Play Fosters Creativity. In directing our company, Kagan Publishing and Professional Development, I am struck by how much play produces superior outcomes. For example, our graphic design team will play with a book cover design or a page layout, tweaking it this way and that, not knowing exactly which design elements will end up in the final version. By allowing themselves the opportunity to play with the elements of design, they end up with a superior book cover or page layout. They don't know from the outset what they will find; they allow themselves a process rather than outcome orientation. At Kagan, we regularly brainstorm possible solutions to a problem. We play with the ideas that emerge, tweaking ideas, combining ideas, bouncing off the ideas to create new ideas. None of us knows what will eventually emerge from playing with the ideas, but the end product is better than any one of us could have come up with on our own.

Play Develops Practical Intelligence. A play orientation allows discovery of alternatives that would not otherwise be discovered. Those who have had experience playing as youth, are more successful later because they are more open to find novel solutions to problems. By playing with things, we develop the ability to conceptualize alternative ways to construct and destruct objects, skills essential to creativity. We also develop our imagination and the ability to imagine how a project if implemented, will turn out. This is

When JPL's management team analyzed the difference between those who were being successful and those who were not, it was youthful play!

ten count

Can your group count to ten? It is harder than it sounds!

1 Players Form Groups
Players form groups of about a dozen.

2 The Count Begins
Any player in the group starts off the count, saying "One." Any player can say "two" at any time. The goal is for the group to count to 10.

3 Tie? Try Again
Any time two players call out a number at the same time, the group must start over. Although this game sounds easy and does not sound like much fun, players are surprised, both by how difficult it is and how much fun it is. Interesting strategies and group dynamics evolve.

Game 124

crazy challenges

Source: Dr. Spencer Kagan • *Silly Sports & Goofy Games*
Kagan Publishing
1 (800) 933-2667
www.KaganOnline.com

demonstrated dramatically by the experience of JPL's management team. JPL is Cal Tech's Jet Propulsion Laboratory, the engineering/research center that has developed major components of every United States space mission. They have dreamed up, built, and operated the robot vehicles that have successfully explored other planets.

In the late 1990s, many of JPL's engineers and scientists were retiring and JPL found that even though they hired graduates with the highest grades from the top engineering schools like MIT, Stanford, and Cal Tech, many of the new hires were not being successful. They were great at theoretical, mathematical problems, but they could not manage the practical aspects of complex projects. They could not move from theory to practice. When JPL's management team analyzed the difference between those hires who were being successful and those who were not, it was youthful play! They went back and looked at their own retirees, and found the same pattern: those able to problem solve and take projects from theory to practice

> …in their youth had taken apart clocks to see how they worked, or made soapbox derby racers, or built hi-fi stereos, or fixed appliances. The young engineering school graduates who had also done these things, who had played with their hands, were adept at the kinds of problem solving that management sought. Those who hadn't, generally were not. From that point on, JPL made questions about applicants' youthful projects and play a standard part of job interviews.[54]

Challenge Games Develop Practical Intelligence. The category of Silly Sports and Goofy Games most aligned with the development of intelligence are the challenge games. Participants are presented a problem to solve. In **Pretzler-Unpretzler**, they are tied in pretzel shapes for an "unpretzler" to untangle. In **All-On-The-Ball**, participants work against the clock to as quickly as possible get everyone "on the ball." **Ten Count** is a very simple but effective challenge game. The class is challenged to count to ten, with a different person calling out each number. The catch: If two people say the same number at the same time, the class has

to start over. Once the class has devised one of the clever ways to solve this challenge, the difficulty is increased: They must do it again, but this time with eyes closed. See Blackline: Ten Count, p. 6.29.

Tool 4

Furnish Effective Feedback

The neurons in the brain not only send signals out, but also they receive feedback in. For example, neurons constantly receive feedback about how well new sensory input they send corresponds to prior experience.[55] A mismatch between new input and prior experience is a signal to the brain to go into action to reconcile the discrepancy.

Our brains seek not only internal feedback; they constantly seek feedback from the external world. Does what we do make a difference? And if so, what kind of difference? Does an action produce positive, negative, or no feedback? Receiving no feedback or discovering that what we do does not make a difference, can be more devastating than receiving even negative feedback.

If what we do does not make a difference, we stop doing it. The search for feedback is biologically rooted in our need to be an effective organism, to make a difference, to satisfy our needs, to avoid aversive stimuli, to survive. A brain-friendly classroom is feedback rich.

Facts about Feedback
▸ In the largest comparison of meta-analyses ever conducted, involving 800 meta-analyses and 100 factors enhancing educational outcomes, feedback is among the top ten factors influencing student outcomes.[56]
▸ Feedback (giving and getting feedback) is one of the variables that most distinguishes teachers who pass national board certification as "accomplished," from teachers who do not pass.[57]

- Feedback is more effective when it focuses on correct rather than incorrect responses, and when goals are specific, challenging, and not too complex.[58]
- Almost all students like to be praised by the teacher for success, but twice as many prefer quiet, private praise to loud, public praise. Only 10% prefer no praise.[59]
- Students from collectivist cultures (Confucian-based Asian, South Pacific, American Indian) prefer indirect feedback (mentioning to another student or parent how well the student is doing—within earshot of the student) and group-level feedback (complimenting the student's group rather than the student as an individual); students from individualistic cultures (USA) prefer and seek more direct, individual feedback.[60]
- Students differ in how accepting they are of feedback: Students accept, modify, or reject feedback.[61]
- Praise, rewards, and punishment produce little effect compared to formative feedback that focuses students on how to accomplish a task.[62]
- Multifaceted feedback (marking spelling, grammar, paragraph structure, and…) is less effective than feedback focused on one objective.[63]
- Verbal praise does not erode intrinsic motivation.[64]
- Feedback increases effort to the extent it makes the goal clear and obtainable, and when it produces buy-in to the importance of the learning.[65]
- Feedback about task (right or wrong); feedback about process (it would help to use a certain strategy); and feedback about self-evaluation (you can check your answer by…) are all far more effective than personal feedback (you are a good student).[66]
- Feedback that is evaluative without specifying the grounds for the evaluation leads to poor performance.[67]
- Older students often interpret praise after success as indicating the teacher believes they have low ability.[68]
- Feedback that reinforces effort rather than ability produces more learning and more enjoyment of learning.[69]
- Immediate feedback is more effective than delayed feedback for error correction of relatively easy, right-wrong performance; delayed feedback is more effective for difficult and process-oriented performance.[70]
- Approximately 90% of teacher questions are right-wrong informational questions, and most feedback is about the correctness of students' answers rather than the quality of their thinking.[71]

Not All Feedback Helps

Contrary to common belief, not all feedback is helpful to students. In a major review of the effects of feedback, researchers analyzed 131 carefully selected, tightly controlled studies of the effect of feedback and found over one-third of the studies showed negative effects![72] It is not just negative feedback that is detrimental. Positive feedback that is non-contingent reduces motivation and is detrimental to subsequent performance. For example, telling students *"good job"* regardless of the level of performance reduces motivation: *"If I get the same feedback regardless of how hard I try, why try?"*

Dimensions of Feedback

Our job as educators is to create learning. We are responsible for fostering all sorts of learning—acquisition of a daunting array of knowledge and skills including thinking skills, teamwork skills, social skills, and character development. We engage and develop the multiple intelligences and foster the acquisition of emotional intelligence. Feedback is one of the most powerful tools we have as we tackle these momentous tasks. Feedback, given properly, fosters learning.

An overview of feedback in the classroom reveals an incredible array of ways we can and do give feedback. The feedback-rich classroom includes feedback on different types of performance; given at different times; by different people; to different individuals and groups; and in different forms.

Dimensions of Feedback

On What?	Tests, Quizzes, Presentations, Projects, Worksheets, Individual Assignments, Homework, Oral Responses During Q&A, Computer Learning Program, Class Participation, Social Skills, Character Virtues, Thinking
When?	Formative-Summative; Spontaneous-Scheduled; Timely-Delayed; Periodic: Daily, Weekly, Unit Completion, Benchmark Period, Progress Report, Final Grade
By Whom?	Teacher, Class, Teammates, Partner, Principal, Parent, Testing Company, Self
To Whom?	Self, Individual, Pair, Team, Class, Teacher
In What Form?	Grades; Improvement Scoring, Rubrics; Written Comments; Notes; Oral Comments; Oral Questions; Video-, Audio-, and Computer-Assisted Instructional Feedback; In-Class Conferences; Parent Conferences; Comments in Portfolios; Peer Responses within Learning Structures; Nonverbal; Announcements; Celebrations; Praise, Stickers, Stamps

The Power of Feedback

Feedback controls the behavior of rats in the same exact way as it controls the behavior of university professors! More amazing: It allows brains to control computers with no wires attached!

Feedback Controls a Rat. The power of feedback cannot be underestimated. To a large extent, it controls our behavior. I had powerful, firsthand experiences of the power of feedback as a graduate student at UCLA, first with how feedback controls a rat and then how it controls a professor!

As part of our training to become clinical psychologists, we took courses in learning. In one lab, we were assigned to control the behavior of a rat by operant conditioning. The task was to condition a naive rat to press a bar for food, and to do it in as little time as possible. A hungry rat was placed in the middle of a cage he had never been in. The cage was designed to deliver a food pellet whenever the rat depressed a bar located on one side of the cage. When the bar was pressed, food was delivered through a shoot located on a different side of the cage. We each had a clicker that we could press to deliver a food pellet to our rat. If we were successful in training our rat, the hungry rat would know how to press the bar for food, press the bar, run over and eat the delivered food, and then run back to press the bar for more food—all on his own.

Within 10 to 15 minutes, most of us had trained our rats so they were pressing the bar and getting their food. How? Operant conditioning. That is, at first, every time our rat turned even slightly toward the bar, we clicked our clicker to reinforce that behavior. The rat would run over and get his food. When the reinforced behavior (turning toward the bar) occurred again, we delivered another food pellet. After a bit, for us to click our clicker to deliver food, it was not enough for the rat to turn toward the bar, the rat had to take a step or two toward the bar. After we reinforced this new behavior several times, we upped the ante. To get reinforcement, the rat had to walk all the way up to the bar. Next, we would reinforce the rat only if he put a paw on the bar. Finally, the rat had to put enough weight on the bar to press it. At that point, our job was done. The rat pressing the bar delivered the reinforcement, so without our help, the rats would press the bar, run to get food, and then go back to press the bar again. They "got it."

In technical terms, we had "shaped" the behavior of the rat using positive reinforcement. In nontechnical terms: Feedback controls behavior. We were able to shape the rat's behavior by giving and withholding positive feedback. See Table: Dimensions of Feedback.

Arms and Feet Constrained

Feedback Controls a Professor! After experiencing the power of operant conditioning on a rat, a number of us graduate students had a devilish idea. Would the same principle work on our professor? We conspired to try it out during his next lecture. Our plan: Without letting our professor know what we were doing, whenever our professor moved to his right, we would sit up a bit more in our chairs, lean forward a bit more, and look just a tad more interested. If he failed to move or moved to his left, we would look a bit less interested in his lecture. It worked! By the end of the 90-minute lecture, we had our professor delivering his lecture standing all the way to his right in the front corner of the room! He was so passionately involved in his lecture, he didn't even notice!

(Note: Although we performed this informal experiment as a prank in 1969, 10 years later, the impact of student interest on teacher performance was documented in a true experiment.[73])

The Clapping Game. What we did with our rats and our professor is very much like what teammates do in the clapping game.[74] To play the clapping game, one teammate steps out of the room while his or her teammates hide something. When the object is hidden, the seeker reenters the room. Teammates clap higher and louder when the seeker approaches the object and clap lower and softer when the seeker moves from the object. Teammates shape the behavior of the seeker by the feedback they give. See Blackline: Clapping Game, p. 6.34.

Feedback Controls Brains! Some of the most amazing work in brain science is based on the power of feedback. Given appropriate feedback, people can learn to control computer cursors and prosthetic arms just by thinking![75] Using a wide range of technologies to capture brain transmissions, researchers have demonstrated that animals and humans can use feedback to change their brain transmissions in ways that control mechanical devices called brain-controlled interfaces (BCIs).

Some methods record brain activity using noninvasive EEG recordings from the surface of the scalp. Unfortunately, these devises pick up a great deal of noise because the cortex is 2–3 centimeters below the scalp surface and cortex neurons are aligned parallel to the surface of the

scalp—they are designed to send signals to each other, not upward toward EEG recorders.

Various, more invasive technologies have been developed including some recording devices that rest on the surface of the cortex and some that are placed deep within the brain to record the output of single neurons. Using feedback from these more invasive devices, animals and humans quickly learn to perform various actions via prosthetics by just thinking! For example, monkeys had microelectrode arrays placed in their primary motor cortices and then had their arms constrained and a prosthetic arm placed at their shoulder (see graphic). The prosthetic arm and its gripper hand were controlled by the signals from the monkey's motor cortex. After only a brief time, monkeys were able to feed themselves grapes and marshmallows by opening and closing the gripper, navigating the arm smoothly, and making subtle adjustments—much as if it were a real arm and hand! On some tasks, the monkeys achieved 98% accuracy! The researchers conclude:

> This demonstration of multi-degree-of-freedom embodied prosthetic control paves the way towards the development of dexterous prosthetic devices that could ultimately achieve arm and hand function at a near-natural level.[76]

In different Brain Computer Interface (BCI) approaches, paralyzed humans, using only the electrical outputs from their brain, have been able to feed themselves and perform various motor tasks including controlling computer cursors, and communicating.

clapping game

Seekers find helping hands, a hidden object, and a hug! What more could a Seeker seek?

1 Form Groups
Groups of four to six are formed.

2 Seekers Sent Out
One person from each group (the Seeker) is sent out of the room.

3 Helpers
The others in each group (the Helpers) decide on an object that the Seeker can easily find and touch.

4 Seekers Return
When all groups have decided on an object (a different object for each group), Seekers are invited back. Their goal is to find the hidden object.

5 Helping Hands
The Helpers give the Seeker a "helping hand" by clapping. The Helpers may be seated, or may follow the Seeker around the room. They clap low, slow, and quietly if the person is "cold." (far from the object). They clap higher, faster, and louder as the Seeker gets warmer (approaches the object).

6 Celebration
When the Seeker finds the object, the Helpers all give him/her a hug or a pat on the back.

7 New Seekers
A new Seeker is selected for each round.

Source: Dr. Spencer Kagan • *Silly Sports & Goofy Games*
Kagan Publishing
1 (800) 933-2667
www.KaganOnline.com

Game 51

happy helpers

BCI research illustrates the power of feedback. In many of the BCI paradigms, animals and humans use feedback from movement of a cursor on a computer screen or movement of a prosthetic arm to learn to control their brain. They watch what the prosthetic arm or computer cursor does in response to their brain waves, and then learn to change their brain waves to fire in ways that make the arm or cursor function the way they want! Feedback allows us to control our brains.

Imagining Makes It So! Not all BCI is feedback based. An exciting BCI approach takes advantage of the finding that imagining a motor movement stimulates many of the same neurons that are activated during actual movement. Thus, researchers have been able to implant electrodes that capture intention to move, and send that information to prosthetic devices that carry out the intended action. This approach depends on first recording the pattern of electrical signals that are generated when subjects are told to imagine carrying out an action. Then those patterns are programmed to move a cursor or prosthetic in the way imagined. Thus, the paralyzed person has but to think of carrying out an action and the action is performed![77]

> ### Tip
> Have students repeatedly imagine performing a skill you would like them to practice.

Imagination Is Practice. Because imagining an action fires many of the same neurons as does actually carrying out the action, imagination is practice. I had a firsthand experience of the power of imagination to improve performance when I was in Junior High School. It was in my first typing class when we had our first weekly typing test. Most of us scored between 15 and 20 words a minute. One boy in the class scored 55! I asked him if he was practicing at home. He said he did not own a typewriter, but that whenever he had a chance he closed his eyes and pretended he was typing. Because imagining doing something exercises many of the same neural tracks as actually carrying out that action, he was practicing typing frequently during the day!

Having overviewed some of what we know about feedback and having examined the power of feedback to transform behavior, let's examine ways to apply what we know about feedback to make our teaching more brain friendly and more effective.

Giving Effective Feedback

Effective feedback matches the form of the feedback to our intended outcome. It is immediate, contingent, and frequent. Teacher and peer comments are more powerful than grades. Feedback takes many forms.

Match Feedback Form to Intended Outcome. When we consider giving feedback, the first question should be the function of the feedback. What do we hope to accomplish with the feedback? For example, if our goal is to evaluate or rank students, a grade will probably accomplish the task. As we will see, however, compared to other forms of feedback, grades alone do not promote learning. If our goal is to motivate students and direct their attention toward their learning process or specific aspects of their product, in-class conferences are more appropriate. If our goal is to direct students to different dimensions of their projects, a rubric is the feedback form of choice. If we want to shape our class through feedback, spontaneous positive, public feedback to a well-performing individual or group is powerful. Teacher competence includes knowing a range of feedback options and when to use each. Examining all these options is beyond the scope of this book. We can, however, highlight some dimensions and forms of feedback that are particularly powerful in fostering learning and a sense of personal control in our students. Let's first examine the incredible power of feedback to influence performance.

Immediate Feedback. Neurons that fire together wire together. It is contiguity, neurons firing at the same time, that determines many types of learning. Thousands of research studies prove that immediate feedback is more powerful than delayed feedback if the goal is a learning connection. Immediate feedback means neurons firing in association with the feedback, are firing at almost the same time as the neurons firing in association with the performance. Neurons that fire together wire together, so the feedback is linked to the performance. Too much delay and the neurons don't fire together and so don't wire together.

We don't need research studies to know immediate feedback leads to learning whereas delayed feedback does not. We touch a hot stove, and immediately feel pain. The connection is made, and we have learned not to touch a hot stove. If the pain occurred an hour later, we would not make the connection and no learning would occur.

Delayed Feedback Allows Bad Habits to Persist. It is the lack of immediate feedback that makes it difficult to break many bad habits. If every time someone drank alcohol they immediately felt a severe hangover, they would be less likely to drink. Because the hangover does not occur until the next morning, the hangover is not as powerful in curbing the drinking. Delayed feedback allows the drinking habit to continue. Lack of immediacy of feedback makes dieting difficult. We do not see the weight accumulate immediately after overeating. Many bad habits, like smoking, are difficult to break because in the short term they make us feel good even though we know in the long term they are harmful. The power of feedback is increased tremendously when it is immediate.

Applying the power of immediate feedback to the classroom guides us toward more powerful ways of giving feedback. Let's contrast two ways of giving feedback to students as they practice a new skill: Traditional Worksheet Work v. **RallyCoach.**

Traditional Worksheet Work Provides Delayed Feedback. To practice a skill or review facts, the teacher has demonstrated, worksheet practice is common. Students are given an individual worksheet and are instructed to solve the problems or to fill in the blanks. Students work alone on the worksheet, worksheets are collected and graded, and worksheets are returned to students graded and corrected. With traditional

Tip
Structure practice so students receive immediate feedback.

worksheet work, students receive feedback when the teacher has had time to correct the papers. Feedback is so delayed, students may have forgotten doing the problems, focusing on the grade, not the process of solving the problems. It is summative feedback: The feedback does not serve to improve the process of solving the worksheet problems as the student works on the worksheet.

Kagan Structures Provide Immediate Feedback. The Kagan mastery structures all provide immediate feedback. For example, in **Sage-N-Scribe,** there is one worksheet and one pencil for each pair of students. The Sage tells the Scribe what to do, but the Scribe is to give the Sage feedback through the process. If the sage tells the scribe a wrong step or answer, the Scribe makes a polite correction: *"Let's review the procedure."* With the mastery-oriented Kagan Structures, students receive immediate feedback during and following each problem they do. The focus is not on a grade but on the process of obtaining correct answers. It is formative feedback, allowing students to improve their process as they practice.

See Structures Section
17. Sage-N-Scribe

Contingent Feedback. Noncontingent feedback produces helplessness. If students know that their feedback will be the same no matter what they do, they discover there is no reason to do anything. They lose motivation and fall into helplessness.

Frequent Feedback. Traditional worksheet work and **Sage-N-Scribe** differ in a second very important way: the frequency of feedback. In the traditional format, students receive feedback one

Kagan Structures That Provide Immediate Feedback

Structures	Structure Section
AllWrite Consensus	1
Both Record RallyRobin	2
Flashcard Game	5
Listen Right!	8
PairUp Review	11
Paraphrase Passport	12
Quiz-Quiz-Trade	13
RallyQuiz	14
Sage-N-Scribe	18
SeeOne–DoOne–TeachOne	19
Team-Pair-Solo	24
Traveling Heads Together	27

time, after each worksheet. In **Sage-N-Scribe**, they receive very frequent feedback, at least once after every problem they solve and often multiple times from their Scribe as they solve the problem. Frequent feedback is far more powerful than infrequent feedback.

Frequent Testing. A meta-analysis examined the effect of frequency of testing in 35 research studies.[78] In 83% of the studies, students receiving more frequent testing scored better on the final exam, and in 100% of the studies, frequent testing resulted in more positive student attitudes.

Exam-A-Day. Frank C. Leeming, a psychology professor, took the research on frequency of testing to heart and decided to test his students every class period. As most of us have experienced, infrequent testing in college leads to putting off studying and cramming before tests. This pattern has been called the "procrastination scallop."[79]

Leeming compared his Exam-A-Day procedure to the more traditional four exams per course, in four of his undergraduate courses.[80] The course material and final exams were identical in the four exams per semester and the Exam-A-Day courses. In the Exam-A-Day courses, exams were short so as not to steal too much time from instruction.

In courses in which Exam-A-Day was used, students reported the procedure led to:
▶ More studying
▶ Keeping up better with course material
▶ Greater learning
▶ Greater liking for the course
▶ Better time management in other courses

The students performed significantly better academically when tested every day. In the Exam-A-Day courses, final semester grades were significantly higher and the percentage of D's and F's dropped precipitously. With the traditional four exams per course format, the average percentage of D's and F's was 21%; with Exam-A-Day, it was 2%! Percentage of A's increased from 22% to 43%!

To test long-term retention, a 2-hour retention test (short essay, multiple-choice, and fill-in-the-blank questions) was given 6 weeks after the first four chapters of the course content had been covered. The students in the traditional format had only one test on the content by that time, whereas those in the Exam-A-Day course had thirteen short tests on the content. Those in the Exam-A-Day course performed significantly better.

Tip

Give frequent quizzes to ensure students are keeping up with the material. The quiz can be as simple as one or two problems from homework. Knowing there is likely to be a quiz, students are more likely to review the content.

Even though the daily tests were more brief, giving a test each day did take more time than giving just four tests a semester, but Dr. Leeming reported,

"...it was necessary for me to eliminate some material from my usual lectures the first time the procedure was used in both courses, but the major effect was to reduce redundancy rather than to omit basic material. I believe that, if anything, my lectures are now better and more focused than they were when exams were widely spaced."

Teacher Comments Trump Letter Grades.

After taking a test, students get feedback in the form of a letter grade and/or a comment. In a classic test of the added value of teacher comments, 74 secondary teachers were randomly assigned to give one of three types of feedback to their 2,139 students:[81]

Condition 1: No Comment
Teachers gave Letter Grades Only:
A, B, C, D, or F

Condition 2: Specified Comment:
A: Excellent! Keep it up.
B: Good work. Keep at it.
C: Perhaps try to do still better.
D: Let's bring this up.
F: Let's raise this grade!

Condition 3: Free Comment
Teachers were instructed: *"Write anything that occurs to you in the circumstances. There is not any 'right' or 'wrong' comment for this study. A comment is 'right' for the study if it conforms with your own feelings and practices."*

The results were extremely clear. To test the impact on students of the three types of feedback, the researcher analyzed student scores on their next test. Students who received the free

> **Tip**
> Give personalized, contingent comments rather than just letter grades.

comments performed best, those who received the canned comment scored next best, and those who received only a letter grade scored worst. This pattern of results was highly significant and was consistent for students across school years from grades 7 to 12, across twelve different secondary schools, and held up for high-, middle-, and low-achieving students. The finding is consistent with research showing simply receiving a grade with no comments does not improve subsequent performance.[82] We could not ask for a clearer set of findings.

We can interpret these results in terms of personal control. By responding to students via comments, students had an experience of learned effectiveness: What they did impacted on their teacher. Those who received personalized comments had more of an impact on their teacher than those who received only specified comments. Those who received only a grade, influenced their teacher least.

> **Tip**
> Give individualized, personal attention in some way to each student.

All of us can relate to the power of personalized attention. In workshops, I ask teachers to think of a teacher that gave them some special, personal attention. I then ask them to stand up if they tried harder in that class. Almost every teacher stands up!

Choose Your Audience. While monitoring the class doing a worksheet, a teacher notices two or three students using the wrong procedure. The teacher stops the class and models the correct procedure. For most of the class, this is non-contingent feedback. Most students feel *"I am doing this right and don't need corrective feedback. This feedback has nothing to do with what I am doing."* Thus, the teacher might have been more effective by asking those few students to gather around his desk so he could model the correct procedure. He could go in more depth and better

Improvement Scoring

	Week 1	Week 2	Week 3	Week 4	Week 5
Student 1	8	8	8	8	8
Student 2	2	3	4	5	6

field questions, rather than teaching the whole class while most of the class did not need that instruction. The students selected as audience for the feedback receive contingent feedback and the rest of the class does not receive noncontingent feedback. Choosing our audience for feedback is one way of increasing the amount of contingent feedback.

> ### Tip
> Choose your audience carefully. If possible, give corrective feedback to only those needing it.

Improvement Scoring. One way to ensure that every student receives optimal contingent feedback is to use improvement scoring. Rather than comparing each student to other students in the class, we can compare each student to himself or herself. Is the student improving, regardless of where that student stands in relation to others? If so, the student deserves positive feedback. Comparing students to each other promotes helplessness at both ends of the achievement continuum. The high achiever knows he or she can get a good mark with little effort and the low achiever knows no matter how hard he or she tries, he or she will not match the performance of the high achievers. Improvement scoring maximizes the opportunity for contingent feedback.

Let's examine sample student scores to see why improvement scoring is superior to normative scoring. Let's imagine students take a test each week and can score from 1 to 10 (the numbers could just as well be 0–100 or any other scores). See Table: Improvement Scoring. Looking vertically at each week, Student 1 looks to be doing better than Student 2, and we might be tempted to give that student better feedback.

Looking horizontally at the weeks, Student 1 is not improving at all whereas Student 2 needs recognition for improvement. Improvement scoring and recognition for improvement would be more motivating for both students. Student 1 needs a prod, *"You can do better; I think if you try harder you can improve and bring up your score."* Student 2 needs reinforcement of the remarkable improvement he or she is making, *"You are really putting in more effort each week; keep up the great improvement."*

TV Feedback! Some schools have classroom televisions and some principals use that for announcement time. Melissa Wincel describes live news coverage from the principal that served as positive feedback for her kindergarten students:

> Choosing a student of the week was a way to give students feedback. We chose a new student every week based on our PBS (positive behavior support) expectations; Be Respectful, Be Responsible, Be a Learner, Be Safe. They received a certificate on our live news coverage from the principal, a student of the week pencil, a sticker, and they could choose a reward coupon: lunch with the teacher, sit on the bean bag chair during carpet time, read to the class, or pick the Silly Sports of the day.

> ### Tip
> When possible, focus the attention of students on how their performance compares to their own prior performance, not the performance of others.

Compliment Jar. Melissa's classroom was positive feedback-rich. Her compliment jar served to reinforce positive behaviors:

> I had a compliment jar to help reinforce line behavior, cafeteria behavior, and special class behavior. If another teacher, administrator, or special area teacher gave us an unsolicited positive compliment, I would add 5 marbles to our jar. I would record with tally marks to include math into it. Students would count by 5's and when we got to 50 we would celebrate. One of their favorites was lunch with the teacher outside, picnic style.

Spontaneous Feedback. I recommend to teachers that they always be on the lookout for positive academic performance and positive behaviors. It is almost magic how powerful it is to hold up as an example, behavior we would like to see more often. With regard to positive social behaviors (helping, working quietly, staying on task, asking for help…), I recommend a three-pronged approach: Modeling, Reinforcement, and Practice. For example, as we are monitoring our class, we see a student compliment another student, saying, *"You did a really good job on that!"* At that moment, we do three things:

Modeling: *"Class, I want you to hear what I just heard. Johnny please turn to Pedro and tell him again what you just told him."*

Reinforcement: *"I appreciate hearing that kind of praise. We all need support and it creates a positive tone in our class."*

Practice: *"I want everyone in the class to turn to their shoulder partner and say, 'You did a really good job on that!'"*

Modeling paints a concrete picture in the minds of students as to what the desired behavior is. Reinforcement increases the probability of having more of that behavior. Via mirror neurons, every student has received a bit of reinforcement as they watch a student receive positive feedback for positive behavior. It is vicarious reinforcement. Finally, by having all students turn to someone and practice the desired behavior, we disinhibit that behavior. Having done the behavior once, increases dramatically the probability of repeating it.

Silent Feedback. Nonverbal communication is most of the message in face-to-face interactions. We can't expect to be believed if we tell a student we like them when in fact we don't. If we have a difficult student and we want to communicate caring, we need to find something about that student we like or feel positive about when we communicate with the student.

If, as we walk around and monitor the class, we focus on the positive, if we find things we like, those feelings get communicated. A smile from a teacher goes a mile. Our tone of voice, body language, facial expressions, nods, are all forms of feedback. Students work hard in a class where they feel appreciated.

Feedback to Teacher. In the feedback-rich classroom, feedback is two-way. When we solicit feedback from our students we accomplish two things: (1) We receive information that can improve our teaching; and (2) We empower our students.

If a student offers feedback that we respond to, the student has had an experience of personal control—they have acted in a way that determined their outcomes. They feel better about themselves (*"I make a difference"*) and have changed their environment in some way rather than passively accepting the situation. This inoculates them against helplessness and makes it more likely they will be proactive in the future.

As we receive feedback from students, it allows an additional vehicle for our own self-evaluation. Our perception of what is happening in our classrooms may differ rather dramatically from the perceptions of our students. For example, research revealed that about 70% of teachers claimed they provided detailed feedback often or always, whereas only 45% of students felt so.[83]

There are many ways we can have students provide feedback on the content and process of our lessons. Doing so creates an "our class" feeling; students feel on the same side with the teacher, trying to improve teaching and learning. One simple approach is a "Ticket Out the Door" that students fill out following a lesson. See Blackline: Ticket Out the Door, p. 6.41.

Ticket Out the Door

Directions: Please take a moment to reflect on today's lesson. Respond to the four questions below. Your name is optional. Leave your ticket on the table as you leave class.

1. Something I learned. _____

_____

_____

_____

2. Something that helped me learn. _____

_____

_____

_____

3. Something I could do to learn more. _____

_____

_____

_____

4. Something the teacher could do to help me learn

more. _____

_____

_____

_____

_____ _____
                                    Name

Class Goals Put Students on the Same Side

"We had class goals. For example, when 90% of our class got 100% on the mad minute math addition/subtraction facts, we would celebrate with a Silly Sport. I loved this because students would help each other practice using Flashcard Game as a sponge activity. They were supporting one another rather than in competition."

—Melissa Wincel
Kindergarten
Trafalgar Elementary School
Cape Coral, FL

Another approach to eliciting feedback from students is a "parking lot." The Parking Lot is a place in the room students can post sticky notes. With a Post-A-Note bulletin board with four areas (+, Δ, ?, and !), students are encouraged to post sticky notes with comments, questions, and concerns. See Blackline: Post-A-Note, p. 6.43.

Personal Control Questions. Because a sense of personal control among students is critical for fostering motivation and effort, it is valuable for us to get feedback from our students regarding their sense of personal control and to elicit suggestions. Students might be a bit hesitant to answer in front of the whole class, so a brief anonymous questionnaire like the How Is It Going? Questionnaire is likely to produce more informative answers. See Blackline: How Is It Going?, p. 6.44

Peer Feedback. For many students, feedback from their peers is more important than feedback from their teacher. Most feedback students obtain in

any day in classrooms is from other students, and most of this feedback is incorrect![84] That most feedback comes from peers is not remarkable when we consider that a student in a class of thirty has twenty-nine fellow students but only one teacher.

There are a number of things we can do to make feedback from peers more frequent, more positive, and more accurate.

Class Goals. Class goals set students on the same side so they are likely to encourage each other and give each other positive feedback. When we have a class goal, all students appreciate the progress of any student because the success of one moves all students closer to their shared goal. Teachers who grade on a curve or who recognize only the best students inadvertently, sets students against each other. If there can be only seven A's on a test, I am hoping you don't get an A because that increases the chances that I will. If, in contrast, all our points are summed as progress toward a class goal, I am hoping you will do as well. I will encourage you and give you positive feedback for your success. Your success increases the chances for all of us to obtain the goal.

Feedback Captain. If we have students working on a project in teams, we can assign a role of Feedback Captain. The goal of the Feedback Captain is not to provide all the feedback, but rather to encourage positive feedback from teammates to individuals and to the team as a whole. When we first assign the role of Feedback Captain, we need to introduce the kinds of gambits the Feedback Captain can use to elicit positive feedback. For examples:

▶ *"Let's stop for a moment and evaluate our progress."*
▶ *"That idea helps us; who would like to give Jennifer some positive feedback?"*
▶ *"Let's pause. Who deserves some positive feedback for their contributions?"*

Post-A-Note

Directions: Write your comments in the boxes below. Or, if a Post-A-Note board is in your classroom, use sticky notes to post your notes.

 I Like...

I Wish We Could Change...

 My Questions...

My Comments...

How Is It Going?

Directions: Please help me be a better teacher by filling out the questions below. How is our class going?

What do you enjoy about class? _____

_____

_____

What in class you would like to do more? _____

_____

_____

What in class you would like to do less? _____

_____

_____

What would you like your teacher to do more? _____

_____

_____

What would you like your teacher to do less? _____

_____

_____

What can you do differently to learn more, and enjoy class more? _____

_____

_____

Brain-Friendly Teaching • Dr. Spencer Kagan
Kagan Publishing • 800.933.2667 • www.KaganOnline.com

Generating Feedback Gambits. Students are not born with positive feedback gambits. Feedback gambits are learned. To foster positive feedback, we can begin by providing examples, and then have the class generate additional gambits. For example, we can say,

> *"As you are working, your team will function better if you provide each other frequent positive feedback. For example you might say, 'That idea really opened a new way of thinking.'—or 'Thank you for figuring out how to solve that.' Class, what are some positive feedback phrases you can use?"*

Posting Feedback Gambits. As the class generates feedback gambits, you or a student can record them on the whiteboard or on a flip chart, and leave them posted. A positive feedback poster can be created by the students and permanently posted.

Modeling and Praising Positive Peer Feedback. While students are working in their teams, we can circulate, listening for positive feedback. When we hear positive feedback we can stop the class for a moment and say, *"Class, I want you all to hear what I just heard."* After the student repeats the positive feedback, we can then compliment the student, *"That is very supportive feedback. That is the kind of feedback I like to hear."*

Processing Peer Feedback. Sometime, about half way through a project, you can ask the students to stop and process their progress in giving each other positive feedback.

> *"Class, let's put our projects down for a moment and reflect on how well you have been giving each other positive feedback. What is some of the positive feedback you have heard?"*

Planning Positive Peer Feedback. There are two times that lend themselves to having students plan how they will give positive feedback. At the outset of the project: Before students begin work, we can ask students to take a few minutes and plan how they will give each other positive feedback. Planning is looking forward: How can we do better? Have students make a plan. The second time is midway in the project: Have students stop and reflect on the feedback they have gotten. Reflection is looking back: How well have we done?

Feedback Gambit Chips. Students can be provided with, or can generate, positive feedback Gambit Chips. The chips are either dealt out for students to use during their work together, or can be placed in the center of the table for students to draw from. Gambit Chips are simple phrases or sentence starters.

Sample Positive Feedback Gambit Chips
▶ We should be proud of…
▶ We are making good progress!
▶ Your idea helped because…
▶ The reason I like…

Generic v. Specific Feedback. It is helpful to have students distinguish generic feedback from specific feedback, and encourage specific feedback. Generic feedback is something you can say to any performance. Specific feedback is something you can say only to the specific performance you are responding to. This difference is critical because generic feedback can be insincere, given with little or no thought, and does not focus recipients on the positive aspects of their performance. For example, a comment like *"Great idea!"* can be said of any idea and is not nearly as thoughtful or informative as, *"Your idea helped us focus on…."*

Stickers and Stamps. With her kindergarten students, Melissa Wincel would not only stamp their papers as a form of feedback—she would stamp her students too! *"Sometimes I would even stamp their hands with a 'WOW' or 'Great Job!' They were always flashing their hands."*

Self-Evaluation

One of the most powerful yet under-utilized forms of feedback is self-evaluation. Having students evaluate their own work is having them practice a life-skill. Self-evaluation can be as simple as checking an answer key to grade one's own paper or as complex as repeated meta-cognitive processing in the course of constructing complex knowledge.[85]

At the higher end of the self-evaluation continuum, students create error-detection skills, self-monitoring habits, self-assessment methods, and internal feedback systems.[86] Self-evaluation creates a positive habit of mind. An internalized habit of self-evaluation is what distinguishes those with a drive for excellence from those who approach tasks half-heartily and who are satisfied with mediocre work. Self-evaluation places the locus of evaluation in the most important place —within the person creating the work.

> ### Tip
> Have students choose what to put in their portfolio and to write about why they chose that item. Have them include self-evaluations of their work.

Portfolios. Portfolios are a powerful tool for self-evaluation. Students choose which items to put in their portfolios. Students look back at their own work and write about it. Students take an objective look at their work, writing mini-essays to discuss its strengths and weaknesses. Students meet with their teacher to guide them in the process of self-evaluation. Students are encouraged to include in their portfolio a range of sample work, videos of performances, and pictures of completed projects.

Valedictory Scrapbooks are created by high school seniors at Republic High School, Republic Missouri. It is a culminating statement to and about oneself as they complete their high school career. Some contributions to the scrapbook are required, and others are optional. Students are given 100 prompts from which they select 50.

Sample Required Entries
- ▶ Letter of appreciation to a significant adult
- ▶ Letter to self
- ▶ List of thirty "I Remember" statements
- ▶ An "I Believe…" statement
- ▶ Resume

Sample Optional Prompts
- ▶ Interview with a grandparent
- ▶ Describe a typical day at the lunch table with your "lunch buddies"
- ▶ Description of what you hope to gain from your education
- ▶ Define and defend your idea of success
- ▶ Bucket list—things you want to do before you die
- ▶ Description of the ideals to which you are committed

Rubrics. Self-evaluation rubrics provide students guidelines and a differentiated way to evaluate their own work along a number of dimensions. There are many types of rubrics,[87] but all of them can be used to promote self-evaluation. When first introducing a rubric, it is helpful to explain the rubric to the class by using it to evaluate sample products. After students understand the rubric, to promote self-evaluation, they use it during planning, mid-way through their project, and for a final evaluation of their project. The student and teacher can then compare how they each independently evaluated the project using the same rubric. More advanced students take self-evaluation to the next step by learning how to create their own rubrics for self-evaluation.

> ### Tip
> Provide students with rubrics for self-evaluation, or work with the class so students create their own.

Self-evaluation can be included during or following any performance or any project. Self-evaluation forms can facilitate the process.

The PMI Form. A Plus, Minus, Interesting (PMI) Form encourages students to reflect on the strengths, weaknesses, and other aspects of their work. See Blackline: PMI Form, p. 6.48.

The Self-Evaluation Form. Students can create or the teacher can provide self-evaluation forms to encourage students to reflect on the process they engaged in and develop paths to self-improvement. See Blackline: Project Self-Evaluation Form, p. 6.49.

Tool 5

Catch Them Being Good!

We all crave positive feedback, and so any teacher has the power to shape his class by giving positive attention to those behaviors the teacher would like to promote.

Shaping Our Classes through Positive Feedback

The power of feedback to control behavior has direct implications for us as teachers. We shape our class by the feedback we give. The classroom is a feedback-hungry place. There is only one teacher, but there are about thirty students. If we tried to give a minute of feedback to each student each hour, we would be spending half our time giving students feedback! The only way we can solve this dilemma is to give feedback to the whole class or to teams and to have students give each other feedback as they solve problems or present their work to each other.

Shaping a Noisy Class. Let me share an experience that occurred over 30 years ago when I first began training teachers in cooperative learning. The experience illustrates the power we have to shape the behavior of our classes.

Catch them Being Good
The Listening Signal

The most powerful way to motivate students to consistently give their attention, in my experience, is sincere praise every time students give you their attention. When you notice your students being particularly attentive, stop in the middle of your lesson and compliment them. It helps to build the "we're all in this together" attitude—a powerful and wonderful dynamic in a classroom.

Early in the instructional period, I might say, *"Thanks for helping us get off to a good start, today, I really appreciate it."*

During the lesson I used different gambits: *"Thanks for the great listening, you're making this very easy."*

"Almost everyone is giving me eye contact, thank you very much!"

"Thanks for your attention and cooperation. You're making this fun."

"You really motivate me with the way you listen."

At the end of a period, I might say, *"Great day today! Thanks!"*

I'd look for students using, "the knowing nod" when I was making important points. I would stop and explain what it is and have that student model it. Then I would explain how encouraging it is for teachers when they know their students are "with them." It was really funny. At times, from the front of the room, it looked as if I was teaching a room full of bobble head dolls after I'd make those comments. It'd be hard to keep from smiling.

—*Dan Kuzma*
U.S. History
Indian Hills Regional High School
Oakland, NJ

I was working with the teachers at Chaparral Middle School in Diamond Bar, California. After teaching the faculty cooperative learning methods in a series of workshops, I visited each classroom to help teachers implement cooperative learning.

When I visited one classroom, I saw a teacher struggling to implement the complex **Double Expert Group Jigsaw** structure I had taught. The problem was not with the structure; the

PMI Form
(Plus, Minus, Interesting)

Directions: What are the strengths, the weaknesses, and other interesting features of your work?

+

**Plus
Strengths**

_____

_____

_____

_____

−

**Minus
Weaknesses**

_____

_____

_____

_____

I

**Interesting
Features**

_____

_____

_____

_____

Brain-Friendly Teaching • Dr. Spencer Kagan
Kagan Publishing • 800.933.2667 • www.KaganOnline.com

Project Self-Evaluation Form

Directions: Take some time to look back on your project. Record your reflections on this form.

1. What am I most proud of? Why?

2. What would I change in the final project if I did it again? Why?

3. What were difficult parts of making the project?

4. What parts came easily?

5. How could I have done the project more easily or more efficiently?

6. If I were to put more effort into the project, on which parts would I work harder?

teacher knew the steps and was well prepared. The problem was with management. This was the first time the teacher had students in teams, and she was frustrated by their behavior. The students were enthusiastic. In fact they were too enthusiastic. One team would talk loudly, and the next team would talk even louder to hear themselves. This in turn led other teams to talk even louder yet. Noise escalated.

The teacher was trying to manage the noise level by using the quiet signal. She would raise her hand to get all the students quiet, which they did readily, and then she would plead with them to talk more quietly. It wasn't working. The students would talk quietly for a few minutes, but then noise would again escalate. The teacher was beginning to look like a puppet with her hand pulled up by an invisible string every 5 minutes as she repeatedly tried to quiet her room.

While the students were working, the teacher walked over to me and with some desperation asked what she should do. I said, *"Go over and observe the quietest team for a minute and then give the quiet signal to the class. Once you have full attention of the whole class, compliment the one team on how they are working quietly, not disturbing other teams."* She looked at me with even more desperation on her face, whispering, *"There are no quiet teams!"* I whispered back, *"Lie. Just go over to any team and try it."* Although she was clearly skeptical, she tried it.

When she complimented the one team for using their inner voice (a voice that only their teammates could hear), there was a bit of a strange look on the face of many of the students in the class. This was different. The students remained quieter for a longer time than when she had pleaded with the class to interact quietly. But then noise escalated again. I told the teacher to try it again with a different team. After the third time that hour that she complimented a team for using their inner voice, we had quiet cooperative learning!

What is the take-away from this incident? Catch them being good! In a feedback-hungry environment, anything we pay attention to is reinforcing. By paying attention to the quiet groups, the teacher was communicating that the

> ## Tip
> Catch them being good! Look for, pay attention to, and compliment individuals and teams performing as you would like. We get more of whatever we pay attention to.

way to get positive attention is to work quietly. The other groups, wanting positive attention, began to work quietly.

What happened in that Chaparral classroom was just like what happened to our graduate school professor who wanted his lecture to be well received and so ended up lecturing from the corner of the room. We shaped his behavior by positive feedback, just as the teacher at Chaparral Middle School shaped the behavior of her class by giving positive feedback to groups behaving the way she liked. Positive attention is very powerful reinforcement—especially in a feedback-hungry environment.

Feedback Explains a Mystery

Some educators complain of a mystery: Each year, the same teachers seem to get all the disruptive students while others get angels. That we get more of whatever we pay attention to explains this mystery. One teacher is looking for the positive behavior, and finds it. That teacher's students notice that the way to get attention is to behave positively. The other teacher is on guard against misbehavior. Looking for it, she finds it, and reprimands the misbehaving student or students. The message she inadvertently conveys: In this class, the way to get attention is to misbehave. Over time, there is a lot of responsible behavior in one class and a lot of disruptive behavior in the other. For some students, attention, even negative attention, is better than no attention.

Tool 6

Recommend Biofeedback

Feedback is the path to improvement. Biofeedback is feedback about otherwise unconscious biological functions. Instruments can be hooked up to give participants feedback on EEG, muscle action potentials, skin temperature, skin conductance (sweating), blood flow, blood pressure, heart rate, respiratory rate, CO_2 expelled, or amount of oxygenated and unoxygenated blood in the brain.

Lester the Feedback Mouse

"When I taught first grade, I had a challenging group, so I had a pretend school mouse that lived in our classroom. His name was Lester and Lester was always watching. No one ever saw him, though many of the children claimed to. Every morning, Lester would leave notes on my student's desks or write one to the whole class giving them positive feedback about something: "I was really proud of your awesome job of coaching Joey yesterday" or "I really liked that you held the door for Mrs. Vetter.""

"Students loved coming in to see who Lester left a note for. I would ask the special area teacher, lunch ladies, etc., if anyone did something nice or was exceptionally well behaved so Lester could leave a note. It sure did improve the behavior in my class. It worked like a charm!"

—*Melissa Wincel*
Kindergarten, Trafalgar Elementary
Cape Coral, FL

By responding to biofeedback, participants learn to control many things that otherwise were out of conscious control, including brainwaves, heartbeat, blood pressure, asthma, skin temperature, sweating, stress, anxiety, pain, headaches, joint disorders, incontinence, and even visual acuity.[88] It seems there is little we cannot control if we have feedback. Research shows we can control specific neuronal groups via biofeedback,[89] offering help to epilepsy patients[90] and victims of stroke.[91]

Although these studies are not directly relevant to classroom practice, they do indicate the power of feedback in general and biofeedback specifically. More directly relevant to classroom practice are studies showing the effectiveness of biofeedback for controlling the symptoms of attention deficit disorder and learning disabilities.[92]

Biofeedback and ADHD

Both case studies and experimental studies demonstrate the power of biofeedback to reduce ADHD. See Box: Biofeedback.

Case Studies. There are numerous case studies showing dramatic improvement in ADHD symptoms following biofeedback training.[93] Improvements include decreases in undesirable behaviors including off-task behaviors, oppositional behaviors, emotional outbursts, and

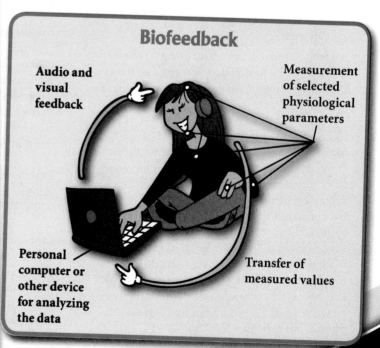

Biofeedback

Audio and visual feedback

Measurement of selected physiological parameters

Personal computer or other device for analyzing the data

Transfer of measured values

distractibility. The case studies find increases in desirable behaviors including cooperation, completion of schoolwork, report card marks, and improved scores on tests of attention, impulse control, and IQ.

Case studies are generally suspect (other variables could cause the improvements). Evidence in at least one case study, however, argues strongly that it is biofeedback training rather than any other variable responsible for the improvements: Using a design in which the training was turned off and turned on again, it was demonstrated that symptom improvements paralleled increases and decreases in biofeedback training.[94]

Ten year follow-up studies[95] have shown sustained gains including control over symptoms of hyperactivity and emotional control. The follow-up studies found sustained improvement in homework completion and report card grades.

Experimental Studies. Controlled experimental studies leave no doubt about the effectiveness of biofeedback training for students with symptoms of ADHD.

Biofeedback v. No Treatment. In a controlled experiment comparing students who were diagnosed with ADHD and recommended for medication, students were randomly assigned to biofeedback or a no-treatment waiting control. Compared to control group students, those receiving biofeedback showed significant reduction of symptoms of inattention as well as gains in IQ.[96]

Biofeedback v. Ritalin. In a comparison of biofeedback and Ritalin on 43 students, both treatment approaches produced gains for over 80% of students on a wide variety of ADHD-related behaviors, behavioral problems, and tests of attention. Improvements for the two approaches were not significantly different.[97] A 12-week study comparing the effectiveness of Ritalin and biofeedback supports the same conclusion: Both treatments were found to be effective, but there was no significant difference between them.[98] Children received biofeedback training three times a week for 30 to 60 minutes per session. Biofeedback and Ritalin produced equally significant improvements in computerized tests of attention as well as behavioral rating scales.

> **Tip**
> Parents and educators wanting an alternative to Ritalin can consider biofeedback as a treatment option!

Ritalin Treats Symptoms; Biofeedback Retrains the Brain. In order to test if biofeedback has benefits beyond Ritalin, experimenters assigned 100 students to either of two conditions.[99] Half received only Ritalin and a parenting program; the other half received Ritalin and the parenting program plus biofeedback. The question: Was there an added value of biofeedback?

The study lasted one year. Biofeedback sessions were 40 minutes long and were discontinued after a month or two (from 33 to 50 sessions; average = 43 sessions) when students reached the criterion of brain waves within one standard deviation of peer norms. All participants continued to take Ritalin for the full year. At the end of the year, all participants took a battery of tests under two conditions: (1) while still taking Ritalin, and (2) one week after discontinuing Ritalin. The tests included behavioral measures of ADHD; the Continuous Performance Test (CPT) designed to measure sustained attention and impulse control; and brain wave measures.

On the basis of this research we can recommend biofeedback for ADHD students, even if they are taking Ritalin.

Results are extremely revealing. Significant improvement was noted for both groups while still taking Ritalin. When Ritalin was discontinued, however, large differences between the two groups emerged. Those that did not have the initial biofeedback training relapsed on all measures; those that had the biofeedback training maintained sustained gains on all measures. This pattern of results supports a very important conclusion: Ritalin treats symptoms, but biofeedback changes basic brain functioning and leads to sustained improvement! On the basis of this research, we can recommend biofeedback for ADHD students, even if they are taking Ritalin.

Notes of Caution

In the face of the positive results of published studies of biofeedback for ADHD students, it is tempting to recommend widespread use of biofeedback, and even to recommend it instead of Ritalin. We need, however, to be cautious. A wide range of types of biofeedback training methods have been used across the biofeedback studies.[100] There is also a wide range of types of ADHD, each with very different patterns of brain over- and underactivation in different brain structures and neural tracks.[101] Some biofeedback methods involve teaching people to decrease activity in overactive parts of the brain; others involve increasing activity in underactive structures. Clearly to enhance the probability of success there needs to be a careful match of type of biofeedback training with type of ADHD. Research testing which biofeedback methods produce which kinds of results for which kinds of ADHD is critical.

A second reason for caution: We cannot extrapolate with any certainty from significant differences between treated and untreated experimental groups to individuals. Significant differences among groups are based on averages that mask individual differences. Across the experimental studies, approximately 75% of students receiving biofeedback training show improvements in ADHD symptoms. While this is sufficient to produce significant experimental effects, it does not guarantee success for any particular individual student. If we were to roll out biofeedback generally in schools and districts, we would likely have a success rate lower than 75% and possibly much lower. Experiments are conducted with motivated volunteer participants under the best of treatment conditions. These research studies demonstrate what is possible, but do not tell us what is probable in less than perfect school or district settings where not all ADHD students are highly motivated and treatments may not be administered under tightly controlled experimental conditions.

Tool 7
Illustrate with Images

The brain processes information as concrete visual images. In workshops, I ask participants to close their eyes and see what comes to mind when I say a word. I say the word *"table."* I then ask them to open their eyes and raise their hands if they saw the word, "table." Almost no one raises a hand. I then ask participants if they pictured a table. Almost everyone raises a hand. We form visual images to process information. This does not apply only to concrete objects. When I perform the experiment again and ask people what comes to mind when I say the word, *"justice,"* most everyone again has a concrete picture. Some see a judge in a black robe, others see the scales of justice, others see only a judge's gavel. One participant reported seeing O. J. Simpson behind bars, yet others have more complicated pictures to symbolize justice. But the point is that almost everyone responds with a visual image, not the word, "justice." If we want to teach with the stimuli that the brain naturally attends to and retains, the implication is clear: We need to illustrate with visual images!

Research supports the power of images to improve achievement: For both young and older subjects, visual presentation of content results in greater later recognition and recall than does verbal presentation. This is true even for those students who have been identified as verbal learners![102]

Almost Unlimited Memory for Photos!

A series of experiments were conducted to test the power of visual memory. The results are almost unbelievable, but they have been replicated in a number of experiments. In 1965, Raymond S. Nickerson performed a rather simple experiment that transformed our understanding of memory.[103] He presented 600 8 x 10 inch photographs for 5 seconds each to 56 subjects. The pictures "represented a broad spectrum of subject matter, selected from photography periodicals." After the first 200 pictures, half the subsequent 400 photos were duplicates, occurring for the second time in the series. Subjects were asked not to respond to the first 200 photos, but for each of the 400 subsequent photos, subjects were asked to designate if the photo was new or previously seen.

The results: Everyone recognized when a picture came up a second time! *"The general performance level was almost perfect: 95% of all responses were correct! The lowest*

Everyone recognized pictures they had seen: 95% of all responses were correct!

scoring subject was correct on better than 80% of the trials." There was a slight decline as the somewhat exhausting procedure progressed, but even after a lag (number of pictures between first and second appearance) of 200 photos, 87% of the previously viewed items were identified correctly! See Graph: Recognition of Photos.

Why Is this Finding Transformative?
Prior to this research, psychologists had focused on the extreme limits of short-term memory. Miller had published his formative research on the magical number seven, showing that the average person could remember only six to eight randomly ordered items after seeing them or hearing them once.[104] It did not matter if the items were words, nonsense syllables, letters, or digits.[105] In contrast, the photo recognition study indicated we have almost unlimited memory capacity, not just a capacity for six to eight items.

Explaining the Finding.
There are two reasons for this huge discrepancy: (1) reproduction v. recognition; (2) nonsense v. meaning.

Reproduction v. Recognition. The photo experiments only asked people to recognize if a photo had appeared before; the magical seven research asked people to reproduce the digits or words. Recognition is much easier than reproduction. We all easily recognize a penny, but cannot reproduce with any degree of accuracy what is on the penny or where the objects on the penny are located.[106] See Box: Penny Drawings by U.S. Citizens, p. 6.98.

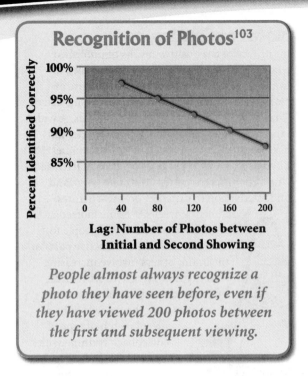

Recognition of Photos[103]

People almost always recognize a photo they have seen before, even if they have viewed 200 photos between the first and subsequent viewing.

Nonsense v. Meaning. The magical seven experiments asked people to recall meaningless letters or digits. The brain cannot make associative links to meaningless digits, so they are not remembered. In contrast, the photo recognition studies presented meaningful content to which everyone can make associative links, making later recognition easy. Recognition rates drop dramatically if meaningless rather than meaningful stimuli are presented. When subjects are presented meaningless visual stimuli rather than real photos, instead of unlimited memory, recognition rates drop to chance after just fifteen items.[107]

Follow-Up Research
Following Nickerson's experiment, a series of experiments revealed most people have near perfect and almost unlimited memory for meaningful visual images.

2,560 Slides with 90% Accuracy! A series of four experiments demonstrated amazing, near perfect recall for photographs.[108]

▶ 1,100 Photos, 10 Seconds Each. In the first experiment, 1,100 photographs (8 x 10 inches) taken from news, travel, and sports magazines were presented to two subjects for 5 seconds each and to two subjects for 10 seconds each. This took from 2 to 4 hours. After a 30-minute rest, subjects were given 100 test trials. Tests were pairs of pictures, one from those presented and one new. Subjects were to say which one had been in the original set of 1,100 pictures. Results: Those who saw the pictures for 10 seconds each averaged 97% correct; those who saw the pictures for 5 seconds averaged 96% correct!

▶ **2,560 Slides, 10 Seconds Each.** In the second experiment, 2,560 35mm slides were projected for 10 seconds each. Slides were of humans, animals, vegetation, city scenes, and mechanical objects. To view that many slides, subjects were shown the slides either over 4 days or over 2 days with rest periods each hour. Results: Those shown the slides over 4 days averaged 91% correct; those shown the slides over two days averaged 89.5% correct!

▶ **120 Slides, 1 Second Each.** Subjects were shown 120 slides for only 1 second each, given 30 minutes of rest, and then tested to see if they could distinguish the slide they had seen from one they had not. (New slides were of the same type as old slides). Result: 91% accuracy!

▶ **Slides Flipped, 24 Hours Later.** In the final experiment in this series, subjects were shown 120 slides for 2 seconds each and tested after either 30 minutes or 24 hours. Further, some of the slides were flipped horizontally and subjects were asked to identify if the slides were as they had seen them originally or if they were reversed. Results: With the exception of one of the eight subjects, all subjects scored between 92% and 100% in identifying which slides they had seen before regardless of whether the slide had been reversed or not!

10,000 Pictures, Memory Almost Limitless!
Another series of studies involving up to 10,000 photographs established that the memory capacity for pictures is almost limitless.[109] Percentage retained when required to remember huge numbers of photos drops only slightly in spite of the "extremely grueling and unpleasant" task of remaining vigilant over the 5 days of viewing. The number of pictures recognized becomes incredible, leading the researchers to conclude, "memory capacity is almost limitless."

Long-Term Memory for Photos. To test how long people remember if they have seen a picture before, subjects were tested 1 year after briefly viewing photographs.[110] Memory was substantial; memory for photos is enduring.

Recognition v. Reproduction

Although our main focus here is why it is brain friendly to illustrate with images, we will take a bit of a detour to detail some implications for educators of the finding that recognition is easy and reproduction is difficult. It is tempting to look at the truly phenomenal results of the photo recognition studies and overestimate the ability of the human brain to store visual images. In fact, while the studies demonstrate a magnificent ability to recognize visual images, they do not indicate the images have been stored in a way they can be reproduced in any detail. Ability to recognize is not the same as the ability to reproduce. To recognize something, we only need to be able to identify one critical feature. To reproduce something, we need to remember all its details. This distinction between recognition and reproduction has important implications for us as educators.

When teaching a concept, we can scaffold for success by teaching for and testing for recognition before teaching and testing for production. For example, imagine we are teaching the distance from the sun to the planets in the solar system. As we do, we point to a planet and have the students answer back in unison the name of the planet. At the recognition level, we might ask, *"Is this planet Mars or Venus?* At the production level we might ask, *"What is the name of this planet?"* If we teach for and test for recognition before production, we scaffold for success. See Table: Teaching and Testing for Recognition v. Production, p. 6.56.

Teaching and Testing for Recognition v. Production

Content	Example	Recognition	Production
Science	Land Forms	"Is this a plateau?"	"What is the name of this land form (pointing to picture of plateau)?"
Language Arts	Parts of Speech	"Is this a verb or an adverb?"	"What part of speech is this word (pointing to it in a sentence)?"
Math	Formulas	"Is this the formula for the area of a triangle?"	"What is the formula for the area of a triangle?"
Social Studies	Government	"Are these steps of moving a bill to a law in the correct order?"	"What are the steps of moving a bill to a law?"

Test Construction: Recognition Before Production. The recognition v. production distinction has implication for how best to construct a test. Forced Choice, Matching, and True-False test items are recognition questions. Recognition questions have the answer provided, and the student need only choose the right answer from among alternatives. Short Answer, Write-A-Definition, Label-the-Parts are production items. Production items do not have the answer provided—the student must produce the answer from memory.

Because recognition items are easier, it is best to place them before the production items. Why? The probability of the student finishing the test is much greater and we get a better assessment of their knowledge. If we place difficult production items first, the student may spend a great deal of time on those items, never getting to the recognition items that they would have answered correctly if they had gotten to them. By placing the easy items first, students can answer more items and we have a better assessment.

Further, by placing items first that the student has a high probability of answering correctly, the student is in a better mood when coming to the more difficult items. As we have seen, a good mood promotes thinking and problem solving. So for two reasons, probability of answering more questions and probability of answering them more correctly, placing easy recognition items first in a test is good test construction practice. See Table: Types of Test Questions In Order of Difficulty, p. 6.57.

Tip

In constructing a test, order the items by difficulty, from easiest to most difficult. Place recognition items before production items. Students will finish more items, experience early success which reduces anxiety, and will feel better about their performance.

Types of Test Questions In Order of Difficulty

True-False	
Multiple-Choice	Recognition
Matching	
Fill In the Blanks	
Short Answer	Production
Essay	

Illustrate with Images: Implications for Educators

Returning to our main focus, given the brain's natural tendency to attend to and create visual images, let's look at ways to include visual images as we present content. When presenting using a whiteboard or flip chart, include visual images.

Simultaneity Counts. Neurons that fire together, wire together. To maximize the power of presenting with images, to the extent possible, we want to present the images *at the same time* as the verbal instruction. Thus, a PowerPoint slide that contains the image and the text is better than one slide with text followed by a slide with an image. By presenting the visual image with the written or verbal instruction simultaneously, we dramatically increase the probability of building dendrite connections between the auditory and visual cortices. Thus, a teacher who can draw a diagram or image as he or she lectures will be more effective than one who shows an image after lecturing. See ways to avoid the split attention effect, in Tool 6: Avoid Distractions, in Principle 5: Attention, p. 5.38.

Drawing or showing their drawings to the class intimidates many teachers, but there is a very simple solution. In his inexpensive, approachable book, *Make a World*,[111] Ed Emberley has created a simple step-by-step approach that allows any teacher to become comfortable with creating simple drawings to illustrate any content.

Mind Maps

Perhaps the strongest approach to illustrating with images is Mind Mapping.[112] Mind maps are a visual representation of our cognitive maps. By including arrows, boxes, images, words, white space, symbols, and text of different sizes, mind maps represent our thoughts. Concepts of more importance are larger, representing their relative importance. The arrows and links let us see a glance which ideas lead to, support, and link to other concepts.

Tony Buzan relates the story of Edward Hughes. Edward was a C and B student. He learned mind mapping and proclaimed he would get all A's and go to Cambridge. His teachers said he was "daft," and proclaimed that even if he worked very hard he would only get B's. The school refused to pay for his entrance exams saying it was a waste of school money and Edward's time. Edward persisted, but had to pay his own entrance fee.

Describing how he prepared for the very difficult exams Edward said,

> "I summarized my last two years of school notes neatly into Mind Maps. I then coloured them, highlighted them, and produced giant Master Mind Maps for each of the courses, and in some instances for each major section of each course. In this way, I could see where and how the more detailed elements fitted together, and in addition, get a good overview, thus enabling me to be able to 'just flick through' giant sections of the course with completely accurate recall."[113]

Edward passed all his exams with A's or distinction and in one was the best student ever! When he went on to Cambridge, he used the same mind map techniques to study and performed at excellent levels in all courses except one in which he only passed, but in that course, half the students failed. In one final exam, he received the highest mark ever given by the University for that subject!

We can't attribute this remarkable turnaround only to mind mapping as Edward was very dedicated, studied hard and consistently, and began running 2 to 3 miles two or three times

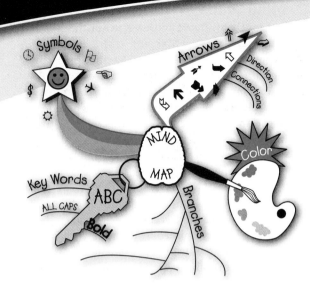

per week, and began working out. As he stated, consistent with the research we reviewed in Principle 1: Nourishment, *"I became better physically, which I found helped my concentration enormously."* Nevertheless, Edward attributed much of his remarkable success to Mind Mapping.

Mind Maps Are More Brain Friendly than Outlines.
Mind maps parallel brain functioning in two important ways: (1) Connections; and (2) Focus on Big Picture and Details.

Mind Maps Allow Connections. Neurons reach out and make dendrite connections to other neurons stimulated by the same content, forming neural networks. That is how we build our perceptual and cognitive worlds. While mind mapping if we see a connection, we draw a link, just as neurons do between related content. This allows a visual map that shows relations between object, events, and concepts that is not possible in the traditional outline. In the traditional outline, there is no way to show a link between item IIIb and item IVc. Seeing that connection while mind mapping, we just draw an arrow.

Mind Maps Are Details within the Big Picture. To function, the brain must integrate details within a big picture. This is hardwired into the structure of the brain with the left hemisphere specializing in details while the right hemisphere specializes in grasping the big picture. So too is it with Mind Maps. As Edward said, *"In this way, I could see where and how the more detailed elements fitted together, and in addition get a good*

overview...." At a glance, the mind map allows a view of both global and analytic thinking.

Functions of Mind Maps. Mind maps can be used in many ways including teacher presentations, student note-taking, prewriting, journaling, brainstorming, test prep, and assessment/evaluation.

Mind Maps for Teacher Presentations. Mind maps are used by the teacher to record at the board or flip chart the ideas they are presenting and for ideas shared by students during a class discussion. Once a teacher is fluent in mind mapping, the teacher uses mind mapping to plan a lesson or a presentation.

Mind Maps for Student Note-Taking. After the teacher has modeled and taught the students how to mind map, student can be encouraged to use mind maps to take their own notes.

Mind Maps for Prewriting, Journaling. Mind maps are great for prewriting. Writing from a mind map ensures that the writing conveys all the elements and connections in the mind map. Students may use mind maps also for personal journaling.

Mind Maps for Brainstorming. Teams may create a large mind map on flip chart paper. Each student adds to the map in his or her own color, allowing accountability.

Overlap Maps for Test Prep: One of the strongest ways for students to prepare for a test is a structure called **Overlap Map**. Students first create a mind map on a topic, or study a mind map the teacher has provided. The mind map is then set out of sight and the student attempts to draw it from memory. Students then check their map against the original and color in the missing elements in a bright color. Students then use the new mind map to study for a test. Because the elements they are most likely to miss are in a bright color, those elements become objects of focus and so become memorable.

Team Mind Maps. When teams work together to create a mind map, after the main topic is placed in the center of a large piece of chart paper, students seek consensus before creating at least four core concepts on their mind map. Following that, they all work simultaneously using a variety of elements to symbolize the content, including:

- ▶ Colors
- ▶ Connecting lines
- ▶ Different size print
- ▶ Doodles
- ▶ Illustrations
- ▶ Symbols

Team Mind Maps for Assessment, Evaluation. Mind maps created by teams or individuals give a window onto their level of conceptual understandings and differentiation. A map that provides more weight to core concepts and which has many supporting elements to each core concept indicates a rich understanding of both the big picture and the details. If students are free to contribute in any way they want to a team mind map, and are limited to just their own color, we can see at a glance how the team is functioning. If a student adds only supporting elements and no core concepts, we might infer that student has an analytic style. Conversely, if a student adds only core concepts, we might infer a global style. If a student adds a core concept and all the supporting details to just that one concept and no other students add to or link to that core concept, we can infer a cognitive isolate. If all colors are spread over the entire mind map, we can infer a team with good integration: Students are relating to each others' ideas.

Word Webs

Word Webs are the anemic brothers of mind maps. Word Webs allow lines or arrows to connect words, but they do not contain symbols and images. A common format is to draw a rectangle around the main idea to be webbed. From that rectangle, draw lines radiating out and at the end of each line, write a related main concept, and encircle them with an oval. Finally, draw lines out from each oval and write ideas related to each main concept. Drawing lines to connect related ideas creates more sophisticated Word Webs. A bridge may be drawn over any line that is to be crossed. See Box: Word Web, Brain-Friendly Teaching, p. 6.60.

Graphic Organizers

Graphic organizers are a visual representation of the relation of ideas. Mind Maps and Word Webs are but two types of graphic organizers—ways to illustrate the relations among concepts. They are unique in the family of graphic organizers because they allow illustrating the relation of any item with any other item by drawing connectors. The remaining graphic organizers are ways of placing items in categories. For example, in the traditional Venn Diagram, there are four areas, A, B, A and B, and neither A nor B. Each item is placed in one of the four categories, but there is no way to show the relation of individual items to each other.

There are many graphic organizers[114] including:

- ▶ Cause-Effect Organizers
- ▶ Classification Organizers
- ▶ Compare/Contrast Organizers
- ▶ Concept Development Organizers
- ▶ Cyclical Organizers
- ▶ Evaluation Organizers
- ▶ Planning Organizers
- ▶ Relational Organizers
- ▶ Sequence Organizers

Within each category of organizer, there are a number of different graphic organizers. For example, within the category of compare/contrast organizers we find Venn Diagrams, T-Charts, and Compare/Contrast Charts. Graphic organizers come in a wide range of types adapted to specific curriculum; they are used for every Common Core standard.[115] See Box: Graphic Organizers, p. 6.61.

Graphic Organizers Are Brain Friendly. All graphic organizers are brain friendly for three main reasons. First, they illustrate the big picture and provide details, responding to the analytic—global left and right hemisphere modes of processing information. Second, they are visual

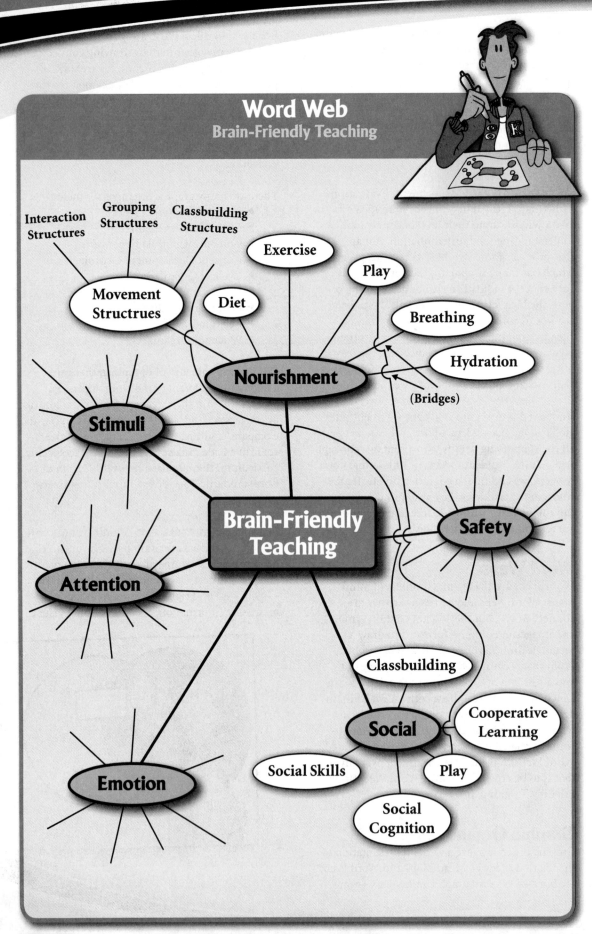

Word Web
Brain-Friendly Teaching

Interaction Structures
Grouping Structures
Classbuilding Structures

Movement Structrues

Diet

Exercise

Play

Breathing

Hydration

(Bridges)

Nourishment

Stimuli

Attention

Brain-Friendly Teaching

Safety

Classbuilding

Cooperative Learning

Social

Social Skills

Play

Social Cognition

Emotion

Graphic Organizers

Sequence Organizers
Chains

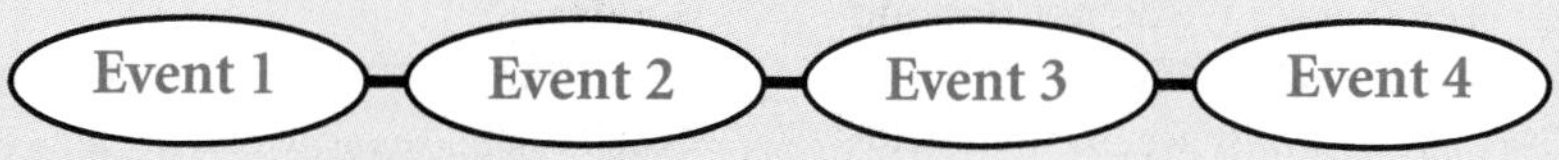

$$\text{Event 1} - \text{Event 2} - \text{Event 3} - \text{Event 4}$$

Concept Development Organizers
Concept Map

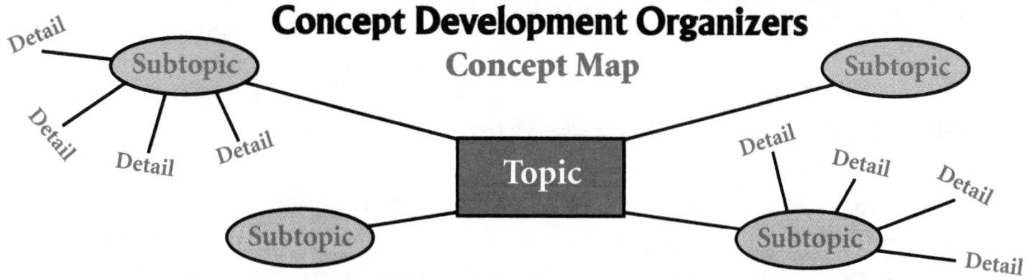

Detail — Subtopic — Detail Detail Detail — **Topic** — Subtopic — Detail Detail Detail Detail

Subtopic — Subtopic

Compare/Contrast Organizers
Venn Diagrams

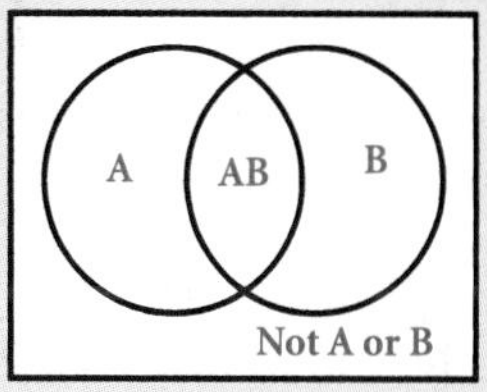

A | AB | B
Not A or B

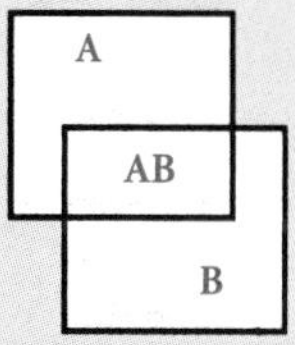

A
AB
B

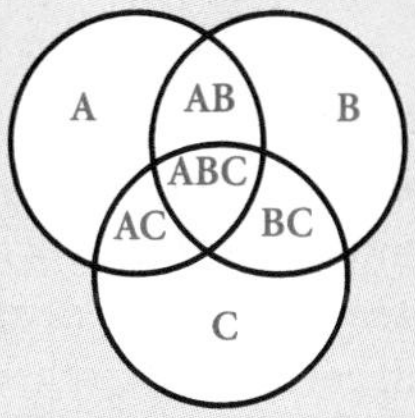

A | AB | B
ABC
AC | BC
C

Evaluation Organizers
Charts

P	M	I
Plus	Minus	Interesting

PMI Chart

+	−
Positive or Like or Agree	Negative or Dislike or Disagree

Plus/Minus T-Chart

Relational Organizers
Charts

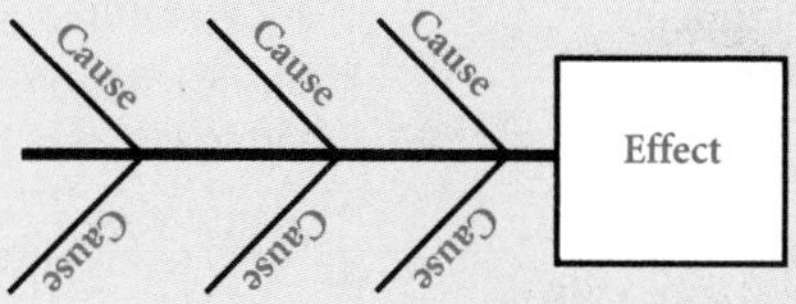

Cause Cause Cause
Cause Cause Cause
Effect

Fish Bone

Whole
Part
Part | Part

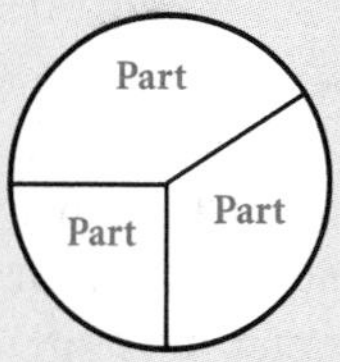

Pie Chart

Categorize/Classify Organizers
Categories

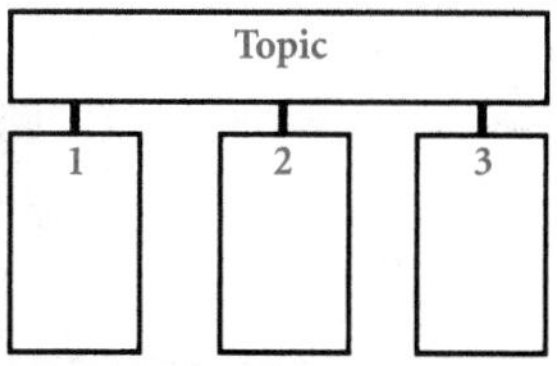

Topic
1 | 2 | 3

Topic
1
2
3

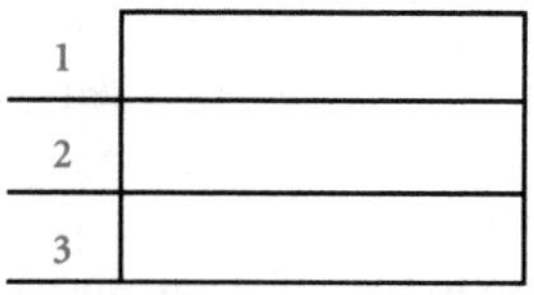

images, which in itself makes them easy to attend to and remember. Third, the brain naturally creates categories and stores information in those categories. For example, let's say we encounter an insect we have not seen before. We do not respond to the insect as a unique creature unrelated to all other creatures. Rather, mentally we immediately categorize the new insect within the category of insects, and compare and contrast it with other insects. Graphic organizers mirror this mental process.

Benefits of Graphic Organizers. A graphic organizer is a memory aide. The brain retains visual images and can recall visual images far more readily than auditory information. Graphic organizers provide a way to organize concepts and so create a framework to use as new information is encountered—new information is added to an existing mental graphic organizer. Graphic organizers help cope with information overload. Instead of coping with long lists of items, we can more comfortably deal with categories of items. Research demonstrates graphic organizers aid comprehension and recall.[116]

Visual Presentations

As we present, we can create visual images in many ways. In her book, *Dynamic Trainer*,[117] Laurie Kagan lists many visual/spatial presentation modes as well as ways to make the classroom environment visual/spatial friendly. See Box: Visual Presentation Methods.

Visual Activities

One of an infinite number of possible visual activities is Pizza Math. Students first use a file folder to draw a colorful Pizza Parlor with prices posted. For example, different sized pizzas have different prices: small, $5; medium, $10; and large, $15. So too do different sized drinks. Different numbers of toppings have different prices as well. There may also be specials. For example: Buy a medium pizza with two toppings and a drink for only $11.50. Students then create problem cards. For example: How much change do I receive from $50 if I buy one medium pizza special, one trip to the salad bar, and four additional small drinks? After creating problem

cards with a question on the front and the answer on the back, teams pass the Pizza Parlor and Question Cards to another team to solve. See Box: Visual Activity Centers, p. 6.63.

Student Presentations and Projects. Students create more memorable presentations, for themselves and the class, if they are encouraged to include visually rich presentation modes. They may incorporate a visual project in their presentation. Dramas, plays, tableaus, and simulations are particularly rich visually. See Box: Visual Projects, p. 6.63.

Classroom Environment. A visually rich classroom environment makes class more inviting and content more memorable. Some elements to include: Bulletin boards, particularly interactive and 3-D bulletin boards; Word Walls; posters; mobiles; and posted student work. A visually rich classroom environment has crayons or markers and clean paper readily available.

Handouts and Worksheets. Handouts and worksheets become more attractive by including borders, diagrams, and images.

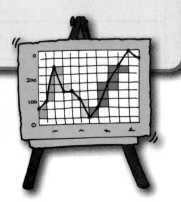

Visual Presentation Methods

- ▶ Display charts, graphs, diagrams, maps, signs
- ▶ Give demonstrations
- ▶ Have students imagine/pretend
- ▶ Incorporate visual aids
- ▶ Play movies, videos
- ▶ Show slides
- ▶ Use drawings, paintings
- ▶ Lead guided imagery, visualizations
- ▶ Incorporate flip charts, overheads, PowerPoint slides
- ▶ Show cartoons and video clips
- ▶ Mind Map
- ▶ Model directions

Visual Activity Centers

- Same-Different
- Match Mine
- Copy a Painting
- Sculpture
- Charcoal
- Cut-n-Paste
- Tear Art
- Simultaneous RoundTable
- Build-A-Robot

Kagan Structures Engage Visual Processing

Dozens of the Kagan Structures provide visual images of the content so are aligned with the call to illustrate with images. See Box: Kagan Visual Instructional Strategies.

Brain Rationale for Illustrating with Images

Although we experience consciousness as unified, our brain is divided. The right hemisphere specializes in visual information and the left hemisphere specializes in verbal information. The teacher who presents information only verbally is teaching to half a brain. The rationale for illustrating with images is firmly established by studies of hemisphere specialization.

Visual Projects

Students can build, draw, or design any number of projects that provide a visual representation of the curriculum, including

- Books
- Brochures
- Business cards
- Cartoons
- Catalogs
- CD covers
- Collages
- Comic books
- Diagrams
- Dioramas
- Flowcharts
- Hats
- Letterheads
- Logos
- Magazines
- Covers
- Montages
- Murals
- Pictures
- Posters
- Sculptures
- Shirts
- Videos
- Blueprints
- Maps
- Models

Kagan Visual Instructional Strategies

Many Kagan Instructional strategies emphasize visual processing of the content. Most of the visual Kagan Structures listed below can be found in two sources, *Kagan Cooperative Learning*,[118] and *Multiple Intelligences: The Complete MI Book*.[119]

- Blind Sequencing
- Collective Memory
- Draw It!
- Draw-What-I-Write
- Fill-A-Frame
- Flashcard Game
- Flashcard Star
- Formations
- Guided Imagery
- Line-Ups
- Listen-Sketch-Draft
- Look-Write-Discuss
- Match Mine
- Mind Mapping
- Observe-Draw-RallyRobin
- Observe-Write-RoundRobin
- Overlap Map
- Pantomime
- Picture Links
- Reservoir Room
- Same-Different
- Tableau
- Team Charades
- Team Overlap Map
- Team Mind-Mapping
- Team Window
- Team Word-Webbing
- Transparency Slide Show: Flashback
- Visualization
- Vocab Toons
- Window Paning
- Word Webbing

Hemisphere Specialization

Many experiments reveal that the left hemisphere is superior to the right hemisphere in processing most types of verbal stimuli whereas the right hemisphere is superior in processing most types of visual/spatial stimuli.

In 1981, Roger Sperry won the Nobel Prize for his work demonstrating the functional specialization of the hemispheres. He worked with patients who had had a corpus callosotomy. That is, to alleviate symptoms of epilepsy, their corpus callosum (the bundle of neural tracks that carries communication between the right

Presenting Information to the Left v. Right Hemispheres

A word is flashed briefly to the right field of view, and the patient is asked what he saw.

Because the left hemisphere is dominant for verbal processing, the patient's answer matches the word.

A word is flashed to the left field of view, and the patient is asked what he saw.

The right hemisphere cannot share information with the left, so the patient is unable to say what he saw, but he can draw it.

and left hemispheres) was cut, so the right and left hemispheres functioned independently. This surgery (which is almost never performed today) allowed researchers to present stimuli to only the left or only the right hemisphere to determine how each processes information. Researchers present information very quickly to only the left or right visual field. If the stimuli is presented quickly enough, the person cannot move their eyes, so the stimuli reaches only one visual field. Stimuli projected to the left visual field is received only by the right hemisphere, and stimuli in the right visual field is received only by the left hemisphere. See Box: Presenting Information to the Left v. Right Hemispheres.

Left Hemisphere: Superior in Verbal. In one fascinating experiment, researchers quickly flashed the word "face" to either the left or right visual field of split-brain subjects. Split-brain subjects respond very differently depending on whether the word "face" is shown to the left hemisphere or the right hemisphere. When the left hemisphere receives the word, subjects respond normally: When they are asked what they saw, they said the word "face." When the same word is shown to the right hemisphere, subjects act very strangely: They say they have not seen anything! Or sometimes say they have seen only a flash of light. More peculiarly, when asked to draw what they have seen, even though they say they saw nothing, they draw a face![120] The right hemisphere has the ability to decode and respond

to the word nonverbally—without the conscious experience of having seen the word! The right hemisphere is not conscious of verbal stimuli per se, yet can process and respond to them!

This right hemisphere ability to understand a word without being able to verbalize it or even being conscious of having seen it, has been demonstrated in a number of ways. For example, when the word "key" is presented only to the right hemisphere, people with a split-brain cannot say the word "key;" some say they have not seen anything. Yet when asked to identify what they have seen, with their left hand (controlled by their right hemisphere), they correctly pick out a key from many objects! Their right hand cannot find the key because the left hemisphere (which controls the right hand) has not seen the word key. The same pattern is true if a picture of a key is projected rather than the word key. In the split-brain person one hemisphere is unaware of what the other has perceived.[121]

Recent research in normal, non-split-brain patients has revealed that when asked to distinguish words from non-words (actual words v. strings of letters that sound like words, but which are not real words), the left hemisphere performs the task more quickly and more accurately.[122] When the task is presented to the right hemisphere, the person performs more slowly because his or her brain must send the information across the corpus callosum to the left hemisphere to be processed. The corpus callosum shows more activity when a word is shown to the right hemisphere than the left. It is as if the right hemisphere says, *"I can't deal with this, I'll send it to you, left hemisphere, you specialize in words."* Because the information has to travel across the corpus callosum, it takes a bit more time to process verbal stimuli presented to the right hemisphere than information presented directly to the left hemisphere.

Both Hemispheres Process Verbal Stimuli. It is an overgeneralization to categorize the right hemisphere as visual and the left hemisphere as verbal. The right and left hemispheres both process words—they simply process words differently. As we have seen, when the right hemisphere sees the word key, it can recognize and find a key from among many objects. It decodes the word unconsciously so it cannot verbalize what it has seen. The left hemisphere is superior to the right in processing the logical relations between words and the denotation of words,[123] but the right hemisphere is superior in processing associations between words.[124] To cite some examples, the right hemisphere is superior to the left in:

- ▶ Recognizing words are in the same category. For example, recognizing that the words "car" and "driver" are related.[125]
- ▶ Detecting a relationship between words that refer to things that occur in the same location. For example, that "eagle" and "sun" are related because they both can be located in the sky.
- ▶ Recognizing whole-part relations. For example, that the words "eagle" and "beak" are related.[126]
- ▶ Understanding the connotation of words.[127]

In sum, the difference between how the right and left hemispheres process words is the same as how they process stimuli in general: The left hemisphere is logical and sequential whereas the right hemisphere is more global and relational. The right hemisphere connects the dots, creating a whole; the left hemisphere focuses more narrowly on the parts.

Right Hemisphere: Superior in Visual/ Spatial. The right hemisphere specializes in visual/spatial stimuli. When individuals with a split-brain are given blocks and are asked to assemble them in the same way as a group of blocks arranged on the table, their right hand, which is controlled by the left hemisphere, cannot do the task. The person fumbles with the blocks but cannot manage to arrange them correctly. The left hemisphere does not have spatial ability. When the person is told to use only his or her left hand, which is controlled by the right hemisphere, he or she performs the task easily, indicating the right hemisphere specializes in spatial relational skills. Intriguingly, when the split-brain person is told to use both hands in the block arrangement task, both hands actually squabble, one interfering with the other as the hemispheres work independently, one not knowing what the other is doing!

Additional evidence that the right hemisphere is superior in processing visual stimuli comes from face recognition tasks. The right hemisphere is excellent at face recognition, a skill the left hemisphere lacks.

Both Hemispheres Process Visual Stimuli. As with verbal stimuli, we need to caution against overgeneralization. Both hemispheres process visual stimuli, they just process the stimuli differently. The original experiments by Roger Sperry demonstrated hemisphere specialization in processing of visual images. When a visual image was projected to only the left hemisphere, split-brain subjects described what they saw, but could not draw it. When the image was projected to the right hemisphere, the subjects drew the image, but could not verbalize what they saw, stating they cannot recall what they have seen. It appears that the two hemispheres process the same image in very different ways: The right hemisphere as a visual image; the left hemisphere as a verbal description.

In the original split-brain experiments with animals, different visual stimuli were projected to the right and left hemispheres at the same time. For example, the left hemisphere was presented a circle on the left and a cross on the right, while the right hemisphere was presented the cross on the left and the circle on the right as a signal that food was available. Later, when the stimuli were presented to the left and right hemispheres separately, each hemisphere had learned the opposite cue for the availability of food. The two hemispheres both responded to visual stimuli, but the animal functioned as if it had two completely independent brains, each having learned the opposite thing![128]

Tool 8

Teach with Tunes

Lyrical Lessons

"Transforming lessons into songs is the most enjoyable and productive way of teaching and raising students' levels and results. With my students' help, I change some lessons into simple songs for the students to memorize. I remember when one of my students scored 23 out of 25 in English Social Studies. I was so proud of him. He looked at me one day and said that he had cheated during the exam. I couldn't believe my ears and I asked him to explain how. He said, 'I was reciting the song of the lesson as I was answering the questions.' I laughed and I told him that it wasn't cheating; it was a good way to memorize the information."

—*Mahmoud Al Shariti*
7th Grade, Liwa International School
Al Ain, Abu Dhabi
United Arab Emirates

The power of music to increase academic achievement is enormously underestimated by most educators. Students of all ages come to class having memorized all of the words to complex songs, but we struggle getting them to memorize simple multiplication facts. Five-year-olds enter school having memorized 26 non-meaningful items—in order! How are parents routinely accomplishing this amazing learning feat with their little ones? They simply rely on the power of song. We are shutting our eyes (plugging our ears?) to the obvious. We can boost retention of much of our curriculum if we do with our curriculum what parents do with the alphabet—put it to song. Before looking at some ways teachers are being successful teaching their curriculum through song, let's explore a bit of brain science behind music.

Pitch on the Left; Melody on the Right. There are many dimensions of processing music and each is processed with a variety of brain structures, some in the right hemisphere and some in the left. Some aspects of music are located more in the right hemisphere and some more in the left. For example, processing pitch is more of a left hemisphere task[129] whereas remembering the melody of a song is more of a right hemisphere task.[130] These differences are consistent with the left hemisphere specializing in details in contrast to the right hemisphere, which processes more globally, dealing with the relation of elements to each other.

Music: A Model of Neuroplasticity. Different aspects of music recognition, appreciation, memory, composition, and production involve myriad parts of the brain—in both left and right hemispheres.[131] There is greater development of grey matter in the motor, auditory, cerebellum, and visual-spatial brain regions of professional musicians compared to amateur musicians, and greater development in those areas in amateur musicians compared to those who play no

music.[132] The areas that show a correlation with music practice correspond to finger movements, finger-hand representation, translating musical notation into motor movements, and music processing. Music follows the general rule of brain plasticity: There are strong links between the development of specialized skills and the development of particular brain structures. Use it and it develops.

At the same time, that use develops the brain. For music, like other specialized skills, practice leads to efficiency, so musicians require fewer neurons and expend less energy to perform music-related finger movements.[133] This too is a general finding. As they improve in skill, Tetris players use less and less brain energy.[134] With practice, the brain becomes more efficient, dedicating fewer neurons to perform a skill.

Listening to Music: Experienced Musicians on the Left; Amateurs on the Right. Traditionally, brain theorists thought people processed music with their right hemisphere. They were correct, but only for those who are naive to music. Listening to music neatly follows the pattern of movement from right to left hemisphere processing with practice.[135] Experienced musicians process music with the left hemisphere more than amateurs, who process music more with their right hemisphere. Novices process music primarily with the right hemisphere. This is consistent with the right hemisphere as more global and the left hemisphere as more analytic. Novices process music more globally; experienced listeners processing more analytically, discerning discrete elements lost to the naive listener.

Memory for Music: Novel on the Right; Familiar on the Left. Memory for music follows the general pattern of greater right hemisphere activation for novel and episodic aspects of music and greater left hemisphere activation for familiar and semantic aspects of music.[136] In general, the left hemisphere specializes in semantic memory (memory for discrete facts) whereas the right hemisphere specializes in episodic memory (memory for many integrated elements).[137]

Hemisphere Specialization: Novel on the Right; Familiar on the Left

That experienced musicians compared to amateurs process music more with their left hemisphere and the left hemisphere is more active for familiar aspects of music, follow a more general principle of hemisphere specialization: In general, the right hemisphere specializes in novel stimuli and the left hemisphere specializes in practiced or familiar stimuli.

Hemisphere Specialization: Novel v. Familiar. The right hemisphere is more active processing novel stimuli and the left hemisphere processes familiar, practiced sequences.[138] Language is familiar, we run off practiced sequences. Early on, the child processes language with both hemispheres, but with age, as language becomes a practiced sequence, it becomes localized in the left hemisphere. That is why children receiving a left hemispherectomy

(removal of the left hemisphere) recover their language skills, but adults receiving the same operation, lose their ability to verbalize. By adulthood, language skills have become practiced and are located more exclusively in the left hemisphere. Consistently, adults with a left hemisphere stroke generally become aphasic, lose verbal abilities; those with a right hemisphere stroke generally do not.

The specialization of the left hemisphere in language is a special case of a much more general brain principle: Novelty is processed primarily by the right hemisphere. With repeated exposure or practice, novel stimuli and behaviors become familiar, and there is a transition to left hemisphere dominance. As Robert Sylwester puts it: *"Processing novel stimuli with the right hemisphere and moving it to the left when it becomes a practiced sequence is like moving data from RAM to the hard drive. When the processing becomes practiced, by moving the processing to the left hemisphere we free up space in the right hemisphere to process new novel stimuli."*

Support for the conclusion that the right hemisphere specializes in novel stimuli and the left hemisphere specializes in familiar or practiced stimuli comes in many forms:

▶ Damage to left hemisphere in the very young leads to few disabilities; damage to the right is devastating. The reverse is true in adults.[139] In the young, little information is located exclusively in the left hemisphere; in adults, the hemispheres have specialized so damage to the left hemisphere means catastrophic loss of information exclusively located there.

▶ Those experienced with listening to music process the music primarily in the left hemisphere; naive listeners process the same music primarily in the right hemisphere.[140]

▶ The right hemisphere is superior for face recognition in general, but the left hemisphere is superior for recognizing very familiar faces (famous individuals).[141]

▶ When people are shown pictures they have never before seen, there is greater activation in the right hemisphere than the left; when shown familiar pictures, activation is greater in the left hemisphere than the right.[142]

▶ A novelty processing network in the brain has been located. It is transmodal: responding to novel visual and auditory stimuli. It is located in the right limbic system.[143]

> ### Tip
>
> Practice makes perfect. To routinize any skill, students need massive practice. Practice rewires the brain so it performs a skill with a fraction of the effort. If students are working hard at a skill, it is not yet time to move on.

Caution Warranted. As with any generalization regarding the brain, we must be cautious. Both hemispheres are activated by both novel and familiar stimuli. There are specific structures and neural tracks on the right that respond more to novel stimuli and specific structures and neural tracks on the left that respond more to familiar stimuli. But to say the right hemisphere is for novel stimuli and the left is for familiar stimuli is an overgeneralization.

For example, in the response to new v. old pictures, areas of both right and left hemispheres show increased activity in response to familiar pictures. Picture recognition involves many structures in the brain—the shift from novel stimuli to familiar stimuli does not override the fact that the right hemisphere is responsible for many aspects of picture recognition. Similarly, as players practice the game Tetris, there is a seven-fold increase in proficiency, and a very substantial decrease in brain activity. Experienced players exert far less energy while becoming far more efficient. Players who improved the most in Tetris showed the greatest decrease in brain energy.[144] Nevertheless, the decrease in energy exerted occurs in a variety of areas in both the right and left hemispheres, not a movement from left to right as we might predict if a transition from right to left occurred with familiarity. This may occur because Tetris is a visual/spatial game, 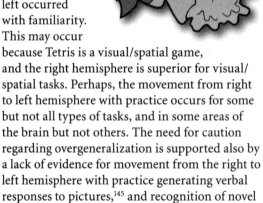 and the right hemisphere is superior for visual/spatial tasks. Perhaps, the movement from right to left hemisphere with practice occurs for some but not all types of tasks, and in some areas of the brain but not others. The need for caution regarding overgeneralization is supported also by a lack of evidence for movement from the right to left hemisphere with practice generating verbal responses to pictures,[145] and recognition of novel v. familiar sentences.[146]

Lyrical Lessons: Making Curriculum Memorable

Teachers are harnessing the power of music to deliver the curriculum by using **Lyrical Lessons**, a Kagan Structure. Students and/or the teacher simply put the curriculum to familiar tunes and have students sing it. The power of music takes over. The steps are straightforward: The teacher assigns the curriculum topic to teams. Each team may have a different topic, or all teams may create their song on the same topic. Teams brainstorm words and phrases relating to their topic. Teams select a familiar tune and sing the original lyrics several times to refresh their memory and to get set to put the curriculum words and phrases into

The Heart Dance

"I teach the pathway for the flow of blood through the heart using sign language, Donna Summer's song, "Last Dance" (Karaoke version), and movement to the music beat. I teach students letters in sign ("A" for Arteries and Atrium; "V" for Ventricles and Veins; "B" for Body; "L" for Lungs, and "C" for Capillaries). We start with our right hand raised and the symbol "A" for "Right Atrium. We follow the music counting 4 beats. Then we move down to the Right Ventricle using the symbol for "V." Four beats in that ventricle. Crossing our arms across the chest and using the letter "L" for the Lungs – 4 beats. Then with our left hand and symbol for "A" we're in the Left Atrium for 4 beats. Next down to the Left Ventricle for 4 beats and symbol for "V." Then both hands go out to the side using the symbol for "B" signifying the blood moves to the body for 4 beats. To stay with the music, we alternate hands for 2 beats each with the symbols "A" for Arteries, "C" for Capillaries, "V" for Veins. Then we squeeze each hand onto itself and say "push–push" for 2 beats because the blood is being forced back into the Right Atrium with the muscles squeezing on the Veins. The cycle begins again.

"Six years after a student was in my class, the student wrote to me, thanking me for the dance. The student took the EMT Test for NYS and two of the questions on the heart referred to the pathway of the flow of blood and he remembered the dance."

—**Kevin McIntyre**
High School Biology Teacher
Washingtonville, NY

Encounter in Dress Barn

I had a math student years ago who I bumped into last year at the Dress Barn as she now works there part time. She told me she still remembers the songs and they help her with the math she now does.

—**Heather DeMao**
Pre-Algebra & Honors Algebra Teacher
McIntosh Middle School
Sarasota, FL

- ▶ Molecular Genetics
- ▶ Chinese Dynasties
- ▶ Adding and Subtracting Decimals
- ▶ Memorizing the Quadratic Formula
- ▶ Creating a Flowchart Proof

Lyrical Lessons can be thought of as a mnemonic—a memory aide. As students do a procedure, they remind themselves of the steps by recalling the **Lyrical Lesson**. A number of teachers and Kagan trainers comment that they used **Lyrical Lessons** in their own classrooms, and saw big gains. Some relate how they have met students years later and discovered that the students remember the songs.

Tool 9

Communicate with Gestures

the tune. After creating their new song, teams share their song with another team or with the class.

When I asked Kagan trainers to share examples of **Lyrical Lessons** they had seen as they observed classrooms, they gave me far too many examples to share here. Topics of the **Lyrical Lessons** included:

- ▶ Cellular Respiration
- ▶ Biochemical Processes

Multimodal theorists have placed heavy emphasis on visual and auditory learning. Until recently, among theorists and educators, kinesthetic learning has been something of a stepchild. There is a growing body of research, however, indicating gesturing is extremely important in cognition, problem solving, and cognitive development. Students who are taught to gesture as they learn, learn more. Merely observing the

*"Great ideas originate
in the muscles."*
—*Thomas Alva Edison
(1847–1931)*

teacher gesturing during instruction increases achievement. Before examining these findings in more depth, let's overview one approach to harnessing the power of gesturing: **Kinesthetic Symbols**.

Kinesthetic Symbols: Harnessing the Power of Gesturing

For quite a few years, we have been training teachers in the use of **Kinesthetic Symbols**. Teachers have students symbolize content with their hands, bodies, and gestures. Functions of a president, parts of speech, steps of an algorithm, and stages of cell life, are all samples of content taught not just with words, but also with gestures. Teachers in the classrooms and trainers in their workshops consistently report very positive results. Teachers are boosting their vocabulary test scores from an average of 75 to an average of 95 by having students create and practice a kinesthetic symbol for the meaning of each word. I am amused by one result: A boy shyly admitted to his teacher that he had cheated on the vocabulary test. She asked how. *"I put my hands in the desk and did the kinesthetic symbols to remember."*

Most teachers encourage students to use **Kinesthetic Symbols** as memory aides during recall. Sarah Backner, a Kagan trainer, recalls that as a teacher,

> *"I had a high population of second-language learners in my classroom and found that Kinesthetic Symbols had a big impact on helping students raise their test scores. I knew that Kinesthetic Symbols played a role in raising scores because during their weekly vocabulary quiz, I could see students doing the Kinesthetic Symbols at their desk as they were going through the quiz to remind themselves what the words meant."*

Amal Mahmoud Al Shariti at Liwa International School in Al Ain, Abu Dhabi, United Arab Emirates, teaches her English-as-a-second-

language students a kinesthetic symbol for each vocabulary word. For example, when introduced to the word "reliable," students learn to say the word while giving themselves a pat on the shoulder. As they say "sociable," they intertwine their fingers like many people interacting.

See Structures Section
7. Kinesthetic Symbols

As they say "astounded," students put both hands under their jaws and open their mouths wide in an exaggerated expression of surprise. The students now receive very high marks on their vocabulary words, whereas prior to using **Kinesthetic Symbols**, their performance was substantially lower. Amal writes,

> After attending one of Mrs. Laurie Kagan's workshops in which she used Kinesthetic Symbols in training Kagan Structures, I decided to use them in my class. I started using them with vocabulary lessons, and the results were awesome—one of the students whose average score was 11 out of 20 showed a great improvement and could achieve a score of 19 out of 20. After that, I started using Kinesthetic Symbols in all my classes. I am teaching grade seven right now, but I have used Kinesthetic Symbols with all levels, and the results are always unbelievable. Using the Kinesthetic Symbols is full of fun, and it is effective in keeping energy levels high and in recalling information on tests. The part I enjoy most is when all the students are involved in creating their own kinesthetic symbols and giving me ideas to make the actions either easier or harder, as that stimulates their critical thinking.

Ways to Use Kinesthetic Symbols

There are various ways teachers are using **Kinesthetic Symbols**, differing in who makes up the symbols and how they are used.

 Brain-Friendly Teaching • Dr. Spencer Kagan
Kagan Publishing • 800.933.2667 • www.KaganOnline.com

Who Makes Up the Symbols? The teacher may make up the symbols and then teach them to the students. Alternatively, each team may make up its own symbols. Or in some cases, teachers have students each create their own unique symbols. There is something to be said for each approach. For the class to use the symbols as response modes, it is important the whole class has the same set of symbols. The process of having teams make up their own symbols serves as teambuilding. See Table: Kinesthetic Symbols for Punctuation. Individuals making up their own unique symbols gives them practice in translating from a verbal symbol system to a kinesthetic symbol system. Given the advantages of each approach, age permitting, I would recommend that teachers incorporate each approach at different times.

How to Use Kinesthetic Symbols. There are many ways **Kinesthetic Symbols** are used, including as response modes, for isolated content, for sequences of content, as signals, and to reinforce verbal instruction. They serve primarily, for students to practice content and as a memory aide in recall.

Kinesthetic Symbols as Response Modes. **Kinesthetic Symbols** are handy (literally) as response modes. After students have practiced the symbols and are fluent with them, the teacher can then post or project a sentence with missing punctuation marks, point to each missing punctuation in turn, and on cue, have students respond with the appropriate kinesthetic symbol. For example, the teacher might post the following:

> If Jonny has enough money ___
> he will buy a new bike___

The teacher says, *"When I snap my fingers, everyone give me the kinesthetic symbol for the punctuation that belongs in the first blank."*

Kinesthetic Symbols for Isolated Content. Sometimes the symbols are used in isolation as when a symbol is created for each vocabulary word, the names of types of rocks, the names of elements, the names of geometric forms, or the branches of government. Some teachers have used the symbols to help students remember

Kinesthetic Symbols for Punctuation

Period	Fist
Colon	Two fists, one above the other
Comma	Hand curved in shape of letter C
Semicolon	Fist above + hand curved below
Exclamation Point	Fist below elbow of raised forearm

the class rules: Misty Higgins, another Kagan trainer, taught biology at Anderson County High School in Lexington, Kentucky. She stated, *"I used Kinesthetic Symbols for class rules at the beginning of the year."* Misty, used the symbols for a range of content during the school year, including anatomical terminology in anatomy and physiology. In her words,

> "The most important thing I believe the Kinesthetic Symbols did was to give students something to anchor their thinking, to connect with the content. It helped them to conceptualize abstract concepts. Basically, providing for more linkages in the brain around specific content."

While coaching in a middle school science classroom, Sarah Backner, a Kagan trainer, saw a teacher using **Kinesthetic Symbols** to help students remember the part of a cell.

> "For each part of the cell, students had a kinesthetic symbol that reminded them of the function. For example, when they talked about the mitochondria as the power of the cell, students flexed their muscles. When they talked about the nucleus, students tapped their brains."

Melissa Wincel provides a powerful example of how teaching **Kinesthetic Symbols** for isolated content improved both reading and writing. She taught her kindergarten students at Trafalgar Elementary School in Cape Coral, Florida, the 70 sounds associated with the letters in the alphabet. She describes the results,

> "Kinesthetic Symbols were key to the children remembering the sounds of the letters. Every one of my students

walked out of my kindergarten class reading. I had some kindergartners reading at a third grade level! When my students came to a word they couldn't read by sight, I would see them using the kinesthetic symbols to decode unknown words.

"Not only did it impact reading significantly, but also their writing. The program gave them the confidence to sound words out and write the sounds they heard. Having Kinesthetic Symbols made it less inhibiting to their writing and creativity. Students didn't constantly ask 'how do you spell…?'"

Kinesthetic Symbols for Sequences. Often the symbols are used to remember a sequence of items in order as when the students are memorizing the Ten Amendments in the Bill of Rights, the steps of how a bill becomes a law, the parts of a letter, or the steps of a math algorithm. By practicing the sequence repeatedly, it becomes automatic, and even fairly long sequences can be recalled in order perfectly. Misty used the symbols for sequences like chromosomal movement during the stages of cell division, stages of photosynthesis, and cellular respiration.

Angela Pinkerton, a Kagan trainer, used **Kinesthetic Symbols** with her first-grade students to help them remember the sequence of steps for tackling word problems, a strategy called CUBES. In her words:

"I taught my students a problem-solving strategy for word problems called CUBES. Before solving the word problem, we would stand up and review each letter's meaning with a corresponding kinesthetic symbol.

"**C** Circle the numbers (we drew a large circle in the air as we said the phrase).

U Underline the key words (we drew a straight line across our bodies horizontally as we said, 'underline,' as we said, 'key,' we pretended to put a key in the door, then twisted the key as we said, 'words').
B Box the question (we drew a box in the air, saying one word or syllable at a time as we drew each side of the square).
E X out Extra info (we put our arms in an X across our bodies for X, then dropped them down on 'out,' then threw our right thumbs over our right shoulders when saying, 'extra info.'
S Show your work (we drew a giant S in the air as we said the phrase).

"Then students sat down and followed each step with a word problem in their math journal. We did this as a daily math warm up, and my first graders never forgot the strategy."

Kinesthetic Symbols as Signals. Some teachers teach their students to silently convey information to the teacher. *"I need help," "Please slow down," "I need a restroom break,"* and *"I don't understand,"* are some common examples. The flip side of the coin is the teacher may use **Kinesthetic Symbols** to signal the class. *"Please work quieter," "You are working really well,"* or *"Please come see me,"* are examples. Without disturbing the other students, a teacher can silently signal an individual or a team.

Kinesthetic Symbols as Coaching Tips. Sarah Backner provides an example of how her students used **Kinesthetic Symbols** to scaffold support for each other within the Kagan Structures:

"I used Kinesthetic Symbols in my second-grade classroom at Martinez Elementary School in North Las Vegas, Nevada, each week for my vocabulary words. On Monday, I would introduce the class to the words with kinesthetic symbols. Then as the week went on and we reviewed our vocabulary words using structures, students had their coaching tips ready to go. For example, in Quiz-Quiz-Trade, if your partner is stuck on the definition, Tip #1: Demonstrate the kinesthetic symbol.

Kinesthetic Symbols to Recall Steps of Structures. Some teachers have used **Kinesthetic Symbols** to have students remember the steps of a cooperative learning structure. Kindergarten students easily recall the steps of **Mix-Pair-Share** once they have learned the symbol for each step.

Content Examples of Kinesthetic Symbols. In the Table: Academic Content Taught with Kinesthetic Symbols, are examples of academic content taught with **Kinesthetic Symbols**.

Kinesthetic Symbols for Kinesthetic Learners. Although I strongly advocate teaching all students with **Kinesthetic Symbols**, **Kinesthetic Symbols** can have an amazingly liberating impact on students who are especially strong in the bodily/kinesthetic intelligence.

For two examples of how it can be life changing for students if we teach with **Kinesthetic Symbols**, and respect the need for some students to learn and express themselves kinesthetically, see Paula's Story (p. 6.85)[147] and Gillian's Story (p. 6.86).[190]

Academic Content Taught with Kinesthetic Symbols

Language Arts	Math	Social Studies	Science
▸ Simile v. Metaphor ▸ Punctuation Marks ▸ Proofreading Marks ▸ Parts of Speech ▸ Literary Techniques ▸ Vocabulary Words ▸ Figures of Speech	▸ Forms of Linear Equations ▸ Angles ▸ Geometric Figures ▸ Math Symbols: (Plus, Minus, Equal, Divide, Multiply, Exponent...) ▸ Order of Operations ▸ Patterns ▸ Steps of an Algorithm	▸ Land Forms ▸ Branches of Government ▸ Accomplishments of a Person ▸ Historical Figure ▸ Bill of Rights ▸ Events in Sequence ▸ Functions of the President ▸ Steps: Bill Becomes a Law	▸ Geologic Regions ▸ Types of Rocks ▸ States of Matter ▸ Classes of Animals ▸ Body Systems ▸ Measurement Units ▸ Stages of Cell Life

Gestures and Kinesthetic Symbols Accelerate Learning

Teachers use **Kinesthetic Symbols** and gestures while teaching. Whereas the hand symbols created during the structure **Kinesthetic Symbols** are deliberately created and often involve considerable thought, gestures are spontaneous symbolization of ideas, often created unconsciously.

There is a growing body of research indicating gestures and **Kinesthetic Symbols** used by teachers are powerful symbol systems that promote learning, retention, and transfer of learning. Gesturing is extremely important in cognition, problem solving, and cognitive development. Students who are taught to gesture as they learn, learn more. Merely observing the teacher gesturing during instruction increases achievement. Before presenting that research, let's list some of what is known about gesturing:

- ▶ Gesturing is not merely imitation and does not need to be learned by watching others. Congenitally blind individuals gesture.[148]

- ▶ Young children spontaneously use hand gestures while telling stories,[149] solving problems,[150] and during conversation.[151]

- ▶ Memory for action words is increased when the corresponding action is performed as the word is said.[152]

- ▶ Making a gesture that improperly represents a subsequent action, interferes with ability to perform that action quickly or accurately.[153]

- ▶ Watching someone make a gesture while explaining an action determines how the viewer will perform the action.[154]

- ▶ If we have performed an action, when we hear that action described in words, our premotor cortex becomes active. The more we have performed the action, the more

our premotor cortex activates upon hearing the word. The implication: Comprehension of action speech is facilitated by the motor cortex.[155]

- ▶ Training gesturing is associated with improved skills in mental rotation and spatial transformation. Spontaneous gesturing during mental rotation tasks predicts higher performance.[156]

- ▶ Gesturing not only represents thought, it influences thought, and may express thought of which we are unaware.[157]

- ▶ Gesturing represents an independent cognitive symbol system that enriches understanding and increases learning and retention.[158]

- ▶ Teachers who gesture while giving instructions increase the probability of students' gesturing, which in turn leads to increased learning.[159]

- ▶ When the same verbal lecture is given with and without gestures, students in the gesture condition rate the lecture as more understandable and are more confident they have answered correctly questions testing comprehension and retention of the lecture.[160]

Gesturing and Executive Function. Executive function is more important than general intelligence with regard to problem solving and cognitive development. Executive function refers to the cognitive processes that we use to control our thinking and behavior when trying to achieve a goal or solve a problem. It is dependent on four factors: (1) short-term memory: holding content in memory, (2) working memory: manipulating content mentally, (3) impulse control: inhibiting interfering thoughts and impulses, and (4) cognitive flexibility: shifting from one perspective to another or from one problem solving strategy to another. In short, executive function is smarts. Whereas general intelligence includes the information we have accumulated and is dependent on learning and culture, executive function describes the most important pure cognitive abilities. As such, it is better than IQ in predicting a person's ability to learn and problem solve. Executive function develops from infancy through late adolescence.[161]

The use of gestures predicts the development of executive function even better than does age! In an extraordinarily revealing study, children ages 2.5 to 6 years of age were given a test of executive function, and their gesturing was carefully videotaped and analyzed.[162] Results indicated that gesturing predicted executive function better than did age:

"…both gesturing and age contributed significantly to task performance. However, gesturing was the stronger predictor of accuracy…." Further, spontaneous gesturing predicted accuracy better than spontaneous verbalization:

"Whereas 97% of the spontaneous gestures on a given trial resulted in correct sorts on that trial, only 69% of spontaneous verbalizations resulted in correct sorts." Interestingly, those children who used gestures most did better on the cognitive tasks even when they were not using gesturing. It is possible that gesturing, like speech, is internalized. When children learn to read, they move from subvocal speech to internalized speech or silent reading. Perhaps children who have learned to gesture internalize the gestures, moving from performing the gestures to merely visualizing them or remembering them nonverbally in the pre-motor cortex, without a need to carry out the action.

Gesturing Predicts Cognitive Leaps.

Gesturing predicts which students are ready to make a cognitive leap. In a classic Piaget conservation task, water is poured from a short, wide beaker into a tall, thin beaker and children are asked where there was more water. Those children that have acquired conservation of liquid say the amount of water is the same; those that have not, say the tall thin beaker held more water. Gesturing predicts which children will show more improvement when they are

> **Tip**
> Gesture while teaching. Draw students' attention to your gestures. Have students mimic your gestures.

subsequently taught! Among the children who lacked quantity invariance, when asked to explain their reasoning, those who spontaneously showed with their hands the decrease in width of the taller beaker, showed the greater improvement following subsequent training.[163]

Teacher Gestures Improve Student Achievement. Instruction that includes speech and gestures produces more learning than speech alone.[164] Students who mimic their teacher's hand gestures while solving math problems are more likely to obtain correct solutions.[165] Preschool children who watch an instructor produce meaningful gestures while teaching about symmetry obtain the symmetry concept better than those who receive the same instruction without gestures.[166] First-grade students obtain conservation better from a videotaped lesson if the instructor uses gestures.[167] Observing teacher gestures facilitates different types of learning.[168]

Teacher Gestures Facilitate Student Retention and Transfer. Not only do teacher gestures improve immediate acquisition of content, they also improve consolidation and retention of content and transfer of concepts to new problems. In a very tightly controlled gesturing study, experimenters gave second- and third-grade students instruction in mathematical equivalence via videotaped lessons in which the instructor either used gestures while teaching or gave the same audio instruction without gestures.[169] Students were given a pretest, and those who could not solve the math equivalence problems were included in the study. Students were tested immediately after instruction and then 24 hours later. To test retention and transference, the delayed posttest included not only problems like those on which the students were instructed, but also problems that required transferring the concept of equivalence to a different type problem.

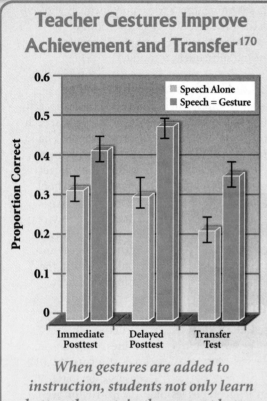

Teacher Gestures Improve Achievement and Transfer[170]

When gestures are added to instruction, students not only learn better, they retain the concept better, and are better able to apply the concept in a new context.

Many students mistake the equal sign as a sign to add numbers.[170] When students are taught to add with problems like $8 + 6 =$ ___, many interpret the equal sign as merely a sign to display a sum, not understanding that it is a sign to show equivalence. Many students obtain the correct answer, but they have only procedural knowledge; they lack conceptual knowledge. That is, they do not understand the equal sign is a sign to make the two sides of the equation equivalent. To test for acquisition of conceptual knowledge, the researchers used problems like $8 + 6 + 2 =$ ___ $+ 2$.

In the instruction video, the instructor said, "I want to make one side equal to the other side. Eight plus six plus two is sixteen, and fourteen plus two is sixteen. So, one side is equal to the other side." For audio only instruction, the instructor kept her hands to her

Students instructed with gestures performed better on the immediate posttest, delayed posttest, and on transfer tests.

sides. For the audio plus gesture instruction, whenever the teacher said the words, *"one side,"* she swept her left hand back and forth beneath the left side of the equation, and whenever she referred to *"the other side"* she swept her right hand back and forth beneath the right half of the equation.

Results: Students who were instructed with gestures performed better than those who received the same instruction without gestures. They performed significantly better on the immediate posttest, delayed posttest (24 hours later), and on transfer tests. See Graph: Teacher Gestures Improve Achievement and Transfer.

There are two very important implications to note about these results beyond simply that gestures boost achievement. The results strongly support the conclusions that: (1) gestures foster consolidation of new learning during sleep, or at least retention of new learning, and (2) gestures foster concept attainment.

Gestures Increase Retention. The brain consolidates new learning during sleep.[171] It may be that gestures help in this consolidation process: The audio-plus-gesture group showed higher performance following sleep whereas the audio-only group did not. (Difference between the two groups at immediate testing was $p < .01$; Difference after sleep, $p < .0001$). We cannot say with certainty that sleep consolidation is the cause of the increased retention in the gesture group, but it seems likely. At minimum, we can say with certainty: Gestures increase retention.

Gestures Foster Concept Attainment. The results of the transfer test are particularly telling. During instruction and during the immediate posttest, equations contained the same numbers on the right and left side of the equation. Problems were of the following type: $7 + 2 + 9 = 7 +$ ___. Students could learn to solve these problems with procedural, but not conceptual knowledge. That is, they could learn to ignore the numbers that were the same on both sides of the equation (the 7s in the example) and simply add the remaining numbers to get an answer. They could obtain the right answer without having grasped the concept of equivalence. To test for transfer of the equivalence concept, the second-grade students were given problems in which no number was repeated on both the right and left sides of the equation. For example, their problems were of this type: $4 + 5 + 7 = 3 +$ ___. Additionally, the third-grade students were given a test of even further transference. They were given multiplication problems of this type: $6 \times 2 \times 3 = 6 \times$ ___. That gestures facilitated transference to both types of new problems indicates that gestures are not merely a procedural aide; gestures actually foster concept acquisition!

Student Gestures Accelerate Achievement.
Children learn more if they gesture while learning.[172] It is not simply that better students gesture: Controlled research proves that teaching students to gesture while acquiring new information and skills improves comprehension and retention.[173] Students who are instructed to move their hands like their instructor's gestures are better able to verbalize the mathematical reasoning behind the gestures, even when that reasoning is never verbalized by the instructor.[174]

Symbolization of Content v. Hand Movements.
Researchers designed an experiment to test if the positive effect of gesturing is due to simply creating more active engagement via hand movements or if it is due to symbolization of the content. They instructed third and fourth graders in a math problem-solving strategy using three conditions: No gestures, hand movements that did not gesture the problem-solving strategy, and hand movements that gestured the problem-solving strategy. Students who were instructed with the correct hand movement gestures learned more than children required to produce partially correct gestures or no gestures.[175] The interpretation is clear: Gains from gesturing are caused by symbolizing the concept kinesthetically, not just by hand movements. The researchers concluded, *"We may be able to lay foundations for new knowledge simply by telling learners how to move their hands."*

Hand movements are processed in a very different way than gestures. The brain integrates gestures with speech to enhance meaning; hand movements during speech are not integrated with speech.[176]

Student Gestures Increase Retention of Learning.
By having students gesture during the acquisition of a math concept, the concept is retained longer. In the same experiment just described, on immediate recall following instruction, the group that did not gesture learned the concept as well as the group that did gesture. However, at a 4-week follow-up test, those who were taught to use gestures performed better than those who were not, indicating gestures help consolidate learning into long-term memory.[177] This finding using student gestures parallels the finding that teacher gestures also lead to more retained learning.

Why Gestures and Kinesthetic Symbols Boost Comprehension and Retention

Gestures represent a parallel communication system. Whereas language is processed primarily in the left hemisphere, gestures are processed primarily by the right hemisphere.[178] To say it crudely: Gestures say it another way. They use a different symbol system, enriching the communicative message. **Kinesthetic Symbols** communicate aspects of the curriculum that are difficult or even impossible to communicate with words alone.

Short-term memory can retain only a limited amount of information. By practicing a sequence of gestures, the sequence is moved from short-term to procedural memory. We say there is "memory in the muscles." Actually, muscle memory is merely procedural memory. When first learning a sequence of actions, there is considerable activity in the motor and somatosensory cortices of the brain to encode and carry out those actions. There is also considerable action in the prefrontal and frontal areas of the brain as we have to direct and maintain our attention on the task. As the task is repeatedly practiced, however, activation in those areas decreases and we see an increased activation of the basal ganglia and cerebellum, sites responsible for procedural memory. At that point, we can run off the sequence of actions without prefrontal activation, without thinking. We say the behavior is "overlearned" or that we have obtained "unconscious competence." To use a computer analogy, we move the behavior from RAM to hard drive where the behavior can be run off without occupying short-term memory.

We all experienced this process when we learned to ride a bike, drive a car, or use a computer keyboard. At first, we had to think about those actions, but now we can perform those actions without thought or while thinking about something else. So too is it with **Kinesthetic Symbols**. Because kinesthetic symbols are associatively linked to verbal content, a student triggers semantic recall as they enact a set of kinesthetic symbols.

To ensure that link, it is important that when students first acquire a kinesthetic symbol for a word or concept, we have students verbalize the meaning of the symbol *while* they are performing it. *Neurons that fire together wire together*. By having students make the symbol while simultaneously verbalizing its meaning, we ensure dendrite connections are formed between the motor cortex movement and the temporal lobe verbalization. Repeating the symbol and the word at the same time, a number of times, strengthens the link.

Kinesthetic Symbols: Three Modalities in One! If a teacher has students say their new vocabulary word while doing their **Kinesthetic Symbols**, they are engaging three modalities at once. *Auditory*: Students say the word. *Visual*: Students see the symbol they and others are making. *Kinesthetic*: Students are symbolizing the word with their hands. Not only is our content stored in those three areas of the brain, it is stored in the dendrite interconnections among them! Because neurons that fire together wire together, the neurons in the temporal lobe (auditory) are making dendrite connections with neurons in the occipital lobe (visual), and neurons in both these areas are sending out dendrites to connect to neurons in the posterior portion of the frontal lobe, the motor cortex (kinesthetic). Literally, students are rewiring their brains! With so many dendrite connections, it is no wonder that **Kinesthetic Symbols** are so powerful in boosting retention and recall.

In Conclusion

We have known for years that teaching with **Kinesthetic Symbols** is powerful, promoting learning and retention. The research on gesturing provides empirical evidence proving that teacher and student gestures provide increased comprehension, recall, and transfer of concepts. For years, most educators have relied almost exclusively on the verbal and visual symbol systems to communicate concepts. We can improve student outcomes dramatically by communicating also with gestures and teaching with **Kinesthetic Symbols**.

Tool 10
Make It Multimodal

The brain is specialized. Different parts of the brain process visual, auditory, tactile, and kinesthetic stimuli. Students differ not only in their abilities to process and retain these different types of stimuli, but they differ also in their preferences. Whereas some prefer to attend to and learn well with visual stimuli, others more readily attend to and retain auditory stimuli.

If I ask you how many windows there are in your house, in your mind's eye you are likely to walk through the house and "see" the windows as you count them. You are exercising your visual memory. If instead I ask you who has a more resonant voice, Ronald Reagan or Barack Obama, to make the comparison you call up an auditory memory of each of them speaking. Some individuals have stronger auditory memories; others have stronger visual memories. There is an association between how readily we create and retain auditory and visual memories and our preferred learning styles.

A published study claims that 82% of undergraduate engineers are visual learners and 94% of their faculty are visual learners![179] If you Google "Visual Learners," you will find wildly differing estimates of how common it is to be a visual learner. Estimates range from 65% of all learners down to 40%. You will find also many unsubstantiated claims like, *"visual learners are good at spelling but forget names." "Visual*

learners struggle during essay exams because they can't remember material that was heard in a lecture." This stereotyping of students in some cases has gone to extreme: *"Some school districts actually require students wear buttons identifying themselves as visual or verbal learners."*[180] These kinds of estimates, generalizations, and applications are not research based and warrant caution. Even among some who study modality preferences, there are poorly defined definitions of what it means to be a visual v. an auditory learner.

Let's take a peek at the complexity. Imagine we present two types of content to two learners. We present pictures to remember and verbal lecture content to remember. We measure the percent of content they remember from each presentation mode and their scores come out as follows: See Table: Visual v. Auditory Learners, Outcome 1.

Given this first outcome, we would have no problem labeling Student 1 a visual learner and Student 2 an auditory learner. In reality, the situation is never that clear. Consider the scores in a second example. See Table: Visual v. Auditory Learners, Outcome 2, p. 6.80.

Would we still be comfortable labeling Student 1 a visual learner and Student 2 an auditory learner? Both students retain about the same percentage from both modalities. Many students are neither visual nor auditory learners; they may have just a slightly greater memory for content in one modality or another, and that difference may not hold across different types of content.

Given Outcome 2, p. 6.80, the situation gets even more complex. Compare Student 1 to Student 2. Student 1 is more of a visual learner than an auditory learner, but retains far less visual

Visual v. Auditory Learners
Outcome 1

	Visual Memory	Auditory Memory
Student 1	95%	12%
Student 2	12%	95%

Visual v. Auditory Learners
Outcome 2

	Visual Memory	Auditory Memory
Student 1	55%	50%
Student 2	80%	85%

content than Student 2, who is presumably more of an auditory learner than a visual learner. Our visual learner does not come close to our auditory learner in retaining visual content, and our auditory learner is far better than our visual learner in retaining visual content! Given this, it seems fairly silly to label students as visual or auditory learners.

This labeling process gets even more questionable. Our results will come out very differently if the test for auditory learning includes an animated lecturer who has voice changes, dramatic pauses, and who speaks directly to each student compared to a monotone lecturer who looks down the whole time he presents. With the animated lecturer, our tests might show most learners are auditory learners; with the monotone lecturer, our test would probably show most learners are not auditory learners and retain more of the visual information. The truth is that no learner is just a visual learner or an auditory learner; we all learn in all four modalities. How much we learn in each modality is to a tremendous extent a function of the relevance of the content being presented and how well it is presented in that modality.

All this being said, educators converge on the generalization that students retain a greater percentage of visual information than information presented in the other three modalities. Prominent educational theorists estimate,

> Approximately 20% to 30% of the school-aged population remembers what is heard; 40% recall well visually the things that are seen or read; many must write or use their fingers in some manipulative way to help them remember basic facts; other people cannot internalize information or skills unless they use them in real-life activities such as actually writing a letter to learn the correct format.[181]

The same theorists claim percentages differ by age:

> Children enter kindergarten as kinesthetic and tactile learners, moving and touching everything as they learn. By second or third grade, some students have become visual learners. During the late elementary years, some students, primarily females, become auditory learners. Yet, many adults, especially males, maintain kinesthetic and tactual strengths throughout their lives.[182]

To indicate "many" adults maintain kinesthetic and tactual strengths, implies not all do. This is silly. All adults and children, save those with severe brain damage, process content in all modalities.

Caution! Content Overrides Modality Preference. There is another reason we need to be cautious in labeling individuals as "verbal learners" or "auditory learners" and then teaching them in the presumed modality preference. Content usually overrides modality preference. How best to teach a given content is often determined by the content itself, not the modality preferences of students.

Let's assume Peter is a visual learner. That is, he has an excellent visual memory, draws well, and is attentive to visual stimuli. Let's assume further that his classmate, Sally, is an auditory learner. She attends to and retains lecture content well and loves to prepare and give oral reports. Now, our task is to teach Peter and Sally long division. If we over-apply modality theory, we might conclude Peter would benefit most by being shown a diagram of the steps of long division and Sally would benefit most by having the steps described in an oral presentation. We would be wrong in both cases!

Learning the steps of long division, like most step-by-step skills, involves creating a procedural memory. Procedural memories are best acquired neither by hearing a lecture nor by seeing a diagram—procedural memories are created by repeated practice of the target skill. To teach long division via a lecture or a diagram is akin to teaching a student how to ride a bike by giving the student a lecture or showing the student a film. Procedural memories are acquired via repeated practice, by doing rather than listening or seeing. Often, the type of learning, not the modality preference of the student, best predicts which instructional strategy will be most efficient.

If we want to teach students about the meaning of the stock market crash of 1929, we could lecture about it or show pictures of people at the time. It would be far more powerful, however, to create a simulation in which students accumulate play money they can trade for rewards, but then suddenly have the money lose its value. If we want to create an episodic memory, we need to create simulations, episodes in our classroom.

> **Tip**
> Attempt to match instruction to learning style for different students only as a last resort. Instead, first analyze the content and determine how it can be presented best to be memorable for all students.

The general principle: Different types of content are best learned by instructional strategies that correspond to that particular content. This is true for all learners regardless of their modality preference. More often than not, efficient teaching matches instructional strategy to the content to be acquired, not to the learning style of individuals.

Stretch All Modalities

Given that all students learn in all modalities, rather than teaching individuals exclusively in their dominant modality, we best prepare

> **Tip**
> Applying universal brain processes are a better predictor of teaching success than attempting to tailor instruction to individual differences.

students for life by having them exposed to and gain competence learning in all modalities. In spite of the common idea that students should be taught in their preferred modality, there is no empirical evidence supporting that notion.[183] Not only is the notion impractical, it retards full development of students. Workplace competence involves receiving information in all modalities. To tailor the learning experience of each student to their preferred learning modality leaves them with weaker employability skills. We create richer lessons, more fully develop the brain, and better prepare students with a full complement of skills by teaching all students through all learning modalities.

Simultaneous v. Sequential Multimodal Input. Both brain theory and empirical evidence support the superiority of simultaneous over sequential multimodal input. One of the most fundamental principles of brain science is that neurons that fire together wire together. In learning theory, the superiority of simultaneous presentation of stimuli is called the *Contiguity Principle*. It explains why reinforcement is most powerful when it occurs at the same time or immediately following the behavior we wish to reinforce. Any delay between performance and reinforcement makes the reinforcement far less powerful. Connections are made in the brain when things happen at the same time. Thus, if we use gestures at the same time as giving our verbal instructions, the kinesthetic and auditory input form dendrite connections so later stimulation of one causes the other to fire. This increases the probability of subsequent memory: The content is now in two places in the brain plus in the interconnections. If the stimuli do not occur at the same time, connection between them is less likely to be made.

> # Tip
> To increase learning, present multimodal input simultaneously. Avoid the split attention effect: See Principle 5: Attention, Tool 6: Avoid Distractions.

Teachers who gesture while they give their oral instructions produce higher concept attainment. This, however, does not prove simultaneous presentation is superior; it proves only that multimodal presentation is superior. To test the contiguity principle, researchers have presented multimodal instruction both simultaneously and sequentially. The results: Simultaneous presentations are superior:

- ▶ Students who receive multiframe illustrations containing verbal descriptions within each frame are better able to solve transfer problems than students who receive the verbal information separated from the illustration.[184]

- ▶ Students who view an animation along with narration perform better on transfer problems than those who view the animation following the narration.[185]

The closer two modes of presentation are in time and space, the greater the probability of association resulting in deeper understanding and better retention of the content.

Multimodal Presentations Fit Today's Youth.
The need for multimodal input is greater among today's youth than it was a generation ago, because they have become accustomed to a steady diet of multimodal input including MTV, DVDs, YouTube, video games, and the Internet. The pace of stimulation has increased exponentially. To view, literally view, how the pace of stimulation has multiplied, simply watch a movie made 30 years ago. Everything moves slowly. We become bored, anticipating action that does not happen. So too is it with today's youth in a lecture. They are bored, having become accustomed to

fast-moving multimedia stimulation. Whereas yesterday's instructor could hold the attention of students with straight instructor talk (because that was the most stimulating game in town), today's instructors rarely can.

Because there is a strong need for multimodal input, and the brain is a parallel processer, if academic content is presented in only one channel, say instructor talk, the rest of the student's processing capacity will likely focus on nonacademic content including doodling, memories, fantasies, and attention to the hem line of the student in the seat in the next row! The more content is presented in the range of modalities, the more it will fully occupy the attention and processing capacity of students, and the more it will be retained. See Table: Teaching to All Modalities, p. 6.83.

Kagan Structures Are Multimodal.
This need for multimodal input is one reason cooperative learning structures are so powerful: They are multimodal events. They involve interaction, drawing, writing, discussing, music, movement, constructing, manipulating spinners, rolling dice, and building with hands-on manipulatives. For example, there may be a quiet *Think Time* followed by a rapid-paced pair interaction in the form of a **RallyRobin** followed by the team constructing a **Kinesthetic Symbol**. With each structure, and often with each step within a structure, different parts of the brain are engaged, so there is more stimulation. The content is approached in more ways, and the brain is allowed to function as it is designed to function —as a multimodal parallel processor.

Kagan Structures are designed to structure the interaction of students with the content, with peers, and with the teacher. Structures are content free and can be used to deliver any academic content. Because different structures engage

Brain-Friendly Teaching • Dr. Spencer Kagan
Kagan Publishing • 800.933.2667 • www.KaganOnline.com

Teaching to All Modalities

Modality	Sample Instructional Strategies
Visual	**Present Content Using:** Diagrams; Charts; Graphs; Pictures; Symbols; Movies; Illustrations; PowerPoint; Concept Maps; Handouts, Cloze Sentences in Handouts; Flip Charts; Guided Imagery; Visualization, Lists of what will be covered **Have Students:** Sketch; Draw Pictures; Make Maps, Outlines, Lists, Use Computer Graphics; Take Pictures; Color-Code, Circle, Highlight, Underline Words; Use Flashcards; Take Notes; Mind-Map; Word-Web; Create Graphic Organizers; Use Visual Mnemonics (Loci, Pegs)
Auditory	**Present Content Using:** Lectures; Guest Lectures; Audiotapes; Podcasts; Descriptions; Videos; Call-Backs, Answer Back; Poems, Rhymes, Jingles; Auditory Description of what will be learned in the lesson; Auditory Descriptions of what has been learned **Have Students:** Give Speeches, Oral Reports; Engage in Discussions; Debate; Create Lyrical Lessons; Teach each other; Summarize their learning to a partner; Read; Use Auditory Mnemonics (Acronyms; Acrostics, Rhymes)
Tactile	**Present Content Using:** Manipulatives, (Fraction Bars, Base-10 Blocks, Algebra Tiles); Labs; Props; Models; Hands-On Learning Centers; Applications **Have Students:** Build Models; Manipulate Think Pad Slips, Learning Cubes, Spinners; Use Tactile Mnemonics (Peg to Body Parts)
Kinesthetic	**Present Content Using:** Simulations; Field Trips; Drama; Formations; Corners; Similarity Groups; Line-Ups **Have Students:** Role Play; Move, Take Stretch Breaks; Dance; Create Plays; Make Mobiles, Mazes; Kinesthetic Symbols

different modalities, a teacher can make any lesson multimodal by selecting the appropriate structures for the lesson. Structures to engage the four modalities are presented here. See Table: Kagan Structures for Multimodal Teaching, p. 6.84. Detailed descriptions of the structures as well as sample activities for each are available in *Kagan Cooperative Learning*,[186] *Multiple Intelligences: The Complete MI Book*,[187] as well as in over 100 structure-based books available online: www.KaganOnline.com.

Multiple Intelligences

Like modality theory, Multiple Intelligences (MI) theory postulates that different students are attracted to and skilled with different types of stimuli and that a match of instructional strategy with stimuli preference will lead to enhanced achievement. Howard Gardner's theory of multiple intelligences, however, goes beyond the focus on sense modalities, including a broader range of stimuli to which students are attracted. It is more differentiated: Instead of lumping all auditory stimuli, it distinguishes attraction to words from attraction to music. Further, it includes stimuli that are not directly linked to the senses like the feelings of others (interpersonal) and patterns (logical/mathematical). MI theory postulates that attraction to different types of stimuli leads to skill in dealing with that type of stimuli, which in turn leads to different specialties or end states. A student strong in the bodily/kinesthetic intelligence, for example, is attracted to and practices the skills associated with that intelligence, and may become an athlete or dancer. See Table: Intelligences, Stimuli, Skills, and End States, p. 6.85.

Kagan Structures for Multimodal Teaching

Modality	Sample Instructional Strategies
Visual	Collective Memory, Draw It!, Draw-What-I Write, Listen-Sketch-Draft, Look-Write-Discuss, Observe-Write-RoundRobin, Same-Different, Team Mind Mapping, Team Overlap Maps, Visualization, VocabToons, Window Panes
Auditory	Answer Back, Circle-the-Sage, Debate, Dialogues, Echoing, Gambit Chips, Listen Up!, Listen Write!, Lyrical Lessons, Match Mine, Paraphrase Passport, Poems for Two Voices, Traveling RallyInterview, RoundRobin, Team Interview, Telephone, Three-Step Interview, Timed Pair Share
Tactile	Blind Sequencing, Draw What I Write, Draw-A-Chip, Find-A-Frame, Spend-A-Buck, Spin-N-Review, Spin-N-Think, Talking Chips, Team Projects, Turn Toss
Kinesthetic	Kinesthetic Symbols, Formations, StandUp–HandUp–PairUp, Traveling Heads Together, One Stray, Three Stray, Stroll Pair Share, Team Stand-N-Share, Traveling Star, Similarity Groups, Corners, Stir-the-Class, Team Charades, Value Lines, Agree-Disagree Line-Ups, Tableau

According to MI theory, each intelligence corresponds to a different type of stimuli and to some extent is processed by different parts of the brain or different sets of brain structures. A brain-compatible classroom includes experiences that stimulate and develop each of these intelligences.

Kagan MI Structures. In our own work with multiple intelligences, we developed 84 MI instructional strategies, called structures.[188] Each time one of these instructional strategies is used, it engages and develops one or more of the intelligences. Thus, by using MI structures as part of any lesson, the teacher is creating an MI classroom—engaging and developing different part of the brain. An advantage of the structural approach to MI is there is no need to develop special MI lessons or activities; MI is integrated into every lesson.

Each of the 84 multiple intelligences structures is designed to engage and develop different intelligences. For examples, **Formations** engage the bodily/kinesthetic intelligence whereas **Paraphrase Passport** engages the interpersonal and verbal linguistic intelligences. Because we advocate using each of the MI structures with the whole class, any time a structure is used, it "matches" some students and "stretches" others. For example, when **Formations** is used, students for whom the bodily/kinesthetic intelligence is strong are *matched*, they are receiving the content in their preferred modality. Students for whom the kinesthetic intelligence is weak, are *stretched*. That is, they are exercising and developing a nondominant intelligence. Similarly, when **Paraphrase Passport** is used, those students strong in the interpersonal/social intelligence and/or the verbal/linguistic intelligence are matched, and those weak in those intelligences are stretched. Each time we use an MI structure, we are delivering the curriculum in the preferred way for those who are matched, and we are developing a nondominant intelligence for those who are stretched.

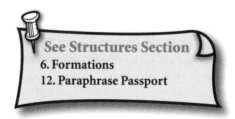

See Structures Section
6. Formations
12. Paraphrase Passport

Intelligences, Stimuli, Skills, and End States

Intelligence	Stimuli	Skills	End State
Verbal/Linguistic	Written and Spoken Words	Listening, speaking, reading, writing encoding and decoding language	Orator Journalist
Logical/Mathematical	Patterns, Relations, Numbers, Symbols	Problem solving, reasoning, logic, numerical skills	Scientist Mathematician
Visual/Spatial	Color, Shape, Distance	Sense of direction, architecture, painting, sculpting, arranging, decorating	Navigator Sculptor
Musical/Rhythmic	Rhythm, Pitch, Timbre	Composing, performing, appreciating, recognizing music	Composer Pianist
Bodily/Kinesthetic	Bodily Cues	Dancing, catching, throwing, jumping, handling objects moving with grace and precision	Athlete Dancer
Naturalist	Flora, Fauna, Rocks, Clouds	Green thumb, animal husbandry, discriminating, recognizing, categorizing, analyzing	Biologist Gardener
Interpersonal	Desires, Motivation, Feelings of Others	Accurate social map, empathy, organize and lead groups, understand and connect with others, conflict resolution and consensus-seeking skills, good team member	Counselor Salesperson
Intrapersonal	Emotions, Impulses, Moods, Deeper Thoughts	Self-knowledge, accurate self-concept, evaluation, self-direction, impulse control	Philosopher Religious Figure

Three MI Success Stories

Paula's Story. Paula's story illustrates how knowing the cognitive, or learning, style of a student can powerfully accelerate learning.[189] Early in her school career, Paula was assessed as learning disabled; she developed a very low self-esteem and a dislike for school. By fifth grade, Paula was several grade levels behind her classmates. Paula attempted suicide in the summer before sixth grade.

Her sixth-grade teacher noticed Paula moved with poise and dignity. Following her hunch that Paula would benefit from kinesthetic instruction, Paula's teacher asked her to create a "movement alphabet"—movements to form the letters of the alphabet. Paula responded. Not only did she create letters, she sequenced them into a dance. Paula went on to dance her name, the words on the blackboard, spelling words, and even entire sentences. She performed for her class. Paula's self-esteem and liking for school increased. By the end of sixth grade, Paula reached grade level in reading and writing. In seventh grade, she was mainstreamed in all classes and received above-average grades!

Had her teacher not recognized Paula's unique learning style, Paula's academic career (and possibly her life) would not have been saved. Paula's story is one of many that illustrate the power of adapting how we teach to how students best learn.

Gillian's Story. Let's take another example, the story of Gillian Lynne. Gillian grew up in the 1930s in Britain. She was doing terribly in school; she was always fidgeting and never paid attention to lessons. School officials told Gillian's parents that she was mentally disabled.

Gillian and her mother went to see a specialist, who talked to Gillian about school while the girl sat on her hands, trying not to fidget. After 20 minutes, the doctor asked to speak to Gillian's mother alone in the hallway. As they were leaving the office, the doctor flipped on the radio. When they were in the hallway, the doctor pointed through the widow back into the office. *"Look,"* he said, and directed the mother's attention to Gillian, who had gotten up and started moving to the music as soon as they left. *"Mrs. Lynne,"* said the doctor, *"your daughter's not sick, she's a dancer."*[190]

At the doctor's recommendation, Gillian was enrolled in dance school. There she found people like herself, who, as she describes it, *"people who had to move to think."* Gillian Lynne went on to become a principal dancer in the Royal ballet; founded her own dance company; created Collages, the first original dance show in England that was a mixture of jazz, classical, and words; began working with Andrew Lloyd Webber and other producers; and was the choreographer for the musicals *Cats* and *Phantom of the Opera.*

Jill's Story. MI success stories are not limited to kinesthetic learning. Bruce Campbell tells the story of a student we will call Jill who simply could not memorize her multiplication facts, no matter how much time she spent with her multiplication flashcards. Noting Jill's talent for drawing, Bruce suggested she draw a picture on each flashcard. After completing the pictures, Jill knew all the multiplication facts perfectly.

By coincidence, a year later while shopping, Bruce met Jill in the aisle of a supermarket. On the spot, he quizzed her on the multiplication facts. She still knew them perfectly! One of the most basic principles of brain science is that neurons that fire together wire together. By drawing on her flashcards, Jill was connecting an area of weakness to an area of strength. The math facts were so strongly linked to the pictures, Jill could not forget them.

What Do These Stories Tell Us?

Clearly, if we recognize the type of stimuli students are attracted to and skilled with, and tailor a learning experience to those special skills, we can help learners blossom, who otherwise would be struggling or failing. The stories encourage us to give special attention to struggling learners and to find ways to reach them.

Why Not Tailor Instruction to Each Learner?

The stories do not tell us to assess every student and attempt to tailor unique learning experiences for each student. There are four reasons to caution against assessing students and attempting to teach each in their dominant intelligence: (1) It Is Not Practical; (2) It Narrows Learning; (3) Assessment Is Fraught with Problems; and (4) It Limits Brain Development.

1. Not Practical. It is simply not practical to assess every student and tailor learning experiences to each. It would mean designing each lesson in many ways. Designing each lesson in one powerful way is a task daunting enough. To multiply that task by the number of learning modalities would mean spending each night planning and each day teaching, without time to do anything else! This is especially true at secondary where teachers see students in many classes each day.

2. Narrows Learning.
To teach each student only one way narrows our curriculum and narrows the learning experience for students. If each lesson is taught to all students, but contains a range of modalities, each lesson is richer for each student.

3. Modality Assessment Is Fraught with Problems.
As we have indicated, assessment of modality preferences is a tricky business. How we assess modality preference will determine our results (contrast the animated v. monotone lecturer). Further, some students may be strong (or weak) in several modalities. How should we label and teach them? Yet further, some students may be strong in one modality but prefer another—ability and preference are not perfectly correlated.

4. Limits Brain Development.
Because engagement of each modality and each intelligence is associated with activity in different brain structures, we are actually developing different parts of the brain when we teach in ways that engage the various intelligences. It can be argued that we maximize brain development not be teaching students in their strongest modality or intelligence, but in their weakest!

Brain neuroplasticity is well established. Brains are constantly rewiring themselves depending on which parts of the brain are frequently used and which fall into disuse.[191] For example, when a blind person touches Braille dots, neurons in the *visual* cortex respond. Why does the visual cortex respond to tactile stimuli in the blind? Because in the blind person, the visual cortex is not used, while touch is frequently used. The brain of the blind person rewires itself to make use of the unused parts of the brain. When a finger is amputated, within a few months neurons that received input from that finger are receiving input from surrounding fingers. Thus, it is not too much of a stretch to conclude that by using nondominant modalities we are actually rewiring brains—developing parts of the brain

that otherwise would be underdeveloped. Schools have implemented multiple intelligences theory in different ways and the positive academic and non-academic outcomes have been extraordinary.[192]

Some Limits to MI Theory
Some original claims for Multiple Intelligences theory merit reexamination. Those claims have been analyzed in depth in our book on Multiple Intelligences.[193] Let's briefly overview three questionable claims: (1) Intelligences exist as discrete entities; (2) Students can be labeled as being strong or weak in an intelligence; and (3) Intelligences have a location in the brain.

Do Intelligences Exist? As odd as this question sounds, intelligences do not exist as discrete entities. Intelligences are categories of skills, not all of which hang together. Let's take one intelligence as an example. We speak of the Visual/Spatial intelligence as if it were one thing. In fact, it is a label for a host of different, mostly independent skills including, among many things, finding one's way around, being able to recognize and remember visual stimuli, estimating distance, color coordination, solving jigsaw puzzles, forming mental images, reading maps, production and appreciation of visual art, and so on.

Each of these facets of the Visual/Spatial intelligence is performed by different collections of neurons in the brain. Because these collections of neurons are largely independent of each other, the skills do not necessarily correlate with each other. For example, if I come to school each day immaculately color coordinated, it does not mean I will be skilled at parallel parking! A good sense of direction may or may not be associated with ability to draw.

Although having categories of skills like visual/spatial and verbal/linguistic is helpful, we should not be seduced into thinking "visual/spatial intelligence" or any of the other MI intelligences as discrete, measurable attributes. Each student is high on some and low on other facets within each of the intelligences.

Is It Meaningful to Categorize Students?

I cringe a bit when I hear an educator refer to Susie as a "visual/spatial learner," or say Johnny is "bodily/kinesthetic." I cringe even more when I learn the teacher is planning to use different instructional strategies to teach Susie than Johnny. We have reviewed four pitfalls of attempting to tailor instruction to student modality preference: (1) It is not practical; (2) It narrows learning; (3) Classifying students is fraught with problems; and (4) It short changes brain development. Here we can add a fifth problem: (5) Students are not strong or weak in any intelligence. Because there are so many facets to each intelligence, each student is strong in some facets and weak in other facets of each intelligence. This is all the more reason not to label students as strong or weak in an intelligence and not to try to teach each student according to their strongest intelligence. The answer is to teach all students with a full range of instructional strategies to match and stretch all students.

Can Intelligences Be Located in the Brain?

Intelligences do not reside in specific places in the brain. The brain is mini-modular. That is, different facets of each intelligence are located in specific areas or sets of areas. Even though we speak of one intelligence called the Visual/Spatial intelligence, sense of direction is located in an entirely different part of the brain than color recognition. In turn, there are distinct parts of the brain dealing with different facets of dealing with color.

My favorite example of just how mini-modular the brain is comes from research locating the sites of two different types of logic. Deductive reasoning is processed primarily by neurons in the right hemisphere whereas probabilistic reasoning is processed primarily in the left hemisphere.[194] This finding indicates each intelligence, in this case the Logical/Mathematical intelligence, does not reside in a specific area of the brain.[195] Different facets

Brainiac Box

Question:
Where is the ability to deal with color located in the brain?

Answer:
The brain is mini-modular. *Anomia*, the inability to name colors correctly, occurs when there is damage to the temporal segment of the left lingual gyrus. *Achromatopsia*, the inability to perceive or imagine colors occurs when there is damage to the occipital and subcalcarine portions of the left and right lingual gyri. Inability to pronounce color words occurs following damage to the left posterior temporal and inferior parietal cortex.

of each intelligence are located in different parts of the brain. A student can be very strong in geometry and fall flat in algebra, or vice versa. There is not one thing called Logical/Mathematical intelligence.

Brain Base for Modality Theories

Common to both modality theory and MI theory are two modalities for which there is a firm rationale in brain science: Visual/spatial stimuli and verbal/linguistic stimuli. The brain science rationale for distinguishing these modalities is hemisphere functional specialization. That is, the left hemisphere of the cerebral cortex specializes in most aspects of verbal/linguistic stimuli and the right hemisphere specializes in most aspects of visual/spatial stimuli. There are, however, important exceptions to this general rule: Both hemispheres process both verbal and auditory stimuli. See p. 6.65.

Lumping music with verbal stimuli under the category of auditory stimuli, however, does not receive support from brain science. As we have seen, music, unlike verbal stimuli, is not located in one hemisphere or another, and, is located in the hemispheres differently for musicians and non-musicians.

Tool 11

Teach with Styles

Modality and multiple intelligences theories emphasize individual differences in *what* students are attracted to. Cognitive style theories emphasize individual differences in *how* students attend to and process learning content.

As we saw when we examined how to capture and hold attention, students have different cognitive styles. When presented with the same large L made up of a number of small D's, some students first see the large letter L and others first see the small D's that form the L. (See Tool 9: Respond to Attention Styles, in Principle 5: Attention). Those with a global cognitive style focus first and primarily on the big picture (one large L); those with an analytic cognitive style focus first and primarily on the details (many small D's). The Analytic/Global style dimension is but one of many style dimensions that have been proposed and researched. See Table: Cognitive Style Dimensions, p. 6.90. A number of these style theories are rooted in, or at least claim to be rooted in, brain science. For example, a Global Style is linked to right-hemisphere processing and an Analytic Style is linked to left-hemisphere processing.

The preference for one style over another can be so strong that a student will convert content presented in one style into his or her preferred style. For example, when presented pictures, some students with an auditory style convert that content into a linguistic representation. Some students with a strong visual style convert auditory stimuli into visual images.

The notion of cognitive style has a long history. In 1857, Charles Darwin noted two distinct styles in classifying species: "Those who make many species are the 'splitters,' and those who make few are the 'lumpers.'" The distinction between lumpers and splitters has been applied to styles of classification in biology, history, software modeling, language classification, liturgical studies, and philosophy. McKusick's analysis of lumping v. splitting approaches to the classification of diseases is an excellent example of applying the Lumper-Splitter distinction.[197]

A review of nine cognitive style dimensions indicated some measure ability rather than style, others have scant empirical evidence, and yet others appear to be developmental stages rather than a stable style difference.[198] Field-Dependence/Independence has a very high correlation with IQ subscales and is better thought of as an ability measure.

Many of the dimensions reveal a great deal of overlap. It is as if most of the theorists are trying in different ways to capture right v. left hemisphere differences. The left hemisphere focuses on details and also runs practiced routines with familiar stimuli. The right hemisphere focuses on the big picture and processes novel stimuli. It seems the various cognitive style theorists have focused either on the Analytic/Global or the Familiar/Novel dimensions and so their dimensions can be classified as Left/Right hemisphere dimensions.

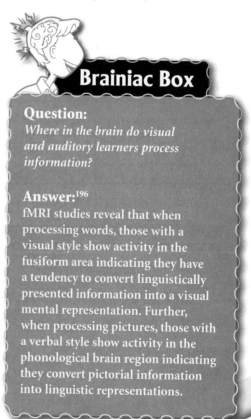

Brainiac Box

Question:
Where in the brain do visual and auditory learners process information?

Answer:[196]
fMRI studies reveal that when processing words, those with a visual style show activity in the fusiform area indicating they have a tendency to convert linguistically presented information into a visual mental representation. Further, when processing pictures, those with a verbal style show activity in the phonological brain region indicating they convert pictorial information into linguistic representations.

Cognitive Style Dimensions

Cognitive Style	Description
Analytic/Global	Focus on details v. Focus on the big picture
Impulsive/Reflective	Act on impulse; Quick decisions v. Reflect before acting; Deliberate before deciding
Visual/Verbal	Focus on images v. Focus on words
Leveler/Sharpener	Simplify, gloss over distinctions v. Perceive in complex, differentiated manner
Lumper/Splitter	Focus on similarities v. Focus on differences
Field-Dependence/Independence	Inability to separate details from context; Global perception v. Ability to separate items from context; Analytic perception
Divergent/Convergent Thinker	Creative, Preference: open-ended, no right answer tasks v. Data-driven, logical, Preference: Structured correct answer tasks
Holist/Serialist Thinker	Global, big picture, simultaneous, random thinker v. Detail, linear, step-by-step sequential thinker
Concrete/Abstract	Sensory based v. Concept based
Random/Sequential	Random: Unstructured, responds to various stimuli v. Sequential: Structured, step-by-step, one stimuli at a time
Explorer/Assimilator	Seeks: Novelty, new ideas, and low structure v. Seeks: Familiarity, low ideation, and structure
Innovator/Adaptor	Do things differently; Invent new responses v. Do things better; Improve practiced sequences;
Sensing/Intuition	Concrete: Sensory based, detail oriented v. Abstract: Generalizations, big picture oriented

With just a bit of a stretch, the many style dimensions correspond to the two hemisphere styles. See Table: Left/Right Hemisphere Style Dimensions, p. 6.91.

A Brain-Based Approach to Style

Ways of cutting the style pie have come and gone. In education, they have faded primarily for lack of practicality. Teachers were told to assess individual students and to teach each student differently according to the student's individual style. Teachers simply do not have time on a daily basis to design different lessons for different learners. How then is the style research relevant to us as educators?

I believe the style research is an important guide, encouraging us to teach all students in the most important styles. The result is to maximize brain development and to make lessons appealing to students of all style orientations.

Given this approach, the question becomes, which of the many style dimensions should we

Brain-Friendly Teaching • Dr. Spencer Kagan
Kagan Publishing • 800.933.2667 • www.KaganOnline.com

Left/Right Hemisphere Style Dimensions

Left Hemisphere: Analytic/Familiar	Right Hemisphere: Global/Novel
Verbal	Imaging
Sharpener	Leveler
Splitter	Lumper
Field Independent	Field Dependent
Convergent	Divergent
Serialist	Holist
Assimilator	Explorer
Adaptor	Innovator
Sensing	Intuition
Sequential	Random
Concrete	Abstract

apply? My guess is that the style dimensions that are most firmly rooted in brain science will be the most enduring. Two style dimensions built into the structure of the brain are right-left and top-down. A left-right hemisphere style is (Analytic/Global); a top-bottom style is (Reflective/Impulsive). Reflective corresponds to the prefrontal cortex which is located above the impulse-driven subcortical system below.

Left/Right = Analytic/Global Style

There is considerable evidence that the left hemisphere processes details whereas the right hemisphere processes the big picture. The evidence comes from both split-brain research in which the same stimuli is presented to each hemisphere independently, from lesion studies that examine what happens when one or the other hemisphere is damaged, and from studies that present stimuli to one or the other hemisphere in normal individuals.[199] The lesion studies reveal that when the left hemisphere is damaged, patients have trouble or inability in seeing details;

when the right hemisphere is damaged, patients have trouble or inability in putting the details into a meaningful whole.

Addition, Subtraction, Multiplication, Division Problems: Left Hemisphere. One type of split-brain research presents content to only one hemisphere at a time in order to determine how each hemisphere functions. For example, in one experiment, multiplication, division, addition, and subtraction problems were presented to a split-brain person. After the problem was presented, two answers (one correct; one false) were projected either to the right or to the left hemisphere. The left hemisphere picked the correct answer 90% of the time; the right hemisphere performed at chance.[200] This supports the conclusion that the left hemisphere processes calculations. Calculations are one of many examples of analytic, sequential reasoning. The left hemisphere specializes in sequential, step-by-step procedures. It does not look at the whole, but rather takes one part at a time. It is analytic, breaking the whole into its parts.

Brainiac Box

Question:
When we look at a large L made up of small D's, which parts of the brain process the big L and which parts process the small D's?

Answer:[201]
Experimenters used a number of large letters each composed of small letters. They had people direct their attention either to the large letter (Global, Big Picture Processing) or the small letters (Analytic, Detail Processing).

Results: Focusing on the large letter activated the right lingual gyrus; attention to the small letters activated the left inferior occipital cortex. This finding is consistent with the generalization that the right hemisphere processes globally and the left hemisphere processes analytically.

Block Assembly: Right Hemisphere. In contrast, the right hemisphere specializes in global processing skills. As we have seen, in a split-brain person, when given blocks and asked to assemble them in the same way as another set of blocks on the table, the right hand, which is controlled by the left hemisphere, cannot do the task; the left hand does the task easily, indicating spatial relational skills are right-hemisphere functions. The right hemisphere processes wholes—relations among objects; the left focuses only on discrete details so cannot arrange the blocks in correct relation to each other.

Given the strong support for hemisphere styles, we can feel comfortable that the Analytic/Global style dimension is here to stay. Further, we have support for the idea that when we engage both the analytic and the global styles in our classrooms, we are fostering fuller brain development than if we engage just one style.

Top/Bottom = Reflective/Impulsive Style

A second brain-based cognitive style is Reflective/Impulsive. The Reflective/Impulsive style dimension corresponds to the top-down brain specialization. Reflective corresponds to the prefrontal cortex residing in the top portion of the brain, and impulsive corresponds to the limbic system residing underneath. Our impulses to act are generated in the limbic system along with our feelings. The prefrontal cortex can inhibit impulses. It is the inability of the development of the prefrontal cortex to keep pace with the development of the limbic system in teenagers that makes them so impulsive. They leap before they look, often later regretting their actions. Later they ask themselves, *"How could I have been so dumb?"* Only after the teen years have passed is the prefrontal cortex sufficiently developed to consistently inhibit risky impulses.

The Quadrant Style Map

Years ago as a clinical psychologist, I began wrestling with how to conceptualize cognitive styles. I overviewed the various dimensions of cognitive and perceptual styles, trying to integrate the various dimensions with my experience as a clinician. I settled on a Quadrant Style Map that integrates what I thought are the most important style dimensions. The Quadrant Style Map fits nicely with both the Analytic/Global and the Reflective/Impulsive dimensions.

The approach began with my work with clients and my observation that thinking and feeling seemed to be opposite poles of a dimension. Some clients would come in talking a lot about what was going on in their life, analyzing their situation, trying to figure it out. I learned to say, *"Please stop talking and let yourself feel whatever emerges."* When the client would stop thinking, feelings would well up—often sadness or anger.

I began to think of thinking and feeling as opposite ends of a continuum. You can process either the feeling component of an experience or you can think about that experience, but it seems you can't do both at the same time. Thinking and feeling are two end points along a processing dimension. After I go to a movie, I can focus on the feelings the movie left me (*"What a sad movie"*; *"That movie left me in an upbeat mood…".*) or I can focus on any number of thoughts about the movie (*"Why did an actor say a certain line?" "Was that scene intentional foreshadowing?"*). I can't keep feeling deeply when I am thinking intensely, and I can't keep thinking logically while I am feeling deeply. Why? Thinking occurs in the prefrontal cortex and feeling is a function of the limbic system. We now know there are many inhibitory neural tacks between the two, so we can shut off feelings by thinking and shut off thinking by feeling.[202] At any moment, we process a stimulus by focusing on the feelings it generates or by focusing on the thoughts it elicits. Individuals differ in how much they focus on feelings v. thoughts. We all know people who are very reactive emotionally and we know others who are very cerebral.

A second bipolar dimension is what we do when confronted with a stimulus. Either we can take it in, perceive it—listen and observe, or we can react by doing something. For example, as my wife tells me about a difficult situation, I can either listen empathetically, or I can give her advice. I can take in or put out. Much was made of this dichotomy in the book *Men Are from Mars, Women Are from Venus*.[203] The author claims problems arise between men and women because women want men to listen empathetically whereas men want to suggest what to do to solve the problem. She feels frustrated: He is not listening. He feels frustrated: She is rejecting or ignoring my advice. This Perceiving/Acting style dimension also corresponds to distinct parts of the brain. We perceive stimuli mainly using our auditory, visual, and parietal cortices; actions are generated and carried out via our premotor and motor cortices.

We can symbolize these two style dimensions as follows, creating a quadrant style map. See Quadrant Style Map 1.

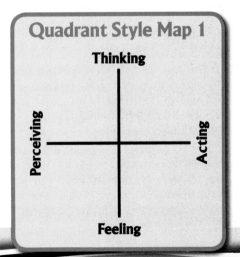

The Analytic/Global Style

Students who are strong in perceiving and feeling (bottom-left quadrant) are more likely to take in the big picture; they are more global in their style. Those strong in thinking and acting (upper-right quadrant) are more analytic. Analytic thinking is action oriented; it literally acts on the stimulus, breaking it into its components. Thus, thinking and acting are aligned with an analytic style; perceiving and feeling are aligned with a global style. This allows us to map the Analytic/Global style onto the quadrant map. See Quadrant Style Map 2.

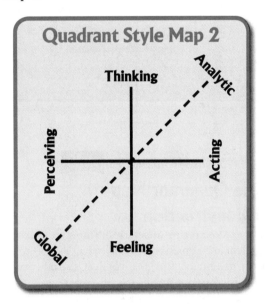

As we have seen, the Analytic/Global style dimension corresponds to left hemisphere/right hemisphere functioning.

The Reflective/Impulsive Style

The Reflective/Impulsive dimension also maps nicely onto the Quadrant Style Map. Emotion is motivation to act. If we are angry, we are motivated to fight; if we are fearful, we are motivated to run or hide; if we feel love, we are motivated to hug…. Those who are strong in feelings are motivated to act on their feelings (lower-right quadrant) so are more impulsive. Their motto: *"He who hesitates is lost."* In contrast, those strong in thinking and perceiving (upper-left quadrant) are more reflective.

Their motto: *"Look before you leap."* Thus, it is meaningful to map the Reflective/Impulsive dimension onto our quadrant map. See Quadrant Style Map 3.

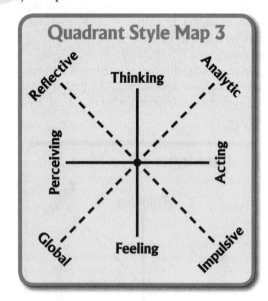

The Quadrant Map and Instruction

Rather than trying to determine the style of each student and somehow tailor different lessons to each, an efficient way to apply the Quadrant Style Map is to make sure our lessons respond to the four core styles. That is, if we want to match the style of all students, our lessons should contain questions to think about, content that evokes emotion, things to observe, and things to do. Further, early in a lesson, we need to provide students both the big picture and intriguing details: Where we are going and some of the interesting things we will learn along the way.

The Quadrant Map as a Corrective.

Following a lesson or lessons, we can take out the Quadrant Style Map and ask if we have been meeting the needs of all styles. For example, we might note we are giving students plenty of content to think about, but have not had content that evokes any emotion. This might lead us to consider ways to make the content more personally relevant, to connect it to students' concerns and feelings, to allow self-expression, opinions. Conversely, we might note there has been a ton of practice (acting), but no big picture or things to observe and reflect on. This might lead us to consider ways to focus on aspects of the content that are puzzling, or to ask questions that

are designed to have students think deeply about the meaning of the content. Not every lesson needs to respond to every style, but over time, if we want to respond to all styles, we want to include content that engages the range of styles.

Style Dimensions: Issues to Consider

When thinking about style, it is important to recognize that not everyone has preferred styles, and that ability does not always predict style.

Not Everyone Has a Preferred Style. It is tempting to classify everyone. Are you strong in thinking or feeling? Reflecting or acting? Are you analytic or global? In fact, this is foolish. We all use all the styles and there is every possibility. Some students might be weak in both analytic and global skills, some strong in both, and others strong in one, but not the other. A noble goal of education would be to make all students strong in all styles.

Style v. Ability. We need to be careful to distinguish style from ability. Strength in an ability is not perfectly correlated with a preference for the corresponding style. A person may be quite able to find the embedded figures, that is, have strong analytic skills, yet have a global style.

As we saw with the large L made of small D's, about half of us approached that stimuli with an analytic style (first seeing the small D's) and about half of us approached that stimuli with a global style (first seeing the large L). But within seconds, almost everyone had seen it both ways. The *ability* to see it both ways describes what we are capable of; our preference for how we approach the stimuli is our *style*.

Analytic Ability. There are tests of analytic abilities.

The Embedded Figures Test. The Sample Embedded Figures Test Item (see Box, p. 6.95), assesses how well a person can find a figure embedded within another figure.

The embedded figure is more or less hidden across the various test items. How many items a person can find and how quickly they can find them tests analytic skills—the ability to break a complex figure into its components.

Brain-Friendly Teaching • Dr. Spencer Kagan
Kagan Publishing • 800.933.2667 • www.KaganOnline.com

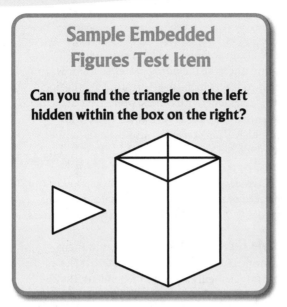

Sample Embedded Figures Test Item

Can you find the triangle on the left hidden within the box on the right?

show fragments of an object, and the test measures how long it takes for subjects to discover the object. See Box: What Is This?

Some people immediately see the helicopter and the car; others take some time; yet others do not find the hidden objects without having the pictures explained to them.

The Gollin Incomplete Figures Test. The Gollin Test is a second approach to assessing global ability. Each picture is presented first in separate tiny fragments. On each successive presentation more of the picture is filled in. The question: How quickly can a person make a meaningful whole of the fragments? Some people are very quick to form the big picture; others need more clues. See Box: Gollin Incomplete Figures Test.

A caution: Although the Embedded Figures Test is taken to be a test of general analytic skills, a person who can readily find the embedded figures in a visual/spatial task may or may not be able to efficiently analyze an oral argument to find its flaws. Visual/spatial skills may not generalize to analytic verbal/linguistic skills. Skills are mini-modular and we need to resist the temptation to overgeneralize.

Global Ability. There are also tests of global abilities; they assess how well we can put stimuli together to make a meaningful whole.

Cloze Pictures. One approach to testing global ability is to present cloze pictures. Cloze pictures

What Is This?

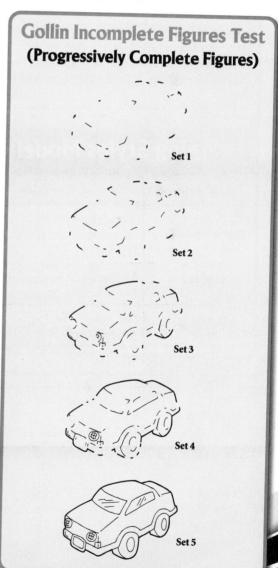

Gollin Incomplete Figures Test
(Progressively Complete Figures)

Set 1

Set 2

Set 3

Set 4

Set 5

Combining Modality Theory and Cognitive Style Theory: Dunn & Dunn

The most comprehensive learning style approach has been that of Rita and Kenneth Dunn.[204] They distinguish 21 elements of style! Their theory bridges multimodal theories and cognitive style theories. That is, some of the 21 elements draw from multimodal theory, indicating *what* stimuli students prefer (background sound, temperature, room arrangement, peer interaction…) and others of the 21 elements draw from cognitive style theory, indicating *ways* students deal with stimuli (Global/Analytic, Impulsive/Reflective…).

The Dunn & Dunn learning style approach defines five dimensions of stimuli each of which has a number of elements of style resulting in the 21 different style elements! See Table: Learning Styles Model.

Learning Styles Model

Type of Stimuli	Style Elements
Environmental	Sound; Light; Temperature; Furniture Design
Emotional	Motivation; Persistence; Responsibility; Structure
Sociological	Self; Pair; Peers; Team; Adult; Varied
Physiological	Perceptual; Intake; Time; Mobility
Psychological	Global/Analytic; Hemisphericity; Impulsive/Reflective

The Dunn & Dunn model is extremely comprehensive including preferences for warm/cold room temperature, furniture arrangement, working alone/with others, preferring movement/sedentary, as well as Global/Analytic and Impulsive/Reflective cognitive styles. I am tempted to call it the "everything but the kitchen sink" approach! It leaves me wondering how a classroom teacher could possibly respond to the pattern of style elements it generates for each student. One solution is to identify style clusters.

Style Clusters. Dunn & Dunn and their coworkers provide some evidence that these 21 style elements are not independent; they have identified two clusters: Analytic/Left Hemisphere v. Global/Right Hemisphere.[205] That is, students who tend to be analytic also tend to avoid external input, like bright lights, no interruptions, and to be more verbal. Students who tend to be global tend toward the opposite on those dimensions. See Table: Style Clusters, p. 6.97.

Some of these style dimensions seem to hang together in a logical way. For example, avoiding interruptions fits with working alone, avoiding background music and talk, and not eating snacks while working. Simply put: Some students prefer to avoid extraneous external stimuli while learning.

Other dimensions seem not to hang together in as logical a way. For example, my wife, Laurie, is the most persistent person I know when it comes to studying and learning. She can work steadily for a great many hours at a stretch. At the same time while she works alone, she enjoys music and snacks and is not bothered by others talking. She tolerates interruptions well. She draws from both style clusters. My learning preferences are different from Laurie's, but also draw from both clusters: I take more frequent breaks and enjoy snacks while working, but I am very sequential and can't work well if others are talking. I do not tolerate interruptions well. Both of us have style elements from both clusters, indicating a need for caution before generalizing or assuming the elements of the clusters hang together for individual students.

Style Clusters

Analytic/Left Hemisphere	Global/Right Hemisphere
Analytic, Detail Oriented	Global, Big Picture Oriented
Persistent	Take Frequent Breaks
Prefer Bright Light	Prefer Soft Light
Prefer Quiet Environment; Avoid Interruptions	Enjoy Background Music, Talk; Snacks While Working
Prefer Formal Seating	Prefer Informal Seating
Work Alone	Welcome Peer Interaction
Verbal	Tactile
Sequential	Holistic
Deductive	Inductive

Now That We Know About Modalities and Styles, What Should We Do?

Most theorists who have written extensively about style differences have advocated first assessing the styles of each student and then teaching students differently depending on their styles. Whereas this might be a good idea theoretically, as I have indicated, it is not practical. To teach each student differently or even groups of students differently for each lesson is simply not feasible.

In our own work in the areas of multiple intelligences, modalities, and styles we have advocated teaching each lesson to the whole class using a range of instructional strategies that engage and develop the range of cognitive and learning styles. This approach is spelled out in detail in our approach to engaging and developing all of the multiple intelligences for all students.[206] We recommend the same approach with regard to styles. Teaching in a variety of styles to all students makes for far richer lessons for all students and more fully develops their brains.

The more ways we teach, the more students we reach— and the more ways we reach each.

Tool 12

Establish Relevance

If I told you that your house is burning down, that would be very relevant to you. If I told you that your neighbor's house is burning down, that would be relevant to you also, but somewhat less. If I told you someone's house is burning down somewhere in a remote place in the world, that would be far less relevant to you. The brain is always asking: Will this affect my outcomes? If so, the brain lights up. The brain seeks relevance: Will this help me get what I want and avoid what I don't want? This selective attention to relevant stimuli is a by-product of the brain's most important function: Survival.

Stimuli that are personally relevant, useful, or potentially useful, are attended to and retained; stimuli are ignored if they are not relevant to our functioning or to our identity. An example of how we ignore irrelevant stimuli was provided by a simple series of experiments involving the United States penny.[207] The researchers asked how well twenty United States citizens could recall what is on a penny. They gave people circles and instructed them, "to draw from memory what is on each side of a United States penny." Subjects were asked to include all the pictorial and alphanumeric detail they could, and they were allowed to draw as many versions of each side as they wanted.

To score the results, the researchers did not count the quality of the drawings, but rather how many elements of the penny the people included in their drawings. People could score from 0 to 8 depending on whether they included the following elements:

Front: (1) Lincoln head, (2) "In God We Trust," (3) "Liberty," and (4) Date

Back: (5) Building, (6) "United States of America," (7) *E Pluribus Unum,"* and (8) "One Cent"

The penny, of course, is something U.S. citizens see frequently, and have seen for many years. Yet, performance was, as the authors described it, "remarkably poor." See Box: Penny Drawings by U.S. Citizens. The authors stated:

Not counting the Lincoln head and the Lincoln Memorial, the median number of recalled and correctly located features was one! Only four of our twenty subjects got as many as half of the features correct. One person did get all eight, but that person was an avid penny collector.

Penny Drawings by U.S. Citizens[207]

Although U.S. citizens see pennies frequently, and have done so for many years, they do not recall what is on the penny.

The Importance of Relevance

The penny experiment is an excellent demonstration of the importance of relevance. We remember what is relevant, useful to us. It is important for people to recognize a penny from either side, thus the high proportion of people who include the Lincoln head and the Lincoln Memorial. Beyond that, the details on a penny are not personally relevant. Knowing and remembering them do not help us accomplish anything we want to accomplish. The one exception was the avid penny collector for whom the details on a penny are very relevant because a penny collector must examine each detail carefully to rate the condition of a penny. For the others, in spite of seeing pennies daily for years, they did not remember the presence of or location of the details on a penny. Those details are not relevant; they do not affect the outcomes of non-collectors. *We remember only what is relevant!*

We can apply the relevance tool to create greater attention to and retention of our academic content. We simply need to show students how our academic content is personally relevant. Too many teachers attempt to create relevance by saying *"This will be on the test."* If scoring well on a test is not itself personally relevant, the student will not be invested in learning. Even if getting a good test score is important and motivating to a student, by using the test to create relevance, we have relegated learning to a mere means, the real goal of which is a grade. If when we ask students why they are learning, they respond, *"to get a good grade,"* or *"to pass the test,"* then we have demoted the importance of learning to a mere means to getting a grade—not the true purpose of education. In contrast, if we make our curriculum personally relevant for students, they become more invested in learning as the goal, not merely the means. If we then ask them why they are learning, they answer *"because I want to learn this."*

We can make our curriculum relevant by showing students how acquiring the academic curriculum relates to their personal interests and concerns, and that the curriculum empowers them to be more effective in their present and future life. There are numerous ways to make content more relevant. Let's explore five: We can design content that (1) is Empowering; (2) Links to Student Interests; (3) Addresses Student Concerns; (4) Facilitates Identification; and (5) Elicits Emotion.

These five ways of enhancing relevance are not independent. Some activities create relevance in two or more of five ways. For example, when Laurie Kagan taught fourth grade, she went to a Baskins-Robbins 31 Flavors Ice Cream store and asked for a menu. She made a copy of the menu for each student. Her math problems were menu-based: *"If you buy a triple scoop ice cream cone and an ice cream sundae, and pay with a $20 bill, not counting tax, how much change should you receive?"*

The activities that were based on the ice cream menu created relevance in at least three ways: (1) students could see knowing how much change to get back would be useful to them; (2) students are interested in ice cream; and (3) the very idea of being able to purchase ice cream elicits emotion.

Let's examine in more detail each of the five ways to make content relevant.

1. Content Students Feel Is Empowering

If, at the outset of a lesson introducing the concept and skills of subtraction, students learn that subtraction skills will make the difference between running out of money or having money to spend because they can balance their checkbooks, they will be more attentive when we teach our subtraction lesson. When Dawn Odum taught fourth grade, to introduce subtraction she partnered with the local bank. They were happy to talk about banking and brought each student his or her own a checkbook and discussed the relevance of math skills. Every time she introduced a new math concept, the class discussed *"Why do we need to know this?"* or *"Have you ever seen an adult doing...."*

Relevance is equivalent to anticipation of reward—to say something is relevant is to say

Why Do I Need to Know This?

"I remember when my nephew came home from school one day and told me he was sent to the office because he asked the math teacher, 'Why do I need to know this?' This was an eye-opener for me. I wondered how many of my students were asking the same question.

"As a result, when I start each new math concept I always try to help them understand, 'Why do I need to know this?'

"When I introduced measurement, I had students in pairs RallyRobin, 'What task do you do in your daily life that requires measurement?' I also asked, 'What jobs would require you to have mastered measurement skills?'

"I asked these same questions with every new concept. I asked it at the start of the lesson, but sometimes I also used it to wrap up a math lesson. Often times the responses were very different."

—*Dawn Odum*
4th Grade, Berkley Elementary School
Auburndale, FL

it will help us get what we want sometime in the future. Anticipation of reward, like novelty, activates the dopamine reward center that in turn increases attention and motivation.[208] Specific neurons respond to the anticipation of reward rather than reward itself.[209] Thus, to make our lessons memorable, we need to make the link between what is to be learned and how it will be rewarding for every student. Students verbalize this principle; they tell us lack of relevance produces lack of attention. *"I'll never use this, so why bother paying attention?"*

Why do we teach what we teach? Presumably, we choose content that students will find useful during their lives. To have students better attend to and remember academic content, we need to make salient the usefulness of the content.

Money: An Empowering Commodity.

Students know that money is useful. It can get them things they want. If we draw a link between learning and having money, students will see the usefulness of school achievement. The Bureau of Labor Statistics compiles data we can use in creating the link between school achievement and money.

Earnings go up and unemployment goes down as a linear function of level of education. Compared to students who make it all the way through the educational system, unemployment is five times greater among students who do not complete high school. Earnings for those not completing high school are $471 a week. Those who complete college earn over $1,000 a week. Ask students if they would like to earn $24,000 a year for the rest of their life or $55,000 a year. See Graph: Earnings and Unemployment Rates by Educational Attainment.

The Weather: Useful Data. In North

Carolina, a fifth-grade science objective is to predict upcoming weather events from weather data collected through observation and measurements. Rob Jutras helped his students reach that objective by making the content more personally relevant for them. He had them work in groups to generate reasons why predicting the weather would be useful. The students then moved to analyzing which kind of weather information would help them reach the goal of more accurately predicting the weather. Rob engaged students in conversations about the weather, making the usefulness link salient. In his words:

"Results from the conversations included learning the names of the clouds so they can match weather condition to cloud condition to determine if the clouds were effective predictors of those matched conditions. Well, after the unit on weather, students would make comments about the weather conditions as we walked around the campus. Their involvement and understanding of the objective became a lifelong comprehension of weather concepts."

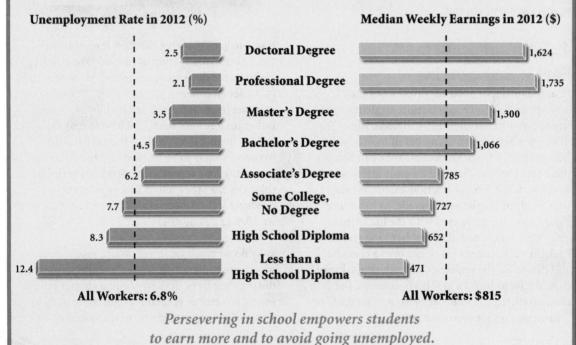

Earnings and Unemployment Rates by Educational Attainment

Unemployment Rate in 2012 (%)		Median Weekly Earnings in 2012 ($)
2.5	Doctoral Degree	1,624
2.1	Professional Degree	1,735
3.5	Master's Degree	1,300
4.5	Bachelor's Degree	1,066
6.2	Associate's Degree	785
7.7	Some College, No Degree	727
8.3	High School Diploma	652
12.4	Less than a High School Diploma	471

All Workers: 6.8%   All Workers: $815

Persevering in school empowers students to earn more and to avoid going unemployed.

Source: United States Department of Labor; Bureau of Labor Statistics; Employment Projections; Earnings and Unemployment Rates by Educational Attainment. www.bls.gov/emp/ep_chart_001.htm

Career Journal. A fourth-grade teacher in Martinez Elementary School, Las Vegas, Nevada, created relevance by having each student keep a career journal. Sarah Backner, a Kagan trainer, describes the process:

"Each week, students picked a new profession to research and as they learned a new concept, they journaled how the skill would be applied to their chosen profession. So, for example, this week a student might choose to explore the career of a professional baseball player. As we learn about converting fractions to decimals, the student would journal how to use this skill to convert batting averages, and other stats. What made it so interesting is the student next to the baseball player that week might have been an accountant. Every student in the room created their own relevance of the skill to the career of their choice. They shared with others, making what they learned relevant to their future."

Reveal How Curriculum Empowers. As we introduce a new skill, we enhance relevance to the extent we show what that skill will allow students to do—how it will empower them. For example, we make the empowerment of multiplication salient by showing how it will help us.

- ▶ **Calculating Earnings:** How much will we have saved in 3 months if we save $14 a week?
- ▶ **Calculating Spending:** How much will we spend on candy in a year if we buy three candy bars a week and candy bars cost $1.50?
- ▶ **Calculating Savings:** How much will we save in a year, if we can buy our candy bars for $1.25 instead of $1.50?
- ▶ **Party Planning:** How many people can sit at eight tables if each table seats seven people?
- ▶ **Driving:** How far we can travel before we need to fill up if our car has only three gallons of gas left and it gets 27 miles to the gallon?

One of the most powerful ways to make curriculum relevant is to have students see they can use their new skills to solve problems they are likely to encounter, or obtain rewards they seek. Linking the skills to being able to talk with a friend, cook a treat, plant a successful garden, purchase ice cream, or take an exciting trip are a few of the many possible examples.

Talking with a Friend. To understand time zones and to practice time zone conversions, students are told their best friend is in California and they are in Iowa. The friend says, *"Call me at 2:00 p.m. California time."* What time will it be in Iowa when they need to make the call?

Cooking. What could be more relevant and empowering to a student than being able to make something tasty? Dawn Odum gives the recipe:

"I often used cooking in the classroom. Following recipes requires math and reading skills. About every other month I gave the team a recipe. I used a variety of recipes. Anything from cookies to pudding. Students completed recipes as a team. I used RoundTable Consensus during cooking activities. Student 1 read the first direction, told team what he or she was going to do, got the OK from team. Student 2 followed next step and so on. When we were done, we looked at what math skills were used. We also discussed what would have happened if we couldn't have read and understood the directions. Sometimes I had them half or double a recipe emphasizing even more math skills. There were also times I used poor directions. I let them get partway through the recipe and we stopped and discussed the importance of writing

clear directions. Around Mother's Day, I let them each write their own recipe and we made a recipe book for mom."

Gardening. Showing how academic skills allow students to accomplish things they could not otherwise accomplish, creates relevance and motivates students to hone those skills. For example, when teaching how to calculate the area of rectangles, the teacher tells students to imagine they are going to put in a new lawn, and sod is sold by the square foot. They are then asked how much sod to buy given a diagram of the lawn area that is laid out in a way it can be divided into rectangles.

Dawn Odum describes how she had students use their math and reading skills as they created their class garden:

> "I tied the garden to multiple skills. We used calculating perimeter to build a fence. We used multiplication to determine how many plants were planted. We used measurement as we planted plants (depth of seeds planted and distance). Students saw the importance of being able to read the directions on the seed packs. We looked at the growth of the plants as a function of watering, and identified parts of plants."

Ice Cream Menu: Teaching Percentages.
When Laurie Kagan was teaching her students percentages, she had students use their ice cream parlor menus. She gave students a series of problems like: *"If you buy an ice cream sundae plus a double-scoop cone, and the tax rate is 6.5%, how much will you have to pay?" "How much would you pay for the same things if the tax rate were 8%?"*

Traveling. Students want autonomy. Think of the excitement students have when learning to drive, and being able to travel on their own. To link this drive for autonomy to the curriculum, students are assigned an age-appropriate "Team Trip." Students in teams are given $1,000 to spend on a road trip. They use the Internet to download maps and sites of interest. They need to carefully calculate how many miles they can reasonably travel each day given speed limits. They need to calculate gas expenses given a car that gets 36 miles per gallon on the road and 20 miles per gallon on city streets. They need to check the cost of gas, hotel prices, and food prices. Their team trip write-up must include a detailed budget, a map showing their route, and an essay by each student on a different point of interest they visited on their imaginary trip.

Running a Business. What could be more empowering than seeing that the skills acquired in school allow you to run a business. Denise Goevert describes how her students each year run a small counter-service restaurant. See Box: The Pit Stop, p. 6.103.

2. Content Linked to Student Interests

We enhance the relevance of our curriculum for students by linking the curriculum to their interests. When students are interested in a topic, their minds wander less, they take better notes, and they score higher academically.[210] Text passages that are more interesting to students are better comprehended and recalled.[211] The importance of interest in grabbing and holding attention as well as in promoting comprehension of content has been underestimated.[212] In fact, interest is as powerful as text difficulty in predicting reading comprehension![213] With easy but uninteresting text, minds wander and comprehension suffers. With difficult but interesting text, readers work their way through the difficulty to master the content.

How then can we enhance student interest?

Empirical research provides evidence that students find text more interesting if it contains surprise, coherence, concreteness, vividness, and ease of comprehension.[214] There are three categories of stimuli that stimulate interest: Affective Interest, Cognitive Interest, and Personal Interest. Affective and Cognitive Interest

The Pit Stop

"The Pit Stop is a small business operated by the Business Management and Entrepreneurship students at Hesston High School, Hesston, Kansas. Opened in 2003, the business has evolved from a coffee and snack shop with limited hours to a small counter-service restaurant, open before, during, and after school for activities. The desire to give students real-world experience in starting and operating a business lead to the opening of The Pit Stop. The school district and numerous donors funded the original project; however, The Pit Stop is now self-supporting with limited funding from the district.

"Career and Technical Education initiatives provided the structure for the sequence of courses. Students are required to take one introductory business course prior to enrollment in Business Management. Application and instructor permission are required for enrollment, with approximately 25–30 students enrolling in Business Management and/or Entrepreneurship each year. Student learning is evaluated based on performance objectives and a participation rubric, as well as weekly assignments. While a text is used for both courses and state competencies are followed, the majority of learning comes from the daily operation of the business.

"The course sequence for The Pit Stop is to enroll in Business Management for the first year, followed by Entrepreneurship for the second year. This allows for some continuity in the day-to-day operations of the business. One of the biggest challenges is the transition from one year to the next. Each new school year brings a new group of students that must be trained quickly in the management of the business. The second-year students have learned about employee retention and the value of work experience! Another challenge for The Pit Stop is our location. While it has been a benefit to be the only option for our market (staff and students)

"In The Pit Stop you learn so much more than a book can teach you. I've learned all aspects of a business that I hope to utilize in my own business one day."

—Rachel Shogren, Class of 2013

to purchase drinks and snacks during the school day, we must also be conscious of pricing and the nutritional content of menu items. Prices are set at a level to cover costs and profit margin, yet remain affordable to students and staff. Nutritional guidelines are set by the federal and district Wellness Policy guidelines. If this business were located outside of a school, the pricing structure and menu could look very different. This challenge has provided students with the opportunity to problem solve and be creative with our menu.

"One of the primary benefits of having The Pit Stop is the change in climate at Hesston High. Having a place for students to come to that is run by the students, has created a positive atmosphere. They are excited to show off 'their' business to visitors and students from surrounding schools, creating a sense of pride throughout the building.

"I have enjoyed the challenge of educating students through the operation of The Pit Stop because of the relationships that can be formed, both student-to-student and teacher-to-student. Teaching kids to work with, resolve conflict

"Having a class like The Pit Stop helped me appreciate a hands-on learning style rather than a traditional style. It made school seem more like real life. The experiences I had in The Pit Stop have transferred to everyday life."

—Molly Easley, Class of 2011

with, and have fun with their peers is something that will stick with them beyond their high school experience. They are developing life-long skills that will stay with them, as they become successful employees and managers in their chosen careers. These skills do not come from a textbook, but the daily operation of The Pit Stop."

—**Denise Goevert**
Business/CTE Teacher
Hesston High School, Hesston, KS

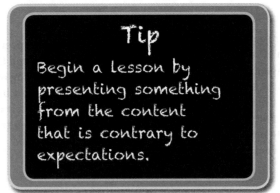
> **Tip**
> In teaching history, literature, and science, link the curriculum to topics related to survival and pleasure.

are common to all humans—they are based in our biology and the way the brain makes sense of the world. Personal Interest is based on individual genes and experiences.

Affective Interest. Content is inherently interesting if it relates to obtaining what we want and avoiding what we don't want. We are biologically set to attend to things that promote our survival—that allow us to obtain pleasure and avoid pain. Things that create affective interest include:

- ▶ **Survival-Related Stimuli:** Violence, Death, Injury, Power, Money, and Competition
- ▶ **Pleasure-Related Stimuli:** Food, Love, Cooperation, Sensuality, and Sex

Cognitive Interest. We are interested in anything that causes us to revise our set of expectations about how things behave. We are constantly making predictions, and when something doesn't conform to one of our predictions, we become interested because we need to revise our picture of the world. If we turn on the kitchen faucet and no water comes out, we suddenly become interested. Anything that violates our expectations demands our interest. Novelty, surprise, and uncertainty all demand additional cognitive effort as we try to reconcile present with past experience and/or predict what will happen next. We are biologically geared to attend to novelty

> **Tip**
> Begin a lesson by presenting something from the content that is contrary to expectations.

because it may be a threat or an opportunity. Things that create cognitive interest include:

- ▶ Violation of expectations
- ▶ Novelty
- ▶ Surprise
- ▶ Uncertainty

The unexpected grabs our attention; it demands we revise our expectations. To take a simple example, read each of the following two sentences, and then ask yourself which one grabs your interest more:

Sentence 1: John, who is 12 years old, walks across the street and hits Bill.

Sentence 2: John, who is 12 years old, walks across the street and hits a policeman.

Why is sentence 2 more interesting? Twelve-year-old kids sometimes hit another kid, but they simply do not walk across the street to hit policemen. We wonder why he did such an unusual thing, and what might be the consequence.

As simple as is this example, it has implications for us as teachers. If we embed the unexpected in our curriculum, we can grab the attention of our students.

Personal Interest. Students each have their own areas of interest. Many students have interests in sports, clothes, a TV series, actors, and/or types of music. Some students have interests not commonly held—butterflies, France, stamp collecting, model airplanes. The more we can link our curriculum to the interests of our students, the greater will be their liking for class, and memory for content. Not all curricula lend themselves to linking to specific interests, but with a bit of imagination, we can make that link. For example, in teaching the golden ratio, Rochelle Shumaker of Republic Middle School in Republic, Missouri, linked the content to something all students are interested in—their own body.

Relevance Boosts Engagement

"With word problems, I try to create an example that relates to a job that students might have and the wages they can expect to earn by working a certain number of regular hours and overtime hours. With fractions, we talk about credit cards and interest rates and what paying the minimum amount each month really translates to. If I can make it relevant to what goes on in their world, it makes a huge difference in their understanding and reduces their anxiety levels."

—Mark Dahlsten
Mathematics, Hesston High School
Hesston, KS

"We did the 'Golden Ratio' this week and that has sparked discussions which I didn't even think about related to body image, self-esteem, and being in middle school. The students work in groups of four and have to measure eight parts of their bodies, which are broken into four sections. For example, person 1 measures the length of the leg and then the hip to the knee and tells the group the ratio. He measures everyone in his group. So each person in the group gets a section to measure for everyone. Once the group gets the ratios done, individually they calculate the decimal form of their ratio and compare it to the Golden Ratio decimal. I give them the Golden Ratio, but I also give them a range to see if they fit the Golden Ratio. After all the calculations are done, they then discuss their results."

I am reminded of a time I was asked to do a demonstration lesson on Greek history to a group of students who had no interest in the topic. At the outset of the lesson, I asked students to do a **RoundTable** listing all the sports they could think of. Next, I had students **RoundTable** all the TV programs and movies they could. Finally, I asked the students to take turns putting happy faces, sad faces, or both next to each TV program depending on how the show made them feel. I then explained how what they had done had its roots in Greek history. Many of the sports they had listed had their roots in the ancient Olympic Games. The tradition of making comedy and tragedy core to entertainment is rooted in ancient Greek theater. Because I had linked the academic content to their personal interests (sports and TV), students became interested in ancient Greece—it was relevant to their personal interests.

The theory of multiple intelligences goes a long way toward explaining personal interests. Different individuals are attracted to and thereby become skilled with different types of stimuli. Howard Gardner originally postulated seven intelligences:[215]

> **Verbal/Linguistic**
> **Logical/Mathematical**
> **Visual/Spatial**
> **Musical/Rhythmic**
> **Bodily/Kinesthetic**
> **Interpersonal/Social**
> **Intrapersonal/Introspective**

Relevance via Remodeling

"With our floor plan project, kids have to "remodel" a house. They have to find the area of rooms and figure the cost to perform specific tasks. Most students enjoy this project because they can picture how they may actually do this in their future."

—Alana Cutbirth
Mathematics, Rebuplic High School
Republic, MO

He later added an additional intelligence, the naturalist intelligence and speculated about the existence of a spiritual intelligence as well.

Gardner originally proposed using different instructional strategies to teach students strong in different intelligences, and even to assign them to different classes depending on their strongest intelligences. In our response and extension of the theory, Miguel Kagan and I proposed a different approach.[216] Rather than using different strategies to teach students who are strong in different intelligences, we have taken the approach of teaching all students with strategies that engage and develop each of the intelligences. We developed structures, instructional strategies, to engage and develop each of the intelligences. The structures can be used at any grade and with almost any academic content. The three main advantages of this approach: (1) Students become well rounded, developing all intelligences; (2) Students are not tracked or stereotyped, and (3) The teacher does not have to develop different lessons for students with different intelligences.

> **Tip**
> To the extent we engage the multiple intelligences, our students will be more motivated to learn.

In our extension of the theory of multiple intelligences, we pointed out that as much evidence exists for a mechanical intelligence and a culinary intelligence as for the original seven intelligences, and that different students can be attracted to and skilled with specific types of stimuli not included in the set of intelligences postulated by Gardner.

Discovering Student Interests. If we have the time, it is very helpful to chat with each student to discover their personal interests.

Kagan Structures Reveal Student Interests. Kagan Structures allow students to reveal their

> **Tip**
> Discover the personal interests of students who are low in motivation, and link the curriculum to their topics of interest.

interests to each other, and by listening in, the teacher gets to know his or her students. Teachers consistently report that once they begin using the Kagan Structures, they have more contact with their students—they know them better and have an improved relationship. There are several reasons for this. If a teacher's role is to stand in front of the class and present information, social distance is created between a teacher and his or her students. If, in contrast, the teacher's role is to circulate among teams and listen in while they interact, the teacher comes to know the students much better. This is especially true if sometimes the teacher has students do a **Three-Step Interview** or a **Timed Pair Share** to share personal interests, hobbies, and aspirations. Although mostly used for academic content, **Swap Talk** and **Traveling RallyInterview** are used with personal information (especially at the beginning of the semester) to have classmates get to know each other. If the teacher circulates during this time, the teacher comes to know his or her students.

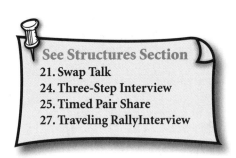

See Structures Section
21. Swap Talk
24. Three-Step Interview
25. Timed Pair Share
27. Traveling RallyInterview

The Interest Survey. It can be helpful to survey students to discover their particular interests. In introducing the survey to students, we might say, *"We will spend time together in this class, and I would like to know more about you as a person. If you are willing, it would help me if you to tell me about your personal interests."* Almost all students appreciate their teacher taking a personal interest in them. See Blackline: Internet Survey, p. 6.107.

Interest Survey

Directions: Answer the questions about your personal interests.

1. **If you could have any profession, what would it be? Why?** _____
_____
_____

2. **List your hobbies.** _____
_____

3. **Do you enjoy making things? If so, what?** _____
_____
_____

4. **Which sports do you enjoy watching? Which sports do you like to play?** _____
_____
_____

5. **Do you have favorite teams? If so, which teams?** _____
_____

6. **Do you like listening to music? If so, what type? Who are your favorite bands? Do you have a favorite singer?** _____
_____
_____

7. **Do you play a musical instrument or sing? Please describe.** _____
_____

8. **List your favorite TV programs.** _____
_____

9. **Do you have any collections? If so, what do you collect?** _____
_____

10. **Are you curious about something? Please describe.** _____
_____
_____

After students complete the Interest Survey, you can have students share their interests with the class or within their teams in a variety of ways. For example, focusing on Question 2, Hobbies, you can have students do a **Similarity Groups** activity. They can group by their favorite hobbies sharing within groups to get to know others with a similar hobby and the groups can share out with the rest of the class so that class see the range of hobbies classmates have.

To share within teams, you might focus on Question 6, Music, and have students do a **RallyRobin** with a partner naming favorite bands. Focusing on Question 10, What are you curious about?, you might have students **RoundRobin** within teams things that capture their interest.

Collect the Interest Surveys and read through them to discover individual interests of students as well as class trends. For example, if Bob is a reluctant learner and you find he has a particular interest in skateboarding, you can integrate skateboarding into math or physics problems. If a particular interest is common among students, that can be the basis for a writing topic.

Increasing Student Interest.

We can increase student interest by expressing our own interest in the content; by posing puzzling questions; by having students experience an unexpected outcome; by providing choices, hands-on activities, field trips, and challenges; and by having students generate questions, predictions, postdictions, and estimates. In addition, using a variety of instructional strategies increases student interest.

Teacher Interest. One of the most powerful tools we have for generating student interest in our content is our own interest. How we feel about the content speaks to our students louder than what we say. Through mirror neurons, interest becomes contagious. If you are not terribly interested in some lesson content you must teach, take the time to find something in the lesson that interests you. Begin the lesson by sharing your own interest.

Puzzling Questions. A question is like an itch, demanding our attention. Once we have a question, we want an answer. Thus, one way to generate student interest is to have students puzzle over a question to which they don't have an answer. Tool 1: Stimulate with Surprise and Novelty, p. 6.4, lists a number of imponderables to capture an hold interest—questions like,

> ▶ *"If horses and hippos have the same diet, why do they grow up so different?"*
> ▶ *"Why does a giraffe know how to stand and walk as soon as it is born, but human infants take a year to learn those skills?"*
> ▶ *"Why don't spiders stick to their own webs?"*

Unexpected Outcomes. Tool 1: Stimulate with Surprise and Novelty, pp. 6.4–6.13, provides a number of ways to stimulate interest by presenting students with unexpected outcomes across the curriculum areas.

Student Generated Questions. A powerful way to stimulate interest is to have students form a habit of mind of asking questions. At any moment, we can look around and ask questions of what we see: *"How does my computer work? Who decided on the color to paint this room? How could this room be made more functional? Prettier?"* Posing a question is the first step in generating interest. Questioning too often has been the domain of the teacher, and the type of question has too often been a right-wrong question. Teachers' questions too often are not true questions. A true question is one to which we do not know the answer. Teachers' questions too often are mini quizzes. The teacher knows the answer and asks the question to check for student understanding. We can foster interest by posing true questions—asking questions to which we do not know the answer. By modeling our own curiosity, we generate curiosity in our students.

The Question Dice and Spinners. We can foster questioning as a habit of mind in our students by having students generate true questions on a regular basis—questions to which they do not know the answer. Powerful tools to help students generate true questions are the Question Dice and Question Spinners.[217] Each time students role the two Question Dice or spin the two Question Spinners, they generate 1 of 36 question prompts. Seeing the question prompts (How did...?, Who can...?, When will...?, etc.), questions about the content pop to mind. The Question Dice can be used to generate questions about almost any academic content. In the process, students become more interested in the content and develop questioning as a habit of mind.

Hands-On Activities. Students who are bored with algebra become intensely interested when we have them manipulate algebra tiles. The light goes on for many students when they work at the concrete level; students who just "don't get" borrowing, immediately grasp the concept when they are allowed to manipulate base-ten blocks. Their interest skyrockets. Students are highly successful in the Singapore Math program in part because the program relies heavily on students drawing math problems. The visual helps students grasp concepts that would be beyond them otherwise.

Hands-on activities are not limited to math. Book reports become more interesting for students if they draw a picture and explain their picture. Science experiments generate interest. Creating and manipulating time lines with objects representing events make history more memorable. Hands-on activities create greater involvement and interest.

Field Trips and Multimedia. Learning about beavers from a book pales compared to visiting a beaver dam and watching beavers in action. If there are no beaver dams in the area, videos are the second-best alternative. With the proliferation of web-based videos, videos are readily available on almost any topic. Creating team or class videos on a topic and having students post their videos online is another way to generate and hold student interest. The more senses that are involved in an activity, the greater the interest.

Having students build a beaver dam or having them do a bodily-kinesthetic simulation, forming the dam, adds additional senses and so heightens interest.

Challenges. Challenge piques interest. Challenges can be of the class, of teams, or of individuals. When you give a challenge to teams or to the class, it is important to assign roles or divide the labor so everyone contributes. Otherwise, we run the risk of having free-riders who sit back and let others do the work. A few of the many possible challenges:

▶ *"How large of a square of lawn would it take to contain a million blades of grass?"*
▶ *"If each generation is 25 years, how many generations ago was the Declaration of Independence signed?"*
▶ *"What are all the arguments you can make for and against the theory of evolution?"*
▶ *"Which way of folding paper will create a paper airplane that will travel farthest?"*
▶ *"How many words can you find that rhyme with the word 'Fun?'"*

With more advanced students, teams can come up with content-related challenges to present to other teams.

Challenges can be used as class energizers. The *Silly Sports & Goofy Games* book includes thirteen crazy challenges.[218] For example, in the challenge game **Magic 11**, students form groups of four to six. They hold their right hand behind their back. With their left hand held in a fist, in unison they chant, *"One, Two, Three, 11!"* As they say 11, they bring their right hand forward revealing one to five fingers. The Challenge: Have all the fingers of the group sum exactly to 11. If students don't succeed, they try again. When they succeed, they celebrate. If they succeed early, they try a different number.

Student-Generated Predictions, Postdictions, and Estimates. When we make a prediction, postdiction, or estimate, immediately we become more interested in the answer. We want to know if our guess is confirmed or not.

Predictions. Teachers can generate more interest in a book they are about to read to the class or a book they will have students read if they simply hold up the cover and ask students to turn to a partner and each make a prediction: *"What is the book about? What will happen in the story?"* Half way through the book, teachers can sustain interest by stopping at a suspenseful moment and have students again make a prediction, this time about what will happen next.

In teaching a unit on the weather, we boost interest in the topic by having students make and record their predictions on number of rainy days in the next month, number of days the temperature will exceed 80 degrees (or whatever is about ten degrees above average for that month in your area), and/or how many days wind will exceed 15 miles an hour.

Postdictions. Postdictions are informed guesses about the outcome of events that have already occurred. Like predictions, they are powerful tools to increase interest. During a lesson on a historical decade, we might ask students to guess the popular vote margin and the electoral college margin on a given presidential election; how many states had a ban on mixed race marriage in a given year; what percent of the U.S. budget was spent on military and on welfare; or what percent of families were on welfare at the beginning of the Bush presidency and at the end.

Estimates. Estimates stimulate interest in the same way as do predictions and postdictions. Once we make an estimate, we want to know the answer. Students can estimate what percent of the class have a family dog, how long it will take to drive from California to New York at 60 miles an hour if there were a completely straight road, the combined weight of all the students in the class in kilos, the height of the tallest building. An estimate is like an itch. Once made, it begs to be scratched. Students become invested in knowing the answer.

Student Choices. The more students are allowed to choose what to study, how to study, and how to demonstrate their learning, the more they will self-align the content with their interests. Students allowed to choose which book to read for a book report, which current event to report on, or which science topic to investigate, become more interested in the content than students assigned topics.

Student projects lend themselves to intense interest because students naturally choose topics, ways to investigate those topics, and how to present their projects in ways aligned with their interests. For example, there are many choices student teams make as they prepare a simulation for the class.

See Structures Section
19. Simulations

Varied Instructional Strategies. By mixing up the instructional strategies we use, we create interest. Using a variety of instructional strategies creates uncertainty; students do not know which strategy will be used next. Students are more alert because instruction is not entirely predictable. Voice changes pique interest—shift to a whisper as you lecture; students will be drawn in. Novelty of any sort creates interest. Reforming base teams and frequent use of breakout teams also generates interest. A wide range of cooperative learning structures and team formation methods are provided in *Kagan Cooperative Learning*.[219]

3. Addressing Student Concerns

Concerns are different from interests. Concerns create anxiety. Most students have some things that preoccupy their attention, things they worry about. Concerns differ among students. The victim of an abusive parent or a school bully is concerned about safety. A student applying to colleges is concerned about grades, letters of recommendations, and living on his or her own for the first time. There are certain concerns that are fairly universal among students. By successfully addressing the concerns of our students, we free up energy for learning. And if we link our curriculum to student concerns, we create far more interest in our academic content.

Common Concerns. The list of common concerns among students includes safety, inclusion, love, achievement, autonomy, and identity.

Safety. We have extensively addressed safety in Principle 2: Safety. If we think of Maslow's hierarchy of needs, until a student feels safe, there is not much energy left for academics or creativity. The brain takes care of its most basic needs first.

Inclusion. We have extensively addressed the need for inclusion in Principle 3: Social. Students spend a great deal of energy attempting to be "in." The need for inclusion is related to the need for safety—there is safety in numbers.

Love. Students need to feel loved, cared about. This need is in relation to family, friends, and teacher. Feeling loved, like inclusion, is related to the need for safety. If I am loved, someone will be there to nourish and protect me. Attention-seeking often is a thinly disguised bid for love. Even negative attention means someone is there for me, so negative attention is better than no attention.

Achievement. Students want to do well in school. Even many of those who pretend to themselves and others that they do not care about school, secretly wish they were doing well. A student wants to feel smart, and academic success is a measure of that. Factor analysis of self-esteem measures consistently show academic success is a major factor in self-esteem.

Autonomy. As students mature, there is a growing need for autonomy. Students want to feel they can make independent decisions, that they are not just a pawn doing what they are told. The concern over autonomy can take very positive forms as when a student proves they can do something difficult on their own. It can also take negative forms as when a student refuses to do what the teacher asks in an attempt to prove that *"no one tells me what to do."*

Identity. Forming one's identity is answering the question, *"Who am I?"* The concern for identity is behind the need for students to define themselves as an athlete, a scholar, nerd, or hippie. Students spend a great deal of energy deciding how to dress as a sign of their identity. The drive to join a club, team, or gang is related to the concern over inclusion, but also is a solution to the problem of creating identity.

The Miracle Workers

Mark Phillips has designed an approach called *The Miracle Workers* to help teachers assess the concerns of their students, help students address their own concerns, and to link student concerns with academic content. A full presentation of *The Miracle Workers* is presented on the Web.[220] Mark and Edutopia[221] have kindly granted permission to include excerpts from *The Miracle Workers* in this book. See Box: The Miracle Workers, pp. 6.112–6.113. See Blackline: The Miracle Worker, p. 6.114.

4. Fostering Identification with Content

Why do we get so excited when our favorite professional sports team wins? Why do we wear their colors when we go to the game, or even just on game day? Once we have identified with a team, when they are playing it is as if we are playing; their success is our success; their failure is our failure; the team is an extension of ourself. The team becomes part of our identity. We are a Red Sox fan. That is part of who we are. We identify with the team.

If students can identify with the feelings and life situation of Romeo and Juliet as they read the play, they are "into" the play at a much deeper level. They are invested in the outcome. The outcomes for the characters in the play are felt like outcomes for oneself. The outcomes for the character become relevant to students because it is as if they are the character.

The Miracle Workers
Mark Phillips

Preparation. Students are given a list of fictitious miracle workers and told to imagine that each one can work a miracle for them. See Blackline: The Miracle Workers, p. 6.114. Students are asked to select the three who would be most valuable to them and to designate one of those as their primary choice. The names of each are designed to be humorous. For instance, Sir Vival provides street smarts and "Pop" Larity…well, you get it!

Begin by telling your class that you'd like them to imagine they have the opportunity to have some miracle performed that will instantly improve the quality of each of their lives. These miracle workers will provide that miracle free of charge and almost instantly. Tell students to enjoy the fantasy for a few moments. Emphasize the fact that these miracle workers will provide them with a miracle that will improve their present and future lives.

Next, hand out the list of miracle workers. Tell students not to put their names on the paper. I hand it to students, have them anonymously make their selections, and also write these selections in their journals. Students who have a concern that they think was omitted can add it and even come up with the name of a new miracle worker if they'd like. I collect the sheets and tabulate the concerns to determine which are dominant. Since students will be interested in the results, I spend time sharing and discussing them the next day.

How to Apply the Miracle Workers.
So now what? Once you know student concerns, you need to incorporate them into your lessons.

Language Arts. In language arts classes, it's easy to find readings that relate to the concerns of the students. There are many superb young adult novels that specifically address the concerns of kids. Most of them are so good that adults can also appreciate them.

If you're required to teach a book that doesn't relate to the lives of your students, at least find a way of providing supplementary options. Use any wiggle room you have! There are no formulaic answers to any of this, which means doing the minimal online searching needed to find books they can relate to, or consulting with your school librarian.

Equally important, writing assignments and video productions are great ways of addressing your students' concerns. As one example, the California Film Institute's My Place program helps kids tell their stories through video. The work is illustrative of what could be done in schools as well.

History. In history classes, consider organizing your curriculum around issues. If you do this rather than relying purely on chronology, it becomes easier for your students to find significant connections. Issues related to equality, violence, and power versus powerlessness are just a few of the many learning approaches that you can connect to learner concerns.

Science, Math, and Art. In the sciences, there will be opportunities to address concerns related to health, diseases and diet, or natural disasters. In math, the greatest concern is usually the subject itself. Math anxiety is something that needs to be

(continued)

The Miracle Workers (continued)

addressed by every math teacher. There are numerous ways of engaging students in art projects, especially drawing, painting, and collages, to express their concerns.

Directly Addressing Student Concerns.

One other way of attending to student concerns is the direct route. Although that's an extensive subject, here are a few preliminary ideas.

In my classes, I had students imagine a dialogue with their primary miracle worker in which they told the miracle worker why they needed the miracle. One option is to have them imagine that they have a dialogue with the miracle worker in which the worker asks: "Why do you need my miracle? How will it improve your life?" You could also include the question: "Would this miracle help you sleep better or worry less?"

This dialogue could be written or could be shared with another student with whom they feel comfortable. It also could be in a short paper that they hand in to you. Clearly you have to decide whether the climate in your class is one that makes self-disclosure safe and comfortable, both with other students and with you. I would not recommend ever having these responses shared with the class as a whole, except in extraordinarily open environments.

I also had them address the question, "Since there are no miracle workers, what personal resources do you have for dealing with your concern, and how can you help make this 'miracle' happen?"

That latter question became the subject for considerable exploration, individually, with a partner or two, and sometimes with me.

This also points to the importance of creating an environment of openness and trust, a subject I'll revisit in more depth in a future blog post. In this type of classroom environment, there will be many opportunities for students to talk about their concerns directly, both with you and with other students around whom they feel safe.

This is a vast and rich territory. To explore it and apply what we discover begins with an understanding of why we're exploring. Discovering the concerns of our students provides us with an opportunity to increase their motivation and help them take more control over their own lives."
© 2013 Mark Phillips

The Miracle Workers

Directions: Put a check in the box by the three miracle workers who would be most valuable to you in your life, and put a star by the one who will be the most valuable.

☐ **Madame Yin Yang**—She will provide you with perfect health and protection from injury throughout your life.

☐ **Jedediah Methuselah**—He guarantees you a long life of up to 200 years, with your aging slowed down proportionately. At the age of 80, you will look and feel like 40.

☐ **Bea Utiful**—A magically gifted plastic surgeon, she will utilize a painless and rapid technique to make you look exactly as you want to look. She also uses her magic to alter your body structure and size. Your ideal physical appearance will be an almost instant reality.

☐ **Rocky Fellah**—His guaranteed financial schemes will bring you millions within a few weeks.

☐ **Studia Wurkis**—From her home on a Greek island, Studia will send you a miraculous formula that guarantees you the college and/or job of your choice. Your future academic and work life will be instantly ensured.

☐ **"Pop" Larity**—He guarantees that you will have the friends you want both now and in the future. You will be instantly well liked by everyone.

☐ **Dr. Hwei Que**—A world-renowned Chinese neuropsychologist, she will apply her groundbreaking technique to increase your intelligence to genius levels within a few days.

☐ **Haim Okay Yorok**—This great Israeli miracle worker provides guaranteed self-confidence. You will never question your worth again and will be confident in all situations.

☐ **Sir Vival**—He provides perfect skills in dealing with bureaucracies and unlimited "street smarts." You'll have no trouble handling any challenges that might get in the way of your success in the world.

☐ **Stu Denpower**—Stu is an expert on authority and will make sure that you will never again be bothered by authorities. His miracle gift will make you immune to all unfair controls imposed by the school, the police, and the government.

☐ **Claire Voyant**—All of your questions about the future will be answered through your instant mind meld with this renowned mystic.

☐ **Moma Dada**—The world's most renowned family therapist, she applies a breakthrough approach to ensure that you will never have any problem with your parents again. In two days, you will learn how to interact with them in a way that instantly resolves all conflicts whenever they occur.

Brain-Friendly Teaching • Dr. Spencer Kagan
Kagan Publishing • 800.933.2667 • www.KaganOnline.com

Simulations. We can release the power of identification as we teach much of our academic content. A powerful tool to create identification: Simulations. Students role-play being the character or object of study. In the process, they identify with the content.

Social Studies. As a set for a unit on the westward movement, we have students imagine they are packing their things into the covered wagon. They decide what to take and what to leave behind. They describe their hopes and fears as their wagon joins the wagon train, not knowing if they will make it, or what exactly awaits them.

Math. Rather than giving students a worksheet full of multiplication problems, we can have students identify with each problem by putting them in the place of a person needing an answer: *"You want to put tile on the floor of your bedroom. Tiles are 1-foot square. The room is 12 feet by 10 feet. Assuming you won't crack or destroy any, how many tiles do you need to buy?"*

Science. Role-play is not limited to playing people. Students can research and then pretend to be an element, an atom, a planet, or whatever the content, describing themselves in the first person. Pairs or teams of students can role play interaction: *"We are the moon revolving around the earth, while we both revolve around the sun."* Two teams can work together to demonstrate why a convex meniscus forms when mercury is placed in a glass beaker or tube: *"We are mercury atoms and we are more attracted to each other (cohesion) than to the glass (adhesion), so watch what happens."*

Language Arts. Much of the impact of literature is based on identification. The author attempts to have the reader identify with the characters so the reader will feel what happens to the character. Students can discuss which characters they identify with and why, making the content more relevant.

5. Content that Elicits Emotion

Any stimulus that elicits emotion in a student becomes relevant for the student. As we have seen in Principle 4: Emotion, emotion is the signal that something is relevant, it is the signal that something is good or bad, pleasurable

Making Migration Meaningful

"When I taught immigration, migration, or colonization, I would create heterogeneous teams based on the number of times students had moved. (I would do a Line-Up with the students based on the number of times they moved and then fold the line to create heterogeneous teams.) That placed at least one student that had moved on each team.

"I'd start the lesson by having students think about and then answer the question: 'What are the advantages and disadvantages of moving to a new place to live?' I'd let all students answer in a RoundRobin, whether they had moved or not. That seemed to personalize the topic and a good place to start."

—*Dan Kuzma*
U.S. History
Indian Hills Regional High School
Oakland, NJ

or painful, worthy of memory. If there is no emotion, there is no relevance. Anything that elicits positive emotion activates the dopamine rewards centers, which in turn activate the hippocampus, enhancing long-term memory. If the hippocampus could talk, it would say, *"This is generating emotion; it is relevant to me; I better remember it."*

Tip

Emotion is the litmus test for relevance. If the content generates emotion in our students, we have created relevance.

Tool 13
Construct Meaning

The more meaningful the content, the better it is remembered. Content, which is meaningful to the learner, is processed in a deeper way. The cognitive work of constructing meaning results in more synaptic connections promoting memory. One of the clearest experimental examples of the power of meaning had college students process words in four ways, increasing in depth of meaningful processing.[222] At a very low level of meaning the students simply stated if the word was written in capital or lower case. At a very high level of meaning, the students had to determine if the word fit well in a blank in a sentence. The students answered yes or no to each question and thought the experiment was to determine how fast they could respond. Afterwards they received a surprise test to determine if they could recall if they had seen the word during the experiment. Results indicate as meaningfulness of processing increases, so too does subsequent memory. See Table: Meaning Makes Memory.

Many studies have demonstrated that the greater the meaningfulness of processing, the greater the recall. To cite a few:

▶ Students were asked to rate either the pronouncability or the image-evoking potential of a series of sentences. In the surprise recall test, students recalled 65% of the sentences for which they had rated if the sentence easily evoked an image, but recalled only 25% of those sentences rated for pronouncability.[223]

▶ Participants were asked to fill in the blank in a sentence or to simply read the sentence with the word filled in. For example: Elevators stop at every _____. v. Elevators stop at every floor. Participants that had the word supplied remembered about 10% fewer sentences compared to those who had to come up with the missing word.[224]

▶ College students read definitions of difficult, unfamiliar words such as cuprous, palliate, and xanthous. They then answered multiple-choice questions requiring them to identify examples of the concepts. Half were required in addition to create and say a sentence containing the word. The other half spent the same amount of time reading the definition three times. Percent recalled: Say the definition three times: 44%; Create a sentence containing the word: 65%.[225]

▶ Rating paragraphs for clarity or difficulty leads to substantially better recall than counting four-letter words or number of personal pronouns in the paragraph.[226]

▶ Medical graduate students enrolled in a course on genomics and personalized medicine who choose to undergo personal genotyping, show a significantly greater increase in pre- to post-course scores on knowledge of course content compare

Meaning Makes Memory

Level of Meaning	Visual Memory	Percent Recalled
Very Low	Is the word in capital or lowercase?	16%
Low	Does the word rhyme with (another word)?	57%
High	Does the word belong in (a given category)	78%
Very High	Does the word fit in the blank in a given sentence?	90%

> **Tip**
> Teach for understanding, not for memory. Paradoxically, teaching for understanding creates more memory than teaching for memory.

on preparing our students to score well on state tests or focus on fostering understanding of concepts. Scoring well as an end is a dead end. Mindlessly carrying out the steps of an algorithm to arrive at the correct answer, does not lead to understanding, application, or creativity with the concept. A 5-year-old that sings as she counts by 5s may have no understanding of the meaning of successive addition. The same child who just sang her 5s to 100 perfectly, may have no clue when we ask, *"If three people each give me 5 marbles, how many will I have?"* As teachers, we need to look beyond correct answers and teach for understanding.

to those not undergoing the personal genotyping. Seventy percent reported a better understanding of human genetics on the basis of having taken the testing. Caution is warranted in interpreting the data because students self-selected to undergo the personal genotype testing.[227]

▶ After reading each passage explaining a psychological principle, high school students were either asked to apply the principle to a new example, identify an example of the principle, or name the psychologist associated with the principle. Applying the principle produced the highest test performance, next highest was identifying the principle. Naming the psychologist produced performance even below just reading the passages![228]

▶ Recall of text is more a function of how meaningful it is as opposed to its readability.[229]

▶ Later recognition rates drop very dramatically if meaningless rather than meaningful stimuli are presented.[230]

▶ Students instructed to take notes on the meaningful elements as they listened to a prose passage when tested 1 week later recalled 34% of those elements they had taken notes on, and 5% of those elements on which they had not taken notes.[231]

Constructing meaning is among the most important, if not the single most important, goals of teaching. The pressure to boost test scores has obscured this goal. As educators, we can focus

Making Meaning Hands On

"Each time I introduced a new science topic I tried to find a hands-on way to develop meaning. Often this was done in the form of a science experiment. For example, when I taught about friction we built ramps. Each ramp was covered with a different substance. One ramp was covered in rock, one was covered in carpet, and one was left unfinished. Each team raced cars and recorded times. Students made conclusions based on the observations."

—*Dawn Odum*
4th Grade, Berkley Elementary School
Auburndale, FL

For much of our curriculum we have a choice: Focus on having students get the right answer, or focus on having students construct meaning. For example, it has no meaning to tell students the commutative property tells us that 2 x 3 = 3 x 2. In contrast, if I have students construct an array and then spin it so they can see that two 3s is just another way of looking at three 2s, and then do that with several arrays, and then have them construct their own arrays and spin

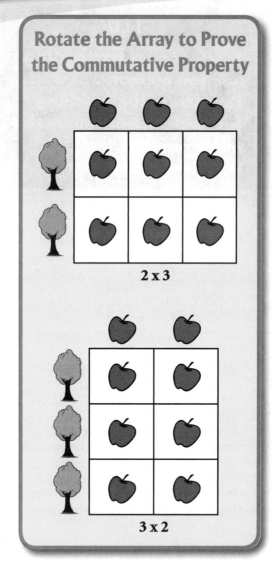

Rotate the Array to Prove the Commutative Property

2 x 3

3 x 2

> Tip
> Provide many concrete examples to facilitate acquisition of an abstract concept. Allow students to discover the rule by repeated experiences.

them and label them, then the commutative property comes alive. Not only have students constructed meaning, they will remember what the commutative property is, and hopefully use it. See Box: Rotate the Array to Prove the Commutative Property.

Constructing Meaning: Induction

Repeated experience leads students to construct meaning. For example, when we first introduce multiplication, we have three alternatives: (1) Have students create flashcards and begin memorizing their multiplication facts; (2) Have them do a series of repeated addition problems and then show them multiplication is the same thing; and (3) Have them do a series of repeated addition problems until students derive the meaning of multiplication.

To take another example, to have students understand the difference between adjectives and adverbs, instead of beginning with the definitions, we might use a Kagan Structure, **Find My Rule**, to have them induce the meaning of those concepts. In **Find My Rule**, first we place one sentence in Box 1 and one sentence in Box 2, and have students work in pairs and teams to make guesses about what distinguishes Box 1 sentences from Box 2 sentences.

As more and more sentences appear, students discover the difference—in this case, Box 1 sentences have a word that modifies a noun and Box 2 sentences have a word that modifies a verb. Only after students have figured out the

difference between Box 1 and Box 2 sentences, do we write the words "Adverb Sentences" above Box 1 and write "Adjective Sentences" above Box 2. In the process of discovering the difference, students have constructed meaning. See Table: Two-Box Induction: Adverbs v. Adjectives, p. 6.119.

Constructing Meaning: Concrete Examples

The brain processes and retains concrete visual images far more easily than abstract concepts. Applying this finding to construction of meaning, we help students construct meaning by giving them concrete visual images to associate with a construct.

A few days ago, my daughter asked me to give her 6-year-old son his new word for the day. I suggested several words, but he already knew

Two-Box Induction: Adverbs v. Adjectives

Box 1	Box 2
Johnny ran fast.	Johnny wore red shoes.
Sue cut the grass quickly.	Sue cut the green grass.
Jesus drove carefully.	Jesus drove a fast car.
Melinda laughed loudly.	Melinda watched a funny movie.

them. Then I suggested the word "amiable." He had never heard that word. To introduce that word to him, I said,

"I want you to picture a boy walking down the street. Another boy comes up to him and says, 'Let's play.' The boy who was walking down the street frowns, [here I frown] and says, 'No way! I don't want to play with you!' and keeps walking.

"Now I want you to picture a different boy walking down the street. A boy comes up to him and says, 'Let's play.' The boy who was walking stops walking, smiles, [here I smile] and says, 'Sure, let's play.'

"Now I want you to guess: Which boy is more amiable [here I smile]—the one who frowned [here I frown] and kept walking or the one who smiled [here I smile] and stopped to play?"

After my grandson proudly answered correctly, I had him come up with some examples of being amiable. I am certain his memory for the meaning of the word is far greater than if I had just given him the definition, or even if I had given him the definition and some examples. I had him construct meaning via a concrete example which I had him visualize.

Some students simply don't "get" the meaning of X^2 until we have them manipulate the algebra tiles and define X as a line and X^2 as a square with the X line as the length of each side.

To this day I remember the word "onomatopoeia" because my teacher introduced it after using prolonged Ss to say "Slithering Snake." After

Concrete Visual Images Create Meaning

"When I was teaching 2nd grade at Martinez Elementary in Las Vegas, NV, I used to teach all math concepts at the concrete level with manipulatives to help students create meaning. Then we would connect manipulatives to the numbers and symbols so students would know what the numbers actually meant.

"Also when teaching vocabulary to 2nd graders, I would bring in real world examples that students could see. After they saw examples, students would draw a picture in their journal with the definition to help create meaning rather than just telling them what the word meant.

"Most of my students were second language learners so I would try to bring in physical examples. If the vocabulary word was sprout, I would find a plant that was sprouting so they could see it. Or if the word was camouflage, we would go outside and find examples of things that are blending into the environment around them. The more they could see concrete examples, the better they seemed to understand the meaning."

—*Sarah Backner*
2nd Grade, Martinez Elementary
Las Vegas, NV

having students say why hiccup, hum, knock, screech, and smack are onomatopoeic words, to have students construct meaning we might challenge them to find other onomatopoeia words or even to create their own!

Constructing Meaning: Throughlines

Overarching goals, or throughlines,[232] describe the most important understandings that students should develop during an entire course. The teaching for understanding goals for particular lessons and units should be aligned with one or more of these overarching understanding goals of the course. By establishing throughlines and having individual lessons and units align with those core ideas, the lessons with units and units within a course "add up," allowing student to construct meaning not just within lessons, but within the course as a whole. See Box: Sample Throughlines.

> **Tip**
> Use themes to unify learning.

Constructing Meaning: Personal Experience

Personal experience is the natural way in which we construct meaning. By designing relevant experiences, we can set the stage for students to construct meaning. For example, a simulation of the stock market crash of 1929 or the bust of the housing bubble of 2006–2012 allows an opportunity for students to construct the meaning of those events far more than reading about those events. Rather than having students read a scene in a Shakespeare play, they construct far more meaning by role-playing the characters interacting in the scene. To provide an even greater opportunity to construct meaning, allow students to begin in role verbatim as the scene is written, but then having them "take off" to interact in role without a script.

Sample Throughlines

▶ **For an American history course:** "How does our historical past make us who we are today?"

▶ **For a general science course:** "Students will understand that 'doing science' is not the process of finding facts, but of constructing and testing theories."

▶ **For an algebra course:** "How can we use what we know to figure out what we don't know?"

▶ **For a literature course:** "Students will understand how metaphors shape the way we experience the world."

Source: http://learnweb.harvard.edu/alps/tfu/info3b.cfm

Constructing Meaning: Linking to Prior Knowledge

Educators have long known that new knowledge is better understood and retained if it is linked to prior knowledge. Brain science explains this: Dendrite connections are made between the new and prior knowledge, creating associative links. Thus, when the student thinks about the topic, the old, well-established knowledge is stimulated which in turn brings up the new knowledge via the links that have been established. A broader set of neurons has been stimulated, constructing a larger knowledge base.

To apply this principle, in introducing new knowledge, we first have students think about or interact over related knowledge or experience so the new knowledge has something to connect to. By activating the prior knowledge, we are literally activating the neurons to which we want the new knowledge to connect. For examples,

▶ In introducing fractions, we might first have students remember cutting a pizza into equal parts, and then define one part as a numerator and the total number of parts as the denominator.

▶ In introducing new spelling words, we have students focus on the smaller, familiar words within the new words and how compound words are made up of familiar words put together.

▶ In introducing time zones, we might ask students if they have a relative living in a different time zone and to describe how they figure out what time it is for them.

- In introducing the First Amendment of the Bill of Rights, we might ask students if it is okay for them to say anything at all in school, or whether certain speech is prohibited.
- In introducing the difference between a mixture and a compound, we might mix table salt and pepper on a table. We repeatedly run a comb through our hair, saying that we are creating static electricity. We then show how by waving the comb charged with static electricity over the mixture, we can separate the pepper from the salt. Finally, we point out that we cannot separate the sodium and chlorine that makes the salt compound.

Social Interaction Facilitates Construction of Meaning

Through social interaction we construct meaning. Each of us has our own knowledge base and our own conceptual framework for organizing that knowledge. There is cognitive inertia: We maintain our knowledge and our way of organizing it until we bump into something that forces us to add new knowledge and/or revise the way we think about the knowledge. Experience can do that as when Einstein discovered as a child that the needle of a compass always pointed north. The world worked in a way that forced Einstein to revise his model of how objects behave. Primary encounters with physical phenomena are one way we are pushed to construct meaning. Encounters with others are, however, the primary way we construct meaning. Because each of us has a different knowledge base and different conceptual systems, interaction between and among individuals necessarily creates cognitive friction. Following an encounter I add to my knowledge base and/or revise my conceptual framework. Social interaction is the royal road to constructing meaning.

"Through others, we become ourselves."
—Lev S. Vygotsky

Constructing Meaning: Kindergarten Shapes Lesson

"**Objective:** Students will be able to identify and describe shapes. Students will be able to analyze, compare, create, and compose shapes.

"**Lesson Sequence:** Students bring in solid objects from the environment or home for Shape Show and Tell. They are encouraged to bring in spheres, cones, cubes, pyramids, cylinders, or a rectangular prism. Students present their shapes to their teammates using a Timed RoundRobin. They share the name of the shape. If it has a special meaning to them, they share that as well as its characteristics and math facts: number of sides, number of vertices, if it could combine it with another shape to make something, does it roll, stack, or slide?

"We use their show and tell items for Quiz-Quiz-Trade, Mix-Freeze-Group, Talking Chips, and Turn Toss throughout the week. This lesson is much more meaningful to them and connected with their schema, rather than me getting out the 3D shape blocks."

—*Melissa Wincel*
Kindergarten, Trafalgar Elementary
Cape Coral, FL

Students, both of whom are not yet at the level of conservation of liquid, but who have different conceptual models, interact. Following that, they move up to understand conservation. It is not one teaching the other that is the stimulus for revising their conceptual framework. It is the interaction with someone with a different conceptual framework.

Two of the most influential educators of all time placed social interaction at the heart of cognitive development. John Dewey[233] emphasized that true education was not accomplished by a teacher dispensing knowledge, but rather by a teacher helping construct social situations from which a child learns. Education in Dewey's view is a social and interactive process. Lev Vygotsky believed cognitive development advanced through imitative learning, instructed learning, and collaborative learning.[234]

"The only true education comes through the stimulation of the child's powers by the demands of the social situations in which he finds himself."

—*John Dewey*
My Pedagogic Creed, 1897

Kagan Structures for Constructing Meaning

A number of Kagan Structures help students in their process of constructing meaning. These structures have been described in detail in other Kagan publications.[235] Four types of structures foster construction of meaning: Processing Structures, Categorizing Structures, Metacognition Structures, and Concept Development Structures. Sample structures of each type are described briefly below.

Processing Structures.

Instructors working in the Kagan model are encouraged to have students process the content very regularly, by writing, drawing, discussing, and debating the content. Structures like **Timed Pair Share** and **Timed RoundRobin** are designed to have students interact over and reflect on the content immediately after it is presented—essentially to construct meaning of the content for themselves.

Timed Pair Share. Students are in pairs. Student A shares for a predetermined time while Student B listens. B responds. Partners switch roles.

Timed RoundRobin. Students are in teams, usually teams of four. Students take turns each sharing for a predetermined time.

Categorizing Structures.
Facts learned in isolation are soon forgotten; facts that are part of a coherent whole, which have meaning, are retained. Making meaning involves examining relationships, relating stimuli to other stimuli, and categories of stimuli, constructing conceptual models.

Team Mind Mapping. In **Team Mind Mapping**, students in teams each work with a different colored marker to create one large Mind Map of the content. They begin by putting the main idea in the center of a piece of chart paper. They draw lines out from the main idea and write or symbolize core concepts. Supporting details are added to the core concepts. Use of colors, pictures, symbols, arrows, and other graphic elements offer more ways of organizing information and creating meaning than does the traditional outline. In the process of negotiating agreement on how to construct the Mind Map, the students construct meaning much more than if they worked alone. See Mind Maps in Tool 7: Illustrate with Images, p. 6.57.

Find-A-Frame. Students begin with the names of many items, each written on a separate slip of paper. Students move the items about, grouping them until they reach consensus on how best to organize the items, using a Venn Diagram, a 2 x 2 matrix, placing the items on a time line or a size line, or creating an original organizer. Afterwards, students deal out the items and take turns placing them in the organizer and explaining their thinking.

Metacognitive Structures.
Some structures facilitate students thinking about their own thinking. *Metacognition* is another form of constructing meaning. As students ask themselves how they are thinking about a problem or issue, they give meaning to the content.

Journal Reflections. Students write in their journal, at times on a topic provided by the teacher and at other times on a topic of their choosing.

SeeOne–DoOne–TeachOne. Students see a procedure modeled, usually by the teacher. They then practice the procedure on their own. Finally, they teach the procedure to a partner, explaining their thinking as they teach.

Concept Development Structures. Some concept development structures like **Team Statements** have students construct a meaningful definition of a broad concept like democracy, gratefulness, or the scientific inquiry process. There is no right or wrong, only the meaning students create. Other concept development structures like **Odd One Out** and **Find My Rule** focus on having students construct a rule that captures the properties common to objects or ideas.

AllWrite Consensus. As students interact to reach consensus they clarify and refine their own thinking. They take in new ideas from others, which helps them in their own concept development.

See Structures Section
1. AllWrite Consensus
16. RoundRobin
18. SeeOne–DoOne–TeachOne
25. Timed Pair Share

Team Statements. Students are given a topic and pair up to share their ideas on the topic. For example, first they complete a sentence like: *"Democracy is…"* *"Multiplication is useful because…"* *"I am grateful for…"* Students individually write their sentence and then read their sentence to the group using **RoundRobin**. Students then work as a group to come up with a single statement that all of them can endorse more fully than their own individual statement, something that captures the place from which each individual statement sprang.

Odd One Out. Students sit in teams of four. The teacher displays four items numbered 1–4 corresponding to student numbers 1–4. Three items have a common characteristic such as three mammals and one is the odd one out—an animal that is not a mammal. Each student writes either *"I'm Out"* or *"I Fit,"* depending on whether the item that corresponds to their number fits the concept common to the other items. Students **RoundRobin** share what they have written and their thinking. Students then celebrate if they have correctly developed the concept.

Having constructed meaning, the concept becomes part of a memorable schema. This, in part, is why structures improve academic achievement. The structures are brain-compatible because they assist the brain in its natural search to construct meaning. Instruction that promotes identification of patterns and construction of meaning is brain-friendly instruction.

Conclusion

The idea is simple. If the brain seeks some kinds of stimuli and tends to ignore other kinds, our students will be more successful if we teach with brain-friendly stimuli.

Much of what is recommended in this principle is well-known by good teachers. These teachers provide novelty and predictability, furnish feedback frequently, catch their students being good, make their content personally relevant, and use visual images to make abstract ideas understandable and memorable. The brain science and experimental studies provide additional rationale for these powerful practices. We are encouraged to redouble our efforts to become brain-friendly teachers.

We have known for years that distributed practice trumps massed practice, but in the press to "cover the curriculum," we abandon that proven practice, jumping to the next content to cover rather than returning to something we have presented, to cement learning. Similarly, we teach to boost test scores rather than to foster construction of meaning. The result: We buy short-term memory at the expense of long-term understanding and content acquisition. The review of the research provides ammunition for those of us who would like to counter the trend of providing a curriculum that is a mile wide but only an inch deep. We are encouraged to redouble our efforts to make our curriculum personally relevant and to have our students construct meaning.

Not everything emerging from the research is intuitively obvious or generally applied. It is not intuitively obvious that gesturing while teaching, and teaching students to gesture, helps students construct meaning and boosts retention and transference. It is obvious that recognition is easier than recall, but we have not applied that principle as fully as would be optimal to instruction and test construction. Based on the research we now know, it is not the amount of rewards that motivate students; rather, it is the contingency of rewards. We stand warned against telling a student he or she is smart, or complimenting students on their products regardless of effort or performance. We serve our students far better by complimenting their effort, and getting them to believe it is their effort that counts. The research and theory on styles and modalities encourages us to broaden how we teach, including the range of modality preferences and cognitive styles.

In looking over the thirteen tools, each of us can pat ourselves on the back for those tools we are now using regularly, be encouraged to more often implement some tools we are using only occasionally, and begin experimenting with tools that are new to us. Every teacher can find within the thirteen tools new ways to make their instruction more effective by incorporating stimuli to which brains naturally attend.

Thirteen Tools to Supply Brain-Friendly Stimuli

1. Stimulate with Surprise and Novelty
2. Provide Predictability
3. Allow Play
4. Furnish Effective Feedback
5. Catch Them Being Good!
6. Recommend Biofeedback
7. Illustrate with Images
8. Teach with Tunes
9. Communicate with Gestures
10. Make it Multimodal
11. Teach with Styles
12. Establish Relevance
13. Construct Meaning

References

[1] Bunzeck, N. & Düzel, E. *Absolute coding of stimulus novelty in the human substantia nigra/VTA.* **Neuron**, 2006, 51(3), 369–379.

[2] Fried, I., MacDonald, K.A. & Wilson, C.L. *Single neuron activity in human hippocampus and amygdala during recognition of faces and objects.* **Neuron**, 1997, 18(5), 753–765.

[3] Bunzeck, N., Doeller, C.F., Dolan, R.J. & Duzel, E. *Contextual interaction between novelty and rewards processing within the mesolimbic system.* **Human Brain Mapping**, 2012, 33(6), 1309–1324.

Wittmann, B.C., Bunzeck, N., Dolan, R.J. & Duzel, E. *Anticipation of novelty recruits reward system and hippocampus while promoting recollection.* **Neuroimage**, 2007, 38(1–9), 194–202.

[4] Addessi, E., Mancini, A., Crescimbene, L., Ariely, D. & Visalberghi, E. *How to spend a token? Trade-offs between food variety and food preference in tufted capuchin monkeys (Cebus apella).* **Behavioural Processes**, 2010, 83(3), 267–275.

[5] Reichel, C.M. & Bevins, R.A. *Competition Between novelty and cocaine conditioned reward is sensitive to drug dose and retention interval.* **Behavioral Neuroscience**, 2010, 124(1), 141–151.

[6] Slater, A., Morison, V. & Rose, D. *Habituation in the newborn.* **Infant Behavior and Development**, 1984, 7(2), 183–200.

[7] Tobler, P.N., Fiorillo, C.D. & Schultz, W. *Adaptive coding of reward value by dopamine neurons.* **Science**, 2005, 307(5715), 1642–1645.

[8] Bunzeck, N. & Düzel, E. *Absolute coding of stimulus novelty in the human substantia nigra/VTA.* **Neuron**, 2006, 51(3), 369–379.

[9] Strange, B.A. & Dolan, R.J. *Adaptive anterior hippocampal responses to oddball stimuli.* **Hippocampus**, 2001, 11(6), 690–698.

Strange, B.A., Henson, R.N.A., Friston, K.J. & Dolan, R.J. *Brain mechanisms for detecting perceptual, semantic, and emotional deviance.* **NeuroImage**, 2000, 12(4), 425–433.

[10] Berns, G.S., McClure, S.M., Pagnoni, G. & Montague, P.R. *Predictability modulates human brain response to reward.* **The Journal of Neuroscience**, 2001, 21(8), 2793–2798.

[11] Berns, G.S., McClure, S.M., Pagnoni, G. & Montague, P.R. *Predictability Modulates Human Brain Response to Reward.* **The Journal of Neuroscience**, 2001, 21(8), 2793-2798.

[12] Feldman, D. **Why Do Clocks Run Clockwise? And Other Imponderables.** New York, NY: Harper & Row, 1987.

[13] Kagan, S. **Cooperative Learning.** San Clemente, CA: Kagan Publishing, 1995.

[14] Kagan, S. **Silly Sports & Goofy Games.** San Clemente, CA: Kagan Publishing, 2000.

[15] Kagan S. & Kagan, M. **Multiple Intelligences: The Complete MI Book.** San Clemente, CA: Kagan Publishing, 1998.

[16] Reim, B., Glass, D.C. & Singer, J.E. *Behavioral consequences of exposure to uncontrollable and unpredictable noise.* **Journal of Applied Social Psychology**, 1971, 1(1), 44–56.

[17] Lockard, J.S. *Choice of warning signal or no warning signal in an unavoidable shock situation.* **Journal of Comparative and Physiological Psychology**, 1963, 56(3), 526–630.

Perkins, C.C., Levin, D. & Seymann, R. *Preference for signal-shock versus shock-signal.* **Psychological Reports**, 1963, 13(3), 735–738.

Pervin, L.A. *The need to predict and control under conditions of threat.* **Journal of Personality**, 1963, 31(4), 570–587.

[18] Berns, G.S., McClure, S.M., Pagnoni, G. & Montague, P.R. *Predictability Modulates Human Brain Response to Reward.* **The Journal of Neuroscience**, 2001, 21(8), 2793–2798.

[19] Hawkins, J. **On Intelligence.** New York, NY: Holt, 2004.

[20] Gopnik, A., Meltzoff, A.N. & Kuhl, P.K. **The Scientist in the Crib.** New York, NY: William Morrow, 1999.

[21] Averill, J.R. *Personal control over aversive stimuli and its relationship to stress.* **Psychological Bulletin**, 1973, 80(4), 286–303.

[22] Geer, J.H. & Maisel, E. *Evaluating the effects of the prediction-control confound.* **Journal of Personality and Social Psychology**, 1972, 23(3), 314–319.

Reim, B., Glass, D.C. & Singer, J.E. *Behavioral consequences of exposure to uncontrollable and unpredictable noise.* **Journal of Applied Social Psychology**, 1971, 1(1), 44–56.

[23] Schulz, R. *Effects of control and predictability on the physical and psychological well-being of the institutionalized aged.* **Journal of Personality and Social Psychology**, 1976, 33(5), 563–573.

[24] Macknik, S.L. & Martinez-Conde, S. **Sleights of Mind. What the Neuroscience of Magic Reveals about Our Everyday Deceptions.** New York, NY: Henry Holt, Picador, 2010, 8.

[25] Nickerson R.S. *Confirmation bias: A ubiquitous phenomenon in many guises.* **Review of General Psychology**, 1998, 2(2), 175–220.

[26] Westen, D., Blagov, P.S., Harenski, K., Kilts, C. & Hamann, S. *Neural bases of motivated reasoning: An fMRI study of emotional constraints on partisan political judgment in the 2004 U.S. presidential election.* **Journal of Cognitive Neuroscience**, 2006, 18(11), 1947–1958.

27 Young, A.I., Ratner, K.G. & Fazio, R.H. *Political attitudes bias the mental representation of a presidential candidate's face.* **Psychological Science OnlineFirst**, 2013, 1–8.

28 Mahoney, M.J. *Scientist as Subject: The Psychological Imperative.* Cambridge, MA: Ballinger, 1976.

Mitroff, I. *The Subjective Side of Science.* Amsterdam, NL: Elsevier, 1974.

29 Roszak, T. *The Cult of Information: The Folklore of Computers and the True Art of Thinking.* New York, NY: Pantheon Books, 1986.

30 Crabtree, S (July 6, 1999). *New poll gauges Americans' general knowledge levels: Four-fifths know earth revolves around sun.* **GALLUP**. Retrieved on February 3, 3014 from http://www.gallup.com/poll/3742/New-Poll-Gauges-Americans-General-Knowledge-Levels.aspx

31 Rosenthal, R. & Jacobson, L. *Pygmalion in the classroom (Expanded Edition).* New York, NY: Irvington, 1992.

32 Spitz, H.H. *Beleaguered Pygmalion: A history of the controversy over claims that teacher expectancy raises intelligence.* **Intelligence**, 1999, 27(3), 199–234.

33 Brophy, J.E. *Research on the self-fulfilling prophecy and teacher expectations.* **Journal of Educational Psychology**, 1983, 75(5), 631–661.

Good, T.L. *Two decades of research on teacher expectations: Findings and future directions.* **Journal of Teacher Education**, 1987, 38(4), 32–47.

Mitman, A.L. *Teachers' differential behavior toward higher and lower achieving students and its relation to selected teacher characteristics.* **Journal of Educational Psychology**, 1985, 77(2), 149–161.

34 Baron, R.M., Tom, D.Y.H. & Cooper, H.M. *Social Class, Race and Teacher Expectations.* In J. Dusek (Ed.), **Teacher Expectancies**, 251–270. Hillsdale, NJ: Lawrence Erlbaum Associates, 1985.

35 Darley, J.M. & Gross, P.H. *A hypothesis-confirming bias in labeling effects.* **Journal of Personality and Social Psychology**, 1983, 44(1), 20–33.

36 Feldman, R.S. & Prohaska, T. *The student as Pygmalion: Effect of student expectation on the teacher.* **Journal of Educational Psychology**, 1979, 71(4), 485–493.

37 Kagan, S., Kyle, P. & Scott, S. *Win-Win Discipline.* San Clemente, CA: Kagan Publishing, 2004.

38 Kagan, S., Kyle, P. & Scott, S. *Win-Win Discipline.* San Clemente, CA: Kagan Publishing, 2004.

39 Kagan, S. & Kagan, M. *Kagan Cooperative Learning.* San Clemente, CA: Kagan Publishing, 2009. www.KaganOnline.com

Kagan S. & Kagan, M. *Multiple Intelligences: The Complete MI Book.* San Clemente, CA: Kagan Publishing, 1998. www.KaganOnline.com

Bride, B. *Cooperative Learning & Algebra.* San Clemente, CA: Kagan Publishing, 2007. www.KaganOnline.com

Stites, R. & Buethe, A. *Cooperative Mathematics.* San Clemente, CA: Kagan Publishing, 2008. www.KaganOnline.com

Candler, L. *Hands-On Science.* San Clemente, CA: Kagan Publishing, 1995. www.KaganOnline.com

Michels, M., Manzi, A. & Mele, J. *Cooperative Learning & Science.* **High School Activities.** San Clemente, CA: Kagan Publishing, 2003. www.KaganOnline.com

Taylor, B. *Vocabulary: Making it Memorable.* San Clemente, CA: Kagan Publishing, 2011. www.KaganOnline.com

Agnew, M. & McKoy, S. *Cooperative Learning & Grammar.* San Clemente, CA: Kagan Publishing, 2011. www.KaganOnline.com

Millwood, R. *Experience U.S. History.* San Clemente, CA: Kagan Publishing, 2007. www.KaganOnline.com

Millwood, R. *Adventures through World History.* San Clemente, CA: Kagan Publishing, 2007. www.KaganOnline.com

40 Kagan, S. & Kagan, M. *Kagan Cooperative Learning.* San Clemente, CA: Kagan Publishing, 2009. www.KaganOnline.com

TeamMats: ManageMats & Fan-N-Pick Mats. San Clemente, CA: Kagan Publishing, 2009. www.KaganOnline.com

41 Kagan, S. *Spin-N-Review Spinner (MSSNR).* San Clemente, CA: Kagan Publishing, 1997. www.KaganOnline.com

Kagan, S. *Spin-N-Think Spinner (MSSNT).* San Clemente, CA: Kagan Publishing, 1997. www.KaganOnline.com

42 Wiederhold, C. *Higher Level Thinking Book and Class Manipulative Set (BWCTM).* San Clemente, CA: Kagan Publishing, 20012. www.KaganOnline.com

Wiederhold, C. *Question Dice Class Set (CMLQ).* San Clemente, CA: Kagan Publishing, 2005. www.KaganOnline.com

Wiederhold, C. *Question Spinner (MSQQD).* San Clemente, CA: Kagan Publishing, 1997. www.KaganOnline.com

43 Panksepp, J. *Affective Neuroscience. The Foundations of Human and Animal Emotions.* New York, NY: Oxford University Press, 1998, 281–282.

44 Masson, J.M. & McCarthy, S. *When Elephants Weep. The Emotional Lives of Animals.* New York, NY: Dell Publishing, 1995, 129.

45 Beatty, W.W., Dodge, A.M., Dodge, L.J., White, K. & Panksepp, J. *Psychomotor stimulants, social deprivation, and play in juvenile rats.* **Pharamacology Biochemistry and Behavior**, 1982, 16(3), 417–422.

46 Panksepp, J. *Affective Neuroscience. The Foundations of Human and Animal Emotions.* New York, NY: Oxford University Press, 1998, 18.

47 Panksepp, J. *Affective Neuroscience. The Foundations of Human and Animal Emotions.* New York, NY: Oxford University Press, 1998, 291.

48 Panksepp, J. *Affective Neuroscience. The Foundations of Human and Animal Emotions*. New York, NY: Oxford University Press, 1998, 297.

49 Brown, S. *Play. How it shapes the Brain, Opens the Imagination, and Invigorates the Soul*. New York, NY: Avery, 2009.

50 Brown, S. *Play. How it shapes the Brain, Opens the Imagination, and Invigorates the Soul*. New York, NY: Avery, 2009, 49.

51 Brown, S. *Play. How it shapes the Brain, Opens the Imagination, and Invigorates the Soul*. New York, NY: Avery, 2009, 31.

52 Brown, S. *Play. How it shapes the Brain, Opens the Imagination, and Invigorates the Soul*. New York, NY: Avery, 2009, 37.

53 Diamond, M. *Enriching Heredity. The Impact of the Environment on the Anatomy of the Brain*. New York, NY: Macmillian, Inc., 1988.

54 Brown, S. *Play. How it Shapes the Brain, Opens the Imagination, and Invigorates the Soul*. New York, NY: Penguin Group, 2009, 11.

55 Hawkins, J. *On Intelligence*. New York, NY: Holt, 2004.

56 Hattie, J. *Visible Learning. A Synthesis of Over 800 Meta-Analyses Relating to Achievement*. New York, NY: Routledge, 2010.

57 Bond, L., Smith, R., Baker, W.K. & Hattie, J.A. *Certification System of the National Board for Professional Teaching Standards: A Construct and Consequential Validity Study*. Washington, DC: National Board for Professional Teaching Standards, 2000.

58 Kluger, A.N. & DeNisi, A. *The effects of feedback interventions on performance: A historical review, a meta-analysis, and a preliminary feedback intervention theory*. **Psychological Bulletin**, 1996, 119(2), 254–284.

59 Sharp, P. *Behaviour modification in the secondary school: A survey of students' attitudes to rewards and praise*. **Behavioral Approaches with Children**, 1985, 9, 109–112.

60 de Luque, M.F. & Sommer, S.M. *The impact of culture on feed-back-seeking behavior: An integrated model and propositions*. **Academy of Management Review**, 2000, 25(4), 829–849.

61 Kulhavy, R.W. *Feedback in written instruction*. **Review of Educational Research**, 1997, 47(1), 211–232.

62 Hattie, J. *Visible Learning. A Synthesis of Over 800 Meta-Analyses Relating to Achievement*. New York, NY: Routledge, 2010.

63 Clarke, S., Timperley, H. & Hattie, J.A. *Assessing Formative Assessment*. Auckland, New Zealand: Hodder Moa Beckett, 2003.

64 Cameron, J. & Pierce, W.D. *Reinforcement, reward, and intrinsic motivation: A meta-analysis*. **Review of Educational Research**, 1994, 64(3), 363–423.

65 Kluger, A.N., & DeNisi, A. *The effects of feedback interventions on performance: A historical review, a meta-analysis, and a preliminary feedback intervention theory*. **Psychological Bulletin**, 1996, 119(2), 254–284.

66 Hattie, J. & Timperley, H. *The power of feedback*. **Review of Educational Research**, 2007, 77(1), 81–112.

67 Thompson, T. & Richardson, A. *Self-handicapping status, claimed self-handicaps and reduced practice effort following success and failure feedback*. **British Journal of Educational Psychology**, 2001, 71(1), 151–170.

68 Meyer, W. *Indirect communication about perceived ability estimates*. **Journal of Educational Psychology**, 1982, 74(6), 888–897.

Meyer, W., Bachmann, U., Hempelmann, M., Ploger, F. & Spiller, H. *The informational value of evaluation behavior: Influences of praise and blame in perceptions of ability*. **Journal of Educational Psychology**, 1979, 71(2), 259–268.

69 Mueller, C.M. & Dweck, C.S. *Praise for intelligence can undermine children's motivation and performance*. **Journal of Personality and Social Psychology**, 1998, 75(1), 33–52.

70 Clariana, R.B., Wagner, D. & Roher Murphy, L.C. *Applying a connectionist description of feedback timing*. **Educational Technology Research and Development**, 2000, 48(3), 5–21.

71 Airasian, P.W. *Classroom Assessment (3rd Ed.)*. New York, NY: McGraw-Hill, 1997.

72 Kluger, A.N. & DeNisi, A. *The effects of feedback interventions on performance: A historical review, a meta-analysis, and a preliminary feedback intervention theory*. **Psychological Bulletin**, 1996, 119(2), 254–284.

73 Feldman, R.S. & Prohaska, T. *The student as Pygmalion: Effect of student expectation on the teacher*. **Journal of Educational Psychology**, 1979, 71(4), 485–493.

74 Kagan, S. *Silly Sports & Goofy Games*. San Clemente, CA: Kagan Publishing, 2000. www.KaganOnline.com.

75 Schwartz, A.B., Cui, X.T., Weber, D.J. & Moran, D.W. *Brain-controlled interfaces: Movement restoration with neural prosthetics*. **Neuron**, 2006, 52(1), 205–220.

76 Velliste, M., Perel, S., Spalding, M.C., Whitford, A.S. & Schwartz, A.B. *Cortical control of a prosthetic arm for self-feeding*. **Nature**, 2008, 453(7198), 1098–1101.

77 Miller, K.J., Schalk, G., Fetz, E.E., den Nijs, M., Ojemann, J.G. & Rao, R.P.N. *Cortical activity during motor execution, motor imagery, and imagery-based online feedback*. **Proceedings of the National Academy of Sciences of the USA**, 2010, 107(9), 4430–4435.

Schwartz, A.B., Cui, X.T., Weber, D.J. & Moran, D.W. *Brain-controlled interfaces: Movement restoration with neural prosthetics*. **Neuron**, 2006, 52(1), 205–220.

78 Bangert-Drowns, R.L., Kulik, J.A., & Kulik, C.L.C. *Effects of frequent classroom testing*. **Journal of Educational Research**, 1991, 85(2), 89–99.

79 Michael, J. *A behavioral perspective on college teaching*. **The Behavior Analyst**, 1991, 14, 229–239.

[80] Leeming, F.C. *The exam-a-day procedure improves performance in psychology classes.* **Teaching of Psychology**, 2002, 29(3), 210–212.

[81] Page, E.B. *Teacher comments and student performance: A seventy-four classroom experiment in school motivation.* **Journal of Educational Psychology**, 1958, 49(4), 173–181.

[82] Crooks, T.J. *The impact of classroom evaluation on students.* **Review of Educational Research**, 1988, 58(4), 438–481.

[83] Carless, D. *Differing perceptions in the feedback process.* **Studies in Higher Education**, 2006, 31(2), 219–233.

[84] Nuthall, G.A. *The cultural myths and realities of classroom teaching and learning: A personal journey.* **Teachers College Record**, 2005, 107(5), 895–934.

[85] Butler, D.L. & Winne, P.H. *Feedback and self-regulated learning: A theoretical synthesis.* **Review of Educational Research**, 1995, 65(3), 245–281.

[86] Butler, D.L. & Winne, P.H. *Feedback and self-regulated learning: A theoretical synthesis.* **Review of Educational Research**, 1995, 65(3), 245–274.

Paris, S.G & Cunningham, A.E. *Children becoming students.* In D.C. Berliner & R.C. Calfee (Eds.), **Handbook of Educational Psychology**, 117–147. New York, NY: Macmillan, 1996.

[87] Brookhart, S.M. **How to Create and Use Rubrics for Formative Assessment and Grading.** Alexandria, VA: ASCD, 2013.

[88] Florimond, V. **Basics of Surface Electromyography Applied to Physical Rehabilitation and Biomechanics.** Montreal, CA: Thought Technology Ltd., 2009.

Sackett, D.L., Straus, S.E., Richardson, W.S., Rosenberg, W. & Haynes, R.B. (Eds.). **Evidence-based medicine: How to Practice and Teach EBM.** Edinburgh, NY: Churchill Livingstone, 2005.

Tassinary, L.G., Cacioppo, J.T. & Vanman, E.J. *The skeletomotor system: Surface electromyography.* In J.T. Cacioppo, L.G. Tassinary & G.G. Berntson (Eds.), **Handbook of Psychophysiology (3rd Ed.).** New York, NY: Cambridge University Press, 2007.

[89] Harrison V.F. & Mortenson O.A. *Identification and voluntary control of single motor unit activity in the tibialis anterior muscle.* **Anatomical Record**, 1962, 144(2), 109–116.

[90] Sterman M.B. *Neurophysiologic and clinical studies of sensorimotor EEG biofeedback training: Some effects on epilepsy.* **Seminars in Psychiatry**, 1973, 5(4), 507–524.

[91] Wolf, S.L. *Electromyographic biofeedback applications to stroke patients. A critical review.* **Physical Therapy**, 1983, 63(9), 1448–1459.

[92] Budzynski, T.H., Budzynski, H.K., Evans, J.R. & Abarbanel, A. (Eds.). **Introduction to Quantitative EEG and Neurofeedback (2nd Ed.).** Burlington, MA: Academic Press, 2009.

Monastra V., Lynn S., Linden M., Lubar J.F., Gruzelier J. & LaVaque T.J. *Electroencephalographic biofeedback in the treatment of Attention-Deficit/Hyperactivity Disorder.* **Applied Psychophysiology and Biofeedback**, 2005, 30(2), 95–114.

Yucha, C. & Montgomery, D. **Evidence-Based Practice in Biofeedback and Neurofeedback.** Wheat Ridge, CO: AAPB, 2008.

[93] Kaiser, D.A. & Othmer, S. *Effect of neurofeedback on variables of attention in a large multi-center trial.* **Journal of Neurotherapy**, 2000, 4(1), 5–28.

Monastra, V., Lynn, S., Linden, M., Lubar, J.F., Gruzelier, J. & LaVaque, T.J. *Electroencephalographic biofeedback in the treatment of Attention-Deficit/Hyperactivity Disorder.* **Applied Psychophysiology and Biofeedback**, 2005, 30(2), 95–114.

Thompson, L. & Thompson, M. *Neurofeedback combined with training in metacognitive strategies: Effectiveness in students with ADD.* **Applied Psycho-physiology and Biofeedback**, 1998, 23(4), 243–263.

[94] Lubar, J.F. & Shouse, M.N. *EEG and behavioral changes in a hyperkinetic child concurrent with training of the sensorimotor rhythm (SMR): A preliminary report.* **Biofeedback and Self Regulation**, 1976, 1(3), 293–306.

[95] Lubar, J.F. *Neurofeedback for the management of attention deficit disorders.* In M.S. Schwartz & F. Andrasik (Eds.), **Biofeedback: A Practitioner's Guide, 3rd Ed**, 409–437. New York: Guilford Press, 2003.

Tansey, M. *Ten-year stability of EEG biofeedback results for a hyperactive boy who failed the fourth grade perceptually impaired class.* **Biofeedback and Self-Regulation**, 1993, 18(1), 33–38.

[96] Linden, M., Habib, T. & Radojevic, V. *A controlled study of the effects of EEG biofeedback on cognition and behavior of children with attention deficit disorder and learning disabilities.* **Biofeedback and Self-Regulation**, 1996, 21(1), 35–49.

[97] Rossiter, T.R. & LaVaque, T.J. *A comparison of EEG biofeedback and psychostimulants in treating attention deficit/hyperactivity disorders.* **Journal of Neurotherapy**, 1995, 1(1), 48–59.

[98] Fuchs, T., Birbaumer, N., Lutzenberger, W., Gruzelier, J. H. & Kaiser, J. *Neurofeedback treatment for attention-deficit/hyperactivity disorder in children: A comparison with methylphenidate.* **Applied Psychophysiology and Biofeedback**, 2003, 28(1), 1–12.

[99] Monastra, V.J., Monastra, D.M. & George, S. *The effects of stimulant therapy, EEG biofeedback, and parenting style on the primary symptoms of Attention-Deficit/Hyperactivity Disorder.* **Applied Psychophysiology and Biofeedback**, 2002, 27(4), 231–249.

[100] Monastra, V., Lynn, S., Linden, M., Lubar, J.F., Gruzelier, J. & LaVaque, T.J. *Electroencephalographic biofeedback in the treatment of Attention-Deficit/Hyperactivity Disorder.* **Applied Psychophysiology and Biofeedback**, 2005, 30(2), 95–114.

[101] Amen, D.G. **Healing ADD. The Breakthrough Program That Allows You to See and Heal the Six Types of ADD.** New York, NY: Berkley Publishing, 2001.

[102] Constantinidou, F. & Baker, S. *Stimulus modality and verbal learning performance in normal aging.* **Brain and Language**, 2002, 82(3), 296–311.

[103] Nickerson, R.S. *Short-term memory for complex meaningful visual configurations: A demonstration of capacity.* **Canadian Journal of Psychology**, 1965, 19(2), 155–160.

[104] Miller, G.A. *The magical number seven, plus or minus two: some limits on our capacity for processing information.* **Psychological Review**, 1956, 63(2), 81–97.

[105] Brener, R. *An experimental investigation of memory span.* **Experimental Psychology**, 1940, 26(5), 467–482.

Hayes, J.R.M. *Memory span for several vocabularies as a function of vocabulary size.* **Quarterly Progress Report**, 1952, January-March, 338–352.

[106] Nickerson, R.S. & Adams, M.J. *Long-term memory for a common object.* **Cognitive Psychology**, 1979, 11(3) 1979, 287–307.

[107] Mooney, C.M. *Recognition of ambiguous and unambiguous visual configurations with short and longer exposures.* **British Journal of Psychology**, 1960, 51(2), 119–125.

[108] Standing, L., Conezio, J. & Haber, R.N. *Perception and memory for pictures: Single-trial learning of 2500 visual stimuli.* **Psychonomic Science**, 1970, 19(2), 73–74.

[109] Standing, L. *Learning 10,000 Pictures.* **Quarterly Journal of Experimental Psychology**, 1973, 25(2), 207–22.

[110] Nickerson, R.S. *A note on long-term recognition memory for pictorial material.* **Psychonomic Science**, 1968, 11(2), 58.

[111] Emberley, E. *Ed Emberley's Drawing Book: Make a World.* New York, NY: LB Kids, 1972.

[112] Buzan, T. & Buzan, B. **The Mind Map Book. How to Use Radiant Thinking to Maximize Your Brain's Untapped Potential**. New York, NY: Penguin Publishing, 1996.

Harris, I. & Caviglioli, O. **Think it—Map it! How Schools Use Mapping to Transform Teaching and Learning**. Stafford, Great Britain: MPG Books, 2003.

Kagan, M. **Mind Mapping. A Smart Card**. San Clemente, CA: Kagan Publishing, 1998. www.KaganOnline.com

Margulies, N. **Mapping Inner Space. Learning and Teaching Mind Mapping**. Tucson, AZ: Zephyr Press, 1991.

Wycoff, J. **Mindmapping. Your Personal Guide to Exploring Creativity and Problem-Solving**. New York, NY: Berkley Publishing Corporation, 1991.

[113] Buzan, T. **Use Both Sides of Your Brain, 3rd Edition**. New York, NY: Penguin Group, 1989.

[114] Bromley, K. Irwin-De Vitis, L. & Modlo, M. **Graphic Organizers. Visual Strategies for Active Learning**. New York, NY: Scholastic Professional Books, 1995.

Kagan, M. **Graphic Organizers. SmartCard**. San Clemente, CA: Kagan Publishing, 1998. www.KaganOnline.com

[115] Candler, L. **Graphic Organizers for Reading. Teaching Tools Aligned with the Commone Core**. Saint Johnsbury, Vermont: Compass, 2012.

[116] Dunston, P.J. *A critique of graphic organizer research.* **Reading Research and Instruction**. 1992, 31(2), 57–65.

Flood, J. & Lapp, D. *Conceutal mapping strategies for understanding information texts.* **The Reading Teacher**, 1988, 41(8), 780–783.

Heimlich, J.E. & Pittelman, S.D. **Semantic Mapping: Classroom Applications**. Newark, DE: International Reading Association, 1986.

Moore, D.W. & Readance, J.E. *A quantitative and qualitative review of graphic organizer research.* **Journal of Educational Research**, 1984, 78(1), 11–17.

[117] Kagan, L. **Dynamic Trainer**. San Clemente, CA: Kagan Publishing, 2007. www.Kaganonline.com

[118] Kagan, S. & Kagan, M. **Kagan Cooperative Learning**. San Clemente, CA: Kagan Publishing, 2009. www.KaganOnline.com

[119] Kagan, S. & Kagan, M. **Multiple Intelligences: The Complete MI Book**. San Clemente, CA: Kagan Publishing, 1998. www.KaganOnline.com

[120] Gazzaniga, M.S., Bogen, J.E. & Sperry, R.W. *Some functional effects of sectioning the cerebral commissures in man.* **Proceedings of the National Academy of Sciences of the USA**, 1962, 48(10), 1765–1769.

[121] Sperry, R.W., Gazzaniga, M.S. & Bogen, J.E. *Interhemispheric relationships: The neocortical commissures; syndromes of hemisphere disconnection.* **Handbook of Clinical Neurology**, 1969, 4, 273–290.

[122] Doron, K.W., Bassett, D.S. & Gazzaniga, M.S. *Inaugural article: Dynamic network structure of interhemispheric coordination.* **Proceedings of the National Academy of Sciences of the USA**, 2012, 109(46), 18661–18668.

[123] Nocentini, U., Goulet, P., Roberts, P.M. & Joanette, Y. *The effects of left- versus right-hemisphere lesions on the sensitivity to intra- and interconceptual semantic relationships.* **Neuropsychologia**, 2001, 39(5), 443–451.

[124] Abernethy, M. & Coney, J. *Semantic and phonemic priming in the cerebral hemispheres.* **Neuropsychologia**, 1990, 28(9), 933–945.

[125] Chiarello C. & Richards, L. *Another look at categorical priming in the cerebral hemispheres.* **Neuropsychologia**, 1992, 30(4), 381–392.

[126] Nocentini, U., Goulet, P., Roberts, P.M. & Joanette, Y. *The effects of left- versus right-hemisphere lesions on the sensitivity to intra- and interconceptual semantic relationships.* **Neuropsychologia**, 2001, 39(5), 443–451.

[127] Brownell, H.H., Potter, H.H., Michelow, D. & Gardner H. *Sensitivity to lexical denotation and connotation in brain damaged patients: A double dissociation.* **Brain and Language**, 1984, 22(2), 253–265.

[128] Sperry, R.W. *Cerebral organization and behavior.* **Science**, 1961, 133(3466), 1749–1757.

[129] Gaab, N., Gaser, C., Zaehle, T., Jancke, L. & Schlaug, G. *Functional anatomy of pitch memory—an fMRI study with sparse temporal sampling.* **NeuroImage**, 2003, 19(4), 1417–1426.

[130] Platel, H., Baron, J-C., Desgranges, B., Bernard, F. & Eustache, F. *Semantic and episodic memory of music are subserved by distinct neural networks.* **NeuroImage**. 2003, 20(1), 244–256.

[131] Levitin, D.J. ***This is Your Brain on Music. The Science of a Human Obsession***. New York, NY: Penguin Group, 2006.

[132] Gaser, C. & Schlaug, G. *Brain structures differ between musicians and non-musicians.* ***The Journal of Neuroscience***, 2003, 23(27), 9240–9245.

[133] Koeneke, S., Lutz, K., Wüstenberg, T. & Jäncke, L. *Long-term training affects cerebellar processing in skilled keyboard players.* **NeuroReport**, 2004, 15(8), 1279–1282.

Krings, T., Töpper, R., Foltys, H., Erberich, S., Sparing, R., Willmes, K. & Thron, A. *Cortical activation patterns during complex motor tasks in piano players and control subjects. A functional magnetic resonance imaging study.* **Neuroscience Letters**, 2000, 278(3), 189–193.

[134] Haier, R.J., Siegel, B.V.Jr., MacLachlan, A., Soderling, E., Lottenberg, S. & Buchsbaum, M.S. *Regional glucose metabolic changes after learning a complex visuospacial/motor task: A positron emission tomographic study.* **Brain Research**, 1992, 570(1-2), 134–143.

[135] Bever, T.G & Chiarello, R.J. *Cerebral dominance in musicians and nonmusicians.* **Science**, 1974, 185(150), 537–539.

[136] Platel, H., Baron, J-C., Desgranges, B., Bernard, F. & Eustache, F. *Semantic and episodic memory of music are subserved by distinct neural networks.* **NeuroImage**. 2003, 20(1), 244–256.

[137] Tulving, E., Kapur, S., Craik F.I.M., Moscovitch, M. & Houle, S. *Hemispheric encoding/retrieval asymmetry in episodic memory: positron emission tomography findings.* **Proceedings of the National Academy of Sciences of the USA**, 1994, 91(6), 2016–2020.

[138] Goldberg, E. ***The Executive Brain. Frontal Lobes and the Civilized Mind***. Oxford, England: Oxford University Press, 2001.

Goldberg, E. & Costa, L.D. *Hemisphere differences in the acquisition and use of descriptive systems.* **Brain and Language**, 1981, 14(1), 144–173.

[139] Goldberg, E. ***The Executive Brain. Frontal Lobes and the Civilized Mind***. Oxford, England: Oxford University Press, 2001, 42.

[140] Bever, T.G & Chiarello, R.J. *Cerebral dominance in musicians and nonmusicians.* **Science**, 1974, 185(150), 537–539.

[141] Marzi, C.A. & Berlucchi, G. *Right visual field superiority for accuracy of recognition of famous faces in normals.* **Neuropshchologia**, 1977, 15(6), 751–756.

[142] Tulving, E., Markowitsch, H.J., Craik, F.E., Hiabib, R. & Houl, S. *Novelty and familiarity activations in PET studies of memory encoding and retrieval.* **Cerebral Cortex**, 1996, 6(1), 71–79.

[143] Tulving, E., Markowitsch, H.J., Craik, F.I.M., Habib, R. & Houle, S. *Novelty and familiarity activations in PET studies of memory encoding and retrieval.* **Cerebral Cortex**, 1996, 6(1), 71–79.

Tulving, E., Markowitsch, H.J., Kapur, S., Habib, R. & Houle, S. *Novelty encoding networks in the human brain: data from positron emission tomography studies.* **NeuroReport**, 1994, 5(18), 2525–2528.

[144] Haier, R.J., Siegel, B.V.Jr., MacLachlan, A., Soderling, E., Lottenberg, S. & Buchsbaum, M.S. *Regional glucose metabolic changes after learning a complex visuospacial/motor task: a positron emission tomographic study.* **Brain Research**, 1992, 570(1–2), 134–143.

[145] Raichle, M.E., Fiez, J.A., Videen, T.O., MacLeod, A.M., Pardo, J.V., Fox, P.T. & Peterson, S.E. *Practice-related changes in human brain functional anatomy during nonmotor learning.* **Cerebral Cortex**, 1994, 4(1), 26.

[146] Tulving, E., Kapur, S., Markowitsch, H.J., Craik, G., Habib, R. & Houle, S. *Neuroanatomical correlates of retrieval in episodic memory: auditory sentence recognition.* **Proceedings of the National Academy of Sciences of the USA**, 1994, 91(6), 2012–2015.

[147] Campbell, L., Campbell, B. & Dickinson, D. ***Teaching and Learning through Multiple Intelligences***. Needham Heights, MA: Allyn & Bacon, 1996, 1992, 7–8.

[148] Iverson, J.M. & Goldin-Meadow, S. *Why people gesture when they speak.* **Nature**, 1998, 396(6708), 228.

[149] Colletta, J.-M., Pellenq, C. & Guidetti, M. *Age-related changes in co-speech gesture and narrative: Evidence from French children and adults.* **Speech Communication**, 2010, 52(6), 565–576.

[150] Church, R.B. *Using gesture and speech to capture transitions in learning.* **Cognitive Development**, 1999, 14(2), 313–342.

Garber, P., Alibali, M.W. & Goldin-Meadow, S. *Knowledge conveyed in gesture is not tied to the hands.* **Child Development**, 1998, 69(1), 75–84.

[151] Boyatzis, C.J. & Satyaprasad, C. *Children's facial and gestural decoding and encoding: Relations between skills and with popularity.* **Journal of Nonverbal Behavior**, 1994, 18(1), 37–55.

[152] Cohen, R.L. *On the generality of some memory laws.* **Scandinavian Journal of Psychology**, 1981, 22(1), 267–281.

Cohen, R.L. & Stewart, M. *How to avoid developmental effects in free recall.* **Scandinavian Journal of Psychology**, 1982, 23(1), 9–16.

Saltz, E. & Donnenwerth-Nolan, S. *Does motoric imagery facilitate memory for sentences? A selective interference test.* **Journal of Verbal Learning & Verbal Behavior**, 1981, 20(3), 322–332.

[153] Beilock, S. & Goldin-Meadow, S. *Gesture changes thought by grounding it in action.* **Psychological Science**, 2010, 21(11), 1605–1610.

[154] Cook, S.W. & Tanenhaus, M.K. *Embodied communication: Speakers' gestures affect listeners' actions.* **Cognition**, 2009, 113(1), 98–104.

155 Beilock, S.L., Lyons I.M., Mattarella-Micke, A., Nusbaum, H.C. & Small, S.L. *Sports experience changes the neural processing of action language.* **Proceedings of the National Academy of Sciences**, 2008, 105(36), 13269-13273.

156 Chu, M. & Kita, S. *Spontaneous gestures during mental rotation tasks: Insights into the microdevelopment of the motor strategy.* **Journal of Experimental Psychology: General**, 2008, 137(4), 706–723.

Chu, M. & Kita, S. *The nature of gestures' beneficial role in spatial problem solving.* **Journal of Experimental Psychology: General**, 2011, 140(1), 102–116.

Ehrlich, S.B., Levine, S.C. & Goldin-Meadow, S. *The importance of gesture in children's spatial reasoning.* **Developmental Psychology**, 2006, 42(6), 1259–1268.

Hostetter, A.B. & Alibali, M.W. *Raise your hand if you're spatial: Relations between verbal and spatial skills and gesture production.* **Gesture**, 2007, 7(1), 73–95.

157 Goldin-Meadow, S. & Beilock, S.L. *Action's influence on thought: The case of gesture.* **Perspectives on Psychological Science**, 2010, 5(6), 664–674.

158 Goldin-Meadow, S. **Hearing Gesture: How Our Hands Help Us Think**. Cambridge, MA: Harvard University Press, 2003.

159 Cook, S.W. & Goldin-Meadow, S. *The role of gesture in learning: Do children use their hands to change their minds?* **Journal of Cognition & Development**, 2006, 7(2), 211–232.

160 Kelly, S.D. & Goldsmith, L. *Gesture and right hemisphere involvement in evaluating lecture material.* **Gesture**, 2004, 4(1), 25–42.

161 Best, J.R., Miller, P.H. & Jones, L.L. *Executive functions after age 5: Changes and correlates.* **Developmental Review**, 2009, 29(3), 180–200.

162 Miller, P.H. & O'Neil, G. *A show of hands: relations between young children's gesturing and executive function.* **Developmental Psychology**, 2013, 49(8), 1517–1528.

163 Church, R.B. & Goldin-Meadow, S. *The mismatch between gesture and speech as an index of transitional knowledge.* **Cognition**, 1986, 23(1), 43–71.

Perry, M. & Elder, A.D. *Knowledge in transition: Adults' developing understanding of a principle of physical causality.* **Cognitive Development**, 1997, 12(1), 131–157.

164 Church, R.B., Ayman-Nolley, S. & Mahootian, S. *The effects of gestural instruction on bilingual children.* **International Journal of Bilingual Education and Bilingualism**, 2004, 7(4), 303–319.

Perry, M., Berch, D.B. & Singleton, J.L. *Constructing shared understanding: The role of nonverbal input in learning contexts.* **Journal of Contemporary Legal Issues**, 1995, 6, 213–236.

Ping, R. & Goldin-Meadow, S. *Hands in the air: Using ungrounded iconic gestures to teach children conservation of quantity.* **Developmental Psychology**, 2008, 44(5), 1277–1287.

Singer, M.A. & Goldin-Meadow, S. *Children learn when their teachers' gestures and speech differ.* **Psychological Science**, 2005, 16(2), 85–89.

Valenzeno, L., Alibali, M.W. & Klatzky, R. *Teachers' gestures facilitate students' learning: A lesson in symmetry.* **Contemporary Educational Psychology**, 2003, 28(2), 187–204.

165 Cook, S.W. & Goldin-Meadow, S. *The role of gesture in learning: Do children use their hands to change their minds?* **Journal of Cognition and Development**, 2006, 7(2), 211–232.

166 Valenzeno, L., Alibali, M.W. & Klatzky, R. (2003). *Teachers' gestures facilitate students' learning: A lesson in symmetry.* **Contemporary Educational Psychology**, 2003, 28(2), 187–204.

167 Church, R.B., Ayman-Nolley, S. & Mahootian, S. *The role of gesture in bilingual education: Does gesture enhance learning?* **Bilingual Education and Bilingualism**, 2004, 7(4), 303–319.

168 Goldin-Meadow, S., Cook, S.W., & Mitchell, Z.A. *Gesturing gives children new ideas about math.* **Psychological Science**, 2009, 20(3), 267–272.

Perry, M., Berch, D. & Singleton, J. *Constructing shared understanding: The role of nonverbal input in learning contexts.* **Journal of Contemporary Legal Issues**, 1995, 6, 215–235.

Richland, L.E. & McDonough, I.M. *Learning by analogy: Discriminating between potential analogs.* **Contemporary Educational Psychology**, 2010, 35(1), 28–43.

Singer, M.A. & Goldin-Meadow, S. *Children learn when their teachers' gestures and speech differ.* **Psychological Science**, 2005, 16(2), 85–89.

169 Cook, S.W., Duffy, R.G. & Fenn, K.M. *Consolidation and transfer of learning after observing hand gesture.* **Child Development**, 2013, 84(6), 1863–1871.

170 Alibali, M.W. *How children change their minds: Strategy change can be gradual or abrupt.* **Developmental Psychology**, 1999, 35(1), 127–145.

Rittle-Johnson, B. & Alibali, M.W. *Conceptual and procedural knowledge of mathematics: Does one lead to the other?* **Journal of Educational Psychology**, 1999, 91(1), 175–189.

171 Diekelmann, S. & Born, J. *The memory function of sleep.* **Nature Neuroscience**, 2010, 11(2), 114–126.

Margoliash, D. & Fenn, K.M. *Sleep and memory consolidation in audition.* In A. I. Basbaum, A. Kaneko, G.M. Shepherd, & G. Westheimer (Eds.), **The Senses: A Comprehensive Reference (Vol. 3, pp. 895–912)**. San Diego, CA: Academic Press, 2008.

McGaugh, J.L. *Memory: A century of consolidation.* **Science**, 2000, 287(5451), 248–251.

172 Cook, S.W. & Goldin-Meadow, S. *The role of gesture in learning: Do children use their hands to change their minds?* **Journal of Cognition and Development**, 2006, 7(2), 211–232.

Cook, S.W., Mitchell, Z. & Goldin-Meadow, S. *Gesturing makes learning last.* **Cognition**, 2008, 106(2), 1047–1058.

Feyereisen, P. *How could gesture facilitate lexical access?* **Advances in Speech Language Pathology**, 2006, 8(2), 128–133.

[173] Broaders, S., Cook, S.W., Mitchell, Z. & Goldin-Meadow, S. *Making children gesture reveals implicit knowledge and leads to learning.* **Journal of Experimental Psychology: General**, 2007, 136(4), 539–550.

Goldin-Meadow, S., Cook, S.W. & Mitchell, Z.A. *Gesturing gives children new ideas about math.* **Psychological Science**, 2009, 20(3), 267–272.

[174] Goldin-Meadow, S., Cook, S.W. & Mitchell, Z.A. *Gesturing gives children new ideas about math.* **Psychological Science**, 2009, 20(3), 267–272.

[175] Goldin-Meadow, S., Cook, S.W. & Mitchell, Z.A. *Gesturing gives children new ideas about math.* **Psychological Science**, 2009, 20(3), 267–272.

[176] Kelly, S., Healey, M., Ozyurek, A. & Holler, J. *The communicative influence of gesture and action during speech comprehension: Gestures have the upper hand.* **The Journal of the Acoustical Society of America**, 2012, 131(4), 3311–3311.

[177] Cook, S.W., Mitchell, Z. & Goldin-Meadow, S. *Gesturing makes learning last.* **Cognition**, 2008, 106(2), 1047–1058.

[178] McNeill, D. & Pedelty, L.L. Right brain and gesture. In K. Emmorey & J.S. Reilly (Eds.), **Language, Gesture, and Space**, 63–65. Hillsdale, NJ: Lawrence Erlbaum Associates, Inc., 1995.

[179] Felder, R.M. & Brent, R. *Understand student differences.* **Journal of Engineering Education**, 2005, 94(1), 57–72.

[180] University of Pennsylvania. (March 28, 2009). *Visual learners convert words to pictures in the brain and vice versa, says psychology study.* **ScienceDaily.** Retrieved October 4, 2013 from http://www.sciencedaily.com/releases/2009/03/090325091834.htm

[181] Carbo, M., Dunn, R. & Dunn, K. **Teaching Students to Read through Their Individual Learning Styles**, Prentice-Hall, 1986, 13.

[182] Strafford, R. & Dunn, K.J. **Teaching Secondary Students through Their Individual Learning Styles.** Boston, MA: Allyn and Bacon, 1993.

[183] Pashler, H., McDaniel, M., Rohrer, D. & Bjork, R. *Learning styles concepts and evidence.* **Psychological Science in the Public Interest**, 2008, 9(3), 105–119.

[184] Mayer, R.E. *Systematic thinking fostered by illustrations in scientific text.* **Journal of Educational Psychology**, 1989, 81(2), 240–246.

Mayer, R.E. & Gallini, J.K. *When is an illustration worth ten thousand words?* **Journal of Educational Psychology**, 1990, 82(4), 715–726.

[185] Mayer, R.E. & Anderson, R.B. *Animations need narrations: An experimental test of a dual-coding hypothesis.* **Journal of Educational Psychology**, 1991, 83(4), 484–490.

Mayor, R.E. & Anderson, R.B. *The Instructive Animation—Helping students build connections between words and pictures in multimedia learning.* **Journal of Educational Psychology**, 84(4), 1992, 444–452.

[186] Kagan, S. & Kagan, M. **Kagan Cooperative Learning**. San Clemente, CA: Kagan Publishing, 2009.

[187] Kagan, S. & Kagan, M. **Multiple Intelligences. The Complete MI Book**. San Clemente, CA: Kagan Publishing, 1998.

[188] Kagan, S. & Kagan, M. **Multiple Intelligences. The Complete MI Book**. San Clemente, CA: Kagan Publishing, 1998.

[189] Campbell, L., Campbell, B. & Dickinson, D. **Teaching and Learning through Multiple Intelligences**. Needham Heights, MA: Allyn & Bacon, 1996, 1992, 7–8.

[190] Brown, S. **Play. How it Shapes the Brain, Opens the Imagination, and Invigorates the Soul**. New York, NY: Avery, 2009.

[191] Kilgard, M.P. Pandya, P.K., Engineer, N.D. & Moucha, R. *Cortical network reorganization guided by sensory input features,* **Biological Cybernetics**, 2002, 87(5-6), 333–343.

[192] Campbell, L. & Campbell, B. **Multiple Intelligences and Student Achievement. Success Stories from Six Schools**. Alexandria, VA: Association for Supervision and Curriculum Development, 1999.

[193] Kagan, S. & Kagan, M. **Multiple Intelligences. The Complete MI Book**. San Clemente, CA: Kagan Publishing, 1998.

[194] Lawrence, M. & Osherson, D. *New evidence for distinct right and left brain systems for deductive versus probabilistic reasoning.* **Cerebral Cortex**, 2001, 11(10), 954–965.

[195] Kagan, S., Gardner, H. & Sylwester, R. *Trialogue: Brain localization of intelligences.* San Clemente, CA: Kagan Publishing. **Kagan Online Magazine**, Fall 2002. www.KaganOnline.com

[196] Kraemer, D.J.M., Rosenberg, L.M. & Thompson-Schill, S.L. *The neural correlates of visual and verbal cognitive style.* **The Journal of Neuroscience**, 2009, 29(12), 3792–3798.

[197] McKusick, V.A. *On lumpers and splitters, or the nosology of genetic disease.* **Perspectives in Biology and Medicine**, 1969, 12(2), 298–312.

[198] Riding, R. & Rayer, S. **Cognitive Styles and Learning Strategies. Understanding Style Differences in Learning and Behavior**. London, Great Britain: David Fulton Publishers, Ltd, 2001.

[199] Fink, G.R. Halligan, P.W., Marshall, J.C., Frith, C.D., Frackowiak, R.S. & Dolan, R.J. *Neural mechanisms involved in the processing of global and local aspects of hierarchically organized visual stimuli.* **Brain**, 1997, 120(10), 1779–1791.

[200] Funnell, M.G., Colvin, M.K. & Gazzaniga, M.S. *The calculating hemispheres: Studies of a split-brain patient.* **Neuropsychologia**, 2007, 45(10), 2378–2386.

[201] Fink, G.R. Halligan, P.W., Marshall, J.C., Frith, C.D., Frackowiak, R.S. & Dolan, R.J. *Neural mechanisms involved in the processing of global and local aspects of hierarchically organized visual stimuli.* **Brain**, 1997, 120(10), 1779–1791.

[202] Lane, R.D. & L. Nadel, (Eds). **Cognitive Neuroscience of Emotion**. New York, NY: Oxford University Press, 2000.

203 Gray, J. *Men Are from Mars, Women Are from Venus: The Classic Guide to Understanding the Opposite Sex*. New York, NY: Harper Collins, 2009.

204 Stafford, R. & Dunn, K.J. *Teaching Secondary Students through Their Individual Learning Styles*. Boston, MA: Allyn & Bacon, 1993.

Dunn, R. & Dunn, K. *Teaching Elementary Students through their Individual Learning Styles: Practical Approaches for Grades 3–6*. Boston, MA: Allyn & Bacon, 1992.

205 Dunn, R. & Dunn, K. *Teaching Elementary Students through their Individual Learning Styles: Practical Approaches for Grades 3–6*. Boston, MA: Allyn & Bacon, 1992.

206 Kagan, S. & Kagan, M. *Multiple Intelligences. The Complete MI Book*. San Clemente, CA: Kagan Publishing, 1998. www.KaganOnline.com

207 Nickerson, R.S. & Adams, M.J. *Long-term memory for a common object. Cognitive Psychology*, 1979, 11(3) 1979, 287–307.

208 Schultz, W., Dayan, P. & Montague, P.R. *A neural substrate of prediction and reward. Science.* 1997, 275(5306), 1593–1599.

209 Schultz, W. *Predictive reward signal of dopamine neurons. Journal of Neurophysiology*, 1998, 80(1), 1–27.

210 Smallwood, J. & Schooler, J.W. *The restless mind. Psychological Bulletin*, 2006, 132(6), 946–958.

Lindquist, S.I. & McLean, J.P. *Daydreaming and its correlates in an educational environment. Learning and Individual Differences*, 2011, 21(2), 158–167.

211 Hidi, S. & Baird, W. *Strategies for increasing text-based interest and students' recall of expository text. Reading Research Quarterly*, 1988, 23(4), 465–483.

Anderson, R.C., Mason, J. & Shirey, L. *The reading group: An experimental investigation of a labyrinth. Reading Research Quarterly*, 1984, 20(1), 6–37.

Anderson, R.C., Shirey, L., Wilson, P.T. & Fielding, L.G. *Interestingness of children's reading material*. In R.E. Snow & M.J. Farr (Eds.), *Aptitude, Learning and Instruction: Vol. 3. Cognitive and Affective Process Analyses*, 287–299. Hillsdale, NJ: Erlbaum, 1986.

Asher, S.R. *Influence of topic interest on black children's and white children's reading comprehension. Child Development*, 1979, 50(3), 686–690.

212 Hidi, S. & Baird, W. *Interestingness—a neglected variable in discourse processing. Cognitive Science*, 1986, 10(2), 179–194.

213 Estes, T.H. & Vaughn, J.L., Jr. *Reading interest and comprehension: Implications. The Reading Teacher*, 1973, 27(2), 149–153.

214 Schraw, G. *Situational interest in literary text. Contemporary Educational Psychology*, 1997, 22(4), 279–294.

Scraw, G. & Lehan, S. *Situational interest: A review of the literature and directions for future research. Educational Psychology Review*, 2001, 13(1), 23–52.

Silvia, P.J. *What is interesting? Exploring the appraisal structure of interest. Emotion*, 2005, 5(1), 89–102.

Silvia, P.J. *Exploring the Psychology of Interest*. New York, NY: Oxford University Press, 2006.

215 Gardner, H. *Frames of Mind. The Theory of Multiple Intelligences*. New York, NY: Basic Books, 1983.

Gardner, H. *Intelligence Reframed: Multiple Intelligences for the 21st Century*. New York, NY: Basic Books, 1999.

Gardner, H. *Multiple Intelligences. The Theory in Practice*. New York: Basic Books, 1993.

216 Kagan, S. & Kagan, M. *Multiple Intelligences: The Complete MI Book*. San Clemente, CA: Kagan Publishing, 1998. www.KaganOnline.com

217 Wiederhold, C. *Higher Level Thinking Book and Class Manipulative Set*. San Clemente, CA: Kagan Publishing, 20012. www.KaganOnline.com

218 Kagan, S. *Silly Sports & Goofy Games*. San Clemente, CA: Kagan Publishing, 2000. www.KaganOnline.com

219 Kagan, S. & Kagan, M. *Kagan Cooperative Learning*. San Clemente, CA: Kagan Publishing, 2009. www.KaganOnline.com

220 Phillips, M. *The Miracle Workers*. 2013. PDF available on website: http://cdn3.edutopia.org/pdfs/blogs/edutopia-phillips-concerns-miracle.pdf

221 Edutopia: http://www.edutopia.org/

222 Craik, F.I.M. & Tulving, E. *Depth of processing and the retention of words in episodic memory. Journal of Experimental Psychology: General*, 1975, 104(3), 268–294.

223 Anderson, R.C. & Hidde, J.L. *Imagery and sentence learning. Journal of Educational Psychology*, 1971, 62(6), 526–530.

224 Anderson, R.C., Goldberg, S.R. & Hidde, J.L. *Meaninful processing of sentences. Journal of Educational Psychology*, 1971, 62(5), 395–399.

Kane, J.H. & Anderson, R.C. *Depth of processing and interference effects in the learning of and remembering of sentences. Journal of Educational Psychology*, 1978, 70(4), 626–635.

225 Anderson, R.C. & Kulhavy, R.W. *Learning concepts from definitions. American Eduation Research Journal*, 1972, 9(3), 385–390.

226 Schallert, D.L. *Improving memory for prose: The relationship between depth of processing and context. Journal of Verbal Learning and Verbal Behavior*, 1976, 15(6), 621–632.

227 Salari, K., Karczewski, K.J., Hudgins, L. & Ormond, K.E. *Evidence that personal genome testing enhances student learning in a course on genomics and personalized medicine. Public Library of Science ONE*, 8(7), e68853.

228 Watts, G.H. & Anderson, R.C. *Effects of three types of inserted questions on learning from prose.* **Journal of Educational Psychology**, 1971, 62(5), 387–394.

229 Anderson, R.C., Mason, J. & Shirey, L. *The reading group: An experimental investigation of a labyrinth.* **Reading Research Quarterly**, 1984, 20(1), 6–37.

230 Mooney, C.M. *Recognition of ambiguous and unambiguous visual configurations with short and longer exposures.* **British Journal of Psychology**, 1960, 51(2), 119–125.

231 Howe, M.J.A. *Using students' notes to examine the role of the individual learning in acquiring meaningful subject matter.* **Journal of Educational Research**, 1970, 64(2), 61–3.

232 Smith, A. & Call, N. **Accelerated Learning: The ALPS Approach: Brain-Based Methods for Accelerating Motivation and Achievement (Grades K–6)**. San Clemente, CA: Kagan Publishing, 2002.

Smith, A. **Accelerated Learning in Practice: Brain-Based Methods for Accelerating Motivation and Achievement (Grades 6–12)**. San Clemente, CA: Kagan Publishing, 2002.

233 Dewey, J. **Experience and Education**. New York, NY: Touchstone, 1938.

Dewey, J. **Democracy and Education**. Radford, VA: Wilder Publications, LLC. 2008.

234 Vygotsky, L.S. **Mind in Society. The Development of Higher Psychological Processes**. Cambridge, MA: President and Fellows of Harvard College, 1978.

235 Kagan, S. & Kagan, M. **Kagan Cooperative Learning**. San Clemente, CA: Kagan Publishing, 2009. www.KaganOnline.com

Kagan, S. & Kagan, M. **Multiple Intelligences. The Complete MI Book**. San Clemente, CA: Kagan Publishing, 1998. www.KaganOnline.com

Structures

Kagan Structures for Brain-Friendly Teaching

In this section, you will find the steps of the 27 Kagan Structures featured throughout this book. The chart, Kagan Structures for Brain-Friendly Teaching, provides the page numbers for each of the structures described within each of the six principles. At a glance, we can see many structures help us implement a number of principles. For example, **Timed Pair Share** implements the principles of *Safety* (students respond to a teammate, which is safer than responding in front of the whole class), *Social* (students interact and develop empathy), *Emotion* (students praise each other), *Attention* (students learn and practice active listening), and *Stimuli* (the structure provides novelty, predictability, and feedback, and allows students to construct meaning). The structures are powerful tools to implement the six principles of brain-friendly teaching.

Structures Implement the Six Principles

Here, we overview the six principles of brain-friendly teaching and examine how three different structures implement each of the principles in different ways. There are over 200 Kagan Structures, and each one implements different principles of brain-friendly teaching in different ways. The conclusion we can draw: When we are teaching with structures, we are engaged in brain-friendly teaching. Structures are the most powerful and comprehensive set of instructional strategies for brain-friendly teaching.

27 Structures to Implement Brain-Friendly Teaching

Principle 1: Nourishment

Kagan Structures that involve movement improve nourishment to the brain. How? Any major muscle movement increases heart rate as well as breathing rate and volume. This means more blood is pumped to the brain and the blood that is pumped to the brain is better oxygenated. As we have noted, the simple act of walking moves blood more rapidly through the legs, and the valves in the legs pump blood to the heart, which in turn sends a better supply of blood to the brain.

Major muscle movement increases heart rate and breathing rate and volume, sending more nutrients to the brain.

The structures that include movement cannot claim the benefits of intense exercise and should not be seen as a substitute for high-impact exercise. Exercise, especially high-impact exercise, releases epinephrine, norepinephrine, dopamine, and brain-derived neurotrophic factor (BDNF), which are associated with increased alertness and learning, as well as brain growth and development. None of the Kagan Structures involve high-impact exercise. For that, we can turn to the rapid movement generated by the tag games found in *Silly Sports & Goofy Games*.

Many Kagan Structures do, however, increase nourishment of the brain because they involve major muscle movement, which elevates heart rate as well as breathing rate and volume. That the structures energize students is obvious to anyone who has observed the body language, facial expressions, and level of alertness of students before and after a **StandUp–HandUp–PairUp** or any of the other structures that involve student movement. Some of the enhanced alertness is undoubtedly due to novelty and social interaction, but movement plays an important role. Let's examine how **Formations**, **Number Group Mania!**, and **TakeOff-TouchDown** nourish the brain through movement.

Formations (Structure 6). During a math lesson on angles, a teacher wants to energize the class and to have students create a bodily/kinesthetic symbol of the content. She says, *"When I say go, you will stand up and move to form one large right angle triangle. No talking. Go!"* Students silently move about the room to form the figure. The teacher then has students move to form different-sized angles. As students move, their heart rates increase a bit, their breathing rate and volume increases a bit, and their brains are a bit better nourished. (Incidentally, we often ask students to complete their formations without talking because we want to engage the bodily/kinesthetic symbol system rather than allowing the highly verbal or dominant students to simply tell everyone where to stand.)

Number Group Mania! (Structure 9). A teacher has been presenting the events that led up to the Civil War. The teacher wants to cement memory for the events by having students do a **RallyRobin**, taking turns naming and describing the events. The teacher notices the eyes of some students are a bit glazed over and so wants to energize the class. Literally, the teacher wants to pump more oxygen into the brains of the students. So, rather than simply having students turn to their face partner or shoulder partner to do the **RallyRobin**, the teacher says, *"When I say go, you will form groups of two, odd numbers with odd numbers and even numbers with even numbers. Go!"* By having students get up and move about the classroom before interacting, the students' brains are better nourished. The probability of their retaining the content is greater than if they had done the **RallyRobin** in a less energized state.

TakeOff-TouchDown (Structure 22). A teacher wants to poll her class. The poll might be about any topic, such as how many students had protein in their breakfast, completed the homework assignment, know the name of the water channel that separates England from France, or brought in a signed permission slip. The teacher knows that whenever she wants to poll her class, she has a choice. She can use the time-honored method of having students raise their hands (*"Raise your hand if you feel the principle of manifest destiny justified the United States annexing Texas from Mexico."*). Alternatively, she can use **TakeOff-TouchDown**. Instead of having students raise their hands, she can ask students to show their agreement by standing up. By simply having students stand up and sit down, the teacher has included major muscle movement and so the brains of her students are a bit better nourished.

TakeOff-TouchDown produces even more brain nourishment when a teacher asks a series of questions, having students stand each time the question is true of them. For example, a teacher wants to know her class better and asks a series of getting acquainted questions: *"We will do a **TakeOff-TouchDown** to respond: Each time something is true of you, stand up. How many of you,*

> *Walk to school?*
> *Own a pet?*
> *Went to bed before 10:00 p.m. last night?*
> *Own a personal cell phone?*
> *Have visited another country?*
> *Have an after school job?"*

Principle 2: Safety

When brains are safe, the prefrontal cortex is less inhibited, freer to make learning connections, and to be more creative. Almost all Kagan Structures involve safe, supportive social interaction. Students are in teams or pairs and encourage, coach, and praise each other. They feel themselves to be on the same side. They know they will receive positive feedback rather than put-downs. They feel safe. Let's examine how three structures provide safety, **Flashcard Game**, **Team-Pair-Solo**, and **Paraphrase Passport**.

Flashcard Game (Structure 5). The **Flashcard Game** is designed to create a safe context within which to memorize new content. The three rounds are progressive in difficulty to ensure initial success, which helps students feel more confident as they progress. Students prepare for the game by making up flashcards on the content they have missed on a pretest. By making up their own cards with the question on one side and the answer on the other, students become familiar with the content and know what they will be quizzed on. In the first of

Almost all Kagan Structures involve safe, supportive social interaction.

the three rounds, a partner shows the student the front of the first card and reads it to him or her. The partner then shows the student the answer on the back of the first card and reads it. Next, the partner turns the card over so the student sees only the front and asks what is on the back. The student has made up the card and has just seen and heard the answer, so the student is simply repeating the answer from immediate short-term memory. This feels too easy! Having given the right answer, the student wins back the card and receives surprising, delightful praise. Thus, the **Flashcard Game** creates a very safe context for learning. Initial success is almost guaranteed, and successive rounds build on the success of prior rounds so students remain in a safe learning context.

Paraphrase Passport (Structure 12). During an unstructured discussion, there is often disagreement. Often one person puts down the idea of another in an attempt to promote his or her own idea. For example, the student might preface an introduction to his or her own idea by saying, *"What would be better is…,"* or, *"That won't work because…"* Without intending, students have created an unsafe context for creativity. Everyone knows they suggest an idea at the risk of having that idea put down.

In contrast, **Paraphrase Passport**, creates a context in which all ideas are received and understood. Students feel listened to as their partner or teammate begins a paraphrase with gambits like, *"What I understand you to mean is…,"* or, *"What is important to you is…"* Knowing they will be listened to with respect, teammates feel safe to contribute.

Team-Pair-Solo (Structure 23). Like the **Flashcard Game**, **Team-Pair-Solo** ensures initial success that creates a safe context for learning. The team is presented a problem that is not within the capacity of all students to solve working alone. The team is heterogeneous in ability levels, so the problem is within the capacity of at least one teammate. The team is tasked with two jobs: (1) solve the problem, and (2) make sure everyone on the team knows how to solve the problem. Teammates are told to encourage and tutor those who would benefit from coaching.

When the team has solved the problem and feels everyone knows how to solve that type of problem, the team of four breaks into two pairs, advancing to pair work for the next problem. Only after successes in pair work does the pair split up and individuals work alone to solve successive problems. **Team-Pair-Solo** scaffolds for success, providing support for those who need it. A student who would not have felt safe working on his or her own has received support first in his or her team and then with a partner before tackling problems individually. There are other levels of support as well: Any pair experiencing difficulty can move back to teamwork, and students having difficulty working alone can move back to pair work.

Principle 3: Social

The third principle of Brain-Friendly Teaching, Social, is implemented when we structure social interaction, foster social cognition among our students, and when we help students acquire social skills. Social interaction maximizes brain engagement because it involves visual and auditory stimulation, as well as activation of mirror neurons and other parts of the brain to decode social stimuli. Social cognition, thinking about the thoughts, feelings, and intentions of others, occurs naturally as students interact—especially in structures that demand that students become aware of and respond to the communications of others. The structural approach to social skill acquisition embeds social skills within structures, so social skills are acquired as students interact with and master the academic curriculum. Rather than teaching separate lessons on social skills, we take a few moments before, during, and/or after students interact in a structure to model and reinforce the social skills embedded within the structure. Let's see how

Social cognition, thinking about the thoughts, feelings, and intentions of others, occurs naturally as students interact.

this plays out in **AllWrite Consensus**, **Celebrity Interview**, and **Timed Pair Share**.

AllWrite Consensus (Structure 1). When **AllWrite Consensus** is practiced, a student suggests the idea, but no team member can record the idea until all teammates have reached consensus. This fosters social cognition because in order to reach consensus, students need to understand the perspectives of the others in the group. Through the structure, students acquire the social skills of active listening, disagreeing politely, understanding points of view different than their own, and consensus seeking.

Celebrity Interview (Structure 3). Students enjoy **Celebrity Interview**, whether the content is teambuilding or academic. Learning about one's teammates fosters social bonds that facilitate later mutual encouragement and tutoring. Often **Celebrity Interview** is played in role, as students become an author, a scientist, or a historical character. Role-playing develops social cognition—students attempt to understand and portray the mind of another. Students acquire social skills including listening, praising, spontaneous speaking, and interviewing.

Timed Pair Share (Structure 25). Too often during a pair discussion, one person is talking while the other person is thinking about what they want to say. Neither partner is deeply processing what the other is saying. **Timed Pair Share** remedies this. Giving each person a predetermined amount of time to speak, telling the listener not to interrupt, and instructing the listener on the skills of active listening, radically transforms the communication. Rather than allowing their minds to wander, students practice intense focused listening.

Numerous times I have asked students and workshop participants if they found themselves listening more carefully than they would have otherwise because we used **Timed Pair**

Share. Without exception, there is enthusiastic agreement. The structure defines roles clearly so when students are listening, they are just listening rather than thinking about what they want to say, waiting for the other person to finish so they can have a turn. Students acquire the social skills of taking turns and active listening. They acquire response gambits like, *"I enjoyed listening to you because…," "Thanks for sharing…,"* and *"Your most convincing argument was…"* Giving students response gambits that cause them to reflect on the mind of the other fosters social cognition. As students use **Timed Pair Share,** they respond to their partner with phrases like, *"You believe…,"* or, *"What you feel most strongly is…"*

Principle 4: Emotion

Eliciting positive emotion enhances learning in a number of ways. Positive emotion elicits dopamine, which stimulates the motivation and attention centers in the brain. Eliciting positive emotion diminishes anxiety so the amygdalae doesn't interfere with creativity and learning. Positive emotion following success cements learning through retrograde memory enhancement. The mere anticipation of a reward stimulates the reward centers. The Kagan Structures elicit positive emotion through social support, praise, celebrations, and inclusion. Let's examine how three structures harness the power of positive emotion: **PairUp Review, Quiz-Quiz-Trade,** and **Sage-N-Scribe**.

Positive emotion following success cements learning through retrograde memory enhancement.

PairUp Review (Structure 11). **PairUp Review** is a substitute for the traditional approach to having students respond to teacher questions. In the traditional approach, the teacher poses a question and some students raise their hands to be called upon. This traditional Q & A method has obvious pitfalls: It is the high achievers who most often raise their hands to be called on, so we end up calling most on those who least need the practice and calling least on those who most need the practice.

Students begin **PairUp Review** with a **StandUp–HandUp–PairUp**, greeting a partner with a high five and a positive greeting. Mere anticipation of a positive greeting elicits positive emotion even before students find a partner. As we have seen, a high five produces positive emotion in two ways—proximity and touch. The teacher encourages positive greetings (*"Glad to be your partner." "Howdy partner."*), which elicit additional positive emotion.

The teacher poses a review question, and the students stand back to back. Standing back to back adds novelty, stimulating the brain's attention centers. Students each write their best answer on their own, turn around while hiding their AnswerBoards, and wait for the teacher to randomly call for Partners A or B to display their answers to their partners. Because the students don't know which question will be asked or who will be called upon to answer, there are unexpected stimuli, an additional source of stimulation. After students have shown their partners their answers, the teacher displays or announces the correct answer and students celebrate or coach each other, eliciting additional positive emotion. Finally, they repeat the process with a new partner, providing even more novel stimuli and positive emotion.

Quiz-Quiz-Trade (Structure 13). Like **PairUp Review, Quiz-Quiz-Trade** overcomes the pitfalls of the traditional Teacher Question—Student Answer structure. Rather than calling on one student to answer each question while the rest of the class is free to mind-wander, during **Quiz-Quiz-Trade** all students are simultaneously engaged asking and answering questions.

Quiz-Quiz-Trade begins with a **StandUp–HandUp–PairUp** and so elicits the same initial positive emotions as does **PairUp Review**. Unlike **PairUp Review**, however, **Quiz-Quiz-Trade** uses question cards (question on the front; answer on the back) rather than teacher-posed questions.

Students each quiz their partner using their question card, eliciting positive emotion as they praise and coach each other. After quizzing each other, students trade cards, show appreciation for each other, and seek another partner. Students move through the structure at their own pace, so there is no downtime waiting for the teacher to pose the next question. Students enjoy this aspect of the structure: They act independently to become a community of learners, not dependent on the teacher asking questions. Feeling self-directed elicits positive emotion.

Sage-N-Scribe (Structure 17). **Sage-N-Scribe** is a substitute for the traditional approach to worksheet practice. The traditional method has students working in isolation and has the obvious pitfall of students not receiving support when they need it. In the traditional approach, students don't receive feedback until after the teacher has time to correct their worksheet. Not receiving feedback, some students practice the worksheet skill wrong. **Sage-N-Scribe** provides immediate feedback and elicits positive emotion in the process.

In **Sage-N-Scribe**, students take turns with a partner, rotating roles for each problem. One is the Sage (saying how to solve the worksheet problem) and the other is the Scribe (recording the answer). Positive emotion is elicited as the Scribe praises the Sage after completion of a problem. The two students experience themselves on the same side and feel mutual support. The praise immediately following successful completion of a problem cements the procedure in memory via retrograde memory enhancement.

Principle 5: Attention

Almost all Kagan Structures focus attention via social interaction. When a student asks a partner or teammate a question or requests a response, there is little room for mind-wandering. When the structures are used, students keep each other focused and on task. Each Kagan Structure captures and holds the attention of students in different ways. Let's examine three structures: **Listen Right!**, **SeeOne–DoOne–TeachOne**, and **Three-Step Interview**.

Listen Right! (Structure 8). By providing information in small chunks and allowing students to take notes and interact following each chunk, **Listen Right!** focuses attention in a number of ways. Students do not have to divide their attention between listening and note-taking—when they are listening, they are fully focused on listening; when they are taking notes, they are fully focused on taking notes. As we have seen, multitasking decreases performance; **Listen Right!** allows undivided attention during both listening and note-taking. Further, stopping to process each chunk frequently clears working memory, so students attend to each new chunk with more focused attention.

SeeOne–DoOne–TeachOne (Structure 18). Distributed practice produces greater retention than massed practice. This is true in part because distributed practice multiplies the number of primacy and recency effects. It is true also because short, spaced practice sessions hold attention better—the longer a practice session, the more attention wanders. See Principle 5: Attention, Tool 7, Distribute Practice. **SeeOne–DoOne–TeachOne** distributes practice. First, the teacher presents how to solve a type of problem. Next, students solve that type of problem on their own. Finally, students teach another student how to solve that type of problem. Breaking the learning into three sessions, **SeeOne–DoOne–TeachOne** cements learning and increases retention. Attention is enhanced during the first step of the structure because students know steps two and three are coming. They know they will have to perform on their own and then teach another. Knowing they will have to perform in front of a peer increases motivation and attention.

Three-Step Interview (Structure 24). I must admit I was quite proud when I invented **Three-**

When a teammate asks you a question or requests a response, there is little room for mind-wandering.

Step Interview. For some time, I was not satisfied with students just interviewing a partner because students were not being held accountable for listening to their partners and for retaining what they learned. As we have noted, mind-wandering is very common and there is nothing in a pair interview to prevent mind-wandering. **Three-Step Interview** solves this problem by including a **RoundRobin** following the interview, so students are accountable for sharing what they have learned from their partner. In this way, **Three-Step Interview** holds students accountable for listening. Students listen much more attentively when they know they will have to share with teammates what they have learned in their interview.

Partners and teammates provide information a student has never heard before (novelty), and teammates respond in ways a student cannot anticipate (surprise).

Principle 6: Stimuli

Because the Kagan Structures involve social interaction, they include surprise and novelty, both of which focus attention. Partners and teammates provide information that a student has never heard before (novelty), and teammates respond in ways a student cannot anticipate (surprise). The structures, however, are predictable sequences, so students feel safe. Brains crave feedback, and the structures are feedback rich. Further, different structures emphasize drawing, words, gestures, music, social interaction, and/or movement. In this way structures respond to the brain's need for multimodal input and to individual differences in cognitive and perceptual styles. Let's see how three structures provide brain-friendly stimuli: **Kinesthetic Symbols**, **Traveling Heads Together**, and **Simulations**.

Kinesthetic Symbols (Structure 7). Gestures are a spontaneous, natural symbol system found in all peoples, even the blind who have never seen anyone else gesture. Students who gesture achieve more whether the gestures are spontaneous or taught.

Kinesthetic Symbols are intentional rather than spontaneous gestures, serving to symbolize ideas with an alternative symbol system that serves as a memory aide. **Kinesthetic Symbols** harness the power of gestures—stimuli the brain naturally attends to. **Kinesthetic Symbols** can symbolize items or sequences of items or ideas and are created by the teacher, teams, or individual students. They are used as response modes that allow teachers to call on all students at once to respond, rather than calling on just one. Students spontaneously use **Kinesthetic Symbols** during tests to help them remember the content.

Simulations (Structure 19). **Simulations** allow students to act out the content, making it memorable for the students who create the simulation and for the students who view it. Students are encouraged to elicit emotion in their audience during the simulation to release the power of retrograde memory enhancement. Because **Simulations** can involve acting, talking, music, drawing, and the creation of a range of props, they are multimodal stimulation for the actors and their audience. Simulations respond to the needs of students to express themselves and learn content in their preferred modality.

Traveling Heads Together (Structure 26). The brain craves feedback. Most Kagan Structures provide peer feedback in the form of praise or coaching. **Traveling Heads Together** provides three levels of feedback: Teacher, teammates, and classmates. The teacher poses a question and students, seated in teams, write their own answer without help from teammates. Teammates then stand and compare answers, correcting and adding to their own answers, given the feedback of their teammates. This is the first form of feedback in **Traveling Heads Together**. When they feel they have a complete, correct answer, students sit down. The teacher then calls a student number to travel to a new team, to stand and share their answer. When finished, students sit at their new teams and the teacher announces the correct answer, a second form of feedback. Those students who had the correct answer receive applause from their new teammates, a third form of feedback. Feedback is a type of stimuli brains crave, and Kagan Structures are feedback rich.

Kagan Structures are Empowering

Kagan Structures are empowering. There are two reasons for this. First, the structures are content-free so they can be used repeatedly and with any academic content. Second, the structures deliver an embedded curriculum, making an otherwise impossible job possible. Let's briefly overview these two characteristics of Kagan Structures: Kagan Structures are content-free, and they deliver an embedded curriculum.

Structures Are Content-Free. Any Kagan Structure can be used to deliver a wide range of content. For example, **Kinesthetic Symbols** improves memory for almost any content. In math, the teacher may use **Kinesthetic Symbols** to help students remember the steps of an algorithm; in language arts **Kinesthetic Symbols** can symbolize punctuation marks, which are then used as response modes; in science **Kinesthetic Symbols** may represent the steps of the scientific inquiry process; in social studies **Kinesthetic Symbols** help students remember in order the amendments in the Bill of Rights.

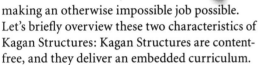

Once the steps of any structure are mastered, the structure can be used on the fly to deliver an infinite range of curriculum.

Once the steps of any structure are mastered, the structure can be used on the fly to deliver an infinite range of curricula. The teacher does not have to make up new activities for each curriculum objective; the teacher needs only to present that curriculum via a structure to generate an engaging and memorable activity. In creating structure-based activities, we work with a basic formula: *Structure + Content = Activity*. The structure is the constant in the formula. Each time we deliver new content via a structure, we generate a new activity. This empowers teachers to generate an infinite number of engaging activities with little planning and little effort. All a teacher needs to do is drop his or her content into an existing structure. The best part: Students are fully engaged, enjoy class and content more, and achieve at an accelerated rate.

Structures Deliver an Embedded Curriculum.

Traditionally, educators have made a clear distinction between curriculum and instruction. In teacher training courses across the nation, student teachers take some courses in curriculum and other courses in instruction. Many schools and districts have two sets of experts. Some occupy positions called Curriculum Specialists; others are Directors of Instruction. Outside consultants are hired to give either curriculum workshops (math, science, language arts, social studies…) or workshops on instruction (how to use cooperative learning, how to align instruction with the latest in brain science, how to apply the elements of effective instruction…). On the one hand we have our curriculum; on the other hand we have instructional strategies to deliver that curriculum.

Thus, teaching in this traditional view can be conceptualized with a simple formula:

Teaching = Curriculum (What we teach) +
Instruction (How we teach)

The formula changes when we teach with structures because there is a curriculum embedded in instruction. When we use the instructional strategy **Paraphrase Passport**, students are learning a social skill—active listening. When we teach with **Find My Rule**, students learn a thinking skill—inductive reasoning. **Logic Line-Ups** teaches deductive reasoning. **AllWrite Consensus** teaches how to strive for and reach consensus. **Kinesthetic Symbols** develops the ability to encode and decode an alternative symbol system. These skills, an additional curriculum, are acquired by students while they are learning the academic curriculum.

Because this additional curriculum is embedded in the structures, we conceptualize teaching differently:

Teaching = *Curriculum* (What we teach) + *Instruction* (How we teach + The Embedded Curriculum)

Kagan Structures change how we teach, not what we teach.

The presentation of structures in this book illustrates how we can create brain-friendly classrooms not by changing what we teach, but by changing how we teach. Brain-friendly teaching is embedded in the structures. The structures are an instructional approach to making our classrooms more brain friendly.

Creating a brain-friendly classroom through structures is an addition to what has become a long list of curricula embedded in structures. By using structures, educational challenges are met via the curriculum embedded in structures, rather than by creating a new curriculum. In the traditional, curriculum-based approach to educational reform, if we want to develop character virtues among our students, we develop a character program—curriculum to teach the virtues. If we want to develop thinking skills among our students, we develop a thinking skills program—curriculum to teach thinking skills. Each new educational innovation is rolled out as a new curriculum to teach.

The structures represent an instructional rather than curricular approach to meeting the expanding demands placed on educators.

The structures are not a new curriculum program; they are a better way to teach any program.[1] When a range of structures is used on a regular basis, students acquire thinking skills,[2] character virtues,[3] and social and life skills.[4] Rather than developing special multiple intelligences lessons, teachers using the structures engage and develop all the multiple intelligences.[5] Rather than teaching diversity skills, teachers using the structures improve race relations.[6] While delivering very rich embedded curricula, the structures accelerate achievement and close the achievement gap.[7] For the evidence that structures accelerate and reduce the achievement gap, see Principle 3: Social, Tool 3, Structure Cooperative Interaction. The achievement data presented there demonstrates structures dramatically accelerate achievement and close the achievement gap.

The most important educational challenges are met when a teacher uses a range of Kagan Structures because a response to the most important educational mandates is embedded in the structures.[8] The structures represent an instructional, rather than curricular, approach to meeting the expanding demands placed on educators. The mandate to align how we teach with how brains best learn can be met without adopting a new curriculum, but by changing how we teach. Structures represent a powerful set of instructional strategies that meet the challenge to make teaching more brain friendly.

References

[1] Kagan, S. *Kagan structures—not one more program, a better way to teach any program.* **Kagan Online Magazine**, Fall 2000. www.KaganOnline.com

[2] Kagan, S. *Kagan structures for thinking skills.* **Kagan Online Magazine**, Fall 2003. www.KaganOnline.com

[3] Kagan, S. *Teaching for character and community.* **Educational Leadership**, 2001, 59(2), 50–55.

[4] Kagan, S. *Addressing the life skills crisis.* **Kagan Online Magazine**, Summer 2003. www.KaganOnline.com

[5] Kagan, S. *Cooperative learning and multiple intelligences: What are the connections?* **Kagan Online Magazine**, Fall 1998. www.KaganOnline.com

Kagan, S. & Kagan, M. *Multiple intelligences structures—opening doors to learning.* **Kagan Online Magazine**, Summer 2006. www.KaganOnline.com

Kagan, S. & Kagan, M. **Multiple Intelligences: The Complete MI Book**. San Clemente, CA: Kagan Publishing, 1998.

[6] Kagan, S. *Cooperative learning, the power to transform race relations.* **Teaching Tolerance**, 2006, 53.

[7] Kagan, S. *Excellence & equity.* **Kagan Online Magazine**, Summer 2010. www.KaganOnline.com

[8] Kagan, S. *The embedded curriculum.* **Kagan Online Magazine**, Spring 2002. www.KaganOnline.com

1. AllWrite Consensus

In teams, students take turns stating an answer. If there is consensus, all teammates write the answer.

1 Teacher provides a question with multiple possible answers or multiple questions, then selects a student on each team to begin.

2 Selected student suggests the first answer.

3 Teammates put thumbs up, down, or sideways to indicate agreement, disagreement, or doubt.

4 If teammates agree, all students write the answer on their own paper. If there is disagreement or doubt, the team discusses the answer until agreement is reached.

5 Process is continued, each student in turn suggesting an answer.

• **Related Structures.** RoundRobin has teammates take turns sharing, but does not require consensus or recording of ideas.

Implementing Brain-Friendly Teaching Principles

▶ **Nourishment.** To increase nourishment to the brain, students express their agreement by standing up, rather than using the more traditional symbol, a thumb up. Students who agree stand up. Students who disagree and those not sure remain seated. Students continue discussing until all are standing. At that point, all sit to write the idea on their own paper.

▶ **Safety.** Students are taught polite gambits for disagreement. *"In my opinion, …" "It seems to me…" "We may need to agree to disagree on that point…".* As students reach consensus they bond, building a more inclusive team.

▶ **Social.** Students learn consensus-seeking skills, appreciation of points of view different from their own, and polite ways to disagree.

Students activate their social cognition network as they process the ideas of their teammates.

▶ **Emotion.** Students may do a cheer each time they reach consensus or when complete. Positive emotion is elicited each time students reach consensus.

▶ **Attention.** Students attend carefully to the ideas of their teammates because they must respond. **AllWrite Consensus** can be used to process presentation content. For example, midway through a lecture, students reach consensus on the key points of the lecture, clearing working and short-term memory.

▶ **Stimuli.** Students are attending to novel stimuli and constructing meaning.

2. Both Record RallyRobin

Partners take turns stating ideas or answers, both recording each idea or answer on their own paper.

1 Teacher poses a problem to which there are multiple possible responses or solutions.

2 In pairs, students take turns stating responses or solutions, each recording each answer on their own paper.

• **Variation.** RallyTable is the written form of **RallyRobin**: Partners take turns recording their ideas on a common piece of paper rather than just stating their ideas.

• **Related Structures.** There is a family of "Rally" structures—structures in which partners take turns. See **RallyQuiz** and **Traveling RallyInterview**.

Implementing Brain-Friendly Teaching Principles

▶ **Nourishment.** To increase nourishment, students may be asked to stand each time they contribute an idea.

▶ **Safety.** Students share their ideas with a partner, usually a supportive teammate, rather than in front of the whole class.

▶ **Social.** Students learn turn-taking and listen with respect to the ideas of their teammates.

▶ **Emotion.** Students may do a high five after recording each idea, or after completing the list.

▶ **Attention.** Students listen carefully to the ideas of others to be able to record the idea accurately. **Both Record RallyRobin** may be used to process presentation content, clearing short-term and working memory.

▶ **Stimuli.** **RallyRobin** is fast paced, providing frequent stimulation. The ideas of others are often novel. Working with another provides more stimulation than generating ideas alone. Hearing an idea of a partner may stimulate an idea that otherwise would not have occurred.

3. Celebrity Interview

Students generate questions for teammates who each become "The Celebrity," receiving applause after sequencing and answering the questions.

1 A Celebrity is randomly chosen.

2 The other teammates generate one or two questions to ask the Celebrity, writing each question on a different slip of paper.

3 Teammates pass their slips of paper to the Celebrity.

4 The Celebrity sequences the slips, deciding the order in which to answer the questions.

5 The Celebrity answers the questions, receiving appreciation.

6 The process is repeated for each teammate in random order.

• **Related Structures. Three-Step Interview** and **RoundRobin** also allow students to take turns sharing information.

Implementing Brain-Friendly Teaching Principles

▶ **Nourishment.** Celebrities stand while sharing and sit when finished, generating a bit of movement, increasing nourishment to the brain.

▶ **Safety.** Celebrities share within the safe context of a team knowing they will receive appreciation for their ideas. Teammates get to know, accept, and appreciate each other, creating a safe context for learning. Teambuilding content creates positive social interaction and a more inclusive team.

▶ **Social.** Students get to know each other better, promoting bonding.

▶ **Emotion.** Celebrities receive appreciation. Teammates are encouraged to give the Celebrity "wild applause" when they first stand and when they finish sharing. Positive emotion is generated

as students share about themselves and receive attention from their teammates.

▶ **Attention.** Celebrities attend to the question cards provided by teammates. If students are interviewed in role (as a character from literature or history, for example), they pay closer attention as they study that character, knowing they will impersonate that character.

▶ **Stimuli.** The brain seeks predictability. Like all structures, **Celebrity Interview** is a predictable sequence: Each teammate in turn stands to become the Celebrity, responds to the question cards, and then receives appreciation—students know exactly what is coming next. The brain seeks novelty. Like all structures, **Celebrity Interview** includes novelty within the predictable sequence: The responses of each Celebrity provide novel stimuli.

4. Choral Practice

At a cue from the teacher, students respond in unison.

1 Teacher asks a question or assigns a choral piece.

2 At a cue from the teacher, students practice in unison.

3 Example: *"Class, let's say the alphabet together."* *"Class, let's recite the Gettysburg Address."*

● **Variations.** **Choral Practice** is used to have students recite in unison works to memorize, such as poems or the Pledge of Allegiance. In contrast, **Answer Back** is used to have classmates answer short-answer questions in unison. For example, the teacher may ask, *"The First Amendment guarantees …,"* and students answer back, *"Freedom of Speech."* **Echoing** is used to have classmates recite back in unison what the teacher has just said or chanted. For example, to help students remember the order of operations in math, the teacher might chant, *"Parentheses precede multiplication and division. Save addition and subtraction for dessert."* To cement memory, classmates then echo those same words. The brain is more active when talking than listening. Students remember more of what they say than what they hear, so **Choral Practice**, **Answer Backs,** and **Echoing** all increase retention of content.

Implementing Brain-Friendly Teaching Principles

▶ **Nourishment.** Students may be asked to stand up while practicing.

▶ **Safety.** Students perform as a group and are not called upon as individuals so there is no potential for failure or embarrassment. Responding in unison helps create a more inclusive class.

▶ **Social.** Classmates bond because they are performing in unison.

▶ **Emotion.** Positive emotion is generated as students coordinate their oral practice.

▶ **Attention.** Students must closely attend to the teacher's words and to the voices of classmates in order to avoid getting out of sync.

▶ **Stimuli.** The voices of classmates provide the stimuli to which students must attend.

5. Flashcard Game

Partners proceed through three rounds as they quiz each other with flashcards, mastering the content to win cards.

Setup: Students each have their own set of flashcards.

1 In pairs, the Tutee gives his or her flashcards to the Tutor.

2 **Round 1: Maximum Cues**
The Tutor shows the question on the first card, reads the question, and shows and reads the answer written on the back of the card. The Tutor then turns the card back over and again reads the question on the front of the card, asking the Tutee to answer from memory.

3 The Tutee answers. If correct, Tutee wins the card back and receives surprising, delightful praise from the Tutor. If wrong, the Tutor shows the Tutee the answer side of the card and coaches. The card is then returned to stack to try again later.

4 When the Tutee wins all the cards, partners switch roles. When the new Tutee wins all his or her cards, partners advance to Round 2.

5 **Round 2: Few Cues**
The process is repeated, except the Tutor shows only the question on the front of each card and asks the Tutee to answer from memory.

6 **Round 3: No Cues**
The process is repeated, except the Tutor quizzes Tutee on each question without showing the Tutee the flashcards.

• **Hint.** For young students, limit each round to no more than five cards. If a student has won all cards, he or she can add bonus cards.

• **Related Structures.** The **Flashcard Game** is used for initial memorization of isolated facts and information—placing the content into semantic memory. Structures that are used for practice of acquired skills—strengthening procedural memory—include **PairUp Review**, **Quiz-Quiz-Trade**, **RallyQuiz**, and **Sage-N-Scribe**.

Implementing Brain-Friendly Teaching Principles

▶ **Safety.** Students are assured initial success because they have just seen and just heard the card content and have only to repeat it back from immediate short-term memory. Students feel, *"I can't fail."* Safe evaluation is created via the game-like format and the emphasis on coaching rather than evaluating. Students feel themselves to be on the same side, helping each other reach their goals.

▶ **Social.** Students are working with a partner who provides encouragement, coaching, and praise.

▶ **Emotion.** Partners give surprising, delightful praise. Students feel rewarded as they win back their cards. As students work through their deck of cards, their success is tangible and they feel a sense of accomplishment.

▶ **Attention.** Tutors hold the attention of their Tutees as they show them the card, read it to them, and ask for a response.

▶ **Stimuli.** The **Flashcard Game** is multimodal: The cards provide visual stimuli; making the cards involves writing, a form of kinesthetic stimuli; and the partner reading the card provides auditory stimuli. In addition, the **Flashcard Game** is feedback rich. Immediately following each answer, a student receives feedback. This is in contrast to traditional worksheet work in which a student does not receive feedback until after papers are graded. Immediate feedback is far more effective than delayed feedback.

6. Formations

Students work together to "form" symbols and shapes.

1 Teacher announces (or displays) an object or shape for students to form.

2 All students move to stand in position to form the object or shape.

> • **Related Structures.** Kinesthetic Symbols also engages and develops the bodily/kinesthetic intelligence.

Implementing Brain-Friendly Teaching Principles

▶ **Nourishment.** There is major muscle movement as students move around the room, causing heart and breathing rates and volume to increase. More blood is pumped to the brain, and the blood that is pumped to the brain is more fully oxygenated.

▶ **Safety.** Students work together, experiencing themselves in a mutually supportive social context. Everyone is included in each formation, helping form a more inclusive class.

▶ **Social.** If no talking is allowed, students develop their nonverbal communication skills. **Formations** is a strong classbuilding structure.

▶ **Emotion.** Students experience excitement while creating the formations and a rush of joy when they complete each formation. The teacher may call for a celebration with the completion of each formation.

▶ **Attention.** Students must attend carefully to the positions of their classmates in order to place themselves correctly.

▶ **Stimuli.** The structure allows students to symbolize the content with a bodily/kinesthetic symbol system. The structure breaks the routine of teacher talk, providing novel stimuli.

7. Kinesthetic Symbols

Students create and practice gestures or body movements to symbolize the content.

1 Students or the teacher create kinesthetic symbols for the content.

2 Students practice the symbols.

• **Optional Step.** Symbols are used as response modes to answer questions by the teacher.

• **Related Structures. Formations** also engages and develops the bodily/kinesthetic intelligence. **Formations** engages gross-motor movement whereas **Kinesthetic Symbols** usually involves only fine-motor movement.

Implementing Brain-Friendly Teaching Principles

▶ **Nourishment.** To increase nourishment, students can be encouraged to stand while creating their gestures and to incorporate movement into their gestures. Often, movement is included at the outset as well as students are told to stand and find a partner to create and practice their **Kinesthetic Symbols.**

▶ **Safety. Kinesthetic Symbols** are a natural symbol system. By encouraging **Kinesthetic Symbols,** students feel safe to express themselves using this natural symbol system.

▶ **Social.** Student teams are encouraged to make up their own kinesthetic symbols, encouraging team identity and bonding.

▶ **Emotion.** Students can be encouraged to celebrate when they develop their team kinesthetic symbols.

▶ **Attention.** Students naturally attend to this alternative symbol system, reinforcing and augmenting the message provided verbally.

▶ **Stimuli.** The research on gesturing reveals that kinesthetic symbols are a distinct and extremely important symbol system. Teachers who use gestures have students who learn more and who are more confident of their learning. Students who spontaneously gesture are smarter and achieve more. Students who are taught to gesture learn more. As students use gestures and words at the same time to symbolize the content, dendrite connections are made between neurons in the motor cortex and the temporal lobe.

Brain-Friendly Teaching • Dr. Spencer Kagan
Kagan Publishing • 800.933.2667 • www.KaganOnline.com

8. Listen Right!

During a lecture the teacher stops. Students write the main points, compare with a partner, and celebrate.

1 Teacher gives information in small chunks. Students, with pencils down, listen carefully for the key words, phrases, or ideas.

2 Teacher stops.

3 Students write or draw key points.

4 Students share with a partner, checking for accuracy and making corrections on their own papers.

5 Teacher announces key points.

6 Students celebrate if right; or make corrections.

7 Students put pencils down and process is repeated from Step 1.

• **Related Structures.** Paraphrase Passport, **Three-Step Interview**, and **Traveling RallyInterview** also develop active listening skills.

Implementing Brain-Friendly Teaching Principles

▶ **Safety. Listen Right!** provides a safety net. If a student has not grasped a main point during a lecture chunk, the student can get it from her or his peer, or from the teacher afterwards. Safety from negative evaluation is created because the emphasis is on making sure everyone on the team has grasped the main points, not on evaluation.

▶ **Social.** Students check with teammates and receive coaching. This is in contrast to traditional note-taking, which is an isolated act. Students hone their active listening skills.

▶ **Emotion.** Students celebrate when they have grasped the main points.

▶ **Attention.** By not dividing student attention, **Listen Right!** provides more focused attention for both listening and note-taking. Because the teacher frequently stops to have students process the prior presentation chunk, the structure frequently clears working memory. Mind-wandering increases with the length of a presentation. By breaking the presentation into chunks, **Listen Right!** prevents the most prevalent form of distraction—mind-wandering.

▶ **Stimuli.** Students are encouraged to take notes not just with words but also with visual images or mind maps.

9. Number Group Mania!

By announcing the group size and which student numbers should be in each group, the teacher has students form random groups.

Setup: Students each have a number, from 1 to 4.

 1 Teacher announces: (1) group size, and (2) the student numbers in the group.

Examples:
- *"Form pairs with a classmate with the same number as you."*
- *"Form teams of four with a number 1, 2, 3, and 4—all from different teams."*

 2 Students stand up, use fingers to show student number (1 to 4), and group accordingly.

3 Teacher presents the problem or task for the new random groups.

- **Related Structures.** StandUp–HandUp–PairUp is another grouping structure, used to form pairs.

Implementing Brain-Friendly Teaching Principles

▶ **Nourishment.** Students move about the classroom forming groups of the announced size and composition. In the process, they pump more nutrients to the brain.

▶ **Safety.** Teachers are encouraged to have students do some brief teambuilding every time new groups are formed to ensure safety. Teambuilding can be as brief as conducting a **RoundRobin** during which students share their name and something fun they like to do over the weekend. Positive social interaction is enhanced by teaching students welcoming gambits like, *"Come join us,"* and, *"We need you in our group." "Glad you are in our group."*

▶ **Social.** Students acquire different social skills in different groups. By re-forming groups, students have an opportunity to interact with and learn from different classmates.

▶ **Emotion.** Excitement is generated as students rush to find their new groupmates. Students are encouraged to welcome their new groupmates with compliments and/or greetings.

▶ **Attention.** Students are more alert following **Number Group Mania!** because of the novelty as well as the movement.

▶ **Stimuli.** Variety lights up the brain. **Number Group Mania!** provides variety in the form of new teammates with whom to interact.

10. Pair Share

Partners take turns sharing and listening.

Setup: Students are in pairs.

1 Teacher announces the topic.

2 Teacher provides Think Time.

3 One partner shares while his or her partner listens.

4 **Switch roles:** The other partner shares while his or her partner listens.

• **Related Structures.** Pair Share is excellent for very brief answers. **Timed Pair Share** is the structure of choice for longer answers. Without time limits for long answers, equal participation is very unlikely.

Implementing Brain-Friendly Teaching Principles

▶ **Nourishment.** Students may be encouraged to stand up, put a hand up, and pair up prior to a **Pair Share**, to include movement, which pumps a bit more oxygen to the brain.

▶ **Safety.** Pair work is the safest interaction group size. Students who do not feel safe risking possible failure by responding in front of the whole class are quite comfortable sharing with just one other student. **Pair Share** can be used with getting acquainted content, helping create a safe, inclusive class.

▶ **Social.** Although very brief, **Pair Share** offers an opportunity for social interaction and social cognition.

▶ **Emotion.** Students may be encouraged to praise the idea of their partner. Students enjoy being the focus of peer attention.

▶ **Attention.** Students are encouraged to practice active listening: Looking at their partner, making eye contact, facing their partner, not interrupting their partner, and showing nonverbal interest. **Pair Share** may be used to process lecture content, clearing working memory. The teacher stops lecturing and has students do a **Pair Share** to answer questions like, *"What is a key point of the lecture so far?"*

▶ **Stimuli.** Social stimuli grab and hold the attention of students because often it is novel and because we all naturally gravitate to engaging the social cognition network.

11. PairUp Review

In this review session, everyone responds to every question, but partners never know which one will have to show their answer.

Setup: The teacher prepares review questions and answers. Each student needs a response board and marker (or something else to write on).

1 Teacher tells students to, *"Stand up, put a hand up, and pair up."*

2 Teacher asks or displays a review question.

3 Partners stand back to back and independently write their answers. When finished, they face their partners.

4 Teacher randomly selects Partner A or Partner B to share his or her answer with his or her partner.

5 Teacher tells or displays the answer.

6 Students celebrate or coach their partners.

7 Students put up a hand and find a new partner for the next problem.

• **Related Structures.** Quiz-Quiz-Trade, **RallyQuiz**, **Sage-N-Scribe**, **SeeOne–DoOne–TeachOne**, and **Traveling Heads Together** all are used for review and practice. In **Traveling RallyQuiz** students ask each other questions and move at their own pace. In **PairUp Review** both students answer each question and move to a new partner at the direction of the teacher.

Implementing Brain-Friendly Teaching Principles

▶ **Nourishment.** The first step of **PairUp Review** involves movement as students walk around seeking a partner. Walking sends more blood to the brain, nourishing the brain. Students walk to a new partner for each new problem.

▶ **Safety.** Students have a safety net: If they have not arrived at the right answer, their partner coaches them. Evaluation is within the safe context of a supportive partner.

▶ **Social.** Students are on the same side, coaching if necessary, and celebrating each other's successes.

▶ **Emotion.** Students are encouraged to develop novel, creative ways to praise each other.

▶ **Attention.** Knowing they are accountable for writing their own answer, and that they will be accountable for what they write, students pay close attention.

▶ **Stimuli.** The brain craves feedback. **PairUp Review** is feedback rich. Students receive feedback from the teacher following each problem. Coaching, when necessary, provides another form of feedback.

12. Paraphrase Passport

Students earn a passport to speak by accurately paraphrasing the prior speaker.

1 Teacher assigns a discussion topic.

2 One person in the pair or team shares an idea.

3 Any student can go next to share an idea, but first he or she must paraphrase the person who spoke immediately before, checking for accuracy before sharing his or her own idea.

● **Related Structures.** For additional structures to develop listening skills see **Listen Right!**, **Three-Step Interview**, and **Traveling RallyInterview**.

Implementing Brain-Friendly Teaching Principles

▶ **Safety.** Students feel safe because they know their ideas will be understood and received with respect. This is in contrast to unstructured discussion in which students' ideas may be met by criticism or may be put down.

▶ **Social. Paraphrase Passport** develops tolerance of and appreciation of diversity as students listen to and paraphrase the ideas of others. Students learn mutual respect. Understanding the ideas, values, and intentions of others develops the social cognition network. **Paraphrase Passport** creates positive social interaction and a safe context for learning.

▶ **Emotion.** Being listened to and understood is rewarding. Positive emotion is elicited as students have an opportunity to express their ideas and to be received with the respect implied in a paraphrase.

▶ **Attention.** Students must pay close attention to the ideas of others because they are held accountable for paraphrasing. This is in contrast to an unstructured group discussion in which everyone is waiting their turn to talk with no one carefully listening to the ideas of others.

▶ **Stimuli.** Often there is surprise and novelty because students cannot anticipate what a partner or teammate may say. The brain craves feedback, and the quality of a paraphrase provides feedback to students about how well they communicated their ideas. As students are listened to without interruption and with respect, they feel comfortable developing their ideas, constructing meaning.

13. Quiz-Quiz-Trade

Students quiz a partner, get quizzed by a partner, and then trade cards to repeat the process with a new partner.

Setup: *The teacher prepares a set of question cards for the class, or each student creates a question card.*

1 Teacher tells students to, *"Stand up, put a hand up, and pair up."*

2 Partner A quizzes B.

3 Partner B answers.

4 Partner A praises or coaches.

5 Partners switch roles.

6 Partners trade cards and thank each other.

7 Students put up a hand and seek a new partner, continuing through the process until time is called.

• **Related Structures.** For additional practice structures see **PairUp Review**, **RallyQuiz**, **Sage-N-Scribe**, and **Traveling Heads Together**.

Implementing Brain-Friendly Teaching Principles

▶ **Nourishment.** Students repeatedly trade partners, activating major muscle movement that increases nourishment to the brain.

▶ **Safety.** Students are quizzed by and respond to one other person; they are not asked to respond to a teacher's question while the whole class is watching. Thus, the potential for embarrassment is diminished by a factor of 30. Further, students answer to a fellow classmate who is supportive, offering coaching if needed. Evaluation is within the safe context of supportive coaching.

▶ **Social.** Students work with many partners. Receiving support from many classmates is a form of classbuilding. The teacher may

have the students practice greeting gambits (*"How are you doing?" "Glad you are my next partner."*) and/or parting gambits (*"Thanks for working with me." "I appreciate your help."*).

▶ **Emotion.** Students receive praise. Praise following success cements learning via retrograde memory enhancement.

▶ **Attention.** The variety of many new partners heightens attention.

▶ **Stimuli.** Input is multimodal as students see the cards (visual input) as the question is asked of them (auditory input). There is variety in working with many partners. The structure provides immediate feedback.

14. RallyQuiz

Students take turns quizzing their partner.

1 Teacher provides a list of questions, or students generate a list of questions.

2 Partner A asks a thought or review question of Partner B.

3 Partner B answers.

4 For thought questions: Partner A praises the thinking:
For review questions: Partner A checks.
  • If correct, Partner A praises.
  • If not, Partner A coaches, re-asks, then praises.

5 Students switch roles so Partner B quizzes, and then praises or coaches.

6 Process is repeated with additional questions.

• **Optional.** Individuals or teams may write their own questions before playing **RallyQuiz**, or may be provided the questions by the teacher.

• **Variation.** In **RallyQuiz** students stay with one partner; in **Traveling RallyQuiz** students travel to a new partner for each new question.

• **Related Structures.** For additional structures used for practice see **PairUp Review**, **Quiz-Quiz-Trade**, **Sage-N-Scribe**, and **Traveling Heads Together**.

Implementing Brain-Friendly Teaching Principles

▶ **Nourishment.** In the variation, **Traveling RallyQuiz**, students find a new partner for each question, introducing movement that nourishes the brain.

▶ **Safety.** Students work in supportive pairs. Knowing they will receive coaching if needed, students are assured success. The emphasis is on coaching, not evaluation.

▶ **Social.** Students practice and become more proficient at praising and coaching.

▶ **Emotion.** Praise and anticipation of praise both stimulate the reward centers in the brain.

▶ **Attention.** Students cannot tune out or mind-wander because each is engaged throughout. Their partner is either awaiting their answer or it is their turn to ask the next question. The structure focuses attention.

▶ **Stimuli.** The structure includes immediate feedback. If questions are written on cards or are posted on the whiteboard, the structure is multimodal as it includes auditory input (partner asking the question) as well as visual input (seeing the question).

15. RallyRobin

In pairs, students take turns responding orally.

1 Teacher poses a problem to which there are multiple possible responses or solutions, and provides Think Time.

2 Students take turns stating responses or solutions.

• **Related Structures.** There are many turn-taking structures. In **RoundRobin** teammates take turns sharing; in **RallyRobin** partners take turns sharing. In **RallyTable** partners take turns writing their answers on a common piece of paper. In **Simultaneous RallyTable** students each have a piece of paper and trade papers each time they add to a list. For example, one paper might be labeled "Democracy" and the other paper labeled "Communism." Students list things true of one form of government that is not true of the other. Each time students receive a paper, they read what has been added by their partner and then add another item to the list. Trading papers up and back makes students aware of the ideas of their partner, and both students contribute to both lists. Additional turn-taking structures include: **Both Record RallyRobin**, **RallyQuiz**, **RoundRobin**, and **Traveling RallyInterview.**

Implementing Brain-Friendly Teaching Principles

▶ **Nourishment.** To increase nourishment via fast-paced movement, students can be asked to stand each time they contribute an idea, sitting down when done.

▶ **Safety.** Responding with a partner is safer than responding in front of the whole class—especially if the partner is a supportive teammate. Students experience themselves as on the same side, working together to generate an oral list.

▶ **Social.** Students practice turn-taking and listening to the ideas of others. Students bond, working together to generate an oral list.

▶ **Emotion.** Students are excited due to the fast-paced up-and-back of a **RallyRobin**. They say it is fun, activating the reward circuits in the brain.

▶ **Attention.** Students must listen to their partner so as not to repeat something their partner has said.

▶ **Stimuli.** **RallyRobin** is useful for review. Allowing the students to verbalize what they remember helps clear working and short-term memory.

Brain-Friendly Teaching • Dr. Spencer Kagan
Kagan Publishing • 800.933.2667 • www.KaganOnline.com

16. RoundRobin

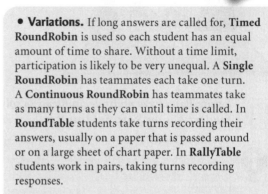

In teams, students take turns responding orally.

1 Teacher poses a problem to which there are multiple possible responses or solutions, and provides Think Time.

2 Students take turns stating responses or solutions.

- **Variations.** If long answers are called for, **Timed RoundRobin** is used so each student has an equal amount of time to share. Without a time limit, participation is likely to be very unequal. A **Single RoundRobin** has teammates each take one turn. A **Continuous RoundRobin** has teammates take as many turns as they can until time is called. In **RoundTable** students take turns recording their answers, usually on a paper that is passed around or on a large sheet of chart paper. In **RallyTable** students work in pairs, taking turns recording responses.

- **Related Structures.** In **AllWrite Consensus** teammates take turns suggesting ideas, but the structure includes consensus seeking and recording ideas.

Implementing Brain-Friendly Teaching Principles

▶ **Nourishment.** To include movement during **RoundRobin**, students stand each time it is their turn, sitting down when finished.

▶ **Safety.** Students share their ideas within the safety of a team, rather than being called upon to answer in front of the whole class. **RoundRobin** lends itself to teambuilding content which creates a safe context for learning. That each teammate has a turn creates a more inclusive team and creates a norm for positive social interaction.

▶ **Social.** Students learn turn-taking and patient waiting. If the teacher calls for each teammate to compliment the student who shared before them, students learn to appreciate the ideas of others. As students listen to the ideas, feelings, and intentions of their teammates, they exercise their social cognition network.

▶ **Emotion.** Students may be encouraged to applaud and/or cheer for each student as they stand to share, generating positive emotion. Students literally look up to the student who is standing to share, affording that student more status and enhanced self-worth.

▶ **Attention.** By having the student who is sharing stand, attention is more likely to be sustained on that student. **RoundRobin** is an excellent structure to allow students to process presentation content, clearing short-term and working memory.

▶ **Stimuli.** The responses of others provide novelty and variety. Each student sharing in turn provides predictability.

17. Sage-N-Scribe

Partners take turns being the Sage and Scribe.

Setup: Pairs have multiple problems to solve. Student A is the Sage; Student B is the Scribe.

1 The Sage gives the Scribe step-by-step instructions how to perform a task or solve a problem.

2 The Scribe records the Sage's solution step-by-step in writing, coaching if necessary.

3 The Scribe praises the Sage.

4 Students switch roles for the next problem or task.

• **Related Structures.** Additional structures used to practice skills include: **PairUp Review**, **Quiz-Quiz-Trade**, **RallyQuiz**, and **Traveling Heads Together.**

Implementing Brain-Friendly Teaching Principles

▶ **Safety.** There is safety in performing prescribed roles. The Scribe has the role of following the Sage's instructions. The Sage has the role of giving instructions, but if the Sage veers off track, the Sage receives help from the Scribe.

▶ **Social.** Scribes exercise their social cognition as they listen to how the Sage thinks through a problem.

▶ **Emotion.** Sages receive praise for each problem they solve.

▶ **Attention.** The Scribe must pay close attention to the Sage in order to follow his or her directions.

▶ **Stimuli. Sage-N-Scribe** is more multi-modal than traditional worksheet work, which is only visual (see the problems) and kinesthetic (write the answers). **Sage-N-Scribe** includes auditory stimuli. By verbalizing his or her thinking, students are more meta-cognitive and are more likely to self-correct. Further, verbalization cements memory.

Brain-Friendly Teaching • Dr. Spencer Kagan
Kagan Publishing • 800.933.2667 • www.KaganOnline.com

18. SeeOne–DoOne–TeachOne

SeeOne

DoOne

TeachOne

After seeing a procedure modeled, students perform on their own until they are ready to teach a partner.

1 Teacher (or student) models a procedure (lab procedure, algorithm, how to fill in a graphic organizer).

2 Students form A-B pairs, and the A's and B's in each pair receive a different problem that can be solved by the procedure modeled by the teacher.

3 Students work alone to solve their problem, making sure they are ready to teach it.

4 A's move to one side of the room and B's move to the other, each taking with them the problem they have solved.

5 A's consult with another A and B's consult with another B, checking for completeness and accuracy.

6 A's and B's move to the center of the room, form A-B pairs, and sit down together.

7 Students each teach their partner how they applied the procedure to solve their problem.

- **Related Structures.** SeeOne–DoOne–TeachOne is used for initial instruction in a skill. Once the skill has been introduced, students can practice the skill using **PairUp Review**, **Quiz-Quiz-Trade**, **RallyQuiz**, or **Traveling Heads Together**.

Implementing Brain-Friendly Teaching Principles

▶ **Nourishment.** Walking to the sides of the room to find a same-problem partner and moving to the center of the room to find a different-problem partner inject movement into the class, and therefore better brain nourishment.

▶ **Safety.** Before teaching a partner, students have a safety net: They check with their same-problem partner and receive coaching if necessary.

▶ **Social.** The social cognition network is engaged as students listen to the thinking of their teaching partner. **SeeOne–DoOne–TeachOne** creates a more cohesive class because students are not working with teammates—they teach fellow classmates. The first step of the structure is modeling—activating mirror neurons.

▶ **Emotion.** Students are encouraged to praise or celebrate at two points: With their same-problem partner when they agree on the procedure and answer, and with their teaching buddy after each one has successfully taught the other.

▶ **Attention.** Students pay closer attention to the teacher's modeling because they know they will have to teach a peer.

▶ **Stimuli.** Students receive feedback from their same-problem partner as well as from watching the impact of their teaching on their teaching buddy. Relevance is established because students know they are learning so they will be able to teach. As students verbalize, they listen to themselves, cementing memory and promoting meta-cognition and construction of meaning.

19. Simulations

Individuals, pairs, or teams enact an event, idea, or process.

Setup: Often costumes or props are created or obtained beforehand to aid the simulation.

1 Students are assigned or create roles for their simulations.

2 Students design and practice their simulation.

3 Students perform the simulation.

Implementing Brain-Friendly Teaching Principles

▶ **Nourishment.** Usually a simulation involves movement during both the planning and the presentation, and movement increases nourishment to the brain.

▶ **Safety.** Students practice their simulation, supporting each other until they feel comfortable performing for another team or the class.

▶ **Social.** Students learn collaborative skills as they work together to create their simulation. They also acquire presentation and performance skills. Students are encouraged to anticipate audience reaction, activating their social cognition network.

▶ **Emotion.** We encourage students to stimulate emotion in their audience to evoke the power of retrograde memory

enhancement. Simulations are one of the strongest strategies we have to link emotion to the content.

▶ **Attention.** Students' motivation and attention to the task are enhanced by knowing they will perform for others.

▶ **Stimuli.** Simulations are multimodal. Performers are encouraged to use auditory and visual stimuli as well as body language, including gestures. Students are encouraged also to include surprise and novelty in their simulations. Students receive feedback from the class and from the teacher, often with an evaluation rubric. Both the performers and the audience are much more likely to construct meaning from a simulation than from a lecture or even a video.

20. StandUp–HandUp–PairUp

Students stand up, put their hands up, and quickly find a partner with whom to share or discuss.

1 Teacher says, *"When I say go, you will stand up, hand up, and pair up!"* Teacher pauses, then says, *"Go!"*

2 Students stand up and keep one hand high in the air until they find the closest partner who's not a teammate. Students do a high five and put their hands down.

3 Teacher may ask a question or give an assignment, and provides Think Time.

4 Partners interact using structures like:
- **RallyRobin**
- **Timed Pair Share**

> • **Hint.** In some classes, it may be necessary to make sure students pair with the classmate they are closest to rather than running to a friend.

> • **Related Structures.** Whereas **StandUp–HandUp–PairUp** is a quick way to form pairs, **Number Group Mania!** forms groups of any size.

Implementing Brain-Friendly Teaching Principles

▶ **Nourishment.** Movement nourishes the brain.

▶ **Safety.** Students feel safer while performing for a partner than while performing in front of the whole class.

▶ **Social.** Students practice greetings, partings, and, if the interaction includes it, praise and celebrations.

▶ **Emotion.** There is emotion generated as students seek and find a new partner.

▶ **Attention.** Attention is enhanced as students seek a new partner.

▶ **Stimuli.** Working with a new partner provides variety.

21. Swap Talk

Students circulate trading cards to introduce their new partners to their prior partners.

1 Students each create a card with information to share (e.g., facts about themselves; facts about a famous person; science or history facts).

2 Teacher tells students to, *"Stand up, put a hand up, and pair up."*

3 Each student shares his or her information with a partner using **Pair Share**.

4 Students swap cards, thank their partners, and put a hand up to find a new partner.

5 Each student shares his or her new card info with a new partner. For examples,
- Info about classmate: *"Let me introduce you to Susie"* (pointing to her)
- Info about event: *"Let me tell you why 1492 is important…"*
- Info about scientist: *"I want to tell you about three inventions by Ben Franklin…"*

6 The process is continued until the teacher calls, *"Stop,"* or, *"Time is up."*

Implementing Brain-Friendly Teaching Principles

▶ **Nourishment.** Students move about the room, which sends more nutrients to the brain.

▶ **Safety.** Students are working in pairs, the safest group size for interaction. Often **Swap Talk** is used to help students better know their classmates, creating a safe context for learning and a more inclusive class.

▶ **Social.** Students thank each other and learn introduction gambits (*"I would like to introduce you to…"*). Students work with many classmates, creating a more inclusive class.

▶ **Emotion.** Students are learning information in what feels to them like a game—**Swap Talk** is fun! This positive emotion facilitates learning.

▶ **Attention.** Students pay close attention to their partner because they know they will have to present that information to their next partner.

▶ **Stimuli.** **Swap Talk** is multimodal, involving reading, listening, and presenting.

22. TakeOff-TouchDown

Students stand and sit to answer questions as the teacher polls the class.

1 Teacher makes a statement.

2 Students to whom the statement applies stand up ("Take Off").

3 Those to whom it does NOT apply remain seated.

4 All students sit down.

5 Steps are repeated for the next question.

Implementing Brain-Friendly Teaching Principles

▶ **Nourishment.** Repeatedly standing and sitting requires major muscle movement, accelerating delivering of nutrients to the brain.

▶ **Stimuli.** Students show their agreement or lack of agreement bodily/kinesthetically, appealing to those strong in the bodily/kinesthetic intelligence. Using **TakeOff-TouchDown** creates variety—students don't always just raise their hands to indicate agreement.

23. Team-Pair-Solo

Students solve problems first as a team, then as a pair, and finally on their own.

Setup: Teacher prepares a set of problems that depend on a common problem-solving strategy.

1 **Team:** Teammates work together solving a problem.

2 Teacher announces the answer and models the strategy.

3 If correct, students advance to pair work. If not, they solve another problem as a team.

4 **Pair:** Students form two pairs within the team to solve additional problems. First, Partner A solves a problem while Partner B checks and praises. The partners switch roles to solve the next problem.

5 If correct, the students advance to solo. If not, they move back to solving problems as a team.

6 **Solo:** Each student works alone to solve new, similar problems.

- **Related Structures.** Like **SeeOne–DoOne–TeachOne**, **Team-Pair-Solo** is most often used to introduce a skill to students. Once the skill has been taught, a number of practice structures can be used to cement memory for the procedure, including: **PairUp Review, Quiz-Quiz-Trade, RallyQuiz, Sage-N-Scribe,** and **Traveling Heads Together.**

Implementing Brain-Friendly Teaching Principles

▶ **Safety.** **Team-Pair-Solo** creates safety: Before doing problems on their own, students have the support first of teammates, and then of a partner.

▶ **Social.** As students listen to and observe the problem-solving strategy of teammates and partners, they engage the social cognition network. The encouragement, coaching, and praising create positive social interaction.

▶ **Emotion.** Students are encouraged to celebrate their successes.

▶ **Attention.** Attention is focused because students know that after teamwork and pair work, they will perform alone. Distributed practice increases achievement, and **Team-Pair-Solo** distributes practice among teamwork, pair work, and individual work.

▶ **Stimuli.** Students receive immediate feedback from their teaching by seeing what their teammates and partners do. Students receive feedback also on their solo work. The structure is multimodal as students receive visual and auditory input. As students move from teamwork through pair work to individual work, they construct meaning— how to solve the type of problem or perform the skill.

24. Three-Step Interview

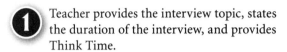

Students interview their partner and then each share with teammates what they learned.

1 Teacher provides the interview topic, states the duration of the interview, and provides Think Time.

2 In pairs, Student A interviews Student B.

3 Pairs switch roles: Student B interviews Student A.

4 RoundRobin: Pairs pair up to form groups of four. Each student, in turn, shares with the team what he or she learned in the interview.

> • **Related Structures.** Additional structures to develop listening skills include **Listen Right!**, **Paraphrase Passport**, and **Traveling RallyInterview**.

Implementing Brain-Friendly Teaching Principles

▶ **Nourishment.** To increase movement (and status), students can be asked to stand while being interviewed. They can be asked to stand also in Step 3 when they are introducing their partner.

▶ **Safety.** Students are interviewed by a teammate who is practicing active listening, creating a safe context within which to share. **Three-Step Interview** is a perfect structure for teambuilding. Teambuilding creates a safe context for learning, positive social interaction, and more inclusive teams.

▶ **Social.** In the first two steps, students develop active listening and oral presentation skills. Students thank their partners for sharing using appreciation gambits like, *"Thank you for sharing,"* and *"One thing I found very interesting was…"* In the third step, while paraphrasing their interview partner, students are improving social cognition as well as oral presentation skills.

▶ **Emotion.** Students are listened to with respect and understanding, making them feel appreciated.

▶ **Attention.** While interviewing their partner, students listen carefully: They know Step 3 is coming and they will be held accountable for sharing what they have learned. **Three-Step Interview** is an effective structure to allow students to clear working and short-term memory.

▶ **Stimuli.** Interest is created as students cannot predict what their partners will share, nor can they predict what their partner will share about them. Students receive feedback on their communication skills as they listen to their partner paraphrase what they have shared. During the uninterrupted sharing, as they speak, students put their thoughts together, constructing meaning. Often the interview topic is relevant to the individual student. With academic topics, students may be interviewed on a project they are building, an experiment they are conducting, or a story or essay they are writing. Teambuilding topics lend themselves to relevance: *"What kind of job do you hope for?" "Do you have a favorite sports team or music group? What is a possession you would hate to lose? Why?"*

25. Timed Pair Share

In pairs, students share with a partner for a predetermined time while the partner listens. Then partners switch roles.

1 Teacher announces a topic, states how long each student will share, and provides Think Time.

2 In pairs, Partner A shares; Partner B listens.

3 Partner B responds with a positive gambit.

4 Partners switch roles.

● **Hint.** The teacher provides positive response gambits to use in Step 3:
Copycat response gambits
  • *"Thanks for sharing!"*
  • *"You are interesting to listen to!"*
Complete the sentence gambits
  • *"One thing I learned listening to you was…"*
  • *"I enjoyed listening to you because…"*
  • *"Your most interesting idea was…"*

● **Related Structures.** **Pair Share** is excellent for very brief answers that do not require a time limit to equalize participation. For longer answers, **Timed Pair Share** is the structure of choice. Using a timer with a predetermined time for each turn limits those who would otherwise dominate and encourages elaboration of thought for those who otherwise would give only brief answers.

Implementing Brain-Friendly Teaching Principles

▶ **Nourishment.** Students may be asked to stand during a **Timed Pair Share**. To increase nourishment, students may walk together during the **Timed Pair Share**, a variation called **Stroll Pair Share**.

▶ **Safety.** Students share in a safe context with a partner who is practicing active listening. Students may be asked to share about themselves with teammates or classmates, helping students get to know and accept each other—creating positive social interaction and a safe context for learning.

▶ **Social.** As students listen to the thoughts, feelings, and intentions of others, they are practicing social cognition.

▶ **Emotion.** Students thank or praise each other with gambits like, *"You are very articulate,"* or *"I enjoy listening to you."*

▶ **Attention.** Attention is more focused when students practice active listening. Listening to just one other person who is in close proximity focuses attention. **Timed Pair Share** is a quick, efficient processing structure to clear working and short-term memory.

▶ **Stimuli.** Students may be asked to communicate with gestures. Topics can be chosen for relevance and meaning.

Brain-Friendly Teaching • Dr. Spencer Kagan
Kagan Publishing • 800.933.2667 • www.KaganOnline.com

26. Traveling Heads Together

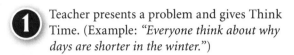

Students travel to new teams to share their team answer.

1 Teacher presents a problem and gives Think Time. (Example: *"Everyone think about why days are shorter in the winter."*)

2 Students privately write their answers.

3 Students lift up from their chairs to put their heads together, show answers, and discuss and teach each other.

4 Students sit down when everyone knows the answer or has something to share.

5 Teacher calls a number. One student on each team with the selected number stands. For example, the teacher calls Student #3 and all Student #3s stand.

6 Teacher instructs the seated students to beckon for one of the standing students to join their team.

7 Traveling students move to a new team, standing behind the chair of the student who just left, and wait for a cue from the teacher to begin sharing.

8 Teacher gives a cue for the standing students to share their answers, and tells them to sit when they have finished.

9 Seated students coach or praise the traveler.

- **Alternative.** Traveling students may rotate a specific number through a pre-established pattern, say 2 teams ahead.

- **Random Team Formation.** If more than one round of **Traveling Heads Together** is used, traveling students are instructed to join a team that their teammates have not already joined. Thus after three rounds, new teams have been formed with no students sitting with prior teammates.

- **Variation.** Students can remain within their teams and not travel to another team to share their answer, in which case the structure is called **Numbered Heads Together**. When a number is called, the student stands to share his or her best answer with teammates.

- **Related Structures.** Structures also used for practice of skills include **PairUp Review**, **Quiz-Quiz-Trade**, **RallyQuiz**, **Sage-N-Scribe**, and **SeeOne–DoOne– TeachOne**. **Traveling Heads Together** is more flexible than the other mastery structures because it is sometimes used to practice a skill (procedural memory), while at other times it is used to formulate ideas (working memory).

Implementing Brain-Friendly Teaching Principles

▶ **Nourishment.** Movement is built into the structure in two ways. Students stand during heads together, and a quarter of the students travel to a new team on each question.

▶ **Safety.** Before sharing with a new team, students have supportive teammates to help them formulate their answers.

▶ **Social.** Students bond. They are all on the same side, hoping everyone on the team can formulate a good answer. They know the person who travels represents their team. As they listen to the thoughts of their teammates, they activate social cognition.

▶ **Emotion.** Recognition is afforded to individuals with correct answers in the form of high fives and pats on the back. During the travel time, students are encouraged to "wildly beckon" for a new teammate, generating excitement.

▶ **Attention.** The structure has built-in suspense and variety. When the teacher is about to call a student number, students wait in anticipation to see who will travel. Students pay close attention to their teammates during the "heads together" step because they know they might be called upon to share their answers with another team.

▶ **Stimuli.** The structure is feedback rich: Students receive feedback during the "heads together" step as students share what they have written on their own. The students receive feedback again as the teacher announces the correct answer. Those students with a strong interpersonal intelligence find the structure matches their style. As students put their heads together to formulate their best answer, they are constructing meaning.

27. Traveling RallyInterview

Students pair up repeatedly to interview classmates.

Setup: The teacher poses an interview question, displays question(s), or students create interview questions.

1 The teacher tells students to, *"Stand up, put a hand up, and pair up."*

2 Partner A interviews Partner B.

3 Partner B interviews Partner A.

4 Students "travel" to a new partner for the next interview.

- **Hint.** The teacher determines the interview duration or number of interview questions each student asks.

- **Variation.** Students can remain with the same partner, often a shoulder partner or face partner within their team, in which case, the structure is simply **RallyInterview**.

- **Related Structures.** RallyInterview is the same as **Traveling RallyInterview** except students remain with the same partner. **Three-Step Interview** is another interview structure and has the advantage of holding students accountable for listening because in the third step they share what they learned in the interview. Rather than taking turns interviewing each other, in **RallyQuiz** students take turns quizzing each other. In **Traveling RallyQuiz** students travel to a new partner for each new question.

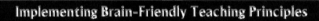

Implementing Brain-Friendly Teaching Principles

▶ **Nourishment.** Students travel to new partners for each interview, increasing heart rate, breathing rate, and volume, pumping more nutrients to the brain.

▶ **Safety.** Students feel safe sharing with just one other, rather than before the whole class. The interview content may be getting-acquainted content or interviews on fun topics, helping classmates know and accept each other, creating a safe context for learning.

▶ **Social.** Teachers may include social skills, including greeting, parting, and appreciation gambits. Appreciation gambits may be "copy cat" gambits like, *"Thank you for sharing,"* or

compete this sentence gambits like, *"I enjoy interviewing you because…"*. As students interview a number of classmates, a more cohesive class is created.

▶ **Emotion.** If appreciation gambits are included, students find them rewarding. Emotion is generated because students never know who their next partner will be.

▶ **Stimuli.** Unexpected and novel stimuli are built into the structure because students cannot anticipate who their next partner will be or what they will say.

Kagan Structures for Brain-Friendly Teaching

Structures	Principles					
	1. Nourishment	2. Safety	3. Social	4. Emotion	5. Attention	6. Stimuli
1. AllWrite Consensus			3.37–3.38	4.9	5.19, 5.24, 5.30, 5.50	6.37, 6.123
2. Both Record RallyRobin			3.38		5.19, 5.24, 5.29, 5.50	6.37
3. Celebrity Interview		2.16	3.25, 3.37–3.38	4.9	5.19, 5.49	6.10
4. Choral Practice		2.18	3.37–3.38		5.19, 5.24, 5.29, 5.50	
5. Flashcard Game		2.13	3.24–3.25, 3.37–3.38	4.9, 17	5.19, 5.24, 5.29, 5.40, 5.45, 5.50	6.10, 6.37, 6.63
6. Formations	1.28		3.37–3.38	4.9	5.19	6.10–6.11, 6.63, 6.83–6.84
7. Kinesthetic Symbols			3.37–3.38		5.19, 5.24, 5.45	6.10, 6.70–6.74, 6.77–6.78, 6.82–6.84
8. Listen Right!			3.37–3.38	4.9	5.17–5.19, 5.24, 5.28–5.30, 5.45	6.11, 6.20, 6.37
9. Number Group Mania!	1.28	2.17–2.18		4.9	5.19	
10. Pair Share			3.37–3.38		5.45	
11. PairUp Review	1.29		3.37–3.38	4.9	5.19, 5.24, 5.30, 5.50	6.37
12. Paraphrase Passport		2.14	3.24, 3.37–3.38	4.9	5.18–5.20, 5.24, 5.30	6.37, 6.84
13. Quiz-Quiz-Trade	1.28–1.30		3.25, 3.37–3.38	4.9	5.19, 5.24, 5.45, 5.50	6.10, 6.37
14. RallyQuiz		2.13	3.37–3.38	4.9	5.19, 5.24, 5.45, 5.50	6.10–6.11, 6.37
15. RallyRobin	1.28	2.17–2.18	3.23, 3.28, 3.37–3.38		5.19–5.20, 5.28–5.29, 5.36, 5.48, 5.50	6.11, 6.82, 6.108
16. RoundRobin	1.29	2.16–2.17	3.37–3.38	4.33	5.48–5.50	6.10–6.11, 6.84, 6.108, 6.123
17. Sage-N-Scribe		2.13	3.8, 3.37–3.38	4.9–4.10	5.19, 5.24, 5.45, 5.50	6.10, 6.36–6.37
18. SeeOne–DoOne–TeachOne		2.18	3.19, 3.24, 3.37–3.38	4.9	5.24, 5.30, 5.50	6.37, 6.123
19. Simulations			3.37–3.38	4.9	5.24	6.10, 6.83, 6.110, 6.115
20. StandUp–HandUp–PairUp	1.28–1.29	2.17–2.18	3.25	4.44		6.84
21. Swap Talk	1.28	2.17–2.18	3.25, 3.37–3.38	4.10		6.11, 6.106
22. TakeOff–TouchDown	1.29					6.10
23. Team-Pair-Solo		2.13	3.37–3.38	4.10	5.24, 5.44–5.45, 5.50	6.11, 6.23, 6.37
24. Three-Step Interview		2.16–2.17	3.25, 3.37–3.38	4.10	5.18–5.19, 5.24, 5.40–5.41, 5.45, 5.49	6.10, 6.84, 6.106
25. Timed Pair Share	1.28	2.13, 2.18	3.28, 3.36–3.38	4.10, 4.30–4.31	5.19–5.20, 5.24, 5.30, 5.49	6.10–6.11, 6.84, 6.106, 6.122–6.123
26. Traveling Heads Together	1.29–1.30		3.37–3.38	4.10	5.19, 5.24, 5.30, 5.38, 5.50	6.10, 6.20, 6.37, 6.84
27. Traveling RallyInterview	1.29	2.17–2.18	3.37–3.38		5.19, 5.24, 5.30	6.84, 6.106

Kagan Structures are multi-functional. Many structures implement a number of principles of brain-friendly instruction.

Attention Deficit Disorder (ADD)
   biofeedback, 6.51–53
   brain games, 5.55
   meditation, 2.33, 5.56
   working memory, 5.66
Attraction, neurotransmitter effects on, 4.4
Attribution shift, 4.15–16
Audience
   feedback, 6.38–39
   social cognition, 3.23
Auditory information/learners
   Instructional strategies, 6.83
   Kinesthetic Symbols, 6.78
   stimuli, 6.88
   visuals v., 6.62, 6.79, 6.82
Autism, 3.4, 3.5, 6.14
Autonomy, student concerns about, 6.111
Awareness, 5.9. *See also* Attention;
   Consciousness
Awe, 4.31

B

Babies
   abused, 3.18
   cooperation, 3.17, 3.18
   mortality and social interaction, 3.10
   orphans, 3.11
   predictions, 6.15
   premature, 3.11
Balance games, 1.15
Behavior
   approach, 3.7
   demonstrating, 3.19
   exercise and diet, 1.20
   feedback shaping, 6.32, 6.47–50
   impression based on, 3.6
   recess, 1.20
Beliefs, and confirmation bias, 6.16–19
Bell work, 6.21
Belongingness, 2.15, 2.16, 3.14–15
Beta-endorphins, 4.27, 4.38
Biases
   attention, 5.65–66
   confirmation, 6.16–19
Big picture
   attention to, 5.45–47, 6.95
   brain hemispheres, 6.91
   global cognitive style, 6.89, 6.91, 6.93
   graphic organizers, 6.59
   mind maps, 6.58, 6.59
   test of focus on, 6.95
Biofeedback, 6.51–53
Blessings, counting, 4.33, 4.34
Blindness, and inattention, 5.11–12
Blood flow
   attention, 5.51
   brain nourishment, 1.27
   breathing, 1.25
   exercise, 1.6, 5.51
Blood lactate, and meditation, 2.33
Blood pressure
   animal petting, 4.38
   breathing, 2.28
   cortisol, 4.43
   laughter, 2.22
   relaxation, 2.8
   threats, 2.5
Blood sugar levels, 1.16
Board responses, 5.44
Bodily/kinesthetic intelligence, 6.73, 6.85

Body language, and social cognition, 3.7, 3.8
Bonding, 3.15, 3.43
Boredom, 2.11
   Kagan Structures counteracting, 5.53
   novelty, 6.9
   task difficulty, 5.43
Bottom-down orienting, 5.12–13
Brain
   blood flow, 1.27
   default mode, 3.4
   density, 5.69
   function. See Brain function
   IQ mapping, 5.68
   parallel processing, 6.82
   pleasure center, 4.30
   praise, 4.16
   social cognition network, 3.3–49
Brain breaks, 1.14
Brain-controlled interfaces, 6.33
Brain-derived neurotrophic factor, 2.20
Brain function
   animal petting, 4.38
   attention, 5.4, 5.5, 5.12–14, 5.33, 5.35, 5.46,
   5.51, 5.57
   brain games, 5.54–55
   cognitive styles, 6.89–92
   confirmation bias, 6.17
   emotion influencing, 4.3–5, 4.27
   exercise, 5.51
   feedback, 6.30, 6.33, 6.35–36
   gestures, 6.74–75, 6.77–78
   graphic organizers, 6.59–62
   Kinesthetic Symbols, 6.78
   meditation, 2.33, 2.34, 5.56
   mind maps, 6.58
   music, 6.67
   nature, 4.38
   novelty, 6.4–5
   pain, 5.7
   play, 3.40–41, 3.46–47, 6.27
   processing, 5.36, 5.37–38, 5.57
   prosthetics, 6.33–35
   quiet signal, 5.16–17
   safety. See Safety
   short-term memory, 5.25, 5.66
   visuals, 6.58, 6.59–65
   working memory, 5.25, 5.66, 5.68–70
Brain plasticity. See Neuroplasticity
Brainstorming, mind maps for, 6.58
Brain structure
   ADD, 6.53
   multimodal teaching, 6.82, 6.87–88
   music, 6.66–67
Breadth, and attention, 5.57, 5.59, 5.61
Breakfast, 1.18–20
Breathing
   brain nourishment, 1.24–27
   diaphragmatic, 2.27
   meditation, 2.32–33, 5.56
   relaxation, 2.8, 2.28, 4.40
   threats, 2.5
Broaden-and-build theory, 4.26
Bulletin boards, 6.62
Bullying, 2.7, 2.8, 2.34, 3.12
Business, running a, 6.102

C

Caffeine, 4.4
Calendars, 6.24

Calmness
   attention, 5.55, 5.56
   breathing, 1.25, 2.28
   games for, 1.15
   meditation, 2.35
   relaxation response, 2.8–9
   touch, 2.25
   voice, 2.25
Calories, brain's need for, 1.3
Candle roblem, 4.21
Candle Solution, 4.21
Captions, 5.39
Carbohydrates, 1.16, 1.17
Cardio exercises, 1.10
Career. See Working/workplace
Career journal, 6.101
Caregiving, and positive emotion, 4.38
Caring, hard-wired, 3.20, 3.21
Categorization
   graphic organizers, 6.62
   positive emotion, 4.22
Causality, correlation v., 4.26
Celebrations
   before performance, 4.28, 4.29
   memory enhancement, 4.8
   success, 4.18
Cell phones, 3.7, 5.10
Challenge
   achievement, 2.10
   arousal, 2.11
   flow, 5.43–44
   games, 1.15
   motivation, 4.16
   passion, 4.7
   play, 6.30
   student interest, 6.109
Character virtues, 3.37, 3.38
Check-off lists, 5.38
Cheers
   attention, 5.31
   before performance, 4.28, 4.29
   emotion, 4.18, 4.19
   eliciting passion, 4.6
Choices, and student interests, 6.110
Chunks of information, 5.18, 5.27, 5.38, 5.71
Classbuilding
   belongingness, 3.14
   incentives, 4.44
   safety, 2.16–18
   social cognition, 3.24–26
   movement, 1.27–28
Classification, and style theories, 6.89
Class meetings, 3.26
Classroom
   inclusive, 2.16–18
   tag game in, 1.14
   visitors, 6.22
Classroom environment
   exercise, 1.9
   meditation, 2.35
   threats, 2.7
   visually rich, 6.62
Classroom management
   attention, 5.9
   cooperative learning, 3.31–32
   predictability, 6.22–25
Closure
   attention, 5.21
   clearing working memory, 5.29

Desks, clearing, 5.38
Details
    focus on, 5.45, 6.89, 6.91
    mind maps, 6.59
    relevance, 6.98
Diagrams, 5.39
Diaphragmatic breathing, 1.24–27, 2.27
Dichotic listening, 5.5, 5.40
Diet
    attention, 5.13
    brain function, 1.16–22
    costs of healthy, 1.22
    exercise, 1.20–21
    quality, 1.18
    school contribution to, 1.21
Differentiated instruction, 5.43, 5.44
Digestion, and breathing, 1.25
Directions, bite-sized, 5.38
Discipline
    exercise and diet, 1.20
    meditation, 2.36
    predictable, 6.24
    teams, 3.30
    win-win, 2.12
Discovery, effects on emotion of, 4.10
Discrete attention systems, 5.12–14
Discussions
    attention, 5.18, 5.33, 5.36
    closure, 5.49
    mindreading, 3.24
Disease
    cortisol, 4.43
    negative emotions, 4.24–25
Disruptions
    feedback, 6.50
    play, 6.27
Distractions, 5.3, 5.4
    ADD, 5.51
    anxiety, 5.56
    flow, 5.44
    group work, 5.53
    Kagan Structures, 5.40–41
    short-term memory, 5.77
    ways to avoid, 5.38–41
    working memory, 5.67
Distributed practice, 5.41–42
Dominance
    play for, 3.44–46
    testosterone, 4.43
Dopamine
    ADD, 5.52
    animal petting, 4.38
    attention, 1.14, 5.13, 5.70
    cocaine, 5.52
    diet, 1.16
    emotions, 4.4, 4.27
    exercise, 1.7
    motivation, 1.14
    music, 4.29
    novelty, 4.30, 6.5, 6.6–7
    play, 3.44, 4.45
    positive emotions, 6.115
    praise, 4.16
    rewards, 4.28, 6.99
    smiles, 4.17
    unanticipated rewards, 4.28
Drawing, by teachers, 6.57
Driving, attention while, 5.10
Dropout, 3.21

Drugs
    cocaine, 4.4, 5.52
    dopamine, 4.4
    pain, 5.6
    Ritalin, 4.4, 5.51–53, 6.52
Dunn & Dunn model, 6.96

E

Echoing, 2.18
Economics, linking emotion to, 4.13
Effectiveness, learned, 5.13, 6.38
Efficiency, and practice, 1.3
Embarrassment, public, 2.12
Embedded Figures test, 6.94–95
Emotion, 4.1–49
    attention, 5.17
    belonging, 3.14–15
    brain function, 4.3–5
    celebrate success, 4.18
    content eliciting, 6.115
    controlling with biofeedback, 6.52
    elicit passion, 4.6–7
    elicit positive, 4.19–45
    hormones, 4.4
    identifying with, 6.111
    irrational thinking, 2.6
    linking to content, 4.7–14
    meditation, 2.34
    memory, 4.3, 4.8, 4.45, 5.36, 5.66
    mirror neurons, 3.18–19
    negative v. positive, 4.20
    neurochemicals, 1.5
    play, 1.12, 4.20, 4.45–48, 5.51
    positive. See Emotion, positive
    praise, 4.15–17
    sadness, 4.7, 4.20, 4.29
    sensitivity to, 3.20
    short-term v. long-term memory, 4.8
    social interaction, 2.25
    in teaching, 4.6, 4.9
    test-taking, 6.56
    thinking about others', 3.4, 3.6, 3.22–23, 3.24
    thinking v., 6.92–93
    working memory, 5.66
    See also Structures Section, S.1–36
Emotion, positive
    attention, 5.56
    dopamine, 6.115
    effects, 4.3
    eliciting, 4.19–45
    list of, 4.31
    play, 5.51
Emotion, negative, 4.20
    disease and, 4.24–25
Emotional intelligence
    feedback, 6.31
    meditation, 2.36
Emotional maturity, 2.5
Empathy
    abuse, 3.43
    brain activity, 3.10, 3.21
    hospital clowns, 2.26
    Kagan Structures for, 3.38
    oxytocin, 2.34, 3.17
    teaching, 3.14
    toddlers, 3.17, 3.18
Empowerment, and relevant content, 5.48–49, 6.99–102
Endorphins, 1.5

Energy
    breathing, 1.25
    diet, 1.16, 1.17
    hydration, 1.22
    levels, 1.15
    music, 4.30
    positive emotion, 4.19
    tag games releasing, 1.14
Epinephrine, 1.7
Episodic memory. See Memory, episodic
Equal participation, 3.27, 3.28, 3.29
Evaluation
    class meetings, 3.26
    mind maps for, 6.59
    notes, 5.24
    praise, 4.16–17
    processing, 5.32
    safe, 2.14–15
    self- and feedback, 6.31, 6.40, 6.46–47
    teacher, 6.33, 6.40–42
    working memory, 5.25, 5.66
Events, communicating upcoming, 6.23, 6.24
Evolution, and play, 6.27
Examples, concrete, 6.118–120
Exams. See Test(s)
Exclusion, social, 2.7, 2.8, 2.15, 3.14–15, 6.111
Executive function
    attention, 5.12, 5.13, 5.14, 5.17, 5.67, 5.69
    brain games, 5.55
    defined, 6.74
    exercise, 1.9, 1.11
    gestures, 6.74–75
    meditation, 2.33, 5.56
    premature infants, 3.11
    working memory, 5.66
Exercise
    achievement, 5.50–51
    attention, 5.13, 5.31, 5.51
    brain nourishment, 1.6–11
    concentration, 6.58
    diet, 1.20–21
    dopamine, 4.4
    encouraging, 1.11
    equipment, 1.22
    intense, 1.6–7
    longevity, 4.26
    stress, 2.20
    tag games, 1.12
    timing, 1.11
    See also Sports
Exhalation, 1.25, 1.26
Expectations
    about teachers, 6.19
    confirmation bias, 6.16–17
    IQ, 6.18–19
    novelty, 6.104
    positive emotion raising, 4.23
    predictability, 6.20
    stimuli, 6.6, 6.7–9
    two-way communication, 6.24
Experience
    adding knowledge, 6.121
    confirmation bias, 6.16–17
    constructing meaning, 6.118, 6.120
    fluid intelligence, 5.68
    neuronal feedback, 6.30
    processing, 6.66–67
    short-term memory, 5.25
Exploration, and positive emotion, 4.20, 4.26

F

Face(s)
  brain hemispheres, 6.68
  confirmation bias, 6.17–18
  expressions, 3.7
  feedback, 6.40
  mirror neurons, 5.37
  recognition, 3.8–9
  threats, 2.5
Face blindness, 3.9
Face partners, 3.32
Facts, memory for, 2.11, 5.36
Failure, and competition, 2.14
Fairness, teaching, 3.17
Fantasy, 3.46, 4.32
Far transfer, 5.71–72, 5.75
Fatty foods, 1.21
Fear
  brain, 2.4
  learning through, 4.20, 4.45
  memory of, 4.5, 4.7
  touch, 2.26
  See also Fight or flee; Safety
Feedback
  bio-, 6.51–53
  contingent, 6.36
  dimensions, 6.31–32
  effective, 6.35–45
  external, 6.30
  formative, 6.31, 6.36
  frequent, 6.36–37
  immediate, 6.35–37
  internal, 6.30
  motivation, 4.15
  negative, 6.31
  safe, 2.14
  shaping behavior, 6.47–50
  threats, 2.7
  timing, 6.31, 6.35–37
Feelings. See Emotion
Fiber, 1.16
Field trips, 4.7, 6.22, 6.109
Fight, and play, 3.42
Fight or flee, 2.3–8
  humans v. primates, 3.20
  mirror neurons, 3.18
  negative emotions, 4.20
Fire drill, 6.22
FitnessGram, 1.8
Fleeing. See Fight or flee
Flexible thinking, 4.21, 4.22, 4.23, 4.27
Flight. See Fight or flee
Flow, 5.42–45
Fluid intelligence. See Intelligence, fluid
Fluid thinking, 4.27
Flying, fear of, 2.23
Focus
  diet, 1.16
  dopamine, 4.4
  emotion, 4.3, 4.4–5, 4.23
  games, 1.15
  social cognition, 3.8
  See also Attention; Concentration
Food. See Diet
Forced choice tests, 6.56
Freedom, and laughter, 4.22
Free reading, 4.32

Free time, 4.31
Friends
  kindness, 3.11–12
  positive emotion, 4.19
Frontloading, 5.17, 5.38
Frustration, 4.20
Fun
  anticipation of, 4.32
  flow, 5.43
  surprise, 6.9
Fusiform gyrus, 3.8, 3.9

G

GABA, 4.4
Games
  brain function, 5.54–55
  brain nourishment, 1.12–15
  pain distraction, 5.6–7
  See also Play
Gardening, relevance of, 6.102
Gene expression, and positive emotion, 4.26
Generosity, and oxytocin, 3.15, 3.17
Gestures
  concept attainment, 6.82
  safe, 2.25
  teaching with, 6.69–78
Glial cells, 1.4
Global abilities, tests of, 6.95
Global cognitive style, 5.46, 5.61, 6.89, 6.91–92, 6.93
Glucocorticoids, 2.10
Glucose, 1.4, 1.16
Goals
  brain structure, 5.69
  constructing meaning, 6.120
  feedback, 6.31, 6.42
  incentives, 4.44–45
  overarching, 6.120
  relevant stimuli, 6.98
Golin Incomplete Figures test, 6.95
Grades
  announcing, 2.12
  curve, 3.21
  online reporting, 6.22
  teacher comments v., 6.38
Graphic organizers, 5.28, 5.32, 6.59–62
Gratitude
  meditation, 4.42
  health, 4.26
  kindness, 4.39
  as positive emotion, 4.31, 4.45
  writing about, 4.33
Groups
  cooperative learning v., 3.28, 3.29
  feedback, 6.31
  forming, 1.29, 1.30
  movement, 1.30
  structures, 1.28
  See also Team(s)
Guesses, interest and, 6.110
Guided imagery, 4.40, 4.41, 5.31
Guided practice, 5.49–50

H

Habits
  attention, 5.45
  feedback, 6.36
  meta-attention, 5.59–60
  repetition forming, 1.27
Handouts, 6.62

Handshakes
  attention, 5.31
  brain function, 2.26–27
  culture, 2.27
  emotions, 4.18, 4.37
  positive social contact, 2.25
  power, 4.43
  social cognition network, 3.7, 3.8
  team, 2.15, 3.31
Happiness
  action, 4.20
  incentives v., 4.45
  kindness, 4.39
  music, 4.29
  performance experience, 4.26–27
  success, 4.27
  survival, 4.7
Happy recall, 4.30
Health
  positive emotion, 4.19, 4.23–26
  school contribution to, 1.21
  spending time in nature, 4.38–39
  weight, 1.21
  See also Immune system
Heart
  breathing, 1.25
  negative emotions, 4.25
Heart rate
  animal petting, 4.38
  brain nourishment, 1.27
  breathing, 2.28
  exercise, 1.6
  lecture length, 5.36
  meditation, 5.56
  neurotransmitter effects, 4.4
  relaxation, 2.8
  threats, 2.5
Help/helping
  asking for, 2.12
  anticipating, 4.39
  brain activity, 3.7
  games, 1.15, 2.20
  infants, 3.17
  Kagan Structures for, 3.38
  recalling, 4.39
Helplessness
  feedback, 6.39, 6.40
  learned, 3.10, 5.13
High fives, 2.27, 4.18, 4.37
History, linking emotion to, 4.13
Hobbies, 4.33
Home, threats in, 2.7
Homework, 5.44, 5.53
Homogeneous groups, and flow, 5.44
Hope, 4.31, 4.32, 4.42
Hormones
  adrenalin, 2.4
  animal petting, 4.38
  anxiety, 4.5
  bonding, 3.15
  cooperation, 3.14, 3.15–17
  emotions, 4.4, 4.27
  human growth, 2.22
  insulin, 1.16
  love, 3.15
  norepinephrine, 1.16, 3.13, 4.4, 5.13
  oxytocin, 2.25, 2.26, 3.14, 3.15–17, 4.26, 4.37, 4.38
  neuropeptides, 4.4, 4.5, 6.27
  prolactin, 4.38

Brain-Friendly Teaching • Dr. Spencer Kagan
Kagan Publishing • 800.933.2667 • www.KaganOnline.com

stress, 2.4, 2.10, 2.19, 4.5, 4.37
Hospital clowns, 2.22
Hostility, and humor, 2.23
Human growth factor, 4.27
Human growth hormone, and humor, 2.22
Humor
    anxiety, 4.31
    creativity, 4.21–22
    positive emotion, 4.21–22, 4.32
    stress, 2.22–24
    See also Amusement
Hydration, 1.22–23, 2.25
Hyperactivity, 1.16. *See also* ADD
Hyperventilation, 1.24
Hypothalamus, 1.6, 2.4, 2.8

I

Ideas, exchange of, 2.14
Identity, student concerns about, 6.111
Image. See Visual(s)
Imagery, guided, 4.40, 4.41
Imagination
    play, 6.28
    practice using, 6.35
    short–term memory, 5.25
Imitative learning, 6.122
Immune system
    breathing, 1.25
    cortisol, 4.43
    humor, 2.22
    meditation, 2.34
    positive emotion, 4.25, 4.26
    stress effects, 2.8
    touch, 2.25
Impossible, imagining, 4.22
Improvement scoring, 6.39
Impulse/impulse control
    brain training, 5.55, 5.70
    executive function, 6.74
    learning style, 6.92
    relaxation, 2.9
    serotonin, 1.16
    threats, 2.5–6
    working memory, 5.69
Incentives, eliciting positive emotion v., 4.43–45
Incidents, memory for, 2.11, 5.36
Inclusion, 3.14–15, 6.111
Inclusive classrooms, 2.16–18
Inclusive teams, 2.15–16
Income, and positive emotion, 4.23
Individual accountability, 3.27, 3.28, 3.29
Infants. See Babies
Inflammation, and positive emotion, 4.26
Inspiration, 4.31
Instructed learning, 6.122
Instruction. See Teaching
Insulin, 1.16
Integration, and positive emotion, 4.26
Intelligence
    attention training, 5.54
    confirmation bias, 6.18
    crystallized, 5.68
    fluid. See Intelligence, fluid
    glial cells, 1.4
    happiness, 4.20
    kinesthetic, 6.73
    matched, 6.84
    multiple. See Intelligences, multiple
    neurons, 1.4
    play, 3.41, 6.28–30

predictive abilities, 6.14–15
    stretched, 6.84
    working memory, 5.27, 5.69, 5.70, 5.71, 5.72–73
Intelligence, fluid
    brain structure, 3.3, 3.4, 3.6, 5.69
    order of information, 3.6
    tests of, 5.68, 5.72
    training, 5.72–5.73
Intelligences, multiple
    feedback, 6.31
    instructional strategies, 2.14, 6.83–88
    personal interests, 6.105–106
    variety, 6.11
Intention
    brain looking for, 3.6
    social cognition, 3.4
Interaction. See Cooperative interaction;
    Social interaction
Interdependence, positive, 3.27, 3.28–29
Interest, 4.31
    meditation, 4.42
    See also Attention; Relevance
Interpersonal intelligence, 6.85
Interviews, getting acquainted using, 3.25
Intrapersonal intelligence, 6.85
IQ
    aloneness, 3.14
    confirmation bias, 6.18–19
    exercise, 1.9
    measuring, 5.68
    meditation, 2.33
    non–social, 3.4, 3.5
    social, 3.4, 3.5
    style dimensions, 6.89
    working memory, 5.67–68

J

Journals
    career, 6.101
    kindness, 4.39
    mind maps, 6.58
    reflection using, 6.123
Joy, 4.4, 4.31

K

Kagan Structures
    attention, 5.17–19
    clear short-term memory, 5.28–31
    constructing meaning, 6.122–123
    distractions, 5.40–41
    eliciting emotion, 4.9–10
    feedback, 6.36–37
    flow, 5.43–45
    mirror neurons, 3.19
    movement, 1.27–30
    multimodal, 6.82–83, 6.84
    multiple intelligences, 6.84
    novelty, 6.9, 6.25
    praise, 4.17
    predictability, 6.20
    principles, 3.27–29
    safety, 2.13–14
    student interests, 6.106–107
    variety, 6.10–11
    visuals, 6.63
    See also Cooperative learning
Kangaroo Care, 3.11
Keep away game, 3.46

Kindness
    popularity, 3.11–12
    positive emotion, 4.39
Kinesthetic learners, 6.83
Kinesthetic Symbols, 6.70–74
Knowledge
    activating, 5.47–48
    fluid intelligence, 5.68
    prior, 5.5, 5.33, 6.120–121
    revising thoughts about, 6.121

L

Language. See Speaking
Language arts
    attention styles, 5.47
    Kinesthetic Symbols, 6.73
    linking emotion to, 4.13, 4.14
    simulations, 6.115
    social cognition, 3.22, 3.23
    stimuli, 6.8
Laughter, 2.22–24, 4.21–22
Leadership, and testosterone, 4.43
Learned effectiveness, 5.13, 6.38
Learned helplessness, 3.10, 5.13
Learning
    brain nourishment, 1.12–15
    breathing promoting, 1.27
    concrete, 6.109
    cooperative. See Cooperative learning
    Dunn & Dunn model, 6.96
    executive function, 6.75
    exercise, 1.6–7
    feedback fostering, 6.31
    humor, 2.23
    hydration, 1.22
    Kinesthetic Symbols, 6.74
    modalities, 6.79–88
    multiple intelligences. See Intelligences, multiple
    multi-tasking, 5.11
    novelty, 6.26
    oxygen, 1.3–4
    parasympathetic arousal, 2.9
    positive emotion, 4.19
    safe context for, 2.12–14
    state-conditioned, 5.42
    threat effects, 2.7
Learning disorders, and attention, 5.60
Lectures
    attention during, 5.47–50, 5.53
    pre-questions, 5.22, 5.24
Leg muscles, 1.27
Lesson maps, 5.38, 5.47
Lesson plan
    attention, 5.47–50
    predictability, 6.20, 6.24
Lesson set, and unexpected stimuli, 6.8–9
Life skills, and working memory, 5.71
Listening
    accountability for, 5.18, 5.21
    active. See Listening, active
    brain activation, 3.7
    dichotic, 5.5, 5.40
    interviews, 2.16
    note taking, 5.17, 5.21–25
    retention, 3.33
    structures for, 3.37, 3.38
Listening, active
    attention, 5.20–25, 5.36, 5.59
    safety, 2.13

Nature
    multiple intelligences, 6.85
    positive emotion, 4.38–39
    sounds, 4.40
N-back research, 5.69, 5.72–73, 5.74
Near-transfer, 5.71
Negative emotion. See Emotion, negative
Negative feedback, 6.31
Neural networks
    computer games, 5.54
    mind maps, 6.58
    play affecting, 3.41–42, 6.27
Neuroception, 2.3
Neurons
    emotion, 4.4, 4.5, 4.45
    energy needs, 1.4
    enriched environments, 3.41
    exercise, 1.6
    feedback, 6.30, 6.35–36
    firing together, 5.47–48, 6.35–36, 6.57, 6.78, 6.81
    images, 6.57
    learning repetition, 5.49
    linking to prior knowledge, 6.120
    mind maps, 6.58
    mirror. See Neurons, mirror
    multiple intelligences, 6.87
    new connections, 3.19
    prosthetics, 6.33–35
    receptors, 1.4–5, 4.4
    rewards, 6.99
    social cognition, 3.19, 3.21
    socially responsive, 3.8
    social stimuli, 3.9–10
    water needs, 1.22
Neurons, mirror
    interests and, 6.108
    laughter, 2.22
    processing, 5.37–38
    quiet signal, 5.17
    reinforcement, 6.40
    social stimuli, 3.10, 3.18–19, 3.21
    teaching with passion, 4.6
Neuropeptides, 4.4, 4.5, 6.27
Neuroplasticity
    capacity of, 5.54
    multimodal teaching, 6.87
    music, 6.66
    Ritalin, 5.51
    social cognition, 3.19, 3.41
    working memory, 5.70
Neurotransmitters
    animal petting, 4.38
    attention, 5.4, 5.13
    exercise, 1.7
    hydration, 1.22
    nutrition, 1.16
    play, 6.27
    positive emotion, 4.4, 4.27
    serotonin. See Serotonin
Noisy class, shaping, 6.47–48
Noradrenalin, 2.4, 2.19, 5.13
Norepinephrine, 1.16, 3.13, 4.4, 5.13
Note taking
    attention, 5.17, 5.18, 5.21–25, 5.28, 5.36
    Cloze, 5.21, 5.22–24, 5.25, 5.28
    Cornell, 5.22–24
    mind maps, 6.58
    mind-wandering, 5.33
    predictability, 6.24

Nourishment, 1.1–30
    breathing, 1.24–27
    diet, 1.16–22
    exercise, 1.6–11
    hydration, 1.22–23
    introduction to, 1.3–5
    movement structures, 1.27–30
    play, 1.12–15
    See also Structures Section, S.1–36
Novelty
    balancing predictability and, 6.25–26
    brain hemispheres, 6.67, 6.68
    dopamine, 4.29
    interest and, 6.104, 6.108
    play, 6.9, 6.28
    positive emotion, 4.30
    stimuli, 5.17, 5.37, 5.40, 6.4–13
    surprise, 4.17
Nutrition. See Diet; Nourishment

O

Observational learning, and mirror neurons, 3.19
Oddball response, 6.6
Operant conditioning, 6.32
Opioid system, 3.12, 3.13
Oral reports
    social cognition, 3.23
    threats, 2.7
Organization, and working memory, 5.25
Orienting system, and attention, 5.12, 5.13, 5.16–17
Orphans, 3.11
Outcomes
    feedback, 6.30, 6.35
    play, 3.39–40
    relevance, 6.97
    teams, 3.27
    unexpected, 6.108
Outlines, mind maps v., 6.58
Overt closure, 5.49
Overt set, 5.48
Oxygen
    brain consumption, 1.3
    meditation, 2.33
    movement supplying, 1.27
    optimum, 1.24–27
    water needs, 1.22
    See also Breathing
Oxytocin, 2.25, 2.26, 3.14, 3.15–17, 4.26, 4.37, 4.38

P

Pain
    attention to, 5.6–7
    memory of, 4.5, 4.7
    power, 4.43
    vicarious perception, 3.10
Parallel communication, 6.77
Paraphrase
    active listening, 5.20–21
    Kagan Structures for, 3.38
Parasympathetic nervous system, 2.8–9, 2.25, 4.26
Parents, and breakfast, 1.18
Parking lot, 6.42
Participation
    equal, 3.27, 3.28, 3.29
    sets, 5.47, 5.48
Passion, teaching with, 4.6
Pats on the back, 2.27, 4.18, 4.37

Peers
    class meetings, 3.26
    feedback from, 6.45
    kindness, 3.12
    rejection by, 2.7, 2.8, 2.15, 3.12–15
    tutoring by, 3.34
Peptide hormones, 4.4, 4.5, 6.27
Perceiving/Acting style, 6.93
Perception
    action v., 6.93
    attention, 5.3, 5.14
    confirmation bias, 6.16–19
    exercise, 1.9
    IQ, 5.68
    mind maps, 6.58
    positive emotion, 4.19, 4.20, 4.22–23, 4.27
    safety, 2.3, 2.4–5, 2.7, 6.14
    social contact, 3.21
Performance
    being called on as threat, 2.7
    embarrassment, 2.12
    individual accountability, 3.28, 3.29
    play as, 3.46
    positive emotion, 4.28, 4.29, 4.44
    practice, 1.3
    predictability, 6.15
    recall of happy experience, 4.26–27
    reinforcement, 6.81
    teaching skills, 5.53–54
Personal control, and feedback, 6.40–42
Personal relevance. See Relevance
Personal space, 2.12
Perspective, and executive function, 6.74
Pets, and positive emotion, 4.37–38
Photos, memory for, 6.53–55
Physical fitness tests, 1.7
Physical stimuli
    brain development, 3.40
    infants, 3.10–11
    See also Exercise; Play; Touch
PIES, 3.27–29
Pit Stop, 6.103
Planning
    class meetings, 3.26
    lesson, 5.47–50, 6.20, 6.24
    threats, 2.5, 2.6
Plants, and positive emotion, 4.38
Play
    animals, 3.40–46
    benefits of, 3.46–49
    brain nourishment, 1.12–15
    cooperative, 3.39–49
    emotion, 4.26, 4.45–48, 5.51
    novelty, 6.9, 6.28
    performance, 3.46
    positive emotion, 4.26, 4.45–48, 5.51
    pretend, 3.46
    safety, 2.20
    stimuli, 6.9, 6.27–30
Pleasure
    dopamine, 4.4
    memory of, 4.5, 4.7, 4.45
    motivation, 4.15
    music, 4.30
    praise, 4.16
    stimuli, 6.104
Plus, Minus, Interesting Form, 6.47
PMI Form, 6.47
Pop quizzes stress, 2.13
Popularity, and kindness, 3.11–12

Brain-Friendly Teaching • Dr. Spencer Kagan
Kagan Publishing • 800.933.2667 • www.KaganOnline.com

Kinesthetic Symbols, 6.77
movement, 1.27
relevance, 6.98
selective attention, 5.5
social cognition, 3.21–22
social interaction, 3.32–33
See also Memory
Retrograde memory enhancement, 4.3, 4.7–8, 4.15
Review
clearing short-term memory, 5.28
closure, 5.49
notes, 5.24, 5.25
recall, 5.22
Rewards
anticipation of, 6.99
arousal, 2.11
brain activity, 3.7, 3.10
cooperative interaction, 3.11
dopamine, 6.99
extrinsic, 4.15–16
formative feedback v., 6.31
incentives, 4.43–45
long-term memory, 6.115
motivation, 4.15–16
non-contingent, 4.29
novelty, 6.5, 6.6–7, 6.14
play, 3.44, 6.27
relative, 6.5
relevant content, 6.4
Ritalin, 5.51
texting, 5.10
unanticipated, 4.28
Ritalin, 4.4, 5.51–53, 6.52
Role play, 3.19
emotion, 4.13
identification, 6.115
social cognition, 3.23
Routines, predictable, 6.14, 6.19–26
Rubrics, self-evaluation using, 6.46
Rules
creativity, 4.22
sports, 3.47

S

Sadness
learning through, 4.20
music, 4.29
survival, 4.7
Safety, 2.1–37
attention, 5.10–11, 5.16–17
breathing, 1.27
driving, 5.10–11
fight or flight. See Fight or flee
hydration, 2.25
meditation, 2.31–36
memory, 2.11–12
optimal stress, 2.9–11
parasympathetic arousal, 2.8–9
play, 1.12–14
positive emotion, 4.37
praise, 4.16
predictability, 6.14, 6.19
social cues, 3.7
social interaction, 2.25–27
stress, 2.11–12
student concerns, 6.111
teams, 3.31
threat-free classroom, 2.12–36
tools, 2.12–36
See also Structures Section, S.1–36

Science
attention styles, 5.47
confirmation, 6.18
Kinesthetic Symbols, 6.73
linking emotion to, 4.14
simulations, 6.115
social cognition, 3.23
stimuli, 6.7
Seating
attention, 5.35
flow, 5.44
traditional, 3.23
Self-esteem, and meditation, 2.33
Self-evaluation
feedback, 6.40, 6.46–47
praise, 4.16–17
Self-expression, Kagan Structures for, 3.38
Self-image, and homogeneous groups, 5.44
Semantic memory, 2.11, 2.13, 2.18, 5.36–37
Sequence
of gestures, 6.78
and Kinesthetic Symbols, 6.72
multimodal input, 6.81–82
Serenity, 4.31, 4.42
Serotonin, 1.16
attention, 5.13, 5.50
spending time in nature, 4.38
Sets
attention, 5.47
and predictability, 6.21
Sharing
about self, 3.25
discouraging, 3.21
safety, 2.13
teams, 2.16
Shootings, school, 2.8
Short-term memory. See Memory, short-term
Shoulder partners, 3.32
Shyness, 3.9, 3.13, 5.13
Signals, Kinesthetic Symbols as, 6.72
Simulations
episodic memory, 6.81
identification, 6.115
teaching with emotion, 4.9
Simultaneous interaction, 3.27, 3.28, 3.29
Simultaneous multimodal input, 6.81–82
Skills
brain energy, 1.3
categories of, 6.87–88
flow, 5.42–44
multiple intelligences, 6.83–88
personal relevance, 6.101, 6.105
Skin-to-skin contact, 3.11
Sleep, consolidation of learning during, 6.76
Sleepiness, 1.16
Smiles, 2.8, 2.25
dopamine, 4.17
feedback, 6.40
social cognition network, 3.7, 3.8
Snacks, 1.21
Social awareness, and class meetings, 3.26
Social brain, tools to teach, 3.21–49
Social cognition, 3.1–49
activating, 3.21–24
classbuilding, 3.24–26
competition, 3.4–5
cooperation, 3.4–5, 3.26–36, 3.39–49
introduction to, 3.1–21
lack of, 3.5
play, 3.39–49

social interaction, 6.121–122
social skills, 3.36–39
See also Structures Section, S.1–36
Social encoding advantage, 3.6, 3.21–24
Social exclusion, 2.7, 2.8, 2.15, 3.14–15, 6.111
Social interaction
attention, 5.17, 5.53
brain activity, 3.7
classbuilding, 3.24–26
constructing meaning, 6.121–122
cooperative play, 3.40
default mode, 3.4, 3.7
mindreading, 3.24
play, 1.12
safe, 2.25–27
simultaneous, 3.27, 3.28, 3.29
social cognition, 3.6
structures, 1.29–30
Socialization
play, 3.42–43
structures, 3.39
Social rejection, pain of, 3.12–15
Social relations, positive emotion, 4.26. *See also*
Relationships
Social separation, 3.13–14
Social skills
feedback, 6.31
safety, 2.14
teaching, 3.36–39
Social stimuli
brain development, 3.40
neurons, 3.9–10
social contact, 3.21
vigilance for, 3.7–8
See also Stimuli
Social studies
attention styles, 5.47
Kinesthetic Symbols, 6.73
linking emotion to, 4.14
simulations, 6.115
social cognition, 3.22
stimuli, 6.8
Socioeconomic background, and teacher
expectations, 6.19
Soft drinks, 1.21
Spaced practice, 5.41–42
Spatial stimuli
brain hemispheres, 6.65
gestures, 6.74
Speaking
action, 6.74
attention, 5.16, 5.20–21, 5.36
brain function, 3.7, 6.67
cooperative learning, 3.31
retention, 3.33
See also Conversations; Discussions
Speech. See Speaking
Spelling, exercise effects, 5.51
Split-attention effect, 5.38–41
Splitters, 6.89
Sponge activity, 1.14, 5.43–44
Spontaneity, and feedback, 6.40
Sports
emotion, 4.5
outcomes, 3.39–40
rules, 3.47
student interest, 6.105, 6.111
tasks, 2.10, 2.11
See also Exercise
Stamina, and arousal, 2.10

Name Index

A

Aarnoudse-Moens, C.S.H., 3.11
Aase, H., 5.52
Abarbanel, A., 6.51
Abel, L., 1.3
Abernethy, M., 6.65
Abrams, A., 5.56
Abrams, A.I., 2.31, 2.33
Achor, S., 4.27
Ackerman, P.L., 5.67, 5.68
Adams, A-M., 5.70
Adams, A.M., 5.67, 5.68
Adams, J., 1.18
Adams, M.J., 6.54, 6.97
Addessi, E., 6.5
Adlard, P.A., 1.6, 2.20
Adolphs, R., 2.25, 3.18, 4.5, 5.68
Agnew, M., 6.25
Ahlström, H.H., 2.33
Ahmadi, S., 3.15, 3.17
Ahnert, L., 2.26
Aiken, C., 5.15, 5.62, 5.65
Airasian, P.W., 6.31
Akert, K., 2.4, 2.8
Al Shariti, M., 6.66
Albright, T.D., 5.4
Alderson, A.L., 2.11
Alexander, A.L., 2.6, 4.26
Alexander, C., 2.19
Alexander, C.N., 2.33, 5.67
Algoe, S.B., 4.26
Alibali, M.W., 6.74, 6.75, 6.76
Allan, W., 3.11
Allison J.D., 1.9
Allison, K.R., 1.9
Alloway, R.G., 5.68
Alloway, T.P., 5.66, 5.67, 5.68, 5.70
Alluri, V., 4.29
Alvarez-Icaza, R., 1.4
Amen, D.G., 2.25, 5.14, 5.76, 6.53
Amir, A., 1.4
Amir, N., 5.65
Anderson, A.K., 4.23
Anderson, N., 5.27, 5.32, 5.35
Anderson, R.B., 6.82
Anderson, R.C., 6.102, 6.116, 6.117
Andersson, M., 5.70
Andreopoulos, A., 1.4
Angrist, B., 5.52
Anthenien, L., 2.19
Antoun, N., 3.18
Apostolos, D., 1.7
Appuswamy, R., 1.4
Apthorp, H.S., 3.33
Araujo, J., 3.34
Arcangelos Chamber Ensemble, 2.19
Arcelin, R., 1.9
Argo J.J., 2.27, 3.8
Ariely, D., 6.5
Armstrong, R.B., 5.51
Armstrong, T., 5.53
Aronson, J.A., 5.67
Arp, L., 3.34
Arriaga, P., 2.22
Arthur, J., 1.4
Asbridge, M., 1.18
Ascough, J.C., 2.24

Ashby, F.G., 4.27
Asher, S.R., 6.102
Ashford, J.W., 1.3
Atkinson, M., 2.19
Austin B.P., 1.9
Averill, J.R., 6.15
Ayman-Nolley, S., 6.75

B

Bachmann, U., 6.31
Bäckman, L., 5.70, 5.72, 5.75, 5.76
Backner, S., 2.17, 3.42, 6.119
Baddeley, A., 5.69
Baird, B., 5.35
Baird, W., 6.102
Baker, C.R., 2.26
Baker, S., 3.12, 6.53
Baker, W.K., 6.30
Bakiri, S., 5.11
Bakwin, H., 2.25, 3.10
Ballard, D., 5.26, 5.68, 5.69
Ballard, G.C., 5.55
Balota, D.A., 5.68
Banaji, M.R., 3.6
Bangert-Drowns, R.L., 6.37
Banich, M.T., 1.11
Barch, D., 1.4
Bardell, L., 1.11
Barden, R.C., 4.23
Barefoot, J.C., 4.24
Bargh, J.A., 3.34
Bar-Haim, Y., 5.65
Barker, S.B., 4.38
Barnes, D.E., 1.6
Barnes, V., 2.33
Barnes, V.A., 2.36
Barnhofer, T., 2.33
Baron, J-C., 6.66, 6.67
Baron, R.M., 6.19
Baros, D.M., 4.8
Basilico, N., 1.4
Bassett, D.S., 6.64
Bateh, M., 2.33, 5.56, 5.67
Batmanghelidj, F., 1.22
Baudry, M., 2.6, 4.26
Bauer, R.M., 3.9
Baughman, F.A., Jr., 5.53
Baumann, N., 4.23
Baumann, S., 1.16
Baumeister, R.F., 3.14
Baumgartner, T., 2.25, 3.14, 3.15, 3.17, 4.37
Baun, M.M., 4.38
Bauza, L., 2.33
Baverstock, A., 2.22
Beard, C., 5.65
Beattie, B.L., 1.3
Beatty, W.W., 6.27
Beauchemin, J., 2.33
Becker, E.S., 5.65
Becker, R.E., 1.3
Beech, E.M., 5.35
Beesley, A.D., 3.33
Begley, S., 5.54
Beier, M.E., 5.67, 5.68
Beilock, S., 6.74
Beilock, S.L., 2.11, 6.74
Benn, R., 2.36
Benovoy, M., 4.29
Benson, H., 2.31, 2.33, 2.34, 4.24
Berch, D., 6.75

Berch, D.B., 6.75
Berchtold, N.C., 1.6, 1.9
Berent, S., 1.3
Berger, C., 3.15, 3.17
Berger, J.S., 5.26, 5.68, 5.69
Bergeron, J.D., 1.24
Bergman, S., 5.70
Berk, D., 2.22
Berk, L.S., 2.22, 4.27, 4.32
Berlucchi, G., 6.68
Berman, M., 4.39
Bernard, F., 6.66, 6.67
Berns, G.S., 6.14, 6.6
Best, J.R., 6.75
Bevins, R.A., 6.5
Bickel, H., 1.11
Bills, A.R., 5.7
Binder, J.R., 5.34
Birbaumer, N., 6.52
Bird, S., 5.41
Bishop, D., 2.6
Bjork, R., 6.81
Black, S.A., 4.25
Blagov, .S., 6.16
Blairy, S., 3.18
Blakemore, C., 2.4, 4.26
Bleckley, K.M., 5.67
Bligh, D.A., 5.36
Blizzard, L., 1.7, 1.9
Bloem, G.M., 2.19
Blough, D., 5.7
Blough, D.K., 5.7
Blumenthal, J.D., 5.66
Board, A., 5.10
Bobbitt, T., 3.34
Boesch, C., 3.17
Boesch-Achermann, H., 3.17
Bogen, J.E., 6.64
Bogert, B., 4.29
Bohlin, G., 5.70
Bohns, V.K., 4.43
Boileau, R.A., 1.11
Bomyea, J., 5.65
Bonci, A., 5.51
Bond, L., 6.30
Bonus, K., 5.56
Bookheimer, S.Y., 2.3
Born, J., 6.76
Borum, R., 2.8
Boss, S.M., 5.12
Bossaerts, P., 3.10
Bosshard, C., 2.19
Bouhuys, A.L., 2.19
Boutelle, K.N., 5.65
Bouvard, M.P., 5.11
Boyatzis, C.J., 6.74
Boyle, M.O., 5.67, 5.68
Brach, J.S., 1.6
Bradley, B.P., 4.23
Branigan, C., 4.22, 4.24, 4.25
Brantley, M., 4.26
Brattico, E., 4.29
Braver, T.S., 5.69
Breedlove, S.M., 3.41
Breitenstein, C., 1.6
Bremner, J.D., 2.7
Brener, R., 6.54
Brennemnn, J., 3.10
Brent, R., 6.79
Brezun, J.M., 5.51

Brain-Friendly Teaching • Dr. Spencer Kagan
Kagan Publishing • 800.933.2667 • www.KaganOnline.com

Bride, B., 6.25
Bridges, M.W., 4.24
Bridle, R., 5.65
Brisswalter, J., 1.9
Britton, J.C., 5.65
Broadbent, D., 5.5
Broaders, S., 6.77
Brod, J., 2.7
Brodsky, W., 5.11
Bromley, K., 6.59
Brookhart, S.M., 6.46
Brophy, J.E., 6.18
Brosnan, S.F., 3.17
Brothers, L., 3.8
Brown, J.A., 5.51
Brown, J.D., 2.27
Brown, L., 5.66
Brown, L.E., 5.67
Brown, M., 3.37
Brown, R.P., 1.25
Brown, S., 3.42, 3.44, 6.28, 6.30, 6.86
Brownell, H.H., 6.65
Browning, H.L., 1.3
Bruner, J.S., 3.40
Bryan, J., 4.23, 4.30
Bryan, T., 4.23, 4.30
Buchanan, T.W., 2.11, 4.5
Buchsbaum, M.S., 1.3, 6.66, 6.68
Buchtel, H.A., 1.3
Buck, S.M., 1.7, 1.9, 5.51
Budzynski, H.K., 6.51
Budzynski, T.H., 6.51
Buethe, A., 6.25
Buhle, J., 5.12, 5.13
Buitelaar, J., 5.14
Bunce, D.M., 5.34, 5.35, 5.36
Bunney, B.G., 5.57
Bunting, M.F., 5.67
Bunzeck, N., 4.30, 5.37, 6.4, 6.6
Burns, A.S., 5.55
Burns, G., 4.26
Burns, G.A., 2.4
Burns, M., 5.65
Buschkuehl, M., 5.27, 5.70, 5.72, 5.73, 5.75
Butcher, M., 5.21
Butler, D.L., 6.46
Butterworth, B., 5.63
Buzan, B., 6.57
Buzan, T., 6.57
Byers, J.A., 3.41
Bystritsky, P., 5.70

C

Cabeza, R., 4.5
Cacioppo, J.T., 6.51
Caggiano, J.M., 5.12
Cahn, B.R., 5.57
Cain, S., 4.43
Calder, A.J., 3.18
Caldwell, K., 3.15
California Department of Education, 1.7
Call, N., 6.120
Callan, D.E., 5.42
Cameron, J., 4.15, 6.31
Cameron, P., 5.34
Campbell, B., 6.85
Campbell, L., 5.65, 6.85
Candler, L., 6.25, 6.59
Cannon, W.B., 2.4
Caprilli, S., 2.22

Carbo, M., 6.80
Cardoner, N., 3.4
Carless, D., 6.40
Carlson, J., 5.65
Carlson, R.L., 5.57
Carnevale, P.J.D., 4.21
Carney, D., 4.42
Carpenter, M., 3.17
Carpenter, P.A., 5.69
Carpenter, S., 5.12
Carpin, S., 1.4
Carré, J.M., 4.43
Carro, E., 1.6
Carrougher, G.J., 5.7
Carson, T., 1.18
Carta, J.J., 3.34
Carter, C.S., 2.26, 3.15
Carter, R., 3.7, 3.11, 3.40, 5.46
Cassidy, A., 1.4
Castellanos, F.X., 5.66
Castelli, D.M., 1.7, 1.9, 5.50, 5.51
Catalino, L.I., 4.26
Caterino, M.C., 1.9
Cattell, R.B., 5.68
Caviglioli, O., 6.57
cbesa.org., 2.34
Cebrian, M., 3.36
Cepeda, N.J., 5.41
Chabris, C.F., 5.12, 5.69
Chan, C.K.K., 3.26
Chandler, P., 5.38
Chandra, S., 1.4
Chang, S.W.C., 3.10
Chang, W., 2.35
Chant, R., 2.33
Chaparro, A., 5.10
Chaplin, W.F., 2.27
Chase, W.G., 5.71
Chason, J., 1.11
Chein, J.M., 5.70
Chen, Q., 2.25, 2.26, 3.14, 3.15, 4.37
Chen, X., 3.15
Chenier, T., 4.20
Cherry, E.C., 5.5
Chesnoff, E., 6.22
Chetana, M., 3.10
Chiarello C., 6.65
Chiarello, R.J., 6.67
Chinn, C.A., 3.26
Christie, L-A., 1.6
Christoff, K., 5.34
Chu, M., 6.74
Church, R.B., 6.74, 6.75
Clanton, N.R., 2.27
Clariana, R.B., 6.31
Clark, L., 1.16, 1.18
Clarke, L.W., 2.19
Clarke, S., 6.31
Clasen, L.S., 5.66
Clay, Z., 3.20
Clayborne, B.M., 2.33, 5.67
Clifford, E., 5.12
Coburn, K.L., 1.3
Coburn, N., 5.41
Cochran, K.F., 5.68
Cockerton, T., 2.19
Coda, B., 5.7
Coda, B.A., 5.7
Coe, D.P., 1.7
Coffee, K.A., 4.42

Coffey, K.A., 4.26
cogmed.com, 5.70
cognifit.com, 5.70
Cohen, G.L., 3.15
Cohen, J.D., 5.67
Cohen, M.X., 3.15, 3.17
Cohen, N.J., 1.11
Cohen, R.L., 6.74
Cohen-Kettenis, P., 5.14
Cohn, M.A., 4.26, 4.42
Colbert, R., 2.33, 5.56
Colcombe, A., 1.11
Colcombe, S., 1.9
Coleman, M., 3.5
Collardeau, M., 1.9
Colletta, J.-M., 6.74
Collier, R.W., 2.33
Colvin, M.K., 6.91
Cone, J.J., 5.51
Coney, J., 6.65
Conezio, J., 6.54
Congreve, W., 4.29
Constantinidou, F., 6.53
Contrand, B., 5.11
Conway, A., 4.39
Conway, A.R., 5.68
Conway, A.R.A., 5.67
Cook, S.W., 6.74, 6.75, 6.77
Cooper, H.M., 6.19
Cooper, J.M., 5.10, 5.12
Corbetta, M., 5.63
Coricelli, G., 3.5
Cornell, D., 2.8
Cosin-Tomas, M., 2.34
Costa, L.D., 6.67
Côté, S., 4.39
Cotman, C.W., 1.6, 1.9, 2.20
Cotten, S., 5.11
Cottrell, L.A., 1.9
Cours, M., 5.11
Cowan, N., 5.27, 5.40, 5.67, 5.71
Cowper, W., 6.10
Crabtree, S., 6.18
Craft, S., 2.11
Craig, A.D., 3.10
Craigen, J., 3.31
Craik, F.E., 6.68
Craik, F.I.M., 6.67, 6.68, 6.116
Craik, G., 6.68
Crane, C., 2.33
Cranson, R.W., 2.33, 5.67
Crescimbene, L., 6.5
Crocker, J.K., 3.12
Crockett, D.J., 1.3
Crockett, M.J., 1.16, 1.18
Crooks, T.J., 6.38
Csikszentmihalyi, M., 5.42
Cuddy, A.J.C., 4.42
Cui, X.T., 6.33
Cunningham, A.E., 6.46
Cutbirth, A., 6.105

D

Dagher, A., 4.29, 4.30
Dahlin, E., 5.70, 5.72, 5.75, 5.76
Dahlsten, M., 6.105
Dahlström, K., 5.66, 5.72
Dahlstrom, W.G., 4.24
Dajani, S., 5.55
Damasio, A., 4.4

Brain-Friendly Teaching • Dr. Spencer Kagan
Kagan Publishing • 800.933.2667 • www.KaganOnline.com

Frackowiak, R.S., 5.46, 6.91
Frager, R., 2.16
Franceschi, D., 5.52
Francis, A.D., 5.56
Franklin, H., 4.38
Frantz, R., 2.26
Fredrick, T., 2.33
Fredrickson, B., 4.31, 4.42
Fredrickson, B.L., 4.20, 4.22, 4.24, 4.25, 4.26, 4.39, 4.42
Fried, I., 3.8, 6.5
Friesen, W.V., 4.24
Friston, K.J., 3.4, 6.6
Frith, C.D., 3.10, 5.46, 6.91
Fromm, P.J., 3.46
Fromme, A., 1.6
Frongillo, E.A., 1.9
Fu, Q., 1.6
Fuchs, T., 6.52
Funnell, M.G., 6.91
Furness, T.A., III, 5.7
Furrer, C., 3.15

G

Gaab, N., 6.66
Gabaude, C., 5.11
Gabbard, C., 1.9
Gackenbach, J., 2.33, 5.67
Gaëlle D., 2.34
Gage, F.H., 3.41
Gaillard, R.C., 2.19
Gainotti, G., 3.9
Galera, C., 5.11
Galinsky, A.D., 4.43
Gallhofer, B., 2.25, 2.26, 3.14, 3.15, 4.37
Gallinat, J., 3.15, 3.17
Gallini, J.K., 6.82
Gao, Z., 3.10
Garber, P., 6.74
Garcia, R., 2.6, 4.26
Gardner H., 6.65, 6.88, 6.105
Gariépy, J-F., 3.10
Garza, C., 1.21
Gaser, C., 2.33, 2.34, 6.66
Gately, S.J., 5.52
Gathercole, S.E., 5.66, 5.67, 5.68, 5.70, 5.72
Gatley, S., 5.52
Gatley, S.J., 5.52
Gaylord-King, C., 2.33
Gazzaniga, M.S., 6.64, 6.91
Geer, J.H., 6.15
Geerligs, T., 5.36
Gelderloos, P., 2.33
George, C., 3.18, 3.43
George, S., 6.52
Gepshteina, S., 5.4
Gerace, D., 2.33, 5.56
Gerasimov, M., 5.52
Gerbarg, P.L., 1.25
Giambra, L.M., 5.34
Gibbs, J., 3.25
Giedd, J.N., 5.66
Gielen, A., 5.14
Gifford, A., 5.52
Gifford, A.N., 5.52
Gilbert, D.T., 5.34
Gillberg, C., 3.5
Gillberg, C.G., 5.66, 5.72
Gillespie, P., 3.26
Gillin, C.J., 2.11

Ginsburg-Block, M.D., 3.34
Giordani, B., 1.3
Girard, B.L., 1.18
Giuntoli, D., 5.34
Gladstones, W.H., 5.11
Gläscher, J., 5.68
Glaser, R., 5.41
Glass, D.C., 6.14
Glatstein, M., 2.22
Godeli, M.R., 2.19
Godfrey, C.N., 5.10
Godfrey, D.A., 5.51
Goel, R., 2.22
Goevert, D., 6.103
Golan, G., 2.22
Golchert, J., 5.35
Gold, S., 2.8
Goldberg, E., 6.67
Goldberg, S.R., 6.116
Goldberger, A., 2.34
Goldeoot, D.A., 5.5
Goldin-Meadow, S., 6.74, 6.75, 6.77
Goldsmith, L., 6.74
Golec, L., 2.19
Goleman, D., 2.3, 2.31, 5.3, 5.55, 5.56
Gomes, C.M., 3.17
Gomez-Pinilla, F., 5.51
Good, T.L., 6.18
Goodall, J., 3.17
Goodwin, J.S., 4.25
Gopnik, A., 6.15
Gordon, A.M., 5.34
Gorgolewski, K.J., 5.35
Gould, E., 2.20
Goulet, P., 6.65
Grabowski, T., 5.68
Grafton, S.T., 5.34, 5.36
Grahn, J.A., 5.55
Grannis, J.C., 2.7
Grant, J., 2.35
Gray, J.R., 2.34, 5.69
Grayshield, L., 2.33, 5.56
Graziano, M.S.A., 5.57
Green, H., 1.21
Greene, T.R., 4.21, 4.22
Greenfield, D., 1.21
Greenstein, D.K., 5.66
Greenwood, C.R., 3.34
Greer, S., 4.24
Greischar, L.L., 5.56
Greischer, L.L., 2.34
Greve, D.N., 2.34
Grey, J., 6.93
Griffith, J.W., 2.34
Grimmer, K.A., 5.6
Grodstein, F., 1.6
Groothuis, T.G., 2.19
Gross, P.H., 6.19
Grossman, K.E., 2.26
Grosswald, S., 2.33, 5.56, 5.67
Gruber, A., 2.22
Gruenfeld, D.H., 4.43
Grueter, M., 3.9
Grueter, T., 3.9
Gruppe, H., 2.25, 2.26, 3.14, 3.15, 4.37
Gruzelier, J., 6.51, 6.53
Gruzelier, J.H., 6.52
Gu, X., 3.10
Gucht, K., 2.34
Guidetti, M., 6.74

Guillory, L.E., 4.43
Gustafsson, P., 5.66, 5.72
Gutmann, D.H., 5.51

H

Haaga, D., 2.33
Haber, R.N., 6.54
Habib, R., 6.68
Habib, T., 6.52
Hagelin, J., 2.33, 5.56
Hahn, S., 1.11
Haier, R.J., 1.3, 6.66, 6.68
Haislip, G.R., 5.52
Hall, E.E., 5.50
Hall, J., 2.19
Hall, P., 2.33
Hall, R.V., 3.34
Hall, S., 1.21
Halligan, P.W., 5.46, 6.91
Hallion, L.S., 5.65
Halpern, D.V., 5.34
Hamann, S., 6.16
Hamburger, S.D., 5.66
Hamilton, D.L., 3.6
Hammerstein, O., 4.24
Hampshire, A., 5.55
Hampton, A.N., 3.10
Han, M., 1.9
Han, S.S., 1.9
Handy, T.C., 5.35
Haney, T.L., 4.24
Hanna Damasio, H., 5.68
Hanson, E., 4.14
Hanson, P.G., 5.51
Harenski, K., 6.16
Hariri, A., 2.3
Harlow, H.E., 2.25, 2.26
Harlow, H.F., 2.26
Harlow, J.M., 2.6
Harper, G.F., 3.34, 3.35, 5.53
Harrington, A., 5.56
Harris, I., 6.57
Harris, T.B., 1.6
Harrision, B.J., 3.4
Harrison, V.F., 6.51
Harrison, C.R., 1.11
Hart, A.J., 2.3
Hartmann, O., 2.22
Hastings, J.L., 1.6
Hatta, A., 5.51
Hattie, J., 3.33, 6.30, 6.31
Hattie, J.A., 6.30
Hauck, W.E., 2.23
Hauger, R.L., 2.11
Hausdorff, J., 4.25
Hausdorff, J.M., 2.34
Haviv, E., 2.22
Hawes, A., 3.41, 3.42, 3.44
Hawkins, J., 6.14, 6.30
Haydon, T., 3.34, 3.35, 5.53
Haynes, R.B., 6.51
Hazlett, E., 1.3
Hazlett, K.E., 3.12
Healey, M., 6.77
Heaton, D.P., 2.33
Hedlund, S., 1.6
Heeren, A., 5.65
Heider, F., 3.4
Heimlich, J.E., 6.62

Kivipelto, M., 1.11
Klatzky, R., 6.75
Klein, S.A., 1.9
Kleinman, R.E., 1.21
Klin, A., 3.4
Klingberg, T., 5.66, 5.68, 5.69, 5.70, 5.72, 5.74
Klissouras, V., 1.7, 1.9
Kluger, A.N., 6.31
Knecht, S., 1.6
Knight, R.T., 3.10
Koeneke, S., 6.66
Koeppe, R.A., 3.12, 5.68, 5.69
Kohn, A., 4.15
Kok, B.E., 4.26
Kollins, S.H., 5.52
Komuro, N., 5.69, 5.74
Konig, S., 5.14
Korn, J.H., 5.35
Korsukewitz, C., 1.6
Korycinski, S.T., 3.12
Korzeck-Ramirez, K., 1.21
Kosfeld, M., 2.26, 3.15
Kotovksy, K., 5.67
Kovacevic, N., 4.30
Kozak, M.N., 2.11
Kraemer, D.J.M., 6.89
Kramer, A.F., 1.9, 1.11, 5.50
Krings, T., 6.66
Krueger, K., 1.6
Kuckertz, J.M., 5.65
Kuhl, J., 4.23
Kuhl, P.K., 6.15
Kuhn, C., 4.37
Kuhn, H.G., 3.41
Kulhavy, R.W., 6.31, 6.116
Kulik, C.L.C., 6.37
Kulik, J.A., 6.37
Kunkel, S.R., 4.25
Kuntz, D., 4.13
Kuraev, G.A., 2.19
Kuroiwa, K., 5.51
Kurzban, R., 2.26, 3.15, 3.16
Kusnitz, J.A., 1.4
Kuzma, D., 4.46, 6.47, 6.115
Kwapil, T.R., 5.67
Kwong, K.K., 4.37
Kyle, P., 2.12, 3.26, 3.31, 4.40, 6.22
Kyllonen, P.C., 5.66

L

LaBar, K.S., 4.5
LaBarre, R., 1.9
LaBerge, D., 5.57
Laborey, M., 5.11
Lacey, A., 2.8
Lacson, R., 4.14
Lagarde, E., 5.11
Laine, M., 5.70
Lamb, G., 2.19, 5.40
Lamb, M.E., 2.26
Lamont, E., 5.68
Landers, D.M., 1.9
Landrith, G.S., 2.33
Lane, R.D., 6.93
Lange, K.M., 5.14
Lange, K.W., 5.14
Langenecker, S.A., 3.12
Lantieri, L., 5.57
Lantz, G., 5.10
Lapp, D., 6.62

Larcher, K., 4.29
Larsson, A., 5.72, 5.75, 5.76
Laughlin, M.H., 5.51
Lavallee, H., 1.9
LaVaque, T.J., 6.51, 6.52, 6.53
Lawrence, M., 6.88
Lawton, C.L., 1.18
Layous, K., 3.11
Lazar, S., 2.34
Lazarus, R., 1.7, 1.9
Lease, J., 5.26, 5.68, 5.69
Le Baudour, C., 1.24
Leber, A.B., 5.13
Lechtermann, A., 1.6
Lee, H.J., 2.26
Lee, H.S., 1.9
Lee, P.P., 5.66
Lee, R.B., 5.11
Leeming, F.C., 6.37
Leeuwen, E., 1.14
Lehan, S., 6.102
Lehtinen, S., 1.3
Leibel, R.L., 1.21
Leibenluft, E., 5.65
Leibowitz, J.M., 4.38
Leirer, V.O., 3.6
Lemercier, C., 5.11
Lenton, S., 2.22
Lepore, N., 2.33, 2.34
Lerner, N., 3.26
Lesmesb, L.A., 5.4
Levenson, R.W., 4.24
Levin, D., 6.14
Levine, B.D., 1.6
Levine, S.C., 6.74
Levitin, D.J., 6.66
Levy, B.R., 4.25
Lewis, D., 1.25
Lewis, N.L., 1.21
Li, D., 3.15
Li, S.-C., 5.72
Lieberman, J., 5.52
Lieberman, M.D., 1.16, 1.18, 2.3, 3.3, 3.4, 3.6, 3.14
Liegeois-Chauvel, C., 4.29
Liegeois-Chauvel, J-L.A., 4.29
Lievens, L., 5.65
Likhtik, E., 2.6
Lin, S.Y., 3.10
Linden, M., 6.51, 6.52, 6.53
Lindenberger, U., 5.72
Lindenmeyer, J., 5.65
Lindquist, S.I., 5.34, 5.35, 6.102
Lindqvist, S., 5.70
Lipsey, M.W., 3.33
Lis, S., 2.25, 2.26, 3.14, 3.15, 4.37
Lissek, S., 5.65
Little, J.C., 5.67
Liu, J., 4.37
Liu, X., 3.10
Liu-Ambrose, T., 1.9
Lockard, J.S., 6.14
Loeb, S., 5.10
Logan, J., 5.52
Loosli, S.V., 5.70, 5.72
Lopez-Sola, M., 3.4
Lottenberg, S., 1.3, 6.66, 6.68
Lovallo, W.R., 2.11
Love, T.M., 3.12
Lu, Q., 2.34, 5.56
Lubar, J.F., 6.51, 6.52, 6.53

Lucas, R.E., 4.23
Luders, E., 2.33, 2.34
Luk, J.W., 2.8
Lum, T.E., 5.12
Lupien, S.J., 2.10, 2.11
Lutz, A., 2.34
Lutz, K., 6.66
Lutzenberger, W., 6.52
Luu, T.M., 3.11
Lyman, F., Jr., 3.43
Lyman, F.T., 3.28
Lynn, S., 6.51, 6.53
Lyons, I.M., 6.74
Lyubomirsky, S., 3.11, 4.19, 4.39

M

Ma, Y., 2.34, 5.56
Macbeth, A.H., 2.26
MacDonald, K.A., 3.8, 6.5
Mach, R.H., 5.51
Macknik, S.L., 5.9, 6.16
MacLachlan, A., 1.3, 6.66, 6.68
MacLeod, A.M., 6.68
MacLeod, C., 5.65
Macrae, C.N., 3.6, 5.34, 5.36
Maheady, L., 3.34, 3.35, 5.53
Maheu, F., 2.10
Mahoney, M.J., 6.18
Mahootian, S., 6.75
Maier, W., 3.15, 3.17
Main, M., 3.18, 3.43
Maisel, E., 6.15
Malina, R.M., 1.7
Mallette, B., 3.34, 3.35, 5.53
Malyarenko, T.N., 2.19
Malyarenko, Y.E., 2.19
Mancini, A., 6.5
Mancso, R.A., 4.24, 4.25
Manes, F., 3.18
Mangano, C., 2.22
Manini, T.M., 1.6
Manson, J.E., 1.6
Manzi, A., 6.25
Mar, R.A., 3.4
Margoliash, D., 6.76
Margulies, D.S., 5.35
Margulies, N., 6.57
Marina, O., 4.37
Markel, D., 1.3
Markides, K.S., 4.25
Markowitsch, H.J., 6.68
Marks, E., 2.19
Marquetti, G.P., 2.19
Marra, C., 3.9
Marriott, A., 3.7
Marsh, W.L., 5.66
Marshall, J.C., 5.46, 6.91
Marshuetz, C., 5.68, 5.69
Martinez-Conde, S., 5.9, 6.16
Maruyama, G., 3.33
Marzi, C.A., 6.68
Maslow, A.H., 2.16
Mason, J., 6.102, 6.117
Mason, M.F., 5.34, 5.36
Masson, F., 5.11
Masson, J.M., 3.44, 3.46, 6.27
Master, J.C., 4.23
Mateo, J., 2.11
Mathews, R., 1.21
Mattarella-Micke, A., 2.11, 6.74

Orriols, L., 5.11
Ortega, A., 6.5
Ortiz, H., 3.4
Osherson, D., 6.88
Ostberg, V., 3.12
Ostir, G.V., 4.25
Otake, K., 4.39
Othmer, S., 6.51
Otsui, K., 4.39
Ovid, 3.39
Oviedo-Lim, D., 2.33, 5.56
Owen, A.M., 5.55
Owens, R.J.Q., 5.22
Ozyurek, A., 6.77

P
Pace, T.W.W., 2.34
Paek, J., 1.3
Pagani, J.H., 2.26
Pagano, M.E., 1.21
Page, E.B., 6.38
Page, M., 5.51
Pagnoni, G., 6.6, 6.14
Palmer, M.D., 1.6
Pandya, P.K., 6.87
Panksepp, J., 3.41, 4.20, 6.27, 6.28
Pantelis, C., 3.4
Papousek, I., 2.22
Pappas, N.R., 5.52
Pardo, J.V., 6.68
Pare, D., 2.6
Park, J.W., 2.25, 2.26, 4.37
Park, Y., 2.22
Parks, R.W., 1.3
Pashler, H., 5.11, 5.41, 6.81
Passolunghi, M.C., 5.70
Patin, A., 3.15, 3.17
Patterson, D.R., 5.7
Patterson, F., 2.33
Patton, K., 1.21
Pauk, W., 5.22
Paul, L.K., 5.68
Pawelczack, S., 5.65
Paz R., 2.6
Pedelty, L.L., 6.77
Pedersen, C.A., 3.15
Pek, J., 4.42
Pellenq, C., 6.74
Pelletier, J.G., 2.6
Pellis, S.M., 3.41
Penfield, W., 5.4
Peng, C.K., 2.34
Penney, J.B., 1.3
Pennington, E.C., 5.12
Pereira M.A., 1.18
Perel, A., 2.22
Perel, S., 6.33
Perkins, C.C., 6.14
Perrig, W.J., 5.27, 5.70, 5.72, 5.73
Perry, M., 6.75
Perth, C.B., 1.5, 4.4
Pervin, L.A., 6.14
Petersen, S.E., 5.63, 5.68, 6.68
Petruzello, S.J., 1.9
Philippot, P., 3.18, 5.65
Phillips, J.B., 2.27
Phillips, M., 6.112
Piazza, M., 5.63
Pickering, S.J., 5.66, 5.67, 5.68
Pierce, W.D., 4.15, 6.31

Pieruzzini, P.R., 2.20
Pine, D.S., 5.65
Ping, R., 6.75
Piper, E., 2.25, 2.26, 4.37
Pittelman, S.D., 6.62
Pitts, F.N., Jr., 2.33
Pivarnik, J.M., 1.7
Plailly, J., 3.18
Platel, H., 6.66, 6.67
Platt, M.L., 3.10
Ploger, F., 6.31
Plotnick, G.D., 2.22
Polak, E.D., 1.9
Polich, J., 5.57
Pollitt, E., 1.21
Pontifex, M.B., 5.50, 5.51
Popkin, B.M., 1.18, 1.21
Poppert, H., 1.11
Porges, S.W., 2.3, 2.8, 2.25, 2.26
Posner, M.I., 2.34, 5.12, 5.13, 5.14, 5.56, 5.57
Posnter, M.I., 5.54
Post, S.G., 4.39
Postle, B.R., 5.26, 5.68, 5.69
Postle, R.R., 5.26, 5.69
Potteiger, J.A., 1.20
Potter, H.H., 6.65
Potts, R., 1.3
Powys, M., 4.23
Prange, A.J., Jr., 3.15
Prasad, A., 1.6
Preissl, R., 1.4
Prevo, G., 4.14
Price, C.J., 5.63
Prohaska, T., 6.19, 6.33
Proverbs, 3.40
Pujol, J., 3.4

Q
Quinn, B.T., 2.34
Quirk, G.J., 2.6

R
Rabah, D., 3.10
Rada, P., 2.20
Radojevic, V., 6.52
Radosevich, D.J., 5.41
Raes, F., 2.34
Raichie, M.E., 5.68
Raichle, M.E., 5.13, 6.68
Raife, E.A., 5.68
Raine, L.B., 5.50
Rainforth, M., 2.33, 2.35, 5.56
Rainforth, M.V., 2.33
Raison, C.L., 2.34
Rajic, M., 1.9
Rampersaud G.C., 1.18
Randazzo, W., 1.8
Rao, R.P.N., 6.35
Rapoport, J.L., 5.66
Ratey, J., 1.7, 1.8, 5.26
Ratner, K.G., 6.18
Rauch, S.L., 2.3, 2.34
Rawlings, N.B., 2.34
Rawlinson, H., 4.23
Rayer, S., 6.89
Raz, A., 5.12, 5.13
Rea, C.P., 5.41
Readance, J.E., 6.62
Reber, P.J., 5.67

Recarte, M.A., 5.10
Reddy, M., 2.8
Redelmeier, D.A., 5.10
Redick,T.S., 5.70
Reed, N., 5.10
Rees, B., 2.33
Reese, H.E., 5.65
Reeves, M.J., 1.7
Regan, M.A., 5.11
Regnstrom, O., 1.6
Reichel, C.M., 6.5
Reichle, E.D., 5.34, 5.69
Reim, B., 6.14
Rein, G., 2.19
Rene, A., 1.9
Reuter-Lorenz, P.A., 5.68, 5.69
Rewerts, S., 4.13
Reynolds, J.H., 5.41
Rhodes, T., 3.32
Ribéreau-Gayon, R., 5.11
Ricard, M., 2.34
Richards, A.L., 5.7
Richards, K., 2.11
Richards, L., 6.65
Richards, T.L., 5.7
Richardson, A., 6.31
Richardson, W.S., 6.51
Richland, L.E., 6.75
Rickards, J.P., 5.22
Riding, R., 6.89
Rilling, J.K., 3.11
Rimon, A., 2.22
Rinck, M., 5.65
Rinne, J.O., 5.70
Risk, W.P., 1.4
Risko, E.F., 5.27, 5.32, 5.35
Rittle-Johnson, B., 6.76
Rizzolatti, G., 3.18
Robbins, R., 5.10
Robbins, T.W., 1.16, 1.18
Roberts, P.M., 6.65
Robertson, L., 2.16, 3.25
Robinson, G.F., 4.22
Röcke, C., 5.72
Rocker, L., 2.19
Rodgers, R., 4.24
Rogers, B.L., 1.21
Rogers, P.J., 1.22
Roher Murphy, L.C., 6.31
Rohrbeck, C.A., 3.34
Rohrer, D., 5.41, 6.81
Rondell, B., 5.10
Rorden, C., 5.68
Rosaen, C., 2.36
Rose, D., 6.5
Rosen, B.R., 4.37
Rosenberg, K.M., 3.40
Rosenberg, L.M., 6.89
Rosenberg, W., 6.51
Rosenkranz, M., 5.56
Rosenkranz, M.A., 2.34
Rosenthal, R., 6.18
Rosenthal, Z., 3.11
Rosenzweig, A.S., 4.20
Ross, C.D., 5.51
Rossiter, T.R., 6.52
Roszak, T., 6.18
Rothbart, M.K., 2.34, 5.14, 5.56
Rovio, S., 1.11
Royet, J.P., 3.18

Brain-Friendly Teaching • Dr. Spencer Kagan
Kagan Publishing • 800.933.2667 • www.KaganOnline.com

Sweller, J., 5.38
Sylwester, R., 6.88

T

Tabibnia, G., 1.16, 1.18
Takeuchi, H., 5.69, 5.74
Taki, Y., 5.69, 5.74
Tan, S.A., 2.22, 4.27, 4.32
Tanaka, H., 2.22
Tanaka-Matsumi, J., 4.39
Tanenhaus, M.K., 6.74
Tang, C., 1.3
Tang, Y., 2.34, 5.56
Tanner, M., 2.33
Tansey, M., 6.52
Taras, H.L., 1.18
Tarumi, T., 2.22
Tassinary, L.G., 6.51
Tavor, O., 2.22
Taylor, B., 6.25
Taylor, C.T., 5.65
Telang, F.W., 5.52
Tennie, C., 3.20
Terkel, J., 4.37
Tervaniemi, M., 4.29
Themanson, J.T., 5.51
Thomas, B.H., 5.6
Thomas, J.W., 2.23
Thomas, R., 5.52
Thomas, S.N., 1.6
Thompson, L., 6.51
Thompson, M., 6.51
Thompson, R.F., 2.6, 4.26
Thompson, T., 6.31
Thompson-Schill, S.L., 6.89
Thorell, L.B., 5.70
Thorndike, E.L., 5.71
Thron, A., 6.66
Tibshirani, R.J., 5.10
Tighe, P., 2.22
Timperley, H., 6.31
Tobler, P.N., 6.5
Toga, A.W., 2.33, 2.34
Tom, D.Y.H., 6.19
Tomasello, M., 3.17, 3.20
Tomasi, D., 5.52
Tomporowsi, P.D., 1.9
Tomporowski, P.D., 1.9
Töpper, R., 6.66
Toppino, T.C., 5.41
Torres-Aleman, I., 1.6
Tothbart, M.K., 5.54
Tranel, D., 3.18, 4.5, 5.68
Travis, F., 2.33, 2.34, 5.56, 5.67
Treadway, M.T., 2.34
Treaster, R., 1.30, 2.19, 2.23, 4.18
Treiber, F., 2.33
Treiber, F.A., 2.36
Trejo, J.L., 1.6
Tremblay, M.S., 1.7, 1.9
Tu, M., 2.10
Tucha, L., 5.14
Tucha, O., 5.14
Tucker, D.M., 4.23
Tuckman, B.W., 1.9
Tugade, M.M., 4.24, 4.25
Tulving, E., 6.67, 6.68, 6.116
Tunbridge, R.J., 5.10
Tuokko, H., 1.3
Tuomilehto, J., 1.11

Turken, U., 4.27
Turnbull, M.J., 2.33
Twain, M., 5.31
Twenge, J.M., 3.14
Tye, K.M., 5.51
Tye, L.D., 5.51
Tylavsky, F., 1.6

U

Ulrich, R.S., 4.38, 4.39
Unsworth, N., 5.67
Urbanowski, F., 5.56
Uvnas-Moberg, K., 2.26

V

Vacharkulksemsuk, T., 4.26
Vagnoli, L., 2.22
Vaish, A., 3.17
Vaituzis, A.C., 5.66
Vakil, E., 1.11
Valenzeno, L., 6.75
Valosek, L., 2.35
van den Boom, D.C., 3.12
van den Bosch, I., 4.30
Van Engeland, H., 5.14
Van Goudoever, J.B., 3.11
Van Horn, J.D., 5.34, 5.36
Van Leeuwen, E.J.C., 3.42
Vanman, E.J., 6.51
Van Oostrom, T., 5.7
Van Overwalle, F., 3.4
Vaquero, L.M., 3.36
Varrone, A., 5.70
Vartiainen, N., 4.29
Vaughn, J.L., Jr., 6.102
Vaynman, S., 5.51
Velliste, M., 6.33
Vercambre, M-N., 1.6
Veugelers, P., 1.18
Viadero, D., 1.9
Videen, T.O., 6.68
Viitanen, M., 1.11
Vincent, J.D., 2.7
Vinski, M.T., 5.35
Virta, J., 5.70
Visalberghi, E., 6.5
Vittorio Gallese, V., 3.18
Vo, M.L-H., 5.12
Voelker, K., 1.6
Vogel, R.A., 2.22
Vohr, B.R., 3.11
Volkow, N., 5.52
Volkow, N.D., 5.52
Volle, M., 1.9
Vollert, J., 2.19
Volokhov, R., 5.66, 5.76
Voss, M.W., 1.9
Vossekuil, B., 2.8
Vouimba, R.M., 2.6, 4.26
Vul, E., 5.41
Vygotsky, L.S., 6.121, 6.122

W

Wadlinger, H.A., 4.23
Wager, T., 4.39
Wagner, D., 6.31
Wagner, M., 3.15, 3.17
Walberg, H.J., 3.33
Walker, S.J., 3.12
Wallace, A.B., 2.34

Wallace, B.A., 5.3
Wallace, R.K., 2.33
Walter, J.M., 5.66
Walton, K., 2.33
Walton, G.M., 3.15
Wang, G-J., 5.52
Wang, G-J., 5.52
Wang, H., 3.12
Wang, J., 2.34, 5.56
Wang, X., 3.10
Ward, C., 3.31
Ward, R.M., 1.20
Warneken, F., 3.17
Wasaka, T., 5.51
Wasserman, R.H., 2.34
Waterhouse, B., 5.51
Watkins, A.D., 2.19
Watts, G.H., 6.117
Weber, D.J., 6.33
Weber, G., 5.65
Wegner, D.M., 5.34, 5.36
Wei, J., 4.25
Weiner, B., 5.21
Weisglas-Kuperus, N., 3.11
Weitzman, M., 1.21
Welker, K.M., 4.43
Welling, B., 3.9
Wentzek, S., 3.9
Wentzel, K.R., 3.12, 3.15
Westen, D., 6.16
Westerberg, H., 5.66, 5.68, 5.69, 5.70, 5.72, 5.74
Whalen, P.J., 2.3, 2.6, 4.26
White, K., 6.27
Whitford, A.S., 6.33
Wicker, B., 3.18
Wiederhold, C., 6.26, 6.109
Wiers, R.W., 5.65, 5.67, 5.76
Wigal, T.L., 5.52
Wilkerson, M.K., 5.51
Williams, J.K., 5.57
Williams, J.M.G., 2.33, 2.34
Williams, R.B., Jr., 4.24
Willis, C., 5.68, 5.70
Willis, C.S., 5.67
Willmes, K., 6.66
Willms, J.D., 1.7, 1.9
Wilson, C.L., 3.8, 6.5
Wilson, D.B., 3.33
Wilson, K., 5.35
Wilson, P.T., 6.102
Wiltermuth, S.S., 4.43
Winblad, B., 1.11
Wincel, M., 3.30, 3.39., 6.39., 6.42, 6.51., 6.121
Winkielman, P., 4.20
Winne, P.H., 6.46
Winston, J.S., 2.25
Winter, B., 1.6
Wire, N., 3.7
Wise, B.M., 5.12
Wittberg, R.A., 1.9
Wittmann, B.C., 4.30, 6.4
Wixted, J.T., 5.41
Woeltge, A., 5.64
Wolf, S.L., 6.51
Wolfe, J.M., 5.12
Wolyniez, I., 2.22
Womack, C.J., 1.7
Won, H.S., 1.9
Wong, C.T., 5.52
Wong, T.M., 1.4

Brain-Friendly Teaching • Dr. Spencer Kagan
Kagan Publishing • 800.933.2667 • www.KaganOnline.com

Notes

Notes

Notes

Notes